Derivatives and Alternative Investments

LEVEL I
2007

CFA® PROGRAM CURRICULUM · VOLUME 6

Printed in the United States of America

10 9 8 7 6 5 4 3 2

ISBN 0-536-17613-2

2005160774

BK/JS

Please visit our web site at *www.pearsoncustom.com*

PEARSON CUSTOM PUBLISHING
75 Arlington Street, Suite 300, Boston, MA 02116
A Pearson Education Company

CONTENTS

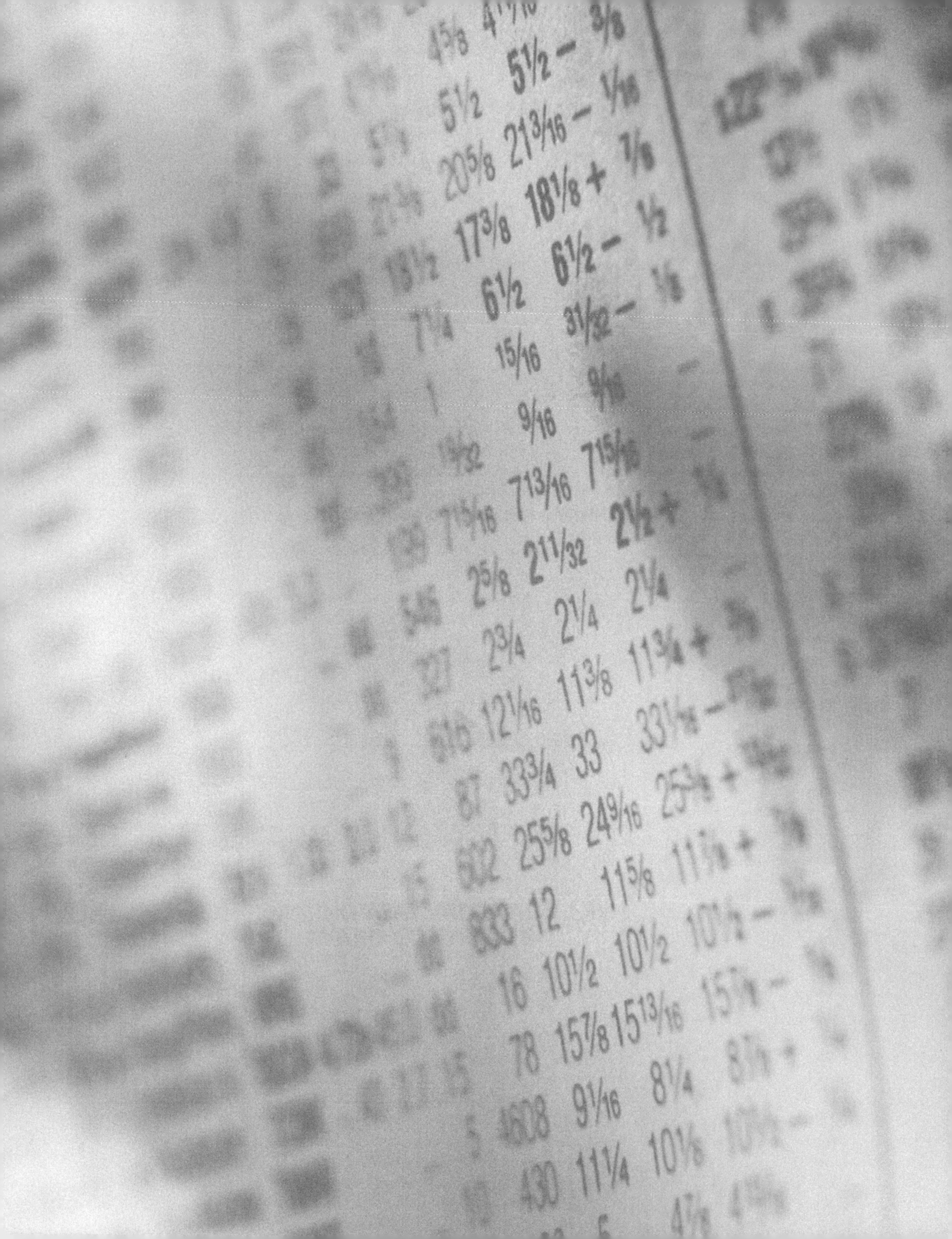

4⅝ 4?/16 3/8
5½ — 3/8
5½ 5½ — 1/16
20⅝ 21³/₁₆ — 1/16
18⅛ + 7/8
17⅜ 18⅛ +
13½ 6½ — ½
6½ 6½ —
7¼ 31/32 —
15/16
9/16
9/16
1/32
7¹³/₁₆ 7¹⁵/₁₆
7¹¹/₁₆
2⅝ 2¹¹/₃₂ 2½ +
2¾ 2¼ 2¼
12¹/₁₆ 11⅜ 11¾ +
33¾ 33 33⅛ —
25⅝ 24⁹/₁₆ 25⅜ +
12 11⅝ 11⅞ +
16 10½ 10½ 10½ —
78 15⅞ 15¹³/₁₆ 15⅞ —
9¹/₁₆ 8¼ 8⅞ +
11¼ 10⅛

HOW TO USE THE CFA PROGRAM CURRICULUM

Congratulations on your decision to enter the Chartered Financial Analyst (CFA®) Program. This exciting and rewarding program of study reflects your desire to become a serious investment professional. You are embarking on a program noted for its requirement of ethics and breadth of knowledge, skills, and abilities.

The credential you seek is respected around the world as a mark of accomplishment and dedication, and each level of the program represents a distinct achievement in professional development. Successful completion of the program is rewarded with membership in a prestigious global community of investment professionals. CFA charterholders are dedicated to life-long learning and maintaining currency with the ever-changing dynamics of a challenging profession.

Curriculum Development

The CFA Program curriculum is grounded in the practice of the investment profession. CFA Institute regularly conducts a practice analysis survey of investment professionals around the world to determine the knowledge, skills, and abilities that are relevant to the profession. The survey results define the Candidate Body of Knowledge (CBOK™), an inventory of knowledge and responsibilities expected of the investment management professional at the level of a new CFA charterholder. The survey also determines how much emphasis each of the major topic areas receives on the CFA examinations.

A committee made up of practicing charterholders, in conjunction with CFA Institute staff, designs the CFA Program curriculum to deliver the CBOK to candidates. The examinations, also written by practicing charterholders, are designed for you to demonstrate mastery of the CBOK as set forth in the CFA Program curriculum. As you structure your personal study program, you should emphasize mastery of the CBOK and the practical application of that knowledge. For more information on the practice analysis, CBOK, and development of the CFA Program curriculum, please visit www.cfainstitute.org/course.

Organization

The 2007 Level I CFA Program curriculum is organized into 10 topic areas. Each topic area begins with a topic level learning outcome that summarizes the broad objective of the material to follow and indicates the depth of knowledge expected. Each topic area is then divided into one or more study sessions, each devoted to a sub-topic (or group of sub-topics) within that topic area. The 2007 Level I curriculum is organized into 18 study sessions. Each study session begins with a purpose statement defining the content structure and objective of that session. Finally, each study session is further divided into reading assignments. *The outline on the inside front cover of each volume should further illustrate this important hierarchy.*

The reading assignments are the basis for all examination questions. The readings are selected or developed specifically to teach candidates the CBOK. Readings are drawn from textbook chapters, professional journal articles, research analyst reports, CFA Program-commissioned content, and cases. Many readings include problems and solutions as well as appendices to help you learn.

Reading-specific Learning Outcome Statements (LOS) are listed in the study session opener page as well as prior to each reading. Reading-specific LOS indicate what you should be able to accomplish after studying the reading. It is important, however, not to interpret LOS narrowly by focusing on a few key sentences in a reading. Readings, particularly CFA Program-commissioned readings, provide context for the learning outcome and enable you to apply a principle or concept in a variety of scenarios. Thus, you should use the LOS to guide and focus your study, as each examination question is based explicitly on one or more LOS. We encourage you to thoroughly review how to properly use LOS and the list and descriptions of commonly used LOS command words at www.cfainstitute.org/toolkit. The command words signal the depth of learning you are expected to achieve from the reading.

Features for 2007

▶ **Required vs. Optional segments** - Several reading assignments use only a portion of the original source textbook chapter or journal article. In order to allow you to read the assignment within its full context, however, we have reprinted the entire chapter or article in the curriculum. When an optional segment begins, you will see an icon. A vertical solid bar in the outside margin will continue until the optional segment ends, symbolized by another icon. Unless the material is specifically noted as optional, you should assume it is required. Keep in mind that the optional material is provided strictly for your convenience and will not be tested. *You should rely on the required segments and the reading-specific LOS in preparing for the examination.*

▶ **Problems/Solutions** - When appropriate, we have developed and assigned problems after readings to demonstrate practical application and reinforce understanding of the concepts presented. The solutions to the problems are provided in an appendix at the back of each volume. Candidates should consider all problems and solutions required material as your ability to solve these problems will prepare you for exam questions.

▶ **Margins** - We have inserted wide margins throughout each volume to allow for easier note taking.

 ▶ **Two-color format** - To enrich the visual appeal and clarity of the exhibits, tables, and required vs. optional treatments, we have printed the curriculum in two-color format.

 ▶ **Six- volume structure** - To improve the portability of the curriculum, we have spread the material over six volumes versus the four we had last year.

▶ **Glossary and Index** - For your convenience, we have printed a comprehensive glossary and index in each volume. Throughout the curriculum, a **bolded blue** word in a reading denotes a glossary term.

Designing your personal study program:

Create a schedule - An orderly, systematic approach to preparation is critical to successful completion of the examination. You should dedicate a consistent block of time every week to reading and studying. Complete all reading assignments and the associated problems and solutions in each study session. Review the LOS both before and after you study each reading to ensure that you have mastered the applicable content and can complete the action(s) specified. Upon completion of each study session, review the session's purpose statement and confirm that you thoroughly understand the subject matter. When you complete a topic area, review the topic level learning outcome and verify that you have mastered the objectives.

CFA Institute estimates that you will need to devote a minimum of 10-15 hours per week for 18 weeks to study the assigned readings. Allow a minimum of one week for each study session spread over several days, with completion scheduled for at least 30-45 days prior to the examination. This schedule will allow you to spend the final four to six weeks before the examination reviewing the assigned material and taking multiple on-line sample examinations. At CFA Institute, we believe that candidates need to commit to a *minimum* of 250 hours reading and reviewing the curriculum and taking online sample exams to master the material. This recommendation, however, may substantially underestimate the hours needed for appropriate exam preparation depending on individual circumstances and academic background.

You will undoubtedly adjust your study time to conform to your own strengths and weaknesses and academic background, and you will probably spend more time on some study sessions than on others. You should allow ample time for both in-depth study of all topic areas and additional concentration on those topic areas for which you feel least prepared.

Preliminary Readings - The reading assignments in Economics and Financial Statement Analysis assume candidates already have a basic mastery of the concepts typically presented in introductory university-level economics and accounting courses. Information on suggested readings to improve your knowledge of these topics precedes these study sessions.

Candidate Preparation Toolkit - We have created the online toolkit to provide a single comprehensive location for resources and guidance for candidate preparation. In addition to in-depth information on study program planning, the CFA Program curriculum, and the online sample exams, the toolkit also contains curriculum errata, printable study session outlines. sample exam questions, and more. We encourage you to use the toolkit as your central preparation resource during your tenure as a candidate. Visit the toolkit at www.cfainstitute.org/toolkit.

Online Sample Exams - After completing your study of the assigned curriculum, use the CFA Institute online sample exams to measure your knowledge of the topics and improve your exam-taking skills. After each question, you will receive immediate feedback noting the correct response and indicating the assigned curriculum for further study. The sample exams are designed by the same people who create the actual CFA exams, and reflect the question formats, topics, and level of difficulty of the actual CFA examinations, in a timed environment. Aggregate data indicate that the CFA examination pass rate was higher among candidates who took one or more online sample examinations than for candidates who did not take the online sample exams. For more information on the online sample exams, please visit www.cfainstitute.org/toolkit.

Review Programs - After you enroll in the CFA Program, you may receive numerous solicitations for preparatory courses and review materials. Although preparatory courses and notes may be helpful to some candidates, you should view these resources as *supplements to the assigned CFA Program curriculum*. The CFA exams reference *only* the 2007 CFA Institute assigned curriculum; no preparatory course or review course materials are consulted or referenced.

Furthermore, CFA Institute does not endorse, promote, review, or warrant the accuracy of the products or services offered by preparatory organizations. CFA Institute does not verify or endorse the pass rates or other claims made by these organizations.

Feedback

At CFA Institute, we are committed to delivering a comprehensive and rigorous curriculum for the development of competent, ethically grounded investment professionals. We rely on candidate and member feedback as we work to incorporate content, design, and packaging improvements. You can be assured that we will continue to listen to your suggestions. Please send any comments or feedback to curriculum@cfainstitute.org. Ongoing improvements in the curriculum will help you prepare for success on the upcoming examinations, and for a lifetime of learning as a serious investment professional.

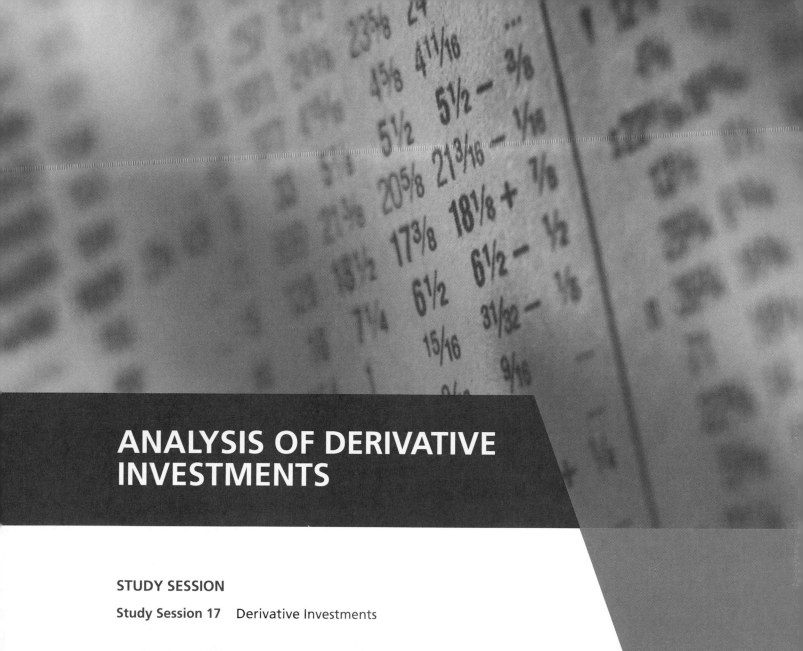

ANALYSIS OF DERIVATIVE INVESTMENTS

TOPIC LEVEL LEARNING OUTCOME

The candidate should be able to demonstrate a working knowledge of the analysis of derivative investments, including forwards, futures, options, and swaps.

	4⁵⁄₈	4⁷⁄₁₆		9⁄₁₆
	5½	5½	−	9⁄₁₆
5½	5½	21³⁄₁₆	−	1⁄₁₆
20⁵⁄₈	21³⁄₁₆			7⁄₈
17³⁄₈	18⅛	+		7⁄₈
6½	6½	−		½
6½	31³⁄₃₂	−		⅛
7¼	15⁄₁₆			
	9⁄₁₆	9⁄₁₆		
⁷⁄₃₂	7¹³⁄₁₆	7¹⁵⁄₁₆		
7¹⁵⁄₁₆	2⁵⁄₈	2¹¹⁄₃₂	2½	+
2¾	2¼	2¼		
2¾	12¹⁄₁₆	11³⁄₈	11¾	+
6½	33¾	33	33⅛	−
87	25⁵⁄₈	24⁹⁄₁₆	25⅜	+
602	12	11⁵⁄₈	11⅜	+
833	10½	10½	10½	−
16	15⁷⁄₈	15¹³⁄₁₆	15⅝	−
78	9¹⁄₁₆	8¼	8⅜	+
4808	11¼	10⅛		
430			4⅞	

STUDY SESSION 17
DERIVATIVE INVESTMENTS

READING ASSIGNMENTS

Reading 73 Derivative Markets and Instruments
Reading 74 Forward Markets and Contracts
Reading 75 Futures Markets and Contracts
Reading 76 Option Markets and Contracts
Reading 77 Swap Markets and Contracts
Reading 78 Risk Management Applications of Option Strategies

Derivatives, financial instruments that offer a return based on the return of some underlying asset, have become increasingly important and fundamental in effectively managing financial risk and creating synthetic exposures to asset classes. As in other security markets, arbitrage and market efficiency play a critical role in establishing prices and maintaining parity.

This study session builds the conceptual framework for understanding derivative investments (forwards, futures, options, and swaps), derivative markets, and the use of options in risk management.

LEARNING OUTCOMES

Reading 73: Derivative Markets and Instruments
The candidate should be able to:

a. define a derivative and differentiate between exchange-traded and over-the-counter derivatives;

b. define a forward commitment, identify the types of forward commitments, and describe the basic characteristics of forward contracts, futures contracts, options (calls and puts), and swaps;

c. discuss the purposes and criticisms of derivative markets;

d. explain the concept of arbitrage and the role it plays in determining prices and in promoting market efficiency.

Reading 74: Forward Markets and Contracts

The candidate should be able to:

a. discuss the differences between the positions held by the long and short parties to a forward contract in terms of delivery/settlement and default risk;

b. describe the procedures for settling a forward contract at expiration, and discuss how a party to a forward contract can terminate a position prior to expiration as well as how credit risk is affected by the way in which a position is terminated;

c. differentiate between a dealer and an end user of a forward contract;

d. describe the characteristics of equity forward contracts and forward contracts on zero-coupon and coupon bonds;

e. explain the characteristics of the Eurodollar time deposit market, define LIBOR and Euribor, and describe the characteristics of forward rate agreements (FRAs);

f. calculate and interpret the payment at expiration of an FRA and explain each of the component terms, when provided with the formula;

g. describe the characteristics of currency forward contracts.

Reading 75: Futures Markets and Contracts

The candidate should be able to:

a. identify the institutional features that distinguish futures contracts from forward contracts and describe the characteristics of futures contracts;

b. differentiate between margin in the securities markets and margin in the futures markets; and define initial margin, maintenance margin, variation margin, and settlement price;

c. describe how a futures trade takes place;

d. describe price limits and the process of marking to market and compute and interpret the margin balance, given the previous day's balance and the new futures price;

e. describe how a futures contract can be terminated by a close-out (i.e., offset) at expiration (or prior to expiration), delivery, an equivalent cash settlement, or an exchange-for-physicals;

f. describe the characteristics of the following types of futures contracts: Eurodollar, Treasury bond, stock index, and currency.

Reading 76: Option Markets and Contracts

The candidate should be able to:

a. define European option, American option, moneyness, payoff, intrinsic value, and time value and differentiate between exchange-traded options and over-the-counter options;

b. identify the different types of options in terms of the underlying instruments;

c. compare and contrast interest rate options to forward rate agreements (FRAs);

d. explain how option payoffs are determined, and show how interest rate option payoffs differ from the payoffs of other types of options;

e. define interest rate caps and floors;

f. identify the minimum and maximum values of European options and American options; calculate and interpret the lowest prices of European and American calls and puts based on the rules for minimum values and lower bounds;

g. describe the relationship between options that differ only by exercise price;

h. explain how option prices are affected by the time to expiration of the option;

i. explain put-call parity for European options, given the payoffs on a fiduciary call and a protective put;

j. explain the relationship between American options and European options in terms of the lower bounds on option prices and the possibility of early exercise;

k. explain how cash flows on the underlying asset affect put-call parity and the lower bounds of option prices;

l. identify the directional effect of an interest rate change or volatility change on an option's price.

Reading 77: Swap Markets and Contracts

The candidate should be able to:

a. describe the characteristics of swap contracts and explain how swaps are terminated;

b. define and give examples of currency swaps, plain vanilla interest rate swaps, and equity swaps, and calculate and interpret the payments on each, when provided with the formulas.

Reading 78: Risk Management Applications of Option Strategies

The candidate should be able to:

a. determine the value at expiration, profit, maximum profit, maximum loss, breakeven underlying price at expiration, and general shape of the graph of the strategies of buying and selling calls and buying and selling puts, and explain each strategy's characteristics;

b. determine the value at expiration, profit, maximum profit, maximum loss, breakeven underlying price at expiration, and general shape of the graph of the covered call strategy and the protective put strategy, and explain each strategy's characteristics.

	4⅝	4	⅜
	5½	5½	− ⅜
5⅛	5½	213/16	− 1¼
	20⅝	213/16	− ⅛
	17⅜	18⅛	+ ⅞
18½	6½	6½	− ½
7¼	6½	31/32	− ⅛
		15/16	
	9/16	9/16	
	11/32		
715/16	713/16	715/16	
	2⅝	211/32	2½ +
	2¾	2¼	2¼
6	12 1/16	11⅜	11¾ +
87	33¾	33	33⅛ −
602	25⅝	249/16	25⅜ +
8333	12	11⅝	11⅞ +
16	10½	10½	10½ −
78	15⅞	1513/16	15⅞ −
4608	91/16	8¼	8⅛ +
430	11¼	10⅛	10⅛

DERIVATIVE MARKETS AND INSTRUMENTS
by Don M. Chance

LEARNING OUTCOMES

The candidate should be able to:

a. define a derivative and differentiate between exchange-traded and over-the-counter derivatives;

b. define a forward commitment, identify the types of forward commitments, and describe the basic characteristics of forward contracts, futures contracts, options (calls and puts), and swaps;

c. discuss the purposes and criticisms of derivative markets;

d. explain the concept of arbitrage and the role it plays in determining prices and in promoting market efficiency.

INTRODUCTION 1

The concept of risk is at the heart of investment management. Financial analysts and portfolio managers continually identify, measure, and manage risk. In a simple world where only stocks and bonds exist, the only risks are the fluctuations associated with market values and the potential for a creditor to default. Measuring risk often takes the form of standard deviations, betas, and probabilities of default. In the above simple setting, managing risk is limited to engaging in stock and bond transactions that reduce or increase risk. For example, a portfolio manager may hold a combination of a risky stock portfolio and a risk-free bond, with the relative allocations determined by the investor's tolerance for risk. If for some reason the manager desires a lower level of risk, the only transactions available to adjust the risk downward are to reduce the allocation to the risky stock portfolio and increase the allocation to the risk-free bond.

But we do not live in a simple world of only stocks and bonds, and in fact investors can adjust the level of risk in a variety of ways. For example, one way to reduce risk is to use insurance, which can be described as the act of paying someone to assume a risk for you. The financial markets have created their own way of offering insurance against financial loss in the form of contracts called **derivatives.** *A derivative is a financial instrument that offers a return based on the return of some other underlying asset.* In this sense, its return is *derived* from another instrument—hence, the name.

As the definition states, a derivative's performance is based on the performance of an underlying asset. This underlying asset is often referred to simply as the **underlying.**[1] It trades in a market in which buyers and sellers meet and decide on a price; the seller then delivers the asset to the buyer and receives payment. The price for immediate purchase of the underlying asset is called the **cash price** or **spot price** (in this book, we will use the latter term). A derivative also has a defined and limited life: A derivative contract initiates on a certain date and terminates on a later date. Often the derivative's payoff is determined and/or made on the expiration date, although that is not always the case. In accordance with the usual rules of law, a derivative contract is an agreement between two parties in which each does something for the other. In some cases, as in the simple insurance analogy, a derivative contract involves one party paying the other some money and receiving coverage against potential losses. In other cases, the parties simply agree that each will do something for the other at a later date. In other words, no money need change hands up front.

We have alluded to several general characteristics of derivative contracts. Let us now turn to the specific types of derivatives that we will cover in this book.

2   TYPES OF DERIVATIVES

In this section, we take a brief look at the different types of derivative contracts. This brief treatment serves only as a short introduction to familiarize you with the general ideas behind the contracts. We shall examine these derivatives in considerable detail in later readings.

Let us start by noting that derivative contracts are created on and traded in two distinct but related types of markets: exchange traded and over the counter. Exchange-traded contracts have standard terms and features and are traded on an organized derivatives trading facility, usually referred to as a futures exchange or an options exchange. Over-the-counter contracts are any transactions created by two parties anywhere else. We shall examine the other distinctive features of these two types of contracts as we proceed.

Derivative contracts can be classified into two general categories: forward commitments and contingent claims. In the following section, we examine for-

---

[1] On behalf of the financial world, we apologize to all English teachers. "Underlying" is not a noun, but in the world of derivatives it is commonly used as such. To be consistent with that terminology, we use it in that manner here.

ward commitments, which are contracts in which the two parties enter into an agreement to engage in a transaction at a later date at a price established at the start. Within the category of forward commitments, two major classifications exist: exchanged-traded contracts, specifically futures, and over-the-counter contracts, which consist of forward contracts and swaps.

2.1 Forward Commitments

The **forward contract** is an agreement between two parties in which one party, the buyer, agrees to buy from the other party, the seller, an underlying asset at a future date at a price established at the start. The parties to the transaction specify the forward contract's terms and conditions, such as when and where delivery will take place and the precise identity of the underlying. In this sense, the contract is said to be *customized*. Each party is subject to the possibility that the other party will default.

Many simple, everyday transactions are forms of forward commitments. For example, when you order a pizza for delivery to your home, you are entering into an agreement for a transaction to take place later ("30 minutes or less," as some advertise) at a price agreed on at the outset. Although default is not likely, it could occur—for instance, if the party ordering the pizza decided to go out to eat, leaving the delivery person wondering where the customer went. Or perhaps the delivery person had a wreck on the way to delivery and the pizza was destroyed. But such events are extremely rare.

Forward contracts in the financial world take place in a large and private market consisting of banks, investment banking firms, governments, and corporations. These contracts call for the purchase and sale of an underlying asset at a later date. The underlying asset could be a security (i.e., a stock or bond), a foreign currency, a commodity, or combinations thereof, or sometimes an interest rate. In the case of an interest rate, the contract is not on a bond from which the interest rate is derived but rather on the interest rate itself. Such a contract calls for the exchange of a single interest payment for another at a later date, where at least one of the payments is determined at the later date.[2]

As an example of someone who might use a forward contract in the financial world, consider a pension fund manager. The manager, anticipating a future inflow of cash, could engage in a forward contract to purchase a portfolio equivalent to the S&P 500 at a future date—timed to coincide with the future cash inflow date—at a price agreed on at the start. When that date arrives, the cash is received and used to settle the obligation on the forward contract.[3] In this manner, the pension fund manager commits to the position in the S&P 500 without having to worry about the risk that the market will rise during that period. Other common forward contracts include commitments to buy and sell a foreign currency or a commodity at a future date, locking in the exchange rate or commodity price at the start.

The forward market is a private and largely unregulated market. Any transaction involving a commitment between two parties for the future purchase/sale of an asset is a forward contract. Although pizza deliveries are generally not considered forward contracts, similar transactions occur commonly in the financial world. Yet we cannot simply pick up *The Wall Street Journal* or *The Financial Times* and read

---

[2] These instruments are called forward rate agreements and will be studied in detail in Reading 74.

[3] The settling of the forward contract can occur through delivery, in which case the buyer pays the agreed-upon price and receives the asset from the seller, or through an equivalent cash settlement. In the latter case, the seller pays the buyer the difference between the market price and the agreed-upon price if the market price is higher. The buyer pays the seller the difference between the agreed-upon price and the market price if the agreed-upon price is higher.

about them or determine how many contracts were created the previous day.[4] They are private transactions for a reason: The parties want to keep them private and want little government interference. This need for privacy and the absence of regulation does not imply anything illegal or corrupt but simply reflects a desire to maintain a prudent level of business secrecy.

Recall that we described a forward contract as an agreement between two parties in which one party, the buyer, agrees to buy from the other party, the seller, an underlying asset at a future date at a price agreed upon at the start. A **futures contract** is a variation of a forward contract that has essentially the same basic definition but some additional features that clearly distinguish it from a forward contract. For one, a futures contract is not a private and customized transaction. Instead, it is a public, standardized transaction that takes place on a futures exchange. A futures exchange, like a stock exchange, is an organization that provides a facility for engaging in futures transactions and establishes a mechanism through which parties can buy and sell these contracts. The contracts are standardized, which means that the exchange determines the expiration dates, the underlying, how many units of the underlying are included in one contract, and various other terms and conditions.

Probably the most important distinction between a futures contract and a forward contract, however, lies in the default risk associated with the contracts. As noted above, in a forward contract, the risk of default is a concern. Specifically, the party with a loss on the contract could default. Although the legal consequences of default are severe, parties nonetheless sometimes fall into financial trouble and are forced to default. For that reason, only solid, creditworthy parties can generally engage in forward contracts. In a futures contract, however, the futures exchange guarantees to each party that if the other fails to pay, the exchange will pay. In fact, the exchange actually writes itself into the middle of the contract so that each party effectively has a contract with the exchange and not with the other party. The exchange collects payment from one party and disburses payment to the other.

The futures exchange implements this performance guarantee through an organization called the clearinghouse. For some futures exchanges, the clearinghouse is a separate corporate entity. For others, it is a division or subsidiary of the exchange. In either case, however, the clearinghouse protects itself by requiring that the parties settle their gains and losses to the exchange on a daily basis. This process, referred to as the **daily settlement** or marking to market, is a critical distinction between futures and forward contracts. With futures contracts, profits and losses are charged and credited to participants' accounts each day. This practice prevents losses from accumulating without being collected. For forward contracts, losses accumulate until the end of the contract.[5]

One should not get the impression that forward contracts are rife with credit losses and futures contracts never involve default. Credit losses on forward contracts are extremely rare, owing to the excellent risk management practices of participants. In the case of futures contracts, parties do default on occasion. In fact, it is likely that there are more defaults on futures contracts than on forward

---

[4] In Section 4 of this reading, we will look at some ways to measure the amount of this type of trading.

[5] Although this process of losses accumulating on forward contracts until the expiration day is the standard format for a contract, modern risk management procedures include the possibility of forcing a party in debt to periodically pay losses accrued prior to expiration. In addition, a variety of risk-reducing techniques, such as the use of collateral, are used to mitigate the risk of loss. We discuss these points in more detail in Reading 74.

contracts.[6] Nonetheless, the exchange guarantee has never failed for the party on the other side of the transaction. Although the possibility of the clearinghouse defaulting does exist, the probability of such a default happening is extremely small. Thus, we can generally assume that futures contracts are default-free. In contrast, the possibility of default, although relatively small, exists for forward contracts.

Another important distinction between forward contracts and futures contracts lies in the ability to engage in offsetting transactions. Forward contracts are generally designed to be held until expiration. It is possible, however, for a party to engage in the opposite transaction prior to expiration. For example, a party might commit to purchase one million euros at a future date at an exchange rate of $0.85/€. Suppose that later the euro has a forward price of $0.90/€. The party might then choose to engage in a new forward contract to sell the euro at the new price of $0.90/€. The party then has a commitment to buy the euro at $0.85 and sell it at $0.90. The risk associated with changes in exchange rates is eliminated, but both transactions remain in place and are subject to default.[7]

In futures markets, the contracts have standardized terms and trade in a market that provides sufficient liquidity to permit the parties to enter the market and offset transactions previously created. The use of contracts with standardized terms results in relatively widespread acceptance of these terms as homogeneous agreed-upon standards for trading these contracts. For example, a U.S. Treasury bond futures contract covering $100,000 face value of Treasury bonds, with an expiration date in March, June, September, or December, is a standard contract. In contrast, if a party wanted a contract covering $120,000 of Treasury bonds, he would not find any such instrument in the futures markets and would have to create a nonstandard instrument in the forward market. The acceptance of standardized terms makes parties more willing to trade futures contracts. Consequently, futures markets offer the parties liquidity, which gives them a means of buying and selling the contracts. Because of this liquidity, a party can enter into a contract and later, before the contract expires, enter into the opposite transaction and offset the position, much the same way one might buy or sell a stock or bond and then reverse the transaction later. This reversal of a futures position completely eliminates any further financial consequences of the original transaction.[8]

A **swap** is a variation of a forward contract that is essentially equivalent to a series of forward contracts. Specifically, a swap is an agreement between two parties to exchange a series of future cash flows. Typically at least one of the two series of cash flows is determined by a later outcome. In other words, one party agrees to pay the other a series of cash flows whose value will be determined by the unknown future course of some underlying factor, such as an interest rate, exchange rate, stock price, or commodity price. The other party promises to make a series of payments that could also be determined by a second unknown factor or, alternatively, could be preset. We commonly refer to swap payments as being "fixed" or "floating" (sometimes "variable").

---

[6] Defaults are more likely for futures contracts than for forward contracts because participants in the forward markets must meet higher creditworthiness standards than those in the futures markets. Indeed, many individuals participate in the futures markets; forward market participants are usually large, creditworthy companies. But the forward markets have no guarantor of performance, while the futures markets do. Therefore, participants in the forward markets have incurred credit losses in the past, while participants in the futures markets have not.

[7] It is possible for the party engaging in the first transaction to engage in the second transaction with the same party. The two parties agree to cancel their transactions, settling the difference in value in cash and thereby eliminating the risk associated with exchange rates as well as the possibility of default.

[8] A common misconception is that, as a result of their standardized terms, futures contracts are liquid but nonstandardized forward contracts are illiquid. This is not always the case; many futures contracts have low liquidity and many forward contracts have high liquidity.

We noted that a forward contract is an agreement to buy or sell an underlying asset at a future date at a price agreed on today. A swap in which one party makes a single fixed payment and the other makes a single floating payment amounts to a forward contract. One party agrees to make known payments to the other and receive something unknown in return. This type of contract is like an agreement to buy at a future date, paying a fixed amount and receiving something of unknown future value. That the swap is a *series* of such payments distinguishes it from a forward contract, which is only a single payment.[9]

Swaps, like forward contracts, are private transactions and thus not subject to direct regulation.[10] Swaps are arguably the most successful of all derivative transactions. Probably the most common use of a swap is a situation in which a corporation, currently borrowing at a floating rate, enters into a swap that commits it to making a series of interest payments to the swap counterparty at a fixed rate, while receiving payments from the swap counterparty at a rate related to the floating rate at which it is making its loan payments. The floating components cancel, resulting in the effective conversion of the original **floating-rate loan** to a fixed-rate loan.

Forward commitments (whether forwards, futures, or swaps) are firm and binding agreements to engage in a transaction at a future date. They obligate each party to complete the transaction, or alternatively, to offset the transaction by engaging in another transaction that settles each party's financial obligation to the other. Contingent claims, on the other hand, allow one party the flexibility to not engage in the future transaction, depending on market conditions.

2.2 Contingent Claims

Contingent claims are derivatives in which the payoffs occur if a specific event happens. We generally refer to these types of derivatives as options. Specifically, an **option** is a financial instrument that gives one party the right, but not the obligation, to buy or sell an underlying asset from or to another party at a fixed price over a specific period of time. An option that gives the right to buy is referred to as a call; an option that gives the right to sell is referred to as a put. The fixed price at which the underlying can be bought or sold is called the exercise price, strike price, striking price, or strike, and is determined at the outset of the transaction. In this book, we refer to it as the exercise price, and the action of buying or selling the underlying at the exercise price is called exercising the option. The holder of the option has the right to exercise it and will do so if conditions are advantageous; otherwise, the option will expire unexercised. Thus, the payoff of the option is contingent on an event taking place, so options are sometimes referred to as contingent claims.

In contrast to participating in a forward or futures contract, which represents a *commitment* to buy or sell, owning an option represents the *right* to buy or sell. To acquire this right, the buyer of the option must pay a price at the start to the option seller. This price is called the **option premium** or sometimes just the option price. In this book, we usually refer to it as the option price.

Because the option buyer has the right to buy or sell an asset, the seller of the option has the potential commitment to sell or buy this asset. If the option

---

[9] A few other distinctions exist between swaps and forward contracts, such as the fact that swaps can involve both parties paying a variable amount.

[10] Like all over-the-counter derivatives transactions, swaps are subject to indirect regulatory oversight in that the companies using them could be regulated by securities or banking authorities. In addition, swaps, like all contracts, are subject to normal contract and civil law.

buyer has the right to buy, the option seller may be obligated to sell. If the option buyer has the right to sell, the option seller may be obligated to buy. As noted above, the option seller receives the amount of the option price from the option buyer for his willingness to bear this risk.

An important distinction we made between forward and futures contracts was that the former are customized private transactions between two parties without a guarantee against losses from default. The latter are standardized contracts that take place on futures exchanges and are guaranteed by the exchange against losses from default. For options, both types of contracts—over-the-counter customized and exchange-listed standardized—exist. In other words, the buyer and seller of an option can arrange their own terms and create an option contract. Alternatively, the buyer and seller can meet directly, or through their brokers, on an options exchange and trade standardized options. In the case of customized options, the buyer is subject to the possibility of the seller defaulting when and if the buyer decides to exercise the option. Because the option buyer is not obligated to do anything beyond paying the original price, the seller of any type of option is not subject to the buyer defaulting. In the case of a standardized option, the buyer does not face the risk of the seller defaulting. The exchange, through its clearinghouse, guarantees the seller's performance to the buyer.

A variety of other instruments contain options and thus are forms of contingent claims. For instance, many corporations issue convertible bonds offering the holder an optionlike feature that enables the holder to participate in gains on the market price of the corporation's stock without having to participate in losses on the stock. Callable bonds are another example of a common financial instrument that contains an option, in this case the option of the issuer to pay off the bond before its maturity. Options themselves are often characterized in terms of standard or fairly basic options and more advanced options, often referred to as exotic options. There are also options that are not even based on assets but rather on futures contracts or other derivatives. A very widely used group of options is based on interest rates.

Another common type of option is contained in asset-backed securities. An asset-backed security is a claim on a pool of securities. The pool, which might be mortgages, loans, or bonds, is a portfolio assembled by a financial institution that then sells claims on the portfolio. Often, the borrowers who issued the mortgages, loans, or bonds have the right to pay off their debts early, and many choose to do so when interest rates fall significantly. They then refinance their loans by taking out a new loan at a lower interest rate. This right, called a prepayment feature, is a valuable option owned by the borrower. Holders of asset-backed securities bear the risk associated with prepayment options and hence are sellers of those options. The holders, or option sellers, receive a higher promised yield on their bond investment than they would have received on an otherwise equivalent bond without the option.

With an understanding of derivatives, there are no limits to the types of financial instruments that can be constructed, analyzed, and applied to achieve investment objectives. What you learn from this book and the CFA Program will help you recognize and understand the variety of derivatives that appear in many forms in the financial world.

Exhibit 73-1 presents a classification of the types of derivative contracts as we have described them. Note that we have partitioned derivatives into those that are exchange-traded and those that trade in the over-the-counter market. The exhibit also notes some other categories not specifically mentioned above. These instruments are included for completeness, but they are relatively advanced and not covered in this first reading.

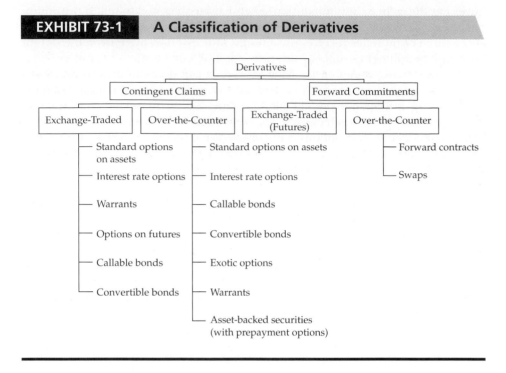

EXHIBIT 73-1   A Classification of Derivatives

We have now looked at the basic characteristics of derivative contracts. In order to better understand and appreciate derivatives, we should take a quick look at where they came from and where they are now. Accordingly, we take a brief look at the history and current state of derivative markets.

3   DERIVATIVE MARKETS: PAST AND PRESENT

Derivative markets have an exciting and colorful history. Examining that history gives insights that help us understand the structure of these markets as they exist today.

The basic characteristics of derivative contracts can be found throughout the history of humankind. Agreements to engage in a commercial transaction as well as agreements that provide the right to engage in a commercial transaction date back hundreds of years. In medieval times, contracts for the future delivery of an asset with the price fixed at the time of the contract initiation were frequent. Early indications of futures markets were seen in Japan many hundreds of years ago. The futures markets generally trace their roots, however, to the 1848 creation of the Chicago Board of Trade, the first organized futures market. Its origins resulted from the burgeoning grain markets in Chicago, which created a need for a farmer to secure a price at one point in time, store the grain, and deliver it at a later point in time. At around the same time, customized option transactions were being offered, including some by the well known financier Russell Sage, who found a clever way to offer combinations of customized options that replicated a loan at a rate that exceeded the maximum allowable rate under the then-existing usury laws.[11]

---

[11] Sage was perhaps the first options arbitrageur. Of course, usury laws are rare these days and most investors understand put–call parity, so do not expect to make any money copying Sage's scheme.

In the century that followed, the futures industry grew rapidly. Institutions such as the Chicago Board of Trade, the Chicago Mercantile Exchange, and later, the New York Mercantile Exchange and the Chicago Board Options Exchange became the primary forces in the global derivatives industry. These exchanges created and successfully marketed many innovative derivative contracts.[12] Although the first 100 years of futures exchanges were dominated by trading in futures on agricultural commodities, the 1970s saw the introduction of futures on financial instruments such as currencies, bonds, and stock indices. These "financial futures," as well as newly introduced options on individual stocks, currencies, bonds, and stock indices, ushered in a new era in which financial derivatives dominated agricultural derivatives—a situation that continues today. Although the commodity derivatives market includes very active contracts in oil and precious metals, financial derivatives have remained the primary force in the worldwide derivatives market.

Exchange-listed standardized derivatives, however, have hardly been the only instruments in the derivatives world. As noted, customized options have been around since at least the 19th century. The customized-options market flourished until the early 1970s, largely as a retail product. With the introduction of standardized options in 1973, however, the customized options market effectively died. But something else was going on at the time that would later revive this market. In the early 1970s, foreign exchange rates were deregulated and allowed to float freely. This deregulation led not only to the development of a futures, and later options, market for currencies but also to a market for customized forward contracts in foreign currencies. This market became known as the interbank market because it was largely operated within the global banking community, and it grew rapidly. Most importantly, it set the stage for the banking industry to engage in other customized derivative transactions.

Spurred by deregulation of their permitted activities during the 1980s, banks discovered that they could create derivatives of all forms and sell them to corporations and institutions that had risks that could best be managed with products specifically tailored for a given situation. These banks make markets in derivative products by assuming the risks that the corporations want to eliminate. But banks are not in the business of assuming unwanted risks. They use their vast resources and global networks to transfer or lay off the risk elsewhere, often in the futures markets. If they successfully lay off these risks, they can profit by buying and selling the derivatives at a suitable bid–ask spread. In addition to banks, investment banking firms also engage in derivatives transactions of this sort. The commercial and investment banks that make markets in derivatives are called **derivatives dealers**. Buying and selling derivatives is a natural extension of the activity these banks normally undertake in financial markets. This market for customized derivatives is what we refer to as the over-the-counter derivatives market.

By the end of the 20th century, the derivatives market reached a mature stage, growing at only a slow pace but providing a steady offering of existing products and a continuing slate of new products. Derivatives exchanges underwent numerous changes, often spurred by growing competition from the over-the-counter market. Some merged; others that were formerly nonprofit corporations have since become profit making. Some derivatives exchanges have even experimented with offering somewhat customized transactions. Nearly all have lobbied heavily for a reduction in the level or structure of the regulations imposed on them. Some derivatives exchanges have altered the manner in which trading takes place, from the old system of face to face on a trading floor (in sections called pits) to off-floor electronic trading in which participants communicate

---

[12] It is probably also important to note that the futures and options exchanges have introduced many unsuccessful contracts as well.

through computer screens. This type of transacting, called electronic trading, has even been extended to the Internet and, not surprisingly, is called e-trading. Pit trading is still the primary format for derivatives exchanges in the United States, but electronic trading is clearly the wave of the future. As the dominant form of trading outside the United States, it will likely replace pit trading in the United States in coming years.

Exhibit 73-2 lists all global derivatives exchanges as of January 2002. Note that almost every country with a reasonably advanced financial market system has a derivatives exchange.

EXHIBIT 73-2   Global Derivatives Exchanges

North America
American Stock Exchange
Bourse de Montreal
BrokerTec Futures Exchange
Chicago Board Options Exchange
Chicago Board of Trade
Chicago Mercantile Exchange
International Securities Exchange
   (New York)
Kansas City Board of Trade
Minneapolis Grain Exchange
New York Board of Trade
New York Mercantile Exchange
Pacific Exchange (San Francisco)
Philadelphia Stock Exchange
Winnipeg Commodity Exchange

Asia
Central Japan Commodity Exchange
Dalian Commodity Exchange
Hong Kong Exchanges & Clearing
Kansai Commodities Exchange (Osaka)
Korea Futures Exchange
Korea Stock Exchange
Malaysia Derivatives Exchange
New Zealand Futures & Options
   Exchange
Osaka Mercantile Exchange
Shanghai Futures Exchange
Singapore Commodity Exchange
Singapore Exchange
Tokyo Commodity Exchange
Tokyo Grain Exchange
Tokyo International Financial Futures
   Exchange
Tokyo Stock Exchange
Zhengzhou Commodity Exchange

Europe
Bolsa de Valores de Lisboa e Porto
Borsa Italiana
Budapest Commodity Exchange
Eurex Frankfurt
Eurex Zurich
Euronext Amsterdam
Euronext Brussels
Euronext Paris
FUTOP Market (Copenhagen)
Helsinki Exchanges Group
International Petroleum Exchange of
   London
London International Financial Futures
   and Options Exchange
London Metal Exchange
MEFF Renta Fija (Barcelona)
MEFF Renta Variable (Madrid)
OM London Exchange
OM Stockholm Exchange
Romanian Commodity Exchange
Sibiu Monetary–Financial and
   Commodities Exchange (Romania)
Tel Aviv Stock Exchange
Wiener Borse AG (Vienna)

South America
Bolsa de Mercadorias & Futuros
   (Sao Paulo)
Mercado a Termino de Buenos Aires
Santiago Stock Exchange

Africa
South African Futures Exchange

Australia
Australian Stock Exchange
Sydney Futures Exchange

Source: Futures [magazine] *2002 Sourcebook.*

We cannot technically identify where over-the-counter derivatives markets exist. These types of transactions can conceivably occur anywhere two parties can agree to engage in a transaction. It is generally conceded, however, that London and New York are the primary markets for over-the-counter derivatives; considerable activity also takes place in Tokyo, Paris, Frankfurt, Chicago, Amsterdam, and many other major world cities.

Now we know where the derivative markets are, but are they big enough for us to care about? We examine this question in Section 4.

HOW BIG IS THE DERIVATIVES MARKET?   4

Good question. And the answer is: We really do not know. Because trading in exchange-listed contracts, such as futures and some options, is recorded, volume figures for those types of contracts are available. Exhibit 73-3 presents summary statistics for contract volume of global futures and options for 2000 and 2001. Note that in 2001, the largest category is equity indices. In 2000, the largest category was individual equities, followed by interest rates. In prior years, the largest category had been interest rates.

Currently, the United States accounts for approximately 35 percent of global futures and options volume. The largest exchange in the world, however, is the Korea Stock Exchange, which trades an exceptionally large volume of options on a Korean stock index. The second-largest exchange (and the largest exchange in terms of futures volume only) is the combined German–Swiss exchange called Eurex. The other largest exchanges (in order of 2001 volume) are the Chicago Mercantile Exchange, the Chicago Board of Trade, the London International Financial Futures and Options Exchange, the Paris Bourse, the New York Mercantile Exchange, the Bolsa de Mercadorias & Futuros of Brazil, and the Chicago Board Options Exchange. All of these exchanges traded at least 70 million contracts in 2001.[13]

EXHIBIT 73-3	Global Exchange-Traded Futures and Options Contract Volume (in millions of contracts)	
Contract Type	2000	2001
Equity indices	674.8	1,470.3
Interest rates	844.3	1,216.1
Individual equities	969.7	1,112.7
Energy	154.8	166.9
Agricultural	185.7	156.5
Nonprecious metals	75.7	70.2
Currencies	47.0	49.2
Precious metals	36.2	39.1
Other	1.3	0.8
Overall Total	2,989.5	4,281.8

Source: Futures Industry (January/February 2002).

---

[13] *Futures Industry* (January/February 2002).

One important factor that must be considered, however, in looking at trading volume as a measure of activity is that the futures and options exchanges influence their own volume by designating a contract's size. For example, a standard option in the United States covers 100 shares of the underlying stock. If an investor takes a position in options on 1,000 shares of stock, the investor would trade 10 options. If the options exchange had designated that the contract size be 200 options, then the investor would trade only five contracts. Although there are often good reasons for setting a contract size at a certain level, volume comparisons must be taken with a degree of skepticism.[14]

The over-the-counter derivatives market is much more difficult to measure. Because the transactions are private, unregulated, and can take place virtually anywhere two parties can enter into an agreement, no official tabulation exists that allows us to identify the size of the market. Information is available, however, from semiannual surveys conducted by the Bank for International Settlements (BIS) of Basel, Switzerland, an international organization of central banks. The BIS publishes this data in its semiannual report "Regular OTC Derivatives Market Statistics," available on its website at www.bis.org/publ/regpubl.htm.

Exhibit 73-4 presents two charts constructed from the 30 June 2001 BIS survey and shows figures for foreign exchange, interest rate, equity, and commodity derivatives transactions. The "other" category, however, does include transactions of these types and reflects the BIS's estimates of positions taken by parties that do not report in this survey. It is used primarily to obtain an estimate for the overall size of the market and is not broken down by category.

For over-the-counter derivatives, notional principal is the most widely used measure of market size. Notional principal measures the amount of the underlying asset covered by a derivative contract. For example, a swap involving interest payments on ¥500 million has a notional principal of ¥500 million. The actual payments made in the swap, however, are merely interest payments on ¥500 million and do not come close to ¥500 million.[15] Thus, although notional principal is a commonly used measure of the size of the market, it can give a misleading impression by suggesting that it reflects the amount of money involved.[16]

Nonetheless, we would be remiss if we failed to note the market size as measured by notional principal. Based on Exhibit 73-4A, the total notional principal summing over these five categories is almost $100 trillion. Also note that interest rate derivatives are the most widely used category by far.

Exhibit 73-4B gives another picture of the size of the market by indicating the market value of over-the-counter derivatives. Market value indicates the

---

[14] For example, in 1999 the volume of Treasury bond futures on the Chicago Board of Trade was about 90 million contracts while the volume of Eurodollar futures on the Chicago Mercantile Exchange was about 93 million contracts. Consequently, at that time these two contracts appeared to have about the same amount of activity. But the Treasury bond contract covers Treasury bonds with a face value of $100,000 while the Eurodollar contract covers Eurodollars with a face value of $1,000,000. Thus, the Eurodollar futures market was arguably 10 times the size of the Treasury bond futures market. In 2002, about three Eurodollar futures contracts were traded for every Treasury bond futures contract traded.

[15] In fact, the payments on a swap are even smaller than the interest payments on the notional principal. Swap interest payments usually equal only the difference between the interest payments owed by the two parties.

[16] The over-the-counter derivatives industry originally began the practice of measuring its size by notional principal. This was a deliberate tactic designed to make the industry look larger so it would be more noticed and viewed as a significant and legitimate force. As it turns out, this tactic backfired, resulting in fears that more money was involved and at risk of loss than really was. Calls for increased scrutiny of the industry by government authorities resulted in the industry backpedaling on its use of notional principal and focusing more on market value as a measure of its size. Nonetheless, notional principal continues to be used as one, if not the primary, measure of the industry's size.

EXHIBIT 73-4A	Outstanding Notional Principal of Global Over-the-Counter Derivatives, 30 June 2001 (billions)

Notional Principal (billions of $)

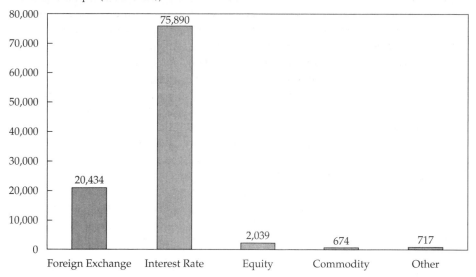

Source: Bank for International Settlements, www.bis.org/publ/regpubl.htm

EXHIBIT 73-4B	Outstanding Market Value of Global Over-the-Counter Derivatives, 30 June 2001 (billions)

Market Value (billions of $)

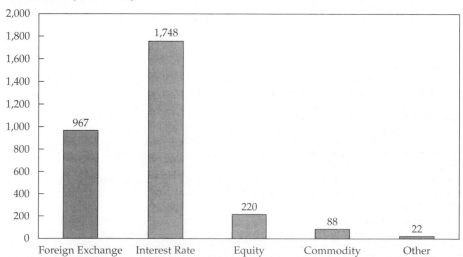

Source: Bank for International Settlements, www.bis.org/publ/regpubl.htm

economic worth of a derivative contract and represents the amount of money that would change hands if these transactions were terminated at the time of the report. The total market value for all categories is about $3 trillion. Market value is a better indication of the size of the market because it more accurately represents the actual money involved. Nonetheless, market value is subject to greater errors in estimation and thus is a less reliable measure than notional principal.

Although it is impossible to determine where these contracts originate, dollar-denominated derivatives represented about 34 percent of the global interest rate derivatives market in 2001, with euro-denominated derivatives accounting for about 27 percent and yen-denominated derivatives representing 17 percent.

Whether notional principal or market value is used, it is clear that the derivatives industry is large by any standard. Derivatives are widely available in global asset markets, and consequently, understanding derivatives is essential to operating in these markets, whether one chooses to use them or not.

Because derivative markets have been created around the world, there must be a reason for their continued existence. Let us now look at why derivative markets exist.

5   THE PURPOSES OF DERIVATIVE MARKETS

Derivative markets serve a variety of purposes in global social and economic systems. One of the primary functions of futures markets is **price discovery.** Futures markets provide valuable information about the prices of the underlying assets on which futures contracts are based. They provide this information in two ways. First, many of these assets are traded in geographically dispersed markets. Recall that the current price of the underlying asset is called the spot price. With geographically dispersed markets, many different spot prices could exist. In the futures markets, the price of the contract with the shortest **time to expiration** often serves as a proxy for the price of the underlying asset. Second, the prices of all futures contracts serve as prices that can be accepted by those who trade contracts in lieu of facing the risk of uncertain future prices. For example, a company that mines gold can hedge by selling a futures contract on gold expiring in two months, which locks in the price of gold two months later. In this manner, the two-month futures price substitutes for the uncertainty of the price of gold over the next two months.[17]

Futures contracts are not, however, the only derivatives that serve this purpose. In fact, forward contracts and swaps allow users to substitute a single locked-in price for the uncertainty of future spot prices and thereby permit the same form of price discovery as do futures.

Options work in a slightly different manner. They are used in a different form of hedging, one that permits the holder to protect against loss while allowing participation in gains if prices move favorably. Options do not so much reveal *prices* as they reveal *volatility*. As we shall see in Reading 76, the volatility of the underlying asset is a critical factor in the pricing of options. It is possible, therefore, to infer what investors feel about volatility from the prices of options.

---

[17] Some people view futures prices as revealing expectations of future spot prices of the underlying asset, and in that sense, leading to price discovery. This view, however, is incorrect. Futures prices are not necessarily expectations of future spot prices. As we discussed above, they allow a substitution of the futures price for the uncertainty of future spot prices of the asset. In that sense they permit the acceptance of a sure price and the avoidance of risk.

Perhaps the most important purpose of derivative markets is **risk management.** We define risk management as the process of identifying the desired level of risk, identifying the actual level of risk, and altering the latter to equal the former. Often this process is described as hedging, which generally refers to the reduction, and in some cases the elimination, of risk. On the other side is the process called speculation. Traditional discussions of derivatives refer to hedging and speculation as complementary activities. In general, hedgers seek to eliminate risk and need speculators to assume risk, but such is not always the case. Hedgers often trade with other hedgers, and speculators often trade with other speculators. All one needs to hedge or speculate is a party with opposite beliefs or opposite risk exposure. For example, a corporation that mines gold could hedge the future sale of gold by entering into a derivative transaction with a company that manufactures jewelry. Both of these companies are hedgers, seeking to avoid the uncertainty of future gold prices by locking in a price for a future transaction. The mining corporation has concerns about a price decrease, and the jewelry manufacturer is worried about a price increase.

An unfortunate consequence of the use of the terms "hedging" and "speculating" is that hedgers are somehow seen as on the high moral ground and speculators are sometimes seen as evil—a distortion of the role of speculators. In fact, there need be very little difference between hedgers and speculators. To restate an example we used when discussing swaps, consider a corporation that currently borrows at a floating rate. A common response to a fear of rising interest rates is for the corporation to use an interest rate swap in which it will make payments at a fixed rate and receive payments at a floating rate. The floating-rate payments it receives from the swap offset the floating-rate payments on the loan, thereby effectively converting the loan to a fixed-rate loan. The company is now borrowing at a fixed rate and, in the eyes of many, hedging.

But is the company really hedging? Or is it simply making a bet that interest rates will increase? If interest rates decrease, the company will be losing money in the sense of the lost opportunity to borrow at a lower rate. From a budgeting and cash flow standpoint, however, its fixed interest payments are set in stone. Moreover, the market value of a fixed-rate loan is considerably more volatile than that of a floating-rate loan. Thus, our "hedging" corporation can be viewed as taking more risk than it originally had.

The more modern view of the reason for using derivatives does not refer to hedging or speculation. Although we shall sometimes use those terms, we shall use them carefully and make our intentions clear. In the grander scheme of things, derivatives are tools that enable companies to more easily practice risk management. In the context of our corporation borrowing at the floating rate, it made a conscious decision to borrow at a fixed rate. Engaging in the swap is simply an activity designed to align its risk with the risk it wants, given its outlook for interest rates. Whether one calls this activity hedging or speculation is not even very important. The company is simply managing risk.

Derivative markets serve several other useful purposes. As we show later when exploring the pricing of derivative contracts, they improve market efficiency for the underlying assets. Efficient markets are fair and competitive and do not allow one party to easily take money from another. As a simple example, buying a stock index fund can be replicated by buying a futures on the fund and investing in risk-free bonds with the money that otherwise would have been spent on the fund. In other words, the fund and the combination of the futures and risk-free bond will have the same performance. But if the fund costs more than the combination of the futures and risk-free bond, investors have the opportunity to avoid the overpriced fund and take the combination.[18] This decreased demand for the fund will lower its price. The benefits to investors who do not even use derivatives should be clear: They can now invest in the fund at a more attractive price, because the derivatives market forced the price back to its appropriate level.

Derivative markets are also characterized by relatively low transaction costs. For example, the cost of investing in a stock index portfolio is as much as 20 times the cost of buying a futures contract on the index and a risk-free bond as described above. One might reasonably ask why derivatives are so much less expensive in terms of transaction costs. The answer is that derivatives are designed to provide a means of managing risk. As we have previously described, they serve as a form of insurance. Insurance cannot be a viable product if its cost is too high relative to the value of the insured asset. In other words, derivatives must have low transaction costs; otherwise, they would not exist.

It would be remiss to overlook the fact that derivative markets have been subject to many criticisms. We next present some of these complaints and the reasons behind them.

6   CRITICISMS OF DERIVATIVE MARKETS

Derivatives have been highly controversial for a number of reasons. For one, they are very complex. Much of the criticism has stemmed from a failure to understand derivatives. When derivatives fail to do their job, it is often the derivatives themselves, rather than the users of derivatives, that take the blame. Yet, in many cases, the critics of derivatives simply do not understand them well enough. As described in Section 2, when homeowners take out mortgages, they usually receive a valuable option: the right to prepay their mortgages. When interest rates fall, homeowners often pay off their mortgages, refinancing them at lower rates. The holders of these mortgages usually sell them to other parties, which can include small organizations and individuals. Thus, we often find unsophisticated investors holding securities based on the payments from mortgages. When homeowners refinance, they capture huge interest savings. Where does this money come from? It comes from the pockets of the holders of mortgage securities. When these unsophisticated investors lose a lot of money, derivatives usually get the blame. Yet these losses went into the pockets of homeowners in the form of interest savings. Who is to blame? Probably the brokers, who sold the securities to investors who did not know what they were buying—which leads us to the next common criticism of derivatives.

The complexity of derivatives means that sometimes the parties that use them do not understand them well. As a result, they are often used improperly, leading to potentially large losses. Such an argument can, however, be used to describe fire, electricity, and chemicals. Used improperly, perhaps in the hands of a child or someone who does not know how to use them, all of these can be extremely dangerous. Yet, we know that sufficient knowledge of fire, electricity, and chemicals to use them properly is not very difficult to obtain. The same is true for derivatives; treat them with respect and healthy doses of knowledge.

Derivatives are also mistakenly characterized as a form of legalized gambling. Although gambling is certainly legal in many parts of the world, derivatives

---

[18] Some investors, called arbitrageurs, will even find ways to sell the fund short to eliminate the risk of holding the futures and the bond, earning a profit from any discrepancy in their prices. We shall cover this type of transaction later in this reading.

are often viewed as a government's sanction of gambling via the financial markets. But there is an important distinction between gambling and derivatives: The benefits of derivatives extend much further across society. By providing a means of managing risk along with the other benefits discussed above, derivatives make financial markets work better. The organized gambling industry affects the participants, the owners of casinos, and perhaps some citizens who benefit from state lotteries. Organized gambling does not, however, make society function better, and it arguably incurs social costs.

We have taken a look at what derivatives are, where they come from, where they are now, why we have them, and what people think of them. Understanding derivatives, however, requires a basic understanding of the market forces that govern derivative prices. Although we shall cover derivative pricing in more detail in later readings, here we take a brief look at the process of pricing derivatives by examining some important fundamental principles.

ELEMENTARY PRINCIPLES OF DERIVATIVE PRICING

7

In this section, we take a preliminary glance at how derivative contracts are priced. First, we introduce the concept of **arbitrage.** Arbitrage occurs when equivalent assets or combinations of assets sell for two different prices. This situation creates an opportunity to profit at no risk with no commitment of money. Let us start with the simplest (and least likely) opportunity for arbitrage: the case of a stock selling for more than one price at a given time. Assume that a stock is trading in two markets simultaneously. Suppose the stock is trading at $100 in one market and $98 in the other market. We simply buy a share for $98 in one market and immediately sell it for $100 in the other. We have no net position in the stock, so it does not matter what price the stock moves to. We make an easy $2 at no risk and we did not have to put up any funds of our own. The sale of the stock at $100 was more than adequate to finance the purchase of the stock at $98. Naturally, many market participants would do this, which would create downward pressure on the price of the stock in the market where it trades for $100 and upward pressure on the price of the stock in the market where it trades for $98. Eventually the two prices must come together so that there is but a single price for the stock. Accordingly, the principle that no arbitrage opportunities should be available is often referred to as the **law of one price.**

Recall that we mentioned in Section 5 that an asset can potentially trade in different geographic markets and, therefore, have several spot prices. This potential would appear to violate the law of one price, but in reality, the law is still upheld. A given asset selling in two different locations is not necessarily the same asset. If a buyer in one location discovered that it is possible to buy the asset more cheaply in another location, the buyer would still have to incur the cost of moving the asset to the buyer's location. Transportation costs could offset any such price differences.[19]

Now suppose we face the situation illustrated in Exhibit 73-5. In Exhibit 73-5A, observe that we have one stock, AXE Electronics, which today is worth $50 and which, one period later, will be worth either $75 or $40. We shall denote these

---

[19] One might reasonably wonder if finding a consumer article selling in Wal-Mart at a lower price than in Target is not a violation of the law of one price. It certainly is, but we make no claim that the market for consumer products is efficient. Our focus is on the financial markets where, for example, Goldman Sachs can hardly offer shares of IBM at one price while Merrill Lynch offers them at another.

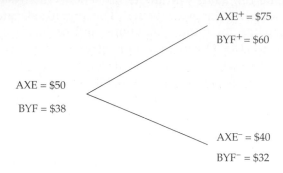

| EXHIBIT 73-5A | Arbitrage Opportunity with Stock AXE, Stock BYF, and a Risk-Free Bond |

$AXE^+ = \$75$

$BYF^+ = \$60$

$AXE = \$50$

$BYF = \$38$

$AXE^- = \$40$

$BYF^- = \$32$

Note: The risk-free rate is 4 percent.

| EXHIBIT 73-5B | Execution of Arbitrage Transaction with Stock AXE, Stock BYF, and a Risk-Free Bond |

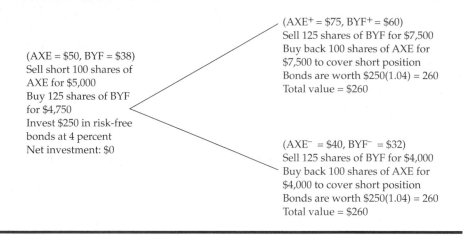

$(AXE = \$50, BYF = \$38)$
Sell short 100 shares of
AXE for \$5,000
Buy 125 shares of BYF
for \$4,750
Invest \$250 in risk-free
bonds at 4 percent
Net investment: \$0

$(AXE^+ = \$75, BYF^+ = \$60)$
Sell 125 shares of BYF for \$7,500
Buy back 100 shares of AXE for
\$7,500 to cover short position
Bonds are worth \$250(1.04) = 260
Total value = \$260

$(AXE^- = \$40, BYF^- = \$32)$
Sell 125 shares of BYF for \$4,000
Buy back 100 shares of AXE for
\$4,000 to cover short position
Bonds are worth \$250(1.04) = 260
Total value = \$260

prices as $AXE = 50$, $AXE^+ = 75$, and $AXE^- = 40$. Another stock, BYF Technology, is today worth \$38 and one period later will be worth \$60 or \$32. Thus, $BYF = 38$, $BYF^+ = 60$, and $BYF^- = 32$. Let us assume the risk-free borrowing and lending rate is 4 percent. We assume no dividends on either stock during the period covered by this example.

The opportunity exists to make a profit at no risk without committing any of our funds, as demonstrated in Exhibit 73-5B. Suppose we borrow 100 shares of stock AXE, which is selling for \$50, and sell short, thereby receiving \$5,000. We take \$4,750 and purchase 125 shares of stock BYF. We invest the remaining \$250 in risk-free bonds at 4 percent. This transaction will not require us to put up any funds of our own: The short sale will be sufficient to fund the investment in BYF and leave money to invest in risk-free bonds.

If the top outcome in Exhibit 73-5 occurs, we sell the 125 shares of BYF for $125 \times \$60 = \$7,500$. This amount is sufficient to buy back the 100 shares of AXE, which is selling for \$75. But we will also have the bonds, which are worth

$250 × 1.04 = $260. If the bottom outcome occurs, we sell the 125 shares of BYF for 125 × $32 = $4,000—enough money to buy back the 100 shares of AXE, which is selling for $40. Again, we will have the risk-free bonds, worth $260. Regardless of the outcome, we end up with $260.

Recall that we put up no money of our own and ended up with a sure $260. It should be apparent that this is an extremely attractive transaction, so everyone would do it. The combined actions of multiple investors would drive down the price of AXE and/or drive up the price of BYF until an equilibrium was reached at which this transaction would not be profitable. Assuming stock BYF's price remained constant, stock AXE would fall to $47.50. Or assuming stock AXE's price remained constant, stock BYF would rise to $40.

Of course, this example is extremely simplified. Clearly a stock price can change to more than two other prices. Also, if a given stock is at one price, another stock may be at any other price. We have created a simple case here to illustrate a point. But as you will learn in Reading 76, when derivatives are involved, the simplification here is relatively safe. In fact, it is quite appropriate.

Now we look at another type of arbitrage opportunity, which involves a forward contract and will establish an appropriate price for the forward contract. Let stock AXE sell for $50. We borrow $50 at 4 percent interest by issuing a risk-free bond, use the money to buy one share of stock AXE, and simultaneously enter into a forward contract to sell this share at a price of $54 one period later. The stock will then move to either $75 or $40 in the next period; the forward contract will require that we deliver the stock and accept $54 for it; and we shall owe $50 × 1.04 = $52 on the loan.

Let us look at the two outcomes. Suppose stock AXE goes to $75. We deliver the stock to settle the obligation on the forward contract and receive $54 for it. We use $52 of the $54 to pay back the loan, leaving a gain of $2. Now suppose AXE goes to $40. We deliver the stock, fulfilling the obligation of the forward contract, and receive $54. Again, we use $52 of the $54 to pay back the loan, leaving a gain of $2.

In either case we made $2, free and clear. In fact, we can even accommodate the possibility of more than two future prices for AXE. The key point is that we faced no risk and did not have to put up any of our own money, but we ended up with $2—clearly a good deal. In fact, this is what we would call an arbitrage profit. But from where did it originate?

It turns out that the forward price we received, $54, was an inappropriate price given current market conditions. In fact, it was just an arbitrary price, made up to illustrate the point. To eliminate the opportunity to earn the $2 profit, the forward price should be $52—equal, not coincidentally, to the amount owed on the loan. It is also no coincidence that $52 is the price of the asset increased by the rate of interest. We will discuss this point further in Reading 74.

In this example, many market participants would do this transaction as long it generates an arbitrage profit. These forces of arbitrage would either force the forward price down or force the price of the stock up until an equilibrium is reached that eliminates the opportunity to profit at no risk with no commitment of one's own funds.

We have just had a taste of not only the powerful forces of arbitrage but also a pricing model for one derivative, the forward contract. In this simple example, according to the pricing model, the forward price should be the spot price increased by the interest rate. Although there is a lot more to derivative pricing than shown here, the basic principle remains the same regardless of the type of instrument or the complexity of the setting: *Prices are set to eliminate the opportunity to profit at no risk with no commitment of one's own funds.* There are no opportunities for arbitrage profits.

Lest we be too naive, however, we must acknowledge that there is a large industry of arbitrageurs. So how can such an industry exist if there are no opportunities for riskless profit? One explanation is that most of the arbitrage transactions are more complex than this simple example and involve estimating information, which can result in differing opinions. Arbitrage involving options, for example, usually requires estimates of a stock's volatility. Different participants have different opinions about this volatility. It is quite possible that two counterparties trading with each other can believe that each is arbitraging against the other.

But more importantly, the absence of arbitrage opportunities is upheld, ironically, only if participants believe that arbitrage opportunities *do* exist. If market traders believe that no opportunities exist to earn arbitrage profits, then they will not follow market prices and compare these prices with what they ought to be, as in the forward contract example given above. Without participants watching closely, prices would surely get out of line and offer arbitrage opportunities. Thus, eliminating arbitrage opportunities requires that participants be vigilant to arbitrage opportunities. In other words, strange as it may sound, disbelief and skepticism concerning the absence of arbitrage opportunities are required in order that it hold as a legitimate principle.

Markets in which arbitrage opportunities are either nonexistent or are quickly eliminated are relatively efficient markets. Recall from your study of portfolio theory and investment analysis that efficient markets are those in which it is not possible, except by chance, to earn returns in excess of those that would be fair compensation for the risk assumed. Although abnormal returns can be earned in a variety of ways, arbitrage profits are definitely examples of abnormal returns, relatively obvious to identify and easy to capture. Thus, they are the most egregious violations of the principle of market efficiency. A market in which arbitrage profits do not exist is one in which the most obvious violations of market efficiency have been eliminated.

Throughout this study session, we shall study derivatives by using the principle of arbitrage as a guide. We will assume that arbitrage opportunities cannot exist for any significant length of time. Thus, prices must conform to models that assume no arbitrage. On the other hand, we do not want to take the absence of arbitrage opportunities so seriously that we give up and believe that arbitrage opportunities never exist. Otherwise, they will arise, and someone else will take them from us.

We have now completed this introductory reading, which has touched only lightly on the world of derivatives. The remainder of the study session is organized as follows: Reading 74 on forwards, Reading 75 on futures, Reading 76 on options, and Reading 77 on swaps provide details describing the types of instruments and how they are priced, Reading 78 is on options. We now proceed to Reading 74, which looks at forward markets and contracts.

SUMMARY

- A derivative contract is a financial instrument with a return that is obtained from or "derived" from the return of another underlying financial instrument.

- Exchange-traded derivatives are created, authorized, and traded on a derivatives exchange, an organized facility for trading derivatives. Exchange-traded derivatives are standardized instruments with respect to certain terms and conditions of the contract. They trade in accordance with rules and specifications prescribed by the derivatives exchange and are usually subject to governmental regulation. Exchange-traded derivatives are guaranteed by the exchange against loss resulting from the default of one of the parties. Over-the-counter derivatives are transactions created by any two parties off of a derivatives exchange. The parties set all of their own terms and conditions, and each assumes the credit risk of the other party.

- A forward commitment is an agreement between two parties in which one party agrees to buy and the other agrees to sell an asset at a future date at a price agreed on today. The three types of forward commitments are forward contracts, futures contracts, and swaps.

- A forward contract is a forward commitment created in the over-the-counter market. A futures contract is a forward commitment created and traded on a futures exchange. A swap is an over-the-counter transaction consisting of a series of forward commitments.

- A contingent claim is a derivative contract with a payoff dependent on the occurrence of a future event. The primary types of contingent claims are options, but other types involve variations of options, often combined with other financial instruments or derivatives.

- An option is a derivative contract giving one party the right to buy or sell an underlying asset at a fixed price over a period of time or at a specific point in time. The party obtaining the right pays a premium (the option price) at the start and receives the right to buy or sell, as prescribed by the contract. The two types of options are a call (the right to buy) and a put (the right to sell).

- The size of the global derivatives market can be measured by notional principal, which is the amount of the underlying on which a derivative is based, and by market value, which is the economic worth of the derivative.

- Derivative markets serve many useful purposes such as providing price discovery, facilitating risk management, making markets more efficient, and lowering transaction costs. Derivatives are often criticized as being excessively dangerous for unknowledgeable investors and have been inappropriately likened to gambling.

- Arbitrage is a process through which an investor can buy an asset or combination of assets at one price and concurrently sell at a higher price, thereby earning a profit without investing any money or being exposed to any risk. The combined actions of many investors engaging in arbitrage results in rapid price adjustments that eliminate these opportunities, thereby bringing prices back in line and making markets more efficient.

PROBLEMS FOR READING 73

1. For all parties involved, which of the following financial instruments is NOT an example of a forward commitment?

   A. Swap

   B. Call option

   C. Futures contract

   D. Forward contract

2. The main risk faced by an individual who enters into a forward contract to buy the S&P 500 Index is that

   A. the market may rise.

   B. the market may fall.

   C. market volatility may rise.

   D. market volatility may fall.

3. Which of the following statements is *most* accurate?

   A. Futures contracts are private transactions.

   B. Forward contracts are marked to market daily.

   C. Futures contracts have more default risk than forward contracts.

   D. Forward contracts require that both parties to the transaction have a high degree of creditworthiness.

4. Which of the following statements is *least* accurate?

   A. Futures contracts are easier to offset than forward contracts.

   B. Forward contracts are generally more liquid than futures contracts.

   C. Forward contracts are easier to tailor to specific needs than futures contracts.

   D. Futures contracts are characterized by having a clearinghouse as an intermediary.

5. A swap is *best* characterized as a

   A. series of forward contracts.

   B. derivative contract that has not gained widespread popularity.

   C. single fixed payment in exchange for a single floating payment.

   D. contract that is binding on only one of the parties to the transaction.

6. Which of the following is *most* representative of forward contracts and contingent claims?

	Forward Contracts	Contingent Claims
A.	Premium paid at inception	Premium paid at inception
B.	Premium paid at inception	No premium paid at inception
C.	No premium paid at inception	Premium paid at inception
D.	No premium paid at inception	No premium paid at inception

7. For the **long position,** the *most likely* advantage of contingent claims over forward commitments is that contingent claims

   A. are easier to offset than forward commitments.

   B. have lower default risk than forward commitments.

   C. permit gains while protecting against losses.

   D. are typically cheaper to initiate than forward commitments.

8. For derivative contracts, the notional principal is *best* described as

   A. the amount of the underlying asset covered by the contract.

   B. a measure of the actual payments made and received in the contract.

   C. tending to underestimate the actual payments made and received in the contract.

   D. being, conceptually and in aggregate, the best available measure of the size of the market.

9. By volume, the most widely used group of derivatives is the one with contracts written on which of the following types of underlying assets?

   A. Financial

   B. Commodities

   C. Energy-related

   D. Precious metals

10. Which of the following is *least* likely to be a purpose served by derivative markets?

    A. Arbitrage

    B. Price discovery

    C. Risk management

    D. Hedging and speculation

11. The *most likely* reason derivative markets have flourished is that

    A. derivatives are easy to understand and use.

    B. derivatives have relatively low transaction costs.

    C. the pricing of derivatives is relatively straightforward.

    D. strong regulation ensures that transacting parties are protected from fraud.

12. If the risk-free rate of interest is 5 percent and an investor enters into a transaction that has no risk, the rate of return the investor should earn in the absence of arbitrage opportunities is

    A. 0%.

    B. between 0% and 5%.

    C. 5%.

    D. more than 5%.

13. If the spot price of gold is $250 per ounce and the risk-free rate of interest is 10 percent per annum, the six-month forward price per ounce of gold, in equilibrium, should be *closest* to

    A. $250.00.

    B. $256.25.

    C. $262.50.

    D. $275.00.

14. Concerning efficient financial (including derivative) markets, the *most appropriate* description is that

    A. it is often possible to earn abnormal returns.

    B. the law of one price holds only in the academic literature.

    C. arbitrage opportunities rarely exist and are quickly eliminated.

    D. arbitrage opportunities often exist and can be exploited for profit.

15. Stock A costs $10.00 today and its price will be either $7.50 or $12.50 next period. Stock B's price will be either $18.00 or $30.00 next period. If risk-free borrowing and lending are possible at 8 percent per period, neither stock pays dividends, and it is possible to buy and sell fractional shares, Stock B's equilibrium price today should be *closest* to

  A. $19.00.

  B. $21.00.

  C. $24.00.

  D. $26.00.

stocks proportionate to its weighting in the index. Consequently, cash settlement is much more practical. Cash-settled forward contracts are sometimes called **NDFs**, for **nondeliverable forwards**, although this term is used predominately with respect to foreign exchange forwards.

1.2 Default Risk and Forward Contracts

An important characteristic of forward contracts is that they are subject to default. Regardless of whether the contract is for delivery or cash settlement, the potential exists for a party to default. In the zero-coupon bond example above, the long might be unable to pay the $98 or the short might be unable to buy the zero-coupon bond and make delivery of the bond to the long. Generally speaking, however, forward contracts are structured so that only the party owing the greater amount can default. In other words, if the short is obligated to deliver a zero-coupon bond selling for more than $98, then the long would not be obligated to make payment unless the short makes delivery. Likewise, in a cash settled contract, only one party—the one owing the greater amount—can default. We discuss the nature of this credit risk in the following section and in Section 5 after we have determined how to value forward contracts.

1.3 Termination of a Forward Contract

Let us note that a forward contract is nearly always constructed with the idea that the participants will hold on to their positions until the contract expires and either engage in delivery of the asset or settle the cash equivalent, as required in the specific contract. The possibility exists, however, that at least one of the participants might wish to terminate the position prior to expiration. For example, suppose a party goes long, meaning that she agrees to buy the asset at the expiration date at the price agreed on at the start, but she subsequently decides to terminate the contract before expiration. We shall assume that the contract calls for delivery rather than cash settlement at expiration.

To see the details of the contract termination, suppose it is part of the way through the life of the contract, and the long decides that she no longer wishes to buy the asset at expiration. She can then re-enter the market and create a new forward contract expiring at the same time as the original forward contract, taking the position of the seller instead. Because of price changes in the market during the period since the original contract was created, this new contract would likely have a different price at which she would have to commit to sell. She would then be long a contract to buy the asset at expiration at one price and short a contract to sell the asset at expiration at a different price. It should be apparent that she has no further exposure to the price of the asset.

For example, suppose she is long to buy at $40 and short to deliver at $42. Depending on the characteristics of the contract, one of several possibilities could occur at expiration. Everything could go as planned—the party holding the short position of the contract on which she is long at $40 delivers the asset to her, and she pays him $40. She then delivers the asset to the party who is long the contract on which she is short at $42. That party pays her $42. She nets $2. The transaction is over.

There is always a possibility that her counterparty on the long contract could default. She is still obligated to deliver the asset on the short contract, for which she will receive $42. But if her counterparty on the long contract defaults, she has to buy the asset in the market and could suffer a significant loss. There is also a possibility that the counterparty on her short contract could fail to pay her the $42. Of course, she would then not deliver the asset but would be exposed to the risk of changes in the asset's price. This type of problem illustrates the credit risk in a forward contract. We shall cover credit risk in more detail in Section 5 of this reading.

To avoid the credit risk, when she re-enters the market to go short the forward contract, she could contact the same counterparty with whom she engaged in the long forward contract. They could agree to cancel both contracts. Because she would be owed $2 at expiration, cancellation of the contract would result in the counterparty paying her the present value of $2. This termination or offset of the original forward position is clearly desirable for both counterparties because it eliminates the credit risk.[3] It is always possible, however, that she might receive a better price from another counterparty. If that price is sufficiently attractive and she does not perceive the credit risk to be too high, she may choose to deal with the other counterparty and leave the credit risk in the picture.

2   THE STRUCTURE OF GLOBAL FORWARD MARKETS

The global market for forward contracts is part of a vast network of financial institutions that make markets in these instruments as well as in other related derivatives, such as swaps and options. Some dealers specialize in certain markets and contracts, such as forward contracts on the euro or forward contracts on Japanese equity products. These dealers are mainly large global banking institutions, but many large non-banking institutions, such as Goldman Sachs and Merrill Lynch, are also big players in this market.

Dealers engage in transactions with two types of parties: end users and other dealers. An end user is typically a corporation, nonprofit organization, or government.[4] An end user is generally a party with a risk management problem that is searching for a dealer to provide it with a financial transaction to solve that problem. Although the problem could simply be that the party wants to take a position in anticipation of a market move, more commonly the end user has a risk it wants to reduce or eliminate.

As an example, Hoffman-LaRoche, the large Swiss pharmaceutical company, sells its products globally. Anticipating the receipt of a large amount of cash in U.S. dollars and worried about a decrease in the value of the dollar relative to the Swiss franc, it could buy a forward contract to sell the dollar and buy Swiss francs. It might seek out a dealer such as UBS Warburg, the investment firm affiliated with the large Swiss bank UBS, or it might approach any of the other large multinational banks with which it does business. Or it might end up dealing with a non-bank entity, like Merrill Lynch. Assume that Hoffman-LaRoche enters into this contract with UBS Warburg. Hoffman-LaRoche is the end user; UBS Warburg is the dealer.

---

[3] This statement is made under the assumption that the parties do not want the credit risk. Credit risk, like other risks, however, can be a risk that some parties want because of the potential for earning attractive returns by using their expertise in measuring the actual credit risk relative to the credit risk as perceived by the market. In addition, credit risk offers diversification benefits.

[4] The U.S. government does not transact in forward contracts or other derivatives, but some foreign governments and central banks do. Within the United States, however, some state and local governments do engage in forward contracts and other derivatives.

Transactions in forward contracts typically are conducted over the phone. Each dealer has a quote desk, whose phone number is well known to the major participants in the market. If a party wishes to conduct a transaction, it simply phones the dealer for a quote. The dealer stands ready to take either side of the transaction, quoting a bid and an ask price or rate. The bid is the price at which the dealer is willing to pay for the future purchase of the asset, and the ask is the price at which the dealer is willing to sell. When a dealer engages in a forward transaction, it has then taken on risk from the other party. For example, in the aforementioned transaction of Hoffman-LaRoche and UBS Warburg, by entering into the contract, UBS Warburg takes on a risk that Hoffman-LaRoche has eliminated. Specifically, UBS Warburg has now committed to buying dollars and selling Swiss francs at a future date. Thus, UBS Warburg is effectively long the dollar and stands to gain from a strengthening dollar/weakening Swiss franc. Typically dealers do not want to hold this exposure. Rather, they find another party to offset the exposure with another derivative or spot transaction. Thus, UBS Warburg is a wholesaler of risk—buying it, selling it, and trying to earn a profit off the spread between its buying price and selling price.

One might reasonably wonder why Hoffman-LaRoche could not avoid the cost of dealing with UBS Warburg. In some cases, it might be able to. It might be aware of another party with the exact opposite needs, but such a situation is rare. The market for financial products such as forward contracts is made up of wholesalers of risk management products who use their technical expertise, their vast network of contacts, and their access to critical financial market information to provide a more efficient means for end users to engage in such risk management transactions.

Dealers such as UBS Warburg lay off the risk they do not wish to assume by transacting with other dealers and potentially other end users. If they do this carefully, quickly, and at accurate prices, they can earn a profit from this market-making activity. One should not get the impression, however, that market making is a highly profitable activity. The competition is fierce, which keeps bid–ask spreads very low and makes it difficult to earn much money on a given transaction. Indeed, many market makers do not make much money on individual transactions—they typically make a small amount of money on each transaction and do a large number of transactions. They may even lose money on some standard transactions, hoping to make up losses on more-complicated, nonstandard transactions, which occur less frequently but have higher bid–ask spreads.

Risk magazine conducts annual surveys to identify the top dealers in various derivative products. Exhibit 74-1 presents the results of those surveys for two of the forward products we cover here, currency and interest rate forwards. Interest rate forwards are called forward rate agreements (FRAs). In the next section, we shall study the different types of forward contracts and note that there are some others not covered in the *Risk* surveys.

One of these surveys was sent to banks and investment banks that are active dealers in over-the-counter derivatives. The other survey was sent to end users. The tabulations are based on respondents' simple rankings of who they think are the best dealers. Although the identities of the specific dealer firms are not critical, it is interesting and helpful to be aware of the major players in these types of contracts. Most of the world's leading global financial institutions are listed, but many other big names are not. It is also interesting to observe that the perceptions of the users of these dealer firms' services differ somewhat from the dealers' self-perceptions. Be aware, however, that the rankings change, sometimes drastically, each year.

EXHIBIT 74-1	*Risk* Magazine Surveys of Banks, Investment Banks, and Corporate End Users to Determine the Top Three Dealers in Currency and Interest Rate Forwards

	Respondents	
Currencies	**Banks and Investment Banks**	**Corporate End Users**
Currency Forwards		
$/€	UBS Warburg	Citigroup
	Deutsche Bank	Royal Bank of Scotland
	JP Morgan Chase	JP Morgan Chase/Bank of America
$/¥	UBS Warburg	Citigroup
	Citigroup	Bank of America
	JP Morgan Chase	JP Morgan Chase/UBS Warburg
$/£	UBS Warburg	Royal Bank of Scotland
	Royal Bank of Scotland	Citigroup
	Hong Kong Shanghai Banking Corporation	UBS Warburg
$/SF	UBS Warburg	UBS Warburg
	Credit Suisse First Boston	Citigroup
	BNP Paribas	Credit Suisse First Boston
Interest Rate Forwards (FRAs)		
$	JP Morgan Chase	JP Morgan Chase
	Bank of America	Royal Bank of Scotland
	Deutsche Bank	Bank of America
€	Deutsche Bank	Royal Bank of Scotland
	Intesa BCI	JP Morgan Chase
	Royal Bank of Scotland	Deutsche Bank
¥	Mizuho Securities	Citigroup
	JP Morgan Chase	Merrill Lynch
	BNP Paribas	Hong Kong Shanghai Banking Corporation
£	Royal Bank of Scotland	Royal Bank of Scotland
	Commerzbank	Bank of America/ING Barings
	Deutsche Bank	
SF	Credit Suisse First Boston	UBS Warburg
	UBS Warburg	Credit Suisse First Boston
	Deutsche Bank	Citigroup/ING Barings

Note: $ = US dollar, € = euro, ¥ = Japanese yen, £ = U.K. pound sterling, SF = Swiss franc.

Source: Risk, September 2002, pp. 30–67 for banks and investment banking dealer respondents, and June 2002, pp. 24–34 for end user respondents. The end user survey provides responses from corporations and asset managers. The above results are for corporate respondents only.

TYPES OF FORWARD CONTRACTS   3

In this section, we examine the types of forward contracts that fall within the scope of this book. By the word "types," we mean the underlying asset groups on which these forward contracts are created. Because the CFA Program focuses on the asset management industry, our primary interest is in equity, interest rate and fixed-income, and currency forwards.

3.1 Equity Forwards

An **equity forward** is a contract calling for the purchase of an individual stock, a stock portfolio, or a stock index at a later date. For the most part, the differences in types of equity forward contracts are only slight, depending on whether the contract is on an individual stock, a portfolio of stocks, or a stock index.

3.1.1 Forward Contracts on Individual Stocks

Consider an asset manager responsible for the portfolio of a high-net-worth individual. As is sometimes the case, such portfolios may be concentrated in a small number of stocks, sometimes stocks that have been in the family for years. In many cases, the individual may be part of the founding family of a particular company. Let us say that the stock is called Gregorian Industries, Inc., or GII, and the client is so heavily invested in this stock that her portfolio is not diversified. The client notifies the portfolio manager of her need for $2 million in cash in six months. This cash can be raised by selling 16,000 shares at the current price of $125 per share. Thus, the risk exposure concerns the market value of $2 million of stock. For whatever reason, it is considered best not to sell the stock any earlier than necessary. The portfolio manager realizes that a forward contract to sell GII in six months will accomplish the client's desired objective. The manager contacts a forward contract dealer and obtains a quote of $128.13 as the price at which a forward contract to sell the stock in six months could be constructed.[5] In other words, the portfolio manager could enter into a contract to sell the stock to the dealer in six months at $128.13. We assume that this contract is deliverable, meaning that when the sale is actually made, the shares will be delivered to the dealer. Assuming that the client has some flexibility in the amount of money needed, let us say that the contract is signed for the sale of 15,600 shares at $128.13, which will raise $1,998,828. Of course when the contract expires, the stock could be selling for any price. The client can gain or lose on the transaction. If the stock rises to a price above $128.13 during the six-month period, the client will still have to deliver the stock for $128.13. But if the price falls, the client will still get $128.13 per share for the stock.

3.1.2 Forward Contracts on Stock Portfolios

Because modern portfolio theory and good common sense dictate that investors should hold diversified portfolios, it is reasonable to assume that forward contracts on specific stock portfolios would be useful. Suppose a pension fund manager knows that in three months he will need to sell about $20 million of stock to make payments to retirees. The manager has analyzed the portfolio and determined the

---

[5] In Section 4, we shall learn how to calculate forward prices such as this one.

precise identities of the stocks he wants to sell and the number of shares of each that he would like to sell. Thus the manager has designated a specific subportfolio to be sold. The problem is that the prices of these stocks in three months are uncertain. The manager can, however, lock in the sale prices by entering into a forward contract to sell the portfolio. This can be done one of two ways.

The manager can enter into a forward contract on each stock that he wants to sell. Alternatively, he can enter into a forward contract on the overall portfolio. The first way would be more costly, as each contract would incur administrative costs, whereas the second way would incur only one set of costs.[6] Assume that the manager chooses the second method. He provides a list of the stocks and number of shares of each he wishes to sell to the dealer and obtains a quote. The dealer gives him a quote of $20,200,000. So, in three months, the manager will sell the stock to the dealer and receive $20,200,000. The transaction can be structured to call for either actual delivery or cash settlement, but in either case, the client will effectively receive $20,200,000 for the stock.[7]

3.1.3 Forward Contracts on Stock Indices

Many equity forward contracts are based on a stock index. For example, consider a U.K. asset manager who wants to protect the value of her portfolio that is a Financial Times Stock Exchange 100 index fund, or who wants to eliminate a risk for which the FTSE 100 Index is a sufficiently accurate representation of the risk she wishes to eliminate. For example, the manager may be anticipating the sale of a number of U.K. blue chip shares at a future date. The manager could, as in our stock portfolio example, take a specific portfolio of stocks to a forward contract dealer and obtain a forward contract on that portfolio. She realizes, however, that a forward contract on a widely accepted benchmark would result in a better price quote, because the dealer can more easily hedge the risk with other transactions. Moreover, the manager is not even sure which stocks she will still be holding at the later date. She simply knows that she will sell a certain amount of stock at a later date and believes that the FTSE 100 is representative of the stock that she will sell. The manager is concerned with the systematic risk associated with the U.K. stock market, and accordingly, she decides that selling a forward contract on the FTSE 100 would be a good way to manage the risk.

Assume that the portfolio manager decides to protect £15,000,000 of stock. The dealer quotes a price of £6,000 on a forward contract covering £15,000,000. We assume that the contract will be cash settled because such index contracts are nearly always done that way. When the contract expiration date arrives, let us say that the index is at £5,925—a decrease of 1.25 percent from the forward price. Because the manager is short the contract and its price went down, the transaction makes money. But how much did it make on a notional principal of £15,000,000?

---

[6] Ignoring those costs, there would be no difference in doing forward contracts on individual stocks or a single forward contract on a portfolio. Because of the non-linearity of their payoffs, this is not true for options. A portfolio of options is not the same as an option on a portfolio, but a portfolio of forward contracts is the same as a forward contract on a portfolio, ignoring the aforementioned costs.

[7] If, for example, the stock is worth $20,500,000 and the transaction calls for delivery, the manager will transfer the stocks to the dealer and receive $20,200,000. The client effectively takes an opportunity loss of $300,000. If the transaction is structured as a cash settlement, the client will pay the dealer $300,000. The client would then sell the stock in the market, receiving $20,500,000 and netting $20,200,000 after settling the forward contract with the dealer. Similarly, if the stock is selling for less than the amount guaranteed by the forward contract, the client will deliver the stock and receive $20,200,000 or, if the transaction is cash settled, the client will sell the stock in the market and receive a cash payment from the dealer, making the effective sale price still $20,200,000.

The index declined by 1.25 percent. Thus, the transaction should make $0.0125 \times £15,000,000 = £187,500$. In other words, the dealer would have to pay £187,500 in cash. If the portfolio were a FTSE 100 index fund, then it would be viewed as a portfolio initially worth £15,000,000 that declined by 1.25 percent, a loss of £187,500. The forward contract offsets this loss. Of course, in reality, the portfolio is not an index fund and such a hedge is not perfect, but as noted above, there are sometimes reasons for preferring that the forward contract be based on an index.

3.1.4 The Effect of Dividends

It is important to note the effect of dividends in equity forward contracts. Any equity portfolio nearly always has at least a few stocks that pay dividends, and it is inconceivable that any well-known equity index would not have some component stocks that pay dividends. Equity forward contracts typically have payoffs based only on the price of the equity, value of the portfolio, or level of the index. They do not ordinarily pay off any dividends paid by the component stocks. An exception, however, is that some equity forwards on stock indices are based on total return indices. For example, there are two versions of the well-known S&P 500 Index. One represents only the market value of the stocks. The other, called the S&P 500 Total Return Index, is structured so that daily dividends paid by the stocks are reinvested in additional units of the index, as though it were a portfolio. In this manner, the rate of return on the index, and the payoff of any forward contract based on it, reflects the payment and reinvestment of dividends into the underlying index. Although this feature might appear attractive, it is not necessarily of much importance in risk management problems. The variability of prices is so much greater than the variability of dividends that managing price risk is considered much more important than worrying about the uncertainty of dividends.

In summary, equity forwards can be based on individual stocks, specific stock portfolios, or stock indices. Moreover, these underlying equities often pay dividends, which can affect forward contracts on equities. Let us now look at bond and **interest rate forward** contracts.

3.2 Bond and Interest Rate Forward Contracts

Forward contracts on bonds are similar to forward contracts on interest rates, but the two are different instruments. Forward contracts on bonds, in fact, are no more difficult to understand than those on equities. Drawing on our experience of Section 3.1, we simply extend the notion of a forward contract on an individual stock, a specific stock portfolio, or a stock index to that of a forward contract on an individual bond, a specific bond portfolio, or a bond index.[8]

3.2.1 Forward Contracts on Individual Bonds and Bond Portfolios

Although a forward contract on a bond and one on a stock are similar, some basic differences nonetheless exist between the two. For example, the bond may pay a coupon, which corresponds somewhat to the dividend that a stock might pay. But unlike a stock, a bond matures, and a forward contract on a bond must

---

[8] It may be useful to review Chapters 1 and 3 of *Fixed Income Analysis for the Chartered Financial Analyst Program* by Frank J. Fabozzi, New Hope, PA: Frank J. Fabozzi Associates (2000).

expire prior to the bond's maturity date. In addition, bonds often have many special features such as calls and convertibility. Finally, we should note that unlike a stock, a bond carries the risk of default. A forward contract written on a bond must contain a provision to recognize how default is defined, what it means for the bond to default, and how default would affect the parties to the contract.

In addition to forward contracts on individual bonds, there are also forward contracts on portfolios of bonds as well as on bond indices. The technical distinctions between forward contracts on individual bonds and collections of bonds, however, are relatively minor.

The primary bonds for which we shall consider forward contracts are default-free zero-coupon bonds, typically called Treasury bills or T-bills in the United States, which serve as a proxy for the risk-free rate.[9] In a forward contract on a T-bill, one party agrees to buy the T-bill at a later date, prior to the bill's maturity, at a price agreed on today. T-bills are typically sold at a discount from par value and the price is quoted in terms of the discount rate. Thus, if a 180-day T-bill is selling at a discount of 4 percent, its price per $1 par will be $1 - 0.04(180/360) = $0.98. The use of 360 days is the convention in calculating the discount. So the bill will sell for $0.98. If purchased and held to maturity, it will pay off $1. This procedure means that the interest is deducted from the face value in advance, which is called **discount interest**.

The T-bill is usually traded by quoting the discount rate, not the price. It is understood that the discount rate can be easily converted to the price by the above procedure. A forward contract might be constructed that would call for delivery of a 90-day T-bill in 60 days. Such a contract might sell for $0.9895, which would imply a discount rate of 4.2 percent because $1 - 0.042(90/360) = $0.9895. Later in this reading, we shall see how forward prices of T-bills are derived.

In addition to forward contracts on zero-coupon bonds/T-bills, we shall consider forward contracts on default-free coupon-bearing bonds, also called Treasury bonds in the United States. These instruments pay interest, typically in semiannual installments, and can sell for more (less) than par value if the yield is lower (higher) than the coupon rate. Prices are typically quoted without the interest that has accrued since the last coupon date, but with a few exceptions, we shall always work with the full price—that is, the price including accrued interest. Prices are often quoted by stating the yield. Forward contracts call for delivery of such a bond at a date prior to the bond's maturity, for which the long pays the short the agreed-upon price.

3.2.2 Forward Contracts on Interest Rates: Forward Rate Agreements

So far in Section 3.2 we have discussed forward contracts on actual fixed-income securities. Fixed-income security prices are driven by interest rates. A more common type of forward contract is the interest rate forward contract, more commonly called a **forward rate agreement** or **FRA**. Before we can begin to understand FRAs, however, we must examine the instruments on which they are based.

There is a large global market for time deposits in various currencies issued by large creditworthy banks. This market is primarily centered in London but also exists elsewhere, though not in the United States. The primary time deposit

---

[9] A government-issued zero-coupon bond is typically used as a proxy for a risk-free asset because it is assumed to be free of default risk. It can be purchased and held to maturity, thereby eliminating any market value risk, and it has no reinvestment risk because it has no coupons. If the bond is liquidated before maturity, however, some market value risk exists in addition to the risk associated with reinvesting the market price.

instrument is called the **Eurodollar**, which is a dollar deposited outside the Unites States. Banks borrow dollars from other banks by issuing Eurodollar time deposits, which are essentially short-term unsecured loans. In London, the rate on such dollar loans is called the London Interbank Rate. Although there are rates for both borrowing and lending, in the financial markets the lending rate, called the **London Interbank Offer Rate** or **LIBOR**, is more commonly used in derivative contracts. LIBOR is the rate at which London banks lend dollars to other London banks. Even though it represents a loan outside of the United States, LIBOR is considered to be the best representative rate on a dollar borrowed by a private, i.e., nongovernmental, high-quality borrower. It should be noted, however, that the London market includes many branches of banks from outside the United Kingdom, and these banks are also active participants in the Eurodollar market.

A Eurodollar time deposit is structured as follows. Let us say a London bank such as NatWest needs to borrow $10 million for 30 days. It obtains a quote from the Royal Bank of Scotland for a rate of 5.25 percent. Thus, 30-day LIBOR is 5.25 percent. If NatWest takes the deal, it will owe $10,000,000 \times [1 + 0.0525(30/360)] = $10,043,750 in 30 days. Note that, like the Treasury bill market, the convention in the Eurodollar market is to prorate the quoted interest rate over 360 days. In contrast to the Treasury bill market, the interest is not deducted from the principal. Rather, it is added on to the face value, a procedure appropriately called **add-on interest**. The market for Eurodollar time deposits is quite large, and the rates on these instruments are assembled by a central organization and quoted in financial newspapers. The British Bankers Association publishes a semi-official Eurodollar rate, compiled from an average of the quotes of London banks.

The U.S. dollar is not the only instrument for which such time deposits exist. Eurosterling, for example, trades in Tokyo, and Euroyen trades in London. You may be wondering about Euroeuro. Actually, there is no such entity as Euroeuro, at least not by that name. The Eurodollar instrument described here has nothing to do with the European currency known as the euro. Eurodollars, Euroyen, Eurosterling, etc. have been around longer than the euro currency and, despite the confusion, have retained their nomenclature. An analogous instrument does exist, however—a euro-denominated loan in which one bank borrows euros from another. Trading in euros and euro deposits occurs in most major world cities, and two similar rates on such euro deposits are commonly quoted. One, called EuroLIBOR, is compiled in London by the British Bankers Association, and the other, called Euribor, is compiled in Frankfurt and published by the European Central Bank. Euribor is more widely used and is the rate we shall refer to in this book.

Now let us return to the world of FRAs. FRAs are contracts in which the underlying is neither a bond nor a Eurodollar or Euribor deposit but simply an interest payment made in dollars, Euribor, or any other currency at a rate appropriate for that currency. Our primary focus will be on dollar LIBOR and Euribor, so we shall henceforth adopt the terminology LIBOR to represent dollar LIBOR and Euribor to represent the euro deposit rate.

Because the mechanics of FRAs are the same for all currencies, for illustrative purposes we shall use LIBOR. Consider an FRA expiring in 90 days for which the underlying is 180-day LIBOR. Suppose the dealer quotes this instrument at a rate of 5.5 percent. Suppose the end user goes long and the dealer goes short. The end user is essentially long the rate and will benefit if rates increase. The dealer is essentially short the rate and will benefit if rates decrease. The contract covers a given notional principal, which we shall assume is $10 million.

The contract stipulates that at expiration, the parties identify the rate on new 180-day LIBOR time deposits. This rate is called 180-day LIBOR. It is, thus, the underlying rate on which the contract is based. Suppose that at expiration in

90 days, the rate on 180-day LIBOR is 6 percent. That 6 percent interest will be paid 180 days later. Therefore, the present value of a Eurodollar time deposit at that point in time would be

$$\frac{\$10,000,000}{1 + 0.06\left(\dfrac{180}{360}\right)}$$

At expiration, then, the end user, the party going long the FRA in our example, receives the following payment from the dealer, which is the party going short:

$$\$10,000,000\left[\frac{(0.06 - 0.055)\left(\dfrac{180}{360}\right)}{1 + 0.06\left(\dfrac{180}{360}\right)}\right] = \$24,272$$

If the underlying rate is less than 5.5 percent, the payment is calculated based on the difference between the 5.5 percent rate and the underlying rate and is paid by the long to the short. It is important to note that even though the contract expires in 90 days, the rate is on a 180-day LIBOR instrument; therefore, the rate calculation adjusts by the factor 180/360. The fact that 90 days have elapsed at expiration is not relevant to the calculation of the payoff.

Before presenting the general formula, let us review the calculations in the numerator and denominator. In the numerator, we see that the contract is obviously paying the difference between the actual rate that exists in the market on the contract expiration date and the agreed-upon rate, adjusted for the fact that the rate applies to a 180-day instrument, multiplied by the notional principal. The divisor appears because when Eurodollar rates are quoted in the market, they are based on the assumption that the rate applies to an instrument that accrues interest at that rate with the interest paid a certain number of days (here 180) later. When participants determine this rate in the London Eurodollar market, it is understood to apply to a Eurodollar time deposit that begins now and matures 180 days later. So the interest on an actual Eurodollar deposit would not be paid until 180 days later. Thus, it is necessary to adjust the FRA payoff to reflect the fact that the rate implies a payment that would occur 180 days later on a standard Eurodollar deposit. This adjustment is easily done by simply discounting the payment at the current LIBOR, which here is 6 percent, prorated over 180 days. These conventions are also followed in the market for FRAs with other underlying rates.

In general, the FRA payoff formula (from the perspective of the party going long) is

$$\text{Notional principal}\left[\frac{(\text{Underlying rate at expiration} - \text{Forward contract rate})\left(\dfrac{\text{Days in underlying rate}}{360}\right)}{1 + \text{Underlying rate at expiration}\left(\dfrac{\text{Days in underlying rate}}{360}\right)}\right]$$

where *forward contract rate* represents the rate the two parties agree will be paid and *days in underlying rate* refers to the number of days to maturity of the instrument on which the underlying rate is based.

One somewhat confusing feature of FRAs is the fact that they mature in a certain number of days and are based on a rate that applies to an instrument maturing in a certain number of days measured from the maturity of the FRA.

EXHIBIT 74-2	FRA Descriptive Notation and Interpretation	
Notation	**Contract Expires in**	**Underlying Rate**
1 × 3	1 month	60-day LIBOR
1 × 4	1 month	90-day LIBOR
1 × 7	1 month	180-day LIBOR
3 × 6	3 months	90-day LIBOR
3 × 9	3 months	180-day LIBOR
6 × 12	6 months	180-day LIBOR
12 × 18	12 months	180-day LIBOR

Note: This list is not exhaustive and represents only the most commonly traded FRAs.

Thus, there are two day figures associated with each contract. Our example was a 90-day contract on 180-day LIBOR. To avoid confusion, the FRA markets use a special type of terminology that converts the number of days to months. Specifically, our example FRA is referred to as a 3 × 9, reflecting the fact that the contract expires in three months and that six months later, or nine months from the contract initiation date, the interest is paid on the underlying Eurodollar time deposit on whose rate the contract is based.[10]

FRAs are available in the market for a variety of maturities that are considered somewhat standard. Exhibit 74-2 presents the most common maturities. Most dealers follow the convention that contracts should expire in a given number of exact months and should be on the most commonly traded Eurodollar rates such as 30-day LIBOR, 60-day LIBOR, 90-day LIBOR, 180-day LIBOR, and so on. If a party wants a contract expiring in 37 days on 122-day LIBOR, it would be considered an exception to the standard, but most dealers would be willing to make a market in such an instrument. Such nonstandard instruments are called *off the run*. Of course, FRAs are available in all of the leading currencies.

The FRA market is large, but not as large as the swaps market. It is important, however, to understand FRAs before trying to understand swaps. As we will show in Reading 77, a swap is a special combination of FRAs. But let us now turn to another large forward market, the market for currency forwards.

3.3 Currency Forward Contracts

Spurred by the relaxation of government controls over the exchange rates of most major currencies in the early 1970s, a currency forward market developed and grew extremely large. Currency forwards are widely used by banks and corporations to manage foreign exchange risk. For example, suppose Microsoft has a European subsidiary that expects to send it €12 million in three months. When Microsoft receives the euros, it will then convert them to dollars. Thus, Microsoft is essentially long euros because it will have to sell euros, or equivalently, it is short dollars because it will have to buy dollars. A currency forward contract is especially useful in this situation, because it enables Microsoft to lock in the rate at which it will sell euros and buy dollars in three months. It can do this by going

[10] The notation "3 × 9" is pronounced "three by nine."

short the forward contract, meaning that it goes short the euro and long the dollar. This arrangement serves to offset its otherwise long-euro, short-dollar position. In other words, it needs a forward contract to sell euros and buy dollars.

For example, say Microsoft goes to JP Morgan Chase and asks for a quote on a currency forward for €12 million in three months. JP Morgan Chase quotes a rate of $0.925, which would enable Microsoft to sell euros and buy dollars at a rate of $0.925 in three months. Under this contract, Microsoft would know it could convert its €12 million to $12,000,000 \times \$0.925 = \$11,100,000$. The contract would also stipulate whether it will settle in cash or will call for Microsoft to actually deliver the euros to the dealer and be paid $11,100,000. This simplified example is a currency forward hedge.

Now let us say that three months later, the spot rate for euros is $0.920. Microsoft is quite pleased that it locked in a rate of $0.925. It simply delivers the euros and receives $11,100,000 at an exchange rate of $0.925.[11] Had rates risen, however, Microsoft would still have had to deliver the euros and accept a rate of $0.925.

A few variations of currency forward contracts exist, but most of them are somewhat specialized and beyond the objectives of this book. Let us now take a very brief look at a few other types of forward contracts.

3.4 Other Types of Forward Contracts

Although this book focuses primarily on the financial derivatives used by asset managers, we should mention here some of the other types. Commodity forwards—in which the underlying asset is oil, a precious metal, or some other commodity—are widely used. In addition, the derivatives industry has created forward contracts and other derivatives on various sources of energy (electricity, gas, etc.) and even weather, in which the underlying is a measure of the temperature or the amount of disaster damage from hurricanes, earthquakes, or tornados.

Many of these instruments are particularly difficult to understand, price, and trade. Nonetheless, through the use of derivatives and indirect investments, such as hedge funds, they can be useful for managing risk and investing in general. They are not, however, the focus of this book.

In the examples and illustrations used, we have made reference to certain prices. Determining appropriate prices and fair values of financial instruments is a central objective of much of the process of asset management. Accordingly, pricing and valuation occupies a major portion of the CFA Program. As such, we turn our attention to the pricing and valuation of forward contracts.

OPTIONAL SEGMENT
BEGINS

4

PRICING AND VALUATION OF FORWARD CONTRACTS

Before getting into the actual mechanics of pricing and valuation, the astute reader might wonder whether we are being a bit redundant. Are pricing and valuation not the same thing?

---

[11] Had the contract been structured to settle in cash, the dealer would have paid Microsoft $12,000,000 \times (\$0.925 - \$0.920) = \$60,000$. Microsoft would have converted the euros to dollars at the current spot exchange rate of $0.920, receiving $12,000,000 \times \$0.920 = \$11,040,000$. Adding the $60,000 payment from the dealer, Microsoft would have received $11,100,000, an effective rate of $0.925.

An equity analyst often finds that a stock is priced at more or less than its fair market value and uses this conclusion as the basis for a buy or sell recommendation.[12] In an efficient market, the price of a stock would always equal its value or the price would quickly converge to the value. Thus, for all practical purposes, pricing and valuation would be the same thing. In general, when we speak of the value and price of an *asset*, we are referring to what that asset is worth and what it sells for. With respect to certain *derivatives*, however, value and price take on slightly different meanings.

So let us begin by defining value: *Value is what you can sell something for or what you must pay to acquire something.* This applies to stocks, bonds, derivatives, and used cars.[13] Accordingly, *valuation is the process of determining the value of an asset or service.* Pricing is a related but different concept; let us explore what we mean by pricing a forward contract.

A forward contract price is the fixed price or rate at which the transaction scheduled to occur at expiration will take place. This price is agreed to on the contract initiation date and is commonly called the **forward price** or **forward rate**. Pricing means to determine the forward price or forward rate. Valuation, however, means to determine the amount of money that one would need to pay or would expect to receive to engage in the transaction. Alternatively, if one already held a position, valuation would mean to determine the amount of money one would either have to pay or expect to receive in order to get out of the position. Let us look at a generic example.

4.1 Generic Pricing and Valuation of a Forward Contract

Because derivative contracts have finite lives, it is important to carefully specify the time frame in which we are operating. We denote time in the following manner: Today is identified as time 0. The expiration date is time T. Time t is an arbitrary time between today and the expiration. Usually when we refer to "today," we are referring to the date on which the contract is created. Later we shall move forward to time t and time T, which will then be "today."

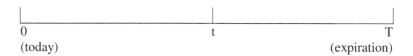

The price of the underlying asset in the spot market is denoted as S_0 at time 0, S_t at time t, and S_T at time T. The forward contract price, established when the contract is initiated at time 0, is F(0,T). This notation indicates that F(0,T) is the price of a forward contract initiated at time 0 and expiring at time T. The value of the forward contract is $V_0(0,T)$. This notation indicates that $V_0(0,T)$ is the value at time 0 of a forward contract initiated at time 0 and expiring at time T. In this book, subscripts always indicate that we are at a specific point in time.

We have several objectives in this analysis. First, we want to determine the forward price F(0,T). We also want to determine the forward contract value today, denoted $V_0(0,T)$, the value at a point during the life of the contract such as time t, denoted $V_t(0,T)$, and the value at expiration, denoted $V_T(0,T)$. Valuation is somewhat easier to grasp from the perspective of the party holding the long position, so

---

[12] From your study of equity analysis, you should recall that we often use the discounted cash flow model, sometimes combined with the capital asset pricing model, to determine the fair market value of a stock.

[13] Be careful. You may think the "value" of a certain used car is $5,000, but if no one will give you that price, it can hardly be called the value.

we shall take that point of view in this example. Once that value is determined, the value to the short is obtained by simply changing the sign.

If we are at expiration, we would observe the spot price as S_T. The long holds a position to buy the asset at the already agreed-upon price of $F(0,T)$. Thus, the value of the forward contract at expiration should be obvious: $S_T - F(0,T)$. If the value at expiration does not equal this amount, then an arbitrage profit can be easily made. For example, suppose the forward price established at the initiation of the contract, $F(0,T)$, is $20. Now at expiration, the spot price, S_T, is $23. The contract value must be $3. If it were more than $3, then the long would be able to sell the contract to someone for more than $3—someone would be paying the long more than $3 to obtain the obligation of buying a $23 asset for $20. Obviously, no one would do that. If the value were less than $3, the long would have to be willing to sell for less than $3 the obligation of buying a $23 asset for $20. Obviously, the long would not do that. Thus, we state that the value at expiration of a forward contract established at time 0 is

$$V_T(0,T) = S_T - F(0,T) \qquad\qquad \textbf{(74-1)}$$

Note that the value of a forward contract can also be interpreted as its profit, the difference between what the long pays for the underlying asset, $F(0,T)$, and what the long receives, the asset price S_T. Of course, we have still not explained how $F(0,T)$ is determined, but the above equation gives the value of the contract at expiration, at which time $F(0,T)$ would certainly be known because it was agreed on at the initiation date of the contract.

Now let us back up to the time when the contract was originated. Consider a contract that expires in one year. Suppose that the underlying asset is worth $100 and that the forward price is $108. We do not know if $108 is the correct forward price; we will simply try it and see.

Suppose we buy the asset for $100 and sell the forward contract for $108. We hold the position until expiration. We assume that there are no direct costs associated with buying or holding the asset, but we must recognize that we lose interest on the $100 tied up in the asset. Assume that the interest rate is 5 percent.

Recall that no money changes hands at the start with a forward contract. Consequently, the $100 invested in the asset is the full outlay. At the end of the year, the forward contract expires and we deliver the asset, receiving $108 for it—not bad at all. At a 5 percent interest rate, we lose only $5 in interest on the $100 tied up in the asset. We receive $108 for the asset regardless of its price at expiration. We can view $108 − $105 = $3 as a risk-free profit, which more than covered the cost. In fact, if we had also borrowed the $100 at 5 percent, we could have done this transaction without putting up any money of our own. We would have more than covered the interest on the borrowed funds and netted a $3 risk-free profit. This profit is essentially free money—there is no cost and no risk. Thus, it is an arbitrage profit, a concept we introduced in Reading 69 and a dominant theme throughout this book. We would certainly want to execute any transaction that would generate an arbitrage profit.

In the market, the forces of arbitrage would then prevail. Other market participants would execute this transaction as well. Although it is possible that the spot price would bear some of the adjustment, in this book we shall always let the derivative price make the full adjustment. Consequently, the derivative price would have to come down to $105.

If the forward price were below $105, we could also earn an arbitrage profit, although it would be a little more difficult because the asset would have to be sold short. Suppose the forward price is $103. If the asset were a financial asset, we could borrow it and sell it short. We would receive $100 for it and invest that $100 at the 5 percent rate. We would simultaneously buy a forward contract. At expiration, we would take delivery of the asset paying $103 and then deliver it to the party from whom we borrowed it. The short position is now covered, and we still have the $100 invested plus 5 percent interest on it. This transaction offers a clear arbitrage profit of $2. Again, the forces of arbitrage would cause other market participants to undertake the transaction, which would push the forward price up to $105.

If short selling is not permitted, too difficult, or too costly, a market participant who already owns the asset could sell it, invest the $100 at 5 percent, and buy a forward contract. At expiration, he would pay $103 and take delivery on the forward contract, which would return him to his original position of owning the asset. He would now, however, receive not only the stock but also 5 percent interest on $100. Again, the forces of arbitrage would make this transaction attractive to other parties who held the asset, provided they could afford to part with it for the necessary period of time.[14]

Going back to the situation in which the forward contract price was $103, an arbitrage profit could, however, be eliminated if the party going long the forward contract were required to pay some money up front. For example, suppose the party going long the forward contract paid the party going short $1.9048. Then the party going long would lose $1.9048 plus interest on this amount. Notice that $1.9048 compounded at 5 percent interest equals precisely $2, which not surprisingly is the amount of the arbitrage profit.

Thus, if the forward price were $103, the value of the contract would be $1.9048. With $T = 1$, this value equals

$$V_0(0,T) = V_0(0,1) = \$100 - \$103/1.05 = \$1.9048$$

Therefore, to enter into this contract at this forward price, one party must pay another. Because the value is positive, it must be paid by the party going long the forward contract to the party going short. Parties going long must pay positive values; parties going short pay negative values.[15]

If the forward price were $108, the value would be

$$V_0(0,T) = \$100 - \$108/1.05 = -\$2.8571$$

In this case, the value is negative and would have to be paid from the short to the long. Doing so would eliminate the arbitrage profit that the short would have otherwise been able to make, given the forward price of $108.

Arbitrage profits can be eliminated with an up-front payment from long to short or vice versa that is consistent with the forward price the parties select. The parties could simply negotiate a forward price, and any resulting market value could be paid from one party to the other. *It is customary, however, in the forward market for the initial value to be set to zero.* This convention eliminates the necessity of either party making a payment to the other and results in a direct and simple determination of the forward price. Specifically, setting $V_0(0,T) = 0$ and letting r represent the interest rate,

$$V_0(0,T) = S_0 - F(0,T)/(1 + r) = 0$$

---

[14] In other words, a party holding the asset must be willing to part with it for the length of time it would take for the forces of arbitrage to bring the price back in line, thereby allowing the party to capture the risk-free profit and return the party to its original state of holding the asset. The period of time required for the price to adjust should be very short if the market is relatively efficient.

[15] For example, when a stock is purchased, its value, which is always positive, is paid from the long to the short. This is true for any asset.

which means that $F(0,T) = S_0(1 + r)$. In our example, $F(0,T) = \$100(1.05) = \$105$, which is the forward price that eliminates the arbitrage profit.

Our forward price formula can be interpreted as saying that the forward price is the spot price compounded at the risk-free interest rate. In our example, we had an annual interest rate of r and one year to expiration. With today being time 0 and expiration being time T, the time $T - 0 = T$ is the number of years to expiration of the forward contract. Then we more generally write the forward price as

$$F(0,T) = S_0(1 + r)^T \tag{74-2}$$

Again, this result is consistent with the custom that no money changes hands at the start of a forward contract, meaning that the value of a forward contract at its start is zero.

Exhibit 74-3 summarizes the process of pricing a forward contract. At time 0, we buy the asset and sell a forward contract for a total outlay of the spot price of the asset.[16] Over the life of the contract, we hold the asset and forgo interest on the money. At expiration, we deliver the asset and receive the forward price for a payoff of $F(0,T)$. The overall transaction is risk free and equivalent to investing the spot price of the asset in a risk-free bond that pays $F(0,T)$ at time T. Therefore, the payoff at T must be the future value of the spot price invested at the risk-free rate. This equality can be true only if the forward price is the spot price compounded at the risk-free rate over the life of the asset.

A contract in which the initial value is intentionally set at a nonzero value is called an **off-market FRA**. In such a contract, the forward price is set arbitrarily in the process of negotiation between the two parties. Given the chosen forward price, the contract will have a nonzero value. As noted above, if the value is positive, the long pays that amount up front to the short. If it is negative, the short pays that amount up front to the long. Although off-market FRAs are not common, we shall use them in Reading 77 when studying swaps.

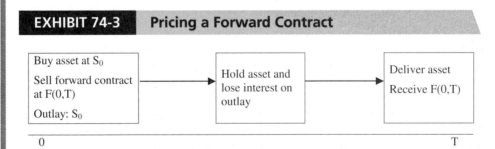

EXHIBIT 74-3   Pricing a Forward Contract

| Buy asset at S_0 |
| Sell forward contract at $F(0,T)$ |
| Outlay: S_0 |

Hold asset and lose interest on outlay

Deliver asset
Receive $F(0,T)$

0   T

The transaction is risk free and should be equivalent to investing S_0 dollars in a risk-free asset that pays $F(0,T)$ at time T. Thus, the amount received at T must be the future value of the initial outlay invested at the risk-free rate. For this equality to hold, the forward price must be given as

$$F(0,T) = S_0(1 + r)^T$$

Example: The spot price is $72.50, the risk-free rate is 8.25 percent, and the contract is for five years. The forward price would be

$$F(0,T) = F(0,5) = 72.50(1.0825)^5 = 107.76$$

---

[16] Remember that in a forward contract, neither party pays anything for the forward contract at the start.

Now suppose we are at a time t, which is a point during the life of the contract. We may want to know the value of the forward contract for several reasons. For one, it makes good business sense to know the monetary value of an obligation to do something at a later date. Also, accounting rules require that a company mark its derivatives to their current market values and report the effects of those values in income statements and balance sheets. In addition, the market value can be used as a gauge of the credit exposure. Finally, the market value can be used to determine how much money one party can pay the other to terminate the contract.

Let us start by assuming that we established a long forward contract at time 0 at the price $F(0,T)$. Of course, its value at time 0 was zero. But now it is time t, and we want to know its new value, $V_t(0,T)$. Let us consider what it means to hold the position of being long at time t a forward contract established at time 0 at the price $F(0,T)$ and expiring at time T:

We will have to pay F(0,T) dollars at T.

We will receive the underlying asset, which will be worth S_T, at T.

At least part of the value will clearly be the present value of a payment of $F(0,T)$, or in other words, $-F(0,T)/(1 + r)^{T-t}$. The other part of the contract value comes from the fact that we have a claim on the asset's value at T. We do not know what S_T (the asset value at T) will be, but we do know that the market tells us its present value is S_t, the current asset price. *By definition, an asset's value today is the present value of its future value.*[17] Thus we can easily value our forward contract at time t during the life of the contract:

$$V_t(0,T) = S_t - F(0,T)/(1 + r)^{(T-t)}$$

(74-3)

Consider our earlier example in which we entered into a one-year forward contract to buy the asset at $105. Now assume it is three months later and the price of the asset is $102. With $t = 0.25$ and $T = 1$, the value of the contract would be

$$V_t(0,T) = V_{0.25}(0,1) = \$102 - \$105/(1.05)^{0.75} = \$0.7728$$

Again, why is this the value? The contract provides the long with a claim on the asset at expiration. That claim is currently worth the current asset value of $102. That claim also obligates the long to pay $105 at expiration, which has a present value of $105/(1.05)^{0.75} = \$101.2272$. Thus, the long position has a value of $102 - \$101.2272 = \$0.7728$.

As noted above, this market value may well affect the income statement and balance sheet. In addition, it gives an idea of the contract's credit exposure, a topic we have touched on and will cover in more detail in Section 5.

Finally, we noted earlier that a party could re-enter the market and offset the contract by paying the counterparty or having the counterparty pay him a cash amount. This cash amount is the market value as calculated here.[18]

Exhibit 74-4 summarizes how we value a forward contract. If we went long a forward contract at time 0 and we are now at time t prior to expiration, we hold a claim on the asset at expiration and are obligated to pay the forward price at

---

[17] This statement is true for any type of asset or financial instrument. It always holds by definition.

[18] If the market value is positive, the value of the asset exceeds the present value of what the long promises to pay. Thus, it makes sense that the short must pay the long. If the market value is negative, then the present value of what the long promises to pay exceeds the value of the asset. Then, it makes sense that the long must pay the short.

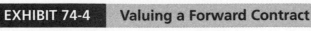

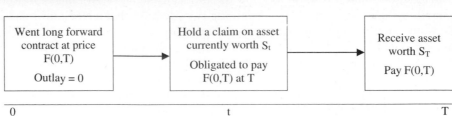

EXHIBIT 74-4   Valuing a Forward Contract

Went long forward contract at price F(0,T) Outlay = 0	→	Hold a claim on asset currently worth S_t Obligated to pay F(0,T) at T	→	Receive asset worth S_T Pay F(0,T)

0 · t · T

The value of the forward contract at t must be the value of what it will produce at T:

$$V_t(0,T) = S_t - F(0,T)/(1 + r)^{(T-t)}$$

Example: A two-year forward contract was established with a price of \$62.25. Now, a year and a half later (t = 1.5), the spot price is \$71.19 and the risk-free rate is 7 percent. The value of the forward contract is

$$V_t(0,T) = V_{1.5}(0,2) = 71.19 - 62.25/(1.07)^{0.5} = 11.01$$

expiration. The claim on the asset is worth its current price; the obligation to pay the forward price at expiration is worth the negative of its present value. Thus, the value of the forward contract is the current spot price minus the forward price discounted from expiration back to the present.

Therefore, we have seen that the forward contract value is zero today: the asset price minus the present value of the forward price at a time prior to expiration, and the asset price minus the forward price at expiration. It may be helpful to note that in general, we can always say that *the forward contract value is the asset price minus the present value of the exercise price*, because given $V_t(0,T) = S_t - F(0,T)/(1 + r)^{(T-t)}$:

If t = 0, $V_t(0,T) = V_0(0,T) = S_0 - F(0,T)/(1 + r)^T = 0$
   because $F(0,T) = S_0(1 + r)^T$

If t = T, $V_t(0,T) = V_T(0,T) = S_T - F(0,T)/(1 + r)^0 = S_T - F(0,T)$

The formulas for pricing and valuation of a forward contract are summarized in Exhibit 74-5.

In our examples, there were no costs or cash flows associated with holding the underlying assets. In the specific examples below for equity derivatives, fixed-income and interest rate derivatives, and currency derivatives, we present cases in which cash flows on the underlying asset will slightly alter our results. We shall ignore any costs of holding assets. Such costs are primarily associated with commodities, an asset class we do not address in this book.

EXHIBIT 74-5   Pricing and Valuation Formulas for a Forward Contract

Today = time 0
Arbitrary point during the contract's life = time t
Expiration = time T

(Exhibit continued on next page ...)

EXHIBIT 74-5   (continued)

Value of a forward contract at any time t:

$$V_t(0,T) = S_t - F(0,T)/(1 + r)^{(T-t)}$$

Value of a forward contract at expiration (t = T):

$$V_T(0,T) = S_T - F(0,T)$$

Value of a forward contract at initiation (t = 0):

$$V_0(0,T) = S_0 - F(0,T)/(1 + r)^T$$

Customarily, no money changes hands at initiation so $V_0(0,T)$ is set equal to zero. Thus,

$$F(0,T) = S_0(1 + r)^T$$

Practice Problem 1

An investor holds title to an asset worth €125.72. To raise money for an unrelated purpose, the investor plans to sell the asset in nine months. The investor is concerned about uncertainty in the price of the asset at that time. The investor learns about the advantages of using forward contracts to manage this risk and enters into such a contract to sell the asset in nine months. The risk-free interest rate is 5.625 percent.

A. Determine the appropriate price the investor could receive in nine months by means of the forward contract.

B. Suppose the counterparty to the forward contract is willing to engage in such a contract at a forward price of €140. Explain what type of transaction the investor could execute to take advantage of the situation. Calculate the rate of return (annualized), and explain why the transaction is attractive.

C. Suppose the forward contract is entered into at the price you computed in Part A. Two months later, the price of the asset is €118.875. The investor would like to evaluate her position with respect to any gain or loss accrued on the forward contract. Determine the market value of the forward contract at this point in time from the perspective of the investor in Part A.

D. Determine the value of the forward contract at expiration assuming the contract is entered into at the price you computed in Part A and the price of the underlying asset is €123.50 at expiration. Explain how the investor did on the overall position of both the asset and the forward contract in terms of the rate of return.

SOLUTIONS

A. $T = 9/12 = 0.75$
$S_0 = 125.72$
$r = 0.05625$

$F(0,T) = 125.72(1.05625)^{0.75} = 130.99$

B. As found in Part A, the forward contract should be selling at €130.99, but it is selling for €140. Consequently, it is overpriced—and an overpriced contract should be sold. Because the investor holds the asset, she will be hedged by selling the forward contract. Consequently, her asset, worth €125.72 when the forward contract is sold, will be delivered in nine months and she will receive €140 for it. The rate of return will be

$$\left(\frac{140}{125.72}\right) - 1 = 0.1136$$

This risk-free return of 11.36 percent for nine months is clearly in excess of the 5.625 percent annual rate. In fact, a rate of 11.36 percent for nine months annualizes to

$$(1.1136)^{12/9} - 1 = 0.1543$$

An annual risk-free rate of 15.43 percent is clearly preferred over the actual risk-free rate of 5.625 percent. The position is not only hedged but also earns an arbitrage profit.

C. $t = 2/12$
$T - t = 9/12 - 2/12 = 7/12$
$S_t = 118.875$
$F(0,T) = 130.99$

$$V_t(0,T) = V_{2/12}(0,9/12) = 118.875 - 130.99/(1.05625)^{7/12} = -8.0$$

The contract has a negative value. Note, however, that in this form, the answer applies to the holder of the long position. This investor is short. Thus, the value to the investor in this problem is positive 8.0.

D. $S_T = 123.50$

$$V_T(0,T) = V_{9/12}(0,9/12) = 123.50 - 130.99 = -7.49$$

This amount is the value to the long. This investor is short, so the value is a positive 7.49. The investor incurred a loss on the asset of 125.72 − 123.50 = 2.22. Combined with the gain on the forward contract, the net gain is 7.49 − 2.22 = 5.27. A gain of 5.27 on an asset worth 125.72 when the transaction was initiated represents a return of 5.27/125.72 = 4.19 percent. When annualized, the rate of return equals

$$(1.0419)^{12/9} - 1 = 0.05625$$

It should come as no surprise that this number is the annual risk-free rate. The transaction was executed at the no-arbitrage forward price of €130.99. Thus, it would be impossible to earn a return higher or lower than the risk-free rate.

4.2 Pricing and Valuation of Equity Forward Contracts

Equity forward contracts are priced and valued much like the generic contract described above, with one important additional feature. Many stocks pay dividends, and the effects of these dividends must be incorporated into the pricing and valuation process. Our concern is with the dividends that occur over the life of the forward contract, but not with those that may come after the contract ends. Following standard procedure, we assume that these dividends are known or are a constant percentage of the stock price.

We begin with the idea of a forward contract on either a single stock, a portfolio of stocks, or an index in which dividends are to be paid during the life of the contract. Using the time notation that today is time 0, expiration is time T, and there is an arbitrary time t during its life when we need to value the contract, assume that dividends can be paid at various times during the life of the contract between t and T.[19]

In the examples that follow, we shall calculate present and future values of this stream of dividends over the life of the forward contract. Given a series of these dividends of $D_1, D_2, \ldots D_n$, whose values are known, that occur at times $t_1, t_2, \ldots t_n$, the present value will be defined as PV(D,0,T) and computed as

$$PV(D,0,T) = \sum_{i=1}^{n} \frac{D_i}{(1 + r)^{t_i}}$$

The future value will be defined as FV(D,0,T) and computed as

$$FV(D,0,T) = \sum_{i=1}^{n} D_i(1 + r)^{T - t_i}$$

Recall that the forward price is established by eliminating any opportunity to arbitrage from establishing a forward contract without making any cash outlay today, as is customary with forward contracts. We found that the forward price is the spot price compounded at the risk-free interest rate. To include dividends, we adjust our formula slightly to

$$F(0,T) = [S_0 - PV(D,0,T)](1 + r)^T \qquad \textbf{(74-4)}$$

In other words, we simply subtract the present value of the dividends from the stock price. Note that the dividends reduce the forward price, a reflection of the fact that holders of long positions in forward contracts do not benefit from dividends in comparison to holders of long positions in the underlying stock.

For example, consider a stock priced at $40, which pays a dividend of $3 in 50 days. The risk-free rate is 6 percent. A forward contract expiring in six months (T = 0.5) would have a price of

$$F(0,T) = F(0,0.5) = [\$40 - \$3/(1.06)^{50/365}](1.06)^{0.5} = \$38.12$$

If the stock had more than one dividend, we would simply subtract the present value of all dividends over the life of the contract from the stock price, as in the following example.

---

[19] Given the way dividends are typically paid, the right to the dividend leaves the stock on the ex-dividend date, which is prior to the payment date. To precisely incorporate this feature, either the dividend payment date should be the ex-dividend date or the dividend should be the present value at the ex-dividend date of the dividend to be paid at a later date. We shall ignore this point here and assume that it would be taken care of in practice.

coupons that must be included in the forward contract pricing calculations. We will let $B_t^c(T + Y)$ represent the bond price at time t, T is the expiration date of the forward contract, Y is the remaining maturity of the bond on the forward contract expiration, and $(T + Y)$ is the time to maturity of the bond at the time the forward contract is initiated. Consider a bond with n coupons to occur before its maturity date. Converting our formula for a forward contract on a stock into that for a forward contract on a bond and letting CI be the coupon interest over a specified period of time, we have a forward price of

$$F(0,T) = [B_0^c(T + Y) - PV(CI,0,T)](1 + r)^T \qquad \textbf{(74-9)}$$

where $PV(CI,0,T)$ is the present value of the coupon interest over the life of the forward contract. Alternatively, the forward price can be obtained as

$$F(0,T) = [B_0^c(T + Y)](1 + r)^T - FV(CI,0,T) \qquad \textbf{(74-10)}$$

where $FV(CI,0,T)$ is the future value of the coupon interest over the life of the forward contract.

The value of the forward contract at time t would be

$$V_t(0,T) = B_t^c(T + Y) - PV(CI,t,T) - F(0,T)/(1 + r)^{(T-t)} \qquad \textbf{(74-11)}$$

at time t; note that the relevant coupons are only those remaining as of time t until expiration of the forward contract. As in the case for stock, this formula will reduce to the appropriate values at time 0 and at expiration. For example, at expiration, no coupons would remain, $t = T$, and $V_T(0,T) = B_T^c(T + Y) - F(0,T)$. At time $t = 0$, the contract is being initiated and has a zero value, which leads to the formula for $F(0,T)$ above.

Consider a bond with semiannual coupons. The bond has a current maturity of 583 days and pays four coupons, each six months apart. The next coupon occurs in 37 days, followed by coupons in 219 days, 401 days, and 583 days, at which time the principal is repaid. Suppose that the bond price, which includes accrued interest, is \$984.45 for a \$1,000 par, 4 percent coupon bond. The coupon rate implies that each coupon is \$20. The risk-free interest rate is 5.75 percent. Assume that the forward contract expires in 310 days. Thus, $T = 310$, $T + Y = 583$, and $Y = 273$, meaning that the bond has 273 days remaining after the forward contract expires. Note that only the first two coupons occur during the life of the forward contract.

The present value of the coupons is

$$\$20/(1.0575)^{37/365} + \$20/(1.0575)^{219/365} = \$39.23$$

The forward price if the contract is initiated now is

$$F(0,T) = (\$984.45 - \$39.23)(1.0575)^{310/365} = \$991.18$$

Thus, we assume that we shall be able to enter into this contract to buy the bond in 310 days at the price of \$991.18.

Now assume it is 15 days later and the new bond price is \$973.14. Let the risk-free interest rate now be 6.75 percent. The present value of the remaining coupons is

$$\$20/(1.0675)^{22/365} + \$20/(1.0675)^{204/365} = \$39.20$$

The value of the forward contract is thus

$$\$973.14 - \$39.20 - \$991.19/(1.0675)^{295/365} = -\$6.28$$

The contract has gone from a zero value at the start to a negative value, primarily as a result of the decrease in the price of the underlying bond.

If the bond is a zero-coupon bond/T-bill, we can perform the same analysis as above, but we simply let the coupons equal zero.

Exhibit 74-7 summarizes the formulas for the pricing and valuation of forward contracts on fixed-income securities.

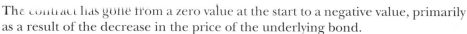

EXHIBIT 74-7	**Pricing and Valuation Formulas for Fixed Income Forward Contracts**

Forward price = (Bond price − Present value of coupons over life of contract)$(1 + r)^T$
or (Bond price)$(1 + r)^T$ − Future value of coupons over life of contract

Price of forward contract on bond with coupons CI:
$$F(0,T) = [B_0{}^c(T + Y) - PV(CI,0,T)](1 + r)^T$$
$$\text{or } [B_0{}^c(T + Y)](1 + r)^T - FV(CI,0,T)$$

Value of forward contract on bond with coupons CI:
$$V_t(0,T) = B_t{}^c(T + Y) - PV(CI,t,T) - F(0,T)/(1 + r)^{(T-t)}$$

Practice Problem 3

An investor purchased a bond when it was originally issued with a maturity of five years. The bond pays semiannual coupons of $50. It is now 150 days into the life of the bond. The investor wants to sell the bond the day after its fourth coupon. The first coupon occurs 181 days after issue, the second 365 days, the third 547 days, and the fourth 730 days. At this point (150 days into the life of the bond), the price is $1,010.25. The bond prices quoted here include accrued interest.

A. At what price could the owner enter into a forward contract to sell the bond on the day after its fourth coupon? Note that the owner would receive that fourth coupon. The risk-free rate is currently 8 percent.

B. Now move forward 365 days. The new risk-free interest rate is 7 percent and the new price of the bond is $1,025.375. The counterparty to the forward contract believes that it has received a gain on the position. Determine the value of the forward contract and the gain or loss to the counterparty at this time. Note that we have now introduced a new risk-free rate, because interest rates can obviously change over the life of the bond and any calculations of the forward contract value must reflect this fact. The new risk-free rate is used instead of the old rate in the valuation formula.

SOLUTIONS

A. First we must find the present value of the four coupons over the life of the forward contract. At the 150th day of the life of the bond, the coupons occur 31 days from now, 215 days from now, 397 days from now, and 580 days from now. Keep in mind that we need consider only the first four coupons because the owner will sell the bond on the day after the fourth coupon. The present value of the coupons is

$$\$50/(1.08)^{31/365} + \$50/(1.08)^{215/365} + \$50/(1.08)^{397/365} + \\ \$50/(1.08)^{580/365} = \$187.69$$

Because we want the forward contract to expire one day after the fourth coupon, it expires in $731 - 150 = 581$ days. Thus, $T = 581/365$.

$$F(0,T) = F(0,581/365) = (\$1,010.25 - \$187.69)(1.08)^{581/365} = \\ \$929.76$$

B. It is now 365 days later—the 515th day of the bond's life. There are two coupons to go, one occurring in $547 - 515 = 32$ days and the other in $730 - 515 = 215$ days. The present value of the coupons is now

$$\$50/(1.07)^{32/365} + \$50/(1.07)^{215/365} = \$97.75$$

To address the value of the forward contract and the gain or loss to the counterparty, note that $731 - 515 = 216$ days now remain until the contract's expiration. Because the bondholder would sell the forward contract to hedge the future sale price of the bond, the bondholder's counterparty to the forward contract would hold a long position. The value of the forward contract is the current spot price minus the present value of the coupons minus the present value of the forward price:

$$\$1,025.375 - \$97.75 - \$929.76/(1.07)^{216/365} = \$34.36$$

Because the contract was initiated with a zero value at the start and the counterparty is long the contract, the value of $34.36 represents a gain to the counterparty.

Now let us look at the pricing and valuation of FRAs. Previously we used the notations t and T to represent the time to a given date. The expressions t or T were, respectively, the number of days to time point t or T, each divided by 365. In the FRA market, contracts are created with specific day counts. We will use the letter h to refer to the day on which the FRA expires and the letter g to refer to an arbitrary day prior to expiration. Consider the time line shown below. We shall initiate an FRA on day 0. The FRA expires on day h. The rate underlying the FRA is the rate on an m-day Eurodollar deposit. Thus, there are h days from today until the FRA expiration and h + m days until the maturity date of the Eurodollar instrument on which the FRA rate is based. The date indicated by g will simply be a date during the life of the FRA at which we want to determine a value for the FRA.

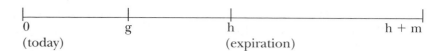

Now let us specify some notation. We let $L_i(j)$ represent the rate on a j-day LIBOR deposit on an arbitrary day i, which falls somewhere in the above period from 0 to h, inclusive. Remember that this instrument is a j-day loan from one bank to another. For example, the bank borrowing \$1 on day i for j days will pay back the amount

$$\$1\left[1 + L_i(j)\left(\frac{j}{360}\right)\right]$$

in j days.

The rate for m-day LIBOR on day h, $L_h(m)$, will determine the payoff of the FRA. We denote the fixed rate on the FRA as FRA(0,h,m), which stands for the rate on an FRA established on day 0, expiring on day h, and based on m-day LIBOR. We shall use a \$1 notional principal for the FRA, which means that at expiration its payoff is

$$\frac{[L_h(m) - FRA(0,h,m)]\left(\dfrac{m}{360}\right)}{1 + L_h(m)\left(\dfrac{m}{360}\right)} \qquad \textbf{(74-12)}$$

The numerator is the difference between the underlying LIBOR on the expiration day and the rate agreed on when the contract was initiated, multiplied by the adjustment factor m/360. Both of these rates are annual rates applied to a Eurodollar deposit of m days; hence, multiplying by m/360 is necessary. The denominator discounts the payoff by the m-day LIBOR in effect at the time of the payoff. As noted earlier, this adjustment is necessary because the rates in the numerator apply to Eurodollar deposits created on day h and paying off m days later. If the notional principal is anything other than \$1, we also must multiply the above payoff by the notional principal to determine the actual payoff.

To derive the formula for pricing an FRA, a specific arbitrage transaction involving Eurodollars and FRAs is required. We omit the details of this somewhat complex transaction, but the end result is that the FRA rate is given by the following formula:

$$FRA(0,h,m) = \left[\frac{1 + L_0(h + m)\left(\dfrac{h + m}{360}\right)}{1 + L_0(h)\left(\dfrac{h}{360}\right)} - 1\right]\left(\frac{360}{m}\right) \qquad \textbf{(74-13)}$$

This somewhat awkward-looking formula is actually just the formula for a LIBOR forward rate, given the interest payment conventions in the FRA market. The numerator is the future value of a Eurodollar deposit of h + m days. The denominator is the future value of a shorter-term Eurodollar deposit of h days. This ratio is 1 plus a rate; subtracting 1 and multiplying by 360/m annualizes the rate.[21]

---

[21] To compare with the traditional method of calculating a forward rate, consider a two-year rate of 10 percent and a one-year rate of 9 percent. The forward rate is $[(1.10)^2/(1.09)] - 1 = 0.1101$. The numerator is the future value of the longer-term bond, and the denominator is the future value of the shorter-term bond. The ratio is 1 plus the rate. We do not need to annualize in this example, because the forward rate is on a one-year bond.

Consider a 3×9 FRA. This instrument expires in 90 days and is based on 180-day LIBOR. Thus, the Eurodollar deposit on which the underlying rate is based begins in 90 days and matures in 270 days. Because we are on day 0, $h = 90$, $m = 180$, and $h + m = 270$. Let the current rates be

$$L_0(h) = L_0(90) = 0.056$$

$$L_0(h + m) = L_0(270) = 0.06$$

In other words, the 90-day rate is 5.6 percent, and the 270-day rate is 6 percent.

With $h = 90$ and $m = 180$, using our formula for the FRA rate, we obtain

$$FRA(0,h,m) = FRA(0,90,180) = \left[\frac{1 + 0.06\left(\frac{270}{360}\right)}{1 + 0.056\left(\frac{90}{360}\right)} - 1 \right]\left(\frac{360}{180}\right) = 0.0611$$

So to enter into an FRA on day 0, the rate would be 6.11 percent.[22]

As noted, the initial outlay for entering the forward contract is zero. Thus, the initial value is zero. Later during the life of the contract, its value will rise above or fall below zero. Now let us determine the value of an FRA during its life. Specifically, we use the notation $V_g(0,h,m)$ to represent the value of an FRA on day g, prior to expiration, which was established on day 0, expires on day h, and is based on m-day LIBOR. Omitting the derivation, the value of the FRA will be

$$V_g(0,h,m) = \frac{1}{1 + L_g(h - g)\left(\frac{h - g}{360}\right)} - \frac{1 + FRA(0,h,m)\left(\frac{m}{360}\right)}{1 + L_g(h + m - g)\left(\frac{h + m - g}{360}\right)} \quad \textbf{(74-14)}$$

This formula looks complicated, but the ideas behind it are actually quite simple. Recall that we are at day g. The first term on the right-hand side is the present value of \$1 received at day h. The second term is the present value of 1 plus the FRA rate to be received on day $h + m$, the maturity date of the underlying Eurodollar time deposit.

Assume that we go long the FRA, and it is 25 days later. We need to assign a value to the FRA. First note that $g = 25$, $h - g = 90 - 25 = 65$, and $h + m - g = 90 + 180 - 25 = 245$. In other words, we are 25 days into the contract, 65 days remain until expiration, and 245 days remain until the maturity of the Eurodollar deposit on which the underlying LIBOR is based. First we need information about the new term structure. Let

$$L_g(h - g) = L_{25}(65) = 0.059$$

$$L_g(h + m - g) = L_{25}(245) = 0.065$$

We now use the formula for the value of the FRA to obtain

$$V_g(0,h,m) = V_{25}(0,90,180) = \frac{1}{1 + 0.059\left(\frac{65}{360}\right)} - \frac{1 + 0.0611\left(\frac{180}{360}\right)}{1 + 0.065\left(\frac{245}{360}\right)} = 0.0026$$

---

[22] It is worthwhile to point out again that this rate is the forward rate in the LIBOR term structure.

Thus, we went long this FRA on day 0. Then 25 days later, the term structure changes to the rates used here and the FRA has a value of $0.0026 per $1 notional principal. If the notional principal is any amount other than $1, we multiply the notional principal by $0.0026 to obtain the full market value of the FRA.

We summarize the FRA formulas in Exhibit 74-8. We have now looked at the pricing and valuation of equity, fixed-income, and interest rate forward contracts. One of the most widely used types of forward contracts is the currency forward. The pricing and valuation of currency forwards is remarkably similar to that of equity forwards.

EXHIBIT 74-8	Pricing and Valuation Formulas for Interest Rate Forward Contracts (FRAs)

Forward price (rate):

$$FRA(0,h,m) = \left[\frac{1 + L_0(h + m)\left(\frac{h + m}{360}\right)}{1 + L_0(h)\left(\frac{h}{360}\right)} - 1 \right]\left(\frac{360}{m}\right)$$

Value of FRA on day g:

$$V_g(0,h,m) = \frac{1}{1 + L_g(h - g)\left(\frac{h - g}{360}\right)} - \frac{1 + FRA(0,h,m)\left(\frac{m}{360}\right)}{1 + L_g(h + m - g)\left(\frac{h + m - g}{360}\right)}$$

Practice Problem 4

A corporate treasurer needs to hedge the risk of the interest rate on a future transaction. The risk is associated with the rate on 180-day Euribor in 30 days. The relevant term structure of Euribor is given as follows:

30-day Euribor	5.75%
210-day Euribor	6.15%

A. State the terminology used to identify the FRA in which the manager is interested.

B. Determine the rate that the company would get on an FRA expiring in 30 days on 180-day Euribor.

C. Suppose the manager went long this FRA. Now, 20 days later, interest rates have moved significantly downward to the following:

10-day Euribor	5.45%
190-day Euribor	5.95%

The manager would like to know where the company stands on this FRA transaction. Determine the market value of the FRA for a €20 million notional principal.

D. On the expiration day, 180-day Euribor is 5.72 percent. Determine the payment made to or by the company to settle the FRA contract.

SOLUTIONS

A. This transaction would be identified as a 1×7 FRA.

B. Here the notation would be h = 30, m = 180, h + m = 210. Then

$$FRA(0,h,m) = FRA(0,30,180) = \left[\frac{1 + 0.0615\left(\frac{210}{360}\right)}{1 + 0.0575\left(\frac{30}{360}\right)} - 1 \right]\left(\frac{360}{180}\right) = 0.0619$$

C. Here g = 20, h − g = 30 − 20 = 10, h + m − g = 30 + 180 − 20 = 190. The value of the FRA for a €1 notional principal would be

$$V_g(0,h,m) = V_{20}(0,30,180) = \frac{1}{1 + 0.0545\left(\frac{10}{360}\right)} - \frac{1 + 0.0619\left(\frac{180}{360}\right)}{1 + 0.0595\left(\frac{190}{360}\right)} = -0.0011$$

Thus, for a notional principal of €20 million, the value would be €20,000,000(−0.0011) = −€22,000.

D. At expiration, the payoff is

$$\frac{[L_h(m) - FRA(0,h,m)]\left(\frac{m}{360}\right)}{1 + L_h(m)\left(\frac{m}{360}\right)} = \frac{(0.0572 - 0.0619)\left(\frac{180}{360}\right)}{1 + 0.0572\left(\frac{180}{360}\right)} = -0.0023$$

For a notional principal of €20 million, the payoff would then be €20,000,000(−0.0023) = −€46,000. Thus, €46,000 would be paid by the company, because it is long and the final rate was lower than the FRA rate.

4.4 Pricing and Valuation of Currency Forward Contracts

Foreign currency derivative transactions as well as spot transactions must be handled with care. The exchange rate can be quoted in terms of units of the domestic currency per unit of foreign currency, or units of the foreign currency per unit of the domestic currency. In this book, we shall always quote exchange rates in terms of units of the domestic currency per unit of the foreign currency, which is also called a direct quote. This approach is in keeping with the way in which other underlying assets are quoted. For example, from the perspective of a U.S. investor, a stock that sells for $50 is quoted in units of the domestic currency per unit (share) of stock. Likewise, if the euro exchange rate is quoted as $0.90, then the euro sells for $0.90 per unit, which is one euro. Alternatively, we could quote that $1 sells for 1/$0.90 = €1.1111—that is, €1.1111 per $1; in this case, units of foreign currency per one unit of domestic currency from the perspective of a U.S. investor. In fact, this type of quote is commonly used and is called an indirect quote. Taking that approach, however, we would quote the stock price as 1/$50 = 0.02 shares per $1, a very unusual and awkward way to quote a stock price.

By taking the approach of quoting prices in terms of units of the domestic currency per unit of foreign currency, we facilitate a comparison of currencies and their derivatives with equities and their derivatives—a topic we have already covered. For example, we have previously discussed the case of a stock selling for S_0, which represents units of the domestic currency per share of stock. Likewise, we shall treat the currency as having an exchange rate of S_0, meaning that it is selling for S_0. We also need the foreign interest rate, denoted as r^f, and the domestic interest rate, denoted as r.[23]

Consider the following transactions executed today (time 0), assuming a contract expiration date of T:

Take $S_0/(1 + r^f)^T$ units of the domestic currency and convert it to $1/(1 + r^f)^T$ units of the foreign currency.[24]

Sell a forward contract to deliver one unit of the foreign currency at the rate F(0,T) expiring at time T.

Hold the position until time T. The $(1 + r^f)^T$ units of foreign currency will accrue interest at the rate r^f and grow to one unit of the currency at T as follows:

$$\left(\frac{1}{1 + r^f}\right)^T (1 + r^f) = 1$$

Thus, at expiration we shall have one unit of the foreign currency, which is then delivered to the holder of the long forward contract, who pays the amount F(0,T). This amount was known at the start of the transaction. Because the risk has been hedged away, the exchange rate at expiration is irrelevant. Hence, this transaction is risk-free. Accordingly, the present value of F(0,T), found by discounting at the domestic risk-free interest rate, must equal the initial outlay of $S_0/(1 + r^f)^T$. Setting these amounts equal and solving for F(0,T) gives

$$F(0,T) = \left[\frac{S_0}{(1 + r^f)^T}\right](1 + r)^T \tag{74-15}$$

The term in brackets is the spot exchange rate discounted by the foreign interest rate. This term is then compounded at the domestic interest rate to the expiration day.[25]

---

[23] We do not use a superscript "d" for the domestic rate, because in all previous examples we have used r to denote the interest rate in the home country of the investor.

[24] In other words, if one unit of the foreign currency costs S_0, then $S_0/(1 + r^f)^T$ units of the domestic currency would, therefore, buy $1/(1 + r^f)^T$ units of the foreign currency.

[25] It is also common to see the above Equation 74-15 written inversely, with the spot rate divided by the domestic interest factor and compounded by the foreign interest factor. This variation would be appropriate if the spot and forward rates were quoted in terms of units of the foreign currency per unit of domestic currency (indirect quotes). As we mentioned earlier, however, it is easier to think of a currency as just another asset, which naturally should have its price quoted in units of the domestic currency per unit of the asset or foreign currency.

Recall that in pricing equity forwards, we always reduced the stock price by the present value of the dividends and then compounded the resulting value to the expiration date. We can view currencies in the same way. The stock makes cash payments that happen to be called dividends; the currency makes cash payments that happen to be called interest. Although the time pattern of how a stock pays dividends is quite different from the time pattern of how interest accrues, the general idea is the same. After reducing the spot price or rate by any cash flows over the life of the contract, the resulting value is then compounded at the risk-free rate to the expiration day.

The formula we have obtained here is simply a variation of the formula used for other types of forward contracts. In international financial markets, however, this formula has acquired its own name: **interest rate parity** (sometimes called covered interest rate parity). It expresses the equivalence, or parity, of spot and forward exchange rates, after adjusting for differences in the interest rates in the two countries. One implication of interest rate parity is that the forward rate will exceed (be less than) the spot rate if the domestic interest rate exceeds (is less than) the foreign interest rate. With a direct quote, if the forward rate exceeds (is less than) the spot rate, the foreign currency is said to be selling at a premium (discount). One should not, on the basis of this information, conclude that a currency selling at a premium is expected to increase or one selling at a discount is expected to decrease. A forward premium or discount is merely an implication of the relationship between interest rates in the two countries. More information would be required to make any assumptions about the outlook for the exchange rate.

If the forward rate in the market does not equal the forward rate given by interest rate parity, then an arbitrage transaction can be executed. Indeed, a similar relationship is true for any of the forward rates we have studied. In the foreign exchange markets, however, this arbitrage transaction has its own name: **covered interest arbitrage**. If the forward rate in the market is higher than the rate given by interest rate parity, then the forward rate is too high. When the price of an asset or derivative is too high, it should be sold. Thus, a trader would 1) sell the forward contract at the market rate, 2) buy $1/(1 + r^f)^T$ units of the foreign currency, 3) hold the position, earning interest on the currency, and 4) at maturity of the forward contract deliver the currency and be paid the forward rate. This arbitrage transaction would earn a return in excess of the domestic risk-free rate without any risk. If the forward rate is less than the rate given by the formula, the trader does the opposite, selling the foreign currency and buying a forward contract, in a similar manner. The combined actions of many traders undertaking this transaction will bring the forward price in the market in line with the forward price given by the model.

In Equation 74-15, both interest rates were annual rates with discrete compounding. In dealing with equities, we sometimes assume that the dividend payments are made continuously. Similarly, we could also assume that interest is compounded continuously. If that is the case, let r^{fc} be the continuously compounded foreign interest rate, defined as $r^{fc} = \ln(1 + r^f)$, and as before, let r^c be the continuously compounded domestic interest rate. Then the forward price is given by the same formula, with appropriately adjusted symbols, as we obtained when working with equity derivatives:

$$F(0,T) = (S_0 e^{-r^{fc}T})e^{r^c T}$$

(74-16)

Now consider how we might value a foreign currency forward contract at some point in time during its life. In fact, we already know how: We simply apply to foreign currency forward contracts what we know about the valuation of equity forwards during the contract's life. Recall that the value of an equity forward is the stock price minus the present value of the dividends over the remaining life of the contract minus the present value of the forward price over the remaining life of the contract. An analogous formula for a currency forward gives us

$$V_t(0,T) = \frac{S_t}{(1 + r^f)^{(T-t)}} - \frac{F(0,T)}{(1 + r)^{(T-t)}} \qquad \textbf{(74-17)}$$

In other words, we take the current exchange rate at time t, S_t, discount it by the foreign interest rate over the remaining life of the contract, and subtract the forward price discounted by the domestic interest rate over the remaining life of the contract. Under the assumption that we are using continuous compounding and discounting, the formula would be

$$V_t(0,T) = (S_t e^{-r^{fc}(T-t)}) - F(0,T)e^{-r^c(T-t)} \qquad \textbf{(74-18)}$$

For example, suppose the domestic currency is the U.S. dollar and the foreign currency is the Swiss franc. Let the spot exchange rate be $0.5987, the U.S. interest rate be 5.5 percent, and the Swiss interest rate be 4.75 percent. We assume these interest rates are fixed and will not change over the life of the forward contract. We also assume that these rates are based on annual compounding and are not quoted as LIBOR-type rates. Thus, we compound using formulas like $(1 + r)^T$, where T is the number of years and r is the annual rate.[26]

Assuming the forward contract has a maturity of 180 days, we have T = 180/365. Using the above formula for the forward rate, we find that the forward price should be

$$F(0,T) = F(0,180/365) = \left[\frac{\$0.5987}{(1.0475)^{180/365}}\right](1.055)^{180/365} = \$0.6008$$

Thus, if we entered into a forward contract, it would call for us to purchase (if long) or sell (if short) one Swiss franc in 180 days at a price of $0.6008.

Suppose we go long this forward contract. It is now 40 days later, or 140 days until expiration. The spot rate is now $0.65. As assumed above, the interest rates are fixed. With t = 40/365 and T − t = 140/365, the value of our long position is

$$V_t(0,T) = V_{40/365}(0,180/365) = \frac{\$0.6500}{(1.0475)^{140/365}} - \frac{\$0.6008}{(1.055)^{140/365}} = \$0.0499$$

So the contract value is $0.0499 per Swiss franc. If the notional principal were more than one Swiss franc, we would simply multiply the notional principal by $0.0499.

If we were working with continuously compounded rates, we would have r^c = ln(1.055) = 0.0535 and r^{fc} = ln(1.0475) = 0.0464. Then the forward price would be F(0,T) = F(0,180/365) = $(0.5987e^{-0.0464(180/365)})e^{0.0535(180/365)}$ = 0.6008, and the value 40 days later would be $V_{40/365}(0,180/365) = 0.65e^{-0.0464(140/365)} - 0.6008e^{-0.0535(140/365)}$ = 0.0499. These are the same results we obtained working with discrete rates.

Exhibit 74-9 summarizes the formulas for pricing and valuation of currency forward contracts.

---

[26] If these were LIBOR-style rates, the interest would be calculated using the factor 1 + [Rate(Days/360)].

| EXHIBIT 74-9 | Pricing and Valuation Formulas for Currency Forward Contracts |

Forward price (rate) = (Spot price discounted by foreign interest rate) compounded at domestic interest rate:

$$\text{Discrete interest: } F(0,T) = \left[\frac{S_0}{(1 + r^f)^T}\right](1 + r)^T$$

$$\text{Continuous interest: } F(0,T) = (S_0 e^{-r^{fc}T}) e^{r^c T}$$

Value of forward contract:

$$\text{Discrete interest: } V_t(0,T) = \left[\frac{S_t}{(1 + r^f)^{(T-t)}}\right] - \frac{F(0,T)}{(1 + r)^{(T-t)}}$$

$$\text{Continuous interest: } V_t(0,T) = [S_t e^{-r^{fc}(T-t)}] - F(0,T) e^{-r^c(T-t)}$$

Note: The exchange rate is quoted in units of domestic currency per unit of foreign currency.

PRACTICE PROBLEM 5

The spot rate for British pounds is $1.76. The U.S. risk-free rate is 5.1 percent, and the U.K. risk-free rate is 6.2 percent; both are compounded annually. One-year forward contracts are currently quoted at a rate of $1.75.

A. Identify a strategy with which a trader can earn a profit at no risk by engaging in a forward contract, regardless of her view of the pound's likely movements. Carefully describe the transactions the trader would make. Show the rate of return that would be earned from this transaction. Assume the trader's domestic currency is U.S. dollars.

B. Suppose the trader simply shorts the forward contract. It is now one month later. Assume interest rates are the same, but the spot rate is now $1.72. What is the gain or loss to the counterparty on the trade?

C. At expiration, the pound is at $1.69. What is the value of the forward contract to the short at expiration?

SOLUTIONS

A. The following information is given:

$$S_0 = \$1.76$$
$$r = 0.051$$
$$r^f = 0.062$$
$$T = 1.0$$

The forward price should be

$$F(0,T) = \left(\frac{\$1.76}{1.062}\right)(1.051) = \$1.7418$$

With the forward contract selling at $1.75, it is slightly overpriced. Thus, the trader should be able to buy the currency and sell a forward contract to earn a return in excess of the risk-free rate at no risk. The specific transactions are as follows:

▶ Take $1.76/(1.062) = $1.6573. Use it to buy 1/1.062 = £0.9416.

▶ Sell a forward contract to deliver £1.00 in one year at the price of $1.75.

▶ Hold the position for one year, collecting interest at the U.K. risk-free rate of 6.2 percent. The £0.9416 will grow to (0.9416)(1.062) = £1.00.

▶ At expiration, deliver the pound and receive $1.75. This is a return of

$$\frac{1.75}{1.6573} - 1 = 0.0559$$

A risk-free return of 5.59 percent is better than the U.S. risk-free rate of 5.1 percent, a result of the fact that the forward contract is overpriced.

B. We now need the value of the forward contract to the counterparty, who went long at $1.75. The inputs are

$$t = 1/12$$
$$S_t = \$1.72$$
$$T - t = 11/12$$
$$F(0,T) = \$1.75$$

The value of the forward contract to the long is

$$V_t(0,T) = \frac{1.72}{(1.062)^{(11/12)}} - \frac{1.75}{(1.051)^{11/12}} = -0.0443$$

which is a loss of $0.0443 to the long and a gain of $0.0443 to the short.

C. The pound is worth $1.69 at expiration. Thus, the value to the long is

$$V_T(0,T) = 1.69 - 1.75 = -0.06$$

and the value to the short is +$0.06. Note the minus sign in the equation $V_T(0,T) = -0.06$. The value to the long is always the spot value at expiration minus the original forward price. The short will be required to deliver the foreign currency and receive $1.75, which is $0.06 more than market value of the pound. The contract's value to the short is thus $0.06, which is the negative of its value to the long.

future purchase or sale of an asset at an agreed-upon price, without the necessity of paying any cash until the asset is actually purchased or sold. In contrast to futures contracts, forward contracts are private transactions, permitting the ultimate in customization. As long as a counterparty can be found, a party can structure the contract completely to its liking. Futures contracts are standardized and may not have the exact terms required by the party. In addition, futures contracts, with their daily marking to market, produce interim cash flows that can lead to imperfections in a hedge transaction designed not to hedge interim events but to hedge a specific event at a target horizon date. Forward markets also provide secrecy and have only a light degree of regulation. In general, forward markets serve a specialized clientele, specifically large corporations and institutions with specific target dates, underlying assets, and risks that they wish to take or reduce by committing to a transaction without paying cash at the start.

As Reading 77 will make clear, however, forward contracts are just miniature versions of swaps. A swap can be viewed as a series of forward contracts. Swaps are much more widely used than forward contracts, suggesting that parties that have specific risk management needs typically require the equivalent of a series of forward contracts. A swap contract consolidates a series of forward contracts into a single instrument at lower cost.

Forward contracts are the building blocks for constructing and understanding both swaps and futures. Swaps and futures are more widely used and better known, but forward contracts play a valuable role in helping us understand swaps and futures. Moreover, as noted, for some parties, forward contracts serve specific needs not met by other derivatives.

In Reading 75 we shall look at futures contracts. We shall demonstrate how similar they are to forward contracts, but the differences are important, and some of their benefits to society are slightly different and less obvious than those of forwards.

OPTIONAL SEGMENT
ENDS

SUMMARY

- ► The holder of a long forward contract (the "long") is obligated to take delivery of the underlying asset and pay the forward price at expiration. The holder of a short forward contract (the "short") is obligated to deliver the underlying asset and accept payment of the forward price at expiration.

- ► At expiration, a forward contract can be terminated by having the short make delivery of the underlying asset to the long or having the long and short exchange the equivalent cash value. If the asset is worth more (less) than the forward price, the short (long) pays the long (short) the cash difference between the market price or rate and the price or rate agreed on in the contract.

- ► A party can terminate a forward contract prior to expiration by entering into an opposite transaction with the same or a different counterparty. It is possible to leave both the original and new transactions in place, thereby leaving both transactions subject to credit risk, or to have the two transactions cancel each other. In the latter case, the party owing the greater amount pays the market value to the other party, resulting in the elimination of the remaining credit risk. This elimination can be achieved, however, only if the counterparty to the second transaction is the same counterparty as in the first.

- ► A dealer is a financial institution that makes a market in forward contracts and other derivatives. A dealer stands ready to take either side of a transaction. An end user is a party that comes to a dealer needing a transaction, usually for the purpose of managing a particular risk.

- ► Equity forward contracts can be written on individual stocks, specific stock portfolios, or stock indices. Equity forward contract prices and values must take into account the fact that the underlying stock, portfolio, or index could pay dividends.

- ► Forward contracts on bonds can be based on zero-coupon bonds or on coupon bonds, as well as portfolios or indices based on zero-coupon bonds or coupon bonds. Zero-coupon bonds pay their return by discounting the face value, often using a 360-day year assumption. Forward contracts on bonds must expire before the bond's maturity. In addition, a forward contract on a bond can be affected by special features of bonds, such as callability and convertibility.

- ► Eurodollar time deposits are dollar loans made by one bank to another. Although the term "Eurodollars" refers to dollar-denominated loans, similar loans exist in other currencies. Eurodollar deposits accrue interest by adding it on to the principal, using a 360-day year assumption. The primary Eurodollar rate is called LIBOR.

- ► LIBOR stands for London Interbank Offer Rate, the rate at which London banks are willing to lend to other London banks. Euribor is the rate on a euro time deposit, a loan made by banks to other banks in Frankfurt in which the currency is the euro.

- ► An FRA is a forward contract in which one party, the long, agrees to pay a fixed interest payment at a future date and receive an interest payment at a rate to be determined at expiration. FRAs are described by a special notation. For example, a 3×6 FRA expires in three months; the underlying is a Eurodollar deposit that begins in three months and ends three months later, or six months from now.

► The payment of an FRA at expiration is based on the net difference between the underlying rate and the agreed-upon rate, adjusted by the notional principal and the number of days in the instrument on which the underlying rate is based. The payoff is also discounted, however, to reflect the fact that the underlying rate on which the instrument is based assumes that payment will occur at a later date.

► A currency forward contract is a commitment for one party, the long, to buy a currency at a fixed price from the other party, the short, at a specific date. The contract can be settled by actual delivery, or the two parties can choose to settle in cash on the expiration day.

► A forward contract is priced by assuming that the underlying asset is purchased, a forward contract is sold, and the position is held to expiration. Because the sale price of the asset is locked in as the forward price, the transaction is risk free and should earn the risk-free rate. The forward price is then obtained as the price that guarantees a return of the risk-free rate. If the forward price is too high or too low, an arbitrage profit in the form of a return in excess of the risk-free rate can be earned. The combined effects of all investors executing arbitrage transactions will force the forward price to converge to its arbitrage-free level.

► The value of a forward contract is determined by the fact that a long forward contract is a claim on the underlying asset and a commitment to pay the forward price at expiration. The value of a forward contract is, therefore, the current price of the asset less the present value of the forward price at expiration. Because no money changes hands at the start, the value of the forward contract today is zero. The value of a forward contract at expiration is the price of the underlying asset minus the forward price.

► Valuation of a forward contract is important because 1) it makes good business sense to know the values of future commitments, 2) accounting rules require that forward contracts be accounted for in income statements and balance sheets, 3) the value gives a good measure of the credit exposure, and 4) the value can be used to determine the amount of money one party would have to pay another party to terminate a position.

► An off-market forward contract is established with a nonzero value at the start. The contract will, therefore, have a positive or negative value and require a cash payment at the start. A positive value is paid by the long to the short; a negative value is paid by the short to the long. In an off-market forward contract, the forward price will not equal the price of the underlying asset compounded at the risk-free rate but rather will be set in the process of negotiation between the two parties.

► An equity forward contract is priced by taking the stock price, subtracting the present value of the dividends over the life of the contract, and then compounding this amount at the risk-free rate to the expiration date of the contract. The present value of the dividends can be found by assuming the dividends are risk-free and calculating their present value using the risk-free rate of interest. Or one can assume that dividends are paid at a constant continuously compounded rate and then discount the stock price by the exponential function using the continuously compounded dividend rate. Alternatively, an equity forward can be priced by compounding the stock price to the expiration date and then subtracting the future value of the dividends at the expiration date. The value of an equity forward contract is the stock price minus the present value of the dividends minus the present value of the forward price that will be paid at expiration.

▶ To price a **fixed-income forward** contract, take the bond price, subtract the present value of the coupons over the life of the contract, and compound this amount at the risk-free rate to the expiration date of the contract. The value of a fixed-income forward contract is the bond price minus the present value of the coupons minus the present value of the forward price that will be paid at expiration.

▶ The price of an FRA, which is actually a rate, is simply the forward rate embedded in the term structure of the FRA's underlying rate. The value of an FRA based on a Eurodollar deposit is the present value of $1 to be received at expiration minus the present value of $1 plus the FRA rate to be received at the maturity date of the Eurodollar deposit on which the FRA is based, with appropriate (days/360) adjustments.

▶ The price, which is actually an exchange rate, of a forward contract on a currency is the spot rate discounted at the foreign interest rate over the life of the contract and then compounded at the domestic interest rate to the expiration date of the contract. The value of a currency forward contract is the spot rate discounted at the foreign interest rate over the life of the contract minus the present value of the forward rate at expiration.

▶ Credit risk in a forward contract arises when the counterparty that owes the greater amount is unable to pay at expiration or declares bankruptcy prior to expiration. The market value of a forward contract is a measure of the net amount one party owes the other. Only one party, the one owing the lesser amount, faces credit risk at any given time. Because the market value can change from positive to negative, however, the other party has the potential for facing credit risk at a later date. Counterparties occasionally mark forward contracts to market, with one party paying the other the current market value; they then reprice the contract to the current market price or rate.

▶ Forward markets play an important role in society, providing a means by which a select clientele of parties can engage in customized, private, unregulated transactions that commit them to buying or selling an asset at a later date at an agreed-upon price without paying any cash at the start. Forward contracts also are a simplified version of both futures and swaps and, therefore, form a basis for understanding these other derivatives.

date at a price agreed on today. Unlike a forward contract, however, a futures contract is not a private and customized transaction but rather a public transaction that takes place on an organized futures exchange. In addition, a futures contract is standardized—the exchange, rather than the individual parties, sets the terms and conditions, with the exception of price. As a result, futures contracts have a secondary market, meaning that previously created contracts can be traded. Also, parties to futures contracts are guaranteed against credit losses resulting from the counterparty's inability to pay. A clearinghouse provides this guarantee via a procedure in which it converts gains and losses that accrue on a daily basis into actual cash gains and losses. Futures contracts are regulated at the federal government level; as we noted in Reading 74, forward contracts are essentially unregulated. Futures contracts are created on organized trading facilities referred to as futures exchanges, whereas forward contracts are not created in any specific location but rather initiated between any two parties who wish to enter into such a contract. Finally, each futures exchange has a division or subsidiary called a clearinghouse that performs the specific responsibilities of paying and collecting daily gains and losses as well as guaranteeing to each party the performance of the other.

In a futures transaction, one party, the long, is the buyer and the other party, the short, is the seller. The buyer agrees to buy the underlying at a later date, the expiration, at a price agreed on at the start of the contract. The seller agrees to sell the underlying to the buyer at the expiration, at the price agreed on at the start of the contract. Every day, the futures contract trades in the market and its price changes in response to new information. Buyers benefit from price increases, and sellers benefit from price decreases. On the expiration day, the contract terminates and no further trading takes place. Then, either the buyer takes delivery of the underlying from the seller, or the two parties make an equivalent cash settlement. We shall explore each of these characteristics of futures contracts in more detail. First, however, it is important to take a brief look at how futures markets came into being.

1.1 A Brief History of Futures Markets

Although vestiges of futures markets appear in the Japanese rice markets of the 18th century and perhaps even earlier, the mid-1800s marked the first clear origins of modern futures markets. For example, in the United States in the 1840s, Chicago was becoming a major transportation and distribution center for agricultural commodities. Its central location and access to the Great Lakes gave Chicago a competitive advantage over other U.S. cities. Farmers from the Midwest would harvest their grain and take it to Chicago for sale. Grain production, however, is seasonal. As a result, grain prices would rise sharply just prior to the harvest but then plunge when the grain was brought to the market. Too much grain at one time and too little at another resulted in severe problems. Grain storage facilities in Chicago were inadequate to accommodate the oversupply. Some farmers even dumped their grain in the Chicago River because prices were so low that they could not afford to take their grain to another city to sell.

To address this problem, in 1848 a group of businessmen formed an organization later named the Chicago Board of Trade (CBOT) and created an arrangement called a "to-arrive" contract. These contracts permitted farmers to sell their grain before delivering it. In other words, farmers could harvest the grain and enter into a contract to deliver it at a much later date at a price already agreed on. This transaction allowed the farmer to hold the grain in storage at some other location besides Chicago. On the other side of these contracts were the businessmen who had formed the Chicago Board of Trade.

It soon became apparent that trading in these to-arrive contracts was more important and useful than trading in the grain itself. Soon the contracts began trading in a type of secondary market, which allowed buyers and sellers to discharge their obligations by passing them on, for a price, to other parties. With the addition of the clearinghouse in the 1920s, which provided a guarantee against default, modern futures markets firmly established their place in the financial world. It was left to other exchanges, such as today's Chicago Mercantile Exchange, the New York Mercantile Exchange, Eurex, and the London International Financial Futures Exchange, to develop and become, along with the Chicago Board of Trade, the global leaders in futures markets.

We shall now explore the important features of futures contracts in more detail.

1.2 Public Standardized Transactions

A private transaction is not generally reported in the news or to any price-reporting service. Forward contracts are private contracts. Just as in most legal contracts, the parties do not publicly report that they have engaged in a contract. In contrast, a futures transaction is reported to the futures exchange, the clearinghouse, and at least one regulatory agency. The price is recorded and available from price reporting services and even on the Internet.[1]

We noted that a futures transaction is not customized. Recall from Reading 74 that in a forward contract, the two parties establish all of the terms of the contract, including the identity of the underlying, the expiration date, and the manner in which the contract is settled (cash or actual delivery) as well as the price. The terms are customized to meet the needs of both parties. In a futures contract, the price is the only term established by the two parties; the exchange establishes all other terms. Moreover, the terms that are established by the exchange are standardized, meaning that the exchange selects a number of choices for underlyings, expiration dates, and a variety of other contract-specific items. These standardized terms are well known to all parties. If a party wishes to trade a futures contract, it must accept these terms. The only alternative would be to create a similar but customized contract on the forward market.

With respect to the underlying, for example, a given asset has a variety of specifications and grades. Consider a futures contract on U.S. Treasury bonds. There are many different Treasury bonds with a variety of characteristics. The futures exchange must decide which Treasury bond or group of bonds the contract covers. One of the most actively traded commodity futures contracts is oil, but there are many different types of oil.[2] To which type of oil does the contract apply? The exchange decides at the time it designs the contract.

The parties to a forward contract set its expiration at whatever date they want. For a futures contract, the exchange establishes a set of expiration dates.

---

[1] The information reported to the general public does not disclose the identity of the parties to transactions but only that a transaction took place at a particular price.

[2] Some of the main types are Saudi Arabian light crude, Brent crude, and West Texas intermediate crude.

The first specification of the expiration is the month. An exchange might establish that a given futures contract expires only in the months of March, June, September, and December. The second specification determines how far the expirations go out into the future. For example, in January of a given year, there may be expirations of March, June, September, and December. Expirations might also be available for March, June, September, and December of the following year, and perhaps some months of the year after that. The exchange decides which expiration months are appropriate for trading, based on which expirations they believe would be actively traded. Treasury bond futures have expirations going out only about a year. Eurodollar futures, however, have expirations that go out about 10 years.[3] The third specification of the expiration is the specific day of expiration. Many, but not all, contracts expire some time during the third week of the expiration month.

The exchange determines a number of other contract characteristics, including the contract size. For example, one Eurodollar futures contract covers $1 million of a Eurodollar time deposit. One U.S. Treasury bond futures contract covers $100,000 face value of Treasury bonds. One futures contract on crude oil covers 1,000 barrels. The exchange also decides on the price quotation unit. For example, Treasury bond futures are quoted in points and 32nds of par of 100. Hence, you will see a price like 104 21/32, which means 104.65625. With a contract size of $100,000, the actual price is $104,656.25.

The exchange also determines what hours of the day trading takes place and at what physical location on the exchange the contract will be traded. Many futures exchanges have a trading floor, which contains octagonal-shaped pits. A contract is assigned to a certain pit. Traders enter the pits and express their willingness to buy and sell by calling out and/or indicating by hand signals their bids and offers. Some exchanges have electronic trading, which means that trading takes place on computer terminals, generally located in companies' offices. Some exchanges have both floor trading and electronic trading; some have only one or the other.

1.3 Homogenization and Liquidity

By creating contracts with generally accepted terms, the exchange standardizes the instrument. In contrast, forward contracts are quite heterogeneous because they are customized. Standardizing the instrument makes it more acceptable to a broader group of participants, with the advantage being that the instrument can then more easily trade in a type of secondary market. Indeed, the ability to sell a previously purchased contract or purchase a previously sold contract is one of the important features of futures contracts. A futures contract is therefore said to have liquidity in contrast to a forward contract, which does not generally trade after it has been created.[4] This ability to trade a previously opened contract allows participants in this market to offset the position before expiration, thereby obtaining exposure to price movements in the underlying without the actual requirement of holding the position to expiration. We shall discuss this characteristic further when we describe futures trading in Section 2.

---

[3] You may be wondering why some Eurodollar futures contracts have such long expirations. Dealers in swaps and forward rate agreements use Eurodollar futures to hedge their positions. Many of those over-the-counter contracts have very long expirations.

[4] The notion of liquidity here is only that a market exists for futures contracts, but this does not imply a high degree of liquidity. There may be little trading in a given contract, and the bid–ask spread can be high. In contrast, some forward markets can be very liquid, allowing forward contracts to be offset, as described in Reading 74.

1.4 The Clearinghouse, Daily Settlement, and Performance Guarantee

Another important distinction between futures and forwards is that the futures exchange guarantees to each party the performance of the other party, through a mechanism known as the clearinghouse. This guarantee means that if one party makes money on the transaction, it does not have to worry about whether it will collect the money from the other party because the clearinghouse ensures it will be paid. In contrast, each party to a forward contract assumes the risk that the other party will default.

An important and distinguishing feature of futures contracts is that the gains and losses on each party's position are credited and charged on a daily basis. This procedure, called **daily settlement** or **marking to market**, essentially results in paper gains and losses being converted to cash gains and losses each day. It is also equivalent to terminating a contract at the end of each day and reopening it the next day at that settlement price. In some sense, a futures contract is like a strategy of opening up a forward contract, closing it one day later, opening up a new contract, closing it one day later, and continuing in that manner until expiration. The exact manner in which the daily settlement works will be covered in more detail later in Section 3.

1.5 Regulation

In most countries, futures contracts are regulated at the federal government level. State and regional laws may also apply. In the United States, the Commodity Futures Trading Commission regulates the futures market. In the United Kingdom, the Securities and Futures Authority regulates both the securities and futures markets.

Federal regulation of futures markets generally arises out of a concern to protect the general public and other futures market participants, as well as through a recognition that futures markets affect all financial markets and the economy. Regulations cover such matters as ensuring that prices are reported accurately and in a timely manner, that markets are not manipulated, that professionals who offer their services to the public are qualified and honest, and that disputes are resolved. In the United States, the government has delegated some of these responsibilities to an organization called the National Futures Association (NFA). An industry self-regulatory body, the NFA was created with the objective of having the industry regulate itself and reduce the federal government's burden.

FUTURES TRADING   2

In this section, we look more closely at how futures contracts are traded. As noted above, futures contracts trade on a futures exchange either in a pit or on a screen or electronic terminal.

We briefly mentioned pit trading, also known as floor-based trading, in Section 1.2. Pit trading is a very physical activity. Traders stand in the pit and shout out their orders in the form of prices they are willing to pay or accept. They also use hand signals to indicate their bids and offers.[5] They engage in

---

[5] Hand signals facilitate trading with someone who is too far away in the pit for verbal communication.

transactions with other traders in the pits by simply agreeing on a price and number of contracts to trade. The activity is fast, furious, exciting, and stressful. The average pit trader is quite young, owing to the physical demands of the job and the toll it takes on body and mind. In recent years, more trading has come off of the exchange floor to electronic screens or terminals. In electronic or screen-based trading, exchange members enter their bids and offers into a computer system, which then displays this information and allows a trader to consummate a trade electronically. In the United States, pit trading is dominant, owing to its long history and tradition. Exchange members who trade on the floor enjoy pit trading and have resisted heavily the advent of electronic trading. Nonetheless, the exchanges have had to respond to market demands to offer electronic trading. In the United States, both pit trading and electronic trading are used, but in other countries, electronic trading is beginning to drive pit trading out of business.[6]

A person who enters into a futures contract establishes either a long position or a short position. Similar to forward contracts, long positions are agreements to buy the underlying at the expiration at a price agreed on at the start. Short positions are agreements to sell the underlying at a future date at a price agreed on at the start. When the position is established, each party deposits a small amount of money, typically called the margin, with the clearinghouse. Then, as briefly described in Section 1.4, the contract is marked to market, whereby the gains are distributed to and the losses collected from each party. We cover this marking-to-market process in more detail in the next section. For now, however, we focus only on the opening and closing of the position.

A party that has opened a long position collects profits or incurs losses on a daily basis. At some point in the life of the contract prior to expiration, that party may wish to re-enter the market and close out the position. This process, called **offsetting**, is the same as selling a previously purchased stock or buying back a stock to close a short position. The holder of a long futures position simply goes back into the market and offers the identical contract for sale. The holder of a short position goes back into the market and offers to buy the identical contract. It should be noted that when a party offsets a position, it does not necessary do so with the same counterparty to the original contract. In fact, rarely would a contract be offset with the same counterparty. Because of the ability to offset, futures contracts are said to be fungible, which means that any futures contract with any counterparty can be offset by an equivalent futures contract with another counterparty. Fungibility is assured by the fact that the clearinghouse inserts itself in the middle of each contract and, therefore, becomes the counterparty to each party.

For example, suppose in early January a futures trader purchases an S&P 500 stock index futures contract expiring in March. Through 15 February, the trader has incurred some gains and losses from the daily settlement and decides that she wants to close the position out. She then goes back into the market and offers for sale the March S&P 500 futures. Once she finds a buyer to take the position, she has a long and short position in the same contract. The clearinghouse considers that she no longer has a position in that contract and has no remaining exposure, nor any obligation to make or take delivery at expiration. Had she initially gone short the March futures, she might re-enter the market in February offering to buy it. Once she finds a seller to take the opposite position, she becomes long and short the same contract and is considered to have offset the contract and therefore have no net position.

---

[6] For example, in France electronic trading was introduced while pit trading continued. Within two weeks, all of the volume had migrated to electronic trading and pit trading was terminated.

THE CLEARINGHOUSE, MARGINS, AND PRICE LIMITS

As briefly noted in the previous section, when a trader takes a long or short position in a futures, he must first deposit sufficient funds in a margin account. This amount of money is traditionally called the margin, a term derived from the stock market practice in which an investor borrows a portion of the money required to purchase a certain amount of stock.

Margin in the stock market is quite different from margin in the futures market. In the stock market, "margin" means that a loan is made. The loan enables the investor to reduce the amount of his own money required to purchase the securities, thereby generating leverage or gearing, as it is sometimes known. If the stock goes up, the percentage gain to the investor is amplified. If the stock goes down, however, the percentage loss is also amplified. The borrowed money must eventually be repaid with interest. The margin percentage equals the market value of the stock minus the market value of the debt divided by the market value of the stock—in other words, the investor's own equity as a percentage of the value of the stock. For example, in the United States, regulations permit an investor to borrow up to 50 percent of the initial value of the stock. This percentage is called the initial margin requirement. On any day thereafter, the equity or percentage ownership in the account, measured as the market value of the securities minus the amount borrowed, can be less than 50 percent but must be at least a percentage known as the maintenance margin requirement. A typical **maintenance margin requirement** is 25 to 30 percent.

In the futures market, by contrast, the word **margin** is commonly used to describe the amount of money that must be put into an account by a party opening up a futures position, but the term is misleading. When a transaction is initiated, a futures trader puts up a certain amount of money to meet the **initial margin requirement**; however, the remaining money is not borrowed. The amount of money deposited is more like a down payment for the commitment to purchase the underlying at a later date. Alternatively, one can view this deposit as a form of good faith money, collateral, or a performance bond: The money helps ensure that the party fulfills his or her obligation.[7] Moreover, both the buyer and the seller of a futures contract must deposit margin.

In securities markets, margin requirements are normally set by federal regulators. In the United States, maintenance margin requirements are set by the securities exchanges and the NASD. In futures markets, margin requirements are set by the clearinghouses. In further contrast to margin practices in securities markets, futures margins are traditionally expressed in dollar terms and not as a percentage of the futures price. For ease of comparison, however, we often speak of the futures margin in terms of its relationship to the futures price. In futures markets, the initial margin requirement is typically much lower than the initial margin requirement in the stock market. In fact, futures margins are usually less than 10 percent of the futures price.[8] Futures clearinghouses set their margin requirements by studying historical price movements. They then establish minimum margin levels by taking into account normal price movements and the fact that accounts are marked to market daily. The clearinghouses thus collect and

---

[7] In fact, the Chicago Mercantile Exchange uses the term "performance bond" instead of "margin." Most other exchanges use the term "margin."

[8] For example, the margin requirement of the Eurodollar futures contract at the Chicago Mercantile Exchange has been less than one-tenth of one percent of the futures price. An exception to this requirement, however, is individual stock futures, which in the United States have margin requirements comparable to those of the stock market.

disburse margin money every day. Moreover, they are permitted to do so more often than daily, and on some occasions they have used that privilege. By carefully setting margin requirements and collecting margin money every day, clearinghouses are able to control the risk of default.

In spite of the differences in margin practices for futures and securities markets, the effect of leverage is similar for both. By putting up a small amount of money, the trader's gains and losses are magnified. Given the tremendously low margin requirements of futures markets, however, the magnitude of the leverage effect is much greater in futures markets. We shall see how this works as we examine the process of the daily settlement.

As previously noted, each day the clearinghouse conducts an activity known as the daily settlement, also called marking to market. This practice results in the conversion of gains and losses on paper into actual gains and losses. As margin account balances change, holders of futures positions must maintain balances above a level called the **maintenance margin requirement**. The maintenance margin requirement is lower than the initial margin requirement. On any day in which the amount of money in the margin account at the end of the day falls below the maintenance margin requirement, the trader must deposit sufficient funds to bring the balance back up to the initial margin requirement. Alternatively, the trader can simply close out the position but is responsible for any further losses incurred if the price changes before a closing transaction can be made.

To provide a fair mark-to-market process, the clearinghouse must designate the official price for determining daily gains and losses. This price is called the **settlement price** and represents an average of the final few trades of the day. It would appear that the closing price of the day would serve as the settlement price, but the closing price is a single value that can potentially be biased high or low or perhaps even manipulated by an unscrupulous trader. Hence, the clearinghouse takes an average of all trades during the closing period (as defined by each exchange).

Exhibit 75-1 provides an example of the marking-to-market process that occurs over a period of six trading days. We start with the assumption that the futures price is $100 when the transaction opens, the initial margin requirement is $5, and the maintenance margin requirement is $3. In Panel A, the trader takes a long position of 10 contracts on Day 0, depositing $50 ($5 times 10 contracts) as indicated in Column 3. At the end of the day, his ending balance is $50.[9] Although the trader can withdraw any funds in excess of the initial margin requirement, we shall assume that he does not do so.[10]

The ending balance on Day 0 is then carried forward to the beginning balance on Day 1. On Day 1, the futures price moves down to 99.20, as indicated in Column 4 of Panel A. The futures price change, Column 5, is −0.80 (99.20 − 100). This amount is then multiplied by the number of contracts to obtain the number in Column 6 of −0.80 × 10 = −$8. The ending balance, Column 7, is the beginning balance plus the gain or loss. The ending balance on Day 1 of $42 is above the maintenance margin requirement of $30, so no funds need to be deposited on Day 2.

---

[9] Technically, we are assuming that the position was opened at the settlement price on Day 0. If the position is opened earlier during the day, it would be marked to the settlement price at the end of the day.

[10] Virtually all professional traders are able to deposit interest-earning assets, although many other account holders are required to deposit cash. If the deposit earns interest, there is no opportunity cost and no obvious necessity to withdraw the money to invest elsewhere.

EXHIBIT 75-1	Mark-to-Market Example

Initial futures price = $100, Initial margin requirement = $5, Maintenance margin requirement = $3

A. *Holder of Long Position of 10 Contracts*

Day (1)	Beginning Balance (2)	Funds Deposited (3)	Settlement Price (4)	Futures Price Change (5)	Gain/ Loss (6)	Ending Balance (7)
0	0	50	100.00			50
1	50	0	99.20	−0.80	−8	42
2	42	0	96.00	−3.20	−32	10
3	10	40	101.00	5.00	50	100
4	100	0	103.50	2.50	25	125
5	125	0	103.00	−0.50	−5	120
6	120	0	104.00	1.00	10	130

B. *Holder of Short Position of 10 Contracts*

Day (1)	Beginning Balance (2)	Funds Deposited (3)	Settlement Price (4)	Futures Price Change (5)	Gain/ Loss (6)	Ending Balance (7)
0	0	50	100.00			50
1	50	0	99.20	−0.80	8	58
2	58	0	96.00	−3.20	32	90
3	90	0	101.00	5.00	−50	40
4	40	0	103.50	2.50	−25	15
5	15	35	103.00	−0.50	5	55
6	55	0	104.00	1.00	−10	45

On Day 2 the settlement price goes down to $96. Based on a price decrease of $3.20 per contract and 10 contracts, the loss is $32, lowering the ending balance to $10. This amount is $20 below the maintenance margin requirement. Thus, the trader will get a margin call the following morning and must deposit $40 to bring the balance up to the initial margin level of $50. This deposit is shown in Column 3 on Day 3.

Here, we must emphasize two important points. First, additional margin that must be deposited is the amount sufficient to bring the ending balance up to the initial margin requirement, not the maintenance margin requirement.[11] This additional margin is called the **variation margin**. In addition, the amount that must be deposited the following day is determined regardless of the price change the following day, which might bring the ending balance well above the initial margin requirement, as it does here, or even well below the maintenance margin requirement. Thus, another margin call could occur. Also note that

---

[11] In the stock market, one must deposit only the amount necessary to bring the balance up to the maintenance margin requirement.

when the trader closes the position, the account is marked to market to the final price at which the transaction occurs, not the settlement price that day.

Over the six-day period, the trader in this example deposited $90. The account balance at the end of the sixth day is $130—nearly a 50 percent return over six days; not bad. But look at Panel B, which shows the position of a holder of 10 short contracts over that same period. Note that the short gains when prices decrease and loses when prices increase. Here the ending balance falls below the maintenance margin requirement on Day 4, and the short must deposit $35 on Day 5. At the end of Day 6, the short has deposited $85 and the balance is $45, a loss of $40 or nearly 50 percent, which is the same $40 the long made. Both cases illustrate the leverage effect that magnifies gains and losses.

When establishing a futures position, it is important to know the price level that would trigger a margin call. In this case, it does not matter how many contracts one has. The price change would need to fall for a long position (or rise for a short position) by the difference between the initial and maintenance margin requirements. In this example, the difference between the initial and maintenance margin requirements is $5 - $3 = 2. Thus, the price would need to fall from $100 to $98 for a long position (or rise from $100 to $102 for a short position) to trigger a margin call.

As described here, when a trader receives a margin call, he is required to deposit funds sufficient to bring the account balance back up to the initial margin level. Alternatively, the trader can choose to simply close out the position as soon as possible. For example, consider the position of the long at the end of the second day when the margin balance is $10. This amount is $20 below the maintenance level, and he is required to deposit $40 to bring the balance up to the initial margin level. If he would prefer not to deposit the additional funds, he can close out the position as soon as possible the following day. Suppose, however, that the price is moving quickly at the opening on Day 3. If the price falls from $96 to $95, he has lost $10 more, wiping out the margin account balance. In fact, if it fell any further, he would have a negative margin account balance. He is still responsible for these losses. Thus, the trader could lose more than the amount of money he has placed in the margin account. The total amount of money he could lose is limited to the price per contract at which he bought, $100, times the number of contracts, 10, or $1,000. Such a loss would occur if the price fell to zero, although this is not likely. This potential loss may not seem like a lot, but it is certainly large relative to the initial margin requirement of $50. For the holder of the short position, there is no upper limit on the price and the potential loss is theoretically infinite.

Practice Problem 1

Consider a futures contract in which the current futures price is $82. The initial margin requirement is $5, and the maintenance margin requirement is $2. You go long 20 contracts and meet all margin calls but do not withdraw any excess margin. Assume that on the first day, the contract is established at the settlement price, so there is no mark-to-market gain or loss on that day.

A. Complete the table below and provide an explanation of any funds deposited.

Day	Beginning Balance	Funds Deposited	Futures Price	Price Change	Gain/Loss	Ending Balance
0			82			
1			84			
2			78			
3			73			
4			79			
5			82			
6			84			

B. Determine the price level that would trigger a margin call.

SOLUTIONS

A.

Day	Beginning Balance	Funds Deposited	Futures Price	Price Change	Gain/Loss	Ending Balance
0	0	100	82			100
1	100	0	84	2	40	140
2	140	0	78	−6	−120	20
3	20	80	73	−5	−100	0
4	0	100	79	6	120	220
5	220	0	82	3	60	280
6	280	0	84	2	40	320

On Day 0, you deposit $100 because the initial margin requirement is $5 per contract and you go long 20 contracts. At the end of Day 2, the balance is down to $20, which is $20 below the $40 maintenance margin requirement ($2 per contract times 20 contracts). You must deposit enough money to bring the balance up to the initial margin requirement of $100 ($5 per contract times 20 contracts). So on Day 3, you deposit $80. The price change on Day 3 causes a gain/loss of −$100, leaving you with a balance of $0 at the end of Day 3. On Day 4, you must deposit $100 to return the balance to the initial margin level.

B. A price decrease to $79 would trigger a margin call. This calculation is based on the fact that the difference between the initial margin requirement and the maintenance margin requirement is $3. If the futures price starts at $82, it can fall by $3 to $79 before it triggers a margin call.

Some futures contracts impose limits on the price change that can occur from one day to the next. Appropriately, these are called **price limits**. These limits are usually set as an absolute change over the previous day. Using the example above, suppose the price limit was $4. This would mean that each day, no transaction could take place higher than the previous settlement price plus $4 or lower than the previous settlement price minus $4. So the next day's settlement price cannot go beyond the price limit and thus no transaction can take place beyond the limits.

If the price at which a transaction would be made exceeds the limits, then price essentially freezes at one of the limits, which is called a **limit move**. If the price is stuck at the upper limit, it is called **limit up**; if stuck at the lower limit, it is called **limit down**. If a transaction cannot take place because the price would be beyond the limits, this situation is called **locked limit**. By the end of the day, unless the price has moved back within the limits, the settlement price will then be at one of the limits. The following day, the new range of acceptable prices is based on the settlement price plus or minus limits. The exchanges have different rules that provide for expansion or contraction of price limits under some circumstances. In addition, not all contracts have price limits.

Finally, we note that the exchanges have the power to mark contracts to market whenever they deem it necessary. Thus, they can do so during the trading day rather than wait until the end of the day. They sometimes do so when abnormally large market moves occur.

The daily settlement procedure is designed to collect losses and distribute gains in such a manner that losses are paid before becoming large enough to impose a serious risk of default. Recall that the clearinghouse guarantees to each party that it need not worry about collecting from the counterparty. The clearinghouse essentially positions itself in the middle of each contract, becoming the short counterparty to the long and the long counterparty to the short. The clearinghouse collects funds from the parties incurring losses in this daily settlement procedure and distributes them to the parties incurring gains. By doing so each day, the clearinghouse ensures that losses cannot build up. Of course, this process offers no guarantee that counterparties will not default. Some defaults do occur, but the counterparty is defaulting to the clearinghouse, which has never failed to pay off the opposite party. In the unlikely event that the clearinghouse were unable to pay, it would turn to a reserve fund or to the exchange, or it would levy a tax on exchange members to cover losses.

4   DELIVERY AND CASH SETTLEMENT

As previously described, a futures trader can close out a position before expiration. If the trader holds a long position, she can simply enter into a position to go short the same futures contract. From the clearinghouse's perspective, the trader holds both a long and short position in the same contract. These positions are considered to offset and, therefore, there is no open position in place. Most futures contracts are offset before expiration. Those that remain in place are subject to either delivery or a final cash settlement. Here we explore this process, which determines how a futures contract terminates at expiration.

When the exchange designs a futures contract, it specifies whether the contract will terminate with delivery or cash settlement. If the contract terminates in delivery, the clearinghouse selects a counterparty, usually the holder of the oldest long contract, to accept delivery. The holder of the short position then delivers the underlying to the holder of the long position, who pays the short the necessary cash for the underlying. Suppose, for example, that two days before expiration, a party goes long one futures contract at a price of $50. The following day (the day before expiration), the settlement price is $52. The trader's margin account is then marked to market by crediting it with a gain of $2. Then suppose that the next day the contract expires with the settlement price at $53. As the end of the trading day draws near, the trader has two choices. She can attempt to close out the position by selling the futures contract. The margin account would then be marked to market at the price at which she sells. If she sells close enough to the expiration, the price she sold at would be very close to the final settlement price of $53. Doing so would add $1 to her margin account balance.

The other choice is to leave the position open at the end of the trading day. Then she would have to take delivery. If that occurred, she would be required to take possession of the asset and pay the short the settlement price of the previous day. Doing so would be equivalent to paying $52 and receiving the asset. She could then sell the asset for its price of $53, netting a $1 gain, which is equivalent to the final $1 credited to her margin account if she had terminated the position at the settlement price of $53, as described above.[12]

An alternative settlement procedure, which we described in Reading 74 on forward contracts, is cash settlement. The exchange designates certain futures contracts as cash-settled contracts. If the contract used in this example were cash settled, then the trader would not need to close out the position close to the end of the expiration day. She could simply leave the position open. When the contract expires, her margin account would be marked to market for a gain on the final day of $1. Cash settlement contracts have some advantages over delivery contracts, particularly with respect to significant savings in transaction costs.[13]

Exhibit 75-2 illustrates the equivalence of these three forms of delivery. Note, however, that because of the transaction costs of delivery, parties clearly prefer a

EXHIBIT 75-2 Closeout versus Physical Delivery versus Cash Settlement

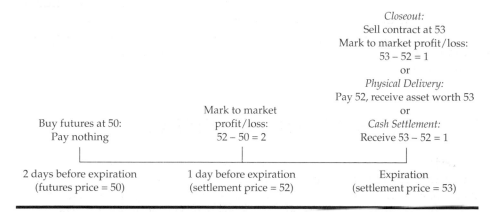

		Closeout: Sell contract at 53 Mark to market profit/loss: 53 – 52 = 1 or *Physical Delivery:* Pay 52, receive asset worth 53
Buy futures at 50: Pay nothing	Mark to market profit/loss: 52 – 50 = 2	or *Cash Settlement:* Receive 53 – 52 = 1
2 days before expiration (futures price = 50)	1 day before expiration (settlement price = 52)	Expiration (settlement price = 53)

---

[12] The reason she pays the settlement price of the previous day is because on the previous day when her account was marked to market, she essentially created a new futures position at a price of $52. Thus, she committed to purchase the asset at expiration, just one day later, at a price of $52. The next day when the contract expires, it is then appropriate that she buy the underlying for $52.

[13] Nonetheless, cash settlement has been somewhat controversial in the United States. If a contract is designated as cash settlement, it implies that the buyer of the contract never intended to actually take possession of the underlying asset. Some legislators and regulators feel that this design is against the spirit of the law, which views a futures contract as a commitment to buy the asset at a later date. Even though parties often offset futures contracts prior to expiration, the possibility of actual delivery is still present in contracts other than those settled by cash. This controversy, however, is relatively minor and has caused no serious problems or debates in recent years.

closeout or cash settlement over physical delivery, particularly when the underlying asset is a physical commodity.

Contracts designated for delivery have a variety of features that can complicate delivery. In most cases, delivery does not occur immediately after expiration but takes place over several days. In addition, many contracts permit the short to choose when delivery takes place. For many contracts, delivery can be made any business day of the month. The delivery period usually includes the days following the last trading day of the month, which is usually in the third week of the month.

In addition, the short often has other choices regarding delivery, a major one being exactly which underlying asset is delivered. For example, a futures contract on U.S. Treasury bonds trading at the Chicago Board of Trade permits the short to deliver any of a number of U.S. Treasury bonds.[14] The wheat futures contract at the Chicago Board of Trade permits delivery of any of several types of wheat. Futures contracts calling for physical delivery of commodities often permit delivery at different locations. A given commodity delivered to one location is not the same as that commodity delivered to another because of the costs involved in transporting the commodity. The short holds the sole right to make decisions about what, when, and where to deliver, and the right to make these decisions can be extremely valuable. The right to make a decision concerning these aspects of delivery is called a **delivery option.**

Some futures contracts that call for delivery require delivery of the actual asset, and some use only a book entry. For example, in this day and age, no one physically handles U.S. Treasury bonds in the form of pieces of paper. Bonds are transferred electronically over the Federal Reserve's wire system. Other contracts, such as oil or wheat, do actually involve the physical transfer of the asset. Physical delivery is more common when the underlying is a physical commodity, whereas book entry is more common when the underlying is a financial asset.

Futures market participants use one additional delivery procedure, which is called **exchange for physicals (EFP)**. In an EFP transaction, the long and short arrange an alternative delivery procedure. For example, the Chicago Board of Trade's wheat futures contracts require delivery on certain dates at certain locations either in Chicago or in a few other specified locations in the Midwest. If the long and short agree, they could effect delivery by having the short deliver the wheat to the long in, for example, Omaha. The two parties would then report to the Chicago Board of Trade that they had settled their contract outside of the exchange's normal delivery procedures, which would be satisfactory to the exchange.

5   FUTURES EXCHANGES

A futures exchange is a legal corporate entity whose shareholders are its members. The members own memberships, more commonly called **seats**. Exchange members have the privilege of executing transactions on the exchange. Each member acts as either a **floor trader** or a **broker**. Floor traders are typically called **locals**; brokers are typically called **futures commission merchants (FCMs)**. Locals are market makers, standing ready to buy and sell by quoting a bid and an ask

---

[14] We shall cover this feature in more detail in Sections 6.2 and 7.2.3.

price. They are the primary providers of liquidity to the market. FCMs execute transactions for other parties off the exchange.

The locals on the exchange floor typically trade according to one of several distinct styles. The most common is called scalping. A **scalper** offers to buy or sell futures contracts, holding the position for only a brief period of time, perhaps just seconds. Scalpers attempt to profit by buying at the bid price and selling at the higher ask price. A **day trader** holds a position open somewhat longer but closes all positions at the end of the day.[15] A **position trader** holds positions open overnight. Day traders and position traders are quite distinct from scalpers in that they attempt to profit from the anticipated direction of the market; scalpers are trying simply to buy at the bid and sell at the ask.

Recall that futures exchanges have trading either on the floor or off the floor on electronic terminals, or in some cases, both. As previously described, floor trading in the United States takes place in pits, which are octagonal, multi-tiered areas where floor traders stand and conduct transactions. Traders wear jackets of specific colors and badges to indicate such information as what type of trader (FCM or local) they are and whom they represent.[16] As noted, to indicate a willingness to trade, a trader shouts and uses a set of standard hand signals. A trade is consummated by two traders agreeing on a price and a number of contracts. These traders might not actually say anything to each other; they may simply use a combination of hand signals and/or eye contact to agree on a transaction. When a transaction is agreed on, the traders fill out small paper forms and turn them over to clerks, who then see that the transactions are entered into the system and reported.

Each trader is required to have an account at a clearing firm. The clearing firms are the actual members of the clearinghouse. The clearinghouse deals only with the clearing firms, which then deal with their individual and institutional customers.

In electronic trading, the principles remain essentially the same but the traders do not stand in the pits. In fact, they do not see each other at all. They sit at computer terminals, which enable them to see the bids and offers of other traders. Transactions are executed by the click of a computer mouse or an entry from a keyboard.

Exhibit 75-3 lists the world's 20 leading futures exchanges in 2001, ranked by trading volume. Recall from Reading 73 that trading volume can be a misleading measure of the size of futures markets; nonetheless, it is the measure primarily used. The structure of global futures exchanges has changed considerably in recent years. Exchanges in the United States, primarily the Chicago Board of Trade and the Chicago Mercantile Exchange, were clearly the world leaders in the past. Note that the volume leader now, however, is Eurex, the combined German–Swiss exchange. Eurex has been so successful partly because of its decision to be an all-electronic futures exchange, whereas the Chicago exchanges are still primarily pit-trading exchanges. Note the popularity of futures trading in Japan; four of the 20 leading exchanges are Japanese.

[15] The term "day trader" has been around the futures market for a long time but has recently acquired a new meaning in the broader financial markets. The term is now used to describe individual investors who trade stocks, often over the Internet, during the day for a living or as a hobby. In fact, the term has even been used in a somewhat pejorative manner, in that day traders are often thought of as naïve investors speculating wildly with money they can ill afford to lose.

[16] For example, an FCM or local could be trading for himself or could represent a company.

EXHIBIT 75-3	The World's 20 Leading Futures Exchanges

Exchange and Location	Volume in 2001 (Number of Contracts)
Eurex (Germany and Switzerland)	435,141,707
Chicago Mercantile Exchange (United States)	315,971,885
Chicago Board of Trade (United States)	209,988,002
London International Financial Futures and Options Exchange (United Kingdom)	161,522,775
Bolsa de Mercadorias & Futuros (Brazil)	94,174,452
New York Mercantile Exchange (United States)	85,039,984
Tokyo Commodity Exchange (Japan)	56,538,245
London Metal Exchange (United Kingdom)	56,224,495
Paris Bourse SA (France)	42,042,673
Sydney Futures Exchange (Australia)	34,075,508
Korea Stock Exchange (Korea)	31,502,184
Singapore Exchange (Singapore)	30,606,546
Central Japan Commodity Exchange (Japan)	27,846,712
International Petroleum Exchange (United Kingdom)	26,098,207
OM Stockholm Exchange (Sweden)	23,408,198
Tokyo Grain Exchange (Japan)	22,707,808
New York Board of Trade (United States)	14,034,168
MEFF Renta Variable (Spain)	13,108,293
Tokyo Stock Exchange (Japan)	12,465,433
South African Futures Exchange (South Africa)	11,868,242

Source: Futures Industry, January/February 2002

6   TYPES OF FUTURES CONTRACTS

The different types of futures contracts are generally divided into two main groups: commodity futures and financial futures. Commodity futures cover traditional agricultural, metal, and petroleum products. Financial futures include stocks, bonds, and currencies. Exhibit 75-4 gives a broad overview of the most active types of futures contracts traded on global futures exchanges. These contracts are those covered by the *Wall Street Journal* on the date indicated.

Our primary focus in this book is on financial and currency futures contracts. Within the financials group, our main interest is on interest rate and bond futures, stock index futures, and currency futures. We may occasionally make reference to a commodity futures contract, but that will primarily be for illustrative purposes. In the following subsections, we introduce the primary contracts we shall focus on. These are U.S. contracts, but they resemble most types of futures contracts found on exchanges throughout the world. Full contract specifications for these and other contracts are available on the Web sites of the futures exchanges, which are easy to locate with most Internet search engines.

| EXHIBIT 75-4 | **Most-Active Global Futures Contracts as Covered by the** *Wall Street Journal*, **18 June 2002** |

Commodity Futures

Corn (CBOT)

Oats (CBOT)

Soybeans (CBOT)

Soybean Meal (CBOT)

Soybean Oil (CBOT)

Wheat (CBOT, KCBT, MGE)

Canola (WPG)

Barley (WPG)

Feeder Cattle (CME)

Live Cattle (CME)

Lean Hogs (CME)

Pork Bellies (CME)

Milk (CME)

Lumber (CME)

Cocoa (NYBOT)

Coffee (NYBOT)

World Sugar (NYBOT)

Domestic Sugar (NYBOT)

Cotton (NYBOT)

Orange Juice (NYBOT)

Copper (NYMEX)

Gold (NYMEX)

Platinum (NYMEX)

Palladium (NYMEX)

Silver (NYMEX)

Crude Oil (NYMEX)

No. 2 Heating Oil (NYMEX)

Unleaded Gasoline (NYMEX)

Natural Gas (NYMEX)

Brent Crude Oil (IPEX)

Gas Oil (IPEX)

Financial Futures

Treasury Bonds (CBOT)

Treasury Notes (CBOT)

10-Year Agency Notes (CBOT)

10-Year Interest Rate Swaps (CBOT)

2-Year Agency Notes (CBOT)

5-Year Treasury Notes (CBOT)

2-Year Treasury Notes (CBOT)

Federal Funds (CBOT)

Municipal Bond Index (CBOT)

Treasury Bills (CME)

1-Month LIBOR (CME)

Eurodollar (CME)

Euroyen (CME, SGX)

Short Sterling (LIFFE)

Long Gilt (LIFFE)

3-Month Euribor (LIFFE)

3-Month Euroswiss (LIFFE)

Canadian Bankers Acceptance (ME)

10-Year Canadian Government Bond (ME)

10-Year Euro Notional Bond (MATIF)

3-Month Euribor (MATIF)

3-Year Commonwealth T-Bonds (SFE)

5-Year German Euro Government Bond (EUREX)

10-Year German Euro Government Bond (EUREX)

2-Year German Euro Government Bond (EUREX)

Japanese Yen (CME)

Canadian Dollar (CME)

British Pound (CME)

Swiss Franc (CME)

Australian Dollar (CME)

Mexican Peso (CME)

Euro (CME)

Euro–Sterling (NYBOT)

Euro–U.S. Dollar (NYBOT)

Euro–Yen (NYBOT)

Dow Jones Industrial Average (CBOT)

Mini Dow Jones Industrial Average (CBOT)

S&P 500 Index (CME)

Mini S&P 500 Index (CME)

S&P Midcap 400 Index (CME)

Nikkei 225 (CME)

Nasdaq 100 Index (CME)

Mini Nasdaq Index (CME)

Goldman Sachs Commodity Index (CME)

Russell 1000 Index (CME)

Russell 2000 Index (CME)

NYSE Composite Index (NYBOT)

U.S. Dollar Index (NYBOT)

Share Price Index (SFE)

CAC 40 Stock Index (MATIF)

Xetra Dax (EUREX)

FTSE 200 Index (LIFFE)

Dow Jones Euro Stoxx 50 Index (EUREX)

Dow Jones Stoxx 50 Index (EUREX)

Exchange codes: CBOT (Chicago Board of Trade), CME (Chicago Mercantile Exchange), LIFFE (London International Financial Futures Exchange), WPG (Winnipeg Grain Exchange), EUREX (Eurex), NYBOT (New York Board of Trade), IPEX (International Petroleum Exchange), MATIF (Marché a Terme International de France), ME (Montreal Exchange), MGE (Minneapolis Grain Exchange), SFE (Sydney Futures Exchange), SGX (Singapore Exchange), KCBT (Kansas City Board of Trade), NYMEX (New York Mercantile Exchange)

Note: These are not the only global futures contracts but are those covered in the *Wall Street Journal* on the date given and represent the most active contracts at that time.

6.1 Short-Term Interest Rate Futures Contracts

The primary short-term interest rate futures contracts are those on U.S. Treasury bills and Eurodollars on the Chicago Mercantile Exchange.

6.1.1 Treasury Bill Futures

The Treasury bill contract, launched in 1976, was the first interest rate futures contract. It is based on a 90-day U.S. Treasury bill, one of the most important U.S. government debt instruments (described in Reading 74, Section 3.2.1). The Treasury bill, or T-bill, is a discount instrument, meaning that its price equals the face value minus a discount representing interest. The discount equals the face value multiplied by the quoted rate times the days to maturity divided by 360. Thus, using the example from Reading 74, if a 180-day T-bill is selling at a discount of 4 percent, its price per $1 par is $1 - 0.04(180/360) = 0.98$. An investor who buys the bill and holds it to maturity would receive $1 at maturity, netting a gain of $0.02.

The futures contract is based on a 90-day $1,000,000 U.S. Treasury bill. Thus, on any given day, the contract trades with the understanding that a 90-day T-bill will be delivered at expiration. While the contract is trading, its price is quoted as 100 minus the rate quoted as a percent priced into the contract by the futures market. This value, 100 − Rate, is known as the IMM Index; IMM stands for International Monetary Market, a division of the Chicago Mercantile Exchange. The IMM Index is a reported and publicly available price; however, it is not the actual futures price, which is

$$100 - (\text{Rate}/100)(90/360)$$

For example, suppose on a given day the rate priced into the contract is 6.25 percent. Then the quoted price will be $100 - 6.25 = 93.75$. The actual futures price would be

$$\$1,000,000[1 - 0.0625(90/360)] = \$984,375$$

Recall, however, that except for the small margin deposit, a futures transaction does not require any cash to be paid up front. As trading takes place, the rate fluctuates with market interest rates and the associated IMM Index price changes accordingly. The actual futures price, as calculated above, also fluctuates according to the above formula, but interestingly, that price is not very important. The same information can be captured more easily by referencing the IMM Index than by calculating the actual price.

Suppose, for example, that a trader had his account marked to market to the above price, 6.25 in terms of the rate, 93.75 in terms of the IMM Index, and $984,375 in terms of the actual futures price. Now suppose the rate goes to 6.50, an increase of 0.25 or 25 basis points. The IMM Index declines to 93.50, and the actual futures price drops to

$$\$1,000,000[1 - 0.065(90/360)] = \$983,750$$

Thus, the actual futures price decreased by $984,375 − $983,750 = $625. A trader who is long would have a loss of $625; a trader who is short would have a gain of $625.

This $625 gain or loss can be arrived at more directly, however, by simply noting that each basis point move is equivalent to $25.[17] This special design of the contract makes it easy for floor traders to do the necessary arithmetic in their heads. For example, if floor traders observe the IMM Index move from 93.75 to 93.50, they immediately know that it has moved down 25 basis points and that 25 basis points times $25 per basis point is a loss of $625. The minimum **tick** size is one-half basis point or $12.50.

T-bill futures contracts have expirations of the current month, the next month, and the next four months of March, June, September, and December. Because of the small trading volume, however, only the closest expiration has much trading volume, and even that one is only lightly traded. T-bill futures expire specifically on the Monday of the week of the third Wednesday each month and settle in cash rather than physical delivery of the T-bill, as described in Section 4.

As important as Treasury bills are in U.S. financial markets, however, today this futures contract is barely active. The Eurodollar contract is considered much more important because it reflects the interest rate on a dollar borrowed by a high-quality private borrower. The rates on T-bills are considered too heavily influenced by U.S. government policies, budget deficits, government funding plans, politics, and Federal Reserve monetary policy. Although unquestionably Eurodollar rates are affected by those factors, market participants consider them much less directly influenced. But in spite of this relative inactivity, T-bill futures are useful instruments for illustrating certain principles of futures market pricing and trading. Accordingly, we shall use them on some occasions. For now, however, we turn to the Eurodollar futures contract.

6.1.2 *Eurodollar Futures*

Recall that in Reading 74, we devoted a good bit of effort to understanding Eurodollar forward contracts, known as FRAs. These contracts pay off based on LIBOR on a given day. The Eurodollar futures contract of the Chicago Mercantile Exchange is based on $1 million notional principal of 90-day Eurodollars. Specifically, the underlying is the rate on a 90-day dollar-denominated time deposit issued by a bank in London. As we described in Reading 74, this deposit is called a Eurodollar time deposit, and the rate is referred to as LIBOR (London Interbank Offer Rate). On a given day, the futures contract trades based on the understanding that at expiration, the official Eurodollar rate, as compiled by the British Bankers Association (BBA), will be the rate at which the final settlement of the contract is made. While the contract is trading, its price is quoted as 100 minus the rate priced into the contract by futures traders. Like its counterpart in the T-bill futures market, this value, 100 − Rate, is also known as the IMM Index.

As in the T-bill futures market, on a given day, if the rate priced into the contract is 5.25 percent, the quoted price will be $100 - 5.25 = 94.75$. With each contract based on $1 million notional principal of Eurodollars, the actual futures price is

$$\$1,000,000[1 - 0.0525(90/360)] = \$986,875$$

Like the T-bill contract, the actual futures price moves $25 for every basis point move in the rate or IMM Index price.

---

[17] Expressed mathematically, $\$1,000,000[0.0001(90/360)] = \$25$. In other words, any move in the last digit of the rate (a basis point) affects the actual futures price by $25.

factor for a given bond. To determine the amount the bond would cost at expiration, one calculates the forward price of the bond, positioned at the delivery date. Of course, this is just a forward computation; circumstances could change by the expiration date. But this forward calculation gives a picture of circumstances as they currently stand and identifies which bond is currently the **cheapest to deliver**. That bond is then considered the bond most likely to be delivered. Recall that one problem with this futures contract is that the identity of the underlying bond is unclear. Traders traditionally treat the cheapest to deliver as the bond that underlies the contract. As time passes and interest rates change, however, the cheapest-to-deliver bond can change. Thus, the bond underlying the futures contract can change, adding an element of uncertainty to the pricing and trading of this contract.

With this complexity associated with the U.S. Treasury bond futures contract, one might suspect that it is less actively traded. In fact, the opposite is true: Complexity creates extraordinary opportunities for gain for those who understand what is going on and can identify the cheapest bond to deliver.

The Chicago Board of Trade's U.S. Treasury bond futures contract covers $100,000 par value of U.S. Treasury bonds. The expiration months are March, June, September, and December. They expire on the seventh business day preceding the last business day of the month and call for actual delivery, through the Federal Reserve's wire system, of the Treasury bond. Prices are quoted in points and 32nds, meaning that you will see prices like 98 18/32, which equals 98.5625. For a contract covering $100,000 par value, for example, the price is $98,562.50. The minimum tick size is 1/32, which is $31.25.

In addition to the futures contract on the long-term government bond, there are also very similar futures contracts on intermediate-term government bonds. The Chicago Board of Trade's contracts on 2-, 5-, and 10-year Treasury notes are very actively traded and are almost identical to its long-term bond contract, except for the exact specification of the underlying instrument. Intermediate and long-term government bonds are important instruments in every country's financial markets. They give the best indication of the long-term default-free interest rate and are often viewed as a **benchmark bond** for various comparisons in financial markets.[21] Accordingly, futures contracts on such bonds play an important role in a country's financial markets and are almost always among the most actively traded contracts in futures markets around the world.

If the underlying instrument is not widely available and not actively traded, the viability of a futures contract on it becomes questionable. The reduction seen in U.S. government debt in the late 1990s has led to a reduction in the supply of intermediate and long-term government bonds, and some concern has arisen over this fact. In the United States, some efforts have been made to promote the long-term debt of Fannie Mae and Freddie Mac as substitute benchmark bonds.[22] It remains to be seen whether such efforts will be necessary and, if so, whether they will succeed.

---

[21] For example, the default risk of a corporate bond is often measured as the difference between the corporate bond yield and the yield on a Treasury bond or note of comparable maturity. Fixed rates on interest rate swaps are usually quoted as a spread over the rate on a Treasury bond or note of comparable maturity.

[22] Fannie Mae is the Federal National Mortgage Association, and Freddie Mac is the Federal Home Loan Mortgage Corporation. These institutions were formerly U.S. government agencies that issued debt to raise funds to buy and sell mortgages and mortgage-backed securities. These institutions are now publicly traded corporations but are considered to have extremely low default risk because of their critical importance in U.S. mortgage markets. It is believed that an implicit Federal government guarantee is associated with their debt. Nonetheless, it seems unlikely that the debt of these institutions could take over that of the U.S. government as a benchmark. The Chicago Board of Trade has offered futures contracts on the bonds of these organizations, but the contracts have not traded actively.

6.3 Stock Index Futures Contracts

One of the most successful types of futures contracts of all time is the class of futures on stock indices. Probably the most successful has been the Chicago Mercantile Exchange's contract on the Standard and Poor's 500 Stock Index. Called the S&P 500 Stock Index futures, this contract premiered in 1982 and has benefited from the widespread acceptance of the S&P 500 Index as a stock market benchmark. The contract is quoted in terms of a price on the same order of magnitude as the S&P 500 itself. For example, if the S&P 500 Index is at 1183, a two-month futures contract might be quoted at a price of, say, 1187. We shall explain how to determine a stock index futures price in Section 7.3.

The contract implicitly contains a multiplier, which is (appropriately) multiplied by the quoted futures price to produce the actual futures price. The multiplier for the S&P 500 futures is $250. Thus, when you hear of a futures price of 1187, the actual price is 1187($250) = $296,750.

S&P 500 futures expirations are March, June, September, and December and go out about two years, although trading is active only in the nearest two to three expirations. With occasional exceptions, the contracts expire on the Thursday preceding the third Friday of the month. Given the impracticality of delivering a portfolio of the 500 stocks in the index combined according to their relative weights in the index, the contract is structured to provide for cash settlement at expiration.

The S&P 500 is not the only active stock index futures contract. In fact, the Chicago Mercantile Exchange has a smaller version of the S&P 500 contract, called the Mini S&P 500, which has a multiplier of $50 and trades only electronically. Other widely traded contracts in the United States are on the Dow Jones Industrials, the S&P Midcap 400, and the Nasdaq 100. Virtually every developed country has a stock index futures contract based on the leading equities of that country. Well-known stock index futures contracts around the world include the United Kingdom's FTSE 100 (pronounced "Footsie 100"), Japan's Nikkei 225, France's CAC 40, and Germany's DAX 30.

6.4 Currency Futures Contracts

In Reading 74 we described forward contracts on foreign currencies. There are also futures contracts on foreign currencies. Although the forward market for foreign currencies is much more widely used, the futures market is still quite active. In fact, currency futures were the first futures contracts not based on physical commodities. Thus, they are sometimes referred to as the first financial futures contracts, and their initial success paved the way for the later introduction of interest rate and stock index futures.

Compared with forward contracts on currencies, currency futures contracts are much smaller in size. In the United States, these contracts trade at the Chicago Mercantile Exchange with a small amount of trading at the New York Board of Trade. In addition there is some trading on exchanges outside the United States. The characteristics we describe below refer to the Chicago Mercantile Exchange's contract.

In the United States, the primary currencies on which trading occurs are the euro, Canadian dollar, Swiss franc, Japanese yen, British pound, Mexican peso, and Australian dollar. Each contract has a designated size and a quotation unit. For example, the euro contract covers €125,000 and is quoted in dollars per euro. A futures price such as $0.8555 is stated in dollars and converts to a contract price of

$$125,000(\$0.8555) = \$106,937.50$$

The Japanese yen futures price is structured somewhat differently. Because of the large number of yen per dollar, the contract covers ¥12,500,000 and is quoted without two zeroes that ordinarily precede the price. For example, a price might be stated as 0.8205, but this actually represents a price of 0.008205, which converts to a contract price of

$$12{,}500{,}000(0.008205) = \$102{,}562.50$$

Alternatively, a quoted price of 0.8205 can be viewed as $1/0.008205 = $¥121.88 per dollar.

Currency futures contracts expire in the months of March, June, September, and December. The specific expiration is the second business day before the third Wednesday of the month. Currency futures contracts call for actual delivery, through book entry, of the underlying currency.

We have briefly examined the different types of futures contracts of interest to us. Of course there are a variety of similar instruments trading on futures exchanges around the world. The purpose of this book, however, is not to provide institutional details, which can be obtained at the Web sites of the world's futures exchanges, but rather to enhance your understanding of the important principles necessary to function in the world of derivatives.

Until now we have made reference to prices of futures contracts. Accordingly, let us move forward and examine the pricing of futures contracts.

7   PRICING AND VALUATION OF FUTURES CONTRACTS

OPTIONAL SEGMENT BEGINS

In Reading 74, we devoted considerable effort to understanding the pricing and valuation of forward contracts. We first discussed the notion of what it means to *price* a forward contract in contrast to what it means to *value* a forward contract. Recall that pricing means to assign a fixed price or rate at which the underlying will be bought by the long and sold by the short at expiration. In assigning a forward price, we set the price such that the value of the contract is zero at the start. A zero-value contract means that the present value of the payments promised by each party to the other is the same, a result in keeping with the fact that neither party pays the other any money at the start. The value of the contract to the long is the present value of the payments promised by the short to the long minus the present value of the payments promised by the long to the short. Although the value is zero at the start, during the life of the contract, the value will fluctuate as market conditions change; the original forward contract price, however, stays the same.

In Reading 74, we presented numerous examples of how to apply the concept of pricing and valuation when dealing with forward contracts on stocks, bonds, currencies, and interest rates. To illustrate the concepts of pricing and valuation, we started with a generic forward contract. Accordingly, we do so here in the futures reading. We assume no transaction costs.

7.1   Generic Pricing and Valuation of a Futures Contract

As we did with forward contracts, we start by illustrating the time frame within which we are working:

| 0 | t − 1 | t | T |

(today) (expiration)

Today is time 0. The expiration date of the futures contract is time T. Times t − 1 and t are arbitrary times between today and the expiration and are the points at which the contract will be marked to market. Thus, we can think of the three periods depicted above, 0 to t − 1, t − 1 to t, and t to T, as three distinct trading days with times t − 1, t, and T being the end of each of the three days.

The price of the underlying asset in the spot market is denoted as S_0 at time 0, S_{t-1} at time t − 1, S_t at time t, and S_T at time T. We denote the futures contract price at time 0 as $f_0(T)$. This notation indicates that $f_0(T)$ is the price of a futures contract at time 0 that expires at time T. Unlike forward contract prices, however, futures prices fluctuate in an open and competitive market. The marking-to-market process results in each futures contract being terminated every day and reinitiated. Thus, we not only have a futures price set at time 0 but we also have a new one at time t − 1, at time t, and at time T. In other words,

$f_0(T)$ = price of a futures contract at time 0 that expires at time T
$f_{t-1}(T)$ = price of a futures contract at time t − 1 that expires at time T
$f_t(T)$ = price of a futures contract at time t that expires at time T
$f_T(T)$ = price of a futures contract at time T that expires at time T

Note, however, that $f_{t-1}(T)$ and $f_t(T)$ are also the prices of contracts newly established at times t − 1 and t for delivery at time T. Futures contracts are homogeneous and fungible. Any contract for delivery of the underlying at T is equivalent to any other contract, regardless of when the contracts were created.[23]

The value of the futures contract is denoted as $v_0(T)$. This notation indicates that $v_0(T)$ is the value at time 0 of a futures contract expiring at time T. We are also interested in the values of the contract prior to expiration, such as at time t, denoted as $v_t(T)$, as well as the value of the contract at expiration, denoted as $v_T(T)$.[24]

7.1.1 The Futures Price at Expiration

Now suppose we are at time T. The spot price is S_T and the futures price is $f_T(T)$. To avoid an arbitrage opportunity, *the futures price must converge to the spot price at expiration*:

$$f_T(T) = S_T \tag{75-1}$$

---

[23] As an analogy from the bond markets, consider a 9 percent coupon bond, originally issued with 10 years remaining. Three years later, that bond is a 9 percent seven-year bond. Consider a newly issued 9 percent coupon bond with seven years maturity and the same issuer. As long as the coupon dates are the same and all other terms are the same, these two bonds are fungible and are perfect substitutes for each other.

[24] It is important at this point to make some comments about notation. First, note that in Reading 74 we use an uppercase F and V for forward contracts; here we use lowercase f and v for futures contracts. Also, we follow the pattern of using subscripts to indicate a price or value at a particular point in time. The arguments in parentheses refer to characteristics of a contract. Thus, in Reading 74 we described the price of a forward contract as F(0,T) meaning the price of a forward contract initiated at time 0 and expiring at time T. This price does not fluctuate during the life of the contract. A futures contract, however, reprices on a daily basis. Its original time of initiation does not matter—it is reinitiated every day. Hence, futures prices are indicated by notation such as $f_0(T)$ and $f_t(T)$. We follow a similar pattern for value, using $V_0(0,T)$, $V_t(0,T)$, and $V_T(0,T)$ for forwards and $v_0(T)$, $v_t(T)$, and $v_T(T)$ for futures.

Consider what would happen if this were not the case. If $f_T(T) < S_T$, a trader could buy the futures contract, let it immediately expire, pay $f_T(T)$ to take delivery of the underlying, and receive an asset worth S_T. The trader would have paid $f_T(T)$ and received an asset worth S_T, which is greater, at no risk. If $f_T(T) > S_T$, the trader would go short the futures, buy the asset for S_T, make delivery, and receive $f_T(T)$ for the asset, for which he paid a lesser amount. Only if $f_T(T) = S_T$ does this arbitrage opportunity go away. Thus, the futures price must equal the spot price at expiration.

Another way to understand this point is to recall that by definition, a futures contract calls for the delivery of an asset at expiration at a price determined when the transaction is initiated. If expiration is right now, a futures transaction is equivalent to a spot transaction, so the futures price must equal the spot price.

7.1.2 Valuation of a Futures

Let us consider how to determine the value of a futures contract. We already agreed that because no money changes hands, the value of a forward contract at the initiation date is zero. For the same reason, *the value of a futures contract at the initiation date is zero*. Thus,

$$v_0(T) = 0 \qquad \text{(75-2)}$$

Now let us determine the value of the contract during its life. Suppose we are at the end of the second day, at time t. In our diagram above, this point would be essentially at time t, but perhaps just an instant before it. So let us call it time t−. An instant later, we call the time point t+. In both cases, the futures price is $f_t(T)$. The contract was previously marked to market at the end of day t − 1 to a price of $f_{t-1}(T)$. An instant later when the futures account is marked to market, the trader will receive a gain of $f_t(T) - f_{t-1}(T)$. We can reasonably ignore the present value difference of receiving this money an instant later. Let us now state more formally that the value of a futures contract is

$$v_{t+}(T) = f_t(T) - f_{t-1}(T) \quad \textit{an instant before the account is marked to market} \qquad \text{(75-3)}$$

$$v_{t-}(T) = 0 \quad \textit{as soon as the account is marked to market}$$

Suppose, however, that the trader is at a time j during the second trading day, between t − 1 and t. The accumulated gain or loss since the account was last marked to market is $f_j(T) - f_{t-1}(T)$. If the trader closes the position out, he would receive or be charged this amount at the end of the day. So the value at time j would be $f_j(T) - f_{t-1}(T)$ discounted back from the end of the day at time t until time j—that is, a fraction of a day. It is fairly routine to ignore this intraday interest. Thus, in general we say that *the value of a futures contract before it has been marked to market is the gain or loss accumulated since the account was last marked to market.*

So to recap, the value of a futures contract is the accumulated gain or loss since the last mark to market. The holder of a futures contract has a claim or liability on this amount. Once that claim is captured or the liability paid through the mark-to-market process, the contract is repriced to its current market price and the claim or liability goes back to a value of zero. Using these results, determining the value of a futures contract at expiration is easy. An instant before expiration, it is simply the accumulated profit since the last mark to market. At expiration, the value goes back to zero. With respect to the value of the futures, expiration is no different from any other day. Exhibit 75-5 summarizes the principles of valuation.

| EXHIBIT 75-5 | The Value of a Futures Contract Before and After Marking to Market |

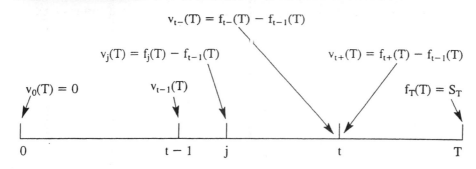

In Reading 74, we devoted considerable effort toward understanding how forward contracts are valued. When holding positions in forward contracts, we are forced to assign values to instruments that do not trade in an open market with widely disseminated prices. Thus, it is important that we understand how forward contracts are valued. When dealing with futures contracts, the process is considerably simplified. Because futures contracts are generally quite actively traded, there is a market with reliable prices that provides all of the information we need. For futures contracts, we see that the value is simply the observable price change since the last mark to market.

7.1.3 Forward and Futures Prices

For all financial instruments, it is important to be able to determine whether the price available in the market is an appropriate one. Hence, we engage in the process of "pricing" the financial instrument. A major objective of this reading is to determine the appropriate price of a futures contract. Given the similarity between futures and forward prices, however, we can benefit from studying forward contract pricing, which was covered in Reading 74. But first, we must look at the similarities and differences between forward and futures contracts.

Recall that futures contracts settle daily and are essentially free of default risk. Forward contracts settle only at expiration and are subject to default risk. Yet both types of contracts allow the party to purchase or sell the underlying asset at a price agreed on in advance. It seems intuitive that futures prices and forward prices would be relatively close to each other.

The issues involved in demonstrating the relationship between futures and forward prices are relatively technical and beyond the scope of this book. We can, however, take a brief and fairly nontechnical look at the question. First let us ignore the credit risk issue. We shall assume that the forward contract participants are prime credit risks. We focus only on the technical distinction caused by the daily marking to market.

The day before expiration, both the futures contract and the forward contract have one day to go. At expiration, they will both settle. These contracts are therefore the same. At any other time prior to expiration, futures and forward prices can be the same or different. If interest rates are constant or at least known, any effect of the addition or subtraction of funds from the marking-to-market process can be shown to be neutral. If interest rates are positively correlated with futures prices, traders with long positions will prefer futures over forwards, because they will generate gains when interest rates are going up, and traders can invest those gains for higher returns. Also, traders will incur losses when interest rates are going down and can borrow to cover those losses at lower rates. Because traders holding long positions prefer the marking to market of futures over forwards when futures prices are positively correlated with interest rates, futures will carry higher prices than forwards. Conversely, when futures prices are negatively correlated with interest rates, traders will prefer not to mark to market, so forward contracts will carry higher prices.

Because interest rates and fixed-income security prices move in opposite directions, interest rate futures are good examples of cases in which forward and futures prices should be inversely related. Alternatively, when inflation is high, interest rates are high and investors oftentimes put their money in such assets as gold. Thus, gold futures prices and interest rates would tend to be positively correlated. It would be difficult to identify a situation in which futures prices are not correlated with interest rates. Zero correlation is rare in the financial world, but we can say that when the correlation is low or close to zero, the difference between forward and futures prices would be very small.

At this introductory level of treatment, we shall make the simplifying assumption that futures prices and forward prices are the same. We do so by ignoring the effects of marking a futures contract to market. In practice, some significant issues arise related to the marking-to-market process, but they detract from our ability to understand the important concepts in pricing and trading futures and forwards.

Therefore, based on the equivalence we are assuming between futures and forwards, we can assume that the value of a futures contract at expiration, before marking to market, is

$$v_T(T) = f_T(T) - f_0(T) = S_T - f_0(T)$$

with the spot price substituted for the futures price at T, given what we know about their convergence.

7.1.4 Pricing Futures Contracts

Now let us proceed to the pricing of futures contracts. As we did with forward contracts, we consider the case of a generic underlying asset priced at $100. A futures contract calls for delivery of the underlying asset in one year at a price of $108. Let us see if $108 is the appropriate price for this futures contract.

Suppose we buy the asset for $100 and sell the futures contract. We hold the position until expiration. For right now, we assume no costs are involved in holding the asset. We do, however, lose interest on the $100 tied up in the asset for one year. We assume that this opportunity cost is at the risk-free interest rate of 5 percent.

Recall that no money changes hands at the start of a futures contract. Moreover, we can reasonably ignore the rather small margin deposit that would be required. In addition, margin deposits can generally be met by putting up interest-earning securities, so there is really no opportunity cost. As discussed in the previous section, we also will assume away the daily settlement procedure; in other words, the value of the futures contract paid out at expiration is the final futures price minus the original futures price. Because the final futures price converges to the spot price, the final payout is the spot price minus the original futures price.

So at the contract expiration, we are short the futures and must deliver the asset, which we own. We do so and receive the original futures price for it. So we receive $108 for an asset purchased a year ago at $100. At a 5 percent interest rate, we lose only $5 in interest, so our return in excess of the opportunity cost is 3 percent risk free. This risk-free return in excess of the risk-free rate is clearly attractive and would induce traders to buy the asset and sell the futures. This arbitrage activity would drive the futures price down until it reaches $105.

If the futures price falls below $105, say to $102, the opposite arbitrage would occur. The arbitrageur would buy the futures, but either we would need to be able to borrow the asset and sell it short, or investors who own the asset would have to be willing to sell it and buy the futures. They would receive the asset price of $100 and invest it at 5 percent interest. Then at expiration, those investors would get the asset back upon taking delivery, paying $102. This transaction would net a clear and risk-free profit of $3, consisting of interest of $5 minus a $2 loss from selling the asset at $100 and buying it back at $102. Again, through the buying of the futures and shorting of the asset, the forces of arbitrage would cause prices to realign to $105.

Some difficulties occur with selling short certain assets. Although the financial markets make short selling relatively easy, some commodities are not easy to sell short. In such a case, it is still possible for arbitrage to occur. If investors who already own the asset sell it and buy the futures, they can reap similar gains at no risk. Because our interest is in financial instruments, we shall ignore these commodity market issues and assume that short selling can be easily executed.[25]

If the market price is not equal to the price given by the model, it is important to note that regardless of the asset price at expiration, the above arbitrage guarantees a risk-free profit. That profit is known at the time the parties enter the transaction. Exhibit 75-6 summarizes and illustrates this point.

The transactions we have described are identical to those using forward contracts. We did note with forward contracts, however, that one can enter into an

EXHIBIT 75-6	The Risk-Free Nature of Long and Short Futures Arbitrage

Asset is priced at $100, futures is priced at $f_0(T)$ and expires in one year. Interest rate over the life of the futures is 5 percent.

Time	Long Asset, Short Futures Arbitrage	Short Asset, Long Futures Arbitrage
Today (time 0)	Buy asset at $100 Sell futures at $f_0(T)$	Sell short asset for $100 Buy futures for $f_0(T)$
Expiration (time T)	Asset price is S_T Futures price converges to asset price	Asset price is S_T Futures price converges to asset price
	Deliver asset	Take delivery of asset
	Profit on asset after accounting for the 5 percent ($5) interest lost from $100 tied up in the investment in the asset: $S_T - 100 - 5$	Profit on asset after accounting for the 5 percent ($5) interest earned on the $100 received from the short sale of the asset: $100 + 5 - S_T$
	Profit on futures: $f_0(T) - S_T$	Profit on futures: $S_T - f_0(T)$
	Total profit: $f_0(T) - 100 - 5$	Total profit: $100 + 5 - f_0(T)$

Conclusion: The asset price at expiration has no effect on the profit captured at expiration for either transaction. The profit is known today. To eliminate arbitrage, the futures price today, $f_0(T)$, must equal $100 + 5 = 105.

---

[25] Keep in mind that there are some restrictions on the short selling of financial instruments, such as uptick rules and margin requirements, but we will not concern ourselves with these impediments here.

off-market forward contract, having one party pay cash to another to settle any difference resulting from the contract not trading at its arbitrage-free value up front. In the futures market, this type of arrangement is not permitted; all contracts are entered into without any cash payments up front.

So in general, through the forces of arbitrage, we say that *the futures price is the spot price compounded at the risk-free rate:*

$$f_0(T) = S_0(1 + r)$$

It is important, however, to write this result in a form we are more likely to use. In the above form, we specify r as the interest rate over the life of the futures contract. In financial markets, however, interest rates are nearly always specified as annual rates. Therefore, to compound the asset price over the life of the futures, we let r equal an annual rate and specify the life of the futures as T years. Then the futures price is found as

$$f_0(T) = S_0(1 + r)^T \tag{75-4}$$

The futures price is the spot price compounded over the life of the contract, T years, at the annual risk-free rate, r. From this point on, we shall use this more general specification.

As an example, consider a futures contract that has a life of 182 days; the annual interest rate is 5 percent. Then $T = 182/365$ and $r = 0.05$. If the spot price is \$100, the futures price would then be

$$f_0(T) = S_0(1 + r)^T$$
$$f_0(182/365) = 100(1.05)^{182/365}$$
$$= 102.46$$

If the futures is selling for more than \$102.46, an arbitrageur can buy the asset for \$100 and sell the futures for whatever its price is, hold the asset (losing interest on \$100 at an annual rate of 5 percent) and deliver it to receive the futures price. The overall strategy will net a return in excess of 5 percent a year at no risk. If the futures is selling for less than \$102.46, the arbitrageur can borrow the asset, sell it short, and buy the futures. She will earn interest on the funds obtained from the short sale and take delivery of the asset at the futures expiration, paying the original futures price. The overall transaction results in receiving \$100 up front and paying back an amount less than the 5 percent risk-free rate, making the transaction like a loan that is paid back at less than the risk-free rate. If one could create such a loan, one could use it to raise funds and invest the funds at the risk-free rate to earn unlimited gains.

7.1.5 Pricing Futures Contracts When There Are Storage Costs

Except for opportunity costs, we have until now ignored any costs associated with holding the asset. In many asset markets, there are significant costs, other than the opportunity cost, to holding an asset. These costs are referred to as **storage costs** or **carrying costs** and are generally a function of the physical characteristics of the underlying asset. Some assets are easy to store; some are difficult. For example, assume the underlying is oil, which has significant storage costs but a very long storage life.[26] One would not expect to incur costs associated with a

---

[26] After all, oil has been stored by nature for millions of years.

decrease in quality of the oil. Significant risks do exist, however, such as spillage, fire, or explosion. Some assets on which futures are based are at risk for damage. For example, cattle and pigs can become ill and die during storage. Grains are subject to pest damage and fire. All of these factors have the potential to produce significant storage costs, and protection such as insurance leads to higher storage costs for these assets. On the other hand, financial assets have virtually no storage costs. Of course, all assets have one significant storage cost, which is the opportunity cost of money tied up in the asset, but this effect is covered in the present value calculation.

It is reasonable to assume that the storage costs on an asset are a function of the quantity of the asset to be stored and the length of time in storage. Let us specify this cost with the variable $FV(SC,0,T)$, which denotes the value at time T (expiration) of the storage costs (excluding opportunity costs) associated with holding the asset over the period 0 to T. By specifying these costs as of time T, we are accumulating the costs and compounding the interest thereon until the end of the storage period. We can reasonably assume that when storage is initiated, these costs are known.[27]

Revisiting the example we used previously, we would buy the asset at S_0, sell a futures contract at $f_0(T)$, store the asset and accumulate costs of $FV(SC,0,T)$, and deliver the asset at expiration to receive the futures price. The total payoff is $f_0(T) - FV(SC,0,T)$. This amount is risk free. To avoid an arbitrage opportunity, its present value should equal the initial outlay, S_0, required to establish the position. Thus,

$$[f_0(T) - FV(SC,0,T)]/(1 + r)^T = S_0$$

Solving for the futures price gives

$$f_0(T) = S_0(1 + r)^T + FV(SC,0,T)$$

(75-5)

This result says that *the futures price equals the spot price compounded over the life of the futures contract at the risk-free rate, plus the future value of the storage costs over the life of the contract.* In the previous example with no storage costs, we saw that the futures price was the spot price compounded at the risk-free rate. With storage costs, we must add the future value of the storage costs. The logic behind this adjustment should make sense. The futures price should be higher by enough to cover the storage costs when a trader buys the asset and sells a futures to create a risk-free position.[28]

Consider the following example. The spot price of the asset is $50, the interest rate is 6.25 percent, the future value of the storage costs is $1.35, and the futures expires in 15 months. Then $T = 15/12 = 1.25$. The futures price would, therefore, be

$$f_0(T) = S_0(1 + r)^T + FV(SC,0,T)$$

$$f_0(1.25) = 50(1.0625)^{1.25} + 1.35$$

$$= 55.29$$

---

[27] There may be reason to suggest that storage costs have an element of uncertainty in them, complicating the analysis.

[28] We did not cover assets that are storable at significant cost when we studied forward contracts because such contracts are less widely used for these assets. Nonetheless, the formula given here would apply for forward contracts as well, given our assumption of no credit risk on forward contracts.

If the futures is selling for more than $55.29, the arbitrageur would buy the asset and sell the futures, holding the position until expiration, at which time he would deliver the asset and collect the futures price, earning a return that covers the 6.25 percent cost of the money and the storage costs of $1.35. If the futures is selling for less than $55.29, the arbitrageur would sell short the asset and buy the futures, reinvesting the proceeds from the short sale at 6.25 percent and saving the storage costs. The net effect would be to generate a cash inflow today plus the storage cost savings and a cash outflow at expiration that would replicate a loan with a rate less than the risk-free rate. Only if the futures sells for exactly $55.29 do these arbitrage opportunities go away.

7.1.6 Pricing Futures Contracts When There Are Cash Flows on the Underlying Asset

In each case we have considered so far, the underlying asset did not generate any positive cash flows to the holder. For some assets, there will indeed be positive cash flows to the holder. Recall that in Reading 74, we examined the pricing and valuation of forward contracts on stocks and bonds and were forced to recognize that stocks pay dividends, bonds pay interest, and these cash flows affect the forward price. A similar concept applies here and does so in a symmetric manner to what we described in the previous section in which the asset incurs a cash cost. As we saw in that section, a cash cost incurred from holding the asset increases the futures price. Thus, we might expect that cash generated from holding the asset would result in a lower futures price and, as we shall see in this section, that is indeed the case. But in the next section, we shall also see that it is even possible for an asset to generate nonmonetary benefits that must also be taken into account when pricing a futures contract on it.

Let us start by assuming that over the life of the futures contract, the asset generates positive cash flows of $FV(CF,0,T)$. It is no coincidence that this notation is similar to the one we used in the previous section for the storage costs of the underlying asset over the life of the futures. Cash inflows and storage costs are just different sides of the same coin. We must remember, however, that $FV(CF,0,T)$ represents a positive flow in this case. Now let us revisit our example.

We would buy the asset at S_0, sell a futures contract at $f_0(T)$, store the asset and generate positive cash flows of $FV(CF,0,T)$, and deliver the asset at expiration, receiving the futures price. The total payoff is $f_0(T) + FV(CF,0,T)$. This amount is risk free and known at the start. To avoid an arbitrage opportunity, its present value should equal the initial outlay, S_0, required to establish the position. Thus,

$$[f_0(T) + FV(CF,0,T)]/(1 + r)^T = S_0$$

Solving for the futures price gives

$$f_0(T) = S_0(1 + r)^T - FV(CF,0,T) \tag{75-6}$$

In the previous example that included storage costs, we saw that the futures price was the spot price compounded at the risk-free rate plus the future value of the storage costs. With positive cash flows, we must subtract the future value of these cash flows. The logic behind this adjustment should make sense. The futures price should be reduced by enough to account for the positive cash flows when a trader buys the asset and sells a futures to create a risk-free position. Otherwise, the trader would receive risk-free cash flows from the asset *and* the equivalent amount from the sale of the asset at the futures price. Reduction of the futures price by this amount avoids overcompensating the trader.

As noted, these cash flows can be in the form of dividends from a stock or coupon interest from a bond. When we specifically examine the pricing of bond and stock futures, we shall make this specification a little more precise and work an example.

7.1.7 Pricing Futures Contracts When There Is a Convenience Yield

Now consider the possibility that the asset might generate nonmonetary benefits that must also be taken into account. The notion of nonmonetary benefits that could affect futures prices might sound strange, but upon reflection, it makes perfect sense. For example, a house is a common and normally desirable investment made by individuals and families. The house generates no monetary benefits and incurs significant costs. As well as being a possible monetary investment if prices rise, the house generates some nonmonetary benefits in the form of serving as a place to live. These benefits are quite substantial; many people consider owning a residence preferable to renting, and people often sell their homes for monetary gains far less than any reasonable return on a risky asset. Clearly the notion of a nonmonetary benefit to owning an asset is one most people are familiar with.

In a futures contract on an asset with a nonmonetary gain, that gain must be taken into account. Suppose, for the purpose of understanding the effect of nonmonetary benefits on a futures contract, we create a hypothetical futures contract on a house. An individual purchases a house and sells a futures contract on it. We shall keep the arguments as simple as possible by ignoring the operating or carrying costs. What should be the futures price? If the futures is priced at the spot price plus the risk-free rate, as in the original case, the homeowner receives a guaranteed sale price, giving a return of the risk-free rate *and* the use of the home. This is clearly a good deal. Homeowners would be eager to sell futures contracts, leading to a decrease in the price of the futures. Thus, any nonmonetary benefits ought to be factored into the futures price and logically would lead to a lower futures price.

Of course, in the real world of standardized futures contracts, there are no futures contracts on houses. Nonetheless, there are futures contracts on assets that have nonmonetary benefits. Assets that are often in short supply, particularly those with seasonal and highly risky production processes, are commonly viewed as having such benefits. The nonmonetary benefits of these assets are referred to as the **convenience yield**. Formally, a convenience yield is the nonmonetary return offered by an asset when in short supply. When an asset is in short supply, its price tends to be high. Holders of the asset earn an implicit incremental return from having the asset on hand. This return enables them, as commercial enterprises, to avoid the cost and inconvenience of not having their primary product or resource input on hand. Because shortages are generally temporary, the spot price can be higher than the futures price, even when the asset incurs storage costs. If a trader buys the asset, sells a futures contract, and stores the asset, the return is risk free and will be sufficient to cover the storage costs and the opportunity cost of money, but it will be reduced by an amount reflecting the benefits of holding the asset during a period of shortage or any other nonmonetary benefits.

Now, let the notation FV(CB,0,T) represent the future value of the costs of storage minus the benefits:

$$FV(CB,0,T) = \text{Costs of storage} - \text{Nonmonetary benefits (Convenience yield)}$$

where all terms are expressed in terms of their future value at time T and are considered to be known at time 0. If the costs exceed the benefits, FV(CB,0,T) is a positive number.[29] We refer to FV(CB,0,T) as the **cost of carry**.[30] The general futures pricing formula is

$$f_0(T) = S_0(1 + r)^T + FV(CB,0,T) \tag{75-7}$$

The futures price is the spot price compounded at the risk-free rate plus the cost of carry. This model is often called the **cost-of-carry model**.

Consider an asset priced at \$75; the risk-free interest rate is 5.15 percent, the net of the storage costs, interest, and convenience yield is \$3.20, and the futures expires in nine months. Thus, T = 9/12 = 0.75. Then the futures price should be

$$f_0(T) = S_0(1 + r)^T + FV(CB,0,T)$$
$$f_0(0.75) = 75(1.0515)^{0.75} + 3.20$$
$$= 81.08$$

As we have always done, we assume that this price will prevail in the marketplace. If it does not, the forces of arbitrage will drive the market price to the model price. If the futures price exceeds \$81.08, the arbitrageur can buy the asset and sell the futures to earn a risk-free return in excess of the risk-free rate. If the futures price is less than \$81.08, the arbitrageur can either sell the asset short or sell it if he already owns it, and then also buy the futures, creating a risk-free position equivalent to a loan that will cost less than the risk-free rate. The gains from both of these transactions will have accounted for any nonmonetary benefits. This arbitrage activity will force the market price to converge to the model price.

The above equation is the most general form of the futures pricing formula we shall encounter. Exhibit 75-7 reviews and illustrates how we obtained this formula and provides another example.

EXHIBIT 75-7   **Pricing a Futures Contract**

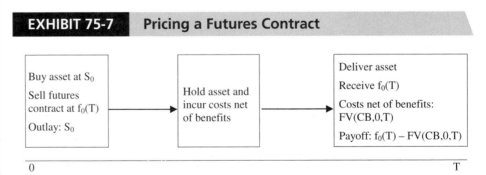

The transaction is risk-free and should be equivalent to investing S_0 dollars in a risk-free asset that pays $f_0(T) - FV(CB,0,T)$ at time T. Therefore, the payoff at T must be the future value of the initial outlay invested at the risk-free rate. For this relationship to hold, the futures price must be given as

$$f_0(T) = S_0(1 + r)^T + FV(CB,0,T)$$

Example: An asset is selling for \$225. A futures contract expires in 150 days (T = 150/365 = 0.411). The risk-free rate is 7.5 percent, and the net cost of carry is \$5.75. The futures price will be

$$f_0(T) = f_0(0.411) = \$225(1.075)^{0.411} + \$5.75 = \$237.54$$

---

[29] In other words, FV(CB,0,T) has to be positive to refer to it as a "cost."

[30] In some cases, such as in inventory storage, it is customary to include the opportunity cost in the definition of cost of carry; but we keep it separate in this text.

Some variations of this general formula are occasionally seen. Sometimes the opportunity cost of interest is converted to dollars and imbedded in the cost of carry. Then we say that $f_0(T) = S_0 + FV(CB,0,T)$; the futures price is the spot price plus the cost of carry. This is a perfectly appropriate way to express the formula if the interest is imbedded in the cost of carry, but we shall not do so in this book.

Another variation of this formula is to specify the cost of carry in terms of a rate, such as y. Then we have $\hat{f}_0(T) = S_0(1 + r)^T(1 + y)^T$. Again, this variation is certainly appropriate but is not the version we shall use.[31]

Note that when we get into the specifics of pricing certain types of futures contracts, we must fine-tune the formulas a little more. First, however, we explore some general characterizations of the relationship between futures and spot prices.

Practice Problem 2

Consider an asset priced at $50. The risk-free interest rate is 8 percent, and a futures contract on the asset expires in 45 days. Answer the following, with questions A, B, C, and D independent of the others.

A. Find the appropriate futures price if the underlying asset has no storage costs, cash flows, or convenience yield.

B. Find the appropriate futures price if the future value of storage costs on the underlying asset at the futures expiration equals $2.25.

C. Find the appropriate futures price if the future value of positive cash flows on the underlying asset equals $0.75.

D. Find the appropriate futures price if the future value of the net overall cost of carry on the underlying asset equals $3.55.

E. Using Part D above, illustrate how an arbitrage transaction could be executed if the futures contract is trading at $60.

F. Using Part A above, determine the value of a long futures contract an instant before marking to market if the previous settlement price was $49.

SOLUTIONS

A. First determine that $T = 45/365 = 0.1233$. Then the futures price is

$$f_0(0.1233) = \$50(1.08)^{0.1233} = \$50.48$$

B. Storage costs must be covered in the futures price, so we add them:

$$f_0(0.1233) = \$50(1.08)^{0.1233} + \$2.25 = \$52.73$$

C. A positive cash flow, such as interest or dividends on the underlying, reduces the futures price:

$$f_0(0.1233) = \$50(1.08)^{0.1233} - \$0.75 = \$49.73$$

---

[31] Yet another variation of this formula is to use $(1 + r + y)^T$ as an approximation for $(1 + r)^T(1 + y)^T$. We do not, however, consider this expression an acceptable way to compute the futures price as it is an approximation of a formula that is simple enough to use without approximating.

D. The net overall cost of carry must be covered in the futures price, so we add it:

$$f_0(0.1233) = \$50(1.08)^{0.1233} + \$3.55 = \$54.03$$

E. Follow these steps:

▶ Sell the futures at $60.

▶ Buy the asset at $50.

▶ Because the asset price compounded at the interest rate is $50.48, the interest forgone is $0.48. So the asset price is effectively $50.48 by the time of the futures expiration.

▶ Incur costs of $3.55.

▶ At expiration, deliver the asset and receive $60. The net investment in the asset is $50.48 + $3.55 = $54.03. If the asset is sold for $60, the net gain is $5.97.

F. If the last settlement price was $49.00 and the price is now $50.48 (our answer in Part A), the value of a long futures contract equals the difference between these prices: $50.48 − $49.00 = $1.48.

7.1.8 Backwardation and Contango

Because the cost of carry, FV(CB,0,T), can be either positive or negative, the futures price can be greater or less than the spot price. Because the costs plus the interest tend to exceed the benefits, it is more common for the futures price to exceed the spot price, a situation called **contango**. In contrast, when the benefits exceed the costs plus the interest, the futures price will be less than the spot price, called **backwardation**. These terms are not particularly important in understanding the necessary concepts, but they are so commonly used that they are worthwhile to remember.

7.1.9 Futures Prices and Expected Spot Prices

An important concept when examining futures prices is the relationship between futures prices and expected spot prices. In order to fully understand the issue, let us first consider the relationship between spot prices and expected spot prices. Consider an asset with no risk, but which incurs carrying costs. At time 0, the holder of the asset purchases it with the certainty that she will cover her opportunity cost and carrying cost. Otherwise, she would not purchase the asset. Thus, the spot price at time 0 is the present value of the total of the spot price at time T less costs minus benefits:

$$S_0 = \frac{S_T - FV(CB,0,T)}{(1 + r)^T}$$

$$= \frac{S_T}{(1 + r)^T} - \frac{FV(CB,0,T)}{(1 - r)^T}$$

Because FV(CB,0,T) is the future value of the carrying cost, $FV(CB,0,T)/(1 + r)^T$ is the present value of the carrying cost. So on the one hand, we can say that the spot price is the future spot price minus the future value of the carrying cost, all discounted to the present. On the other hand, we can also say that the spot price is the discounted value of the future spot price minus the present value of the carrying cost.

If, however, the future price of the asset is uncertain, as it nearly always is, we must make some adjustments. For one, we do not know at time 0 what S_T will be. We must form an expectation, which we will denote as $E_0(S_T)$. But if we simply replace S_T above with $E_0(S_T)$ we would not be acting rationally. We would be paying a price today and expecting compensation only at the risk-free rate along with coverage of our carrying cost. Indeed, one of the most important and intuitive elements of all we know about finance is that risky assets require a risk premium. Let us denote this risk premium with the symbol, $\phi_0(S_T)$. It represents a discount off of the expected value that is imbedded in the current price, S_0. Specifically, the current price is now given as

$$S_0 = \frac{E_0(S_T) - FV(CB,0,T) - \phi_0(S_T)}{(1 + r)^T}$$

where we see that the risk premium lowers the current spot price. Intuitively, investors pay less for risky assets, all other things equal.

Until now, we have worked only with the spot price, but nothing we have said so far violates the rule of no arbitrage. Hence, our futures pricing formula, $f_0(T) = S_0(1 + r)^T + FV(CB,0,T)$, still applies. If we rearrange the futures pricing formula for $FV(CB,0,T)$, substitute this result into the formula for S_0, and solve for the futures price, $f_0(T)$, we obtain $f_0(T) = E_0(S_T) - \phi_0(S_T)$. This equation says that the futures price equals the expected future spot price minus the risk premium.

An important conclusion to draw from this formula is that the futures price does not equal the expectation of the future spot price. The futures price would be biased on the low side. If one felt that the futures price were an unbiased predictor of the future spot price, $f_0(T) = E_0(S_T)$, one could expect on average to be able to predict the future spot price of oil by looking at the futures price of oil. But that is not likely to be the case.

The intuition behind this result is easy to see. We start with the assumption that all units of the asset must be held by someone. Holders of the asset incur the risk of its future selling price. If a holder of the asset wishes to transfer that risk by selling a futures contract, she must offer a futures contract for sale. But if the futures contract is offered at a price equal to the expected spot price, the buyer of the futures contract takes on the risk but expects to earn only a price equal to the price paid for the futures. Thus, the futures trader incurs the risk without an expected gain in the form of a risk premium. On the opposite side of the coin, the holder of the asset would have a risk-free position with an expected gain in excess of the risk-free rate. Clearly, the holder of the asset would not be able to do such a transaction. Thus, she must lower the price to a level sufficient to compensate the futures trader for the risk he is taking on. This process will lead to a futures price that equals the expected spot price minus the risk premium, as shown in the above equation. In effect, the risk premium transfers from the holder of the asset to the buyer of the futures contract.

In all fairness, however, we must acknowledge that this view is not without its opponents. Some consider the futures price an unbiased predictor of the future spot price. In such a case, the futures price would tend to overshoot and undershoot the future spot price but on average would be equal to it. For such a situation to exist would require the unreasonable assumption that there is no risk or that investors are risk neutral, meaning that they are indifferent to risk. There is, however, one other situation in which the risk premium could disappear or even turn negative. Suppose holders of the asset who want to hedge their holdings could find other parties who need to purchase the asset and who would like to hedge by going long. In that case, it should be possible for the two parties to consummate a futures transaction with the futures price equal to the expected spot price. In fact, if the parties going long exerted greater pressure than the parties going short, it might even be possible for the futures price to exceed the expected spot price.

When futures prices are lower than expected spot prices, the situation is called **normal backwardation**. When futures prices are higher than expected spot prices, it is called **normal contango**. Note the contrast with the terms backwardation and contango, which we encountered in Section 7.1.8. Backwardation means that the futures price is lower than the spot price; contango means that the futures price exceeds the spot price. Normal backwardation means that the futures price is lower than the expected spot price; normal contango means that the futures price exceeds the expected spot price.

Generally speaking, we should favor the notion that futures prices are biased predictors of future spot prices because of the transferal of the risk premium from holders of the asset to buyers of futures. Intuitively, this is the more likely case, but the other interpretations are possible. Fortunately, for our purposes, it is not critical to resolve the issue, but we do need to be aware of it.

7.2 Pricing Interest Rate Futures

We shall examine the pricing of three classes of interest rate futures contracts: Treasury bill futures, Eurodollar futures, and Treasury bond futures. In Section 6.1, we described the characteristics of these instruments and contracts. Now we look at their pricing, keeping in mind that we established the general foundations for pricing—the cost-of-carry model—in the previous section. Recall that in the cost-of-carry model, we buy the underlying asset, sell a futures contract, store the asset (which incurs costs and could generate benefits), and deliver the asset at expiration. To prevent arbitrage, the futures price is found in general as

$$\text{Futures price} = \text{Spot price of underlying asset} \times \text{Compounding factor} + \text{Costs net of monetary and nonmonetary benefits}$$

When the underlying is a financial instrument, there will be no nonmonetary benefits and no costs other than the opportunity cost.

7.2.1 Pricing T-Bill Futures

Consider the following time line of our problem:

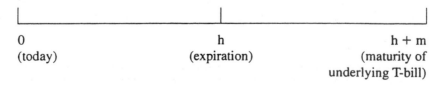

0	h	h + m
(today)	(expiration)	(maturity of underlying T-bill)

Time 0 is today, and time h is the expiration day of the futures contract. The T-bill underlying the contract is an m-day T-bill. Thus, when the futures expires, the T-bill is required to have m days to go before maturity. So from our perspective today, the underlying T-bill is an (h + m)-day T-bill.[32] As in Reading 74 for FRAs,

---

[32] It is common practice in the T-bill futures market to refer to the underlying as an m-day T-bill, but at time 0, the underlying futures must be an (h + m)-day T-bill in order for it to be an m-day T-bill at time h.

h and m represent a particular number of days. In accordance with common practice, m is traditionally 90. We now introduce some necessary notation. First, where necessary, we use a simple expression, r, for the risk-free interest rate. But when pricing Treasury bill futures, we need a more flexible notation. Here we need the rates for T-bills maturing on day h and on day h + m. In addition, because interest rates can change from day 0 to day h, we need notation that distinguishes rates for different maturities and rates at different points in time.[33]

To find the spot price of the underlying asset, we need the discount rate on an (h + m)-day T-bill. Suppose we have

$$r_0^d(h), r_0^d(h + m) = \text{Discount rates in effect on day 0 of h-day and}$$
$$(h + m)\text{-day T-bills}$$

As described in Section 6, these are discount rates and convert to prices by the following formula: $B_0(j) = 1 - r_0^d(j)(j/360)$, where in this case j will either be h or h + m. Thus, the prices of h- and (h + m)-day spot T-bills on day 0 (assuming $1 face amounts) are

$$B_0(h) = 1 - r_0^d(h)\left(\frac{h}{360}\right)$$
$$B_0(h + m) = 1 - r_0^d(h + m)\left(\frac{h + m}{360}\right)$$

In other words, the h- or (h + m)-day discount rate is multiplied by the number of days in the life of the T-bill over 360 and subtracted from the face value of $1.

Now let us turn to the futures market. We define

$$r_0^{df}(h) = \text{implied discount rate on day 0 of futures contract expiring on day}$$
$$\text{h, where the deliverable instrument is an m-day T-bill}$$

$$f_0(h) = \text{price on day 0 of futures contract expiring on day h}$$

The relationship between $r_0^{df}(h)$ and $f_0(h)$ is

$$f_0(h) = 1 - r_0^{df}(h)\left(\frac{m}{360}\right)$$

It is important to note that the futures price, not the implied discount rate, is the more important variable. Like any price, the futures price is determined in a market of buyers and sellers. Any rate is simply a way of transforming a price into a number that can be compared with rates on various other fixed-income instruments.[34] Do not think that a futures contract pays an interest rate. It is more appropriate to think of such a rate imbedded in a futures price as an *implied rate*, hence our use of the term *implied discount rate*. Although knowing this rate does

---

[33] When we assume that the interest rates are the same for all maturities and cannot change over time, which is considered acceptable when working with stock index and currency futures, we can use the simpler notation of r for the rate.

[34] To further reinforce the notion that an interest rate is just a transformation of a price, consider a zero-coupon bond selling at $95 and using 360 days as a year. The price can be transformed into a rate in the manner of $1/0.95 - 1 = 0.0526$ or 5.26 percent. But using the convention of the Treasury bill market, the rate is expressed as a discount rate. Then $0.95 = 1 - \text{Rate} \times (360/360)$, and the rate would be 0.05 or 5 percent. A price can be converted into a rate in a number of other ways, such as by assuming different compound periods. The price of any asset is determined in a market-clearing process. The rate is just a means of transforming the price so that interest rate instruments and their derivatives can be discussed in a more comparable manner.

not tell us any more than knowing the futures price, traders often refer to the futures contract in terms of the rate rather than the price.

Finally, let us note that at expiration, the futures price is the price of the underlying T-bill

$$f_h(h) = B_h(h + m)$$

$$= 1 - r_h^d(h + m)\left(\frac{m}{360}\right)$$

where $B_h(h + m)$ is the price on day h of the T-bill maturing on day $h + m$, and $r_h^d(h + m)$ is the discount rate on day h on the T-bill maturing on day $h + m$.

We now derive the futures price by constructing a risk-free portfolio that permits no arbitrage profits to be earned. This transaction is referred to as a cash-and-carry strategy, because the trader buys the asset in the cash (spot) market and carries (holds) it.

On day 0, we buy the $(h + m)$-day T-bill, investing $B_0(h + m)$. We simultaneously sell a futures contract at the price $f_0(h)$. On day h, we are required to deliver an m-day T-bill. The bill we purchased, which originally had $h + m$ days to maturity, now has m days to maturity. We therefore deliver that bill and receive the original futures price. We can view this transaction as having paid $B_0(h + m)$ on day 0 and receiving $f_0(h)$. Because $f_0(h)$ is known on day 0, this transaction is risk free. It should thus earn the same return per dollar invested as would a T-bill purchased on day 0 that matures on day h. The return per dollar invested from the arbitrage transaction would be $f_0(h)/B_0(h + m)$, and the return per dollar invested in an h-day T-bill would be $1/B_0(h)$.[35] Consequently, we set these values equal:

$$\frac{f_0(h)}{B_0(h + m)} = \frac{1}{B_0(h)}$$

Solving for the futures price, we obtain

$$f_0(h) = \frac{B_0(h + m)}{B_0(h)}$$

In words, the futures price is the ratio of the longer-term bill price to the shorter-term bill price. This price is, in fact, the same as the forward price from the term structure. In fact, as we noted above, futures prices and forward prices will be equal under the assumptions we have made so far and will follow throughout this book.

Recall that we previously demonstrated that the futures price should equal the spot price plus the cost of carry. Yet the above formula looks nothing like this result. In fact, however, it is consistent with the cost-of-carry formula. First, the above formula can be written as

$$f_0(h) = B_0(h + m)\left[\frac{1}{B_0(h)}\right]$$

---

[35] For example, if a one-year \$1 face value T-bill is selling for \$0.90, the return per dollar invested is \$1/\$0.90 = 1.1111.

As noted above, the expression $1/B_0(h)$ can be identified as the return per dollar invested over h days, which simplifies to $[1 + r_0(h)]^{h/365}$, which is essentially a compound interest factor for h days at the rate $r_0(h)$. Note that h is the number of days, assuming 365 in a year. For the period ending at day h, the above formula becomes

$$f_0(h) = B_0(h + m)[1 + r_0(h)]^{h/365}$$ **(75-8)**

and the futures price is seen to equal the spot price of the underlying compounded at the interest rate, which simply reflects the opportunity cost of the money tied up for h days.

Note that what we have been doing is deriving the appropriate price for a futures contract. In a market with no arbitrage opportunities, the actual futures price would be this theoretical price. Let us suppose for a moment, however, that the actual futures price is something else, say $f_0(h)^*$. The spot price is, of course, $B_0(h + m)$. Using these two numbers, we can infer the implied rate of return from a transaction involving the purchase of the T-bill and sale of the futures. We have

$$f_0(h)^* = B_0(h + m)[1 + r_0(h)^*]^{h/365}$$

where $r_0(h)^*$ is the implied rate of return. Solving for $r_0(h)^*$ we obtain

$$r_0(h)^* = \left[\frac{f_0(h)^*}{B_0(h + m)}\right]^{365/h} - 1$$ **(75-9)**

This rate of return, $r_0(h)^*$, has a special name, the **implied repo rate**. It is the rate of return from a cash-and-carry transaction that is implied by the futures price relative to the spot price. Traders who engage in such transactions often obtain the funds to do so in the repurchase agreement (repo) market. The implied repo rate tells the trader what rate of return to expect from the strategy. If the financing rate available in the repo market is less than the implied repo rate, the strategy is worthwhile and would generate an arbitrage profit. If the trader could lend in the repo market at greater than the implied repo rate, the appropriate strategy would be to reverse the transaction—selling the T-bill short and buying the futures—turning the strategy into a source of financing that would cost less than the rate at which the funds could be lent in the repo market.[36]

The implied repo rate is the rate of return implied by the strategy of buying the asset and selling the futures. As noted above, the futures price is often expressed in terms of an implied discount rate. Remember that the buyer of a futures contract is committing to buy a T-bill at the price $f_0(h)$. In the convention of pricing a T-bill by subtracting a discount rate from par value, the implied discount rate would be

$$r_0^{df}(h) = [1 - f_0(h)]\left(\frac{360}{m}\right)$$ **(75-10)**

---

[36] The concepts of a cash-and-carry strategy and the implied repo rate are applicable to any type of futures contract, but we cover them only with respect to T-bill futures.

We can also determine this implied discount rate from the discount rates on the h- and (h + m)-day T-bills as follows:[37]

$$r_0^{df}(h) = \left\{ 1 - \left[\frac{1 - r_0^d(h + m)\left(\frac{h + m}{360}\right)}{1 - r_0^d(h)\left(\frac{h}{360}\right)} \right] \right\} \left(\frac{360}{m}\right)$$

Now let us look at an example. We are interested in pricing a futures contract expiring in 30 days. A 30-day T-bill has a discount rate of 6 percent, and a 120-day T-bill has a discount rate of 6.6 percent. With h = 30 and h + m = 120, we have

$$r_0^d(h) = r_0^d(30) = 0.06$$

$$r_0^d(h + m) = r_0^d(120) = 0.066$$

The prices of these T-bills will, therefore, be

$$B_0(h) = 1 - r_0^d(h)\left(\frac{h}{360}\right)$$

$$B_0(30) = 1 - 0.06\left(\frac{30}{360}\right) = 0.9950$$

$$B_0(h + m) = 1 - r_0^d(h + m)\left(\frac{h + m}{360}\right)$$

$$B_0(120) = 1 - 0.066\left(\frac{120}{360}\right) = 0.9780$$

Using the formula we derived, we have the price of a futures expiring in 30 days as

$$f_0(h) = \frac{B_0(h + m)}{B_0(h)}$$

$$f_0(30) = \frac{B_0(120)}{B_0(30)} = \frac{0.9780}{0.9950} = 0.9829$$

The discount rate implied by the futures price would be

$$r_0^{df}(h) = [1 - f_0(h)]\left(\frac{360}{m}\right)$$

$$r_0^{df}(30) = (1 - 0.9829)\left(\frac{360}{90}\right) = 0.0684$$

In other words, in the T-bill futures market, the rate would be stated as 6.84 percent, which would imply a futures price of 0.9829.[38] Alternatively, the implied futures discount rate could be obtained from the spot discount rates as

---

[37] This formula is found by substituting $1 - r_0^d(h + m)[(h + m)/360]$ for $B_0(h + m)$ and $1 - r_0^d(h)(h/360)$ for $B_0(h)$ in the above equation for $r_0^{df}(h)$. This procedure expresses the spot prices in terms of their respective discount rates.

[38] We should also probably note that the IMM Index would be $100 - 6.84 = 93.16$. Thus, the futures price would be quoted in the market as 93.16.

$$r_0^{df}(h) = \left\{ 1 - \left[\frac{1 - r_0^d(h + m)\left(\frac{h + m}{360}\right)}{1 - r_0^d(h)\left(\frac{h}{360}\right)} \right] \right\} \left(\frac{360}{m}\right)$$

$$r_0^{df}(30) = \left\{ 1 - \left[\frac{1 - 0.066\left(\frac{120}{360}\right)}{1 - 0.06\left(\frac{30}{360}\right)} \right] \right\} \left(\frac{360}{90}\right) = 0.0683$$

with a slight difference due to rounding.

To verify this result, one would buy the 120-day T-bill for 0.9780 and sell the futures at a price of 0.9829. Then, 30 days later, the T-bill would be a 90-day T-bill and would be delivered to settle the futures contract. The trader would receive the original futures price of 0.9829. The return per dollar invested would be

$$\frac{0.9829}{0.9780} = 1.0050$$

If, instead, the trader had purchased a 30-day T-bill at the price of 0.9950 and held it for 30 days, the return per dollar invested would be

$$\frac{1}{0.9950} = 1.0050$$

Thus, the purchase of the 120-day T-bill with its price in 30 days hedged by the sale of the futures contract is equivalent to purchasing a 30-day T-bill and holding it to maturity. Each transaction has the same return per dollar invested and is free of risk.

Suppose in the market, the futures price is 0.9850. The implied repo rate would be

$$r_0(h)^* = \left[\frac{f_0(h)^*}{B_0(h + m)} \right]^{365/h} - 1$$

$$= \left(\frac{0.9850}{0.9780}\right)^{365/30} - 1 = 0.0906$$

Buying the 120-day T-bill for 0.9780 and selling a futures for 0.9850 generates a rate of return of $0.9850/0.9780 - 1 = 0.007157$. Annualizing this rate, $(1.007157)^{365/30} - 1 = 0.0906$. If financing could be obtained in the repo market for less than this annualized rate, the strategy would be attractive. If the trader could lend in the repo market at higher than this rate, he should buy the futures and sell short the T-bill to implicitly borrow at 9.06 percent and lend in the repo market at a higher rate.

Let us now recap the pricing of Treasury bill futures. We buy an (h + m)-day bond and sell a futures expiring on day h, which calls for delivery of an m-day T-bill. The futures price should be the price of the (h + m)-day T-bill compounded at the h-day risk-free rate. That rate is the rate of return on an h-day bill. The futures price can also be obtained as the ratio of the price of the (h + m)-day T-bill to the price of the h-day T-bill. Alternatively, we can express the futures price in terms of an implied discount rate, and we can derive the price in terms of the discount rates on the (h + m)-day T-bill and the h-day T-bill. Finally, remember that the actual futures price in the market relative to the price of the (h + m)-day T-bill implies a rate of return called the implied repo rate. The implied repo rate can be compared with the rate in the actual repo market to determine the attractiveness of an arbitrage transaction.

Exhibit 75-8 summarizes the important formulas involved in the pricing of T-bill futures. We then turn to the pricing of another short-term interest rate futures contract, the Eurodollar futures.

EXHIBIT 75-8 **Pricing Formulas for T-Bill Futures Contract**

Futures price = Underlying T-bill price compounded at risk-free rate

Futures price in terms of spot T-bills:

$$f_0(h) = \frac{B_0(h + m)}{B_0(h)}$$

Futures price as spot price compounded at risk-free rate:

$$f_0(h) = B_0(h + m)[1 + r_0(h)]^{h/365}$$

Discount rate implied by futures price:

$$r_0^{df}(h) = [1 - f_0(h)]\left(\frac{360}{m}\right) = \left\{ 1 - \left[\frac{1 - r_0^d(h + m)\left(\frac{h + m}{360}\right)}{1 - r_0^d(h)\left(\frac{h}{360}\right)} \right] \right\}\left(\frac{360}{m}\right)$$

Implied repo rate:

$$r_0(h)* = \left[\frac{f_0(h)^*}{B_0(h + m)} \right]^{365/h} - 1$$

Practice Problem 3

A futures contract on a Treasury bill expires in 50 days. The T-bill matures in 140 days. The discount rates on T-bills are as follows:

    50-day bill: 5.0 percent
    140-day bill: 4.6 percent

A. Find the appropriate futures price by using the prices of the 50- and 140-day T-bills.

B. Find the futures price in terms of the underlying spot price compounded at the appropriate risk-free rate.

C. Convert the futures price to the implied discount rate on the futures.

D. Now assume that the futures contract is trading in the market at an implied discount rate 10 basis points lower than is appropriate, given the pricing model and the rule of no arbitrage. Demonstrate how an arbitrage transaction could be executed and show the outcome. Calculate the implied repo rate and discuss how it would be used to determine the profitability of the arbitrage.

SOLUTIONS

A. First, find the prices of the 50- and 140-day bonds:

$$B_0(50) = 1 - 0.05(50/360) = 0.9931$$
$$B_0(140) = 1 - 0.046(140/360) = 0.9821$$

The futures price is, therefore,

$$f_0(50) = \frac{0.9821}{0.9931} = 0.9889$$

B. First, find the rate at which to compound the spot price of the 140-day T-bill. This rate is obtained from the 50-day T-bill:

$$[1 + r_0(h)]^{h/365} = \frac{1}{0.9931} = 1.0069$$

We actually do not need to solve for $r_0(h)$. The above says that based on the rate $r_0(h)$, every dollar invested should grow to a value of 1.0069. Thus, the futures price should be the spot price (the price of the 140-day T-bill) compounded by the factor 1.0069:
$$f_0(50) = 0.9821(1.0069) = 0.9889$$

Annualized, this rate would equal $(1.0069)^{365/50} - 1 = 0.0515$.

C. Given the futures price of 0.9889, the implied discount rate is

$$r_0^{df}(50) = (1 - 0.9889)\left(\frac{360}{90}\right)$$
$$= 0.0444$$

D. If the futures is trading for 10 basis points lower, it trades at a rate of 4.34 percent, so the futures price would be

$$f_0(50) = 1 - 0.0434\left(\frac{90}{360}\right)$$
$$= 0.9892$$

Do the following:

▶ Buy the 140-day bond at 0.9821
▶ Sell the futures at 0.9892

This strategy provides a return per dollar invested of

$$\frac{0.9892}{0.9821} = 1.0072$$

which compares favorably with a return per dollar invested of 1.0069 if the futures is correctly priced.

The implied repo rate is simply the annualization of this rate: $(1.0072)^{365/50} - 1 = 0.0538$. The cash-and-carry transaction would, therefore, earn 5.38 percent. Because the futures appears to be mispriced, we could likely obtain financing in the repo market at less than this rate.

7.2.2 Pricing Eurodollar Futures

Based on the T-bill case, it is tempting to argue that the interest rate implied by the Eurodollar futures price would be the forward rate in the term structure of LIBOR. Unfortunately, that is not quite the case. In fact, the unusual construction of the Eurodollar futures contract relative to the Eurodollar spot market means that no risk-free combination of a Eurodollar time deposit and a Eurodollar futures contract can be constructed. Recall that the Eurodollar time deposit is an add-on instrument. Using $L_0(j)$ as the rate (LIBOR) on a j-day Eurodollar time deposit on day 0, if one deposits \$1, the deposit will grow to a value of $1 + L_0(j)(j/360)$ j days later. So, the present value of \$1 in j days is $1/[1 + L_0(j)(j/360)]$. The Eurodollar futures contract, however, is structured like the T-bill contract—as though the underlying were a discount instrument. So its price is stated in the form of $1 - L_0(j)(j/360)$. If we try the same arbitrage with Eurodollars that we did with T-bills, we cannot get the LIBOR that determines the spot price of a Eurodollar at expiration to offset the LIBOR that determines the futures price at expiration.

In other words, suppose that on day 0 we buy an (h + m)-day Eurodollar deposit that pays \$1 on day (h + m) and sell a futures at a price of $f_0(h)$. On day h, the futures expiration, the Eurodollar deposit has m days to go and is worth $1/[1 + L_h(m)(m/360)]$. The futures price at expiration is $f_h(h) = 1 - L_h(m)(m/360)$. The profit from the futures is $f_0(h) - [1 - L_h(m)(m/360)]$. Adding this amount to the value of the m-day Eurodollar deposit we are holding gives a total position value of

$$\frac{1}{1 + L_h(m)\left(\dfrac{m}{360}\right)} + f_0(h) - [1 - L_h(m)]\left(\frac{m}{360}\right)$$

Although $f_0(h)$ is known when the transaction is initiated, $L_h(m)$ is not determined until the futures expiration. There is no way for the $L_h(m)$ terms to offset. This problem does not occur in the T-bill market because the spot price is a discount instrument and the futures contract is designed as a discount instrument.[39] It is,

---

[39] It is not clear why the Chicago Mercantile Exchange designed the Eurodollar contract as a discount instrument when the underlying Eurodollar deposit is an add-on instrument. The most likely reason is that the T-bill futures contract was already trading, was successful, and its design was well understood and accepted by traders. The CME most likely felt that this particular design was successful and should be continued with the Eurodollar contract. Ironically, the Eurodollar contract became exceptionally successful and the T-bill contract now has virtually no trading volume.

nonetheless, common for participants in the futures market to treat the Eurodollar rate as equivalent to the implied forward rate. Such an assumption would require the ability to conduct the risk-free arbitrage, which, as we have shown, is impossible. The differences are fairly small, but we shall not assume that the Eurodollar futures rate should equal the implied forward rate. In that case, it would take a more advanced model to solve the pricing problem. The essential points in pricing interest rate futures on short-term instruments can be understood by studying the T-bill futures market.

This mismatch in the design of spot and futures instruments in the Eurodollar market would appear to make the contract difficult to use as a hedging instrument. We should note that in the above equation for the payoff of the portfolio combining a spot Eurodollar time deposit and a short Eurodollar futures contract, an increase (decrease) in LIBOR lowers (raises) the value of the spot Eurodollar deposit and raises (lowers) the payoff from the short Eurodollar futures. Thus, the Eurodollar futures contract can still serve as a hedging tool. The hedge will not be perfect but can still be quite effective. Indeed, the Eurodollar futures contract is a major hedging tool of dealers in over-the-counter derivatives.

We have now completed the treatment of futures contracts on short-term interest rate instruments. Now let us look at the pricing of Treasury bond futures.

7.2.3 Pricing Treasury Note and Bond Futures

Recall that in Section 6.2, we described the bond futures contract as one in which there are a number of deliverable bonds. When a given bond is delivered, the long pays the short the futures price times an adjustment term called the conversion factor. The conversion factor is the price of a $1 bond with coupon equal to that of the deliverable bond and yield equal to 6 percent, with calculations based on semiannual compounding. Bonds with a coupon greater (less) than 6 percent will have a conversion factor greater (less) than 1. Before we delve into the complexities added by this feature, however, let us start off by assuming a fairly generic type of contract: one in which the underlying is a single, specific bond.

When examining bond forward contracts in Reading 74, we specified a time line and notation. We return to that specific time line and notation, which differs from those we used for examining short-term interest rate futures.

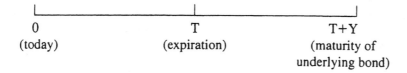

Recall our notation from Reading 74:

$B_0^c(T + Y)$ = price at time 0 of coupon bond that matures at time $T + Y$. The bond has a maturity of Y at the futures expiration.

CI_i = coupon at time t_i, where the coupons occur at times $t_1, t_2, \ldots, t_n$. Note that we care only about coupons prior to the futures expiration at T.

$f_0(T)$ = price at time 0 of futures expiring at time T.

$B_0(T)$ = price at time 0 of zero-coupon bond maturing at T.

We also need to know at time T the accumulated value of all coupons received over the period from 0 to T. We need the compound value from 0 to T of any coupons paid during the time the futures contract is alive. This value is denoted as FV(CI,0,T). We introduced this variable in Reading 74 and showed how to compute it, so you may wish to review that material. It is traditionally assumed that the interest rate at which these coupons are reinvested is known. We also assume that this interest rate applies to the period from 0 to T for money borrowed or lent. We denote this rate as

$r_0(T)$ = Interest rate at time 0 for period until time T

As described in the section on T-bill futures pricing, this is the rate that determines the price of a zero-coupon bond maturing at T.[40] Hence,

$$B_0(T) = \frac{1}{[1 + r_0(T)]^T}$$

The futures price at expiration is the price of the deliverable bond at expiration:

$f_T(T) = B_T(T + Y)$

Now we are ready to price this bond futures contract. On day 0, we buy the bond at the price $B_0^c(T + Y)$ and sell the futures at the price $f_0(T)$. Because the futures does not require any cash up front, its initial value is zero. The current value of the overall transaction is, therefore, just the value of the bond, $B_0^c(T + Y)$. This value represents the amount of money we must invest to engage in this transaction.

We hold this position until the futures expiration. During this time, we collect and reinvest the coupons. On day T, the futures expires. We deliver the bond and receive the futures price, $f_0(T)$. We also have the reinvested coupons, which have a value at T of FV(CI,0,T). These two amounts, $f_0(T)$ and FV(CI,0,T), are known when the transaction was initiated at time 0, so the transaction is risk-free. Therefore, the current value of the transaction, $B_0^c(T + Y)$, should be the discounted value of its value at T of $f_0(T)$ + FV(CI,0,T):

$$B_0^c(T + Y) = \frac{f_0(T) + FV(CI, 0, T)}{[1 + r_0(T)]^T}$$

Note that we are simply discounting the known future value at T of the transaction at the risk-free rate of $r_0(T)$.[41]

We are, of course, more interested in the futures price, which is the only unknown in the above equation. Solving, we obtain

$$f_0(T) = B_0^c(T + Y)[1 + r_0(T)]^T - FV(CI,0,T) \qquad \text{(75-11)}$$

This equation is a variation of our basic cost-of-carry formula. The spot price, $B_0^c(T + Y)$, is compounded at the risk-free interest rate. We then subtract the compound future value of the reinvested coupons over the life of the contract.

---

[40] Keep in mind, however, that this rate is not the discount rate that determines the price of the zero-coupon bond maturing at T. It is the rate of return, expressed as an annual rate. When working with T-bills, the symbol "T" represented Days/365, which is consistent with its use here with T-bonds.

[41] We shall not take up the topic of the implied repo rate again, but note that if the futures is selling for $f_0(T)$, then $r_0(T)$ would be the implied repo rate.

The coupon interest is like a negative cost of carry; it is a positive cash flow associated with holding the underlying bond.

Now let us work an example. Consider a $1 face value Treasury bond that pays interest at 7 percent semiannually. Thus, each coupon is $0.035. The bond has exactly five years remaining, so during that time it will pay 10 coupons, each six months apart. The yield on the bond is 8 percent. The price of the bond is found by calculating the present value of both the 10 coupons and the face value: The price is $0.9594.

Now consider a futures contract that expires in one year and three months: $T = 1.25$. The risk-free rate, $r_0(T)$, is 6.5 percent. The accumulated value of the coupons and the interest on them is

$$\$0.035(1.065)^{0.75} + \$0.035(1.065)^{0.25} = \$0.0722$$

The first coupon is paid in one-half a year and reinvests for three-quarters of a year. The second coupon is paid in one year and reinvests for one-quarter of a year.

Now the futures price is obtained as

$$f_0(T) = B_0^c(T + Y)[1 + r_0(T)]^T - FV(CI,0,T)$$

$$f_0(1.25) = \$0.9594(1.065)^{1.25} - \$0.0722 = \$0.9658$$

This is the price at which the futures should trade, given current market conditions. To verify this result, buy the five-year bond for $0.9594 and sell the futures for $0.9658. Hold the position for 15 months until the futures expiration. Collect and reinvest the coupons. When the futures expires, deliver the bond and receive the futures price of $0.9658. Then add the reinvested coupons of $0.0722 for a total of $0.9658 + $0.0722 = $1.0380. If we invest $0.9594 and end up with $1.0380 15 months later, the return is $1.0380/$0.9594 = 1.0819. For comparison purposes, we should determine the annual equivalent of this rate, which is found as $(1.0819)^{1/1.25} - 1 = 0.065$. This is the same 6.5 percent risk-free rate. If the futures contract trades at a higher price, the above transaction would result in a return greater than 6.5 percent. The amount available at expiration would be higher, clearly leading to a rate of return higher than 6.5 percent. If the futures trades at a lower price, the arbitrageur would sell short the bond and buy the futures, which would generate a cash inflow today. The amount paid back would be at less than the risk-free rate of 6.5 percent.[42]

Unfortunately, we now must complicate the matter a little by moving to the more realistic case with a delivery option. Bond futures contracts traditionally permit the short to choose which bond to deliver. This feature reduces the possibility of unusual price behavior of the deliverable bond caused by holders of short positions scrambling to buy a single deliverable bond at expiration. By allowing more than one bond to be deliverable, such problems are avoided. The contract is structured as though there is a standard hypothetical deliverable bond, which has a given coupon rate. The Chicago Board of Trade's contract uses a 6 percent rate. If the short delivers a bond with a higher (lower) coupon rate, the price received at delivery is adjusted upward (downward). The conversion factor is defined and calculated as the price of a $1 face value bond with a coupon and maturity equal to that of the deliverable bond and a yield of 6 percent. Each deliverable bond has its own conversion factor. The short designates which bond he will deliver, and

---

[42] Again, as in the section on T-bill futures, this analysis could be conducted in terms of the implied repo rate.

that bond's conversion factor is multiplied by the final futures price to determine the amount the long will pay the short for the bond.

The availability of numerous deliverable bonds creates some confusion in pricing the futures contract, arising from the fact that the underlying cannot be uniquely identified, at least not on the surface. This confusion has given rise to the concept that one bond is always the best one to deliver. If a trader buys a given bond and sells the futures, he creates a risk-free hedge. If there are no arbitrage opportunities, the return from that hedge cannot exceed the risk-free rate. That return can, however, be *less* than the risk-free rate. How can this be? In all previous cases, if a return from a risk-free transaction is less than the risk-free rate, it should be a simple matter to reverse the transaction and capture an arbitrage profit. In this case, however, a reverse transaction would not work. If the arbitrageur sells short the bond and buys the futures, she must be assured that the short will deliver the bond from which the potential arbitrage profit was computed. But the short makes the delivery decision and in all likelihood would not deliver that particular bond.

Thus, the short can be long a bond and short futures and earn a return less than the risk-free rate. One bond, however, results in a return closest to the risk-free rate. Clearly that bond is the best bond to deliver. The terminology in the business is that this bond is the cheapest to deliver.

The cheapest-to-deliver bond is determined by selecting a given bond and computing the rate of return from buying that bond and selling the futures to hedge its delivery at expiration. This calculation is performed for all bonds. The one with the highest rate of return is the cheapest to deliver.[43] The cheapest-to-deliver bond can change, however, which can benefit the short and not the long. We ignore the details of determining the cheapest-to-deliver bond and assume that it has been identified. From here, we proceed to price the futures.

Let $CF(T)$ be the conversion factor for the bond we have identified as the cheapest to deliver. Now we go back to the arbitrage transaction described for the case where there is only one deliverable bond. Recall that we buy the bond, sell a futures, and reinvest the coupons on the bond. At expiration, we deliver the bond, receive the futures price $f_0(T)$, and have the reinvested coupons, which are worth $FV(CI,0,T)$. Now, in the case where the futures contract has many deliverable bonds, we must recognize that when the bond is delivered, the long pays $f_0(T)$ times $CF(T)$. This adjustment does not add any risk to this risk-free transaction. Thus, the present value of the amount received at delivery, $f_0(T)CF(T) + FV(CI,0,T)$, should still equal the original price of the bond, which was the amount we invested to initiate the transaction:

$$B_0^c(T + Y) = \frac{f_0(T)CF(T) + FV(CI,0,T)}{[1 + r_0(T)]^T}$$

Solving for the futures price, we obtain

$$f_0(T) = \frac{B_0^c(T + Y)[1 + r_0(T)]^T - FV(CI,0,T)}{CF(T)}$$

(75-12)

Note that when we had only one deliverable bond, the formula did not have the $CF(T)$ term, but a better way to look at it is that for only one deliverable bond, the conversion factor is effectively 1, so Equation 75-12 would still apply.

---

[43] As noted, this rate of return will not exceed the risk-free rate but will be the highest rate below the risk-free rate.

Consider the same example we previously worked, but now we need a conversion factor. As noted above, the conversion factor is the price of a $1 bond with coupon and maturity equal to that of the deliverable bond on the expiration day and yield of 6 percent, with all calculations made assuming semiannual interest payments. As noted, we shall skip the specifics of this calculation here; it is simply a present value calculation. For this example, the 7 percent bond with maturity of three and three-quarter years on the delivery day would have a conversion factor of 1.0505. Thus, the futures price would be

$$f_0(T) = \frac{B_0^c(T + Y)[1 + r_0(T)]^T - FV(CI,0,T)}{CF(T)}$$

$$f_0(1.25) = \frac{0.9594(1.065)^{1.25} - 0.0722}{1.0505} = 0.9193$$

If the futures is priced higher than 0.9193, one can buy the bond and sell the futures to earn more than the risk-free rate. If the futures price is less than 0.9193, one can sell short the bond and buy the futures to end up borrowing at less than the risk-free rate. As noted previously, however, this transaction has a complication: If one goes short the bond and long the futures, this bond must remain the cheapest to deliver. Otherwise, the short will not deliver this particular bond and the arbitrage will not be successful.

Exhibit 75-9 reviews the important formulas for pricing Treasury bond futures contracts.

EXHIBIT 75-9	**Pricing Formulas for Treasury Bond Futures Contract**

Futures price = Underlying T-bond price compounded at risk-free rate less Compound future value of reinvested coupons.

Futures price if underlying bond is the only deliverable bond:

$$f_0(T) = B_0^c(T + Y)[1 + r_0(T)]^T - FV(CI,0,T)$$

Futures price when there are multiple deliverable bonds:

$$f_0(T) = \frac{B_0^c(T + Y)[1 + r_0(T)]^T - FV(CI,0,T)}{CF(T)}$$

Practice Problem 4

Consider a three-year $1 par Treasury bond with a 7.5 percent annual yield and 8 percent semiannual coupon. Its price is $1.0132. A futures contract calling for delivery of this bond only expires in one year. The one-year risk-free rate is 7 percent.

A. Find the future value in one year of the coupons on this bond. Assume a reinvestment rate of 3.75 percent per six-month period.

B. Find the appropriate futures price.

C. Now suppose the bond is one of many deliverable bonds. The contract specification calls for the use of a conversion factor to determine the price paid for a given deliverable bond. Suppose the bond described here has a conversion factor of 1.0372. Now determine the appropriate futures price.

SOLUTIONS

A. One coupon of 0.04 will be invested for half a year at 3.75 percent (half of the rate of 7.5 percent). The other coupon is not reinvested but is still counted. Thus, $FV(CI,0,1) = 0.04(1.0375) + 0.04 = 0.0815$.

B. $f_0(1) = 1.0132(1.07) - 0.0815 = 1.0026$

C. $f_0(1) = \dfrac{1.0132(1.07) - 0.0815}{1.0372} = 0.9667$

7.3 Pricing Stock Index Futures

Now let the underlying be either a portfolio of stocks or an individual stock.[44] The former are normally referred to as stock index futures, in which the portfolio is identical in composition to an underlying index of stocks. In this material, we focus on the pricing of stock index futures, but the principles are the same if the underlying is an individual stock.

In pricing stock index futures, we must account for the fact that the underlying stocks pay dividends.[45] Recall that in our previous discussions about the generic pricing of futures, we demonstrated that the futures price is lower as a result of the compound future value of any cash flows paid on the asset. Such cash flows consist of coupon interest payments if the underlying is a bond, or storage costs if the underlying incurs costs to store.[46] Dividends work exactly like coupon interest.

Consider the same time line we used before. Today is time 0, and the futures expires at time T. During the life of the futures, there are n dividends of D_j, j = 1, 2, . . . , n. We assume these dividends are all known when the futures contract is initiated. Let

$FV(D,0,T)$ = the compound value over the period of 0 to T of all dividends collected and reinvested

We introduced this variable in Reading 74 and showed how to compute it, so you may wish to review that material. The other notation is the same we have previously used:

---

[44] Futures on individual stocks have taken a long time to develop, primarily because of regulatory hurdles. They were introduced in the United States in late 2002 and, as of the publication date of this book, have achieved only modest trading volume. They currently trade in a few other countries such as the United Kingdom and Australia.

[45] Even if not all of the stocks pay dividends, at least some of the stocks almost surely pay dividends.

[46] We also allowed for the possibility of noncash costs, which we called the convenience yield, but there are no implicit costs or benefits associated with stock index futures.

S_0 = current value of the stock index
$f_0(T)$ = futures price today of a contract that expires at T
r = risk-free interest rate over the period 0 to T

Now that we are no longer working with interest rate futures, we do not need the more flexible notation for interest rates on bonds of different maturities or interest rates at different time points. So we can use the simple notation of r as the risk-free interest rate, but we must keep in mind that it is the risk-free rate for the time period from 0 to T.

We undertake the following transaction: On day 0, we buy the stock portfolio that replicates the index. This transaction will require that we invest the amount S_0. We simultaneously sell the futures at the price $f_0(T)$.

On day T, the futures expires. We deliver the stock and receive the original futures price $f_0(T)$.[47] We also have the accumulated value of the reinvested dividends, $FV(D,0,T)$ for a total of $f_0(T) + FV(D,0,T)$. Because this amount is known at time 0, the transaction is risk free. Therefore, we should discount its value at the risk-free rate and set this equal to the initial value of the portfolio, S_0, as follows:

$$S_0 = \frac{f_0(T) + FV(D,0,T)}{(1 + r)^T}$$

Solving for the futures price gives

$$f_0(T) = S_0(1 + r)^T - FV(D,0,T) \qquad \textbf{(75-13)}$$

which is the cost-of-carry formula for stock index futures. Notice that it is virtually identical to that for bond futures. Ignoring the conversion factor necessitated by the delivery option, the only difference is that we use the compound future value of the dividends instead of the compound future value of the coupon interest.

Consider the following example. A stock index is at 1,452.45, and a futures contract on the index expires in three months. Thus, $T = 3/12 = 0.25$. The risk-free interest rate is 5.5 percent. The value of the dividends reinvested over the life of the futures is 7.26. The futures price should, therefore, be

$$f_0(T) = S_0(1 + r)^T - FV(D,0,T)$$
$$f_0(0.25) = 1{,}452.45(1.055)^{0.25} - 7.26$$
$$= 1{,}464.76$$

Thus, if the futures contract is selling for more than this price, an arbitrageur can buy the stocks and sell the futures. The arbitrageur would collect and reinvest the dividends and at expiration would receive a gain that would exceed the risk-free rate of 5.5 percent, a result of receiving more than 1,464.76 for the stocks. If the futures contract is selling for less than this price, the arbitrageur can sell short the stocks and buy the futures. After paying the dividends while holding the stocks,[48] the arbitrageur will end up buying back the stocks at a price that implies that he has borrowed money and paid it back at a rate less than the risk-free rate. The combined activities of all arbitrageurs will force the futures price to 1,464.76.

---

[47] Virtually all stock index futures contracts call for cash settlement at expiration. See the explanation of the equivalence of delivery and cash settlement in Section 4 and Exhibit 75-2.

[48] Remember that a short seller must make restitution for any dividends paid while the position is short.

The stock index futures pricing formula has a number of variations. Suppose we define $FV(D,0,T)/(1 + r)^T$ as the present value of the dividends, $PV(D,0,T)$:

$$FV(D,0,T) = PV(D,0,T)(1 + r)^T$$

Substituting in the futures pricing formula above for $FV(D,0,T)$, we obtain

$$f_0(T) = [S_0 - PV(D,0,T)](1 + r)^T \qquad \textbf{(75-14)}$$

Notice here that the stock price is reduced by the present value of the dividends. This adjusted stock price is then compounded at the risk-free rate over the life of the futures.

In the problem we worked above, the present value of the dividends is found as

$$PV(D,0,T) = \frac{FV(D,0,T)}{(1 + r)^T}$$

$$PV(D,0,0.25) = \frac{7.26}{(1.055)^{0.25}} = 7.16$$

Then the futures price would be

$$f_0(T) = [S_0 - PV(D,0,T)](1 + r)^T$$
$$f_0(0.25) = (1{,}452.45 - 7.16)(1.055)^{0.25}$$
$$= 1{,}464.76$$

Another variation of the formula defines the yield as δ in the following manner:

$$\frac{1}{(1 + \delta)^T} = 1 - \frac{FV(D,0,T)}{S_0(1 + r)^T}$$

The exact solution for δ is somewhat complex, so we shall just leave it in the form above. Using this specification, we find that the futures pricing formula would be

$$f_0(T) = \left(\frac{S_0}{(1 + \delta)^T}\right)(1 + r)^T \qquad \textbf{(75-15)}$$

The stock price is, thus, discounted at the dividend yield, and this adjusted stock price is then compounded at the risk-free rate over the life of the futures.[49]

In the example above, the yield calculation is

$$\frac{1}{(1 + \delta)^T} = 1 - \frac{FV(D,0,T)}{S_0(1 + r)^T}$$

$$\frac{1}{(1 + \delta)^T} = 1 - \frac{7.26}{1{,}452.45(1.055)^{0.25}} = 0.9951$$

---

[49] Sometimes the futures price is written as $f_0(T) = S_0(1 + r - \delta)^T$ where the dividend yield is simply subtracted from the risk-free rate to give a net cost of carry. This formula is a rough approximation that we do not consider acceptable.

Then $(1 + \delta)^T$ is $1/0.9951 = 1.0049$ and the futures price is

$$f_0(T) = \left(\frac{S_0}{(1 + \delta)^T}\right)(1 + r)^T$$

$$f_0(0.25) = \left(\frac{1,452.45}{1.0049}\right)(1.055)^{0.25}$$

$$= 1,464.84$$

The difference between this and the answer we previously obtained is strictly caused by a rounding error.

Another variation of this formula is to express the yield as

$$\delta^* = \frac{PV(D,0,T)}{S_0} = \frac{FV(D,0,T)/(1 + r)^T}{S_0}$$

This means that $FV(D,0,T) = S_0(1 + r)^T\delta^*$. Substituting into our futures pricing formula for $FV(D,0,T)$, we obtain

$$f_0(T) = S_0(1 - \delta^*)(1 + r)^T \qquad \textbf{(75-16)}$$

Here again, the stock price is reduced by the yield, and this "adjusted" stock price is compounded at the risk-free rate.

In the problem we worked above, the yield would be found as

$$\delta^* = \frac{PV(D,0,T)}{S_0}$$

$$\delta^* = \frac{7.16}{1,452.45} = 0.0049$$

Then the futures price would be

$$f_0(T) = S_0(1 - \delta^*)(1 + r)^T$$
$$f_0(0.25) = 1,452.45(1 - 0.0049)(1.055)^{0.25}$$
$$= 1,464.81$$

Again, the difference between the two prices comes from rounding.

A common variation uses the assumption of continuous compounding. The continuously compounded risk-free rate is defined as $r^c = \ln(1 + r)$. The continuously compounded dividend yield is $\delta^c = \ln(1 + \delta)$. When working with discrete dividends, we obtained the relationship

$$\frac{1}{(1 + \delta)^T} = 1 - \frac{FV(D,0,T)}{S_0(1 + r)^T}$$

We calculated $(1 + \delta)^T$. To obtain δ^c, we take the natural log of this value and divide by T: $\delta^c = (1/T)\ln[(1 + \delta)^T]$. The formula for the futures price is

$$f_0(T) = S_0e^{(r^c - \delta^c)T}$$

In the above formula, the opportunity cost, expressed as the interest rate, is reduced by the dividend yield. Thus, the formula compounds the spot price by the interest cost less the dividend benefits. An equivalent variation of the above formula is

$$f_0(T) = (S_0 e^{-\delta^c T}) e^{r^c T} \qquad\qquad\qquad\qquad\qquad \textbf{(75-17)}$$

The expression in parentheses is the stock price discounted at the dividend yield rate. The result is an adjusted stock price with the present value of the dividends removed. This adjusted stock price is then compounded at the risk-free rate. So, as we have previously seen, the stock price less the present value of the dividends is compounded at the risk-free rate to obtain the futures price.

In the previous problem, $(1 + \delta)^T = 1.0049$. Then $\delta^c = (1/0.25)\ln(1.0049) = 0.0196$. The continuously compounded risk-free rate is $\ln(1.055) = 0.0535$. The futures price is, therefore, $f_0(0.25) = (1452.45 e^{-0.0196(0.25)}) e^{0.0535(0.25)} = 1464.81$; again the difference comes from rounding.

Exhibit 75-10 summarizes the formulas for pricing stock index futures contracts. Each of these formulas is consistent with the general formula for pricing futures. They are each based on the notion that a futures price is the spot price compounded at the risk-free rate, plus the compound future value of any other costs minus any cash flows and benefits. Alternatively, one can convert the compound future value of the costs net of benefits or cash flows of holding the asset to their current value and subtract this amount from the spot price before compounding the spot price at the interest rate. In this manner, the spot price adjusted for any costs or benefits is then compounded at the risk-free interest rate to give the futures price. These costs, benefits, and cash flows thus represent the linkage between spot and futures prices.

EXHIBIT 75-10   **Pricing Formulas for Stock Index Futures Contract**

Futures price = Stock index compounded at risk-free rate − Future value of dividends, or (Stock index − Present value of dividends) compounded at risk-free rate.

Futures price as stock index compounded at risk-free rate − Future value of dividends:

$$f_0(T) = S_0(1 + r)^T - FV(D,0,T)$$

Futures price as stock index − Present value of dividends compounded at risk-free rate:

$$f_0(T) = [S_0 - PV(D,0,T)](1 + r)^T$$

Futures price as stock index discounted at dividend yield, compounded at risk-free rate:

$$f_0(T) = \left(\frac{S_0}{(1 + \delta)^T}\right)(1 + r)^T \quad \text{or}$$
$$f_0(T) = S_0(1 - \delta^*)(1 + r)^T$$

Futures price in terms of continuously compounded rate and yield:

$$f_0(T) = S_0 e^{(r^c - \delta^c)T} \qquad\qquad \text{or}$$
$$f_0(T) = (S_0 e^{-\delta^c T}) e^{r^c T}$$

Practice Problem 5

A stock index is at 755.42. A futures contract on the index expires in 57 days. The risk-free interest rate is 6.25 percent. At expiration, the value of the dividends on the index is 3.94.

A. Find the appropriate futures price, using both the future value of the dividends and the present value of the dividends.

B. Find the appropriate futures price in terms of the two specifications of the dividend yield.

C. Using your answer in Part B, find the futures price under the assumption of continuous compounding of interest and dividends.

SOLUTIONS

A. $T = 57/365 = 0.1562$

$$f_0(0.1562) = 755.42(1.0625)^{0.1562} - 3.94 = 758.67$$

Alternatively, we can find the present value of the dividends:

$$PV(D,0,0.1562) = \frac{3.94}{(1.0625)^{0.1562}} = 3.90$$

Then we can find the futures price as $f_0(0.1562) = (755.42 - 3.90)(1.0625)^{0.1562} = 758.67$.

B. Under one specification of the yield, we have

$$\frac{1}{(1 + \delta)^T} = 1 - \frac{3.94}{755.42(1.0625)^{0.1562}} = 0.9948$$

We need the inverse of this amount, which is $1/0.9948 = 1.0052$. Then the futures price is

$$f_0(0.1562) = \left(\frac{755.42}{1.0052}\right)(1.0625)^{0.1562} = 758.66$$

Under the other specification of the dividend yield, we have

$$\delta* = \frac{3.90}{755.42} = 0.0052$$

The futures price is $f_0(0.1562) = 755.42(1 - 0.0052)(1.0625)^{0.1562} = 758.64$, with the difference caused by rounding.

C. The continuously compounded risk-free rate is $r^c = \ln(1.0625) = 0.0606$. The continuously compounded dividend yield is

$$\frac{1}{0.1562}\ln(1.0052) = 0.0332$$

The futures price would then be

$$f_0(0.1562) = 755.42e^{(0.0606-0.0332)(0.1562)}$$
$$= 758.66$$

7.4 Pricing Currency Futures

Given our assumptions about no marking to market, it will be a simple matter to learn how to price currency futures: We price them the same as currency forwards. Recall that in Reading 74 we described a currency as an asset paying a yield of r^f, which can be viewed as the foreign risk-free rate. Thus, in this sense, a currency futures can also be viewed like a stock index futures, whereby the dividend yield is analogous to the foreign interest rate.

Therefore, an arbitrageur can buy the currency for the spot exchange rate of S_0 and sell a futures expiring at T for $f_0(T)$, holding the position until expiration, collecting the foreign interest, and delivering the currency to receive the original futures price. An important twist, however, is that the arbitrageur must be careful to have the correct number of units of the currency on hand to deliver.

Consider a futures contract on one unit of the currency. If the arbitrageur purchases one unit of the currency up front, the accumulation of interest on the currency will result in having more than one unit at the futures expiration. To adjust for this problem, the arbitrageur should take $S_0/(1 + r^f)^T$ units of his own currency and buy $1/(1 + r^f)^T$ units of the foreign currency.[50] The arbitrageur holds this position and collects interest at the foreign rate. The accumulation of interest is accounted for by multiplying by the interest factor $(1 + r^f)^T$. At expiration, the number of units of the currency will have grown to $[1/(1 + r^f)^T]$ $[1 + r^f]^T = 1$. So, the arbitrageur would then have 1 unit of the currency. He delivers that unit and receives the futures price of $f_0(T)$.

To avoid an arbitrage opportunity, the present value of the payoff of $f_0(T)$ must equal the amount initially invested. To find the present value of the payoff, we must discount at the domestic risk-free rate, because that rate reflects the opportunity cost of the arbitrageur's investment of his own money. So, first we equate the present value of the future payoff, discounting at the domestic risk-free rate, to the amount initially invested:

$$\frac{f_0(T)}{(1 + r)^T} = \frac{S_0}{(1 + r^f)^T}$$

Then we solve for the futures price to obtain

$$f_0(T) = \left(\frac{S_0}{(1 + r^f)^T}\right)(1 + r)^T \tag{75-18}$$

This formula is the same one we used for currency forwards.

An alternative variation of this formula would apply when we use continuously compounded interest rates. The adjustment is very slight. In the formula above, dividing S_0 by $(1 + r^f)^T$ finds a present value by discounting at the foreign interest rate. Multiplying by $(1 + r)^T$ is finding a future value by compounding at the domestic interest rate. The continuously compounded analogs to those rates are $r^{fc} = \ln(1 + r^f)$ and $r^c = \ln(1 + r)$. Then the formula becomes

$$f_0(T) = (S_0 e^{-r^{fc}T}) e^{r^c T} \tag{75-19}$$

We also saw this formula in Reading 74.

---

[50] In other words, if S_0 buys 1 unit, then $S_0/(1 + r^f)^T$ buys $1/(1 + r^f)^T$ units.

Consider a futures contract expiring in 55 days on the euro. Therefore, $T = 55/365 = 0.1507$. The spot exchange rate is \$0.8590. The foreign interest rate is 5.25 percent, and the domestic risk-free rate is 6.35 percent. The futures price should, therefore, be

$$f_0(T) = \left(\frac{S_0}{(1 + r^f)^T}\right)(1 + r)^T$$

$$f_0(0.1507) = \left(\frac{0.8590}{(1.0525)^{0.1507}}\right)(1.0635)^{0.1507} = 0.8603$$

If the futures is selling for more than this amount, the arbitrageur can buy the currency and sell the futures. He collects the foreign interest and converts the currency back at a higher rate than 0.8603, resulting in a risk-free return that exceeds the domestic risk-free rate. If the futures is selling for less than this amount, the arbitrageur can borrow the currency and buy the futures. The end result will be to receive money at the start and pay back money at a rate less than the domestic risk-free rate.

If the above problem were structured in terms of continuously compounded rates, the domestic rate would be $\ln(1.0635) = 0.0616$ and the foreign rate would be $\ln(1.0525) = 0.0512$. The futures price would then be

$$f_0(T) = (S_0 e^{-r^{fc}T})e^{r^c T}$$

$$f_0(0.1507) = (0.85890 e^{-0.0512(0.1507)})e^{0.0616(0.1507)} = 0.8603$$

which, of course, is the same price we calculated above.

Exhibit 75-11 summarizes the formulas for pricing currency futures.

EXHIBIT 75-11   Pricing Formulas for Currency Futures Contract

Futures price = (Spot exchange rate discounted by Foreign interest rate) compounded at Domestic interest rate:

Discrete interest: $f_0(T) = \left(\dfrac{S_0}{(1 + r^f)^T}\right)(1 + r)^T$

Continuous interest: $f_0(T) = (S_0 e^{-r^{fc}T})e^{r^c T}$

Practice Problem 6

The spot exchange rate for the Swiss franc is \$0.60. The U.S. interest rate is 6 percent, and the Swiss interest rate is 5 percent. A futures contract expires in 78 days.

A. Find the appropriate futures price.

B. Find the appropriate futures price under the assumption of continuous compounding.

C. Using Part A, execute an arbitrage resulting from a futures price of \$0.62.

SOLUTIONS

$T = 78/365 = 0.2137$

A. $f_0(0.2137) = \dfrac{\$0.60}{(1.05)^{0.2137}}(1.06)^{0.2137} = \$0.6012$

B. The continuously compounded equivalent rates are

$$r^{fc} = \ln(1.05) = 0.0488$$
$$r^c = \ln(1.06) = 0.0583$$

The futures price is

$$f_0(0.2137) = (\$0.60e^{-0.0488(0.2137)})e^{0.0583(0.2137)}$$
$$= \$0.6012$$

C. At \$0.62, the futures price is too high, so we will need to sell the futures. First, however, we must determine how many units of the currency to buy. It should be

$$\frac{1}{(1.05)^{0.2137}} = 0.9896$$

So we buy this many units, which costs $0.9896(\$0.60) = \$0.5938$. We sell the futures at \$0.62. We hold the position until expiration. During that time the accumulation of interest will make the 0.9896 units of the currency grow to 1.0000 unit. We convert the Swiss franc to dollars at the futures rate of \$0.62. The return per dollar invested is

$$\frac{0.62}{0.5938} = 1.0441$$

This is a return of 1.0441 per dollar invested over 78 days. At the risk-free rate of 6 percent, the return over 78 days should be $(1.06)^{0.2137} = 1.0125$. Obviously, the arbitrage transaction is much better.

7.5 Futures Pricing: A Recap

We have now examined the pricing of short-term interest rate futures, intermediate-and long-term interest rate futures, stock index futures, and currency futures. Let us recall the intuition behind pricing a futures contract and see the commonality in each of those special cases. First recall that under the assumption of no marking to market, at expiration the short makes delivery and we assume that the long pays the full futures price at that point. An arbitrageur buys the asset and sells a futures contract, holds the asset for the life of the futures, and delivers it at expiration of the futures, at which time he is paid the futures price. In addition, while holding the asset, the arbitrageur accumulates costs and accrues cash flows, such as interest, dividends, and benefits such as a convenience yield. The value of the position at expiration will be the futures price net of these costs minus benefits and cash flows. The overall value of this transaction at expiration is known when the transaction is initiated; thus, the value at expiration is risk-free. The return from a risk-free transaction should equal the risk-free rate, which is the rate on a zero-coupon bond whose maturity is the futures expiration day. If the return is indeed this risk-free rate, then the futures price must equal the spot price compounded at the risk-free rate plus the compound value of these costs net of benefits and cash flows.

It should also be noted that although we have taken the more natural approach of buying the asset and selling the futures, we could just as easily have sold short the asset and bought the futures. Because short selling is usually a little harder to do as well as to understand, the approach we take is preferable from a pedagogical point of view. It is important, nonetheless, to remember that the ability to sell short the asset or the willingness of parties who own the asset to sell it to offset the buying of the futures is critical to establishing the results we have shown here. Otherwise, the futures pricing formulas would be inequalities— limited on one side but not restricted on the other.

We should remind ourselves that this general form of the futures pricing model also applied in Reading 74 in our discussion of forward contracts. Futures contracts differ from forward contracts in that the latter are subject to credit risk. Futures contracts are marked to market on a daily basis and guaranteed against losses from default by the futures clearinghouse, which has never defaulted. Although there are certain institutional features that distinguish futures from forwards, we consider those features separately from the material on pricing. Because the general economic and financial concepts are the same, for pricing purposes, we treat futures and forwards as the same.

THE ROLE OF FUTURES MARKETS AND EXCHANGES

We conclude this reading with a brief look at the role that futures markets and exchanges play in global financial systems and in society. Virtually all participants in the financial markets have heard of futures markets, but many do not understand the role that futures markets play. Some participants do not understand how futures markets function in global financial systems and often look at futures with suspicion, if not disdain.

In Reading 73, we discussed the purposes of derivative markets. We found that derivative markets provide price discovery and risk management, make the markets for the underlying assets more efficient, and permit trading at low transaction costs. These characteristics are also associated with futures markets. In fact, price discovery is often cited by others as the primary advantage of futures markets. Yet, all derivative markets provide these benefits. What characteristics do futures markets have that are not provided by comparable markets as forward markets?

First recall that a major distinction between futures and forwards is that futures are standardized instruments. By having an agreed-upon set of homogeneous contracts, futures markets can provide an orderly, liquid market in which traders can open and close positions without having to worry about holding these positions to expiration. Although not all futures contracts have a high degree of liquidity, an open position can nonetheless be closed on the exchange where the contract was initiated.[51] More importantly, however, futures contracts

---

[51] Recall that there is no liquid market for previously opened forward contracts to be closed, but the holder of a forward contract can re-enter the market and establish a position opposite to the one previously established. If one holds a long forward contract to buy an asset in six months, one can then do a short forward contract to sell the asset in six months, and this transaction offsets the risk of changing market prices. The credit risk on both contracts remains. In some cases, the offsetting contract can be done with the same counterparty as in the original contract, permitting the two parties to arrange a single cash settlement to offset both contracts.

are guaranteed against credit losses. If a counterparty defaults, the clearinghouse pays and, as we have emphasized, no clearinghouse has ever defaulted. In this manner, a party can engage in a transaction to lock in a future price or rate without having to worry about the credit quality of the counterparty. Forward contracts are subject to default risk, but of course they offer the advantage of customization, the tailoring of a contract's terms to meet the needs of the parties involved.

With an open, standardized, and regulated market for futures contracts, their prices can be disseminated to other investors and the general public. Futures prices are closely watched by a vast number of market participants, many trying to discern an indication of the direction of future spot prices and some simply trying to determine what price they could lock in for future purchase or sale of the underlying asset. Although forward prices provide similar information, forward contracts are private transactions and their prices are not publicly reported. Futures markets thus provide transparency to the financial markets. They reveal the prices at which parties contract for future transactions.

Therefore, futures prices contribute an important element to the body of information on which investors make decisions. In addition, they provide opportunities to transact for future purchase or sale of an underlying asset without having to worry about the credit quality of the counterparty.

In Readings 74 and 75, we studied forward and futures contracts and showed that they have a lot in common. Both are commitments to buy or sell an asset at a future date at a price agreed on today. No money changes hands at the start of either transaction. We learned how to determine appropriate prices and values for these contracts. Now, however, we take a totally different approach and look at contracts that provide not the obligation but rather the right to buy or sell an asset at a later date at a price agreed on today. To obtain such a right, in contrast to agreeing to an obligation, one must pay money at the start. These instruments, called options, are the subject of Reading 76.

OPTIONAL SEGMENT ENDS

SUMMARY

▶ Futures contracts are standardized instruments that trade on a futures exchange, have a secondary market, and are guaranteed against default by means of a daily settling of gains and losses. Forward contracts are customized instruments that are not guaranteed against default and are created anywhere off of an exchange.

▶ Modern futures markets primarily originated in Chicago out of a need for grain farmers and buyers to be able to transact for delivery at future dates for grain that would, in the interim, be placed in storage.

▶ Futures transactions are standardized and conducted in a public market, are homogeneous, have a secondary market giving them an element of liquidity, and have a clearinghouse, which collects margins and settles gains and losses daily to provide a guarantee against default. Futures markets are also regulated at the federal government level.

▶ Margin in the securities markets is the deposit of money, the margin, and a loan for the remainder of the funds required to purchase a stock or bond. Margin in the futures markets is much smaller and does not involve a loan. Futures margin is more like a performance bond or down payment.

▶ Futures trading occurs on a futures exchange, which involves trading either in a physical location called a pit or via a computer terminal off of the floor of the futures exchange as part of an electronic trading system. In either case, a party to a futures contract goes long, committing to buy the underlying asset at an agreed-upon price, or short, committing to sell the underlying asset at an agreed-upon price.

▶ A futures trader who has established a position can re-enter the market and close out the position by doing the opposite transaction (sell if the original position was long or buy if the original position was short). The party has offset the position, no longer has a contract outstanding, and has no further obligation.

▶ Initial margin is the amount of money in a margin account on the day of a transaction or when a margin call is made. Maintenance margin is the amount of money in a margin account on any day other than when the initial margin applies. Minimum requirements exist for the initial and maintenance margins, with the initial margin requirement normally being less than 10 percent of the futures price and the maintenance margin requirement being smaller than the initial margin requirement. Variation margin is the amount of money that must be deposited into the account to bring the balance up to the required level. The settlement price is an average of the last few trades of the day and is used to determine the gains and losses marked to the parties' accounts.

▶ The futures clearinghouse engages in a practice called marking to market, also known as the daily settlement, in which gains and losses on a futures position are credited and charged to the trader's margin account on a daily basis. Thus, profits are available for withdrawal and losses must be paid quickly before they build up and pose a risk that the party will be unable to cover large losses.

▶ The margin balance at the end of the day is determined by taking the previous balance and accounting for any gains or losses from the day's activity, based on the settlement price, as well as any money added or withdrawn.

► Price limits are restrictions on the price of a futures trade and are based on a range relative to the previous day's settlement price. No trade can take place outside of the price limits. A limit move is when the price at which two parties would like to trade is at or beyond the price limit. Limit up is when the market price would be at or above the upper limit. Limit down is when the market price would be at or below the lower limit. Locked limit occurs when a trade cannot take place because the price would be above the limit up or below the limit down prices.

► A futures contract can be terminated by entering into an offsetting position very shortly before the end of the expiration day. If the position is still open when the contract expires, the trader must take delivery (if long) or make delivery (if short), unless the contract requires that an equivalent cash settlement be used in lieu of delivery. In addition, two participants can agree to alternative delivery terms, an arrangement called exchange for physicals.

► Delivery options are features associated with a futures contract that permit the short some flexibility in what to deliver, where to deliver it, and when in the expiration month to make delivery.

► Scalpers are futures traders who take positions for very short periods of time and attempt to profit by buying at the bid price and selling at the ask price. Day traders close out all positions by the end of the day. Position traders leave their positions open overnight and potentially longer.

► Treasury bill futures are contracts in which the underlying is $1,000,000 of a U.S. Treasury bill. Eurodollar futures are contracts in which the underlying is $1,000,000 of a Eurodollar time deposit. Treasury bond futures are contracts in which the underlying is $100,000 of a U.S. Treasury bond with a minimum 15-year maturity. Stock index futures are contracts in which the underlying is a well-known stock index, such as the S&P 500 or FTSE 100. Currency futures are contracts in which the underlying is a foreign currency.

► An expiring futures contract is equivalent to a spot transaction. Consequently, at expiration the futures price must converge to the spot price to avoid an arbitrage opportunity in which one can buy the asset and sell a futures or sell the asset and buy a futures to capture an immediate profit at no risk.

► The value of a futures contract just prior to marking to market is the accumulated price change since the last mark to market. The value of a futures contract just after marking to market is zero. These values reflect the claim a participant has as a result of her position in the contract.

► The price of a futures contract will equal the price of an otherwise equivalent forward contract one day prior to expiration, or if interest rates are known or constant, or if interest rates are uncorrelated with futures prices.

► A futures price is derived by constructing a combination of a long position in the asset and a short position in the futures. This strategy guarantees that the price received from the sale of the asset is known when the transaction is initiated. The futures price is then derived as the unknown value that eliminates the opportunity to earn an arbitrage profit off of the transaction.

► Futures prices are affected by the opportunity cost of funds tied up in the investment in the underlying asset, the costs of storing the underlying asset, any cash flows paid on the underlying asset, such as interest or dividends, and nonmonetary benefits of holding the underlying asset, referred to as the convenience yield.

► Backwardation describes a condition in which the futures price is lower than the spot price. Contango describes a condition in which the futures price is higher than the spot price.

▶ The futures price will not equal the expected spot price if the risk premium in the spot price is transferred from hedgers to futures traders. If the risk premium is transferred, then the futures price will be biased high or low relative to the expected future spot price. When the futures price is biased low (high), it is called normal backwardation (normal contango).

▶ T-bill futures prices are determined by going short a futures contract and going long a T-bill that will have the desired maturity at the futures expiration. At expiration, the T-bill is delivered or cash settled to a price locked in when the transaction was initiated through the sale of the futures. The correct futures price is the one that prohibits this combination from earning an arbitrage profit. Under the assumptions we make, the T-bill futures price is the same as the T-bill forward price.

▶ The implied repo rate is the rate of return implied by a transaction of buying a spot asset and selling a futures contract. If financing can be obtained in the repo market at less than the implied repo rate, the transaction should be undertaken. If financing can be supplied to the repo market at greater than the implied repo rate, the transaction should be reversed.

▶ Eurodollar futures cannot be priced as easily as T-bill futures, because the expiration price of a Eurodollar futures is based on a value computed as 1 minus a rate, whereas the value of the underlying Eurodollar time deposit is based on 1 divided by a rate. The difference is small but not zero. Hence, Eurodollar futures do not lend themselves to an exact pricing formula based on the notion of a cost of carry of the underlying.

▶ Treasury bond futures prices are determined by first identifying the cheapest bond to deliver, which is the bond that the short would deliver under current market conditions. Then one must construct a combination of a short futures contract and a long position in that bond. The bond is held, and the coupons are collected and reinvested. At expiration, the underlying bond is delivered and the futures price times the conversion factor for that bond is received. The correct futures price is the one that prevents this transaction from earning an arbitrage profit.

▶ Stock index futures prices are determined by constructing a combination of a long portfolio of stocks identical to the underlying index and a short futures contract. The stocks are held and the dividends are collected and reinvested. At expiration, the cash settlement results in the effective sale of the stock at the futures price. The correct futures price is the one that prevents this transaction from earning an arbitrage profit.

▶ Currency futures prices are determined by buying the underlying currency and selling a futures on the currency. The position is held, and the underlying currency pays interest at the foreign risk-free rate. At expiration, the currency is delivered and the futures price is received. The correct futures price is the one that prevents this transaction from earning an arbitrage profit.

▶ Futures markets serve our financial systems by making the markets for the underlying assets more efficient, by providing price discovery, by offering opportunities to trade at lower transaction costs, and by providing a means of managing risk. Futures markets also provide a homogeneous, standardized, and tradable instrument through which participants who might not have access to forward markets can make commitments to buy and sell assets at a future date at a locked-in price with no fear of credit risk. Because futures markets are so visible and widely reported on, they are also an excellent source of information, contributing greatly to the transparency of financial markets.

PROBLEMS FOR READING 75

1. **A.** In February, Dave Parsons purchased a June futures contract on the Nasdaq 100 Index. He decides to close out his position in April. Describe how he would do so.

   B. Peggy Smith is a futures trader. In early August, she took a short position in an S&P 500 Index futures contract expiring in September. After a week, she decides to close out her position. Describe how she would do so.

2. A gold futures contract requires the long trader to buy 100 troy ounces of gold. The initial margin requirement is $2,000, and the maintenance margin requirement is $1,500.

   A. Matthew Evans goes long one June gold futures contract at the futures price of $320 per troy ounce. When could Evans receive a maintenance margin call?

   B. Chris Tosca sells one August gold futures contract at a futures price of $323 per ounce. When could Tosca receive a maintenance margin call?

3. A copper futures contract requires the long trader to buy 25,000 lbs of copper. A trader buys one November copper futures contract at a price of $0.75/lb. Theoretically, what is the maximum loss this trader could have? Another trader sells one November copper futures contract. Theoretically, what is the maximum loss this trader with a short position could have?

4. Consider a hypothetical futures contract in which the current price is $212. The initial margin requirement is $10, and the maintenance margin requirement is $8. You go long 20 contracts and meet all margin calls but do not withdraw any excess margin.

   A. When could there be a margin call?

   B. Complete the table below and explain any funds deposited. Assume that the contract is purchased at the settlement price of that day so there is no mark-to-market profit or loss on the day of purchase.

Day	Beginning Balance	Funds Deposited	Futures Price	Price Change	Gain/Loss	Ending Balance
0			212			
1			211			
2			214			
3			209			
4			210			
5			204			
6			202			

   C. How much are your total gains or losses by the end of day 6?

5. Sarah Moore has taken a short position in one Chicago Board of Trade Treasury bond futures contract with a face value of $100,000 at the price of 96 6/32. The initial margin requirement is $2,700, and the maintenance margin requirement is $2,000. Moore would meet all margin calls but would not withdraw any excess margin.

A. Complete the table below and provide an explanation of any funds deposited. Assume that the contract is purchased at the settlement price of that day, so there is no mark-to-market profit or loss on the day of purchase.

Day	Beginning Balance	Funds Deposited	Futures Price	Price Change	Gain/Loss	Ending Balance
0			96-06			
1			96-31			
2			97-22			
3			97-18			
4			97-24			
5			98-04			
6			97-31			

B. How much are Moore's total gains or losses by the end of day 6?

6. A. The IMM index price in yesterday's newspaper for a September Eurodollar futures contract is 95.23. What is the actual price of this contract?

B. The IMM index price in today's newspaper for the contract mentioned above is 95.25. How much is the change in the actual futures price of the contract since the previous day?

4⅝ 4¹¹/₁₆ — ⅜
5½ 5½ — ⅜
5½ 21³/₁₆ — ¼₆
20⅝ 21³/₁₆ + ⅞
17⅜ 18⅛ + ⅞
18½
6½ 6½ — ½
7¼ 6½ 31/₃₂ — ⅛
15/₁₆
9/₁₆ 9/₁₆
⁴/₃₂ 7¹³/₁₆ 7¹⁵/₁₆
7¹⁵/₁₆
2⅝ 2¹¹/₃₂ 2½ —
2¾ 2¼ 2¼
12¹/₁₆ 11⅜ 11¾ +
87 33¾ 33 33¼ —
602 25⅝ 24⁹/₁₆ 25⅝ +
833 12 11⅝ 11⅛ +
16 10½ 10½ 10½ —
78 15⅝ 15¹³/₁₆ 15⅝ —
4608 9¹/₁₆ 8¼ 8⅝
430 11¼ 10⅛ 10⅛

OPTION MARKETS AND CONTRACTS
by Don M. Chance

LEARNING OUTCOMES

The candidate should be able to:

a. define European option, American option, moneyness, payoff, intrinsic value, and time value and differentiate between exchange-traded options and over-the-counter options;

b. identify the different types of options in terms of the underlying instruments;

c. compare and contrast interest rate options to forward rate agreements (FRAs);

d. explain how option payoffs are determined, and show how interest rate option payoffs differ from the payoffs of other types of options;

e. define interest rate caps and floors;

f. identify the minimum and maximum values of European options and American options; calculate and interpret the lowest prices of European and American calls and puts based on the rules for minimum values and lower bounds;

g. describe the relationship between options that differ only by exercise price;

h. explain how option prices are affected by the time to expiration of the option;

i. explain put-call parity for European options, given the payoffs on a fiduciary call and a protective put;

j. explain the relationship between American options and European options in terms of the lower bounds on option prices and the possibility of early exercise;

k. explain how cash flows on the underlying asset affect put-call parity and the lower bounds of option prices;

l. identify the directional effect of an interest rate change or volatility change on an option's price.

Analysis of Derivatives for the CFA® Program, by Don M. Chance, Copyright © 2003 by Association for Investment Management and Research. Reprinted with permission.

1   INTRODUCTION

In Reading 73, we provided a general introduction to derivative markets. In Reading 74 we examined forward contracts, and in Reading 75 we looked at futures contracts. We noted how similar forward and futures contracts are: Both are commitments to buy an underlying asset at a fixed price at a later date. Forward contracts, however, are privately created, over-the-counter customized instruments that carry credit risk. Futures contracts are publicly traded, exchange-listed standardized instruments that effectively have no credit risk. Now we turn to options. Like forwards and futures, they are derivative instruments that provide the opportunity to buy or sell an underlying asset with a specific expiration date. But in contrast, buying an option gives the *right,* not the obligation, to buy or sell an underlying asset. And whereas forward and futures contracts involve no exchange of cash up front, options require a cash payment from the option buyer to the option seller.

Yet options contain several features common to forward and futures contracts. For one, options can be created by any two parties with any set of terms they desire. In this sense, options can be privately created, over-the-counter, customized instruments that are subject to credit risk. In addition, however, there is a large market for publicly traded, exchange-listed, standardized options, for which credit risk is essentially eliminated by the clearinghouse.

Just as we examined the pricing of forwards and futures in the last two readings, we shall examine option pricing in this reading. We shall also see that options can be created out of forward contracts, and that forward contracts can be created out of options. With some simplifying assumptions, options can be created out of futures contracts and futures contracts can be created out of options.

Finally, we note that options also exist that have a futures or forward contract as the underlying. These instruments blend some of the features of both options and forwards/futures.

As background, we discuss the definitions and characteristics of options.

2   BASIC DEFINITIONS AND ILLUSTRATIONS OF OPTIONS CONTRACTS

In Reading 73, we defined an option as a financial derivative contract that provides a party the right to buy or sell an underlying at a fixed price by a certain time in the future. The party holding the right is the option buyer; the party granting the right is the option seller. There are two types of options, a **call** and a **put**. A call is an option granting the right to buy the underlying; a put is an option granting the right to sell the underlying. With the exception of some advanced types of options, a given option contract is either a call, granting the right to buy, or a put, granting the right to sell, but not both.[1] We emphasize that this right to buy or sell is held by the option buyer, also called the long or option holder, and granted by the option seller, also called the short or option writer.

To obtain this right, the option buyer pays the seller a sum of money, commonly referred to as the **option price**. On occasion, this option price is called the **option premium** or just the **premium**. This money is paid when the option contract is initiated.

2.1 Basic Characteristics of Options

The fixed price at which the option holder can buy or sell the underlying is called the **exercise price**, **strike price**, **striking price**, or **strike**. The use of this right to buy or sell the underlying is referred to as **exercise** or **exercising the option**. Like all derivative contracts, an option has an **expiration date,** giving rise to the notion of an option's **time to expiration**. When the expiration date arrives, an option that is not exercised simply expires.

What happens at exercise depends on whether the option is a call or a put. If the buyer is exercising a call, she pays the exercise price and receives either the underlying or an equivalent cash settlement. On the opposite side of the transaction is the seller, who receives the exercise price from the buyer and delivers the underlying, or alternatively, pays an equivalent cash settlement. If the buyer is exercising a put, she delivers the stock and receives the exercise price or an equivalent cash settlement. The seller, therefore, receives the underlying and must pay the exercise price or the equivalent cash settlement.

As noted in the above paragraph, cash settlement is possible. In that case, the option holder exercising a call receives the difference between the market value of the underlying and the exercise price from the seller in cash. If the option holder exercises a put, she receives the difference between the exercise price and the market value of the underlying in cash.

There are two primary exercise styles associated with options. One type of option has **European-style exercise**, which means that the option can be exercised only on its expiration day. In some cases, expiration could occur during that day; in others, exercise can occur only when the option has expired. In either case, such an option is called a **European option**. The other style of exercise is **American-style exercise**. Such an option can be exercised on any day through the expiration day and is generally called an **American option**.[2]

Option contracts specify a designated number of units of the underlying. For exchange-listed, standardized options, the exchange establishes each term, with the exception of the price. The price is negotiated by the two parties. For an over-the-counter option, the two parties decide each of the terms through negotiation.

In an over-the-counter option—one created off of an exchange by any two parties who agree to trade—the buyer is subject to the possibility of the writer defaulting. When the buyer exercises, the writer must either deliver the stock or cash if a call, or pay for the stock or pay cash if a put. If the writer cannot do so for financial reasons, the option holder faces a credit loss. Because the option holder paid the price up front and is not required to do anything else, the seller does not face any credit risk. Thus, although credit risk is bilateral in forward contracts—the long assumes the risk of the short defaulting, and the short assumes the risk of

---

[1] Of course, a party could buy both a call and a put, thereby holding the right to buy *and* sell the underlying.

[2] It is worthwhile to be aware that these terms have nothing to do with Europe or America. Both types of options are found in Europe and America. The names are part of the folklore of options markets, and there is no definitive history to explain how they came into use.

the long defaulting—the credit risk in an option is unilateral. Only the buyer faces credit risk because only the seller can default. As we discuss later, in exchange-listed options, the clearinghouse guarantees payment to the buyer.

2.2 Some Examples of Options

Consider some call and put options on Sun Microsystems (SUNW). The date is 13 June and Sun is selling for $16.25. Exhibit 76-1 gives information on the closing prices of four options, ones expiring in July and October and ones with exercise prices of 15.00 and 17.50. The July options expire on 20 July and the October options expire on 18 October. In the parlance of the profession, these are referred to as the July 15 calls, July 17.50 calls, October 15 calls, and October 17.50 calls, with similar terminology for the puts. These particular options are American style.

EXHIBIT 76-1	Closing Prices of Selected Options on SUNW, 13 June			
Exercise Price	**July Calls**	**October Calls**	**July Puts**	**October Puts**
15.00	2.35	3.30	0.90	1.85
17.50	1.00	2.15	2.15	3.20

Note: Stock price is $16.25; July options expire on 20 July; October options expire on 18 October.

Consider the July 15 call. This option permits the holder to buy SUNW at a price of $15 a share any time through 20 July. To obtain this option, one would pay a price of $2.35. Therefore, a writer received $2.35 on 13 June and must be ready to sell SUNW to the buyer for $15 during the period through 20 July. Currently, SUNW trades above $15 a share, but as we shall see in more detail later, the option holder has no reason to exercise the option right now.[3] To justify purchase of the call, the buyer must be anticipating that SUNW will increase in price before the option expires. The seller of the call must be anticipating that SUNW will not rise sufficiently in price before the option expires.

Note that the option buyer could purchase a call expiring in July but permitting the purchase of SUNW at a price of $17.50. This price is more than the $15.00 exercise price, but as a result, the option, which sells for $1.00, is considerably cheaper. The cheaper price comes from the fact that the July 17.50 call is less likely to be exercised, because the stock has a higher hurdle to clear. A buyer is not willing to pay as much and a seller is more willing to take less for an option that is less likely to be exercised.

Alternatively, the option buyer could choose to purchase an October call instead of a July call. For any exercise price, however, the October calls would be more expensive than the July calls because they allow a longer period for the stock to make the move that the buyer wants. October options are more likely to

---

[3] The buyer paid $2.35 for the option. If he exercised it right now, he would pay $15.00 for the stock, which is worth only $16.25. Thus, he would have effectively paid $17.35 (the cost of the option of $2.35 plus the exercise price of $15) for a stock worth $16.25. Even if he had purchased the option previously at a much lower price, the current option price of $2.35 is the opportunity cost of exercising the option—that is, he can always sell the option for $2.35. Therefore, if he exercised the option, he would be throwing away the $2.35 he could receive if he sold it.

be exercised than July options; therefore, a buyer would be willing to pay more and the seller would demand more for the October calls.

Suppose the buyer expects the stock price to go down. In that case, he might buy a put. Consider the October 17.50 put, which would cost the buyer $3.20. This option would allow the holder to sell SUNW at a price of $17.50 any time up through 18 October.[4] He has no reason to exercise the option right now, because it would mean he would be buying the option for $3.20 and selling a stock worth $16.25 for $17.50. In effect, the option holder would part with $19.45 (the cost of the option of $3.20 plus the value of the stock of $16.25) and obtain only $17.50.[5] The buyer of a put obviously must be anticipating that the stock will fall before the expiration day.

If he wanted a cheaper option than the October 17.50 put, he could buy the October 15 put, which would cost only $1.85 but would allow him to sell the stock for only $15.00 a share. The October 15 put is less likely to be exercised than the October 17.50, because the stock price must fall below a lower hurdle. Thus, the buyer is not willing to pay as much and the seller is willing to take less.

For either exercise price, purchase of a July put instead of an October put would be much cheaper but would allow less time for the stock to make the downward move necessary for the transaction to be worthwhile. The July put is cheaper than the October put; the buyer is not willing to pay as much and the seller is willing to take less because the option is less likely to be exercised.

In observing these option prices, we have obtained our first taste of some principles involved in pricing options.

Call options have a lower premium the higher the exercise price.
Put options have a lower premium the lower the exercise price.
Both call and put options are cheaper the shorter the time to expiration.[6]

These results should be intuitive, but later in this reading we show unequivocally why they must be true.

2.3 The Concept of Moneyness of an Option

An important concept in the study of options is the notion of an option's **moneyness**, which refers to the relationship between the price of the underlying and the exercise price.

We use the terms **in-the-money**, **out-of-the-money**, and **at-the-money**. We explain the concept in Exhibit 76-2 with examples from the SUNW options. Note that in-the-money options are those in which exercising the option would produce a cash inflow that exceeds the cash outflow. Thus, calls are in-the-money when the value of the underlying exceeds the exercise price. Puts are in-the-money when the exercise price exceeds the value of the underlying. In our example, there are no at-the-money SUNW options, which would require that the stock value equal the exercise price; however, an at-the-money option can effectively be viewed as an out-of-the-money option, because its exercise would not bring in more money than is paid out.

---

[4] Even if the option holder did not own the stock, he could use the option to sell the stock short.

[5] Again, even if the option were purchased in the past at a much lower price, the $3.20 current value of the option is an opportunity cost. Exercise of the option is equivalent to throwing away the opportunity cost.

[6] There is an exception to the rule that put options are cheaper the shorter the time to expiration. This statement is always true for American options but not always for European options. We explore this point later.

EXHIBIT 76-2	Moneyness of an Option		
In-the-Money		**Out-of-the-Money**	
Option	**Justification**	**Option**	**Justification**
July 15 call	16.25 > 15.00	July 17.50 call	16.25 < 17.50
October 15 call	16.25 > 15.00	October 17.50 call	16.25 < 17.50
July 17.50 put	17.50 > 16.25	July 15 put	15.00 < 16.25
October 17.50 put	17.50 > 16.25	October 15 put	15.00 < 16.25

Notes: Sun Microsystems options on 13 June; stock price is 16.25. See Exhibit 76-1 for more details. There are no options with an exercise price of 16.25, so no options are at-the-money.

As explained above, *one would not necessarily exercise an in-the-money option, but one would never exercise an out-of-the-money option.*

We now move on to explore how options markets are organized.

3   THE STRUCTURE OF GLOBAL OPTIONS MARKETS

Although no one knows exactly how options first got started, contracts similar to options have been around for thousands of years. In fact, insurance is a form of an option. The insurance buyer pays the insurance writer a premium and receives a type of guarantee that covers losses. This transaction is similar to a put option, which provides coverage of a portion of losses on the underlying and is often used by holders of the underlying. The first true options markets were over-the-counter options markets in the United States in the 19th century.

3.1 Over-the-Counter Options Markets

In the United States, customized over-the-counter options markets were in existence in the early part of the 20th century and lasted well into the 1970s. An organization called the Put and Call Brokers and Dealers Association consisted of a group of firms that served as brokers and dealers. As brokers, they attempted to match buyers of options with sellers, thereby earning a commission. As dealers, they offered to take either side of the option transaction, usually laying off (hedging) the risk in another transaction. Most of these transactions were retail, meaning that the general public were their customers.

As we discuss in Section 3.2 below, the creation of the Chicago Board Options Exchange was a revolutionary event, but it effectively killed the Put and Call Brokers and Dealers Association. Subsequently, the increasing use of swaps facilitated a rebirth of the customized over-the-counter options market. Currency options, a natural extension to currency swaps, were in much demand. Later, interest rate options emerged as a natural outgrowth of interest rate swaps. Soon bond, equity, and index options were trading in a vibrant over-the-counter market. In contrast to the previous over-the-counter options market, however, the current one emerged as a largely wholesale market. Transactions are usually made with institutions and corporations and are rarely conducted directly with individuals. This market is much like the forward market described in Reading 74, with dealers offering to take either the long or short position in options and hedging that risk with transactions in other options or derivatives. There are no guarantees that the seller will perform, hence, the buyer faces credit risk. As such, option buyers must scrutinize sellers' credit risk and may require some risk reduction measures, such as collateral.

As previously noted, customized options have *all* of their terms—such as price, exercise price, time to expiration, identification of the underlying, settlement or delivery terms, size of the contract, and so on—determined by the two parties.

Like forward markets, over-the-counter options markets are essentially unregulated. In most countries, participating firms, such as banks and securities firms, are regulated by the appropriate authorities but there is usually no particular regulatory body for the over-the-counter options markets. In some countries, however, there are regulatory bodies for these markets.

Exhibit 76-3 provides information on the leading dealers in over-the-counter currency and interest rate options as determined by *Risk* magazine in its annual surveys of banks and investment banks and also end users.

EXHIBIT 76-3	*Risk* Magazine Surveys of Banks, Investment Banks, and Corporate End Users to Determine the Top Three Dealers in Over-the-Counter Currency and Interest Rate Options

	Respondents	
Currencies	**Banks and Investment Banks**	**Corporate End Users**
Currency Options		
$/€	UBS Warburg	Citigroup
	Citigroup/Deutsche Bank	Royal Bank of Scotland
		Deutsche Bank
$/¥	UBS Warburg	Citigroup
	Credit Suisse First Boston	JP Morgan Chase
	JP Morgan Chase/Royal Bank of Scotland	UBS Warburg
$/£	Royal Bank of Scotland	Royal Bank of Scotland
	UBS Warburg	Citigroup
	Citigroup	Hong Kong Shanghai Banking Corp.
$/SF	UBS Warburg	UBS Warburg
	Credit Suisse First Boston	Credit Suisse First Boston
	Citigroup	Citigroup
Interest Rate Options		
$	JP Morgan Chase	JP Morgan Chase
	Deutsche Bank	Citigroup

(Exhibit continued on next page ...)

EXHIBIT 76-3	(continued)	

	Respondents	
Currencies	**Banks and Investment Banks**	**Corporate End Users**
Interest Rate Options		
	Bank of America	Deutsche Bank/ Lehman Brothers
€	JP Morgan Chase	JP Morgan Chase
	Credit Suisse First Boston/ Morgan Stanley	Citigroup UBS Warburg
¥	JP Morgan Chase/ Deutsche Bank	UBS Warburg
	Bank of America	Barclays Capital
		Citigroup
£	Barclays Capital	Royal Bank of Scotland
	Societe Generale Groupe	Citigroup
	Bank of America/Royal Bank of Scotland	Hong Kong Shanghai Banking Corp.
SF	UBS Warburg	UBS Warburg
	JP Morgan Chase	JP Morgan
	Credit Suisse First Boston	Goldman Sachs

Notes: $ = U.S. dollar, € = euro, ¥ = Japanese yen, £ = U.K. pound sterling, SF = Swiss franc

Source: Risk, September 2002, pp. 30–67 for Banks and Investment Banking dealer respondents, and June 2002, pp. 24–34 for Corporate End User respondents.

Results for Corporate End Users for Interest Rate Options are from *Risk,* July 2001, pp. 38–46. *Risk* omitted this category from its 2002 survey.

3.2 Exchange Listed Options Markets

As briefly noted above, the Chicago Board Options Exchange was formed in 1973. Created as an extension of the Chicago Board of Trade, it became the first organization to offer a market for standardized options. In the United States, standardized options also trade on the Amex–Nasdaq, the Philadelphia Stock Exchange, and the Pacific Stock Exchange.[7] On a worldwide basis, standardized options are widely traded on such exchanges as LIFFE (the London International Financial Futures and Options Exchange) in London, Eurex in Frankfurt, and most other foreign exchanges. Exhibit 76-4 shows the 20 largest options exchanges in the world. Note, perhaps surprisingly, that the leading options exchange is in Korea.

---

[7] You may wonder why the New York Stock Exchange is not mentioned. Standardized options did trade on the NYSE at one time but were not successful, and the right to trade these options was sold to another exchange.

EXHIBIT 76-4	World's 20 Largest Options Exchanges
Exchange and Location	**Volume in 2001**
Korea Stock Exchange (Korea)	854,791,792
Chicago Board Options Exchange (United States)	306,667,851
MONEP (France)	285,667,686
Eurex (Germany and Switzerland)	239,016,516
American Stock Exchange (United States)	205,103,884
Pacific Stock Exchange (United States)	102,701,752
Philadelphia Stock Exchange (United States)	101,373,433
Chicago Mercantile Exchange (United States)	95,740,352
Amsterdam Exchange (Netherlands)	66,400,654
LIFFE (United Kingdom)	54,225,652
Chicago Board of Trade (United States)	50,345,068
OM Stockholm (Sweden)	39,327,619
South African Futures Exchange (South Africa)	24,307,477
MEFF Renta Variable (Spain)	23,628,446
New York Mercantile Exchange (United States)	17,985,109
Korea Futures Exchange (Korea)	11,468,991
Italian Derivatives Exchange (Italy)	11,045,804
Osaka Securities Exchange (Japan)	6,991,908
Bourse de Montreal (Canada)	5,372,930
Hong Kong Futures Exchange (China)	4,718,880

Note: Volume given is in number of contracts.
Source: Data supplied by *Futures Industry* magazine.

As described in Reading 75 on futures, the exchange fixes all terms of standardized instruments except the price. Thus, the exchange establishes the expiration dates and exercise prices as well as the minimum price quotation unit. The exchange also determines whether the option is European or American, whether the exercise is cash settlement or delivery of the underlying, and the contract size. In the United States, an option contract on an individual stock covers 100 shares of stock. Terminology such as "one option" is often used to refer to one option contract, which is really a set of options on 100 shares of stock. Index option sizes are stated in terms of a multiplier, indicating that the contract covers a hypothetical number of shares, as though the index were an individual stock. Similar specifications apply for options on other types of underlyings.

The exchange generally allows trading in exercise prices that surround the current stock price. As the stock price moves, options with exercise prices around the new stock price are usually added. The majority of trading occurs in options that are close to being at-the-money. Options that are far in-the-money or far out-of-the-money, called **deep-in-the-money** and **deep-out-of-the-money** options, are usually not very actively traded and are often not even listed for trading.

Most exchange-listed options have fairly short-term expirations, usually the current month, the next month, and perhaps one or two other months. Most of the trading takes place for the two shortest expirations. Some exchanges list options with expirations of several years, which have come to be called LEAPS, for **long-term equity anticipatory securities**. These options are fairly actively purchased, but most investors tend to buy and hold them and do not trade them as often as they do the shorter-term options.

The exchanges also determine on which companies they will list options for trading. Although specific requirements do exist, generally the exchange will list the options of any company for which it feels the options would be actively traded. The company has no voice in the matter. Options of a company can be listed on more than one exchange in a given country.

In Reading 75, we described the manner in which futures are traded. The procedure is very similar for exchange-listed options. Some exchanges have pit trading, whereby parties meet in the pit and arrange a transaction. Some exchanges use electronic trading, in which transactions are conducted through computers. In either case, the transactions are guaranteed by the clearinghouse. In the United States, the clearinghouse is an independent company called the Options Clearing Corporation or OCC. The OCC guarantees to the buyer that the clearinghouse will step in and fulfill the obligation if the seller reneges at exercise.

When the buyer purchases the option, the premium, which one might think would go to the seller, instead goes to the clearinghouse, which maintains it in a margin account. In addition, the seller must post some margin money, which is based on a formula that reflects whether the seller has a position that hedges the risk and whether the option is in- or out-of-the-money. If the price moves against the seller, the clearinghouse will force the seller to put up additional margin money. Although defaults are rare, the clearinghouse has always been successful in paying when the seller defaults. Thus, exchange-listed options are effectively free of credit risk.

Because of the standardization of option terms and participants' general acceptance of these terms, exchange-listed options can be bought and sold at any time prior to expiration. Thus, a party who buys or sells an option can re-enter the market before the option expires and offset the position with a sale or a purchase of the identical option. From the clearinghouse's perspective, the positions cancel.

As in futures markets, traders on the options exchange are generally either market makers or brokers. Some slight technical distinctions exist between different types of market makers in different options markets, but the differences are minor and do not concern us here. Like futures traders, option market makers attempt to profit by scalping (holding positions very short term) to earn the bid–ask spread and sometimes holding positions longer, perhaps closing them overnight or leaving them open for days or more.

When an option expires, the holder decides whether or not to exercise it. When the option is expiring, there are no further gains to waiting, so in-the-money options are always exercised, assuming they are in-the-money by more than the transaction cost of buying or selling the underlying or arranging a cash settlement when exercising. Using our example of the SUNW options, if at expiration the stock is at 16, the calls with an exercise price of 15 would be exercised. Most exchange-listed stock options call for actual delivery of the stock. Thus, the seller delivers the stock and the buyer pays the seller, through the clearinghouse, $15 per share. If the exchange specifies that the contract is cash settled, the seller simply pays the buyer $1. For puts requiring delivery, the buyer tenders the stock and receives the exercise price from the seller. If the option is out-of-the-money, it simply expires unexercised and is removed from the books. If the put is cash settled, the writer pays the buyer the equivalent cash amount.

Some nonstandardized exchange-traded options exist in the United States. In an attempt to compete with the over-the-counter options market, some exchanges permit some options to be individually customized and traded on the exchange, thereby benefiting from the advantages of the clearinghouse's credit guarantee. These options are primarily available only in large sizes and tend to be traded only by large institutional investors.

Like futures markets, exchange-listed options markets are typically regulated at the federal level. In the United States, federal regulation of options markets is the responsibility of the Securities and Exchange Commission; similar regulatory structures exist in other countries.

TYPES OF OPTIONS   4

Almost anything with a random outcome can have an option on it. Note that by using the word *anything*, we are implying that the underlying does not even need to be an asset. In this section, we shall discover the different types of options, identified by the nature of the underlying. Our focus in this book is on financial options, but it is important, nonetheless, to gain some awareness of other types of options.

4.1 Financial Options

Financial options are options in which the underlying is a financial asset, interest rate, or a currency.

4.1.1 Stock Options

Options on individual stocks, also called **equity options**, are among the most popular. Exchange-listed options are available on most widely traded stocks and an option on any stock can potentially be created on the over-the-counter market. We have already given examples of stock options in an earlier section; we now move on to index options.

4.1.2 Index Options

Stock market indices are well known, not only in the investment community but also among many individuals who are not even directly investing in the market. Because a stock index is just an artificial portfolio of stocks, it is reasonable to expect that one could create an option on a stock index. Indeed, we have already covered forward and futures contracts on stock indices; options are no more difficult in structure.

For example, consider options on the S&P 500 Index, which trade on the Chicago Board Options Exchange and have a designated index contract multiplier of 100. On 13 June of a given year, the S&P 500 closed at 1241.60. A call option with an exercise price of $1,250 expiring on 20 July was selling for $28. The option is European style and settles in cash. The underlying, the S&P 500, is treated as though it were a share of stock worth $1,241.60, which can be bought, using the call option, for $1,250 on 20 July. At expiration, if the option is in-the-money, the buyer exercises it and the writer pays the buyer the $250 contract multiplier times the difference between the index value at expiration and $1,250.

In the United States, there are also options on the Dow Jones Industrial Average, the Nasdaq, and various other indices. There are nearly always options on the best-known stock indices in most countries.

Just as there are options on stocks, there are also options on bonds.

4.1.3 Bond Options

Options on bonds, usually called **bond options**, are primarily traded in the over-the-counter markets. Options exchanges have attempted to generate interest in options on bonds, but have not been very successful. Corporate bonds are not very actively traded; most are purchased and held to expiration. Government bonds, however, are very actively traded; nevertheless, options on them have not gained widespread acceptance on options exchanges. Options exchanges generate much of their trading volume from individual investors, who have far more interest in and understanding of stocks than bonds.

Thus, bond options are found almost exclusively in the over-the-counter market and are almost always options on government bonds. Consider, for example, a U.S. Treasury bond maturing in 27 years. The bond has a coupon of 5.50 percent, a yield of 5.75 percent, and is selling for $0.9659 per $1 par. An over-the-counter options dealer might sell a put or call option on the bond with an exercise price of $0.98 per $1.00 par. The option could be European or American. Its expiration day must be significantly before the maturity date of the bond. Otherwise, as the bond approaches maturity, its price will move toward par, thereby removing much of the uncertainty in its price. The option could be specified to settle with actual delivery of the bond or with a cash settlement. The parties would also specify that the contract covered a given notional principal, expressed in terms of a face value of the underlying bond.

Continuing our example, let us assume that the contract covers $5 million face value of bonds and is cash settled. Suppose the buyer exercises a call option when the bond price is at $0.995. Then the option is in-the-money by $0.995 − $0.98 = $0.015 per $1 par. The seller pays the buyer 0.015($5,000,000) = $75,000. If instead the contract called for delivery, the seller would deliver $5 million face value of bonds, which would be worth $5,000,000($0.995) = $4,975,000. The buyer would pay $5,000,000($0.98) = $4,900,000. Because the option is created in the over-the-counter market, the option buyer would assume the risk of the seller defaulting.

Even though bond options are not very widely traded, another type of related option is widely used, especially by corporations. This family of options is called **interest rate options**. These are quite different from the options we have previously discussed, because the underlying is not a particular financial instrument.

4.1.4 Interest Rate Options

In Reading 75, we devoted considerable effort to understanding the Eurodollar spot market and forward contracts on the Eurodollar rate or LIBOR, called FRAs. In this reading, we cover options on LIBOR. Although these are not the only interest rate options, their characteristics are sufficiently general to capture most of what we need to know about options on other interest rates. First recall that a Eurodollar is a dollar deposited outside of the United States. The primary Eurodollar rate is LIBOR, and it is considered the best measure of an interest rate paid in dollars on a nongovernmental borrower. These Eurodollars represent dollar-denominated time deposits issued by banks in London borrowing from other banks in London.

Before looking at the characteristics of interest rate options, let us set the perspective by recalling that FRAs are forward contracts that pay off based on the difference between the underlying rate and the fixed rate embedded in the contract when it is constructed. For example, consider a 3 × 9 FRA. This contract expires in three months. The underlying rate is six-month LIBOR. Hence, when the contract is constructed, the underlying Eurodollar instrument matures in nine months. *When the contract expires, the payoff is made immediately,* but the rate on which it is based, 180-day LIBOR, is set in the spot market, where it is assumed that interest will be paid 180 days later. Hence, the payoff on an FRA is discounted by the spot rate on 180-day LIBOR to give a present value for the payoff as of the expiration date.

Just as an FRA is a forward contract in which the underlying is an interest rate, an **interest rate option** is an option in which the underlying is an interest rate. Instead of an exercise price, it has an **exercise rate** (or **strike rate**), which is expressed on an order of magnitude of an interest rate. At expiration, the option payoff is based on the difference between the underlying rate in the market and the exercise rate. Whereas an FRA is a *commitment* to make one interest payment and receive another at a future date, an interest rate option is the *right* to make one interest payment and receive another. And just as there are call and put options, there is also an **interest rate call** and an **interest rate put**.

An interest rate call is an option in which the holder has the right to make a known interest payment and receive an unknown interest payment. The underlying is the unknown interest rate. If the unknown underlying rate turns out to be higher than the exercise rate at expiration, the option is in-the-money and is exercised; otherwise, the option simply expires. *An interest rate put is an option in which the holder has the right to make an unknown interest payment and receive a known interest payment.* If the unknown underlying rate turns out to be lower than the exercise rate at expiration, the option is in-the-money and is exercised; otherwise, the option simply expires. All interest rate option contracts have a specified size, which, as in FRAs, is called the notional principal. An interest rate option can be European or American style, but most tend to be European style. Interest rate options are settled in cash.

As with FRAs, these options are offered for purchase and sale by dealers, which are financial institutions, usually the same ones who offer FRAs. These dealers quote rates for options of various exercise prices and expirations. When a dealer takes an option position, it usually then offsets the risk with other transactions, often Eurodollar futures.

To use the same example we used in introducing FRAs, consider options expiring in 90 days on 180-day LIBOR. The option buyer specifies whatever exercise rate he desires. Let us say he chooses an exercise rate of 5.5 percent and a notional principal of $10 million.

Now let us move to the expiration day. Suppose that 180-day LIBOR is 6 percent. Then the call option is in-the-money. The payoff to the holder of the option is

$$(\$10,000,000)(0.06 - 0.055)\left(\frac{180}{360}\right) = \$25,000$$

This money is not paid at expiration, however; it is paid 180 days later. There is no reason why the payoff could not be made at expiration, as is done with an FRA. The delay of payment associated with interest rate options actually makes more sense, because these instruments are commonly used to hedge floating-rate loans in which the rate is set on a given day but the interest is paid later. We shall see examples of the convenience of this type of structure in Reading 78.

Note that the difference between the underlying rate and the exercise rate is multiplied by 180/360 to reflect the fact that the rate quoted is a 180-day rate but is stated as an annual rate. Also, the interest calculation is multiplied by the notional principal.

In general, the payoff of an interest rate call is

$$(\text{Notional Principal})\,\text{Max}(0,\text{Underlying rate at expiration} - \text{Exercise rate})\left(\frac{\text{Days in underlying rate}}{360}\right) \quad \textbf{(76-1)}$$

The expression Max(0,Underlying rate at expiration − Exercise rate) is similar to a form that we shall commonly see throughout this reading for all options. The payoff of a call option at expiration is based on the maximum of zero or the underlying minus the exercise rate. If the option expires out-of-the-money, then "Underlying rate at expiration − Exercise rate" is negative; consequently, zero is greater. Thus, the option expires with no value. If the option expires in-the-money, "Underlying rate at expiration − Exercise rate" is positive. Thus, the option expires worth this difference (multiplied by the notional principal and the Days/360 adjustment). The expression "Days in underlying rate," which we used in Reading 74, refers to the fact that the rate is specified as the rate on an instrument of a specific number of days to maturity, such as a 90-day or 180-day rate, thereby requiring that we multiply by 90/360 or 180/360 or some similar adjustment.

For an interest rate put option, the general formula is

$$(\text{Notional Principal})\,\text{Max}(0,\text{Exercise rate} - \text{Underlying rate at expiration})\left(\frac{\text{Days in underlying rate}}{360}\right) \quad \textbf{(76-2)}$$

For an exercise rate of 5.5 percent and an underlying rate at expiration of 6 percent, an interest rate put expires out-of-the-money. Only if the underlying rate is less than the exercise rate does the put option expire in-the-money.

As noted above, borrowers often use interest rate call options to hedge the risk of rising rates on floating-rate loans. Lenders often use interest rate put options to hedge the risk of falling rates on floating-rate loans. The form we have seen here, in which the option expires with a single payoff, is not the more commonly used variety of interest rate option. Floating-rate loans usually involve multiple interest payments. Each of those payments is set on a given date. To hedge the risk of interest rates increasing, the borrower would need options expiring on each rate reset date. Thus, the borrower would require a combination of interest rate call options. Likewise, a lender needing to hedge the risk of falling rates on a multiple-payment floating-rate loan would need a combination of interest rate put options.

A combination of interest rate calls is referred to as an **interest rate cap** or sometimes just a **cap**. A combination of interest rate puts is called an **interest rate floor** or sometimes just a **floor**.[8] Specifically, *an interest rate cap is a series of call options on an interest rate, with each option expiring at the date on which the floating loan rate will be reset, and with each option having the same exercise rate.*[9] Each option is independent of the others; thus, exercise of one option does not affect the right to exercise any of the others. Each component call option is called a **caplet**. *An interest rate floor is a series of put options on an interest rate, with each option expiring at the date on which the floating loan rate will be reset, and with each option having the same exercise rate.* Each component put option is called a **floorlet**. The price of an interest rate cap or floor is the sum of the prices of the options that make up the cap or floor.

A special combination of caps and floors is called an **interest rate collar**. *An interest rate collar is a combination of a long cap and a short floor or a short cap and a*

---

[8] It is possible to construct caps and floors with options on any other type of underlying, but they are very often used when the underlying is an interest rate.

[9] Technically, each option need not have the same exercise rate, but they generally do.

long floor. Consider a borrower in a floating rate loan who wants to hedge the risk of rising interest rates but is concerned about the requirement that this hedge must have a cash outlay up front: the option premium. A **collar**, which adds a short floor to a long cap, is a way of reducing and even eliminating the up-front cost of the cap. The sale of the floor brings in cash that reduces the cost of the cap. It is possible to set the exercise rates such that the price received for the sale of the floor precisely offsets the price paid for the cap, thereby completely eliminating the up-front cost. This transaction is sometimes called a **zero-cost collar**. The term is a bit misleading, however, and brings to mind the importance of noting the true cost of a collar. Although the cap allows the borrower to be paid from the call options when rates are high, the sale of the floor requires the borrower to pay the counterparty when rates are low. Thus, the cost of protection against rising rates is the loss of the advantage of falling rates. Caps, floors, and collars are popular instruments in the interest rate markets. We shall explore strategies using them in Reading 78.

Although interest rate options are primarily written on such rates as LIBOR, Euribor, and Euroyen, the underlying can be any interest rate.

4.1.5 Currency Options

As we noted in Reading 74, the currency forward market is quite large. The same is true for the currency options market. A **currency option** allows the holder to buy (if a call) or sell (if a put) an underlying currency at a fixed exercise rate, expressed as an exchange rate. Many companies, knowing that they will need to convert a currency X at a future date into a currency Y, will buy a call option on currency Y specified in terms of currency X. For example, say that a U.S. company will be needing €50 million for an expansion project in three months. Thus, it will be buying euros and is exposed to the risk of the euro rising against the dollar. Even though it has that concern, it would also like to benefit if the euro weakens against the dollar. Thus, it might buy a call option on the euro. Let us say it specifies an exercise rate of $0.90. So it pays cash up front for the right to buy €50 million at a rate of $0.90 per euro. If the option expires with the euro above $0.90, it can buy euros at $0.90 and avoid any additional cost over $0.90. If the option expires with the euro below $0.90, it does not exercise the option and buys euros at the market rate.

Note closely these two cases:

Euro expires above $0.90
 Company buys €50 million at $0.90

Euro expires at or below $0.90
 Company buys €50 million at the market rate

These outcomes can also be viewed in the following manner:

Dollar expires below €1.1111, that is, €1 > $0.90
 Company sells $45 million (€50 million × $0.90) at €1.1111, equivalent to buying €50 million

Dollar expires above €1.1111, that is, €1 < $0.90
 Company sells sufficient dollars to buy €50 million at the market rate

This transaction looks more like a put in which the underlying is the dollar and the exercise rate is expressed as €1.1111. Thus, the call on the euro can be viewed as a put on the dollar. Specifically, a call to buy €50 million at an exercise price of $0.90 is also a put to sell €50 million × $0.90 = $45 million at an exercise price of 1/$0.90, or €1.1111.

Most foreign currency options activity occurs on the customized over-the-counter markets. Some exchange-listed currency options trade on a few exchanges, but activity is fairly low.

4.2 Options on Futures

In Reading 74 we covered futures markets. One of the important innovations of futures markets is options on futures. These contracts originated in the United States as a result of a regulatory structure that separated exchange-listed options and futures markets. The former are regulated by the Securities and Exchange Commission, and the latter are regulated by the Commodity Futures Trading Commission (CFTC). SEC regulations forbid the trading of options side by side with their underlying instruments. Options on stocks trade on one exchange, and the underlying trades on another or on Nasdaq.

The futures exchanges got the idea that they could offer options in which the underlying is a futures contract; no such prohibitions for side-by-side trading existed under CFTC rules. As a result, the futures exchanges were able to add an attractive instrument to their product lines. The side-by-side trading of the option and its underlying futures made for excellent arbitrage linkages between these instruments. Moreover, some of the options on futures are designed to expire on the same day the underlying futures expires. Thus, the options on the futures are effectively options on the spot asset that underlies the futures.

A call option on a futures gives the holder the right to enter into a long futures contract at a fixed futures price. A put option on a futures gives the holder the right to enter into a short futures contract at a fixed futures price. The fixed futures price is, of course, the exercise price. Consider an option on the Eurodollar futures contract trading at the Chicago Mercantile Exchange. On 13 June of a particular year, an option expiring on 13 July was based on the July Eurodollar futures contract. That futures contract expires on 16 July, a few days after the option expires.[10] The call option with exercise price of 95.75 had a price of $4.60. The underlying futures price was 96.21. Recall that this price is the IMM index value, which means that the price is based on a discount rate of $100 - 96.21 = 3.79$. The contract size is $1 million.

The buyer of this call option on a futures would pay $0.046(\$1,000,000) = \$46,000$ and would obtain the right to buy the July futures contract at a price of 95.75. Thus, at that time, the option was in the money by $96.21 - 95.75 = 0.46$ per $100 face value. Suppose that when the option expires, the futures price is 96.00. Then the holder of the call would exercise it and obtain a long futures position at a price of 95.75. The price of the underlying futures is 96.00, so the margin account is immediately marked to market with a credit of 0.25 or $625.[11] The party on the short side of the contract is immediately set up with a short futures contract at the price of 95.75. That party will be charged the $625 gain that the long made. If the option is a put, exercise of it establishes a short position. The exchange assigns the put writer a long futures position.

---

[10] Some options on futures expire a month or so before the futures expires. Others expire very close to, if not at, the futures expiration.

[11] If the contract is in-the-money by $96 - 95.75 = 0.25$ per $100 par, it is in-the-money by $0.25/100 = 0.0025$, or 0.25 percent of the face value. Because the face value is $1 million, the contract is in the money by $(0.0025)(90/360)(\$1,000,000) = \$625$. (Note the adjustment by 90/360.) Another way to look at this calculation is that the futures price at 95.75 is $1 - (0.0425)(90/360) = \$0.989375$ per $1 par, or $989,375. At 96, the futures price is $1 - 0.04(90/360) = \$0.99$ per $1 par or $990,000. The difference is $625. So, exercising this option is like entering into a futures contract at a price of $989,375 and having the price immediately go to $990,000, a gain of $625. The call holder must deposit money to meet the Eurodollar futures margin, but the exercise of the option gives him $625. In other words, assuming he meets the minimum initial margin requirement, he is immediately credited with $625 more.

4.3 Commodity Options

Options in which the asset underlying the futures is a commodity, such as oil, gold, wheat, or soybeans, are also widely traded. There are exchange-traded as well as over-the-counter versions. Over-the-counter options on oil are widely used.

Our focus in this book is on financial instruments so we will not spend any time on commodity options, but readers should be aware of the existence and use of these instruments by companies whose business involves the buying and selling of these commodities.

4.4 Other Types of Options

As derivative markets develop, options (and even some other types of derivatives) have begun to emerge on such underlyings as electricity, various sources of energy, and even weather. These instruments are almost exclusively customized over-the-counter instruments. Perhaps the most notable feature of these instruments is how the underlyings are often instruments that cannot actually be held. For example, electricity is not considered a storable asset because it is produced and almost immediately consumed, but it is nonetheless an asset and certainly has a volatile price. Consequently, it is ideally suited for options and other derivatives trading.

Consider weather. It is hardly an asset at all but simply a random factor that exerts an enormous influence on economic activity. The need to hedge against and speculate on the weather has created a market in which measures of weather activity, such as economic losses from storms or average temperature or rainfall, are structured into a derivative instrument. Option versions of these derivatives are growing in importance and use. For example, consider a company that generates considerable revenue from outdoor summer activities, provided that it does not rain. Obviously a certain amount of rain will occur, but the more rain, the greater the losses for the company. It could buy a call option on the amount of rainfall with the exercise price stated as a quantity of rainfall. If actual rainfall exceeds the exercise price, the company exercises the option and receives an amount of money related to the excess of the rainfall amount over the exercise price.

Another type of option, which is not at all new but is increasingly recognized in practice, is the real option. A real option is an option associated with the flexibility inherent in capital investment projects. For example, companies may invest in new projects that have the option to defer the full investment, expand or contract the project at a later date, or even terminate the project. In fact, most capital investment projects have numerous elements of flexibility that can be viewed as options. Of course, these options do not trade in markets the same way as financial and commodity options, and they must be evaluated much more carefully. They are, nonetheless, options and thus have the potential for generating enormous value.

Again, our emphasis is on financial options, but readers should be aware of the growing role of these other types of options in our economy. Investors who buy shares in companies that have real options are, in effect, buying real options. In addition, commodity and other types of options are sometimes found in investment portfolios in the form of "alternative investments" and can provide significant diversification benefits.

To this point, we have examined characteristics of options markets and contracts. Now we move forward to the all-important topic of how options are priced.

PRINCIPLES OF OPTION PRICING   5

In Readings 74 and 75, we discussed the pricing and valuation of forward and futures contracts. Recall that the value of a contract is what someone must pay to buy into it or what someone would receive to sell out of it. A forward or futures contract has zero value at the start of the contract, but the value turns positive or negative as prices or rates change. A contract that has positive value to one party and negative value to the counterparty can turn around and have negative value to the former and positive value to the latter as prices or rates change. The forward or futures price is the price that the parties agree will be paid on the future date to buy and sell the underlying.

With options, these concepts are different. An option has a positive value at the start. The buyer must pay money and the seller receives money to initiate the contract. Prior to expiration, the option always has positive value to the buyer and negative value to the seller. In a forward or futures contract, the two parties agree on the fixed price the buyer will pay the seller. This fixed price is set such that the buyer and seller do not exchange any money. The corresponding fixed price at which a call holder can buy the underlying or a put holder can sell the underlying is the exercise price. It, too, is negotiated between buyer and seller but still results in the buyer paying the seller money up front in the form of an option premium or price.[12]

Thus, what we called the forward or futures price corresponds more to the exercise price of an option. The option price *is* the option value: With a few exceptions that will be clearly noted, in this reading we do not distinguish between the option price and value.

In this section of the reading, we examine the principles of option pricing. These principles are characteristics of option prices that are governed by the rationality of investors. These principles alone do not allow us to calculate the option price. We do that in Section 6.

Before we begin, it is important to remind the reader that we assume all participants in the market behave in a rational manner such that they do not throw away money and that they take advantage of arbitrage opportunities. As such, we assume that markets are sufficiently competitive that no arbitrage opportunities exist.

Let us start by developing the notation, which is very similar to what we have used previously. Note that time 0 is today and time T is the expiration.

S_0, S_T = price of the underlying asset at time 0 (today) and time T (expiration)

X = exercise price

r = risk-free rate

T = time to expiration, equal to number of days to expiration divided by 365

c_0, c_T = price of European call today and at expiration

C_0, C_T = price of American call today and at expiration

p_0, p_T = price of European put today and at expiration

P_0, P_T = price of American put today and at expiration

On occasion, we will introduce some variations of the above as well as some new notation. For example, we start off with no cash flows on the underlying, but we shall discuss the effects of cash flows on the underlying in Section 5.7.

5.1 Payoff Values

The easiest time to determine an option's value is at expiration. At that point, there is no future. Only the present matters. An option's value at expiration is

---

[12] For a call, there is no finite exercise price that drives the option price to zero. For a put, the unrealistic example of a zero exercise price would make the put price be zero.

called its **payoff**. We introduced this material briefly in our basic descriptions of types of options; now we cover it in more depth.

At expiration, a call option is worth either zero or the difference between the underlying price and the exercise price, whichever is greater:

$$c_T = \text{Max}(0, S_T - X)$$
$$C_T = \text{Max}(0, S_T - X)$$

(76-3)

Note that at expiration, a European option and an American option have the same payoff because they are equivalent instruments at that point.

The expression $\text{Max}(0, S_T - X)$ means to take the greater of zero or $S_T - X$. Suppose the underlying price exceeds the exercise price, $S_T > X$. In this case, the option is expiring in-the-money and the option is worth $S_T - X$. Suppose that at the instant of expiration, it is possible to buy the option for less than $S_T - X$. Then one could buy the option, immediately exercise it, and immediately sell the underlying. Doing so would cost c_T (or C_T) for the option and X to buy the underlying but would bring in S_T for the sale of the underlying. If c_T (or C_T) $< S_T - X$, this transaction would net an immediate risk-free profit. The collective actions of all investors doing this would force the option price up to $S_T - X$. The price could not go higher than $S_T - X$, because all that the option holder would end up with an instant later when the option expires is $S_T - X$. If $S_T < X$, meaning that the call is expiring out-of-the-money, the formula says the option should be worth zero. It cannot sell for less than zero because that would mean that the option seller would have to pay the option buyer. A buyer would not pay more than zero, because the option will expire an instant later with no value.

At expiration, a put option is worth either zero or the difference between the exercise price and the underlying price, whichever is greater:

$$p_T = \text{Max}(0, X - S_T)$$
$$P_T = \text{Max}(0, X - S_T)$$

(76-4)

Suppose $S_T < X$, meaning that the put is expiring in-the-money. At the instant of expiration, suppose the put is selling for less than $X - S_T$. Then an investor buys the put for p_T (or P_T) and the underlying for S_T and exercises the put, receiving X. If p_T (or P_T) $< X - S_T$, this transaction will net an immediate risk-free profit. The combined actions of participants doing this will force the put price up to $X - S_T$. It cannot go any higher, because the put buyer will end up an instant later with only $X - S_T$ and would not pay more than this. If $S_T > X$, meaning that the put is expiring out-of the-money, it is worth zero. It cannot be worth less than zero because the option seller would have to pay the option buyer. It cannot be worth more than zero because the buyer would not pay for a position that, an instant later, will be worth nothing.

These important results are summarized along with an example in Exhibit 76-5. The payoff diagrams for the short positions are also shown and are obtained as the negative of the long positions. For the special case of $S_T = X$, meaning that both call and put are expiring at-the-money, we can effectively treat the option as out-of-the-money because it is worth zero at expiration.

The value $\text{Max}(0, S_T - X)$ for calls or $\text{Max}(0, X - S_T)$ for puts is also called the option's intrinsic value or exercise value. We shall use the former terminology. Intrinsic value is what the option is worth to exercise it based on current conditions. In this section, we have talked only about the option at expiration. Prior to expiration, an option will normally sell for more than its intrinsic value.[13] The difference between the market price of the option and its intrinsic value is called its time value

---

[13] We shall later see an exception to this statement for European puts, but for now take it as the truth.

or speculative value. We shall use the former terminology. The time value reflects the potential for the option's intrinsic value at expiration to be greater than its current intrinsic value. At expiration, of course, the time value is zero.

There is no question that everyone agrees on the option's intrinsic value; after all, it is based on the current stock price and exercise price. It is the time value that we have more difficulty estimating. So remembering that Option price = Intrinsic value + Time value, let us move forward and attempt to determine the value of an option today, prior to expiration.

EXHIBIT 76-5	Option Values at Expiration (Payoffs)

| | | Example (X = 50) | |
Option	Value	$S_T = 52$	$S_T = 48$
European call	$c_T = \text{Max}(0, S_T - X)$	$c_T = \text{Max}(0, 52 - 50) = 2$	$c_T = \text{Max}(0, 48 - 50) = 0$
American call	$C_T = \text{Max}(0, S_T - X)$	$C_T = \text{Max}(0, 52 - 50) = 2$	$C_T = \text{Max}(0, 48 - 50) = 0$
European put	$p_T = \text{Max}(0, X - S_T)$	$p_T = \text{Max}(0, 50 - 52) = 0$	$p_T = \text{Max}(0, 50 - 48) = 2$
American put	$P_T = \text{Max}(0, X - S_T)$	$P_T = \text{Max}(0, 50 - 52) = 0$	$P_T = \text{Max}(0, 50 - 48) = 2$

Notes: Results for the European and American calls correspond to Graph A. Results for Graph B are the negative of Graph A. Results for the European and American puts correspond to Graph C, and results for Graph D are the negative of Graph C.

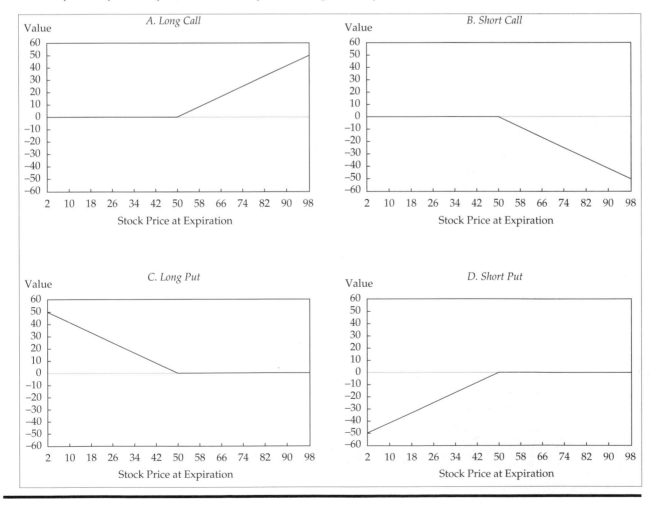

Practice Problem 1

For Parts A through E, determine the payoffs of calls and puts under the conditions given.

A. The underlying is a stock index and is at 5,601.19 when the options expire. The multiplier is 500. The exercise price is
   i. 5,500
   ii. 6,000

B. The underlying is a bond and is at $1.035 per $1 par when the options expire. The contract is on $100,000 face value of bonds. The exercise price is
   i. $1.00
   ii. $1.05

C. The underlying is a 90-day interest rate and is at 9 percent when the options expire. The notional principal is $50 million. The exercise rate is
   i. 8 percent
   ii. 10.5 percent

D. The underlying is the Swiss franc and is at $0.775 when the options expire. The options are on SF500,000. The exercise price is
   i. $0.75
   ii. $0.81

E. The underlying is a futures contract and is at 110.5 when the options expire. The options are on a futures contract covering $1 million of the underlying. These prices are percentages of par. The exercise price is
   i. 110
   ii. 115

For Parts F and G, determine the payoffs of the strategies indicated and describe the payoff graph.

F. The underlying is a stock priced at $40. A call option with an exercise price of $40 is selling for $7. You buy the stock and sell the call. At expiration, the stock price is
   i. $52
   ii. $38

G. The underlying is a stock priced at $60. A put option with an exercise price of $60 is priced at $5. You buy the stock and buy the put. At expiration, the stock price is
   i. $68
   ii. $50

SOLUTIONS

A. **i.** Calls: $\text{Max}(0, 5601.19 - 5500) \times 500 = 50,595$
   Puts: $\text{Max}(0, 5500 - 5601.19) \times 500 = 0$
   ii. Calls: $\text{Max}(0, 5601.19 - 6000) \times 500 = 0$
   Puts: $\text{Max}(0, 6000 - 5601.19) \times 500 = 199,405$

B. **i.** Calls: $\text{Max}(0, 1.035 - 1.00) \times \$100,000 = \$3,500$
   Puts: $\text{Max}(0, 1.00 - 1.035) \times \$100,000 = \$0$

      ii. Calls: $\text{Max}(0,1.035 - 1.05) \times \$100,000 = \$0$
         Puts: $\text{Max}(0,1.05 - 1.035) \times \$100,000 = \$1,500$

  C. **i.** Calls: $\text{Max}(0,0.09 - 0.08) \times (90/360) \times \$50,000,000 = \$125,000$
         Puts: $\text{Max}(0,0.08 - 0.09) \times (90/360) \times \$50,000,000 = \$0$

      ii. Calls: $\text{Max}(0,0.09 - 0.105) \times (90/360) \times \$50,000,000 = \$0$
         Puts: $\text{Max}(0,0.105 - 0.09) \times (90/360) \times \$50,000,000 = \$187,500$

  D. **i.** Calls: $\text{Max}(0,0.775 - 0.75) \times \text{SF}500,000 = \$12,500$
         Puts: $\text{Max}(0,0.75 - 0.775) \times \text{SF}500,000 = \$0$

      ii. Calls: $\text{Max}(0,0.775 - 0.81) \times \text{SF}500,000 = \$0$
         Puts: $\text{Max}(0,0.81 - 0.775) \times \text{SF}500,000 = \$17,500$

  E. **i.** Calls: $\text{Max}(0,110.5 - 110) \times (1/100) \times \$1,000,000 = \$5,000$
         Puts: $\text{Max}(0,110 - 110.5) \times (1/100) \times \$1,000,000 = \$0$

      ii. Calls: $\text{Max}(0,110.5 - 115) \times (1/100) \times \$1,000,000 = \$0$
         Puts: $\text{Max}(0,115 - 110.5) \times (1/100) \times \$1,000,000 = \$45,000$

  F. **i.** $52 - \text{Max}(0,52 - 40) = 40$
     ii. $38 - \text{Max}(0,38 - 40) = 38$

For any value of the stock price at expiration of 40 or above, the payoff is constant at 40. For stock price values below 40 at expiration, the payoff declines with the stock price. The graph would look similar to the short put in Panel D of Exhibit 76-5. This strategy is known as a covered call and is discussed in Reading 78.

  G. **i.** $68 + \text{Max}(0,60 - 68) = 68$
     ii. $50 + \text{Max}(0,60 - 50) = 60$

For any value of the stock price at expiration of 60 or below, the payoff is constant at 60. For stock price values above 60 at expiration, the payoff increases with the stock price at expiration. The graph will look similar to the long call in Panel A of Exhibit 76-5. This strategy is known as a protective put and is covered later in this reading and in Reading 78.

5.2 Boundary Conditions

We start by examining some simple results that establish minimum and maximum values for options prior to expiration.

5.2.1 Minimum and Maximum Values

The first and perhaps most obvious result is one we have already alluded to: *The minimum value of any option is zero.* We state this formally as

$$c_0 \geq 0, C_0 \geq 0$$
$$p_0 \geq 0, P_0 \geq 0$$
         (76-5)

No option can sell for less than zero, for in that case the writer would have to pay the buyer.

    Now consider the maximum value of an option. It differs somewhat depending on whether the option is a call or a put and whether it is European or American. *The maximum value of a call is the current value of the underlying:*

$$c_0 \leq S_0, C_0 \leq S_0$$
         (76-6)

A call is a means of buying the underlying. It would not make sense to pay more for the right to buy the underlying than the value of the underlying itself.

For a put, it makes a difference whether the put is European or American. One way to see the maximum value for puts is to consider the best possible outcome for the put holder. The best outcome is that the underlying goes to a value of zero. Then the put holder could sell a worthless asset for X. For an American put, the holder could sell it immediately and capture a value of X. For a European put, the holder would have to wait until expiration; consequently, we must discount X from the expiration day to the present. Thus, *the maximum value of a European put is the present value of the exercise price. The maximum value of an American put is the exercise price*,

$$p_0 \leq X/(1 + r)^T, P_0 \leq X \tag{76-7}$$

where r is the risk-free interest rate and T is the time to expiration. These results for the maximums and minimums for calls and puts are summarized in Exhibit 76-6, which also includes a numerical example.

EXHIBIT 76-6	Minimum and Maximum Values of Options		
Option	Minimum Value	Maximum Value	Example ($S_0 = 52$, X = 50, r = 5%, T = 1/2 year)
European call	$c_0 \geq 0$	$c_0 \leq S_0$	$0 \leq c_0 \leq 52$
American call	$C_0 \geq 0$	$C_0 \leq S_0$	$0 \leq C_0 \leq 52$
European put	$p_0 \geq 0$	$p_0 \leq X/(1 + r)^T$	$0 \leq p_0 \leq 48.80 \, [48.80 = 50/(1.05)^{0.5}]$
American put	$P_0 \geq 0$	$P_0 \leq X$	$0 \leq P_0 \leq 50$

5.2.2 Lower Bounds

The results we established in Section 5.2.1 do not put much in the way of restrictions on the option price. They tell us that the price is somewhere between zero and the maximum, which is either the underlying price, the exercise price, or the present value of the exercise price—a fairly wide range of possibilities. Fortunately, we can tighten the range up a little on the low side: We can establish a **lower bound** on the option price.

For American options, which are exercisable immediately, we can state that the lower bound of an American option price is its current intrinsic value:[14]

$$C_0 \geq \text{Max}(0, S_0 - X)$$
$$P_0 \geq \text{Max}(0, X - S_0) \tag{76-8}$$

The reason these results hold today is the same reason we have already shown for why they must hold at expiration. If the option is in-the-money and is selling for less than its intrinsic value, it can be bought and exercised to net an immediate

---

[14] Normally we have italicized sentences containing important results. This one, however, is a little different: We are stating it temporarily. We shall soon show that we can override one of these results with a lower bound that is higher and, therefore, is a better lower bound.

risk-free profit.[15] The collective actions of market participants doing this will force the American option price up to at least the intrinsic value.

Unfortunately, we cannot make such a statement about European options—but we can show that the lower bound is either zero or the current underlying price minus the present value of the exercise price, whichever is greater. They cannot be exercised early; thus, there is no way for market participants to exercise an option selling for too little with respect to its intrinsic value. Fortunately, however, there is a way to establish a lower bound for European options. We can combine options with risk-free bonds and the underlying in such a way that a lower bound for the option price emerges.

First, we need the ability to buy and sell a risk-free bond with a face value equal to the exercise price and current value equal to the present value of the exercise price. This procedure is simple but perhaps not obvious. If the exercise price is X (say, 100), we buy a bond with a face value of X (100) maturing on the option expiration day. The current value of that bond is the present value of X, which is $X/(1 + r)^T$. So we buy the bond today for $X/(1 + r)^T$ and hold it until it matures on the option expiration day, at which time it will pay off X. We assume that we can buy or sell (issue) this type of bond. Note that this transaction involves borrowing or lending an amount of money equal to the present value of the exercise price with repayment of the full exercise price.

Exhibit 76-7 illustrates the construction of a special combination of instruments. We buy the European call and the risk-free bond and sell short the underlying asset. Recall that short selling involves borrowing the asset and selling it. At expiration, we shall buy back the asset. In order to illustrate the logic behind the lower bound for a European call in the simplest way, we assume that we can sell short without any restrictions.

EXHIBIT 76-7	A Lower Bound Combination for European Calls		
		Value at Expiration	
Transaction	Current Value	$ST \leq X$	$ST > X$
Buy call	c_0	0	$S_T - X$
Sell short underlying	$-S_0$	$-S_T$	$-S_T$
Buy bond	$X/(1 + r)^T$	X	X
Total	$c_0 - S_0 + X/(1 + r)^T$	$X - S_T \geq 0$	0

In Exhibit 76-7 the two right-hand columns contain the value of each instrument when the option expires. The rightmost column is the case of the call expiring in-the-money, in which case it is worth $S_T - X$. In the other column, the out-of-the-money case, the call is worth zero. The underlying is worth $-S_T$ (the negative of its current value) in either case, reflecting the fact that we buy it back to

---

[15] Consider, for example, an in-the-money call selling for less than $S_0 - X$. One can buy the call for C_0, exercise it, paying X, and sell the underlying netting a gain of $S_0 - X - C_0$. This value is positive and represents an immediate risk-free gain. If the option is an in-the-money put selling for less than $X - S_0$, one can buy the put for P_0, buy the underlying for S_0, and exercise the put to receive X, thereby netting an immediate risk-free gain of $X - S_0 - P_0$.

cover the short position. The bond is worth X in both cases. The sum of all the positions is positive when the option expires out-of-the-money and zero when the option expires in-the-money. Therefore, in no case does this combination of instruments have a negative value. That means that we never have to pay out any money at expiration. We are guaranteed at least no loss at expiration and possibly something positive.

If there is a possibility of a positive outcome from the combination and if we know we shall never have to pay anything out from holding a combination of instruments, the cost of that combination must be positive—it must cost us something to enter into the position. We cannot take in money to enter into the position. In that case, we would be receiving money up front and never having to pay anything out. The cost of entering the position is shown in the second column, labeled the "Current Value." Because that value must be positive, we therefore require that $c_0 - S_0 + X/(1 + r)^T \geq 0$. Rearranging this equation, we obtain $c_0 \geq S_0 - X/(1 + r)^T$. Now we have a statement about the minimum value of the option, which can serve as a lower bound. This result is solid, because if the call is selling for less than $S_0 - X/(1 + r)^T$, an investor can buy the call, sell short the underlying, and buy the bond. Doing so would bring in money up front and, as we see in Exhibit 76-7, an investor would not have to pay out any money at expiration and might even get a little more money. Because other investors would do the same, the call price would be forced up until it is at least $S_0 - X/(1 + r)^T$.

But we can improve on this result. Suppose $S_0 - X/(1 + r)^T$ is negative. Then we are stating that the call price is greater than a negative number. But we already know that the call price cannot be negative. So we can now say that

$$c_0 \geq \text{Max}[0, S_0 - X/(1 + r)^T]$$

In other words, *the lower bound on a European call price is either zero or the underlying price minus the present value of the exercise price, whichever is greater.* Notice how this lower bound differs from the minimum value for the American call, $\text{Max}(0, S_0 - X)$. For the European call, we must wait to pay the exercise price and obtain the underlying. Therefore, the expression contains the current underlying value—the present value of its future value—as well as the present value of the exercise price. For the American call, we do not have to wait until expiration; therefore, the expression reflects the potential to immediately receive the underlying price minus the exercise price. We shall have more to say, however, about the relationship between these two values.

To illustrate the lower bound, let $X = 50$, $r = 0.05$, and $T = 0.5$. If the current underlying price is 45, then the lower bound for the European call is

$$\text{Max}[0, 45 - 50/(1.05)^{0.5}] = \text{Max}(0, 45 - 48.80) = \text{Max}(0, -3.80) = 0$$

All this calculation tells us is that the call must be worth no less than zero, which we already knew. If the current underlying price is 54, however, the lower bound for the European call is

$$\text{Max}(0, 54 - 48.80) = \text{Max}(0, 5.20) = 5.20$$

which tells us that the call must be worth no less than 5.20. With European puts, we can also see that the lower bound differs from the lower bound on American puts in this same use of the present value of the exercise price.

Exhibit 76-8 constructs a similar type of portfolio for European puts. Here, however, we buy the put and the underlying and borrow by issuing the zero-coupon bond. The payoff of each instrument is indicated in the two

EXHIBIT 76-8	A Lower Bound Combination for European Puts		
		Value at Expiration	
Transaction	Current Value	$S_T < X$	$S_T \geq X$
Buy put	p_0	$X - S_T$	0
Buy underlying	S_0	S_T	S_T
Issue bond	$-X/(1 + r)^T$	$-X$	$-X$
Total	$p_0 + S_0 - X/(1 + r)^T$	0	$S_T - X \geq 0$

rightmost columns. Note that the total payoff is never less than zero. Consequently, the initial value of the combination must not be less than zero. Therefore, $p_0 + S_0 - X/(1 + r)^T \geq 0$. Isolating the put price gives us $p_0 \geq X/(1 + r)^T - S_0$. But suppose that $X/(1 + r)^T - S_0$ is negative. Then, the put price must be greater than a negative number. We know that the put price must be no less than zero. So we can now formally say that

$$p_0 \geq Max[0, X/(1 + r)^T - S_0]$$

In other words, *the lower bound of a European put is the greater of either zero or the present value of the exercise price minus the underlying price.* For the American put, recall that the expression was $Max(0, X - S_0)$. So for the European put, we adjust this value to the present value of the exercise price. The present value of the asset price is already adjusted to S_0.

Using the same example we did for calls, let $X = 50$, $r = 0.05$, and $T = 0.5$. If the current underlying price is 45, then the lower bound for the European put is

$$Max(0, 50/(1.05)^{0.5} - 45) = Max(0, 48.80 - 45) = Max(0, 3.80) = 3.80$$

If the current underlying price is 54, however, the lower bound is

$$Max(0, 48.80 - 54) = Max(0, -5.20) = 0$$

At this point let us reconsider what we have found. The lower bound for a European call is $Max[0, S_0 - X/(1 + r)^T]$. We also observed that an American call must be worth at least $Max(0, S_0 - X)$. But except at expiration, the European lower bound is greater than the minimum value of the American call.[16] We could not, however, expect an American call to be worth less than a European call. Thus the lower bound of the European call holds for American calls as well. Hence, we can conclude that

$$c_0 \geq Max[0, S_0 - X/(1 + r)^T]$$
$$C_0 \geq Max[0, S_0 - X/(1 + r)^T]$$

(76-9)

For European puts, the lower bound is $Max[0, X/(1 + r)^T - S_0]$. For American puts, the minimum price is $Max(0, X - S_0)$. The European lower bound is lower than the minimum price of the American put, so the American put lower bound is not changed to the European lower bound, the way we did for calls. Hence,

---

[16] We discuss this point more formally and in the context of whether it is ever worthwhile to exercise an American call early in Section 5.6.

$$p_0 \geq Max[0, X/(1 + r)^T - S_0]$$
$$P_0 \geq Max(0, X - S_0)$$

(76-10)

These results tell us the lowest possible price for European and American options

Recall that we previously referred to an option price as having an intrinsic value and a time value. For American options, the intrinsic value is the value if exercised, $Max(0, S_0 - X)$ for calls and $Max(0, X - S_0)$ for puts. The remainder of the option price is the time value. For European options, the notion of a time value is somewhat murky, because it first requires recognition of an intrinsic value. Because a European option cannot be exercised until expiration, in a sense, all of the value of a European option is time value. The notion of an intrinsic value and its complement, a time value, is therefore inappropriate for European options, though the concepts are commonly applied to European options. Fortunately, understanding European options does not require that we separate intrinsic value from time value. We shall include them together as they make up the option price.

Practice Problem 2

Consider call and put options expiring in 42 days, in which the underlying is at 72 and the risk-free rate is 4.5 percent. The underlying makes no cash payments during the life of the options.

A. Find the lower bounds for European calls and puts with exercise prices of 70 and 75.

B. Find the lower bounds for American calls and puts with exercise prices of 70 and 75.

SOLUTIONS

A. 70 call: $Max[0, 72 - 70/(1.045)^{0.1151}] = Max(0, 2.35) = 2.35$
75 call: $Max[0, 72 - 75/(1.045)^{0.1151}] = Max(0, -2.62) = 0$
70 put: $Max[0, 70/(1.045)^{0.1151} - 72] = Max(0, -2.35) = 0$
75 put: $Max[0, 75/(1.045)^{0.1151} - 72] = Max(0, 2.62) = 2.62$

B. 70 call: $Max[0, 72 - 70/(1.045)^{0.1151}] = Max(0, 2.35) = 2.35$
75 call: $Max[0, 72 - 75/(1.045)^{0.1151}] = Max(0, -2.62) = 0$
70 put: $Max(0, 70 - 72) = 0$
75 put: $Max(0, 75 - 72) = 3$

5.3 The Effect of a Difference in Exercise Price

Now consider two options on the same underlying with the same expiration day but different exercise prices. Generally, the higher the exercise price, the lower the value of a call and the higher the price of a put. To see this, let the two exercise prices be X_1 and X_2, with X_1 being the smaller. Let $c_0(X_1)$ be the price of a European call with exercise price X_1 and $c_0(X_2)$ be the price of a European call with exercise price X_2. We refer to these as the X_1 call and the X_2 call. In Exhibit 75-9, we construct a combination in which we buy the X_1 call and sell the X_2 call.[17]

---

[17] In Reading 78, when we cover option strategies, this transaction will be known as a bull spread.

| | | EXHIBIT 76-9 | Portfolio Combination for European Calls Illustrating the Effect of Differences in Exercise Prices |

		Value at Expiration		
Transaction	Current Value	$S_T \leq X_1$	$X_1 < S_T < X_2$	$S_T \geq X_2$
Buy call ($X = X_1$)	$c_0(X_1)$	0	$S_T - X_1$	$S_T - X_1$
Sell call ($X = X_2$)	$-c_0(X_2)$	0	0	$-(S_T - X_2)$
Total	$c_0(X_1) - c_0(X_2)$	0	$S_T - X_1 > 0$	$X_2 - X_1 > 0$

Note first that the three outcomes are all non-negative. This fact establishes that the current value of the combination, $c_0(X_1) - c_0(X_2)$ has to be non-negative. We have to pay out at least as much for the X_1 call as we take in for the X_2 call; otherwise, we would get money up front, have the possibility of a positive value at expiration, and never have to pay any money out. Thus, because $c_0(X_1) - c_0(X_2) \geq 0$, we restate this result as

$$c_0(X_1) \geq c_0(X_2)$$

This expression is equivalent to the statement that *a call option with a higher exercise price cannot have a higher value than one with a lower exercise price.* The option with the higher exercise price has a higher hurdle to get over; therefore, the buyer is not willing to pay as much for it. Even though we demonstrated this result with European calls, it is also true for American calls. Thus,[18]

$$C_0(X_1) \geq C_0(X_2)$$

In Exhibit 76-10 we construct a similar portfolio for puts, except that we buy the X_2 put (the one with the higher exercise price) and sell the X_1 put (the one with the lower exercise price).

| | | EXHIBIT 76-10 | Portfolio Combination for European Puts Illustrating the Effect of Differences in Exercise Prices |

		Value at Expiration		
Transaction	Current Value	$ST \leq X1$	$X1 < ST < X2$	$ST \geq X2$
Buy put ($X = X_2$)	$p_0(X_2)$	$X_2 - S_T$	$X_2 - S_T$	0
Sell put ($X = X_1$)	$-p_0(X_1)$	$-(X_1 - S_T)$	0	0
Total	$p_0(X_2) - p_0(X_1)$	$X_2 - X_1 > 0$	$X_2 - S_T > 0$	0

---

[18] It is possible to use the results from this table to establish a limit on the difference between the prices of these two options, but we shall not do so here.

Observe that the value of this combination is never negative at expiration; therefore, it must be non-negative today. Hence, $p_0(X_2) - p_0(X_1) \geq 0$. We restate this result as

$$p_0(X_2) \geq p_0(X_1)$$

Thus, *the value of a European put with a higher exercise price must be at least as great as the value of a European put with a lower exercise price.* These results also hold for American puts. Therefore,

$$P_0(X_2) \geq P_0(X_1)$$

Even though it is technically possible for calls and puts with different exercise prices to have the same price, *generally we can say that the higher the exercise price, the lower the price of a call and the higher the price of a put.* For example, refer back to Exhibit 76-1 and observe how the most expensive calls and least expensive puts have the lower exercise prices.

5.4 The Effect of a Difference in Time to Expiration

Option prices are also affected by the time to expiration of the option. Intuitively, one might expect that the longer the time to expiration, the more valuable the option. A longer-term option has more time for the underlying to make a favorable move. In addition, if the option is in-the-money by the end of a given period of time, it has a better chance of moving even further in-the-money over a longer period of time. If the additional time gives it a better chance of moving out-of-the-money or further out-of-the-money, the limitation of losses to the amount of the option premium means that the disadvantage of the longer time is no greater. In most cases, a longer time to expiration is beneficial for an option. We will see that longer-term American and European calls and longer-term American puts are worth no less than their shorter-term counterparts.

First let us consider each of the four types of options: European calls, American calls, European puts, and American puts. We shall introduce options otherwise identical except that one has a longer time to expiration than the other. The one expiring earlier has an expiration of T_1 and the one expiring later has an expiration of T_2. The prices of the options are $c_0(T_1)$ and $c_0(T_2)$ for the European calls, $C_0(T_1)$ and $C_0(T_2)$ for the American calls, $p_0(T_1)$ and $p_0(T_2)$ for the European puts, and $P_0(T_1)$ and $P_0(T_2)$ for the American puts.

When the shorter-term call expires, the European call is worth $\text{Max}(0, S_{T_1} - X)$, but we have already shown that the longer-term European call is worth *at least* $\text{Max}(0, S_{T_1} - X/(1 + r)^{(T_2-T_1)})$, which is at least as great as this amount.[19] Thus, the longer-term European call is worth at least the value of the shorter-term European call. These results are not altered if the call is American. When the shorter-term American call expires, it is worth $\text{Max}(0, S_{T_1} - X)$. The longer-term American call must be worth at least the value of the European call, so it is worth *at least* $\text{Max}[0, S - X/(1 + r)^{T_2-T_1}]$. Thus, the longer-term call, European or American, is worth no less than the shorter-term call when the shorter-term call expires. Because this statement is always true, the longer-term call, European or American, is worth no less than the shorter-term call at any time prior to expiration. Thus,

$$c_0(T_2) \geq c_0(T_1)$$
$$C_0(T_2) \geq C_0(T_1)$$

(76-11)

---

[19] Technically, we showed this calculation using a time to expiration of T, but here the time to expiration is $T_2 - T_1$.

Notice that these statements do not mean that the longer-term call is always worth more; it means that the longer-term call can be worth no less. With the exception of the rare case in which both calls are so far out-of-the-money or in-the-money that the additional time is of no value, the longer-term call will be worth more.

For European puts, we have a slight problem. For calls, the longer term gives additional time for a favorable move in the underlying to occur. For puts, this is also true, but there is one disadvantage to waiting the additional time. When a put is exercised, the holder receives money. The lost interest on the money is a disadvantage of the additional time. For calls, there is no lost interest. In fact, a call holder earns additional interest on the money by paying out the exercise price later. Therefore, it is not always true that additional time is beneficial to the holder of a European put. It is true, however, that the additional time is beneficial to the holder of an American put. An American put can always be exercised; there is no penalty for waiting. Thus, we have

$$p_0(T_2) \text{ can be either greater or less than } p_0(T_1)$$
$$P_0(T_2) \geq P_0(T_1)$$

(76-12)

So for European puts, either the longer-term or the shorter-term option can be worth more. The longer-term European put will tend to be worth more when volatility is greater and interest rates are lower.

Referring back to Exhibit 76-1, observe that the longer-term put and call options are more expensive than the shorter-term ones. As noted, we might observe an exception to this rule for European puts, but these are all American options.

5.5 Put–Call Parity

So far we have been working with puts and calls separately. To see how their prices must be consistent with each other and to explore common option strategies, let us combine puts and calls with each other or with a risk-free bond. We shall put together some combinations that produce equivalent results.

5.5.1 Fiduciary Calls and Protective Puts

First we consider an option strategy referred to as a **fiduciary call**. It consists of a European call and a risk-free bond, just like the ones we have been using, that matures on the option expiration day and has a face value equal to the exercise price of the call. The upper part of the table in Exhibit 76-11 shows the payoffs at expiration of the fiduciary call. We see that if the price of the underlying is below X at expiration, the call expires worthless and the bond is worth X. If the price of the underlying is above X at expiration, the call expires and is worth S_T (the underlying price) − X. So at expiration, the fiduciary call will end up worth X or S_T, whichever is greater.

EXHIBIT 76-11	Portfolio Combinations for Equivalent Packages of Puts and Calls		

		Value at Expiration	
Transaction	Current Value	$S_T \leq X$	$S_T > X$
Fiduciary Call			
Buy call	c_0	0	$S_T - X$

(Exhibit continued on next page ...)

EXHIBIT 76-11	(continued)		

| Transaction | Current Value | Value at Expiration | |
		$S_T \leq X$	$S_T > X$
Buy bond	$X/(1 + r)^T$	X	X
Total	$c_0 + X/(1 + r)^T$	X	S_T
Protective Put			
Buy put	p_0	$X - S_T$	0
Buy underlying asset	S_0	S_T	S_T
Total	$p_0 + S_0$	X	S_T

Value of Fiduciary Call and
Protective Put at Expiration

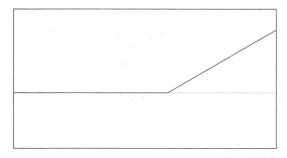

Stock Price at Expiration

This type of combination is called a fiduciary call because it allows protection against downside losses and is thus faithful to the notion of preserving capital.

Now we construct a strategy known as a **protective put**, which consists of a European put and the underlying asset. If the price of the underlying is below X at expiration, the put expires and is worth $X - S_T$ and the underlying is worth S_T. If the price of the underlying is above X at expiration, the put expires with no value and the underlying is worth S_T. So at expiration, the protective put is worth X or S_T, whichever is greater. The lower part of the table in Exhibit 76-11 shows the payoffs at expiration of the protective put.

Thus, the fiduciary call and protective put end up with the same value. They are, therefore, identical combinations. To avoid arbitrage, their values today must be the same. The value of the fiduciary call is the cost of the call, c_0, and the cost of the bond, $X/(1 + r)^T$. The value of the protective put is the cost of the put, p_0, and the cost of the underlying, S_0. Thus,

$$c_0 + X/(1 + r)^T = p_0 + S_0 \qquad \text{(76-13)}$$

This equation is called **put–call parity** and is one of the most important results in options. It does not say that puts and calls are equivalent, but it does show an equivalence (parity) of a call/bond portfolio and a put/underlying portfolio.

Put–call parity can be written in a number of other ways. By rearranging the four terms to isolate one term, we can obtain some interesting and important results. For example,

$$c_0 = p_0 + S_0 - X/(1 + r)^T$$

means that a call is equivalent to a long position in the put, a long position in the asset, and a short position in the risk-free bond. The short bond position simply means to borrow by issuing the bond, rather than lend by buying the bond as we did in the fiduciary call portfolio. We can tell from the sign whether we should go long or short. Positive signs mean to go long; negative signs mean to go short.

5.5.2 Synthetics

Because the right-hand side of the above equation is equivalent to a call, we often refer to it as a **synthetic call**. To see that the synthetic call is equivalent to the actual call, look at Exhibit 76-12:

EXHIBIT 76-12 **Call and Synthetic Call**

| | | Value at Expiration | |
Transaction	Current Value	$S_T \leq X$	$S_T > X$
Call			
Buy call	c_0	0	$S_T - X$
Synthetic Call			
Buy put	p_0	$X - S_T$	0
Buy underlying asset	S_0	S_T	S_T
Issue bond	$-X/(1 + r)^T$	$-X$	$-X$
Total	$p_0 + S_0 - X/(1 + r)^T$	0	$S_T - X$

The call produces the value of the underlying minus the exercise price or zero, whichever is greater. The synthetic call does the same thing, but in a different way. When the call expires in-the-money, the synthetic call produces the underlying value minus the payoff on the bond, which is X. When the call expires out-of-the-money, the put covers the loss on the underlying and the exercise price on the put matches the amount of money needed to pay off the bond.

Similarly, we can isolate the put as follows:

$$p_0 = c_0 - S_0 + X/(1 + r)^T$$

which says that a put is equivalent to a long call, a short position in the underlying, and a long position in the bond. Because the left-hand side is a put, it follows that the right-hand side is a **synthetic put**. The equivalence of the put and synthetic put is shown in Exhibit 76-13.

As you can well imagine, there are numerous other combinations that can be constructed. Exhibit 76-14 shows a number of the more important combinations. There are two primary reasons that it is important to understand synthetic positions in option pricing. Synthetic positions enable us to price options, because they produce the same results as options and have known prices. Synthetic positions also tell

| EXHIBIT 76-13 | Put and Synthetic Put |

| | | Value at Expiration | |
Transaction	Current Value	$S_T \leq X$	$S_T > X$
Put			
Buy put	p_0	$X - S_T$	0
Synthetic Put			
Buy call	c_0	0	$S_T - X$
Short underlying asset	$-S_0$	$-S_T$	$-S_T$
Buy bond	$X/(1+r)^T$	X	X
Total	$c_0 - S_0 + X/(1+r)^T$	$X - S_T$	0

| EXHIBIT 76-14 | Alternative Equivalent Combinations of Calls, Puts, the Underlying, and Risk-Free Bonds |

Strategy	Consisting of	Worth	Equates to	Strategy	Consisting of	Worth
Fiduciary call	Long call + Long bond	$c_0 + X/(1+r)^T$	=	Protective put	Long put + Long underlying	$p_0 + S_0$
Long call	Long call	c_0	=	Synthetic call	Long put + Long underlying + Short bond	$p_0 + S_0 - X/(1+r)^T$
Long put	Long put	p_0	=	Synthetic put	Long call + Short underlying + Long bond	$c_0 - S_0 + X/(1+r)^T$
Long underlying	Long underlying	S_0	=	Synthetic underlying	Long call + Long bond + Short put	$c_0 + X/(1+r)^T - p_0$
Long bond	Long bond	$X/(1+r)^T$	=	Synthetic bond	Long put + Long underlying + Short call	$p_0 + S_0 - c_0$

how to exploit mispricing of options relative to their underlying assets. Note that we can not only synthesize a call or a put, but we can also synthesize the underlying or the bond. As complex as it might seem to do this, it is really quite easy. First, we learn that *a fiduciary call is a call plus a risk-free bond maturing on the option expiration day with a face value equal to the exercise price of the option.* Then we learn that *a protective put is the underlying plus a put.* Then we learn the basic put–call parity equation: *A fiduciary call is equivalent to a protective put:*

$$c_0 + X/(1+r)^T = p_0 + S_0$$

Learn the put–call parity equation this way, because it is the easiest form to remember and has no minus signs.

Next, we decide which instrument we want to synthesize. We use simple algebra to isolate that instrument, with a plus sign, on one side of the equation, moving all other instruments to the other side. We then see what instruments are on the other side, taking plus signs as long positions and minus signs as short positions. Finally, to check our results, we should construct a table like Exhibits 76-11 or 76-12, with the expiration payoffs of the instrument we wish to synthesize compared with the expiration payoffs of the equivalent combination of instruments. We then check to determine that the expiration payoffs are the same.

5.5.3 An Arbitrage Opportunity

In this section we examine the arbitrage strategies that will push prices to put–call parity. Suppose that in the market, prices do not conform to put–call parity. This is a situation in which price does not equal value. Recalling our basic equation, $c_0 + X/(1 + r)^T = p_0 + S_0$, we should insert values into the equation and see if the equality holds. If it does not, then obviously one side is greater than the other. We can view one side as overpriced and the other as underpriced, which suggests an arbitrage opportunity. To exploit this mispricing, we buy the underpriced combination and sell the overpriced combination.

Consider the following example involving call options with an exercise price of $100 expiring in half a year ($T = 0.5$). The risk-free rate is 10 percent. The call is priced at $7.50, and the put is priced at $4.25. The underlying price is $99.

The left-hand side of the basic put–call parity equation is $c_0 + X/(1 + r)^T = 7.50 + 100/(1.10)^{0.5} = 7.50 + 95.35 = 102.85$. The right-hand side is $p_0 + S_0 = 4.25 + 99 = 103.25$. So the right-hand side is greater than the left-hand side. This means that the protective put is overpriced. Equivalently, we could view this as the fiduciary call being underpriced. Either way will lead us to the correct strategy to exploit the mispricing.

We sell the overpriced combination, the protective put. This means that we sell the put and sell short the underlying. Doing so will generate a cash inflow of $103.25. We buy the fiduciary call, paying out $102.85. This series of transactions nets a cash inflow of $103.25 − $102.85 = $0.40. Now, let us see what happens at expiration.

> *The options expire with the underlying above 100:*
> The bond matures, paying $100.
> Use the $100 to exercise the call, receiving the underlying.
> Deliver the underlying to cover the short sale.
> The put expires with no value.
> Net effect: No money in or out.
> *The options expire with the underlying below 100:*
> The bond matures, paying $100.
> The put expires in-the-money; use the $100 to buy the underlying.
> Use the underlying to cover the short sale.
> The call expires with no value.
> Net effect: No money in our out.

So we receive $0.40 up front and do not have to pay anything out. The position is perfectly hedged and represents an arbitrage profit. The combined effects of other investors performing this transaction will result in the value of the protective put going down and/or the value of the covered call going up until the two strategies are equivalent in value. Of course, it is possible that transaction costs might consume any profit, so small discrepancies will not be exploited.

It is important to note that regardless of which put–call parity equation we use, we will arrive at the same strategy. For example, in the above problem, the synthetic put (a long call, a short position in the underlying, and a long bond) is worth $\$7.50 - \$99 + \$95.35 = \$3.85$. The actual put is worth $\$4.25$. Thus, we would conclude that we should sell the actual put and buy the synthetic put. To buy the synthetic put, we would buy the call, short the underlying, and buy the bond—precisely the strategy we used to exploit this price discrepancy.

In all of these examples based on put–call parity, we used only European options. Put–call parity using American options is considerably more complicated. The resulting parity equation is a complex combination of inequalities. Thus, we cannot say that a given combination exactly equals another; we can say only that one combination is more valuable than another. Exploitation of any such mispricing is somewhat more complicated, and we shall not explore it here.

Practice Problem 3

European put and call options with an exercise price of 45 expire in 115 days. The underlying is priced at 48 and makes no cash payments during the life of the options. The risk-free rate is 4.5 percent. The put is selling for 3.75, and the call is selling for 8.00.

A. Identify the mispricing by comparing the price of the actual call with the price of the synthetic call.

B. Based on your answer in Part A, demonstrate how an arbitrage transaction is executed.

SOLUTIONS

A. Using put–call parity, the following formula applies:

$$c_0 = p_0 + S_0 - X/(1 + r)^T$$

The time to expiration is $T = 115/365 = 0.3151$. Substituting values into the right-hand side:

$$c_0 = 3.75 + 48 - 45/(1.045)^{0.3151} = 7.37$$

Hence, the synthetic call is worth 7.37, but the actual call is selling for 8.00 and is, therefore, overpriced.

B. Sell the call for 8.00 and buy the synthetic call for 7.37. To buy the synthetic call, buy the put for 3.75, buy the underlying for 48.00, and issue a zero-coupon bond paying 45.00 at expiration. The bond will bring in $45.00/(1.045)^{0.3151} = 44.38$ today. This transaction will bring in $8.00 - 7.37 = 0.63$.

At expiration, the following payoffs will occur:

	$S_T < 45$	$S_T \geq 45$
Short call	0	$-(S_T - 45)$
Long put	$45 - S_T$	0
Underlying	S_T	S_T
Bond	-45	-45
Total	0	0

Thus there will be no cash in or out at expiration. The transaction will net a risk-free gain of $8.00 - 7.37 = 0.63$ up front.

5.6 American Options, Lower Bounds, and Early Exercise

As we have noted, American options can be exercised early and in this section we specify cases in which early exercise can have value. Because early exercise is never mandatory, the right to exercise early may be worth something but could never hurt the option holder. Consequently, the prices of American options must be no less than the prices of European options:

$$C_0 \geq c_0$$
$$P_0 \geq p_0$$

(76-14)

Recall that we already used this result in establishing the minimum price from the lower bounds and intrinsic value results in Section 5.2.2. Now, however, our concern is understanding the conditions under which early exercise of an American option might occur.

Suppose today, time 0, we are considering exercising early an in-the-money American call. If we exercise, we pay X and receive an asset worth S_0. But we already determined that a European call is worth at least $S_0 - X/(1 + r)^T$—that is, the underlying price minus the present value of the exercise price, which is more than $S_0 - X$. Because we just argued that the American call must be worth no less than the European call, it therefore must also be worth at least $S_0 - X/(1 + r)^T$. This means that the value we could obtain by selling it to someone else is more than the value we could obtain by exercising it. Thus, there is no reason to exercise the call early.

Some people fail to see the logic behind not exercising early. Exercising a call early simply gives the money to the call writer and throws away the right to decide at expiration if you want the underlying. It is like renewing a magazine subscription before the current subscription expires. Not only do you lose the interest on the money, you also lose the right to decide later if you want to renew. Without offering an early exercise incentive, the American call would have a price equal to the European call price. Thus, we must look at another case to see the value of the early exercise option.

If the underlying makes a cash payment, there may be reason to exercise early. If the underlying is a stock and pays a dividend, there may be sufficient reason to exercise just before the stock goes ex-dividend. By exercising, the option holder throws away the time value but captures the dividend. We shall skip the technical details of how this decision is made and conclude by stating that

▶ *When the underlying makes no cash payments, $C_0 = c_0$.*

▶ *When the underlying makes cash payments during the life of the option, early exercise can be worthwhile and CO can thus be higher than c_0.*

We emphasize the word *can*. It is possible that the dividend is not high enough to justify early exercise.

For puts, there is nearly always a possibility of early exercise. Consider the most obvious case, an investor holding an American put on a bankrupt company. The stock is worth zero. It cannot go any lower. Thus, the put holder would exercise immediately. As long as there is a possibility of bankruptcy, the American put will be worth more than the European put. But in fact, bankruptcy is not required for early exercise. The stock price must be very low, although we cannot say exactly how low without resorting to an analysis using option pricing models. Suffice it to say that *the American put is nearly always worth more than the European put: $P_0 > p_0$.*

5.7 The Effect of Cash Flows on the Underlying Asset

Both the lower bounds on puts and calls and the put–call parity relationship must be modified to account for cash flows on the underlying asset. In Readings 74 and 75, we discussed situations in which the underlying has cash flows. Stocks pay dividends, bonds pay interest, foreign currencies pay interest, and commodities have carrying costs. As we have done in the previous readings, we shall assume that these cash flows are either known or can be expressed as a percentage of the asset price. Moreover, as we did previously, we can remove the present value of those cash flows from the price of the underlying and use this adjusted underlying price in the results we have obtained above.

In the previous readings, we specified these cash flows in the form of the accumulated value at T of all cash flows incurred on the underlying over the life of the derivative contract. When the underlying is a stock, we specified these cash flows more precisely in the form of dividends, using the notation $FV(D,0,T)$ as the future value, or alternatively $PV(D,0,T)$ as the present value, of these dividends. When the underlying was a bond, we used the notation $FV(CI,0,T)$ or $PV(CI,0,T)$, where CI stands for "coupon interest." When the cash flows can be specified in terms of a yield or rate, we used the notation δ where $S_0/(1 + \delta)^T$ is the underlying price reduced by the present value of the cash flows.[20] Using continuous compounding, the rate can be specified as dc so that $S_0e^{-\delta^c T}$ is the underlying price reduced by the present value of the dividends. For our purposes in this reading on options, let us just write this specification as $PV(CF,0,T)$, which represents the present value of the cash flows on the underlying over the life of the options. Therefore, we can restate the lower bounds for European options as

$$c_0 \geq \text{Max}\{0, [S_0 - PV(CF,0,T)] - X/(1 + r)^T\}$$
$$p_0 \geq \text{Max}\{0, X/(1 + r)^T - [S_0 - PV(CF,0,T)]\}$$

and put–call parity as

$$c_0 + X/(1 + r)^T = p_0 + [S_0 - PV(CF,0,T)]$$

which reflects the fact that, as we said, we simply reduce the underlying price by the present value of its cash flows over the life of the option.

5.8 The Effect of Interest Rates and Volatility

It is important to know that interest rates and volatility exert an influence on option prices. *When interest rates are higher, call option prices are higher and put option prices are lower.* This effect is not obvious and strains the intuition somewhat. When investors buy call options instead of the underlying, they are effectively buying an indirect leveraged position in the underlying. When interest rates are higher, buying the call instead of a direct leveraged position in the underlying is more attractive. Moreover, by using call options, investors save more money by not paying for the underlying until a later date. For put options, however, higher interest rates are disadvantageous. When interest rates are higher, investors lose more interest while waiting to sell the underlying when using puts. Thus, the opportunity cost of waiting is higher when interest rates are higher. Although these points may not seem completely clear, fortunately they are not critical. Except when the underlying is a bond or interest rate, interest rates do not have a very strong effect on option prices.

---

[20] We actually used several specifications of the dividend yield in Reading 75, but we shall use just one here.

Volatility, however, has an extremely strong effect on option prices. *Higher volatility increases call and put option prices because it increases possible upside values and increases possible downside values of the underlying.* The upside effect helps calls and does not hurt puts. The downside effect does not hurt calls and helps puts. The reason calls are not hurt on the downside and puts are not hurt on the upside is that when options are out-of-the-money, it does not matter if they end up more out-of-the-money. But when options are in-the-money, it does matter if they end up more in-the-money.

Volatility is a critical variable in pricing options. It is the only variable that affects option prices that is not directly observable either in the option contract or in the market. It must be estimated. We shall have more to say about volatility later in this reading.

5.9 Option Price Sensitivities

Later in this reading, we will study option price sensitivities in more detail. These sensitivity measures have Greek names:

▶ **Delta** is the sensitivity of the option price to a change in the price of the underlying.

▶ **Gamma** is a measure of how well the delta sensitivity measure will approximate the option price's response to a change in the price of the underlying.

▶ *Rho* is the sensitivity of the option price to the risk-free rate.

▶ *Theta* is the rate at which the time value decays as the option approaches expiration.

▶ **Vega** is the sensitivity of the option price to volatility.

6   DISCRETE-TIME OPTION PRICING: THE BINOMIAL MODEL

Until now, we have looked only at some basic principles of option pricing. Other than put–call parity, all we examined were rules and conditions, often suggesting limitations, on option prices. With put–call parity, we found that we could price a put or a call based on the prices of the combinations of instruments that make up the synthetic version of the instrument. If we wanted to determine a call price, we had to have a put; if we wanted to determine a put price, we had to have a call. What we need to be able to do is price a put or a call without the other instrument. In this section, we introduce a simple means of pricing an option. It may appear that we oversimplify the situation, but we shall remove the simplifying assumptions gradually, and eventually reach a more realistic scenario.

The approach we take here is called the **binomial model**. The word "binomial" refers to the fact that there are only two outcomes. In other words, we let the underlying price move to only one of two possible new prices. As noted, this framework oversimplifies things, but the model can eventually be extended to encompass all possible prices. In addition, we refer to the structure of this model as **discrete time**, which means that time moves in distinct increments. This is much like looking at a calendar and observing only the months, weeks, or days. Even at its smallest interval, we know that time moves forward at a rate faster than one day at a time. It moves in hours, minutes, seconds, and even fractions of seconds, and fractions of fractions of seconds. When we talk about time moving in the tiniest increments, we are talking about **continuous time**. We will see that the discrete time model can be extended to become a continuous time model. Although we present the continuous time model (Black–Scholes–Merton) in Section 7, we must point out that the binomial model has the advantage of allowing us to price American options. In addition, the binomial model is a simple model requiring a minimum of mathematics. Thus it is worthy of study in its own right.

6.1 The One-Period Binomial Model

We start off by having only one binomial period. This means that the underlying price starts off at a given level, then moves forward to a new price, at which time the option expires. Here we need to change our notation slightly from what we have been using previously. We let S be the current underlying price. One period later, it can move up to S^+ or down to S^-. Note that we are removing the time subscript, because it will not be necessary here. We let X be the exercise price of the option and r be the one period risk-free rate. The option is European style.

6.1.1 The Model

We start with a call option. If the underlying goes up to S^+, the call option will be worth c^+. If the underlying goes down to S^-, the option will be worth c^-. We know that if the option is expiring, its value will be the intrinsic value. Thus,

$$c^+ = \text{Max}(0, S^+ - X)$$
$$c^- = \text{Max}(0, S^- - X)$$

Exhibit 76-15 illustrates this scenario with a diagram commonly known as a **binomial tree**. Note how we indicate that the current option price, c, is unknown.

EXHIBIT 76-15	One-Period Binomial Model

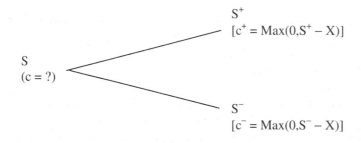

Now let us specify how the underlying moves. We identify a factor, u, as the up move on the underlying and d as the down move:

$$u = \frac{S^+}{S}$$

$$d = \frac{S^-}{S}$$

so that u and d represent 1 plus the rate of return if the underlying goes up and down, respectively. Thus, $S^+ = Su$ and $S^- = Sd$. To avoid an obvious arbitrage opportunity, we require that[21]

$$d < 1 + r < u$$

We are now ready to determine how to price the option. We assume that we have all information except for the current option price. In addition, we do not know in what direction the price of the underlying will move. We start by constructing an arbitrage portfolio consisting of one short call option. Let us now purchase an unspecified number of units of the underlying. Let that number be n. Although at the moment we do not know the value of n, we can figure it out quickly. We call this portfolio a hedge portfolio. In fact, n is sometimes called the **hedge ratio**. Its current value is H, where

$$H = nS - c$$

This specification reflects the fact that we own n units of the underlying worth S and we are short one call.[22] One period later, this portfolio value will go to either H^+ or H^-:

$$H^+ = nS^+ - c^+$$
$$H^- = nS^- - c^-$$

Because we can choose the value of n, let us do so by setting H^+ equal to H^-. This specification means that regardless of which way the underlying moves, the portfolio value will be the same. Thus, the portfolio will be hedged. We do this by setting

$$H^+ = H^-, \text{ which means that}$$
$$nS^+ - c^+ = nS^- - c^-$$

We then solve for n to obtain

$$n = \frac{c^+ - c^-}{S^+ - S^-} \qquad \textbf{(76-15)}$$

Because the values on the right-hand side are known, we can easily set n according to this formula. If we do so, the portfolio will be hedged. A hedged portfolio should grow in value at the risk-free rate.

$$H^+ = H(1 + r), \text{ or}$$
$$H^- = H(1 + r)$$

We know that $H^+ = nS^+ - c^+$, $H^- = nS^- - c^-$, and $H = nS - c$. We know the values of n, S^+, S^-, c^+, and c^-, as well as r. We can substitute and solve either of the above for c to obtain

$$c = \frac{Qc^+ + (1 - Q)c^-}{1 + r} \qquad \textbf{(76-16)}$$

---

[21] This statement says that if the price of the underlying goes up, it must do so at a rate better than the risk-free rate. If it goes down, it must do so at a rate lower than the risk-free rate. If the underlying always does better than the risk-free rate, it would be possible to buy the underlying, financing it by borrowing at the risk-free rate, and be assured of earning a greater return from the underlying than the cost of borrowing. This would make it possible to generate an unlimited amount of money. If the underlying always does worse than the risk-free rate, one can buy the risk-free asset and finance it by shorting the underlying. This would also make it possible to earn an unlimited amount of money. Thus, the risky underlying asset cannot dominate or be dominated by the risk-free asset.

[22] Think of this specification as a plus sign indicating assets and a minus sign indicating liabilities.

where

$$\pi = \frac{1 + r - d}{u - d}$$

(76-17)

We see that the call price today, c, is a weighted average of the next two possible call prices, c^+ and c^-. The weights are π and $1 - \pi$. This weighted average is then discounted one period at the risk-free rate.

It might appear that π and $1 - \pi$ are probabilities of the up and down movements, but they are not. In fact, the probabilities of the up and down movements are not required. It is important to note, however, that π and $1 - \pi$ are the probabilities that would exist if investors were risk neutral. Risk-neutral investors value assets by computing the expected future value and discounting that value at the risk-free rate. Because we are discounting at the risk-free rate, it should be apparent that π and $1 - \pi$ would indeed be the probabilities if the investor were risk neutral. In fact, we shall refer to them as **risk-neutral probabilities** and the process of valuing an option is often called **risk-neutral valuation**.[23]

6.1.2 One-Period Binomial Example

Suppose the underlying is a non-dividend-paying stock currently valued at $50. It can either go up by 25 percent or go down by 20 percent. Thus, u = 1.25 and d = 0.80.

$$S^+ = Su = 50(1.25) = 62.50$$
$$S^- = Sd = 50(0.80) = 40$$

Assume that the call option has an exercise price of 50 and the risk-free rate is 7 percent. Thus, the option values one period later will be

$$c^+ = Max(0,S^+ - X) = Max(0,62.50 - 50) = 12.50$$
$$c^- = Max(0,S^- - X) = Max(0,40 - 50) = 0$$

Exhibit 76-16 depicts the situation.

EXHIBIT 76-16   One-Period Binomial Example

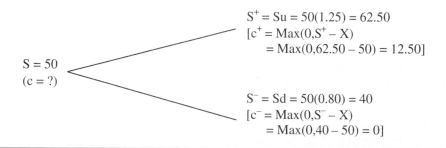

---

[23] It may be helpful to contrast risk neutrality with risk aversion, which characterizes nearly all individuals. People who are risk neutral value an asset, such as an option or stock, by discounting the expected value at the risk-free rate. People who are risk averse discount the expected value at a higher rate, one that consists of the risk-free rate plus a risk premium. In the valuation of options, we are not making the assumption that people are risk neutral, but the fact that options can be valued by finding the expected value, using these special probabilities, and discounting at the risk-free rate creates the *appearance* that investors are assumed to be risk neutral. We emphasize the word "appearance," because no such assumption is being made. The terms "risk neutral probabilities" and "risk neutral valuation" are widely used in options valuation, although they give a misleading impression of the assumptions underlying the process.

First we calculate π:

$$\pi = \frac{1 + r - d}{u - d} = \frac{1.07 - 0.80}{1.25 - 0.80} = 0.6$$

and, hence, $1 - \pi = 0.4$. Now, we can directly calculate the option price:

$$c = \frac{0.6(12.50) + 0.4(0)}{1.07} = 7.01$$

Thus, the option should sell for $7.01.

6.1.3 One-Period Binomial Arbitrage Opportunity

Suppose the option is selling for $8. If the option should be selling for $7.01 and it is selling for $8, it is overpriced—a clear case of price not equaling value. Investors would exploit this opportunity by selling the option and buying the underlying. The number of units of the underlying purchased for each option sold would be the value n:

$$n = \frac{c^+ - c^-}{S^+ - S^-} = \frac{12.50 - 0}{62.50 - 40} = 0.556$$

Thus, for every option sold, we would buy 0.556 units of the underlying. Suppose we sell 1,000 calls and buy 556 units of the underlying. Doing so would require an initial outlay of $H = 556(\$50) - 1,000(\$8) = \$19,800$. One period later, the portfolio value will be either

$$H^+ = nS^+ - c^+ = 556(\$62.50) - 1,000(\$12.50) = \$22,250, \text{ or}$$
$$H^- = nS^- - c^- = 556(\$40) - 1,000(\$0) = \$22,240$$

These two values are not exactly the same, but the difference is due only to rounding the hedge ratio, n. We shall use the $22,250 value. If we invest $19,800 and end up with $22,250, the return is

$$\frac{\$22,250}{\$19,800} - 1 = 0.1237$$

that is, a risk-free return of more than 12 percent in contrast to the actual risk-free rate of 7 percent. Thus we could borrow $19,800 at 7 percent to finance the initial net cash outflow, capturing a risk-free profit of $(0.1237 - 0.07) \times \$19,800 = \$1,063$ (to the nearest dollar) without any net investment of money. Other investors will recognize this opportunity and begin selling the option, which will drive down its price. When the option sells for $7.01, the initial outlay would be $H = 556(\$50) - 1,000(\$7.01) = \$20,790$. The payoffs at expiration would still be $22,250. This transaction would generate a return of

$$\frac{\$22,250}{\$20,790} - 1 \approx 0.07$$

Thus, when the option is trading at the price given by the model, a hedge portfolio would earn the risk-free rate, which is appropriate because the portfolio would be risk free.

If the option sells for less than $7.01, investors would buy the option and sell short the underlying, which would generate cash up front. At expiration, the investor would have to pay back an amount less than 7 percent. All investors would perform this transaction, generating a demand for the option that would push its price back up to $7.01.

Practice Problem 4

Consider a one-period binomial model in which the underlying is at 65 and can go up 30 percent or down 22 percent. The risk-free rate is 8 percent.

A. Determine the price of a European call option with exercise prices of 70.

B. Assume that the call is selling for 9 in the market. Demonstrate how to execute an arbitrage transaction and calculate the rate of return. Use 10,000 call options.

SOLUTIONS

A. First find the underlying prices in the binomial tree. We have u = 1.30 and d = 1 − 0.22 = 0.78.

$$S^+ = Su = 65(1.30) = 84.50$$
$$S^- = Sd = 65(0.78) = 50.70$$

Then find the option values at expiration:

$$c^+ = Max(0, 84.50 − 70) = 14.50$$
$$c^- = Max(0, 50.70 − 70) = 0$$

The risk-neutral probability is

$$\pi = \frac{1.08 − 0.78}{1.30 − 0.78} = 0.5769$$

and $1 − \pi = 0.4231$. The call's price today is

$$n = \frac{0.5769(14.50) + 0.4231(0)}{1.08} = 7.75$$

B. We need the value of n for calls:

$$n = \frac{c^+ − c^-}{S^+ − S^-} = \frac{14.50 − 0}{84.50 − 50.70} = 0.4290$$

The call is overpriced, so we should sell 10,000 call options and buy 4,290 units of the underlying.

Sell 10,000 calls at 9	+90,000
Buy 4,290 units of the underlying at 65	−278,850
Net cash flow	−188,850

So we invest 188,850. The value of this combination at expiration will be

If $S_T = 84.50$,

$$4{,}290(84.50) - 10{,}000(14.50) = 217{,}505$$

If $S_T = 50.70$,

$$4{,}290(50.70) - 10{,}000(0) = 217{,}503$$

These values differ by only a rounding error.
The rate of return is

$$\frac{217{,}505}{188{,}850} - 1 = 0.1517$$

Thus, we receive a risk-free return almost twice the risk-free rate. We could borrow the initial outlay of $188,850 at the risk-free rate and capture a risk-free profit without any net investment of money.

6.2 The Two-Period Binomial Model

In the example above, the movements in the underlying were depicted over one period, and there were only two outcomes. We can extend the model and obtain more-realistic results with more than two outcomes. Exhibit 76-17 shows how to do so with a two-period binomial tree.

EXHIBIT 76-17   Two-Period Binomial Model

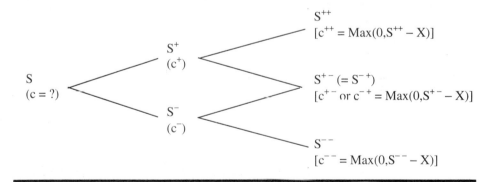

In the first period, we let the underlying price move from S to S^+ or S^- in the manner we did in the one-period model. That is, if u is the up factor and d is the down factor,

$$S^+ = Su$$
$$S^- = Sd$$

Then, with the underlying at S^+ after one period, it can either move up to S^{++} or down to S^{+-}. Thus,

$$S^{++} = S^+u$$
$$S^{+-} = S^+d$$

If the underlying is at S^- after one period, it can either move up to S^{-+} or down to S^{--}.

$$S^{-+} = S^-u$$
$$S^{--} = S^-d$$

We now have three unique final outcomes instead of two. Actually, we have four final outcomes, but S^{+-} is the same as S^{-+}. We can relate the three final outcomes to the starting price in the following manner:

$$S^{++} = S^+u = Suu = Su^2$$
$$S^{+-} \text{ (or } S^{-+}) = S^+d \text{ (or } S^-u) = Sud \text{ (or } Sdu)$$
$$S^{--} = S^-d = Sdd = Sd^2$$

Now we move forward to the end of the first period. Suppose we are at the point where the underlying price is S^+. Note that now we are back into the one-period model we previously derived. There is one period to go and two outcomes. The call price is c^+ and can go up to c^{++} or down to c^{+-}. Using what we know from the one-period model, the call price must be

$$c^+ = \frac{\pi c^{++} + (1 - \pi)c^{+-}}{1 + r}$$

(76-18)

where again we see that the call price is a weighted average of the next two possible call prices, then discounted back one period. If the underlying price is at S^-, the call price would be

$$c^- = \frac{\pi c^{-+} + (1 - \pi)c^{--}}{1 + r}$$

(76-19)

where in both cases the formula for π is still Equation 76-17:

$$\pi = \frac{1 + r - d}{u + d}$$

Now we step back to the starting point and find that the option price is still given as Equation 76-16:

$$c = \frac{\pi c^+ + (1 - \pi)c^-}{1 + r}$$

again, using the general form that the call price is a weighted average of the next two possible call prices, discounted back to the present. Other than requiring knowledge of the formula for π, the call price formula is simple and intuitive. It is an average, weighted by the risk-neutral probabilities, of the next two outcomes, then discounted to the present.[24]

Recall that the hedge ratio, n, was given as the difference in the next two call prices divided by the difference in the next two underlying prices. This will be

---

[24] It is also possible to express the price today as a weighted average of the three final option prices discounted two periods, thereby skipping the intermediate step of finding c^+ and c^-; but little is gained by doing so and this approach is somewhat more technical.

true in all cases throughout the binomial tree. Hence, we have different hedge ratios at each time point:

$$n = \frac{c^+ - c^-}{S^+ - S^-}$$

(76-20)

$$n^+ = \frac{c^{++} - c^{+-}}{S^{++} - S^{--}}$$

$$n^- = \frac{c^{-+} - c^{--}}{S^{-+} - S^{--}}$$

6.2.1 Two-Period Binomial Example

We can continue with the example presented in Section 6.1.2 in which the underlying goes up 25 percent or down 20 percent. Let us, however, alter the example a little. Suppose the underlying goes up 11.8 percent and down 10.56 percent, and we extend the number of periods to two. So, the up factor is 1.118 and the down factor is $1 - 0.1056 = 0.8944$. If the underlying goes up for two consecutive periods, it rises by a factor of $1.118(1.118) = 1.25$ (25 percent). If it goes down in both periods, it falls by a factor of $(0.8944)(0.8944) = 0.80$ (20 percent). This specification makes the highest and lowest prices unchanged. Let the risk-free rate be 3.44 percent per period. The π becomes $(1.0344 - 0.8944)/(1.118 - 0.8944) = 0.6261$. The underlying prices at expiration will be

$$S^{++} = Su^2 = 50(1.118)(1.118) = 62.50$$
$$S^{+-} = Sud = 50(1.118)(0.8944) = 50$$
$$S^{--} = Sd^2 = 50(0.8944)(0.8944) = 40$$

When the options expire, they will be worth

$$c^{++} = Max(0, S^{++} - 50) = Max(0, 62.50 - 50) = 12.50$$
$$c^{+-} = Max(0, S^{+-} - 50) = Max(0, 50 - 50) = 0$$
$$c^{--} = Max(0, S^{--} - 50) = Max(0, 40 - 50) = 0$$

The option values after one period are, therefore,

$$c^+ = \frac{\pi c^{++} + (1 - \pi)c^{+-}}{1 + r} = \frac{0.6261(12.50) + 0.3739(0)}{1.0344} = 7.57$$

$$c^- = \frac{\pi c^{-+} + (1 - \pi)c^{--}}{1 + r} = \frac{0.6261(0) + 0.3739(0)}{1.0344} = 0.0$$

So the option price today is

$$c = \frac{\pi c^+ + (1 - \pi)c^-}{1 + r} = \frac{0.6261(7.57) + 0.3739(0)}{1.0344} = 4.58$$

These results are summarized in Exhibit 76-18.

EXHIBIT 76-18	Two-Period Binomial Example

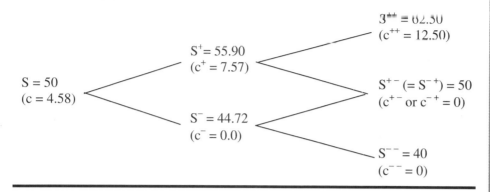

$S^{++} = 62.50$
$(c^{++} = 12.50)$

$S^+ = 55.90$
$(c^+ = 7.57)$

$S = 50$
$(c = 4.58)$

$S^{+-} (= S^{-+}) = 50$
$(c^{+-} \text{ or } c^{-+} = 0)$

$S^- = 44.72$
$(c^- = 0.0)$

$S^{--} = 40$
$(c^{--} = 0)$

We shall not illustrate an arbitrage opportunity, because doing so requires a very long and detailed example that goes beyond our needs. Suffice it to say that if the option is mispriced, one can construct a hedged portfolio that will capture a return in excess of the risk-free rate.

Practice Problem 5

Consider a two-period binomial model in which the underlying is at 30 and can go up 14 percent or down 11 percent each period. The risk-free rate is 3 percent per period.

A. Find the value of a European call option expiring in two periods with an exercise price of 30.

B. Find the number of units of the underlying that would be required at each point in the binomial tree to construct a risk-free hedge using 10,000 calls.

SOLUTIONS

A. First find the underlying prices in the binomial tree: We have $u = 1.14$ and $d = 1 - 0.11 = 0.89$.

$$S^+ = Su = 30(1.14) = 34.20$$
$$S^- = Sd = 30(0.89) = 26.70$$
$$S^{++} = Su^2 = 30(1.14)^2 = 38.99$$
$$S^{+-} = Sud = 30(1.14)(0.89) = 30.44$$
$$S^{--} = Sd^2 = 30(0.89)^2 = 23.76$$

Then find the option prices at expiration:

$$c^{++} = \text{Max}(0, 38.99 - 30) = 8.99$$
$$c^{+-} = \text{Max}(0, 30.44 - 30) = 0.44$$
$$c^{--} = \text{Max}(0, 23.76 - 30) = 0$$

We will need the value of π:

$$\pi = \frac{1.03 - 0.89}{1.14 - 0.89} = 0.56$$

and $1 - \pi = 0.44$. Then step back and find the option prices at time 1:

$$c^+ = \frac{0.56(8.99) + 0.44(0.44)}{1.03} = 5.08$$

$$c^- = \frac{0.56(0.44) + 0.44(0)}{1.03} = 0.24$$

The price today is

$$c = \frac{0.56(5.08) + 0.44(0.24)}{1.03} = 2.86$$

B. The number of units of the underlying at each point in the tree is found by first computing the values of n.

$$n = \frac{5.08 - 0.24}{34.20 - 26.70} = 0.6453$$

$$n^+ = \frac{8.99 - 0.44}{38.99 - 30.44} = 1.00$$

$$n^- = \frac{0.44 - 0}{30.44 - 23.76} = 0.0659$$

The number of units of the underlying required for 10,000 calls would thus be 6,453 today, 10,000 at time 1 if the underlying is at 34.20, and 659 at time 1 if the underlying is at 26.70.

6.3 Binomial Put Option Pricing

In Section 6.2, the option was a call. It is a simple matter to make the option a put. We could step back through the entire example, changing all c's to p's and using the formulas for the payoff values of a put instead of a call. We should note, however, that if the same formula used for a call is used to calculate the hedge ratio, the minus sign should be ignored as it would suggest being long the stock (put) and short the put (stock) when the hedge portfolio should actually be long both instruments or short both instruments. The put moves opposite to the stock in the first place; hence, long or short positions in both instruments are appropriate.

Practice Problem 6

Repeating the data from Practice Problem 4, consider a one-period binomial model in which the underlying is at 65 and can go up 30 percent or down 22 percent. The risk-free rate is 8 percent. Determine the price of a European put option with exercise price of 70.

SOLUTION
First find the underlying prices in the binomial tree. We have $u = 1.30$ and $d = 1 - 0.22 = 0.78$.

$$S^+ = Su = 65(1.30) = 84.50$$
$$S^- = Sd = 65(0.78) = 50.70$$

Then find the option values at expiration:

$$p^+ = Max(0,70 - 84.50) = 0$$
$$p^- = Max(0,70 - 50.70) = 19.30$$
The risk-neutral probability is

$$\pi = \frac{1.08 - 0.78}{1.30 - 0.78} - 0.5769$$

and $1 - \pi = 0.4231$. The put price today is

$$p = \frac{0.5769(0) + 0.423(19.30)}{1.08} = 7.56$$

6.4 Binomial Interest Rate Option Pricing

In the examples above, the applications were appropriate for options on a stock, currency, or commodity.[25] Now we take a brief look at options on bonds and interest rates. A model for pricing these options must start with a model for the one-period interest rate and the prices of zero-coupon bonds.

We look at such a model in Exhibit 76-19. Note that this binomial tree is the first one we have seen with more than two time periods. At each point in the tree, we see a group of numbers. The first number is the one-period interest rate. The second set of numbers, which are in parentheses, represents the prices of $1 face value zero-coupon bonds of various maturities. At time 0, 0.9048 is the price of a one-period zero-coupon bond, 0.8106 is the price of a two-period zero-coupon bond, 0.7254 is the price of a three-period zero-coupon bond, and 0.6479 is the price of a four-period zero-coupon bond. The one-period bond price can be determined from the one-period rate—that is, $0.9048 = 1/1.1051$, subject to some rounding off. The other prices cannot be determined solely from the one-period rate; we would have to see a tree of the two-, three-, and four-period rates. As we move forward in time, we lose one bond as the one-period bond matures.[26] Thus, at time 1, when the one-period rate is 13.04 percent, the two-period bond from the previous period, whose price was 0.8106, is now a one-period bond whose price is $1/1.1304 = 0.8846$. Although we present these prices and rates here without derivation, they were determined using a model that prevents arbitrage opportunities in buying and selling bonds. We do not cover the actual derivation of the model here.

EXHIBIT 76-19	**Binomial Interest Rate Tree**

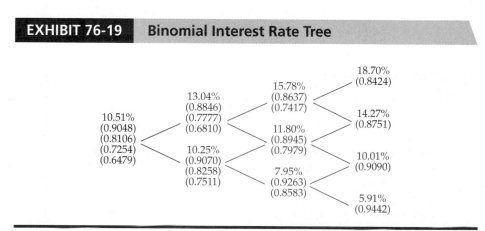

---

[25] We have also been assuming that there are no cash flows on the underlying.

[26] Technically we could show the bond we are losing as a bond with a price of $1.00, its face value, at its point of maturity.

Now let us price a European option on a zero-coupon bond. First note that we need the option to expire before the bond matures, and it should have a reasonable exercise price. We shall work with the four-period zero-coupon bond. Exhibit 76-20 contains its price and the price of a two-period call option with an exercise price of $0.80 per $1 of par, as well as the one-period interest rate. The binomial interest rate tree in Exhibit 76-20 is based on the data in Exhibit 76-19. In parentheses in Exhibit 76-20 are the prices of the call option expiring at time 2.

EXHIBIT 76-20	Four-Period Zero-Coupon Bond and Two-Period Call Option with Exercise Price of 0.80

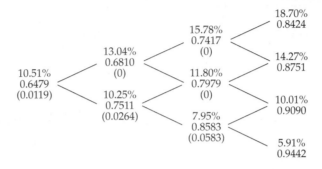

First note that in binomial term structure models, the models are usually fit such that the risk-neutral probability, π, is 0.5. Thus we do not have to calculate π, as in the examples above. We must, however, do one thing quite differently. Whereas we have used a constant interest rate, we must now discount at a different interest rate, the one-period rate, given in Exhibit 76-19, depending on where we are in the tree.

The payoff values at time 2 of the call with exercise price of 0.80 are

$$c^{++} = \text{Max}(0, 0.7417 - 0.80) = 0$$
$$c^{+-} = \text{Max}(0, 0.7979 - 0.80) = 0$$
$$c^{--} = \text{Max}(0, 0.8583 - 0.80) = 0.0583$$

These numbers appear in Exhibit 76-20 at time 2 along with the underlying bond prices and the one-period interest rates. Stepping back to time 1, we find the option prices as follows:

$$c^{+} = \frac{0.5(0) + 0.5(0)}{1.1304} = 0$$

$$c^{-} = \frac{0.5(0) + 0.5(0.0583)}{1.1025} = 0.0264$$

Note how we discount by the appropriate one-period rate, which is 10.25 percent for the bottom outcome at time 1 and 13.04 percent for the top outcome at time 1. Stepping back to time 0, the option price is, therefore,

$$c = \frac{0.5(0) + 0.5(0.0264)}{1.1051} = 0.0119$$

using the one-period rate of 10.51 percent. The call option is thus worth $0.0119 when the underlying zero-coupon bond paying $1 at time 4 is currently worth $0.6479.

Now let us price an option on a coupon bond. First, however, we must construct the tree of coupon bond prices. Exhibit 76-21 illustrates the price of a $1 face value, 11 percent coupon bond maturing at time 4 along with a call option expiring at time 2 with an exercise price of $0.95 per $1 of par.

EXHIBIT 76-21	Four-Period 11 Percent Coupon Bond and Two-Period Call Option with Exercise Price of 0.95

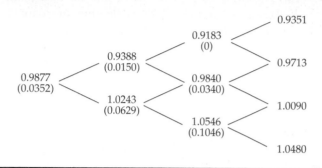

We obtain the prices of the coupon bond from the prices of zero-coupon bonds. For example, at time 0, a four-period 11 percent coupon bond is equivalent to a combination of zero-coupon bonds with face value of 0.11 maturing at times 1, 2, and 3, and a zero-coupon bond with face value of 1.11 maturing at time 4. Thus, its price can be found by multiplying these face values by the prices of one-, two-, three-, and four-period zero-coupon bonds respectively, the prices of which are taken from Exhibit 76-19.

$$0.11(0.9048) + 0.11(0.8106) + 0.11(0.7254) + 1.11(0.6479) = 0.9877$$

At any other point in the tree, we use the same procedure, but of course fewer coupons remain.[27] Of course, pricing a coupon bond by decomposing it into a combination of zero-coupon bonds is basic fixed income material, which you have learned elsewhere in the CFA curriculum.

Now let us find the option prices. At time 2, the prices are

$$c^{++} = Max(0, 0.9183 - 0.95) = 0$$
$$c^{+-} = Max(0, 0.9840 - 0.95) = 0.0340$$
$$c^{--} = Max(0, 1.0546 - 0.95) = 0.1046$$

Stepping back to time 1, the prices are

$$c^{+} = \frac{0.5(0) + 0.5(0.0340)}{1.1304} = 0.0150$$

$$c^{-} = \frac{0.5(0.0340) + 0.5(0.1046)}{1.1025} = 0.0629$$

Stepping back to time 0, the option price is

---

[27] For example, consider the middle node at time 2. The coupon bond is now a two-period bond. The one- and two-period zero-coupon bond prices are 0.8945 and 0.7979, respectively (from Exhibit 76-19). Thus, the coupon bond price is $0.11(0.8945) + 1.11(0.7979) = 0.9840$ as shown in Exhibit 76-21.

$$c = \frac{0.5(0.0150) + 0.5(0.0629)}{1.1051} = 0.0352$$

Now let us look at options on interest rates. Recall that in Section 4.1.4, we illustrated how these options work. Their payoffs are based on the difference between the interest rate and an exercise rate. When the option expires, the payoff does not occur for one additional period. Thus, we have to discount the intrinsic value at expiration by the one-period interest rate. Recall that an interest rate cap is a set of interest rate call options expiring at various points in the life of a loan. The cap is generally set up to hedge the interest rate risk on a floating rate loan.

Exhibit 76-22 illustrates the pricing of a two-period cap with an exercise rate of 10.5 percent. This contract consists of two caplets: a one-period call option on the one-period interest rate with an exercise rate of 10.5 percent, and a two-period call option on the one-period interest rate with an exercise rate of 10.5 percent. We price the cap by pricing these two component options.

EXHIBIT 76-22	Two-Period Cap on One-Period Interest Rate with Exercise Rate of 10.5 Percent

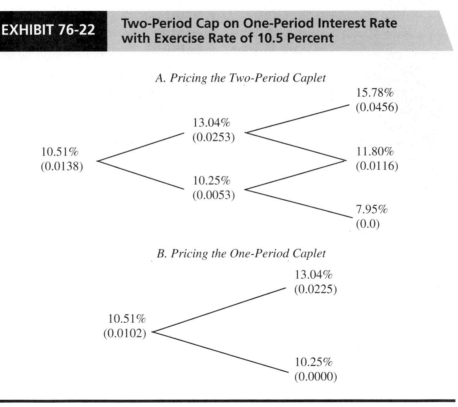

A. Pricing the Two-Period Caplet

B. Pricing the One-Period Caplet

In Panel A, we price the two-period caplet. The values at time 2 are

$$c^{++} = \frac{Max(0, 0.1578 - 0.105)}{1.1578} = 0.0456$$

$$c^{+-} = \frac{Max(0, 0.1180 - 0.105)}{1.1180} = 0.0116$$

$$c^{--} = \frac{Max(0, 0.0795 - 0.105)}{1.0795} = 0.0$$

Note especially that we discount the payoff one period at the appropriate one-period rate, because the payoff does not occur until one period later. Stepping back to time 1:

$$c^+ = \frac{0.5(0.0456) + 0.5(0.0116)}{1.1304} = 0.0253$$

$$c^- = \frac{0.5(0.0116) + 0.5(0.0)}{1.1095} = 0.0053$$

At time 0, the option price is

$$c = \frac{0.5(0.0253) + 0.5(0.0053)}{1.1051} = 0.0138$$

Panel B illustrates the same procedure for the one-period caplet. We shall omit the details because they follow precisely the pattern above. The one-period caplet price is 0.0102; thus the cap costs $0.0138 + 0.0102 = 0.0240$.

If the option is a floor, the procedure is precisely the same but the payoffs are based on the payoffs of a put instead of a call. Pricing a zero-cost collar, however, is considerably more complex. Remember that a zero-cost collar is a long cap and a short floor with the exercise rates set such that the premium on the cap equals the premium on the floor. We can arbitrarily choose the exercise rate on the cap or the floor, but the exercise rate on the other would have to be found by trial and error so that the premium offsets the premium on the other instrument.

Practice Problem 7

The diagram below is a two-period binomial tree containing the one-period interest rate and the prices of zero-coupon bonds. The first price is a one-period zero-coupon bond, the second is a two-period zero-coupon bond, and the third is a three-period zero-coupon bond. As we move forward, one bond matures and its price is removed. The maturity of each bond is then shorter by one period.

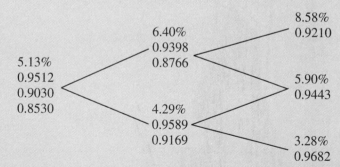

A. Find the price of a European put expiring in two periods with an exercise price of 1.01 on a three-period 6 percent coupon bond with $1.00 face value.

B. Find the price of a European put option expiring at time 2 with an exercise rate of 6 percent where the underlying is the one-period rate.

SOLUTIONS

A. First we have to find the price of the three-period $1.00 par, 6 percent coupon bond at expiration of the option (t = 2). We break the coupon bond up into zero-coupon bonds of one, two, and three periods to maturity. The face values of these zero-coupon bonds are

0.06, 0.06, and 1.06, respectively. The bond price at t = 2 is $1.06 discounted one period at the appropriate discount rate:

Bond prices at time 2:

$$++ \text{ outcome:} \quad 1.06(0.9210) = 0.9763$$
$$+- \text{ outcome:} \quad 1.06(0.9443) = 1.0010$$
$$-- \text{ outcome:} \quad 1.06(0.9682) = 1.0263$$

Now compute the put option values at expiration:

$$++ \text{ outcome:} \quad \text{Max}(0,1.01 - 0.9763) = 0.0337$$
$$+- \text{ outcome:} \quad \text{Max}(0,1.01 - 1.0010) = 0.0090$$
$$-- \text{ outcome:} \quad \text{Max}(0,1.01 - 1.0263) = 0.0000$$

Now step back and compute the option values at time 1:

$$+ \text{ outcome:} \quad \frac{0.5(0.0337) + 0.5(0.0090)}{1.064} = 0.0201$$

$$- \text{ outcome:} \quad \frac{0.5(0.0090) + 0.5(0.0000)}{1.0429} = 0.0043$$

Now step back and compute the option values at time 0:

$$\frac{0.5(0.201) + 0.5(0.0043)}{1.0513} = 0.0116$$

B. First compute the put option values at expiration:

$$p^{++} = \frac{\text{Max}(0,0.06 - 0.0858)}{1.0858} = 0.0000$$

$$p^{+-} = \frac{\text{Max}(0,0.06 - 0.0590)}{1.059} = 0.0009$$

$$p^{--} = \frac{\text{Max}(0,0.06 - 0.0328)}{1.0328} = 0.0263$$

Step back to time 2 and compute the option values:

$$p^{+} = \frac{0.5(0.0000) + 0.5(0.0009)}{1.064} = 0.0004$$

$$p^{-} = \frac{0.5(0.0009) + 0.5(0.0263)}{1.0429} = 0.0130$$

Now step back to time 0 and compute the option price as

$$p = \frac{0.5(0.0004) + 0.5(0.0130)}{1.0513} = 0.0064$$

6.5 American Options

The binomial model is also well suited for handling American-style options. At any point in the binomial tree, we can see whether the calculated value of the option is exceeded by its value if exercised early. If that is the case, we replace the calculated value with the exercise value.[28]

6.6 Extending the Binomial Model

In the examples in this reading, we divided an option's life into a given number of periods. Suppose we are pricing a one-year option. If we use only one binomial period, it will give us only two prices for the underlying, and we are unlikely to get a very good result. If we use two binomial periods, we will have three prices for the underlying at expiration. This result would probably be better but still not very good. But as we increase the number of periods, the result should become more accurate. In fact, in the limiting case, we are likely to get a very good result. By increasing the number of periods, we are moving from discrete time to continuous time.

Consider the following example of a one-period binomial model for a nine-month option. The asset is priced at 52.75. It can go up by 35.41 percent or down by 26.15 percent, so u = 1.3541 and d = 1 − 0.2615 = 0.7385. The risk-free rate is 4.88 percent. A call option has an exercise price of 50 and expires in nine months. Using a one-period binomial model would obtain an option price of 10.0259. Exhibit 76-23 shows the results we obtain if we divide the nine-month option life into an increasing number of periods of smaller and smaller length. The manner in which we fit the binomial tree is not arbitrary, however, because we have to alter the values of u, d, and the risk-free rate so that the underlying price move is reasonable for the life of the option. How we alter u and d is related to the volatility, a topic we cover in the next section. In fact, we need not concern ourselves with exactly how to alter any of these values. We need only to observe that our binomial option price appears to be converging to a value of around 8.62.

In the same way a sequence of rapidly taken still photographs converges to what appears to be a continuous sequence of a subject's movements, the binomial model converges to a continuous-time model, the subject of which is in our next section.

EXHIBIT 76-23	Binomial Option Prices for Different Numbers of Time Periods

Number of Time Periods	Option Price
1	10.0259
2	8.4782
5	8.8305
10	8.6983
25	8.5862
50	8.6438
100	8.6160
500	8.6162
1000	8.6190

Notes: Call option with underlying price of 52.75, up factor of 1.3541, down factor of 0.7385, risk-free rate of 4.88 percent, and exercise price of 50. The variables u, d, and r are altered accordingly as the number of time periods increases.

[28] See Chapter 4 of *An Introduction to Derivatives and Risk Management*, 6th edition, Don M. Chance (South-Western College Publishing, 2004) for a treatment of this topic.

7

CONTINUOUS-TIME OPTION PRICING: THE BLACK–SCHOLES–MERTON MODEL

When we move to a continuous-time world, we price options using the famous Black–Scholes–Merton model. Named after its founders Fischer Black, Myron Scholes, and Robert Merton, this model resulted in the award of a Nobel Prize to Scholes and Merton in 1997.[29] (Fischer Black had died in 1995 and thus was not eligible for the prize.) The model can be derived either as the continuous limit of the binomial model, or through taking expectations, or through a variety of highly complex mathematical procedures. We are not concerned with the derivation here and instead simply present the model and its applications. First, however, let us briefly review its underlying assumptions.

7.1 Assumptions of the Model

7.1.1 The Underlying Price Follows a Geometric Lognormal Diffusion Process

This assumption is probably the most difficult to understand, but in simple terms, *the underlying price follows a lognormal probability distribution as it evolves through time*. A lognormal probability distribution is one in which the log return is normally distributed. For example, if a stock moves from 100 to 110, the return is 10 percent but the log return is $\ln(1.10) = 0.0953$ or 9.53 percent. Log returns are often called *continuously compounded returns*. If the log or continuously compounded return follows the familiar normal or bell-shaped distribution, the return is said to be lognormally distributed. The distribution of the return itself is skewed, reaching further out to the right and truncated on the left side, reflecting the limitation that an asset cannot be worth less than zero.

The lognormal distribution is a convenient and widely used assumption. It is almost surely not an exact measure in reality, but it suffices for our purposes.

7.1.2 The Risk-Free Rate Is Known and Constant

The Black–Scholes–Merton model does not allow interest rates to be random. Generally, we assume that *the risk-free rate is constant*. This assumption becomes a problem for pricing options on bonds and interest rates, and we will have to make some adjustments then.

7.1.3 The Volatility of the Underlying Asset Is Known and Constant

The volatility of the underlying asset, specified in the form of the standard deviation of the log return, is assumed to be known at all times and does not change over the life of the option. This assumption is the most critical, and we take it up again in a later section. In reality, the volatility is definitely not known and must be estimated or obtained from some other source. In addition, volatility is generally not constant. Obviously, the stock market is more volatile at some times than at others. Nonetheless, the assumption is critical for this model. Considerable research has been conducted with the assumption relaxed, but this topic is an advanced one and does not concern us here.

---

[29] The model is more commonly called the Black–Scholes model, but we choose to give Merton the credit he is due that led to his co-receipt of the Nobel Prize.

7.1.4 *There Are No Taxes or Transaction Costs*

We have made this assumption all along in pricing all types of derivatives. Taxes and transaction costs greatly complicate our models and keep us from seeing the essential financial principles involved in the models. It is possible to relax this assumption, but we shall not do so here.

7.1.5 *There Are No Cash Flows on the Underlying*

We have discussed this assumption at great length in pricing futures and forwards and earlier in this reading in studying the fundamentals of option pricing. The basic form of the Black–Scholes–Merton model makes this assumption, but it can easily be relaxed. We will show how to do this in Section 7.4.

7.1.6 *The Options Are European*

With only a few very advanced variations, the Black–Scholes–Merton model does not price American options. Users of the model must keep this in mind, or they may badly misprice these options. For pricing American options, the best approach is the binomial model with a large number of time periods.

7.2 The Black–Scholes–Merton Formula

Although the mathematics underlying the Black–Scholes–Merton formula are quite complex, the formula itself is not difficult, although it may appear so at first glance. The input variables are some of those we have already used: S_0 is the price of the underlying, X is the exercise price, r^c is the continuously compounded risk-free rate, and T is the time to expiration. The one other variable we need is the standard deviation of the log return on the asset. We denote this as σ and refer to it as the volatility. Then, the Black–Scholes–Merton formulas for the prices of call and put options are

$$c = S_0 N(d_1) - Xe^{-r^c T} N(d_2)$$
$$p = Xe^{-r^c T}[1 - N(d_2)] - S_0[1 - N(d_1)]$$

(76-21)

where

$$d_1 = \frac{\ln(S_0/X) + \left[r^c + (\sigma^2/2)\right]T}{\sigma\sqrt{T}}$$

(76-22)

$$d_2 = d_1 - \sigma\sqrt{T}$$

σ = the annualized standard deviation of the continuously compounded return on the stock

r^c = the continuously compounded risk-free rate of return

Of course, we have already seen the terms "ln" and "*e*" in previous readings. We do, however, introduce two new and somewhat unusual looking terms, $N(d_1)$ and $N(d_2)$. These terms represent normal probabilities based on the values of d_1 and d_2. We compute the normal probabilities associated with values of d_1 and d_2 using the second equation above and insert these values into the formula as $N(d_1)$ and $N(d_2)$. Exhibit 76-24 presents a brief review of the normal probability distribution and explains how to obtain a probability value. Once we know how to look up a number in a normal probability table, we can then easily calculate d_1 and d_2, look them up in the table to obtain $N(d_1)$ and $N(d_2)$, and then insert the values of $N(d_1)$ and $N(d_2)$ into the above formula.

EXHIBIT 76-24   The Normal Probability Distribution

The normal probability distribution, or bell-shaped curve, gives the probability that a standard normal random variable will be less than or equal to a given value. The graph below shows the normal probability distribution; note that the curve is centered around zero. The values on the horizontal axis run from $-\infty$ to $+\infty$. If we were interested in a value of x of positive infinity, we would have $N(+\infty) = 1$. This expression means that the probability is 1.0 that we would obtain a value less than $+\infty$. If we were interested in a value of x of negative infinity, then $N(-\infty) = 0.0$. This expression means that there is zero probability of a value of x of less than negative infinity. Below, we are interested in the probability of a value less than x, where x is not infinite. We want $N(x)$, which is the area under the curve to the left of x.

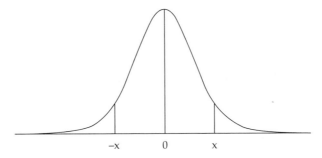

We obtain the values of $N(x)$ by looking them up in a table. Below is an excerpt from a table of values of x (the full table is given as Appendix 76A). Suppose $x = 1.12$. Then we find the row containing the value 1.1 and move over to the column containing 0.02. The sum of the row value and the column value is the value of x.

x	0	0.01	0.02	0.03	0.04	0.05	0.06	0.07	0.08	0.09
0.60	0.7257	0.7291	0.7324	0.7357	0.7389	0.7422	0.7454	0.7486	0.7517	0.7549
0.70	0.7580	0.7611	0.7642	0.7673	0.7704	**0.7734**	0.7764	0.7794	0.7823	0.7852
0.80	0.7881	0.7910	0.7939	0.7967	0.7995	0.8023	0.8051	0.8078	0.8106	0.8133
0.90	0.8159	0.8186	0.8212	0.8238	0.8264	0.8289	0.8315	0.8340	0.8365	0.8389
1.00	0.8413	0.8438	0.8461	0.8485	0.8508	0.8531	0.8554	0.8577	0.8599	0.8621
1.10	0.8643	0.8665	**0.8686**	0.8708	0.8729	0.8749	0.8770	0.8790	0.8810	0.8830
1.20	0.8849	0.8869	0.8888	0.8907	0.8925	0.8944	0.8962	0.8980	0.8997	0.9015

The corresponding probability is seen as the value 0.8686. Thus, $N(1.12) = 0.8686$. This means that the probability of obtaining a value of less than 1.12 in a normal distribution is 0.8686.

Now, suppose the value of x is negative. Observe in the figure above that the area to the left of $-x$ is the same as the area to the right of $+x$. Therefore, if x is a negative number, $N(x)$ is found as $1 - N(-x)$. For example, let $x = -0.75$. We simply look up $N(-x) = N[-(-0.75)] = N(0.75) = 0.7734$. Then $N(-0.75) = 1 - 0.7734 = 0.2266$.

Consider the following example. The underlying price is 52.75 and has a volatility of 0.35. The continuously compounded risk-free rate is 4.88 percent. The option expires in nine months; therefore, $T = 9/12 = 0.75$. The exercise price is 50. First we calculate the values of d1 and d2:

$$d_1 = \frac{\ln(52.75/50) + (0.0488 + (0.35)^2/2)0.75}{0.35\sqrt{0.75}} = 0.4489$$

$$d_2 = 0.4489 - 0.35\sqrt{0.75} = 0.1458$$

To use the normal probability table in Appendix 76A, we must round off d_1 and d_2 to two digits to the right of the decimal. Thus we have $d_1 = 0.45$ and $d_2 = 0.15$. From the table, we obtain

$$N(0.45) = 0.6736$$
$$N(0.15) = 0.5596$$

Then we plug everything into the equation for c:

$$c = 52.75(0.6736) - 50e^{-0.0488(0.75)}(0.5596) = 8.5580$$

The value of a put with the same terms would be

$$p = 50e^{-0.0488(0.75)}(1 - 0.5596) - 52.75(1 - 0.6736) = 4.0110$$

At this point, we should note that the Black–Scholes–Merton model is extremely sensitive to rounding errors. In particular, the process of looking up values in the normal probability table is a major source of error. A number of other ways exist to obtain $N(d_1)$ and $N(d_2)$, such as using Microsoft Excel's function "=normsdist()". Using a more precise method, such as Excel, the value of the call would be 8.619. Note that this is the value to which the binomial option price converged in the example we showed with 1,000 time periods in Exhibit 76-23. Indeed, the Black–Scholes–Merton model is said to be the continuous limit of the binomial model.

Practice Problem 8

Use the Black–Scholes–Merton model to calculate the prices of European call and put options on an asset priced at 68.5. The exercise price is 65, the continuously compounded risk-free rate is 4 percent, the options expire in 110 days, and the volatility is 0.38. There are no cash flows on the underlying.

SOLUTION

The time to expiration will be $T = 110/365 = 0.3014$. Then d_1 and d_2 are

$$d_1 = \frac{\ln(68.5/65) + (0.04 + (0.38)^2/2)(0.3014)}{0.38\sqrt{0.3014}} = 0.4135$$
$$d_2 = 0.4135 - 0.38\sqrt{0.3014} = 0.2049$$

Looking up in the normal probability table, we have

$$N(0.41) = 0.6591$$
$$N(0.20) = 0.5793$$

Plugging into the option price formula,

$$c = 68.5(0.6591) - 65e^{-0.04(0.3014)}(0.5793) = 7.95$$
$$p = 65e^{-0.04(0.3014)}(1 - 0.5793) - 68.5(1 - 0.6591) = 3.67$$

Let us now take a look at the various inputs required in the Black–Scholes–Merton model. We need to know where to obtain the inputs and how the option price varies with these inputs.

7.3 Inputs to the Black–Scholes–Merton Model

The Black–Scholes–Merton model has five inputs: the underlying price, the exercise price, the risk-free rate, the time to expiration, and the volatility.[30] As we have previously seen, call option prices should be higher the higher the underlying price, the longer the time to expiration, the higher the volatility, and the higher the risk-free rate. They should be lower the higher the exercise price. Put option prices should be higher the higher the exercise price and the higher the volatility. They should be lower the higher the underlying price and the higher the risk-free rate. As we saw, European put option prices can be either higher or lower the longer the time to expiration. American put option prices are always higher the longer the time to expiration, but the Black–Scholes–Merton model does not apply to American options.

These relationships are general to any European and American options and do not require the Black–Scholes–Merton model to understand them. Nonetheless, the Black–Scholes–Merton model provides an excellent opportunity to examine these relationships more closely. We can calculate and plot relationships such as those mentioned, which are usually called the option Greeks, because they are often referred to with Greek names. Let us now look at each of the inputs and the various option Greeks.

7.3.1 The Underlying Price: Delta and Gamma

The price of the underlying is generally one of the easiest sources of input information. Suffice it to say that if an investor cannot obtain the price of the underlying, then she should not even be considering the option. The price should generally be obtained as a quote or trade price from a liquid, open market.

The relationship between the option price and the underlying price has a special name: It is called the option **delta**. In fact, the delta can be obtained approximately from the Black–Scholes–Merton formula as the value of $N(d_1)$ for calls and $N(d_1) - 1$ for puts. More formally, the delta is defined as

$$\text{Delta} = \frac{\text{Change in option price}}{\text{Change in underlying price}} \quad \textbf{(76-23)}$$

The above definition for delta is exact; the use of $N(d_1)$ for calls and $N(d_1) - 1$ for puts is approximate. Later in this section, we shall see why $N(d_1)$ and $N(d_2)$ are approximations and when they are good or bad approximations.

Let us consider the example we previously worked, where S = 52.75, X = 50, r^c = 0.0488, T = 0.75, and σ = 0.35. Using a computer to obtain a more precise Black–Scholes–Merton answer, we get a call option price of 8.6186 and a put option price of 4.0717. $N(d_1)$, the call delta, is 0.6733, so the put delta is $0.6733 - 1 = -0.3267$. Given that Delta = (Change in option price/Change in underlying price), we should expect that

Change in option price = Delta × Change in underlying price.

Therefore, for a $1 change in the price of the underlying, we should expect

Change in call option price = 0.6733(1) = 0.6733
Change in put option price = −0.3267(1) = −0.3267

---

[30] Later we shall add one more input, cash flows on the underlying.

This calculation would mean that

Approximate new call option price = 8.6186 + 0.6733 = 9.2919
Approximate new put option price = 4.0717 − 0.3267 = 3.7450

To test the accuracy of this approximation, we let the underlying price move up $1 to $53.75 and re-insert these values into the Black–Scholes–Merton model. We would then obtain

Actual new call option price = 9.3030
Actual new put option price = 3.7560

The delta approximation is fairly good, but not perfect.

Delta is important as a risk measure. *The delta defines the sensitivity of the option price to a change in the price of the underlying.* Traders, especially dealers in options, use delta to construct hedges to offset the risk they have assumed by buying and selling options. For example, recall from Reading 74 that FRA dealers offer to take either side of an FRA transaction. They then usually hedge the risk they have assumed by entering into other transactions. These same types of dealers offer to buy and sell options, hedging that risk with other transactions. For example, suppose we are a dealer offering to sell the call option we have been working with above. A customer buys 1,000 options for 8.619. We now are short 1,000 call options, which exposes us to considerable risk if the underlying goes up. So we must buy a certain number of units of the underlying to hedge this risk. We previously showed that the delta is 0.6733, so we would buy 673 units of the underlying at 52.75.[31] Assume for the moment that the delta tells us precisely the movement in the option for a movement in the underlying. Then suppose the underlying moves up $1:

Change in value of 1,000 long units of the underlying: 673(+$1) = $673
Change in value of 1,000 short options: 1,000(+$1)(0.6733) ≈ $673

Because we are long the underlying and short the options, these values offset. At this point, however, the delta has changed. If we recalculate it, we would find it to be 0.6953. This would require that we have 695 units of the underlying, so we would need to buy an additional 22 units. We would borrow the money to do this. In some cases, we would need to sell off units of the underlying, in which case we would invest the money in the risk-free asset.

We shall return to the topic of delta hedging in Reading 78. For now, however, let us consider how changes in the underlying price will change the delta. In fact, even if the underlying price does not change, the delta would still change as the option moves toward expiration. For a call, the delta will increase toward 1.0 as the underlying price moves up and will decrease toward 0.0 as the underlying price moves down. For a put, the delta will decrease toward −1.0 as the underlying price moves down and increase towards 0.0 as the underlying price moves up.[32] If the underlying price does not move, a call delta will move toward 1.0 if the call is in-the-money or 0.0 if the call is out-of-the-money as the call moves toward the expiration day. A put delta will move toward −1.0 if the put is in-the-money or 0.0 if the put is out-of-the-money as it moves toward expiration.

So the delta is constantly changing, which means that delta hedging is a dynamic process. In fact, delta hedging is often referred to as **dynamic hedging**. In theory, the delta is changing continuously and the hedge should be adjusted continuously, but

---

[31] This transaction would require 673($52.75) = $35,500, less the 1,000($8.619) = $8,619 received from the sale of the option, for a total investment required of $26,881. We would probably borrow this money.

[32] Remember that the put delta is negative; hence, its movement is down toward −1.0 or up toward 0.0.

continuous adjustment is not possible in reality. When the hedge is not adjusted continuously, we are admitting the possibility of much larger moves in the price of the underlying. Let us see what happens in that case.

Using our previous example, we allow an increase in the underlying price of $10 to $62.75. Then the call price should change by $0.6733(10) = 6.733$, and the put option price should change by $-0.3267(10) = -3.267$. Thus, the approximate prices would be

Approximate new call option price = 8.619 + 6.733 = 15.3520
Approximate new put option price = 4.0717 − 3.267 = 0.8047

The actual prices are obtained by recalculating the option values using the Black–Scholes–Merton model with an underlying price of 62.75. Using a computer for greater precision, we find that these prices are

Actual new call option price = 16.3026
Actual new put option price = 1.7557

The approximations based on delta are not very accurate. In general, the larger the move in the underlying, the worse the approximation. This will make delta hedging less effective.

Exhibit 76-25 shows the relationship between the option price and the underlying price. Panel A depicts the relationship for calls and Panel B shows the corresponding relationship for puts. Notice the curvature in the relationship between the option price and the underlying price. Call option values definitely increase the greater the underlying value, and put option values definitely decrease. But the amount of change is not the same in each direction. $N(d_1)$ measures the slope of this line at a given point. As such, it measures only the slope for a very small change in the underlying. When the underlying changes by more than a very small amount, the curvature of the line comes into play and distorts the relationship between the option price and underlying price that is explained by the delta. The problem here is much like the relationship between a bond price and its yield. This first-order relationship between a bond price and its yield is called the duration; therefore, duration is similar to delta.

The curvature or second-order effect is known in the fixed income world as the convexity. In the options world, this effect is called **gamma**. Gamma is a numerical measure of how sensitive the delta is to a change in the underlying—in other words, how much the delta changes. When gamma is large, the delta changes rapidly and cannot provide a good approximation of how much the option moves for each unit of movement in the underlying. We shall not concern ourselves with measuring and using gamma, but we should know a few things about the gamma and, therefore, about the behavior of the delta.

Gamma is larger when there is more uncertainty about whether the option will expire in- or out-of-the-money. This means that *gamma will tend to be large when the option is at-the-money and close to expiration.* In turn, this statement means that delta will be a poor approximation for the option's price sensitivity when it is at-the-money and close to the expiration day. Thus, a **delta hedge** will work poorly. When the gamma is large, we may need to use a gamma-based hedge, which would require that we add a position in another option to the delta-hedge position of the underlying and the option. We shall not take up this advanced topic here.

7.3.2 The Exercise Price

The exercise price is easy to obtain. It is specified in the option contract and does not change. Therefore, it is not worthwhile to speak about what happens when the

| EXHIBIT 76-25 | The Relationship between Option Price and Underlying Price X = 50, r^c = 0.0488, T = 0.75, σ = 0.35 |

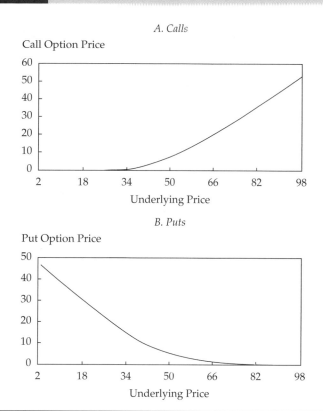

A. Calls

Call Option Price

Underlying Price

B. Puts

Put Option Price

Underlying Price

exercise price changes, but we can talk about how the option price would differ if we choose an option with a different exercise price. As we have previously seen, the call option price will be lower the higher the exercise price and the put option price will be higher. This relationship is confirmed for our sample option in Exhibit 76-26.

| EXHIBIT 76-26 | The Relationship between Option Price and Exercise Price S = 52.75, r^c = 0.0488, T = 0.75, σ = 0.35 |

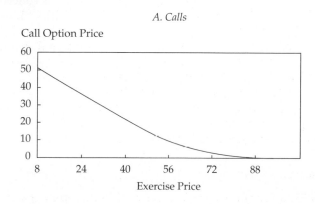

A. Calls

Call Option Price

Exercise Price

(Exhibit continued on next page ...)

EXHIBIT 76-26   **(continued)**

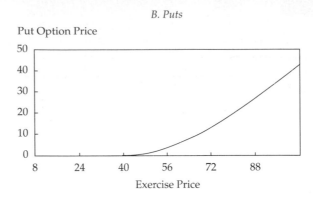

B. Puts

7.3.3 The Risk-Free Rate: Rho

The risk-free rate is the continuously compounded rate on the risk-free security whose maturity corresponds to the option's life. We have used the risk-free rate in previous readings; sometimes we have used the discrete version and sometimes the continuous version. As we have noted, the continuously compounded risk-free rate is the natural log of 1 plus the discrete risk-free rate.

For example, suppose the discrete risk-free rate quoted in annual terms is 5 percent. Then the continuous rate is

$$r^c = \ln(1 + r) = \ln(1.05) = 0.0488$$

Let us recall the difference in these two specifications. Suppose we want to find the present value of \$1 in six months using both the discrete and continuous risk-free rates.

$$\text{Present value using discrete rate} = \frac{1}{(1 + r)^T} = \frac{1}{(1.05)^{0.5}} = 0.9759$$

$$\text{Present value using continuous rate} = e^{-r^c T} = e^{-0.0488(0.5)} = 0.9759$$

Obviously either specification will work. Because of how it uses the risk-free rate in the calculation of d_1, however, the Black–Scholes–Merton model requires the continuous risk-free rate.

The sensitivity of the option price to the risk-free rate is called the **rho.** We shall not concern ourselves with the calculation of rho. Technically, the Black–Scholes–Merton model assumes a constant risk-free rate, so it is meaningless to talk about the risk-free rate changing over the life of the option. We can, however, explore how the option price would differ if the current rate were different. Exhibit 76-27 depicts this effect. Note how little change occurs in the option price over a very broad range of the risk-free rate. Indeed, *the price of a European option on an asset is not very sensitive to the risk-free rate.*[33]

---

[33] When the underlying is an interest rate, however, there is a strong relationship between the option price and interest rates.

EXHIBIT 76-27	The Relationship between Option Price and Risk-Free Rate S = 52.75, X = 50, T = 0.75, σ = 0.35

A. Calls

Call Option Price

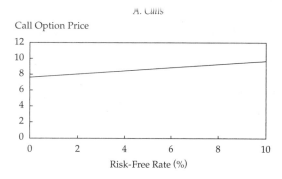

Risk-Free Rate (%)

B. Puts

Put Option Price

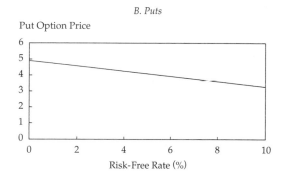

Risk-Free Rate (%)

7.3.4 Time to Expiration: Theta

Time to expiration is an easy input to determine. An option has a definite expiration date specified in the contract. We simply count the number of days until expiration and divide by 365, as we have done previously with forward and futures contracts.

Obviously, the time remaining in an option's life moves constantly towards zero. Even if the underlying price is constant, the option price will still change. We noted that American options have both an intrinsic value and a time value. For European options, all of the price can be viewed as time value. In either case, time value is a function of the option's moneyness, its time to expiration, and its volatility. The more uncertainty there is, the greater the time value. As expiration approaches, the option price moves toward the payoff value of the option at expiration, a process known as **time value decay**. The rate at which the time value decays is called the option's **theta**. We shall not concern ourselves with calculating the specific value of theta, but be aware that if the option price decreases as time moves forward, the theta will be negative. Exhibit 76-28 shows the time value decay for our sample option.

Note that both call and put values decrease as the time to expiration decreases. We previously noted that European put options do not necessarily do this. For some cases, European put options can increase in value as the time to expiration decreases, the case of a positive theta, but that is not so for our put.[34] *Most of the time, option prices are higher the longer the time to expiration. For European puts, however, some exceptions exist.*

---

[34] Positive put thetas tend to occur when the put is deep in-the-money, the volatility is low, the interest rate is high, and the time to expiration is low.

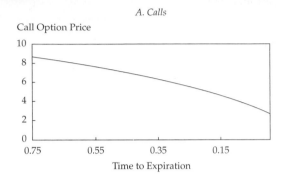

EXHIBIT 76-28 The Relationship between Option Price and Time to Expiration S = 52.75, X = 50, r^c = 0.0488, σ = 0.35. T Starts at 0.75 and Goes toward 0.0

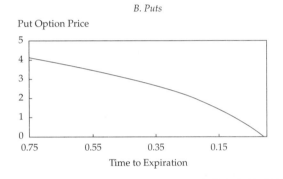

7.3.5 Volatility: Vega

As we have previously noted, volatility is the standard deviation of the continuously compounded return on the stock. We have also noted that the volatility is an extremely important variable in the valuation of an option. It is the only variable that cannot be obtained easily and directly from another source. In addition, as we illustrate here, option prices are extremely sensitive to the volatility. We take up the subject of estimating volatility in Section 7.5.

The relationship between option price and volatility is called the **vega,** which—albeit considered an option Greek—is not actually a Greek word.[35] We shall not concern ourselves with the actual calculation of the vega, but know that the vega is positive for both calls and puts, meaning that if the volatility increases, both call and put prices increase. Also, the vega is larger the closer the option is to being at-the-money.

In the problem we previously worked (S_0 = \$52.75, X = \$50, r^c = 0.0488, T = 0.75), at a volatility of 0.35, the option price was 8.619. Suppose we erroneously use a volatility of 0.40. Then the call price would be 9.446. An error in the volatility of this magnitude would not be difficult to make, especially for a variable that is not directly observable. Yet the result is a very large error in the option price.

Exhibit 76-29 displays the relationship between the option price and the volatility. Note that this relationship is nearly linear and that the option price varies over a very wide range, although this near-linearity is not the case for all options.

---

[35] So that all of these effects ("the Greeks") be named after Greek words, the term *kappa* is sometimes used to represent the relationship between an option price and its volatility. As it turns out, however, vega is used far more often than kappa and is probably easier to remember, given the "v" in vega and the "v" in volatility. Vega, however, is a star, not a letter, and its origin is Latin.

EXHIBIT 76-29	The Relationship between Option Price and Volatility S = 52.75, X = 50, r^c = 0.0488, T = 0.75

A. Calls

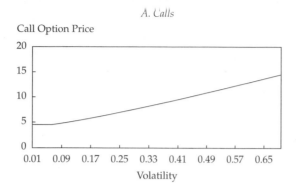

B. Puts

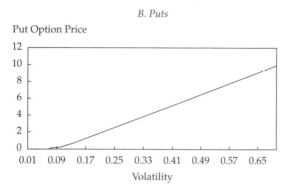

7.4 The Effect of Cash Flows on the Underlying

As we saw in Readings 74 and 75, cash flows on the underlying affect the prices of forward and futures contracts. It should follow that they would affect the prices of options. In studying the option boundary conditions and put–call parity earlier in this reading, we noted that we subtract the present value of the dividends from the underlying price and use this adjusted price to obtain the boundary conditions or to price the options using put–call parity. We do the same using the Black–Scholes–Merton model. Specifically, we introduced the expression PV(CF,0,T) for the present value of the cash flows on the underlying over the life of the option. So, we simply use $S_0 - $ PV(CF,0,T) in the Black–Scholes–Merton model instead of S_0.

Recall that in previous readings, we also used continuous compounding to express the cash flows. For stocks, we used a continuously compounded dividend yield; for currencies, we used a continuously compounded interest rate. In the case of stocks, we let δ^c represent the continuously compounded dividend rate. Then we substituted for $S_0 e^{-\delta^c T}$ for S_0 in the Black–Scholes–Merton formula. For a foreign currency, we let S_0 represent the exchange rate, which we discount using r^{fc}, the continuously compounded foreign risk-free rate. Let us work an example involving a foreign currency option.

Let the exchange rate of U.S. dollars for euros be $0.8475. The continuously compounded U.S. risk-free rate, which in this example is r^c, is 5.10 percent. The continuously compounded euro risk-free rate, r^{fc}, is 4.25 percent. A call option expires in 125 days (T = 125/365 = 0.3425) and has an exercise price of $0.90. The volatility of the continuously compounded exchange rate is 0.055.

The first thing we do is obtain the adjusted price of the underlying: $0.8475e^{-0.0425(0.3425)} = 0.8353$. We then use this value as S_0 in the formula for d_1 and d_2:

$$d_1 = \frac{\ln(0.8353/0.90) + [0.051 + (0.055)^2/2](0.3425)}{0.055\sqrt{0.3425}} = -1.7590$$

$$d_2 = -1.7590 - 0.055\sqrt{0.3425} = -1.7912$$

Using the normal probability table, we find that

$$N(d_1) = N(-1.76) = 1 - 0.9608 = 0.0392$$
$$N(d_2) = N(-1.79) = 1 - 0.9633 = 0.0367$$

In discounting the exercise rate to evaluate the second term in the Black–Scholes–Merton expression, we use the domestic (here, U.S.) continuously compounded risk-free rate. The call option price would thus be

$$c = 0.8353(0.0392) - 0.90e^{-0.051(0.3425)}(0.0367) = 0.0003$$

Therefore, this call option on an asset worth $0.8575 would cost $0.0003.

Practice Problem 9

Use the Black–Scholes–Merton model adjusted for cash flows on the underlying to calculate the price of a call option in which the underlying is priced at 225, the exercise price is 200, the continuously compounded risk-free rate is 5.25 percent, the time to expiration is three years, and the volatility is 0.15. The effect of cash flows on the underlying is indicated below for two alternative approaches:

A. The present value of the cash flows over the life of the option is 19.72.

B. The continuously compounded dividend yield is 2.7 percent.

SOLUTIONS

A. Adjust the price of the underlying to $S_0 - 225 - 19.72 = 205.28$. Then insert into the Black–Scholes–Merton formula as follows:

$$d_1 = \frac{\ln(205.28/200) + [0.0525 + (0.15)^2/2](3.0)}{0.15\sqrt{3.0}} = 0.8364$$

$$d_2 = 0.8364 - 0.15\sqrt{3.0} = 0.5766$$
$$N(0.84) = 0.7995$$
$$N(0.58) = 0.7190$$
$$c = 205.28(0.7995) - 200e^{-0.0525(3.0)}(0.7190) = 41.28$$

B. Adjust the price of the underlying to $S_0 = 225e^{-0.027(3.0)} = 207.49$

$$d_1 = \frac{\ln(207.49/200) + [0.0525 + (0.15)^2/2](3.0)}{0.15\sqrt{3.0}} = 0.8776$$

$$d_2 = 0.8776 - 0.15\sqrt{3.0} = 0.6178$$
$$N(0.88) = 0.8106$$

$$N(0.62) = 0.7324$$
$$c = 207.49(0.8106) - 200e^{-0.0525(3.0)}(0.7324) = 43.06$$

7.5 The Critical Role of Volatility

As we have previously stressed, volatility is an extremely important variable in the pricing of options. In fact, with the possible exception of the cash flows on the underlying, it is the only variable that cannot be directly observed and easily obtained. It is, after all, the volatility over the life of the option; therefore, it is not past or current volatility but rather the future volatility. Differences in opinion on option prices nearly always result from differences of opinion about volatility. But how does one obtain a number for the future volatility?

7.5.1 Historical Volatility

The most logical starting place to look for an estimate of future volatility is past volatility. When the underlying is a publicly traded asset, we usually can collect some data over a recent past period and estimate the standard deviation of the continuously compounded return.

Exhibit 76-30 illustrates this process for a sample of 12 monthly prices of a particular stock. We convert these prices to returns, convert the returns to continuously compounded returns, find the variance of the series of continuously compounded returns, and then convert the variance to the standard deviation. In this example, the data are monthly returns, so we must annualize the variance by multiplying it by 12. Then we take the square root to obtain the historical estimate of the annual standard deviation or volatility.

EXHIBIT 76-30	Estimating Historical Volatility		

Month	Price	Return	Log Return	(Log Return-Average)^2
0	100			
1	102	0.020000	0.019803	0.000123
2	99	−0.029412	−0.029853	0.001486
3	97	−0.020202	−0.020409	0.000847
4	89	−0.082474	−0.086075	0.008982
5	103	0.157303	0.146093	0.018878
6	104	0.009709	0.009662	0.000001
7	102	−0.019231	−0.019418	0.000790
8	99	−0.029412	−0.029853	0.001486
9	104	0.050505	0.049271	0.001646
10	102	−0.019231	−0.019418	0.000790
11	105	0.029412	0.028988	0.000412
12	111	0.057143	0.055570	0.002197
		Sum	0.104360	0.037639
		Average	0.008697	

(Exhibit continued on next page ...)

EXHIBIT 76-30   (continued)

The variance is estimated as follows:

$$\sigma^2 = \frac{\sum_{i=1}^{N} (R_i^c - \overline{R}^c)^2}{N - 1}$$

where R_i^c is the continuously compounded return for observation i (shown above in the fourth column and calculated as $\ln(1 + R_i)$, where i goes from 1 to 12) and R_i is the ith return, $\overline{R}^c$ is the average return over the entire sample, and N is the number of observations in the sample (here, N = 12). Then

$$\sigma^2 = \frac{0.037639}{11} = 0.003422$$

Because this sample consists of monthly returns, to obtain the annual variance, we must multiply this number by 12 (or 52 for weekly, or 250—the approximate number of trading days in a year—for daily). Thus

$$\sigma^2 = 12(0.003422) = 0.041064$$

The annual standard deviation or volatility is, therefore,

$$\sigma = \sqrt{0.041064} = 0.2026$$

So the historical volatility estimate is 20.26 percent.

The historical estimate of the volatility is based only on what happened in the past. To get the best estimate, we must use a lot of prices, but that means going back farther in time. The farther back we go, the less current the data become, and the less reliable our estimate of the volatility. We now look at a way of obtaining a more current estimate of the volatility, but one that raises questions as well as answers them.

7.5.2 Implied Volatility

In a market in which options are traded actively, we can reasonably assume that the market price of the option is an accurate reflection of its true value. Thus, by setting the Black–Scholes–Merton price equal to the market price, we can work backwards to infer the volatility. This procedure enables us to determine the volatility that option traders are using to price the option. This volatility is called the **implied volatility**.

Unfortunately, determining implied volatility is not a simple task. We cannot simply solve the Black–Scholes–Merton equation for the volatility. It is a complicated function with the volatility appearing several times, in some cases as σ^2. There are some mathematical techniques that speed up the estimation of the implied volatility. Here, however, we shall look at only the most basic method: trial and error.

Recall the option we have been working with. The underlying price is 52.75, the exercise price is 50, the risk-free rate is 4.88 percent, and the time to expiration is 0.75. In our previous examples, the volatility was 0.35. Using these values in the Black–Scholes–Merton model, we obtained a call option price of 8.619. Suppose we observe the option selling in the market for 9.25. What volatility would produce this price?

We have already calculated a price of 8.619 at a volatility of 0.35. Because the call price varies directly with the volatility, we know that it would take a volatility greater than 0.35 to produce a price higher than 8.619. We do not know how much higher, so we should just take a guess. Let us try a volatility of 0.40. Using the Black–Scholes–Merton formula with a volatility of 0.40, we obtain a price of 9.446. This is too high, so we try a lower volatility. We keep doing this in the following manner:

Volatility	Black–Scholes–Merton Price
0.35	8.619
0.40	9.446
0.39	9.280
0.38	9.114

So now we know that the correct volatility lies between 0.38 and 0.39, closer to 0.39. In solving for the implied volatility, we must decide either how close to the option price we want to be or how many significant digits we want in the implied volatility. If we choose four significant digits in the implied volatility, a value of 0.3882 would produce the option price of 9.2500. Alternatively, if we decide that we want to be within 0.01 of the option price, we would find that the implied volatility is in the range of 38.76 to 38.88 percent.

Thus, if the option is selling for about 9.25, we say that the market is pricing it at a volatility of 0.3882. This number represents the market's best estimate of the true volatility of the underlying asset; it can be viewed as a more current source of volatility information than the past volatility. Unfortunately, a circularity exists in the argument. If one uses the Black–Scholes–Merton model to determine if an option is over- or underpriced, the procedure for extracting the implied volatility assumes that the market correctly prices the option. The only way to use the implied volatility in identifying mispriced options is to interpret the implied volatility as either too high or too low, which would require an estimate of true volatility. Nonetheless, the implied volatility is a source of valuable information on the uncertainty in the underlying, and option traders use it routinely.

All of this material on continuous-time option pricing has been focused on options in which the underlying is an asset. As we described earlier in this reading, there are also options on futures. Let us take a look at the pricing of options on futures, which will pave the way for a continuous-time pricing model for options on interest rates, another case in which the underlying is not an asset.

8   PRICING OPTIONS ON FORWARD AND FUTURES CONTRACTS AND AN APPLICATION TO INTEREST RATE OPTION PRICING

Earlier in this reading, we discussed how options on futures contracts are active, exchange-traded options in which the underlying is a futures contract. In addition, there are over-the-counter options in which the underlying is a forward contract. In our treatment of these instruments, we assume constant interest rates. As we learned in Readings 74 and 75, this assumption means that futures and forward contracts will have the same prices. European options on futures and forward contracts will, therefore, have the same prices. American options on forwards will differ in price from American options on futures, and we discuss this later.

First we take a quick look at the basic rules that we previously developed for options on underlying assets. If the underlying asset is a futures contract, the payoff values of the options at expiration are

$$c_T = Max[0, f_T(T) - X]$$
$$p_T = Max[0, X - f_T(T)]$$ **(76-24)**

where $f_T(T)$ is the price of a futures contract at T in which the contract expires at T. Thus, $f_T(T)$ is the futures price at expiration. These formulas are, of course, the same as for options when the underlying is an asset, with the futures price substituted for the asset price. When the option and the futures expire simultaneously, the futures price at expiration, $f_T(T)$, converges to the asset price, S_T, making the above payoffs precisely the same as those of the option on the underlying asset.

The minimum and maximum values for options on forwards or futures are the same as those we obtained for options on assets, substituting the futures price for the asset price. Specifically,

$$0 \leq c_0 \leq f_0(T)$$
$$0 \leq C_0 \leq f_0(T)$$
$$0 \leq p_0 \leq X/(1 + r)^T$$ **(76-25)**
$$0 \leq P_0 \leq X$$

We also established lower bounds for European options and intrinsic values for American options and used these results to establish the minimum prices of these options. For options on futures, the lower bounds are

$$c_0 \geq Max\{0, [f_0(T) - X]/(1 + r)^T\}$$
$$p_0 \geq Max\{0, [X - f_0(T)]/(1 + r)^T\}$$ **(76-26)**

where $f_0(T)$ is the price at time 0 of a futures contract expiring at T. Therefore, the price of a European call or put on the futures is either zero or the difference between the futures price and exercise price, as formulated above, discounted to the present. For American options on futures, early exercise is possible. Thus, we express their lowest prices as the intrinsic values:

$$C_0 \geq Max[0, f_0(T) - X]$$
$$P_0 \geq Max[0, X - f_0(T)]$$ **(76-27)**

Because these values are greater than the lower bounds, we maintain these values as the minimum prices of American calls.[36]

As we have previously pointed out, with the assumption of constant interest rates, futures prices and forward prices are the same. We can treat European options on futures the same way as options on forwards. American options on futures will differ from American options on forwards. Now we explore how put–call parity works for options on forwards.

8.1 Put–Call Parity for Options on Forwards

In an earlier section, we examined put–call parity. Now we take a look at the parity between puts and calls on forward contracts and their underlying forward contracts. First recall the notation: $F(0,T)$ is the price established at time 0 for a forward contract expiring at time T. Let c_0 and p_0 be the prices today of calls and puts on the forward contract. We shall assume that the puts and calls expire when the forward contract expires. The exercise price of the options is X. The payoff of the call is $Max(0,S_T - X)$, and the payoff of the put is $Max(0,X - S_T)$.[37] We construct a combination consisting of a long call and a long position in a zero-coupon bond with face value of $X - F(0,T)$. We construct another combination consisting of a long position in a put and a long position in a forward contract. Exhibit 76-31 shows the results.

EXHIBIT 76-31	Portfolio Combinations for Equivalent Packages of Puts, Calls, and Forward Contracts (Put–Call Parity for Forward Contracts		
		Value at Expiration	
Transaction	**Current Value**	$S_T \leq X$	$S_T > X$
Call and Bond			
Buy call	c_0	0	$S_T - X$
Buy bond	$[X - F(0,T)]/(1 + r)^T$	$X - F(0,T)$	$X - F(0,T)$
Total	$c_0 + [X - F(0,T)]/(1 + r)^T$	$X - F(0,T)$	$S_T - F(0,T)$
Put and Forward			
Buy put	p_0	$X - S_T$	0
Buy forward contract	0	$S_T - F(0,T)$	$S_T - F(0,T)$
Total	p_0	$X - F(0,T)$	$S_T - F(0,T)$

As the exhibit demonstrates, both combinations produce a payoff of either $X - F(0,T)$ or $S_T - F(0,T)$, whichever is greater. The call and bond combination is thus equivalent to the put and forward contract combination. Hence, to prevent an arbitrage opportunity, the initial values of these combinations must be the same. The initial value of the call and bond combination is $c_0 + [X - F(0,T)]/(1 + r)^T$. The forward contract has zero initial value, so the initial value of the put and forward contract combination is only the initial value of the put, p_0. Therefore,

---

[36] In other words, we cannot use the European lower bound as the lowest price of an American call or put, as we could with calls when the underlying was an asset instead of a futures.

[37] Recall that the option payoffs are given by the underlying price at expiration, because the forward contract expires when the option expires. Therefore, the forward price at expiration is the underlying price at expiration.

$$c_0 + [X - F(0,T)]/(1 + r)^T = p_0 \qquad\qquad \textbf{(76-28)}$$

This equation is **put–call parity for options on forward contracts.**

Note that we seem to have implied that the bond is a long position, but that might not be the case. The bond should have a face value of $X - F(0,T)$. We learned in Reading 74 that $F(0,T)$ is determined in the market as the underlying price compounded at the risk-free rate.[38] Because there are a variety of options with different exercise prices, any one of which could be chosen, it is clearly possible for X to exceed or be less than $F(0,T)$. If $X > F(0,T)$, we are long the bond, because the payoff of $X - F(0,T)$ is greater than zero, meaning that we get back money from the bond. If $X < F(0,T)$, we issue the bond, because the payoff of $X - F(0,T)$ is less than zero, meaning that we must pay back money. Note the special case when $X = F(0,T)$. The bond is effectively out of the picture. Then $c_0 = p_0$.

Now recall from Reading 75 that with discrete interest compounding and no storage costs, the forward price is the spot price compounded at the risk-free rate. So,

$$F(0,T) = S_0(1 + r)^T$$

If we substitute this result for $F(0,T)$ in the put–call parity equation for options on forwards, we obtain

$$p_0 + S_0 = c_0 + X/(1 + r)^T$$

which is the put–call parity equation for options on the underlying that we learned earlier in this reading. Indeed, put–call parity for options on forwards and put–call parity for options on the underlying asset are the same. The only difference is that in the former, the forward contract and the bond replace the underlying. Given the equivalence of options on the forward contract and options on the underlying, we can refer to put–call parity for options on forwards as **put–call–forward parity**. The equation

$$c_0 + [X - F(0,T)]/(1 + r)^T = p_0$$

expresses the relationship between the forward price and the prices of the options on the underlying asset, or alternatively between the forward price and the prices of options on the forward contract. We can also rearrange the equation to isolate the forward price and obtain

$$F(0,T) = (c_0 - p_0)(1 + r)^T + X$$

which shows how the forward price is related to the put and call prices and to the exercise price.

Now observe in Exhibit 76-32 how a synthetic forward contract can be created out of options. In the top half of the exhibit is a forward contract. Its payoff at expiration is $S_T - F(0,T)$. In the bottom half of the exhibit is a **synthetic forward contract**, which consists of a long call, a short put, and a long risk-free bond with a face value equal to the exercise price minus the forward price. Note that this bond can actually be short if the exercise price of these options is lower than the forward price. The forward contract and synthetic forward contract have the same payoffs, so their initial values must be equal. The initial value of the forward contract is zero, so the initial value of the synthetic forward contract must be zero. Thus,

$$c_0 - p_0 + [X - F(0,T)]/(1 + r)^T = 0$$

---

[38] We are, of course, assuming no cash flows or costs on the underlying asset.

		Value at Expiration	
Transaction	Current Value	$S_T \leq X$	$S_T > X$
Forward Contract			
Long forward contract	0	$S_T - F(0,T)$	$S_T - F(0,T)$
Synthetic Forward Contract			
Buy call	c_0	0	$S_T - X$
Sell put	$-p_0$	$-(X - S_T)$	0
Buy (or sell) bond	$[X - F(0,T)]/(1 + r)^T$	$X - F(0,T)$	$X - F(0,T)$
Total	$c_0 - p_0 + [X - F(0,T)]/(1 + r)^T$	$S_T - F(0,T)$	$S_T - F(0,T)$

EXHIBIT 76-32 Forward Contract and Synthetic Forward Contract

Solving for $F(0,T)$, we obtain the equation for the forward price in terms of the call, put, and bond that was given previously. So a synthetic forward contract is a combination consisting of a long call, a short put, and a zero-coupon bond with face value of $X - F(0,T)$.

Consider the following example: The options and a forward contract expire in 50 days, so $T = 50/365 = 0.1370$. The risk-free rate is 6 percent, and the exercise price is 95. The call price is 5.50, the put price is 10.50, and the forward price is 90.72. Substituting in the above equation, we obtain

$$5.50 - 10.50 + \frac{95 - 90.72}{(1.06)^{0.1370}} = -0.7540$$

which is supposed to be zero. The left-hand side replicates a forward contract. Thus, the synthetic forward is underpriced. We buy it and sell the actual forward contract. So if we buy the call, sell the put, and buy the bond with face value $95 - 90.72 = 4.28$, we bring in 0.7540. At expiration, the payoffs are as follows.

The options and forward expire with the underlying above 95:

The bond matures and pays off $95 - 90.72 = 4.28$.

Exercise the call, paying 95 and obtaining the underlying.

Deliver the underlying and receive 90.72 from the forward contract.

The put expires with no value.

Net effect: No money in or out.

The options and forward expire with the underlying at or below 95:

The bond matures and pays off $95 - 90.72 = 4.28$.

Buy the underlying for 95 with the short put.

Deliver the underlying and receive 90.72 from the forward contract.

The call expires with no value.

Net effect: No money in or out.

So we take in 0.7540 up front and never have to pay anything out. The pressure of other investors doing this will cause the call price to increase and the put price to decrease until the above equation equals zero or is at least equal to the transaction costs that would be incurred to exploit any discrepancy from zero.

Practice Problem 10

Determine if a forward contract is correctly priced by using put–call–forward parity. The option exercise price is 90, the risk-free rate is 5 percent, the options and the forward contract expire in two years, the call price is 15.25, the put price is 3.00, and the forward price is 101.43.

SOLUTION

First note that the time to expiration is T = 2.0. There are many ways to express put–call–forward parity. We use the following specification:

$$p_0 = c_0 + [X - F(0,T)]/(1 + r)^T$$

The right-hand side is the synthetic put and consists of a long call, a short forward contract, and a bond with face value of $X - F(0,T)$. Substituting the values into the right-hand side, we obtain

$$p_0 = 15.25 + (90 - 101.43)/(1.05)^{2.0} = 4.88$$

Because the actual put is selling for 3.00, it is underpriced. So we should buy the put and sell the synthetic put. To sell the synthetic put we should sell the call, buy the forward contract, and hold a bond with face value $F(0,T) - X$. Doing so will generate the following cash flow up front:

Buy put:	−3.00
Sell call:	+15.25
Buy bond:	−(101.43 − 90)/(1.05)^{2.0} = −10.37
Total:	+1.88

Thus the transaction brings in 1.88 up front. The payoffs at expiration are

	$S_T < 90$	$S_T \geq 90$
Long put	$90 - S_T$	0
Short call	0	$-(S_T - 90)$
Long bond	101.43 − 90	101.43 − 90
Long forward	$S_T - 101.43$	$S_T - 101.43$
Total	0	0

Therefore, no money flows in or out at expiration.

Similarly, an option can be created from a forward contract. If a long forward contract is equivalent to a long call, short put, and zero-coupon bond with face value of $X - F(0,T)$, then a long call is a long forward, long put, and a zero-coupon bond with face value of $F(0,T) - X$. A long put is a long call, short forward, and a bond with face value of $X - F(0,T)$. These results are obtained just by rearranging what we learned here about forwards and options.

These results hold strictly for European options; some additional considerations exist for American options, but we do not cover them here.

8.2 Early Exercise of American Options on Forward and Futures Contracts

As we noted earlier, the holder of an American put option may want to exercise it early. For American call options on underlying assets that make no cash payments, however, there is no justification for exercising the option early. If the underlying asset makes a cash payment, such as a dividend on a stock or interest on a bond, it may be justifiable to exercise the call option early.

For American options on futures, it may be worthwhile to exercise both calls and puts early. Even though early exercise is never justified for American calls on underlying assets that make no cash payments, early exercise can be justified for American call options on futures. Deep-in-the money American call options on futures behave almost identically to the underlying, but the investor has money tied up in the call. If the holder exercises the call and establishes a futures position, he earns interest on the futures margin account. A similar argument holds for deep-in-the-money American put options on futures. The determination of the timing of early exercise is a specialist topic so we do not explore it here.

If the option is on a forward contract instead of a futures contract, however, these arguments are overshadowed by the fact that a forward contract does not pay off until expiration, in contrast to the mark-to-market procedure of futures contracts. Thus, if one exercised either a call or a put on a forward contract early, doing so would only establish a long or short position in a forward contract. This position would not pay any cash until expiration. No justification exists for exercising early if one cannot generate any cash from the exercise. Therefore, an American call on a forward contract is the same as a European call on a forward contract, but American calls on futures are different from European calls on futures and carry higher prices.

8.3 The Black Model

The usual model for pricing European options on futures is called the Black model, named after Fischer Black of Black–Scholes–Merton fame. The formula is

$$c = e^{-r^c T}[f_0(T)N(d_1) - XN(d_2)]$$

$$p = e^{-r^c T}(X[1 - N(d_2)] - f_0(T)[1 - N(d_1)])$$

where

$$d_1 = \frac{\ln(f_0(T)/X) + (\sigma^2/2)T}{\sigma\sqrt{T}}$$

$$d_2 = d_1 - \sigma\sqrt{T}$$

$f_0(T)$ = the futures price

and the other terms are those we have previously used. The volatility, σ, is the volatility of the continuously compounded change in the futures price.[39]

---

[39] If we were using the model to price options on forward contracts, we would insert $F(0,T)$, the forward price, instead of the futures price. Doing so would produce some confusion because we have never subscripted the forward price, arguing that it does not change. Therefore, although we could use the formula to price options on forwards at time 0, how could we use the formula to price options on forwards at a later time, say time t, prior to expiration? In that case, we would have to use the price of a newly constructed forward contract that expires at T, $F(t,T)$. Of course, with constant interest rates, these forward prices, $F(0,T)$ and $F(t,T)$, would be identical to the analogous futures price, $f_0(T)$ and $f_t(T)$. So, for ease of exposition we use the futures price.

Although the Black model may appear to give a somewhat different formula, it can be obtained directly from the Black–Scholes–Merton formula. Recall that the futures price in terms of the underlying spot price would be $f_0(T) = S_0 e^{r^c T}$. If we substitute the right-hand-side for $f_0(T)$ in the Black formula for d_1, we obtain the Black–Scholes–Merton formula for d_1.[40] Then if we substitute the right-hand side of the above for $f_0(T)$ in the Black formula for c_0 and p_0, we obtain the Black–Scholes–Merton formula for c_0 and p_0. These substitutions should make sense: The prices of options on futures equal the prices of options on the asset when the options and futures expire simultaneously.

The procedure should be straightforward if you have mastered substituting the asset price and other inputs into the Black–Scholes–Merton formula. Also, note that as with the Black–Scholes–Merton formula, the formula applies only to European options. As we noted in the previous section, early exercise of American options on futures is often justified, so we cannot get away with using this formula for American options on futures. We can, however, use the formula for American options on forwards, because they are never exercised early.

Practice Problem 11

The price of a forward contract is 139.19. A European option on the forward contract expires in 215 days. The exercise price is 125. The continuously compounded risk-free rate is 4.25 percent. The volatility is 0.15.

A. Use the Black model to determine the price of the call option.

B. Determine the price of the underlying from the above information and use the Black–Scholes–Merton model to show that the price of an option on the underlying is the same as the price of the option on the forward.

SOLUTIONS

The time to expiration is $T = 215/365 = 0.5890$.

A. First find d_1 and d_2, then $N(d_1)$ and $N(d_2)$, and then the call price:

$$d_1 = \frac{\ln(139.19/125) + [(0.15)^2/2]0.5890}{0.15\sqrt{0.5890}} = 0.9916$$

$$d_2 = 0.9916 - 0.15\sqrt{0.5890} = 0.8765$$

$$N(0.99) = 0.8389$$

$$N(0.88) = 0.8106$$

$$c = e^{-0.0425(0.5890)}[139.19(0.8389) - 125(0.8106)] = 15.06$$

B. We learned in Reading 74 that if there are no cash flows on the underlying and the interest is compounded continuously, the forward price is given by the formula $F(0, T) = S_0 e^{r^c T}$. We can thus find the spot price as

$$S_0 = F(0,T)e^{-r^c T} = 139.19 e^{-0.0425(0.5890)} = 135.75$$

---

[40] This action requires us to recognize that $\ln(S_0 e^{r^c T}/X) = \ln(S_0/X) + r^c T$.

Then we simply use the Black–Scholes–Merton formula:

$$d_1 = \frac{\ln(135.75/125) + (0.0425 + (0.15)^2/2)(0.5890)}{0.15\sqrt{0.5890}} = 0.9916$$

$$d_2 = 0.9916 - 0.15\sqrt{0.5890} = 0.8765$$

These are the same values as in Part A, so $N(d_1)$ and $N(d_2)$ will be the same. Plugging into the formula for the call price gives

$$c = 135.75(0.8389) - 125e^{-0.0425(0.5890)}(0.8106) = 15.06$$

This price is the same as in Part A.

8.4 Application of the Black Model to Interest Rate Options

Earlier in this reading, we described options on interest rates. These derivative instruments parallel the FRAs that we covered in Reading 74, in that they are derivatives in which the underlying is not a bond but rather an interest rate. Pricing options on interest rates is a challenging task. We showed how this is done using binomial trees. It would be nice if the Black–Scholes–Merton model could be easily used to price interest rate options, but the process is not so straightforward. Pricing options on interest rates requires a sophisticated model that prohibits arbitrage among interest-rate related instruments and their derivatives. The Black–Scholes–Merton model is not sufficiently general to use in this manner. Nonetheless, practitioners often employ the Black model to price interest rate options. Somewhat remarkably, perhaps, it is known to give satisfactory results. Therefore, we provide a quick overview of this practice here.

Suppose we wish to price a one-year interest rate cap, consisting of three caplets. One caplet expires in 90 days, one 180 days, and one in 270 days.[41] The exercise rate is 9 percent. To use the Black model, we use the forward rate as though it were $f_0(T)$.

Therefore, we also require its volatility and the risk-free rate for the period to the option's expiration.[42] Recalling that there are three caplets and we have to price each one individually, let us first focus on the caplet expiring in 90 days. We first specify that $T = 90/365 = 0.2466$. Then we need the forward rate today for the period day 90 to day 180. Let this rate be 9.25 percent. We shall assume its volatility is 0.03. We then need the continuously compounded risk-free rate for

---

[41] A one-year cap will have three individual caplets. The first expires in 90 days and pays off in 180 days, the second expires in 180 days and pays off in 270 days, and the third expires in 270 days and pays off in 360 days. The tendency to think that a one-year cap using quarterly periods should have four caplets is incorrect because there is no caplet expiring right now and paying off in 90 days. It would make no sense to create an option that expires immediately. Also, in a one-year loan, the rate is set at the start and reset only three times; hence, only three caplets are required.

[42] It is important to note here that the Black model requires that all inputs be in continuous compounding format. Therefore, the forward rate and risk-free rate would need to be the continuously compounded analogs to the discrete rates. Because the underlying is usually LIBOR, which is a discrete rate quoted on the basis of a 360-day year, some adjustments must be made to convert to a continuous rate quoted on the basis of a 365-day year. We will not address these adjustments here.

90 days, which we assume to be 9.60 percent. So now we have the following input variables:

$$T = 0.2466$$
$$f_0(T) = 0.0925$$
$$\sigma = 0.03$$
$$X = 0.09$$
$$r^c = 0.096$$

Inserting these inputs into the Black model produces

$$d_1 = \frac{\ln(0.0925/0.09) + [(0.03)^2/2](0.2466)}{0.03\sqrt{0.2466}} = 1.8466$$

$$d_2 = 1.8466 - 0.03\sqrt{0.2466} = 1.8317$$

$$N(1.85) = 0.9678$$

$$N(1.83) = 0.9664$$

$$c_0 = e^{-0.096(0.2466)}[0.0925(0.9678) - 0.09(0.9664)] = 0.00248594$$

(Because of the order of magnitude of the inputs, we carry the answer out to eight decimal places.) But this answer is not quite what we need. The formula gives the answer under the assumption that the option payoff occurs at the option expiration. As we know, interest rate options pay off later than their expirations. This option expires in 90 days and pays off 90 days after that. Therefore, we need to discount this result back from day 180 to day 90 using the forward rate of 9.25 percent.[43] We thus have

$$0.00248594e^{-0.0925(0.2466)} = 0.00242988$$

Another adjustment is necessary. Because the underlying price and exercise price are entered as rates, the resulting answer is a rate. Moreover, the underlying rate and exercise rate are expressed as annual rates, so the answer is an annual rate. Interest rate option prices are always quoted as periodic rates (which are prices for $1 notional principal). We would adjust this rate by multiplying by 90/360.[44] The price would thus be

$$0.00242988(90/360) = 0.00060747$$

Finally, we should note that this price is valid for a $1 notional principal option. If the notional principal were $1 million, the option price would be

$$\$1,000,000(0.00060747) = \$607.47$$

We have just priced the first caplet of this cap. To price the second caplet, we need the forward rate for the period 180 days to 270 days, we would use 180/365 = 0.4932 as the time to expiration, and we need the risk-free rate for 180 days. To price the third caplet, we need the forward rate for the period 270 days to 360 days, we would use 270/365 = 0.7397 as the time to expiration, and we need the

---

[43] Be very careful in this discounting procedure. The exponent in the exponential should have a time factor of the number of days between the option expiration and its payoff. Because there are 90 days between days 90 and 180, we use 90/365 = 0.2466. This value is not quite the same as the time until the option expiration, which today is 90 but which will count down to zero.

[44] It is customary in the interest rate options market to use 360 in the denominator to make this adjustment, even though we have used 365 in other places.

risk-free rate for 270 days. The price of the cap would be the sum of the prices of the three component caplets. If we were pricing a floor, we would price the component floorlets using the Black model for puts.

Although the Black model is frequently used to price interest rate options, binomial models, as we illustrated earlier, are somewhat more widely used in this area. These models are more attuned to deriving prices that prohibit arbitrage opportunities using any of the diverse instruments whose prices are given by the term structure. When you use the Black model to price interest rate options, there is some risk, perhaps minor, of having a counterparty be able to do arbitrage against you. Yet somehow the Black model is used often, and professionals seem to agree that it works remarkably well.

Practice Problem 12

Use the Black model to price an interest rate put that expires in 280 days. The forward rate is currently 6.8 percent, the 280-day continuously compounded risk-free rate is 6.25 percent, the exercise rate is 7 percent, and the volatility is 0.02. The option is based on a 180-day underlying rate, and the notional principal is $10 million.

SOLUTION

The time to expiration is $T = 280/365 = 0.7671$. Calculate the value of d_1, d_2, and $N(d_1)$, $N(d_2)$, and p_0 using the Black model:

$$d_1 = \frac{\ln(0.068/0.07) + [0.02]^2/2]0.7671}{0.02\sqrt{0.7671}} = -1.6461$$

$d_2 = -1.6461 - 0.02\sqrt{0.7671} = -1.6636$

$N(-1.65) = 1 - N(1.65) = 1 - 0.9505 = 0.0495$

$N(-1.66) = 1 - N(1.66) = 1 - 0.9515 = 0.0485$

$p_0 = e^{-0.0625(0.7671)}[0.07(1 - 0.0485) - 0.068(1 - 0.0495)] = 0.00187873$

This formula assumes the option payoff is made at expiration. For an interest rate option, that assumption is false. This is a 180-day rate, so the payoff is made 180 days later. Therefore, we discount the payoff over 180 days using the forward rate:

$e^{-0.068(180/365)}(0.00187873) = 0.00181677$

Interest rate option prices must reflect the fact that the rate used in the formula is quoted as an annual rate. So, we must multiply by 180/360 because the transaction is based on a 180-day rate:

$0.00181677(180/360) = 0.00090839$

Then we multiply by the notional principal:

$\$10,000,000(0.00090839) = \$9,084$

9   THE ROLE OF OPTIONS MARKETS

As we did with futures markets, we conclude the reading by looking at the important role options markets play in the financial system. Recall from Reading 73 that we looked at the purposes of derivative markets. We noted that derivative markets provide price discovery and risk management, make the markets for the underlying assets more efficient, and permit trading at low transaction costs. These features are also associated with options markets. Yet, options offer further advantages that some other derivatives do not offer.

For example, forward and futures contracts have bidirectional payoffs. They have the potential for a substantial gain in one direction and a substantial loss in the other direction. The advantage of taking such a position lies in the fact that one need pay no cash up front. In contrast, options offer the feature that, if one is willing to pay cash up front, one can limit the loss in a given direction. In other words, options have unidirectional payoffs. This feature can be attractive to the holder of an option. To the writer, options offer the opportunity to be paid cash up front for a willingness to assume the risk of the unidirectional payoff. An option writer can assume the risk of potentially a large loss unmatched by the potential for a large gain. In fact, the potential gain is small. But for this risk, the option writer receives money up front.

Options also offer excellent devices for managing the risk of various exposures. An obvious one is the protective put, which we saw earlier and which can protect a position against loss by paying off when the value of the underlying is down. We shall see this and other such applications in Reading 78.

Recall that futures contracts offer price discovery, the revelation of the prices at which investors will contract today for transactions to take place later. Options, on the other hand, provide volatility discovery. Through the implied volatility, investors can determine the market's assessment of how volatile it believes the underlying asset is. This valuable information can be difficult to obtain from any other source.

Futures offer advantages over forwards, in that futures are standardized, tend to be actively traded in a secondary market, and are protected by the exchange's clearinghouse against credit risk. Although some options, such as interest rate options, are available only in over-the-counter forms, many options exist in both over-the-counter and exchange-listed forms. Hence, one can often customize an option if necessary or trade it on an exchange.

In Reading 74, we covered forward contracts; in Reading 75, we covered futures contracts; and in this reading we covered option contracts. We have one more major class of derivative instruments, swaps, which we now turn to in Reading 77. We shall return to options in Reading 78, where we explore option trading strategies.

ENDS

SUMMARY

- Options are rights to buy or sell an underlying at a fixed price, the exercise price, for a period of time. The right to buy is a call; the right to sell is a put. Options have a definite expiration date. Using the option to buy or sell is the action of exercising it. The buyer or holder of an option pays a price to the seller or writer for the right to buy (a call) or sell (a put) the underlying instrument. The writer of an option has the corresponding potential obligation to sell or buy the underlying.

- European options can be exercised only at expiration; American options can be exercised at any time prior to expiration. Moneyness refers to the characteristic that an option has positive intrinsic value. The payoff is the value of the option at expiration. An option's intrinsic value is the value that can be captured if the option is exercised. Time value is the component of an option's price that reflects the uncertainty of what will happen in the future to the price of the underlying.

- Options can be traded as standardized instruments on an options exchange, where they are protected from default on the part of the writer, or as customized instruments on the over-the-counter market, where they are subject to the possibility of the writer defaulting. Because the buyer pays a price at the start and does not have to do anything else, the buyer cannot default.

- The underlying instruments for options are individual stocks, stock indices, bonds, interest rates, currencies, futures, commodities, and even such random factors as the weather. In addition, a class of options called real options is associated with the flexibility in capital investment projects.

- Like FRAs, which are forward contracts in which the underlying is an interest rate, interest rate options are options in which the underlying is an interest rate. However, FRAs are commitments to make one interest payment and receive another, whereas interest rate options are rights to make one interest payment and receive another.

- Option payoffs, which are the values of options when they expire, are determined by the greater of zero or the difference between underlying price and exercise price, if a call, or the greater of zero or the difference between exercise price and underlying price, if a put. For interest rate options, the exercise price is a specified rate and the underlying price is a variable interest rate.

- Interest rate options exist in the form of caps, which are call options on interest rates, and floors, which are put options on interest rates. Caps consist of a series of call options, called caplets, on an underlying rate, with each option expiring at a different time. Floors consist of a series of put options, called floorlets, on an underlying rate, with each option expiring at a different time.

- The minimum value of European and American calls and puts is zero. The maximum value of European and American calls is the underlying price. The maximum value of a European put is the present value of the exercise price. The maximum value of an American put is the exercise price.

- The lower bound of a European call is established by constructing a portfolio consisting of a long call and risk-free bond and a short position in the underlying asset. This combination produces a non-negative value at expiration, so its current value must be non-negative. For this situation to occur, the call price has to be worth at least the underlying price minus the present value of the exercise price. The lower bound of a European put is established by constructing a portfolio consisting of a long put, a long position in the underlying, and the issuance of a zero-coupon bond. This combination produces a non-negative value at expiration so its current value must be non-negative. For this to occur, the put price has to be at least as much as the present value of the exercise price minus the underlying price. For both calls and puts, if this lower bound is negative, we invoke the rule that an option price can be no lower than zero.

▶ The lowest price of a European call is referred to as the lower bound. The lowest price of an American call is also the lower bound of a European call. The lowest price of a European put is also referred to as the lower bound. The lowest price of an American put, however, is its intrinsic value.

▶ Buying a call with a given exercise price and selling an otherwise identical call with a higher exercise price creates a combination that always pays off with a non-negative value. Therefore, its current value must be non-negative. For this to occur, the call with the lower exercise price must be worth at least as much as the other call. A similar argument holds for puts, except that one would buy the put with the higher exercise price. This line of reasoning shows that the put with the higher exercise price must be worth at least as much as the one with the lower exercise price.

▶ A longer-term European or American call must be worth at least as much as a corresponding shorter-term European or American call. A longer-term American put must be worth at least as much as a shorter-term American put. A longer-term European put, however, can be worth more or less than a shorter-term European put.

▶ A fiduciary call, consisting of a European call and a zero-coupon bond, produces the same payoff as a protective put, consisting of the underlying and a European put. Therefore, their current values must be the same. For this equivalence to occur, the call price plus bond price must equal the underlying price plus put price. This relationship is called put–call parity and can be used to identify combinations of instruments that synthesize another instrument by rearranging the equation to isolate the instrument you are trying to create. Long positions are indicated by positive signs, and short positions are indicated by negative signs. One can create a synthetic call, a synthetic put, a synthetic underlying, and a synthetic bond, as well as synthetic short positions in these instruments for the purpose of exploiting mispricing in these instruments.

▶ Put–call parity violations exist when one side of the equation does not equal the other. An arbitrageur buys the lower-priced side and sells the higher-priced side, thereby earning the difference in price, and the positions offset at expiration. The combined actions of many arbitrageurs performing this set of transactions would increase the demand and price for the under-priced instruments and decrease the demand and price for the overpriced instruments, until the put–call parity relationship is upheld.

▶ American option prices must always be no less than those of otherwise equivalent European options. American call options, however, are never exercised early unless there is a cash flow on the underlying, so they can sell for the same as their European counterparts in the absence of such a cash flow. American put options nearly always have a possibility of early exercise, so they ordinarily sell for more than their European counterparts.

▶ Cash flows on the underlying affect an option's boundary conditions and put–call parity by lowering the underlying price by the present value of the cash flows over the life of the option.

- A higher interest rate increases a call option's price and decreases a put option's price.

- In a one-period binomial model, the underlying asset can move up to one of two prices. A portfolio consisting of a long position in the underlying and a short position in a call option can be made risk-free and, therefore, must return the risk-free rate. Under this condition, the option price can be obtained by inferring it from a formula that uses the other input values. The option price is a weighted average of the two option prices at expiration, discounted back one period at the risk-free rate.

- If an option is trading for a price higher than that given in the binomial model, one can sell the option and buy a specific number of units of the underlying, as given by the model. This combination is risk free but will earn a return higher than the risk-free rate. If the option is trading for a price lower than the price given in the binomial model, a short position in a specific number of units of the underlying and a long position in the option will create a risk-free loan that costs less than the risk-free rate.

- In a two-period binomial model, the underlying can move to one of two prices in each of two periods; thus three underlying prices are possible at the option expiration. To price an option, start at the expiration and work backward, following the procedure in the one-period model in which an option price at any given point in time is a weighted average of the next two possible prices discounted at the risk-free rate.

- To calculate the price of an option on a zero-coupon bond or a coupon bond, one must first construct a binomial tree of the price of the bond over the life of the option. To calculate the price of an option on an interest rate, one should use a binomial tree of interest rates. Then the option price is found by starting at the option expiration, determining the payoff and successively working backwards by computing the option price as the weighted average of the next two option prices discounted back one period. For the case of options on bonds or interest rates, a different discount rate is used at different parts of the tree.

- For an option of a given expiration, a greater pricing accuracy is obtained by dividing the option's life into a greater number of time periods in a binomial tree. As more time periods are added, the discrete-time binomial price converges to a stable value as though the option is being modeled in a continuous-time world.

- The assumptions under which the Black–Scholes–Merton model is derived state that the underlying asset follows a geometric lognormal diffusion process, the risk-free rate is known and constant, the volatility of the underlying asset is known and constant, there are no taxes or transaction costs, there are no cash flows on the underlying, and the options are European.

- To calculate the value of an option using the Black–Scholes–Merton model, enter the underlying price, exercise price, risk-free rate, volatility, and time to expiration into a formula. The formula will require you to look up two normal probabilities, obtained from either a table or preferably a computer routine.

- The change in the option price for a change in the price of the underlying is called the delta. The change in the option price for a change in the risk-free rate is called the rho. The change in the option price for a change in the time to expiration is called the theta. The change in the option price for a change in the volatility is called the vega.

▶ The delta is defined as the change in the option price divided by the change in the underlying price. The option price change can be approximated by the delta times the change in the underlying price. To construct a delta-hedged position, a short (long) position in each call is matched with a long (short) position in delta units of the underlying. Changes in the underlying price will generate offsetting changes in the value of the option position, provided the changes in the underlying price are small and occur over a short time period. A delta-hedged position should be adjusted as the delta changes and time passes.

▶ If changes in the price of the underlying are large or the delta hedge is not adjusted over a longer time period, the hedge may not be effective. This effect is due to the instability of the delta and is called the gamma effect. If the gamma effect is large, option price changes will not be very close to the changes as approximated by the delta times the underlying price change.

▶ Cash flows on the underlying are accommodated in option pricing models by reducing the price of the underlying by the present value of the cash flows over the life of the option.

▶ Volatility can be estimated by calculating the standard deviation of the continuously compounded returns from a sample of recent data for the underlying. This is called the historical volatility. An alternative measure, called the implied volatility, can be obtained by setting the Black–Scholes–Merton model price equal to the market price and inferring the volatility. The implied volatility is a measure of the volatility the market is using to price the option.

▶ The payoffs of a call on a forward contract and an appropriately chosen zero-coupon bond are equivalent to the payoffs of a put on the forward contract and the forward contract. Thus, their current values must be the same. For this equality to occur, the call price plus the bond price must equal the put price. The appropriate zero-coupon bond is one with a face value equal to the exercise price minus the forward price. This relationship is called put–call–forward (or futures) parity.

▶ There is no justification for exercising American options on forward contracts early, so they are equivalent to European options on forwards. American options on futures, both calls and puts, can sometimes be exercised early, so they are different from European options on futures and carry a higher price.

▶ The Black model can be used to price European options on forwards or futures by entering the forward price, exercise price, risk-free rate, time to expiration, and volatility into a formula that will also require the determination of two normal probabilities.

▶ The Black model can be used to price European options on interest rates by entering the forward interest rate into the model for the forward or futures price and the exercise rate for the exercise price.

▶ Options are useful in financial markets because they provide a way to limit losses to the premium paid while permitting potentially large gains. They can be used for hedging purposes, especially in the case of puts, which can be used to limit the loss on a long position in an asset. Options also provide information on the volatility of the underlying asset. Options can be standardized and exchange-traded or customized in the over-the-counter market.

APPENDIX 76-A

Cumulative Probabilities for a Standard Normal Distribution
$P(X \le x) = N(x)$ for $x \ge 0$ or $1 - N(-x)$ for $x < 0$

x	0	0.01	0.02	0.03	0.04	0.05	0.06	0.07	0.08	0.09
0.00	0.5000	0.5040	0.5080	0.5120	0.5160	0.5199	0.5239	0.5279	0.5319	0.5359
0.10	0.5398	0.5438	0.5478	0.5517	0.5557	0.5596	0.5636	0.5675	0.5714	0.5753
0.20	0.5793	0.5832	0.5871	0.5910	0.5948	0.5987	0.6026	0.6064	0.6103	0.6141
0.30	0.6179	0.6217	0.6255	0.6293	0.6331	0.6368	0.6406	0.6443	0.6480	0.6517
0.40	0.6554	0.6591	0.6628	0.6664	0.6700	0.6736	0.6772	0.6808	0.6844	0.6879
0.50	0.6915	0.6950	0.6985	0.7019	0.7054	0.7088	0.7123	0.7157	0.7190	0.7224
0.60	0.7257	0.7291	0.7324	0.7357	0.7389	0.7422	0.7454	0.7486	0.7517	0.7549
0.70	0.7580	0.7611	0.7642	0.7673	0.7704	0.7734	0.7764	0.7794	0.7823	0.7852
0.80	0.7881	0.7910	0.7939	0.7967	0.7995	0.8023	0.8051	0.8078	0.8106	0.8133
0.90	0.8159	0.8186	0.8212	0.8238	0.8264	0.8289	0.8315	0.8340	0.8365	0.8389
1.00	0.8413	0.8438	0.8461	0.8485	0.8508	0.8531	0.8554	0.8577	0.8599	0.8621
1.10	0.8643	0.8665	0.8686	0.8708	0.8729	0.8749	0.8770	0.8790	0.8810	0.8830
1.20	0.8849	0.8869	0.8888	0.8907	0.8925	0.8944	0.8962	0.8980	0.8997	0.9015
1.30	0.9032	0.9049	0.9066	0.9082	0.9099	0.9115	0.9131	0.9147	0.9162	0.9177
1.40	0.9192	0.9207	0.9222	0.9236	0.9251	0.9265	0.9279	0.9292	0.9306	0.9319
1.50	0.9332	0.9345	0.9357	0.9370	0.9382	0.9394	0.9406	0.9418	0.9429	0.9441
1.60	0.9452	0.9463	0.9474	0.9484	0.9495	0.9505	0.9515	0.9525	0.9535	0.9545
1.70	0.9554	0.9564	0.9573	0.9582	0.9591	0.9599	0.9608	0.9616	0.9625	0.9633
1.80	0.9641	0.9649	0.9656	0.9664	0.9671	0.9678	0.9686	0.9693	0.9699	0.9706
1.90	0.9713	0.9719	0.9726	0.9732	0.9738	0.9744	0.9750	0.9756	0.9761	0.9767
2.00	0.9772	0.9778	0.9783	0.9788	0.9793	0.9798	0.9803	0.9808	0.9812	0.9817
2.10	0.9821	0.9826	0.9830	0.9834	0.9838	0.9842	0.9846	0.9850	0.9854	0.9857
2.20	0.9861	0.9864	0.9868	0.9871	0.9875	0.9878	0.9881	0.9884	0.9887	0.9890
2.30	0.9893	0.9896	0.9898	0.9901	0.9904	0.9906	0.9909	0.9911	0.9913	0.9916
2.40	0.9918	0.9920	0.9922	0.9925	0.9927	0.9929	0.9931	0.9932	0.9934	0.9936
2.50	0.9938	0.9940	0.9941	0.9943	0.9945	0.9946	0.9948	0.9949	0.9951	0.9952
2.60	0.9953	0.9955	0.9956	0.9957	0.9959	0.9960	0.9961	0.9962	0.9963	0.9964
2.70	0.9965	0.9966	0.9967	0.9968	0.9969	0.9970	0.9971	0.9972	0.9973	0.9974
2.80	0.9974	0.9975	0.9976	0.9977	0.9977	0.9978	0.9979	0.9979	0.9980	0.9981
2.90	0.9981	0.9982	0.9982	0.9983	0.9984	0.9984	0.9985	0.9985	0.9986	0.9986
3.00	0.9987	0.9987	0.9987	0.9988	0.9988	0.9989	0.9989	0.9989	0.9990	0.9990

PROBLEMS FOR READING 76

1. A. Calculate the payoff at expiration for a call option on the S&P 100 stock index in which the underlying price is 579.32 at expiration, the multiplier is 100, and the exercise price is

   i. 450

   ii. 650

B. Calculate the payoff at expiration for a put option on the S&P 100 in which the underlying is at 579.32 at expiration, the multiplier is 100, and the exercise price is

   i. 450

   ii. 650

2. A. Calculate the payoff at expiration for a call option on a bond in which the underlying is at $0.95 per $1 par at expiration, the contract is on $100,000 face value bonds, and the exercise price is

   i. $0.85

   ii. $1.15

B. Calculate the payoff at expiration for a put option on a bond in which the underlying is at $0.95 per $1 par at expiration, the contract is on $100,000 face value bonds, and the exercise price is

   i. $0.85

   ii. $1.15

3. A. Calculate the payoff at expiration for a call option on an interest rate in which the underlying is a 180-day interest rate at 6.53 percent at expiration, the notional principal is $10 million, and the exercise price is

   i. 5 percent

   ii. 8 percent

B. Calculate the payoff at expiration for a put option on an interest rate in which the underlying is a 180-day interest rate at 6.53 percent at expiration, the notional principal is $10 million, and the exercise price is

   i. 5 percent

   ii. 8 percent

4. A. Calculate the payoff at expiration for a call option on the British pound in which the underlying is at $1.438 at expiration, the options are on 125,000 British pounds, and the exercise price is

   i. $1.35

   ii. $1.55

B. Calculate the payoff at expiration for a put option on the British pound where the underlying is at $1.438 at expiration, the options are on 125,000 British pounds, and the exercise price is

   i. $1.35

   ii. $1.55

5. A. Calculate the payoff at expiration for a call option on a futures contract in which the underlying is at 1136.76 at expiration, the options are on a futures contract for $1,000, and the exercise price is

   i. 1130

   ii. 1140

B. Calculate the payoff at expiration for a put option on a futures contract in which the underlying is at 1136.76 at expiration, the options are on a futures contract for $1000, and the exercise price is

   i. 1130

   ii. 1140

6. Consider a stock index option that expires in 75 days. The stock index is currently at 1240.89 and makes no cash payments during the life of the option. Assume that the stock index has a multiplier of 1. The risk-free rate is 3 percent.

   A. Calculate the lowest and highest possible prices for European-style call options on the above stock index with exercise prices of

   i. 1225

   ii. 1255

   B. Calculate the lowest and highest possible prices for European-style put options on the above stock index with exercise prices of

   i. 1225

   ii. 1255

7. **A.** Consider American-style call and put options on a bond. The options expire in 60 days. The bond is currently at $1.05 per $1 par and makes no cash payments during the life of the option. The risk-free rate is 5.5 percent. Assume that the contract is on $1 face value bonds. Calculate the lowest and highest possible prices for the calls and puts with exercise prices of

   i. $0.95

   ii. $1.10

   B. Consider European style call and put options on a bond. The options expire in 60 days. The bond is currently at $1.05 per $1 par and makes no cash payments during the life of the option. The risk-free rate is 5.5 percent. Assume that the contract is on $1 face value bonds. Calculate the lowest and highest possible prices for the calls and puts with exercise prices of

   i. $0.95

   ii. $1.10

8. You are provided with the following information on put and call options on a stock:

   Call price, $c_0 = \$6.64$

   Put price, $p_0 = \$2.75$

   Exercise price, X = $30

   Days to option expiration = 219

   Current stock price, $S_0 = \$33.19$

   Put–call parity shows the equivalence of a call/bond portfolio (fiduciary call) and a put/underlying portfolio (protective put). Illustrate put–call parity assuming stock prices at expiration (S_T) of $20 and of $40. Assume that the risk-free rate, r, is 4 percent.

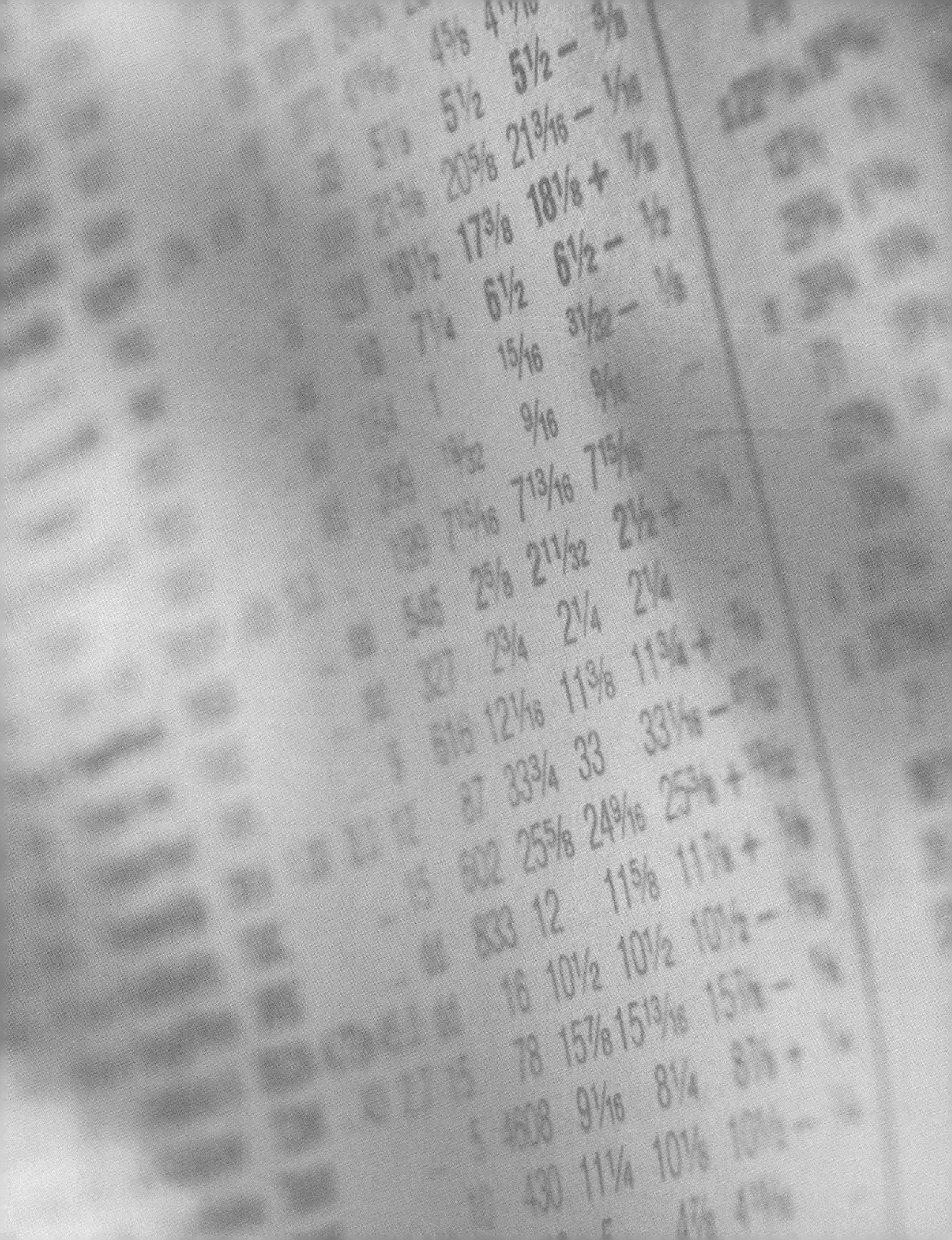

4⅝ 4¹¹/₁₆   ³⁄₈
5½   5½ — ³⁄₈
5½ 2¹³/₁₆ — ¹/₁₆
20⅝ 21³/₁₆
17⅜ 18⅛ + ⅛
18½   6½ — ½
6½ 6½ — ⅛
7¼   31/32 —
15/16
9/16 9/16
1/32
7⁵/₁₆ 7¹³/₁₆ 7¹⁵/₁₆
2⅝ 2¹¹/₃₂ 2½ +
2¾ 2¼ 2¼
12¹/₁₆ 11⅜ 11¾ +
87 33¾ 33 33⅛ —
25⅝ 24⁹/₁₆ 25⅜ +
12 11⅝ 11⅞ +
16 10½ 10½ 10⅛ —
78 15⅞ 15¹³/₁₆ 15⅞ —
9¹/₁₆ 8¼ 8⅝ +
430 11¼ 10⅛

SWAP MARKETS AND CONTRACTS
by Don M. Chance

READING 77

LEARNING OUTCOMES

The candidate should be able to:

a. describe the characteristics of swap contracts and explain how swaps are terminated;

b. define and give examples of currency swaps, plain vanilla interest rate swaps, and equity swaps, and calculate and interpret the payments on each, when provided with the formulas.

INTRODUCTION   1

This reading completes the survey of the main types of derivative instruments. The three preceding readings covered forward contracts, futures contracts, and options. This reading covers swaps. Although swaps were the last of the main types of derivatives to be invented, they are clearly not the least important. In fact, judging by the size of the swap market, they are probably the most important. In Reading 73, we noted that the Bank for International Settlements had estimated the notional principal of the global over-the-counter derivatives market as of 30 June 2001 at $100 trillion. Of that amount, interest rate and currency swaps account for about $61 trillion, with interest rate swaps representing about $57 trillion of that total.[1] Indeed, interest rate swaps have had overwhelming success as a derivative product. They are widely used by corporations, financial institutions, and governments.

In Reading 73, we briefly described the characteristics of swaps, but now we explore this subject in more detail. Recall first that *a swap is an agreement*

---

[1] Equity and commodity swaps account for less than the notional principal of currency swaps.

Analysis of Derivatives for the CFA® Program, by Don M. Chance, Copyright © 2003 by Association for Investment Management and Research. Reprinted with permission.

between two parties to exchange a series of future cash flows. For most types of swaps, one party makes payments that are determined by a random outcome, such as an interest rate, a currency rate, an equity return, or a commodity price. These payments are commonly referred to as variable or *floating*. The other party either makes variable or floating payments determined by some other random factor or makes fixed payments. At least one type of swap involves both parties making fixed payments, but the values of those payments vary due to random factors.

In forwards, futures, and options, the terminology of *long* and *short* has been used to describe buyers and sellers. These terms are not used as often in swaps. The preferred terminology usually designates a party as being the floating- (or variable-) rate payer or the fixed-rate payer. Nonetheless, in swaps in which one party receives a floating rate and the other receives a fixed rate, the former is usually said to be long and the latter is said to be short. This usage is in keeping with the fact that parties who go long in other instruments pay a known amount and receive a claim on an unknown amount. In some swaps, however, both sides are floating or variable, and this terminology breaks down.

1.1 Characteristics of Swap Contracts

Although technically a swap can have a single payment, most swaps involve multiple payments. Thus, we refer to a swap as a *series* of payments. In fact, we have already covered a swap with one payment, which is just a forward contract. Hence, a swap is basically a series of forward contracts. We will elaborate further in Section 4.1.2, but with this idea in mind, we can see that a swap is like an agreement to buy something over a period of time. We might be paying a variable price or a price that has already been fixed; we might be paying an uncertain price, or we might already know the price we shall pay.

When a swap is initiated, neither party pays any amount to the other. Therefore, a swap has zero value at the start of the contract. Although it is not absolutely necessary for this condition to be true, swaps are typically done in this fashion. Neither party pays anything up front. There is, however, a technical exception to this point in regard to currency swaps. Each party pays the notional principal to the other, but the amounts exchanged are equivalent, though denominated in two different currencies.

Each date on which the parties make payments is called a **settlement date**, sometimes called a payment date, and the time between settlement dates is called the **settlement period**. On a given settlement date when payments are due, one party makes a payment to the other, which in turn makes a payment to the first party. With the exception of currency swaps and a few variations associated with other types of swaps, both sets of payments are made in the same currency. Consequently, the parties typically agree to exchange only the net amount owed from one party to the other, a practice called **netting**. In currency swaps and a few other special cases, the payments are not made in the same currency; hence, the parties usually make separate payments without netting. Note the implication that swaps are generally settled in cash. It is quite rare for swaps to call for actual physical delivery of an underlying asset.

A swap always has a **termination date**, the date of the final payment. We can think of this date as its expiration date, as we do with other derivatives. The original time to maturity is sometimes called the *tenor* of a swap.

The swap market is almost exclusively an over-the-counter market, so swaps contracts are customized to the parties' specific needs. Several of the leading futures exchanges have created futures contracts on swaps. These contracts allow participants to hedge and speculate on the rates that will prevail in the swap market at future dates. Of course, these contracts are not swaps themselves but, as derivatives of swaps, they can in some ways serve as substitutes for swaps. These futures contracts have been moderately successful, but their volume is insignificant compared with the over-the-counter market for swaps.

As we have discussed in previous readings, over-the-counter instruments are subject to default risk. Default is possible whenever a payment is due. When a series of payments is made, there is default risk potential throughout the life of the contract, depending on the financial condition of the two parties. But default can be somewhat complicated in swaps. Suppose, for example, that on a settlement date, Party A owes Party B a payment of $50,000 and Party B owes Party A a payment of $12,000. Agreeing to net, Party A owes Party B $38,000 for that particular payment. Party A may be illiquid, or perhaps even bankrupt, and unable to make the payment. But it may be the case that the market value of the swap, which reflects the present value of the remaining payments, could be positive from the perspective of Party A and negative from the perspective of Party B. In that case, Party B owes Party A more for the remaining payments. We will learn how to determine the market value of a swap in Section 4.2 of this reading.

The handling of default in swaps can be complicated, depending on the contract specifications and the applicable laws under which the contract was written. In most cases, the above situation would be resolved by having A be in default but possessing an asset, the swap, that can be used to help settle its other liabilities. We shall discuss the default risk of swaps in more detail in Section 7.

1.2 Termination of a Swap

As we noted earlier, a swap has a termination or expiration date. Sometimes, however, a party could want to terminate a swap before its formal expiration. This scenario is much like a party selling a bond before it matures or selling an exchange-traded option or futures contract before its expiration. With swaps, early termination can take place in several ways.

As we mentioned briefly and will cover in more detail later, a swap has a market value that can be calculated during its life. If a party holds a swap with a market value of $125,000, for example, it can settle the swap with the counterparty by having the counterparty pay it $125,000 in cash. This payment terminates the transaction for both parties. From the opposite perspective, a party holding a swap with a negative market value can terminate the swap by paying the market value to the counterparty. Terminating a swap in this manner is possible only if the counterparties specify in advance that such a transaction can be made, or if they reach an agreement to do so without having specified in advance. In other words, this feature is not automatically available and must be agreed to by both parties.

Many swaps are terminated early by entering into a separate and offsetting swap. For example, suppose a corporation is engaged in a swap to make fixed payments of 5 percent and receive floating payments based on LIBOR, with the payments made each 15 January and 15 July. Three years remain on the swap. That corporation can offset the swap by entering into an entirely new swap in which it makes payments based on LIBOR and receives a fixed rate with the payments made each 15 January and 15 July for three years. The swap fixed rate is determined by market conditions at the time the swap is initiated. Thus, the fixed rate on the new swap is not likely to match the fixed rate on the old swap, but the effect of this transaction is simply to have the floating payments offset; the fixed payments will net out to a known amount. Hence, the risk associated with the floating rate is eliminated. The default risk, however, is not eliminated because both swaps remain in effect.

Another way to terminate a swap early is sell the swap to another counterparty. Suppose a corporation holds a swap worth $75,000. If it can obtain the counterparty's permission, it can find another party to take over its payments. In effect, it sells the swap for $75,000 to that party. This procedure, however, is not commonly used.

A final way to terminate a swap early is by using a **swaption**. This instrument is an option to enter into a swap at terms that are established in advance. Thus, a party could use a swaption to enter into an offsetting swap, as described above. We shall cover swaptions in more detail in Section 6.

2   THE STRUCTURE OF GLOBAL SWAP MARKETS

The global swaps market is much like the global forward and over-the-counter options markets, which we covered in some detail in Readings 73, 74, and 75. It is made up of dealers, which are banks and investment banking firms. These dealers make markets in swaps, quoting bid and ask prices and rates, thereby offering to take either side of a swap transaction. Upon taking a position in a swap, the dealer generally offsets the risk by making transactions in other markets. The counterparties to swaps are either end users or other dealers. The end users are often corporations with risk management problems that can be solved by engaging in a swap—a corporation or other end user is usually exposed to or needs an exposure to some type of risk that arises from interest rates, exchange rates, stock prices, or commodity prices. The end user contacts a dealer that makes a market in swaps. The two engage in a transaction, at which point the dealer assumes some risk from the end user. The dealer then usually lays off the risk by engaging in a transaction with another party. That transaction could be something as simple as a futures contract, or it could be an over-the-counter transaction with another dealer.

Risk magazine conducts annual surveys of participants in various derivative products. Exhibit 77-1 presents the results of those surveys for currency and interest rate swaps. One survey provides opinions of banks and investment banks that are

EXHIBIT 77-1	*Risk* Magazine Surveys of Banks, Investment Banks, and Corporate End Users to Determine the Top Three Dealers in Currency and Interest Rate Swaps

	Respondents	
Currencies	**Banks and Investment Banks**	**Corporate End Users**
Currency Swaps		
$/€	UBS Warburg	Citigroup
	JP Morgan Chase	Royal Bank of Scotland
	Deutsche Bank	Bank of America

(Exhibit continued on next page ...)

EXHIBIT 77-1   **(continued)**

$/¥	JP Morgan Chase	Citigroup
	UBS Warburg	Bank of America
	Credit Suisse First Boston/ Deutsche Bank	JP Morgan Chase
$/£	Royal Bank of Scotland	Royal Bank of Scotland
	JP Morgan Chase	Citigroup
	Goldman Sachs	Deutsche Bank
$/SF	UBS Warburg	UBS Warburg
	Goldman Sachs	Citigroup
	Credit Suisse First Boston	Credit Suisse First Boston

Interest Rate Swaps (2–10 years)

$	JP Morgan Chase	JP Morgan Chase
	Bank of America	Bank of America
	Morgan Stanley	Royal Bank of Scotland
€	JP Morgan Chase	Royal Bank of Scotland
	Deutsche Bank	Deutsche Bank
	Morgan Stanley	Citigroup
¥	JP Morgan Chase	Royal Bank of Scotland
	Deutsche Bank	Barclays Capital
	Bank of America	Citigroup/JP Morgan Chase
£	Royal Bank of Scotland	Royal Bank of Scotland
	Barclays Capital	Barclays Capital
	UBS Warburg	Deutsche Bank
SF	UBS Warburg	UBS Warburg
	Credit Suisse First Boston	Credit Suisse First Boston
	Zürcher Kantonalbank	Zürcher Kantonalbank

Note: $ = U.S. dollar, € = euro, ¥ = Japanese yen, £ = U.K. pound sterling, SF = Swiss franc

Source: Risk, September 2002, pp. 30–67 for banks and investment banking dealer respondents, and June 2002, pp. 24–34 for corporate end user respondents. Ratings for swaps with maturities less than 2 years and greater than 10 years are also provided in the September 2002 issue of *Risk.*

swaps dealers. In the other survey, the respondents are end users. The results give a good idea of the major players in this market. It is interesting to note the disagreement between how dealers view themselves and how end users view them. Also, note that the rankings change, sometimes drastically, from year to year.

TYPES OF SWAPS   3

We alluded to the fact that the underlying asset in a swap can be a currency, interest rate, stock, or commodity. We now take a look at these types of swaps in more detail.

3.1 Currency Swaps

In a currency swap, each party makes interest payments to the other in different currencies.[2] Consider this example. The U.S. retailer Target Corporation (NYSE: TGT) does not have an established presence in Europe. Let us say that it has decided to begin opening a few stores in Germany and needs €9 million to fund construction and initial operations. TGT would like to issue a fixed-rate euro-denominated bond with face value of €9 million, but the company is not very well known in Europe. European investment bankers have given it a quote for such a bond. Deutsche Bank, AG (NYSE: DB), however, tells TGT that it should issue the bond in dollars and use a swap to convert it into euros.

Suppose TGT issues a five-year US$10 million bond at a rate of 6 percent. It then enters into a swap with DB in which DB will make payments to TGT in U.S. dollars at a fixed rate of 5.5 percent and TGT will make payments to DB in euros at a fixed rate of 4.9 percent each 15 March and 15 September for five years. The payments are based on a notional principal of 10 million in dollars and 9 million in euros. We assume the swap starts on 15 September of the current year. The swap specifies that the two parties exchange the notional principal at the start of the swap and at the end. Because the payments are made in different currencies, netting is not practical, so each party makes its respective payments.[3]

Thus, the swap is composed of the following transactions:
15 September:

▶ DB pays TGT €9 million
▶ TGT pays DB $10 million

Each 15 March and 15 September for five years:

▶ DB pays TGT $0.055(180/360)$10 million = $275,000
▶ TGT pays DB $0.049(180/360)$ €9 million = €220,500

15 September five years after initiation:

▶ DB pays TGT $10 million
▶ TGT pays DB €9 million

Note that we have simplified the interest calculations a little. In this example, we calculated semiannual interest using the fraction 180/360. Some parties might choose to use the exact day count in the six-month period divided by 365 days. LIBOR and Euribor transactions, the predominant rates used in interest rate swaps, nearly always use 360 days, as mentioned in previous readings. Exhibit 77-2 shows the stream of cash flows from TGT's perspective.

---

[2] It is important at this point to clear up some terminology confusion. Foreign currency is often called *foreign exchange* or sometimes *FX*. There is another transaction called an *FX swap*, which sounds as if it might be referring to a currency swap. In fact, an FX swap is just a long position in a forward contract on a foreign currency and a short position in a forward contract on the same currency with a different expiration. Why this transaction is called a swap is not clear, but this transaction existed before currency swaps were created. In futures markets, the analogous transaction is called a *spread*, reflecting as it does the risk associated with the spread between the prices of futures contracts with different expirations.

[3] In this example, we shall assume 180 days between payment dates. In practice, exact day counts are usually used, leading to different fixed payment amounts in one six-month period from those of another. In the example here, we are only illustrating the idea behind swap cash flows, so it is convenient to keep the fixed payments the same. Later in the reading, we shall illustrate situations in which the exact day count is used, leading to fixed payments that vary slightly.

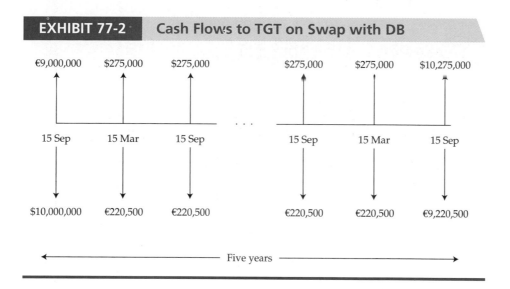

EXHIBIT 77-2   Cash Flows to TGT on Swap with DB

Note that the Target–Deutsche Bank transaction looks just like TGT is issuing a bond with face value of €9 million and that bond is purchased by DB. TGT converts the €9 million to $10 million and buys a dollar-denominated bond issued by DB. Note that TGT, having issued a bond denominated in euros, accordingly makes interest payments to DB in euros. DB, appropriately, makes interest payments in dollars to TGT. At the end, they each pay off the face values of the bonds they have issued. We emphasize that the Target–Deutsche Bank transaction *looks like* what we have just described. In fact, neither TGT nor DB actually issues or purchases a bond. They exchange only a series of cash flows that replicated the issuance and purchase of these bonds.

Exhibit 77-3 illustrates how such a combined transaction would work. TGT issues a bond in dollars (Exhibit 77-3, Panel A). It takes the dollars and passes them through to DB, which gives TGT the €9 million it needs. On the interest payment dates, the swap generates $275,000 of the $300,000 in interest TGT needs to pay its bondholders (Panel B). In turn, TGT makes interest payments in euros. Still, small dollar interest payments are necessary because TGT cannot issue a dollar bond at the swap rate. At the end of the transaction, TGT receives $10 million back from DB and passes it through to its bondholders (Panel C). TGT pays DB €9 million, thus effectively paying off a euro-denominated bond.

TGT has effectively issued a dollar-denominated bond and converted it to a euro-denominated bond. In all likelihood, it can save on interest expense by funding its need for euros in this way, because TGT is better known in the United States than in Europe. Its swap dealer, DB, knows TGT well and also obviously has a strong presence in Europe. Thus, DB can pass on its advantage in euro bond markets to TGT. In addition, had TGT issued a euro-denominated bond, it would have assumed no credit risk. By entering into the swap, TGT assumes a remote possibility of DB defaulting. Thus, TGT saves a little money by assuming some credit risk.

EXHIBIT 77-3   **Issuing a Dollar-Denominated Bond and Using a Currency Swap to Convert a Euro-Denominated Bond**

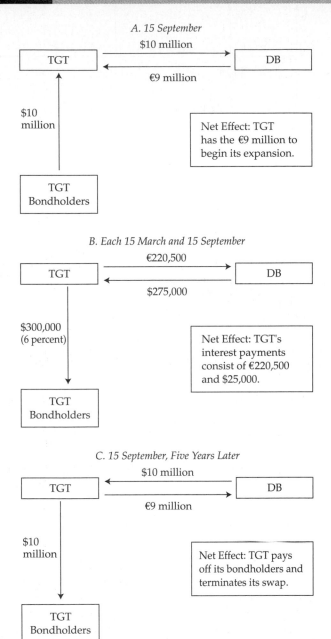

A. 15 September

TGT — $10 million → DB
TGT ← €9 million — DB

$10 million — TGT Bondholders (up to TGT)

Net Effect: TGT has the €9 million to begin its expansion.

B. Each 15 March and 15 September

TGT — €220,500 → DB
TGT ← $275,000 — DB

$300,000 (6 percent) — TGT Bondholders

Net Effect: TGT's interest payments consist of €220,500 and $25,000.

C. 15 September, Five Years Later

TGT ← $10 million — DB
TGT — €9 million → DB

$10 million — TGT Bondholders

Net Effect: TGT pays off its bondholders and terminates its swap.

Returning to the Target swap, recall that Target effectively converted a fixed-rate loan in dollars to a fixed-rate loan in euros. Suppose instead that TGT preferred to borrow in euros at a floating rate. It then would have specified that the swap required it to make payments to DB at a floating rate. Had TGT preferred to issue the dollar-denominated bond at a floating rate, it would have specified that DB pay it dollars at a floating rate.

Practice Problem 1

Consider a currency swap in which the domestic party pays a fixed rate in the foreign currency, the British pound, and the counterparty pays a fixed rate in U.S. dollars. The notional principals are $50 million and £30 million. The fixed rates are 5.6 percent in dollars and 6.25 percent in pounds. Both sets of payments are made on the basis of 30 days per month and 365 days per year, and the payments are made semiannually.

A. Determine the initial exchange of cash that occurs at the start of the swap.

B. Determine the semiannual payments.

C. Determine the final exchange of cash that occurs at the end of the swap.

D. Give an example of a situation in which this swap might be appropriate.

SOLUTIONS

A. At the start of the swap:
   Domestic party pays counterparty $50 million
   Counterparty pays domestic party £30 million

B. Semiannually:
   Domestic party pays counterparty £30,000,000(0.0625)(180/365) = £924,658
   Counterparty pays domestic party $50,000,000(0.056)(180/365) = $1,380,822

C. At the end of the swap:
   Domestic party pays counterparty £30,000,000
   Counterparty pays domestic party $50,000,000

D. This swap would be appropriate for a U.S. company that issues a dollar-denominated bond but would prefer to borrow in British pounds.

Although TGT and DB exchanged notional principal, some scenarios exist in which the notional principals are not exchanged. For example, suppose many years later, TGT is generating €10 million in cash semi-annually and converting it back to dollars on 15 January and 15 July. It might then wish to lock in the conversion rate by entering into a currency swap that would require it to pay a dealer €10 million and receive a fixed amount of dollars. If the euro fixed rate were 5 percent, a notional principal of €400 million would generate a payment of 0.05(180/360)€400 million = €10 million. If the exchange rate is, for example, $0.85, the equivalent dollar notional principal would be $340 million. If the dollar fixed rate is 6 percent, TGT would receive 0.06(180/360)$340 million = $10.2 million.[4] These payments would occur twice a year for the life of the swap.

[4] It might appear that TGT has somehow converted cash flows worth €10 million($0.085) = $8.5 million into cash flows worth $10.2 million. Recall, however, that the €10 million cash flows are generated yearly and $0.85 is the *current* exchange rate. We cannot apply the current exchange rate to a series of cash flows over various future dates. We would apply the respective forward exchange rates, not the spot rate, to the series of future euro cash flows.

TGT might then lock in the conversion rate by entering into a currency swap with notional principal amounts that would allow it to receive a fixed amount of dollars on 15 January and 15 July. There would be no reason to specify an exchange of notional principal. As we previously described, there are four types of currency swaps. Using the original Target–Deutsche Bank swap as an example, the semi-annual payments would be

A. TGT pays euros at a fixed rate; DB pays dollars at a fixed rate.

B. TGT pays euros at a fixed rate; DB pays dollars at a floating rate.

C. TGT pays euros at a floating rate; DB pays dollars at a floating rate.

D. TGT pays euros at a floating rate; DB pays dollars at a fixed rate.

Or, reversing the flow, TGT could be the payer of dollars and DB could be the payer of euros:

E. TGT pays dollars at a fixed rate; DB pays euros at a fixed rate.

F. TGT pays dollars at a fixed rate; DB pays euros at a floating rate.

G. TGT pays dollars at a floating rate; DB pays euros at a floating rate.

H. TGT pays dollars at a floating rate; DB pays euros at a fixed rate.

Suppose we combine Swap A with Swap H. With TGT paying euros at a fixed rate and DB paying euros at a fixed rate, the euro payments wash out and the net effect is

I. TGT pays dollars at a floating rate; DB pays dollars at a fixed rate.

Suppose we combine Swap B with Swap E. Similarly, the euro payments again wash out, and the net effect is

J. TGT pays dollars at a fixed rate; DB pays dollars at a floating rate.

Suppose we combine Swap C with Swap F. Likewise, the euro floating payments wash out, and the net effect is

K. TGT pays dollars at a fixed rate; DB pays dollars at a floating rate.

Lastly, suppose we combine Swap D with Swap G. Again, the euro floating payments wash out, and the net effect is

L. TGT pays dollars at a floating rate; DB pays dollars at a fixed rate.

Of course, the net results of I and L are equivalent, and the net results of J and K are equivalent. What we have shown here, however, is that combinations of currency swaps eliminate the currency flows and leave us with transactions in only one currency. A swap in which both sets of interest payments are made in the same currency is an interest rate swap.

3.2 Interest Rate Swaps

As we discovered in the above paragraph, an interest rate swap can be created as a combination of currency swaps. Of course, no one would create an interest rate swap that way; doing so would require two transactions when only one would suffice. Interest rate swaps evolved into their own market. In fact, the interest rate swap market is much bigger than the currency swap market, as we have seen in the notional principal statistics.

As previously noted, one way to look at an interest rate swap is that it is a currency swap in which both currencies are the same. Consider a swap to pay Currency A fixed and Currency B floating. Currency A could be dollars, and B could be euros. But what if A and B are both dollars, or A and B are both euros? The first case is a dollar-denominated plain vanilla swap; the second is a euro-denominated plain vanilla swap. *A **plain vanilla swap** is simply an interest rate swap in which one party pays a fixed rate and the other pays a floating rate, with both sets of payments in the same currency.* In fact, the plain vanilla swap is probably the most common derivative transaction in the global financial system.

Note that because we are paying in the same currency, there is no need to exchange notional principals at the beginning and at the end of an interest rate swap. In addition, the interest payments can be, and nearly always are, netted. If one party owes $X and the other owes $Y, the party owing the greater amount pays the net difference, which greatly reduces the credit risk (as we discuss in more detail in Section 7). Finally, we note that there is no reason to have both sides pay a fixed rate. The two streams of payments would be identical in that case. So in an interest rate swap, either one side always pays fixed and the other side pays floating, or both sides paying floating, but never do both sides pay fixed.[5]

Thus, in a plain vanilla interest rate swap, one party makes interest payments at a fixed rate and the other makes interest payments at a floating rate. Both sets of payments are on the same notional principal and occur on regularly scheduled dates. For each payment, the interest rate is multiplied by a fraction representing the number of days in the settlement period over the number of days in a year. In some cases, the settlement period is computed assuming 30 days in each month; in others, an exact day count is used. Some cases assume a 360-day year; others use 365 days.

Let us now illustrate an interest rate swap. Suppose that on 15 December, General Electric Company (NYSE: GE) borrows money for one year from a bank such as Bank of America (NYSE: BAC). The loan is for $25 million and specifies that GE will make interest payments on a quarterly basis on the 15th of March, June, September, and December for one year at the rate of LIBOR plus 25 basis points. At the end of the year, it will pay back the principal. On the 15th of December, March, June, and September, LIBOR is observed and sets the rate for that quarter. The interest is then paid at the end of the quarter.[6]

GE believes that it is getting a good rate, but fearing a rise in interest rates, it would prefer a fixed-rate loan. It can easily convert the floating-rate loan to a fixed-rate loan by engaging in a swap. Suppose it approaches JP Morgan Chase (NYSE: JPM), a large dealer bank, and requests a quote on a swap to pay a fixed rate and receive LIBOR, with payments on the dates of its loan payments. The bank prices the swap (a procedure we cover in Section 4) and quotes a fixed rate of 6.2 percent.[7] The fixed payments will be made based on a day count of 90/365, and the floating payments will be made based on 90/360. Current

---

[5] The case of both sides paying floating is called a basis swap, which we shall cover in Section 5.

[6] Again, we assume 90 days in each interest payment period for this example. The exact payment dates are not particularly important for illustrative purposes.

[7] Typically the rate is quoted as a spread over the rate on a U.S. Treasury security with a comparable maturity. Suppose the yield on a two-year Treasury note is 6 percent. Then the swap would be quoted as 20 basis points over the two-year Treasury rate. By quoting the rate in the this manner, GE knows what it is paying over the Treasury rate, a differential called the swap spread, which is a type of credit risk premium we discuss in Section 7. In addition, a quote in this form protects the bank from the rate changing drastically either during the phone conversation or shortly thereafter. Thus, the quote can stay in effect for a reasonable period of time while GE checks out quotes from other dealers.

LIBOR is 5.9 percent. Therefore, the first fixed payment, which GE makes to JPM, is $25,000,000(0.062)(90/365) = $382,192. This is also the amount of each remaining fixed payment.

The first floating payment, which JPM makes to GE, is $25,000,000(0.059)(90/360) = $368,750. Of course, the remaining floating payments will not be known until later. Exhibit 77-4 shows the pattern of cash flows on the swap from GE's perspective.

EXHIBIT 77-4	Cash Flow to GE on Swap with JPM

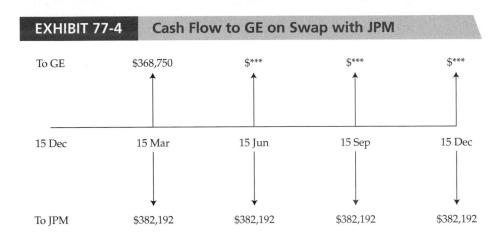

***Computed as $25,000,000(L)90/360, where L is LIBOR on the previous settlement date.

Practice Problem 2

Determine the upcoming payments in a plain vanilla interest rate swap in which the notional principal is €70 million. The end user makes semiannual fixed payments at the rate of 7 percent, and the dealer makes semi-annual floating payments at Euribor, which was 6.25 percent on the last settlement period. The floating payments are made on the basis of 180 days in the settlement period and 360 days in a year. The fixed payments are made on the basis of 180 days in the settlement period and 365 days in a year. Payments are netted, so determine which party pays which and what amount.

SOLUTION
The fixed payments are €70,000,000(0.07)(180/365) = €2,416,438.

The upcoming floating payment is €70,000,000(0.0625)(180/360) = €2,187,500.

The net payment is that the party paying fixed will pay the party paying floating €2,416,438 − €2,187,500 = €228,938.

Note in Exhibit 77-4 that we did not show the notional principal, because it was not exchanged. We could implicitly show that GE received $25 million from JPM and paid $25 million to JPM at the start of the swap. We could also show that the same thing happens at the end. If we look at it that way, it appears as if GE has issued a $25 million fixed-rate bond, which was purchased by JPM, which in turn issued a $25 million floating-rate bond, which was in turn purchased by GE. We say that *it appears* as if this is what happened: In fact, neither party actually issued a bond, but they have generated the cash flows that would occur if GE had issued such a fixed-rate bond, JPM had issued such a floating-rate bond, and each purchased the bond of the other. In other words, we could include the principals on both sides to make each set of cash flows look like a bond, yet the overall cash flows would be the same as on the swap.

So let us say that GE enters into this swap. Exhibit 77-5 shows the net effect of the swap and the loan. GE pays LIBOR plus 25 basis points to Bank of America on its loan, pays 6.2 percent to JPM, and receives LIBOR from JPM. The net effect is that GE pays $6.2 + 0.25 = 6.45$ percent fixed.

EXHIBIT 77-5	GE's Conversion of a Floating-Rate Loan to a Fixed-Rate Loan Using an Interest Rate Swap with JPM

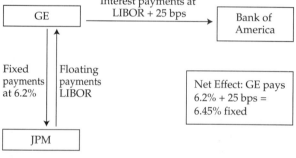

Now, JPM is engaged in a swap to pay LIBOR and receive 6.2 percent. It is exposed to the risk of LIBOR increasing. It would, therefore, probably engage in some other type of transaction to offset this risk. One transaction commonly used in this situation is to sell Eurodollar futures. As discussed in Reading 75, Eurodollar futures prices move $25 in value for each basis point move in LIBOR. JPM will determine how sensitive its position is to a move in LIBOR and sell an appropriate number of futures to offset the risk. Note that Bank of America is exposed to LIBOR as well, but in the banking industry, floating-rate loans are often made because the funding that the bank obtained to make the loan was probably already at LIBOR or a comparable floating rate.

It is possible but unlikely that GE could get a fixed-rate loan at a better rate. The swap involves some credit risk: the possibility, however small, that JPM will default. In return for assuming that risk, GE in all likelihood would get a better rate than it would if it borrowed at a fixed rate. JPM is effectively a wholesaler of risk, using its powerful position as one of the world's leading banks to facilitate the buying and selling of risk for companies such as GE. Dealers profit from the spread between the rates they quote to pay and the rates they quote to receive. The swaps market is, however, extremely competitive and the spreads have been squeezed very tight, which makes it very challenging for dealers to make a profit.

Of course, this competition is good for end users, because it gives them more attractive rates.

3.3 Equity Swaps

By now, it should be apparent that a swap requires at least one variable rate or price underlying it. So far, that rate has been an interest rate.[8] In an equity swap, the rate is the return on a stock or stock index. This characteristic gives the **equity swap** two features that distinguish it from interest rate and currency swaps.

First, the party making the fixed-rate payment could also have to make a variable payment based on the equity return. Suppose the end user pays the equity payment and receives the fixed payment, i.e., it pays the dealer the return on the S&P 500 Index, and the dealer pays the end user a fixed rate. If the S&P 500 increases, the return is positive and the end user pays that return to the dealer. If the S&P 500 goes down, however, its return is obviously negative. In that case, the end user would pay the dealer the *negative return on the S&P 500*, which means that it would receive that return from the dealer. For example, if the S&P 500 falls by 1 percent, the dealer would pay the end user 1 percent, in addition to the fixed payment the dealer makes in any case. So the dealer, or in general the party receiving the equity return, could end up making *both* a fixed-rate payment and an equity payment.

The second distinguishing feature of an equity swap is that the payment is not known until the end of the settlement period, at which time the return on the stock is known. In an interest rate or currency swap, the floating interest rate is set at the beginning of the period.[9] Therefore, one always knows the amount of the upcoming floating interest payment.[10]

Another important feature of some equity swaps is that the rate of return is often structured to include both dividends and capital gains. In interest rate and currency swaps, capital gains are not paid.[11] Finally, we note that in some equity swaps, the notional principal is indexed to change with the level of the stock, although we will not explore such swaps in this book.[12]

Equity swaps are commonly used by asset managers. Let us consider a situation in which an asset manager might use such a swap. Suppose that the Vanguard Asset Allocation Fund (Nasdaq: VAAPX) is authorized to use swaps. On the last day of December, it would like to sell $100 million in U.S. large-cap equities and invest the proceeds at a fixed rate. It believes that a swap allowing it to pay the total return on the S&P 500, while receiving a fixed rate, would achieve this objective. It would like to hold this position for one year, with payments to be made on the last day of March, June, September, and December. It enters into such a swap with Morgan Stanley (NYSE: MWD).

Specifically, the swap covers a notional principal of $100 million and calls for VAAPX to pay MWD the return on the S&P 500 Total Return Index and for MWD to pay VAAPX a fixed rate on the last day of March, June, September, and December for one year. MWD prices the swap at a fixed rate of 6.5 percent. The fixed payments will be made using an actual day count/365 days convention. There are

---

[8] Currency swaps also have the element that the exchange rate is variable.

[9] Technically, there are interest rate swaps in which the floating rate is set at the end of the period, at which time the payment is made. We shall briefly mention these swaps in Section 5.

[10] In a currency swap, however, one does not know the exchange rate until the settlement date.

[11] In some kinds of interest rate swaps, the total return on a bond, which includes dividends and capital gains, is paid. This instrument is called a **total return swap** and is a common variety of a credit derivative.

[12] Some interest rate swaps also have a notional principal that changes, which we shall briefly discuss in Section 5.

90 days between 31 December and 31 March, 91 days between 31 March and 30 June, 92 days between 30 June and 30 September, and 92 days between 30 September and 31 December. Thus, the fixed payments will be

31 March:	$100,000,000(0.065)(90/365) = $1,602,740
30 June:	$100,000,000(0.065)(91/365) = $1,620,548
30 September:	$100,000,000(0.065)(92/365) = $1,638,356
31 December:	$100,000,000(0.065)(92/365) = $1,638,356

Exhibit 77-6 shows the cash flow stream to VAAPX.

Suppose that on the day the swap is initiated, 31 December, the S&P 500 Total Return Index is at 3,517.76. Now suppose that on 31 March, the index is at 3,579.12. The return on the index is

$$\frac{3,579.12}{3,517.76} - 1 = 0.0174$$

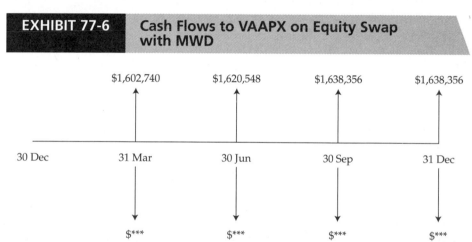

EXHIBIT 77-6   Cash Flows to VAAPX on Equity Swap with MWD

$1,602,740 $1,620,548 $1,638,356 $1,638,356

30 Dec   31 Mar   30 Jun   30 Sep   31 Dec

$*** $*** $*** $***

***Computed as $100,000,000R, where R is the return on the S&P 500 Total Return Index from the previous settlement date.

Thus, the return is 1.74 percent. The equity payment that VAAPX would make to MWD would be $100,000,000(0.0174) = $1,740,000.

Of course, this amount would not be known until 31 March, and only the difference between this amount and the fixed payment would be paid. Then on 31 March, the index value of 3,579.12 would be the base for the following period. Suppose that on 30 June, the index declines to 3,452.78. Then the return for the second quarter would be

$$\frac{3,452.78}{3,579.12} - 1 = -0.0353$$

Therefore, the loss is 3.53 percent, requiring a payment of $100,000,000(0.0353) = $3,530,000.

Because this amount represents a loss on the S&P 500, MWD would make a payment to VAAPX. In addition, MWD would also owe VAAPX the fixed payment of $1,620,548. It is as though VAAPX sold out of its position in stock, thereby avoiding the loss of about $3.5 million, and moved into a fixed-income position, thereby picking up a gain of about $1.6 million.

Practice Problem 3

A mutual fund has arranged an equity swap with a dealer. The swap's notional principal is $100 million, and payments will be made semiannually. The mutual fund agrees to pay the dealer the return on a small-cap stock index, and the dealer agrees to pay the mutual fund based on one of the two specifications given below. The small-cap index starts off at 1,805.20; six months later, it is at 1,796.15.

A. The dealer pays a fixed rate of 6.75 percent to the mutual fund, with payments made on the basis of 182 days in the period and 365 days in a year. Determine the first payment for both parties and, under the assumption of netting, determine the net payment and which party makes it.

B. The dealer pays the return on a large-cap index. The index starts off at 1155.14 and six months later is at 1148.91. Determine the first payment for both parties and, under the assumption of netting, determine the net payment and which party makes it.

SOLUTIONS

A. The fixed payment is $100,000,000(0.0675)182/365 = \$3,365,753$
The equity payment is

$$\left(\frac{1796.15}{1805.20} - 1\right)\$100,000,000 = -\$501,329$$

Because the fund pays the equity return and the equity return is negative, the dealer must pay the equity return. The dealer also pays the fixed return, so the dealer makes both payments, which add up to $3,365,753 + $501,329 = $3,867,082. The net payment is $3,867,082, paid by the dealer to the mutual fund.

B. The large-cap equity payment is

$$\left(\frac{1148.91}{1155.14} - 1\right)\$100,000,000 = -\$539,329$$

The fund owes −$501,329, so the dealer owes the fund $501,329. The dealer owes −$539,329, so the fund owes the dealer $539,329. Therefore, the fund pays the dealer the net amount of $539,329 − $501,329 = $38,000.

Exhibit 77-7 illustrates what VAAPX has accomplished. It is important to note that the conversion of its equity assets into fixed income is not perfect. VAAPX does not hold a portfolio precisely equal to the S&P 500 Total Return Index. To the extent that VAAPX's portfolio generates a return that deviates from the index, some mismatching can occur, which can be a problem. As an alternative, VAAPX can request that MWD give it a swap based on the precise portfolio that VAAPX wishes to sell off. In that case, however, MWD would assess a charge by lowering the fixed rate it pays or raising the rate VAAPX pays to it.[13]

EXHIBIT 77-7   VAAPX's Conversion of an Equity Position into a Fixed-Income Position

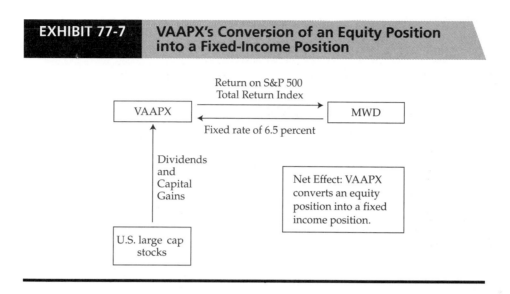

In our previous VAAPX example, the fund wanted to move some money out of a large-cap equity position and invest the proceeds at a fixed rate. Suppose instead that they do not want to move the proceeds into a fixed-rate investment. VAAPX could structure a swap to pay it a floating rate or the return on some other equity index. For example, an asset allocation from U.S. large-cap stocks to U.S. small-cap stocks could be accomplished by having MWD pay the return on the S&P 500 Small Cap 600 Index.

Suppose VAAPX wanted to move out of a position in U.S. stocks and into a position in U.K. large-cap stocks. It could structure the swap to have MWD pay it the return on the FTSE (Financial Times Stock Exchange) 100 Index. Note, however, that this index is based on the prices of U.K. stocks as quoted in pounds sterling. If VAAPX wanted the exposure in pounds—that is, it wanted the currency risk as well as the risk of the U.K. stock market—the payments from MWD to VAAPX would be made in pounds. VAAPX could, however, ask for the payments in dollars. In that case, MWD would hedge the currency risk and make payments in dollars.

Although our focus in this book is on currency, interest rate, and equity products, we shall take a very brief look at some other types of swaps.

3.4 Commodity and Other Types of Swaps

Just as currencies, interest rates, and equities can be used to structure swaps, so too can commodities and just about anything that has a random outcome and to which a corporation, financial institution, or even an individual is exposed. Commodity swaps are very commonly used. For example, airlines enter into swaps to hedge their future purchases of jet fuel. They agree to make fixed payments to a swap dealer on regularly scheduled dates and receive payments determined by the price of jet fuel. Gold mining companies use swaps to hedge future deliveries

---

[13] Note, however, that VAAPX is converting not its entire portfolio but simply a $100 million portion of it.

of gold. Other parties dealing in such commodities as natural gas and precious metals often use swaps to lock in prices for future purchases and sales. In addition, swaps can be based on non-storable commodities, like electricity and the weather. In the case of the weather, payments are made based on a measure of a particular weather factor, such as amounts of rain, snowfall, or weather-related damage.

We have now introduced and described the basic structure of swaps. We have made many references to the pricing and valuation of swaps, and we now move on to explore how this is done.

4   PRICING AND VALUATION OF SWAPS

In Reading 74, we took our first look at the concepts of pricing and valuation when we examined forward contracts on assets and FRAs, which are essentially forward contracts on interest rates. Recall that a forward contract requires no cash payment at the start and commits one party to buy and another to sell an asset at a later date. An FRA commits one party to make a single fixed-rate interest payment and the other to make a single floating-rate interest payment. A swap extends that concept by committing one party to making a series of floating payments. The other party commits to making a series of fixed or floating payments. For swaps containing any fixed terms, such as a fixed rate, pricing the swap means to determine those terms at the start of the swap. Some swaps do not contain any fixed terms; we explore examples of both types of swaps.

All swaps have a market value. Valuation of a swap means to determine the market value of the swap based on current market conditions. The fixed terms, such as the fixed rate, are established at the start to give the swap an initial market value of zero. As we have already discussed, a zero market value means that neither party pays anything to the other at the start. Later during the life of the swap, as market conditions change, the market value will change, moving from zero from both parties' perspective to a positive value for one party and a negative value for the other. When a swap has zero value, it is neither an asset nor a liability to either party. When the swap has positive value to one party, it is an asset to that party; from the perspective of the other party, it thus has negative value and is a liability.

We begin the process of pricing and valuing swaps by learning how swaps are comparable to other instruments. If we know that one financial instrument is equivalent to another, we can price one instrument if we know or can determine the price of the other instrument.

4.1 Equivalence of Swaps and Other Instruments

In this section, we look at how swaps are similar to other instruments. Because our focus is on currency, interest rate, and equity swaps, we do not discuss commodity swaps here.

4.1.1 Swaps and Assets

We have already alluded to the similarity between swaps and assets. For example, a currency swap is identical to issuing a fixed- or floating-rate bond in one currency, converting the proceeds to the other currency, and using the proceeds to purchase a fixed- or floating-rate bond denominated in the other currency. An interest rate swap is identical to issuing a fixed- or floating-rate bond and using the proceeds to purchase a floating- or fixed-rate bond. The notional principal is equivalent to the face value on these hypothetical bonds.

Equity swaps appear to be equivalent to issuing one type of security and using the proceeds to purchase another, where at least one of the types of securities is a stock or stock index. For example, a pay-fixed, receive-equity swap looks like issuing a fixed-rate bond and using the proceeds to buy a stock or index portfolio. As it turns out, however, these two transactions are not exactly the same, although they are close. The stock position in the transaction is not the same as a buy-and-hold position; some adjustments are required on the settlement dates to replicate the cash flows of a swap. We shall take a look at this process of replicating an equity swap in Section 4.2.3. For now, simply recognize that an equity swap is like issuing bonds and buying stock, but not buying and holding stock.

The equivalence of a swap to transactions we are already familiar with, such as owning assets, is important because it allows us to price and value the swap using simple instruments, such as the underlying currency, interest rate, or stock. We do not require other derivatives to replicate the cash flows of a swap. Nonetheless, other derivatives can be used to replicate the cash flows of a swap, and it is worth seeing why this is true.

4.1.2 Swaps and Forward Contracts

Recall that a forward contract, whether on an interest rate, a currency, or an equity, is an agreement for one party to make a fixed payment to the other, while the latter party makes a variable payment to the former. A swap extends this notion by combining a series of forward contracts into a single transaction. There are, however, some subtle differences between swaps and forward contracts. For example, swaps are a series of equal fixed payments, whereas the component contracts of a series of forward contracts would almost always be priced at different fixed rates.[14] In this context we often refer to a swap as a series of off-market forward contracts, reflecting the fact that the implicit forward contracts that make up the swap are all priced at the swap fixed rate and not at the rate at which they would normally be priced in the market. In addition, in interest rate swaps, the next payment that each party makes is known. That would obviously not be the case for a single forward contract. Other subtleties distinguish currency swaps from a series of currency forwards and equity swaps from a series of equity forwards, but in general, it is acceptable to view a swap as a series of forward contracts.

4.1.3 Swaps and Futures Contracts

It is a fairly common practice to equate swaps to futures contracts. This practice is partially correct, but only to the extent that futures contracts can be equated to forward contracts. We saw in Reading 75 that futures contracts are equivalent to forward contracts only when future interest rates are known. Obviously this condition can never truly be met, and because swaps are often used to manage uncertain interest rates, the equivalence of futures with swaps is not always appropriate. Moreover, swaps are highly customized contracts, whereas futures are standardized with respect to expiration and the underlying instrument. Although it is common to equate a swap with a series of futures contracts, this equality holds true only in very limited cases.[15]

---

[14] For example, a series of FRAs would have different fixed rates unless the term structure is flat.

[15] It is possible only in extremely rare circumstances for futures expirations to line up with swap settlement dates and thereby provide perfect equivalence. That does not mean, however, that futures cannot be used to hedge in a delta-hedging sense, as described in Reading 76. A futures price has a given sensitivity to the underlying, and futures are often highly liquid. A dealer, having entered into a swap, can determine the swap's sensitivity to the underlying and execute the appropriate number of futures transactions to balance the volatility of the swap to that of the futures. Indeed, this method is standard for hedging plain vanilla swaps using the Eurodollar futures contract.

4.1.4 *Swaps and Options*

Finally, we note that swaps can be equated to combinations of options. Buying a call and selling a put would force the transacting party to make a net payment if the underlying is below the exercise rate at expiration, and would result in receipt of a payment if the underlying is above the exercise rate at expiration. This payment will be equivalent to a swap payment if the exercise rate is set at the fixed rate on the swap. Therefore, a swap is equivalent to a combination of options with expirations at the swap payment dates. The connection between swaps and options is relatively straightforward for interest rate instruments, but less so for currency and equity instruments. Nonetheless, we can generally consider swaps as equivalent to combinations of options.

In this section, we have learned that swaps can be shown to be equivalent to combinations of assets, combinations of forward contracts, combinations of futures contracts, and combinations of options. Thus, to price and value swaps we can choose any of these approaches. We choose the simplest: swaps and assets.

4.2 Pricing and Valuation

As in previous readings, our goal is to determine the market value of the derivative transaction of interest, in this case, swaps. At the start of a swap, the market value is set to zero. The process of pricing the swap involves finding the terms that force that market value to zero. To determine the market value of a swap, we replicate the swap using other instruments that produce the same cash flows. Knowing the values of these other instruments, we are able to value the swap. This value can be thought of as what the swap is worth if we were to sell it to someone else. In addition, we can think of the value as what we might assign to it on our balance sheet. The swap can have a positive value, making it an asset, or a negative value, making it a liability.

As we noted in Section 4.1, swaps are equivalent to a variety of instruments, but we prefer to use the simplest instruments to replicate the swap. The simplest instruments are the underlying assets: bonds, stocks, and currencies. Therefore, we shall use these underlying instruments to replicate the swap.

To understand the pricing of currency, interest rate, and equity swaps, we shall have to first take a brief digression to examine an instrument that plays an important role in their pricing. We shall see that the floating-rate security will have a value of 1.0, its par, at the start and on any coupon reset date. Recall that we have made numerous references to floating rates and floating payments. Accordingly, we must first obtain a solid understanding of floating-rate notes.

As we did in Reading 74, let us first set up a time line that indicates where we are and where the interest payments on the floating-rate note will occur:

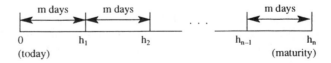

We start at time 0. The interest payments will occur on days $h_1, h_2, \ldots, h_{n-1}$, and h_n, so there are n interest payments in all. Day h_n is the maturity date of the floating-rate note. The time interval between payments is m days. The underlying rate is an m-day interest rate.

For simplicity, we will use LIBOR as the underlying rate and denote it with the symbol we have previously used, $L_i(m)$, which stands for the m-day LIBOR on day i. If i = 1, we are referring to day h_1, which might, for example, be 180 days after day 0. Thus, $h_1 = 180$. $L_0(180)$ is the 180-day LIBOR on day 0. Then h_2 would likely be 360 and $L_0(2m) = L_0(360)$, the 360-day LIBOR on day 0. We denote $B_0(h_j)$ as the present value factor on a zero-coupon instrument paying \$1 at its maturity date. As an example, to discount payments 180 and 360 days later, we multiply the payment amount by the following respective factors:

$$B_0(180) = \frac{1}{1 + L_0(180) \times (180/360)}$$

$$B_0(360) = \frac{1}{1 + L_0(360) \times (360/360)}$$

We can think of these discount factors as the values of spot LIBOR deposits that pay \$1 at maturity, 180 and 360 days later.

On day 0, the floating rate is set for the first period and the interest to be paid at that rate is paid on day h_1. Then on day h_1, the rate is set for the second period and the interest is paid on day h_2. This process continues so that on day h_{n-1} the rate is set for the last period, and the final interest payment and the principal are paid on day h_n. Let the principal be 1.0.

Suppose today is day h_{n-1} and LIBOR on that day is $L_{n-1}(m)$. Remember that this rate is the m-day LIBOR in the market at that time. Therefore, looking ahead to day h_n, we anticipate receiving 1.0, the final principal payment, plus $L_{n-1}(m) \times (m/360)$. What is the value of this amount on day h_{n-1}? We would discount it by the appropriate m-day LIBOR in the following manner:

Value at h_{n-1} = (Payment at h_n)(One-period discount factor)

$$= [1.0 + L_{n-1}(m) \times (m/360)]\left[\frac{1}{1.0 + L_{n-1}(m) \times (m/360)}\right]$$

$$= 1.0$$

The value is 1.0, its par value. Now step back to day h_{n-2}, at which time the rate is $L_{n-2}(m)$. Looking ahead to day h_{n-1} we shall receive an interest payment of $L_{n-2}(m) \times (m/360)$. We do not receive the principal on day h_{n-1}, but it is appropriate to discount the market value on day h_{n-1}, which we just determined is 1.0.[16] Thus, the value of the floating-rate security will be

Value at h_{n-2} = (Payment at h_n−1)(One-period discount factor)

$$= [1.0 + L_{n-2}(m) \times (m/360)]\left[\frac{1}{1.0 + L_{n-2}(m) \times (m/360)}\right]$$

$$= 1.0$$

We continue this procedure, stepping back until we reach time 0. The floating-rate security will have a value of 1.0, its par, at the start and on any coupon reset date.[17] We shall use this result to help us price and value swaps.

---

[16] All we are doing here is discounting the upcoming cash flow and the market value of the security on the next payment date. This procedure is not unique to floating-rate securities; it is standard valuation procedure for any type of security. What is special and different for floating-rate securities is that the market value goes back to par on each payment date.

[17] Floating-rate securities are designed to allow the coupon to catch up with market interest rates on a regularly scheduled basis. The price can deviate from par during the period between reset dates. In addition, if there is any credit risk and that risk changes during the life of the security, its price can deviate from par at any time, including at the coupon reset date. We are assuming no credit risk here.

In previous material in this reading, we have covered currency swaps first. We did so because we showed that an interest rate swap is just a currency swap in which both currencies are the same. A currency swap is thus the more general instrument of the two. For the purposes of this section, however, it will be easier to price and value a currency swap if we first price and value an interest rate swap.

4.2.1 *Interest Rate Swaps*

Pricing an interest rate swap means finding the fixed rate that equates the present value of the fixed payments to the present value of the floating payments, a process that sets the market value of the swap to zero at the start. Using the time line illustrated earlier, the swap cash flows will occur on days $h_1, h_2, \ldots, h_{n-1}$, and h_n, so there are n cash flows in the swap. Day h_n is the expiration date of the swap. The time interval between payments is m days. We can thus think of the swap as being on an m-day interest rate, which will be LIBOR in our examples.

As previously mentioned, the payments in an interest rate swap are a series of fixed and floating interest payments. They do not include an initial and final exchange of notional principals. As we already observed, such payments would be only an exchange of the same money. But if we introduce the notional principal payments as though they were actually made, we have not done any harm. The cash flows on the swap are still the same. The advantage of introducing the notional principal payments is that we can now treat the fixed and floating sides of the swap as though they were fixed- and floating-rate bonds.

So we introduce a hypothetical final notional principal payment of $1 on a swap starting at day 0 and ending on day h_n, in which the underlying is an m-day rate. The fixed swap interest payment *rate*, $FS(0,n,m)$, gives the fixed payment *amount* corresponding to the $1 notional principal. Thus, the present value of a series of fixed interest payments at the swap rate $FS(0,n,m)$ plus a final principal payment of 1.0 is

$$\sum_{j=1}^{n} FS(0,n,m)B_0(h_j) + \$1 \times B_0(h_n), \text{ or}$$

$$FS(0,n,m) \sum_{j=1}^{n} B_0(h_j) + B_0(h_n)$$

Here the summation simply represents the sum of the present value factors for each payment. The expression $B_0(h_n)$ is the present value factor for the final hypothetical notional principal payment of 1.0.

Now we must find the present value of the floating payments, and here we use what we learned about floating-rate notes. Remember that a floating-rate note with $1 face will have a value of $1 at the start and at any coupon reset date. If the swap's floating payments include a final principal payment, we can treat them like a floating-rate note. Hence, we know their value is $1.

Now all we have to do is equate the present value of the fixed payments to the present value of the floating payments

$$FS(0,n,m) \sum_{j=1}^{n} B_0(h_j) + B_0(h_n) = 1.0$$

and solve for the fixed rate $FS(0,n,m)$ that will result in equality of these two streams of payments. The solution is as follows:

$$FS(0,n,m) = \frac{1.0 - B_0(h_n)}{\displaystyle\sum_{j=1}^{n} B_0(h_j)}$$

(77-1)

The swap fixed payment is 1.0 minus the last present value factor divided by the sum of the present value factors for each payment. Thus, we have priced the swap.

One can use several other ways to find the fixed payment on a swap, but this method is unquestionably the simplest. In fact, this formulation shows that the fixed rate on a swap is simply the coupon rate on a par bond whose payments coincide with those on the swap.[18]

Let us now work a problem. Consider a one-year swap with quarterly payments on days 90, 180, 270, and 360. The underlying is 90-day LIBOR. The annualized LIBOR spot rates today are

$L_0(90)$ $= 0.0345$
$L_0(180)$ $= 0.0358$
$L_0(270)$ $= 0.0370$
$L_0(360)$ $= 0.0375$

The present value factors are obtained as follows:

$$B_0(90) = \frac{1}{1 + 0.0345(90/360)} = 0.9914$$

$$B_0(180) = \frac{1}{1 + 0.0358(180/360)} = 0.9824$$

$$B_0(270) = \frac{1}{1 + 0.0370(270/360)} = 0.9730$$

$$B_0(360) = \frac{1}{1 + 0.0375(360/360)} = 0.9639$$

The fixed payment is found as

$$FS(0,n,m) = FS(0,4,90) = \frac{1 - 0.9461}{0.9872 + 0.9737 + 0.9600 + 0.9461} = 0.0092$$

Therefore, the quarterly fixed payment will be 0.0092 for each $1 notional principal. Of course, this rate is quarterly; it is customary to quote it as an annual rate. We would thus see the rate quoted as $0.0092 \times (360/90) = 0.0368$, or 3.68 percent. We would also have to adjust our payment by multiplying by the actual notional principal. For example, if the actual notional principal were $30 million, the payment would be (0.0092)30 million = $276,000.

In determining the fixed rate on the swap, we have essentially found the fixed payment that sets the present value of the floating payments plus a hypothetical notional principal of 1.0 equal to the present value of the fixed payments plus a hypothetical notional principal of 1.0. We have thus made the market value of the swap equal to zero at the start of the transaction. This equality makes sense, because neither party pays any money to the other.

Now suppose we have entered into the swap. Let us move forward into the life of the swap, at which time interest rates have changed, and determine its

---

[18] Technically, bond interest payments are usually found by dividing the annual rate by 2 if the payments are semiannual, whereas swap payments do, on occasion, use day counts such as 181/365 to determine semiannual payments. When we refer to a par bond, we are assuming the payments are structured exactly like those on the swap.

market value. Rather than present mathematical equations for determining its value, we shall work through this example informally. We shall see that the procedure is simple and intuitive. Suppose we have now moved 60 days into the life of the swap. At day 60, we face a new term structure of LIBORs. Because the upcoming payments occur in 30, 120, 210, and 300 days, we want the term structure for 30, 120, 210, and 300 days, which is given as follows:

$$L_{60}(30) = 0.0425$$
$$L_{60}(120) = 0.0432$$
$$L_{60}(210) = 0.0437$$
$$L_{60}(300) = 0.0444$$

The new set of discount factors is

$$B_{60}(30) = \frac{1}{1 + 0.0425(30/360)} = 0.9965$$

$$B_{60}(120) = \frac{1}{1 + 0.0432(120/360)} = 0.9858$$

$$B_{60}(210) = \frac{1}{1 + 0.0437(210/360)} = 0.9751$$

$$B_{60}(300) = \frac{1}{1 + 0.0444(300/360)} = 0.9643$$

We must value the swap from the perspective of one of the parties. Let us look at it as though we were the party paying fixed and receiving floating. Finding the present value of the remaining fixed payments of 0.0092 is straightforward. This present value, including the hypothetical notional principal, is 0.0092(0.9965 + 0.9858 + 0.9751 + 0.9643) + 1.0(0.9643) = 1.0004.

Now we must find the present value of the floating payments. Recall that on day 0, the 90-day LIBOR was 3.45 percent. Thus, the first floating payment will be 0.0345(90/360) = 0.0086. We know that we should discount this payment back 30 days, but what about the remaining floating payments? Remember that we know that the market value of the remaining payments on day 90, including the hypothetical final notional principal, is 1.0. So, we can discount 1.00 + 0.0086 = 1.0086 back 30 days to obtain 1.0086(0.9965) = 1.0051.

The present value of the remaining floating payments, plus the hypothetical notional principal, is 1.0051, and the present value of the remaining fixed payments, plus the hypothetical notional principal, is 1.0004. Therefore, the value of the swap is 1.0051 − 1.0004 = 0.0047 per $1 notional principal. If, for example, the actual swap were for a notional principal of $30 million, the market value would be $30 million(0.0047) = $141,000.

Note that we valued the swap from the perspective of the party paying the fixed rate. From the counterparty's perspective, the value of the swap would be the negative of the value to the fixed-rate payer.

Practice Problem 4

Consider a one-year interest rate swap with semiannual payments.
A. Determine the fixed rate on the swap and express it in annualized terms. The term structure of LIBOR spot rates is given as follows:

Days	Rate
180	7.2%
360	8.0%

B. Ninety days later, the term structure is as follows:

Days	Rate
90	7.1%
270	7.4%

Determine the market value of the swap from the perspective of the party paying the floating rate and receiving the fixed rate. Assume a notional principal of $15 million.

SOLUTIONS

A. First calculate the present value factors for 180 and 360 days:

$$B_0(180) = \frac{1}{1 + 0.072(180/360)} = 0.9653$$

$$B_0(360) = \frac{1}{1 + 0.08(360/360)} = 0.9259$$

The fixed rate is $\frac{1 - 0.9259}{0.9653 + 0.9259} = 0.0392$. The fixed payment would, therefore, be 0.0392 per $1 notional principal. The annualized rate would be $0.0392(360/180) = 0.0784$.

B. Calculate the new present value factors for 90 and 270 days:

$$B_{90}(90) = \frac{1}{1 + 0.071(90/360)} = 0.9826$$

$$B_{90}(270) = \frac{1}{1 + 0.0074(270/360)} = 0.9474$$

The present value of the remaining fixed payments plus the hypothetical $1 notional principal is $0.0392(0.9826 + 0.9474) + 1.0(0.9474) = 1.0231$. The 180-day rate at the start was 7.2 percent, so the first floating payment would be $0.072(180/360) = 0.036$. The present value of the floating payments plus the hypothetical $1 notional principal will be $1.036(0.9826) = 1.0180$. The market value of a pay-floating, receive-fixed swap is, therefore, $1.0231 - 1.0180 = 0.0051$. For a notional principal of $15 million, the market value is $15,000,000(0.0051) = \$76,500$.

Although an interest rate swap is like a series of FRAs, or a long position in an interest rate cap and a short position in an interest rate floor with the exercise rate set at the fixed rate on a swap, pricing and valuing an interest rate swap as either of these instruments is more difficult than what we have done here. To price the swap as a series of FRAs, we would need to calculate the forward rates, which is not difficult but would add another step. If we priced a swap as a combination of caps and floors, we would need to price these options. As we saw in Reading 76, interest rate option pricing can be somewhat complex. In addition, we would have to find the exercise rate on the cap and floor that equated their values, which would require trial and error. What we have seen here is the trick that if we add the notional principal to both sides of an interest rate swap, we do not change the swap payments, but we make the cash flows on each side of the swap equivalent to those of a bond. Then we can price the swap as though it were a pair of bonds, one long and the other short. One side is like a floating-rate bond, which we know is priced at par value at the time of issuance as well as on any reset date. The other side is like a fixed-rate bond. Because the value of the fixed-rate bond must equal that of the floating-rate bond at the start, we know that the coupon on a par value bond is the fixed rate on the swap.

Having discussed the pricing and valuation of interest rate swaps, we can now move on to currency swaps, taking advantage of what we know about pricing interest rate swaps. As we have already noted, an interest rate swap is just like a currency swap in which both currencies are the same.

4.2.2 Currency Swaps

Recall the four types of currency swaps: (1) pay one currency fixed, receive the other fixed, (2) pay one currency fixed, receive the other floating, (3) pay one currency floating, receive the other fixed, and (4) pay one currency floating, receive the other floating. In determining the fixed rate on a swap, we must keep in mind one major point: The fixed rate is the rate that makes the present value of the payments made equal the present value of the payments received. In the fourth type of currency swap mentioned here, both sides pay floating so there is no need to find a fixed rate. But all currency swaps have two notional principals, one in each currency. We can arbitrarily set the notional principal in the domestic currency at one unit. We then must determine the equivalent notional principal in the other currency. This task is straightforward: We simply convert the one unit of domestic currency to the equivalent amount of foreign currency, dividing 1.0 by the exchange rate.

Consider the first type of currency swap, in which we pay the foreign currency at a fixed rate and receive the domestic currency at a fixed rate. What are the two fixed rates? We will see that they are the fixed rates on plain vanilla interest rate swaps in the respective countries.

Because we know that the value of a floating-rate security with $1 face value is $1, we know that the fixed rate on a plain vanilla interest rate swap is the rate on a $1 par bond in the domestic currency. That rate results in the present value of the interest payments and the hypothetical notional principal being equal to 1.0 unit of the domestic currency. Moreover, for a currency swap, the notional principal is typically paid, so we do not even have to call it hypothetical. We know that the fixed rate on the domestic leg of an interest rate swap is the appropriate domestic fixed rate for a currency swap in which the domestic notional principal is 1.0 unit of the domestic currency.

What about the fixed rate for the foreign payments on the currency swap? To answer that question, let us assume the point of view of a resident of the foreign country. Given the term structure in the foreign country, we might be interested in first pricing plain vanilla interest rate swaps in that country. So, we know that the fixed rate on interest rate swaps in that country would make the present value of the interest and principal payments equal 1.0 unit of that currency.

Now let us return to our domestic setting. We know that the fixed rate on interest rate swaps in the foreign currency makes the present value of the foreign interest and principal payments equal to 1.0 unit of the foreign currency. We multiply by the spot rate, S_0, to obtain the value of those payments in our domestic currency: 1.0 times S_0 equals S_0, which is now in terms of the domestic currency. This amount does not equal the present value of the domestic payments, but if we set the notional principal on the foreign side of the swap equal to $1/S_0$, then the present value of the foreign payments will be $S_0(1/S_0) = 1.0$ unit of our domestic currency, which is what we want.

Let us now summarize this argument:

▶ The fixed rate on plain vanilla swaps in our country makes the present value of the domestic interest and principal payments equal 1.0 unit of the domestic currency.

▶ The fixed rate on plain vanilla swaps in the foreign country makes the present value of the foreign interest and principal payments equal 1.0 unit of the foreign currency.

▶ A notional principal of $1/S_0$ units of foreign currency makes the present value of the foreign interest and principal payments equal $1/S_0$ units of the foreign currency.

▶ Conversion of $1/S_0$ units of foreign currency at the current exchange rate of S_0 gives 1.0 unit of domestic currency.

▶ Therefore, the present value of the domestic payments equals the present value of the foreign payments.

▶ The fixed rates on a currency swap are, therefore, the fixed rates on plain vanilla interest rate swaps in the respective countries.

Of course, if the domestic notional principal is any amount other than 1.0, we multiply the domestic notional principal by $1/S_0$ to obtain the foreign notional principal. Then the actual swap payments are calculated by multiplying by the overall respective notional principals.

The second and third types of currency swaps each involve one side paying fixed and the other paying floating. The rate on the fixed side of each of these swaps is, again, just the fixed rate on an interest rate swap in the given country. The payments on the floating side automatically have the same present value as the payments on the fixed side. We again use 1.0 unit of domestic currency and $1/S_0$ units of foreign currency as the notional principal.

For the last type of currency swap, in which both sides pay floating, we do not need to price the swap because both sides pay a floating rate. Again, the notional principals are 1.0 unit of domestic currency and $1/S_0$ units of foreign currency.

In the example we used in pricing interest rate swaps, we were given a term structure for a one-year swap with quarterly payments. We found that the fixed payment was 0.0092, implying an annual rate of 3.68 percent. Let us now work through a currency swap in which the domestic currency is the dollar and the foreign currency is the Swiss franc. The current exchange rate is $0.80. We shall use the same term structure used previously for the domestic term structure: $L_0(90) = 0.0345$, $L_0(180) = 0.0358$, $L_0(270) = 0.0370$, and $L_0(360) = 0.0375$. The Swiss term structure, denoted with a superscript SF, is

$$L_0^{SF}(90) = 0.0520$$
$$L_0^{SF}(180) = 0.0540$$
$$L_0^{SF}(270) = 0.0555$$
$$L_0^{SF}(360) = 0.0570$$

The present value factors are

$$B_0^{SF}(90) = \frac{1}{1 + 0.0520(90/360)} = 0.9872$$

$$B_0^{SF}(180) = \frac{1}{1 + 0.0540(180/360)} = 0.9737$$

$$B_0^{SF}(270) = \frac{1}{1 + 0.0555(270/360)} = 0.9600$$

$$B_0^{SF}(360) = \frac{1}{1 + 0.0570(360/360)} = 0.9461$$

The fixed payment is easily found as

$$FS^{SF}(0, n, m) = FS^{SF}(0,4,90) = \frac{1 - 0.9461}{0.9872 + 0.9737 + 0.9600 + 0.9461} = 0.0139$$

The quarterly fixed payment is thus SF0.0139 for each SF1.00 of notional principal. This translates into an annual rate of $0.0139(360/90) = 0.0556$ or 5.56 percent, so in Switzerland we would quote the fixed rate on a plain vanilla interest rate swap in Swiss francs as 5.56 percent.

Our currency swap involving dollars for Swiss francs would have a fixed rate of 3.68 percent in dollars and 5.56 percent in Swiss francs. The notional principal would be $1.0 and 1/$0.80 = SF1.25. Summarizing, we have the following terms for the four swaps:

Swap 1: Pay dollars fixed at 3.68 percent, receive SF fixed at 5.56 percent.

Swap 2: Pay dollars fixed at 3.68 percent, receive SF floating.

Swap 3: Pay dollars floating, receive SF fixed at 5.56 percent.

Swap 4: Pay dollars floating, receive SF floating.

In each case, the notional principal is $1 and SF1.25, or more generally, SF1.25 for every dollar of notional principal.

As we did with interest rate swaps, we move 60 days forward in time. We have a new U.S. term structure, given in the interest rate swap problem, and a new Swiss franc term structure, which is given below:

$$L_{60}^{SF}(30) = 0.0600$$
$$L_{60}^{SF}(120) = 0.0615$$
$$L_{60}^{SF}(210) = 0.0635$$
$$L_{60}^{SF}(300) = 0.0653$$

The new set of discount factors is

$$B_{60}^{SF}(30) = \frac{1}{1 + 0.0600(30/360)} = 0.9950$$

$$B_{60}^{SF}(120) = \frac{1}{1 + 0.0615(120/360)} = 0.9799$$

$$B_{60}{}^{SF}(210) = \frac{1}{1 + 0.0635(210/360)} = 0.9643$$

$$B_{60}{}^{SF}(300) = \frac{1}{1 + 0.0655(300/360)} = 0.9484$$

The new exchange rate is \$0.82. Now let us value each swap in turn, taking advantage of what we already know about the values of the U.S. dollar interest rate swaps calculated in the previous section. Recall we found that

Present value of dollar fixed payments = 1.0004

Present value of dollar floating payments = 1.0051

Let us find the comparable numbers for the Swiss franc payments. In other words, we position ourselves as a Swiss resident or institution and obtain the values of the fixed and floating streams of Swiss franc payments per SF1 notional principal. The present value of the remaining Swiss fixed payments is

$$0.0139(0.9950 + 0.9799 + 0.9643 + 0.9484) + 1.0(0.9484) = 1.0024$$

Recall that in finding the present value of the floating payments, we simply recognize that on the next payment date, we shall receive a floating payment of $0.052(90/360) = 0.013$, and the market value of the remaining payments will be 1.0.[19] Thus, we can discount 1.0130 back 30 days to obtain $1.0130(0.9950) = 1.0079$.

These two figures are based on SF1 notional principal. We convert them to the actual notional principal in Swiss francs by multiplying by SF1.25. Thus,

Present value of SF fixed payments = 1.0024(1.25) = SF1.2530

Present value of SF floating payments = 1.0079(1.25) = SF1.2599

Now we need to convert these figures to dollars by multiplying by the current exchange rate of \$0.82. Thus,

Present value of SF fixed payments in dollars = 1.2530(\$0.82) = \$1.0275

Present value of SF floating payments in dollars = 1.2599(\$0.82) = \$1.0331

Now we can value the four currency swaps:

Value of swap to pay SF fixed, receive \$ fixed = −\$1.0275 + \$1.0004 = −\$0.0271

Value of swap to pay SF floating, receive \$ fixed = −\$1.0331 + \$1.0004 = −\$0.0327

Value of swap to pay SF fixed, receive \$ floating = −\$1.0275 + \$1.0051 = −\$0.0224

Value of swap to pay SF floating, receive \$ floating = −\$1.0331 + \$1.0051 = −\$0.0280

Note that all of these numbers are negative. Therefore, our swaps are showing losses as a result of the combination of interest rate changes in the two countries as well as the exchange rate change. To the counterparty, the swaps are worth these same numerical amounts, but the signs are positive.

---

[19] The first floating payment was set when the swap was initiated at the 90-day rate of 5.2 percent times 90/360.

Practice Problem 5

Consider a one-year currency swap with semiannual payments. The two currencies are the U.S. dollar and the euro. The current exchange rate is $0.75.

A. The term structure of interest rates for LIBOR and Euribor are

Days	LIBOR	Euribor
180	7.2%	6.0%
360	8.0%	6.6%

Determine the fixed rate in euros and express it in annualized terms. Note that the LIBOR rates are the same as in Practice Problem 4, in which we found that the fixed payment in dollars was 0.0392.

B. Ninety days later, the term structure is as follows:

Days	LIBOR	Euribor
90	7.1%	5.5%
270	7.4%	6.0%

The new exchange rate is $0.70. Determine the market values of swaps to pay dollars and receive euros. Consider all four swaps that are covered in the reading. Assume a notional principal of $20 million and the appropriate amount for euros. Note that the LIBOR rates are the same as in Practice Problem 4, in which we found that the present value of the fixed payments (floating payments) plus the hypothetical $1 notional principal was $1.0231 ($1.0180).

SOLUTIONS

A. The fixed payment in dollars is the same as in Practice Problem 4: 0.0392. To determine the fixed rate in euros, we first compute the discount factors:

$$B_0^{€}(180) = \frac{1}{1 + 0.06(180/360)} = 0.9709$$

$$B_0^{€}(360) = \frac{1}{1 + 0.066(360/360)} = 0.9381$$

The fixed rate in euros is, therefore, $\dfrac{1 - 0.9381}{0.9709 + 0.9381} = 0.0324$.

On an annual basis, this rate would be $0.0324(360/180) = 0.0648$.

B. Recalculate the euro discount factors:

$$B_{90}^{€}(90) = \frac{1}{1 + 0.055(90/360)} = 0.9864$$

$$B_{90}^{€}(270) = \frac{1}{1 + 0.060(270/360)} = 0.9569$$

The present value of the fixed payments plus hypothetical €1 notional principal is €0.0324(0.9864 + 0.9569) + €1.0(0.9569) = €1.0199.

The 180-day rate at the start of the swap was 6 percent, so the first floating payment would be 0.06(180/360) = 0.03. The present value of the floating payments plus hypothetical notional principal of €1 is €1.03(0.9864) = €1.0160.

The euro notional principal, established at the start of the swap, is 1/\$0.75 = €1.3333. Converting the euro payments to dollars at the new exchange rate and multiplying by the euro notional principal, we obtain the following values for the four swaps (where we use the present values of U.S. dollar fixed and floating payments as found in Practice Problem 4, repeated in the statement of Part B above).

▶ Pay \$ fixed, receive € fixed = −\$1.0231 + €1.3333(\$0.70)1.0199 = −\$0.0712

▶ Pay \$ fixed, receive € floating = −\$1.0231 + €1.3333(\$0.70)1.0160 = −\$0.0749

▶ Pay \$ floating, receive € fixed = −\$1.0180 + €1.3333(\$0.70)1.0199 = −\$0.0661

▶ Pay \$ floating, receive € floating = −\$1.0180 + €1.3333(\$0.70)1.0160 = −\$0.0698

Now we turn to equity swaps. It is tempting to believe that we will not use any more information regarding the term structure in pricing and valuing equity swaps. In fact, for equity swaps in which one side pays either a fixed or floating rate, the results we have obtained for interest rate swaps will be very useful.

4.2.3 Equity Swaps

In this section, we explore how to price and value three types of equity swaps: (1) a swap to pay a fixed rate and receive the return on the equity, (2) a swap to pay a floating rate and receive the return on the equity, and (3) a swap to pay the return on one equity and receive the return on another.

To price or value an equity swap, we must determine a combination of stock and bonds that replicates the cash flows on the swap. As we saw with interest rate and currency swaps, such a replication is not difficult to create. We issue a bond and buy a bond, with one being a fixed-rate bond and the other being a floating-rate bond. If we are dealing with a currency swap, we require that one of the bonds be denominated in one currency and the other be denominated in the other currency. With an equity swap, it would appear that a replicating strategy would involve issuing a bond and buying the stock or vice versa, but this is not exactly how to replicate an equity swap. Remember that in an equity swap, we receive cash payments representing the return on the stock, and that is somewhat different from payments based on the price.

Pricing a Swap to Pay a Fixed Rate and Receive the Return on the Equity: By example, we will demonstrate how to price an n-payment m-day rate swap to pay a fixed rate and receive the return on equity. Suppose the notional principal is $1, the swap involves annual settlements and lasts for two years (n = 2), and the returns on the stock for each of the two years are 10 percent for the first year and 15 percent for the second year. The equity payment on the swap would be $0.10 the first year and $0.15 the second. If, however, we purchased the stock instead of doing the equity swap, we would have to sell the stock at the end of the first year or we would not generate any cash. Suppose at the end of the first year, the stock is at $1.10. We sell the stock, withdraw $0.10, and reinvest $1.00 in the stock. At the end of the second year the stock would be at $1.15. We then sell the stock, taking cash of $0.15. But we have $1.00 left over. To get rid of, or off-set, this cash flow, suppose that when we purchased the stock we borrowed the present value of $1.00 for two years. Then two years later, we would pay back $1.00 on that loan. This procedure would offset the $1.00 in cash we have from the stock. The fixed payments on the swap can be easily replicated. If the fixed payment is denoted as $FS(0,n,m)$, we simply borrow the present value of $FS(0,n,m)$ for one year and also borrow the present value of $FS(0,n,m)$ for two years. When we pay those loans back, we will have replicated the fixed payments on the swap.

For the more general case of n payments, we do the following to replicate the swap whose fixed payments are $FS(0,n,m)$:

1. Invest $1.00 in the stock.

2. Borrow the present value of $1.00 to be paid back at the swap expiration, day h_n. This is the amount $B_0(h_n)$.

3. Take out a series of loans requiring that we pay back $FS(0,n,m)$ at time h_1, and also at time h_2, and at all remaining times through time h_n.

Note that this transaction is like issuing debt and buying stock. The amount of money required to do this is

$$\$1 - B_0(h_n) - FS(0,n,m) \sum_{j=1}^{n} B_0(h_j)$$

Because no money changes hands at the start, the initial value of the swap is zero. We set the expression above to zero and solve for the fixed payment $FS(0,n,m)$ to obtain

$$FS(0,n,m) = \frac{1.0 - B_0(h_j)}{\sum_{j=1}^{n} B_0(h_j)}$$

This is precisely the formula (Equation 77-1) for the fixed rate on an interest rate swap or a currency swap.

Pricing a Swap to Pay a Floating Rate and Receive the Return on the Equity: If, instead, the swap involves the payment of a floating rate for the equity return, no further effort is needed because there is no fixed rate for which we must solve. We know from our understanding of interest rate swaps that the present value of the floating payments equals the present value of the fixed payments, which equals the notional principal of 1.0. The market value of the swap is zero at the start, as it should be.

Pricing a Swap to Pay the Return on One Equity and Receive the Return on Another Equity: Let $S_0(1)$ and $S_1(1)$ be the level of Stock Index 1 at times 0 and 1, and let $S_0(2)$ and $S_1(2)$ be the level of Stock Index 2 at times 0 and 1. Assume we pay the return on Index 2 and receive the return on Index 1. We need to replicate the cash flows on this swap by investing in these two stocks using some type of strategy. Suppose we sell short \$1.00 of Index 2, taking the proceeds and investing in \$1.00 of Index 1. Then at time 1, we liquidate the position in Index 1, as described above, withdrawing the cash and reinvesting the \$1.00 back into Index 1. We cover the short position in Index 2, taking the proceeds and re-shorting Index 2. We continue in this manner throughout the life of the swap. This strategy replicates the cash flows on the swap. Thus, going long one stock and short the other replicates this swap. Of course, there is no fixed rate and thus no need to price the swap. The market value at the start is zero as it should be.

Now let us look at how to determine the market values of each of these swaps during their lives. In other words, after the swap has been initiated, we move forward in time. We must take into account where we are in the life of the swap and how interest rates and the equity price have changed.

Valuing a Swap to Pay the Fixed Rate and Receive the Return on the Equity: Let us use the same U.S. term structure we have already been using for interest rate and currency swaps. Our equity swap is for one year and will involve fixed quarterly payments. Recall that the fixed payment on the interest rate swap is 0.0092, corresponding to an annual rate of 3.68 percent. This will be the rate on the swap to pay fixed and receive the equity payment.

Now let us move 60 days into the life of the swap, at which time we have a new term structure as given in the interest rate swap example. We started off with a stock price of S_0, and now the stock price is S_{60}. The stock payment we will receive at the first settlement in 30 days is $S_{90}/S_0 - 1$. Let us write this amount as

$$\left(\frac{1}{S_0}\right)S_{90} - 1$$

Sixty days into the life of the swap, we could replicate this payment by purchasing $1/S_0$ shares of stock, currently at S_{60}. Doing so will cost $(1/S_0)S_{60}$. Then at the first settlement, we shall have stock worth $(1/S_0)S_{90}$. We sell that stock, withdrawing cash of $(1/S_0)S_{90} - 1$. We then take the \$1 left over and roll it into the stock again, which will replicate the return the following period, as described above. This procedure will leave \$1 left over at the end. Thus, sixty days into the swap, to replicate the remaining cash flows, we do the following:

1. Invest $(1/S_0)S_{60}$ in the stock.
2. Borrow the present value of \$1.00 to be paid back at the swap expiration, time h_n. This is the amount $B_{60}(h_n)$.
3. Take out a series of loans requiring that we pay back FS(0,n,m) at time h_1, and also at time h_2, and at all remaining times through time h_n.

For the general case of day t, the market value of the swap is

$$\left(\frac{S_t}{S_0}\right) - B_t(h_n) - FS(0,n,m) \sum_{j=1}^{n} B_t(h_j)$$

(77-2)

The first term reflects the investment in the stock necessary to replicate the equity return. The second term is the loan for the present value of $1.00 due at the expiration date of the swap. The third term is the series of loans of the amount FS(0,n,m) due at the various swap settlement dates. Note that all discounting is done using the new term structure. Of course, the overall market value figure would then be multiplied by the notional principal.

Let us calculate these results for our pay-fixed, receive-equity swap 60 days into its life. Suppose the stock index was at 1405.72 when the swap was initiated. Now it is at 1436.59. We use the same term structure at 60 days that we used for the interest rate swap example. The market value of the swap is

$$\left(\frac{1436.59}{1405.72}\right) - 0.9643 - (0.0092)(0.9965 + 0.9858 + 0.9751 + 0.9643) = 0.0216$$

Thus, 60 days into its life, the market value of this fixed-for-equity swap is positive at $0.0216 per $1 notional principal.

Valuing a Swap to Pay a Floating Rate and Receive the Return on the Equity: We can value this swap in two ways. The first will require that we discount the next floating rate and the par value, as we did with interest rate swaps. We can do this because we recognize that a floating-rate security is worth its par value on the payment date. As long as we add the notional principal, we can assume the floating payments are those of a floating-rate bond. The notional principal offsets the $1 left over at the end from holding the stock and withdrawing all of the profits on each settlement date. The calculation of the market value of this swap is simple. We just determine the value of $1 invested in the stock since the last settlement period, minus the present value of the floating leg. With the upcoming floating payment being 0.0086, the market value of the swap is, therefore,

$$\left(\frac{1436.59}{1405.72}\right) - (1.0086)(0.9965) = 0.0169$$

Another, and probably easier, way to arrive at this answer is to recognize that

▶ a swap to pay fixed and receive the equity return is worth 0.0216, and

▶ a swap to pay floating and receive fixed is worth −0.0047.[20]

If we did both of these swaps, the fixed payments would offset and would leave the equivalent of the equity swap. The value would then be 0.0216 − 0.0047 = 0.0169.

Valuing a Swap to Pay One Equity Return and Receive Another: Now we need to value the swap to pay the return on Index 2 and receive the return on Index 1, 60 days into the swap's life. Let the following be the values of the indices on days 0 and 60.

	Day 0	Day 60
Index 1	1405.72	1436.59
Index 2	5255.18	5285.73

---

[20] In Section 4.2.1, we found the value of a swap to pay fixed and receive floating to be 0.0047. Therefore, a swap to pay floating and receive fixed is worth −0.0047.

As we previously described, this swap can be replicated by going long Index 1 and short Index 2. The market value calculation is simple: We find the value of $1 invested in Index 1 since the last settlement day minus the value of $1 invested in Index 2 since the last settlement day. Thus, the market value of the position is

$$\left(\frac{1436.59}{1405.72}\right) - \left(\frac{5285.73}{5255.18}\right) = 0.0161$$

Of course, all of these results are per $1 notional principal, so we would have to multiply by the actual notional principal to get the overall market value of this equity-for-equity swap.

Practice Problem 6

Consider an equity swap that calls for semiannual payments for one year. The party will receive the return on the Dow Jones Industrial Average (DJIA), which starts off at 10033.27. The current LIBOR term structure is

Days	Rate
180	7.2%
360	8.0%

A. In Practice Problem 4, we determined that the fixed rate for a one-year interest rate swap given the above term structure was 0.0392. Given this term structure data, what is the fixed rate in an equity swap calling for the party to pay a fixed rate and receive the return on the DJIA?

B. Find the market value of the swap 90 days later if the new term structure is

Days	Rate
90	7.1%
270	7.4%

The notional principal of the swap is $60 million. The DJIA is at 9955.14. Again, these are the same rates as in Practice Problem 4, for which we computed $B_{90}(180) = 0.9826$ and $B_{90}(360) = 0.9474$.

C. Recompute the market value under the assumption that the counterparty pays a floating rate instead of a fixed rate.

D. Recompute the market value under the assumption that the counterparty pays the return on the Dow Jones Transportation Index, which started off at 2835.17 and 90 days later is 2842.44.

SOLUTIONS

A. Because this term structure is the same as in Practice Problem 4, the fixed rate is the same at 0.0392. The fact that the party here receives an equity return rather than a floating interest rate does not affect the magnitude of the fixed payment.

B. Using the 180- and 360-day discount factors at 90 days from Practice Problem 4, the market value of the swap to pay a fixed rate and receive the equity return is

$$\left(\frac{9955.14}{10033.27}\right) - 0.9474 - 0.0392(0.9826 + 0.9474) = -0.0309$$

Multiplying by the notional principal of $60 million, we obtain a market value of $60,000,000(-0.0309) = -$1,854,000.

C. Because the first floating payment would be at the rate of 7.2 percent and is, therefore, 0.036, the market value of the swap to pay a floating rate and receive the equity return is

$$\left(\frac{9955.14}{10033.27}\right) - 1.036(0.9826) = -0.0258$$

Adjusting for the notional principal, the market value is $60,000,000(-0.0258) = -$1,548,000.

D. The market value of the swap to pay the return on the Dow Jones Transportation Average and receive the return on the DJIA is

$$\left(\frac{9955.14}{10033.27}\right) - \left(\frac{2842.44}{2835.17}\right) = -0.0104$$

Adjusting for the notional principal, the market value is $60,000,000(-0.0104) = -$624,000.

4.3 Some Concluding Comments on Swap Valuation

Let us review some important results on swap valuation and pricing. Because the market value of the swap when initiated is zero, pricing the swap means to find the terms of the swap that will make its market value be zero. If the swap pays a fixed rate, we must find the fixed rate that makes the present value of the fixed payments equal the present value of the floating payments. If both sides of the swap involve floating payments, there are no terms to determine. For currency swaps, we also have to determine the notional principal in one currency that is equivalent to a given notional principal in another currency.

The market value of a swap starts off at zero but changes to either a positive or negative value as the swap evolves through its life and market conditions change. To determine the market value of a swap, we must determine the present value of the remaining stream of payments, netting one against the other.

The market value of a swap gives a number that represents what the swap is worth to each party. If the market value is positive, the swap is like an asset. The amount due to one party is worth more than the amount that party owes. If it is negative, the swap is like a liability. The amount that party owes is worth more than the amount owed to it. The market value of a swap is also sometimes known as the **replacement value.** This notion views the swap as an instrument whose value can potentially be lost through default. If a party is holding a positive value swap and the other party defaults, that value is lost and would require that amount of money to replace it. We discuss this point further in Section 7.

VARIATIONS OF SWAPS   5

So far we have covered the most common types of swaps: fixed-for-floating interest rate swaps, various combinations of fixed and floating currency swaps, and equity swaps involving fixed payments, floating payments, or the returns on another equity. We must also mention some other types of swaps.

We briefly referred to the **basis swap**, in which both sides pay a floating rate. A typical basis swap involves one party paying LIBOR and the other paying the T-bill rate. As we learned in Reading 75, the term *basis* refers to the spread between two prices, usually the spot and futures prices. Here it is simply the spread between two rates, LIBOR and the T-bill rate. Because LIBOR is always more than the T-bill rate, the two parties negotiate a fixed spread such that the party paying LIBOR actually pays LIBOR minus the spread.[21] LIBOR is the borrowing rate of high-quality London banks, and the T-bill rate is the default-free borrowing rate of the U.S. government. The difference between LIBOR and the T-bill rate is thus a reflection of investors' perception of the general level of credit risk in the market. Basis swaps are usually employed for speculative purposes by end users who believe the spread between LIBOR and the T-bill rate will change.[22] A basis swap of this type is, therefore, usually a position taken in anticipation of a change in the relative level of credit risk in the market. As noted, both sides are floating, and typically both sides use 360-day years in their calculations.[23]

Another type of swap we sometimes encounter is not all that different from a plain vanilla or basis swap. In a **constant maturity swap**, one party pays a fixed rate, or a short-term floating rate such as LIBOR, and the other party pays a floating rate that is the rate on a security known as a **constant maturity treasury (CMT)** security. The transaction is also sometimes known as a CMT swap. This underlying instrument is a hypothetical U.S. Treasury note, meaning that its maturity is in the 2- to 10-year range, with a constant maturity. Obviously the reference to a particular CMT cannot be referring to a single note, because the maturity of any security decreases continuously. As mentioned, the note is hypothetical. For example, for a two-year CMT security, when there is an actual two-year note, that note is the CMT security. Otherwise, the yield on a CMT security is interpolated from the yields of securities with surrounding maturities. The distinguishing characteristic of a constant maturity swap is that the maturity of the underlying security exceeds the length of the settlement period. For example, a CMT swap might call for payments every six months, with the rate based on the one-year CMT security. In contrast, a standard swap settling every six months would nearly always be

---

[21] Alternatively, the counterparty could pay the T-bill rate plus the spread.

[22] The spread between LIBOR and the T-bill rate is called the TED spread. It is considered an indicator of the relative state of credit risk in the markets. LIBOR represents the rate on a private borrower (London banks); the T-bill rate is the U.S. government borrowing rate. When the global economy weakens, the TED spread tends to widen because rates based on the credit risk of private borrowers will increase while the U.S. government remains a risk-free borrower.

[23] Of course, a basis swap need not be based on LIBOR and the T-bill rate, so other conventions can be used.

based on a six-month security. Otherwise, however, a constant maturity swap possesses the general characteristics of a plain vanilla swap.

One interesting variant of an interest rate swap is an **overnight index swap (OIS)**. This instrument commits one party to paying a fixed rate as usual. The floating rate, however, is the cumulative value of a single unit of currency invested at an overnight rate during the settlement period. The overnight rate changes daily. This instrument is used widely in Europe but not in the United States.

Amortizing and **accreting swaps** are those in which the notional principal changes according to a formula related to the underlying. The more common of the two is the amortizing swap, sometimes called an **index amortizing swap**. In this type of interest rate swap, the notional principal is indexed to the level of interest rates. The notional principal declines with the level of interest rates according to a predefined schedule. This feature makes the swap similar to certain asset-backed securities, such as mortgage-backed securities, which prepay some of their principal as rates fall. An index amortizing swap is often used to hedge this type of security.

Diff swaps combine elements of interest rate, currency, and equity swaps. In a typical diff swap, one party pays the floating interest rate of one country and the other pays the floating interest rate of another country. Both sets of payments, however, are made in a single currency. So one set of payments is based on the interest rate of one country, but the payment is made in the currency of another country. This swap is a pure play on the interest rate differential between two countries and is basically a currency swap with the currency risk hedged. Alternatively, in equity diff swaps, the return on a foreign stock index is paid in the domestic currency.

An **arrears swap** is a special type of interest rate swap in which the floating payment is set at the end of the period and the interest is paid at that same time. This procedure stands in contrast to the typical interest rate swap, in which the payment is set on one settlement date and the interest is paid on the next settlement date.

In a **capped swap**, the floating payments have a limit as to how high they can be. Similarly, a **floored swap** has a limit on how low the floating payments can be.

There is no limit to the number of variations that can be found in swaps, and it is not worthwhile to examine them beyond the basic, most frequently used types. We must, however, cover an important variation of a swap that combines elements of both swaps and options.

6   SWAPTIONS

A **swaption** *is an option to enter into a swap*. Although swaptions can be designed in a variety of ways, we shall focus exclusively on the most widely used swaption, the plain vanilla interest rate swaption. This is a swaption to pay the fixed rate and receive the floating rate or the other way around. It allows the holder to establish a fixed rate on the underlying swap in advance and have the option of entering into the swap with that fixed rate or allowing the swaption to expire and entering into the swap at the fixed rate that prevails in the market.

6.1 Basic Characteristics of Swaptions

The two types of swaptions are a **payer swaption** and a **receiver swaption**. A payer swaption allows the holder to enter into a swap as the fixed-rate payer and floating-rate receiver. A receiver swaption allows the holder to enter into a swap as the fixed-rate receiver and floating-rate payer. Therefore, these terms refer to the fixed rate and are comparable to the terms *call* and *put* used for other types of options. Although it is not apparent at this point, a payer swaption is a put and a receiver swaption is a call.

Swaptions have specific expiration dates. Like ordinary options, swaptions can be European style (exercisable only at expiration) or American style (exercisable at any time prior to expiration). A swaption is based on a specific underlying swap. For example, consider a European payer swaption that expires in two years and allows the holder to enter into a three-year swap with semiannual payments every 15 January and 15 July. The payments will be made at the rate of 6.25 percent and will be computed using the 30/360 adjustment. The underlying swap is based on LIBOR, and the notional principal is $10 million. Of course, a swaption has a price or premium, which is an amount paid by the buyer to the seller up front.

Note that this swaption expires in two years and the underlying swap expires three years after that. This arrangement is called a 2×5 swaption, a terminology we used in explaining FRAs. The underlying can be viewed as a five-year swap at the time the swaption is initiated and will be a three-year swap when the swaption expires.

Finally, there are a number of ways to settle a swaption at expiration. Recall that ordinary options can allow for either physical delivery or cash settlement. We will explore the comparable concepts for swaptions in Section 6.3.

6.2 Uses of Swaptions

Swaptions have a variety of purposes, which we shall cover in more detail when we discuss swap applications and strategies. For right now, however, we take a brief glance at why swaptions exist.

Swaptions are used by parties who anticipate the need for a swap at a later date but would like to establish the fixed rate today, while providing the flexibility to not engage in the swap later or engage in the swap at a more favorable rate in the market. These parties are often corporations that expect to need a swap later and would like to hedge against unfavorable interest rate moves while preserving the flexibility to gain from favorable moves.

Swaptions are used by parties entering into a swap to give them the flexibility to terminate the swap. In Section 1.2, we discussed why a party engaged in a swap might wish to terminate it before expiration. Suppose the party in a swap is paying fixed and receiving floating. If it owned a receiver swaption, it could exercise the swaption, thereby entering into a swap to receive a fixed rate and pay a floating rate. It would then have offset the floating parts of the swap, effectively removing any randomness from the position.[24] But the only way the party could do so would require having previously purchased a swaption. Similarly, parties engaged in a receive-fixed, pay-floating swap can effectively offset it by exercising a payer swaption.

Swaptions are used by parties to speculate on interest rates. As with any interest rate sensitive instrument, swaptions can be used to speculate. Their prices move with interest rates and, like all options, they contain significant leverage. Thus, they are appropriate instruments for interest rate speculators.

---

[24] Note, however, that both swaps are still in effect even though the floating sides offset. Because both swaps remain in effect, there is credit risk on the two transactions.

6.3 Swaption Payoffs

When a swaption is exercised, it effectively creates a stream of equivalent payments, commonly referred to in the financial world as an annuity. This stream is a series of interest payments equal to the difference between the exercise rate and the market rate on the underlying swap when the swaption is exercised.

Consider a European payer swaption that expires in two years and is exercisable into a one-year swap with quarterly payments, using 90/360 as the day-count adjustment. The exercise rate is 3.60 percent. The notional principal is $20 million. Now, suppose we are at the swaption expiration and the term structure is the one we obtained when pricing the interest rate swap earlier in this reading. We repeat that information here:

Maturity	Rate	Discount Factor
90 days	3.45%	0.9914
180 days	3.58%	0.9824
270 days	3.70%	0.9730
360 days	3.75%	0.9639

Under these conditions, we found that the swap fixed payment is 0.0092, equating to an annual fixed rate of 3.68 percent.

The holder of the swaption has the right to enter into a swap to pay 3.60 percent, whereas in the market such a swap would require payment at a rate of 3.68 percent. Therefore, here at expiration this swaption does appear to offer an advantage over the market rate. Let us consider the three possible ways to exercise this swaption.

The holder can exercise the swaption, thereby entering into a swap to pay 3.60 percent. The quarterly payment at the rate of 3.60 percent would be $20,000,000 × (0.0360)(90/360) = $180,000. The swaption holder would then be engaged in a swap to pay $180,000 quarterly and receive LIBOR. The first floating payment would be at 3.45 percent[25] and would be $20,000,000(0.0345)(90/360) = $172,500. The remaining floating payments would, of course, be determined later. The payment stream is illustrated in Exhibit 77-8, Panel A.

Alternatively, the holder can exercise the swaption, thereby entering into a swap to pay 3.60 percent, and then enter into a swap in the market to receive fixed and pay floating. The fixed rate the holder would receive is 3.68 percent, the market-determined fixed rate at the time the swaption expires. The quarterly fixed payment at 3.68 percent would be $20,000,000(0.0368)(90/360) = $184,000. Technically, the LIBOR payments are still made, but the same amount is paid and received. Hence, they effectively offset. Panel B illustrates this payment stream. This arrangement would be common if the counterparty to the second swap is not the same as the counterparty to the swaption.

The holder can arrange to receive a net payment stream of $184,000 − $180,000 = $4,000. Panel C illustrates this payment stream. In this case, the counterparty to the second swap is probably the same as the counterparty to the swap created by exercising the swaption, who would be the counterparty to the swaption. Because the floating payments are eliminated, the amount of cash passing between the parties is reduced, which mitigates the credit risk.

---

[25] The first floating payment is at 3.45 percent because this is the 90-day rate in effect at the time the swap is initiated.

The holder can receive an up-front cash payment. We can easily determine the amount. It is simply the present value of the payment stream shown in Panel C, which we can obtain using the discount factors shown above:

$$\$4,000(0.9914 + 0.9824 + 0.9730 + 0.9639) = \$15,643$$

This pure cash settlement is illustrated in Panel D.

EXHIBIT 77-8   **Cash Flows from Swaptions**

A. Exercise of Payer Swaption, Entering into a Pay-Fixed, Receive-Floating Swap

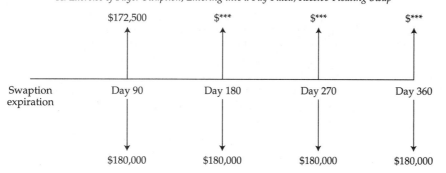

***Computed as $20,000,000(L)90/360, where L is LIBOR on the previous settlement date.

B. Exercise of Payer Swaption, Entering into a Pay-Fixed, Receive-Floating Swap and Entering into a Receive-Fixed, Pay-Floating Swap at the Market Rate

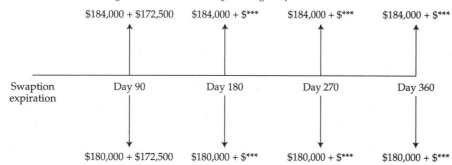

***Computed as $20,000,000(L)90/360, where L is LIBOR on the previous settlement date.

C. Exercise of Swaption with Offsetting Swap Netted

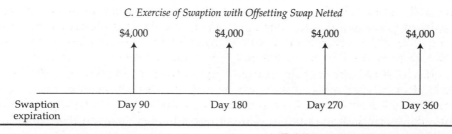

(Exhibit continued on next page ...)

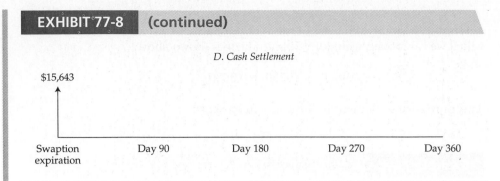

EXHIBIT 77-8   (continued)

D. Cash Settlement

Other than transaction costs and the credit risk associated with the newly created swaps, each of these means of exercising a swaption has the same value. Of course, the two parties would have to agree up front which of these means to use at expiration. Cash settlement is the most common.

Therefore, the payoff of a payer swaption in which the exercise rate is x and the market rate on the underlying swap is FS(0,n,m) is

$$\text{Max}[0, FS(0,n,m) - x] \sum_{j=1}^{n} B_0(h_j) \qquad \text{(77-3)}$$

Similarly, the payoff of a receiver swaption would be

$$\text{Max}[0, x - FS(0,n,m)] \sum_{j=1}^{n} B_0(h_j) \qquad \text{(77-4)}$$

Of course, these figures would be multiplied by the actual notional principal. So we see that a swaption effectively creates an annuity. The present value factors are not relevant in determining whether the swaption will be exercised. Exercise is determined solely on the relationship between the swap rate at expiration and the exercise rate. The present value factors are used to convert the stream of net payments obtained upon exercise of the swap into a current value. Now, let us take a brief look at how a swaption is priced.

6.4 Pricing and Valuation of Swaptions

We shall show here, perhaps somewhat surprisingly, that an interest rate swaption is like an option on a coupon bond. Restating our result given above, the payoff of a payer swaption is

$$\text{Max}[0, FS(0,n,m) - x] \sum_{j=1}^{n} B_0(h_j)$$

This expression finds the present value of the difference between the fixed rate on the swap and the exercise rate on the swaption if that difference is positive. Otherwise, the payoff is zero. Recall from Section 4.2.1 (Equation 77-1) that the fixed rate on an interest rate swap is

$$FS(0,n,m) = \frac{1.0 - B_0(h_n)}{\sum\limits_{j=1}^{n} B_0(h_j)}$$

Substituting the fixed rate into the payoff equation, we obtain

$$\text{Max}\left[0, \frac{1.0 - B_0(h_n)}{\sum\limits_{j=1}^{n} B_0(h_j)} - x \right] \sum\limits_{j=1}^{n} B_0(h_j)$$

which can be rewritten as

$$\text{Max}\left\{ 0, 1.0 - \left[x \sum\limits_{j=1}^{n} B_0(h_j) + B_0(h_N) \right] \right\}$$

Note the term in brackets,

$$x \sum\limits_{j=1}^{n} B_0(h_j) + B_0(h_N)$$

which is the same as the market value at the swaption expiration of a coupon bond of $1.00 par value, in which the coupon is x. Thus, the swaption payoff is effectively Max(0,1.0 − Market value of coupon bond). This amount is the payoff of a put option on a coupon bond with coupon of x, a face value of 1.0, and a maturity of the swap expiration date. The exercise price is the par value of 1.0, and the exercise rate of the swaption is the coupon rate on the bond. Hence, we can value the swaption as though it were simply a put on a bond. In a similar manner, the payoff of a receiver swaption can be shown to be that of a call option on this coupon bond.

Now you can see why, as we stated earlier, a payer swaption is a put option and a receiver swaption is a call option. More specifically, a payer swaption is a put option on a bond and a receiver swaption is a call option on a bond.

Practice Problem 7

Calculate the market value of a receiver swaption at the expiration if the exercise rate is 4 percent and the term structure is given below:

Days	Rate
180	7.2%
360	8.0%

These are the same rates as in Practice Problem 4. The swaption is on a swap that will make payments in 180 and 360 days, and the notional principal is $25 million. Also, show that this payoff is equivalent to that of a call option on a bond.

SOLUTION

Based on a fixed rate of 0.0392 from Practice Problem 4, the market value is Max(0,0.04 − 0.0392)(0.9653 + 0.9259) = 0.0015.

Based on a notional principal of $25 million, this is a market value of 25,000,000(0.0015) = $37,500.

This payoff is equivalent to that of a call option on a bond with an exercise price of 1.0, its par value. At this point in time, the expiration of the option, the bond on which this call is based would have a market value of 0.04(0.9653 + 0.9259) + 1.0(0.9259) = 1.0015.

Therefore, the payoff of a call on this bond is Max(0,1.0015 − 1.0) = 0.0015—the same as that of the swaption.

With that result in mind, we could value the swaption using any of a number of approaches to valuing bond options. We shall not take up the pricing of swaptions here, as it is a somewhat advanced topic and the issues are somewhat complicated. It is not a straightforward matter to apply the Black–Scholes–Merton or Black models to pricing bond options. We discussed the valuation of options on bonds in Reading 76, noting that the binomial model is probably the best way to do so.

6.5 Forward Swaps

We have seen in this book that options represent rights and forward contracts represent commitments. Just as there are options to enter swaps, there are also forward contracts to enter into swaps, called forward swaps. They are not as widely used as swaptions but do offer the advantage, as is always the case with forwards, that one does not have to pay any cash up front as with an option premium. Forward swaps are priced by pricing the swap off of the forward term structure instead of the spot term structure.

7   CREDIT RISK AND SWAPS

In this reading, we have mentioned on a few occasions that swaps are subject to credit risk. Indeed, as we have emphasized throughout the book, *all* over-the-counter derivatives are subject to credit risk. In this section, we examine some of the issues involved in the credit risk of swaps.

Recall that a swap has zero market value at the start. It starts off as neither an asset nor a liability. Once the swap is engaged and market conditions change, the market value becomes positive for one party and negative for the other. The party holding the positive value swap effectively owns an asset, which represents a claim against the counterparty. This claim is a netting of the amount owed by the counterparty and the amount that the party owes, with the former exceeding the latter. The party holding the positive-value swap thus assumes credit risk. The counterparty could declare bankruptcy, leaving the party holding the positive-value swap with a claim that is subject to the legal process of bankruptcy. In most swap arrangements, netting is legally recognized, so the claim has a value based on the net amount. Of course, as we described in the reading, currency swaps are generally not netted so the credit risk is greater on currency swaps.

The party to which the swap has a negative value is not subject to credit risk. It owes more than is owed to it, so the other party faces the risk.

During the life of the swap, however, the market value to a given party can change from positive to negative or vice versa. Hence, the party not facing credit risk at a given moment is not entirely free of risk, because the swap value could turn positive for it later.

The timing of credit risk is in the form of immediate or **current credit risk** and deferred or **potential credit risk**. The former arises when a payment is immediately due and cannot be made by one party. The latter reflects the ever-present possibility that, although a counterparty may currently be able to make payments, it may be unable to make future payments.

Let us work through an example illustrating these points. Consider two parties A and B who are engaged in a swap. At a given payment date, the payment of Party A to Party B is $100,000 and the payment of Party B to Party A is $35,000. As is customarily the case, Party A must pay $65,000 to Party B. Once the payment is made, we shall assume that the market value of the swap is $1,250,000, which is an asset to A and a liability to B.

Suppose Party A is unable to pay and declares bankruptcy. Then Party B does not make any payment to Party A. Party A is bankrupt, but the swap is an asset to A. Given the $65,000 owed by A to B, the claim of A against B is $1,250,000 − $65,000 = $1,185,000. We emphasize in this example that A is the bankrupt party, but the swap is an asset to A, representing its claim against B. If B were holding the positive market value of the swap, it would have a claim of $1,250,000 + $65,000 = $1,315,000 on A as A enters into the bankruptcy process.

Let us change the example a little by having A not be bankrupt on the payment date. It makes its payment of $65,000 to B and moves forward. But a few months later, before the next payment, A declares bankruptcy. Its payment is not immediately due, but it has essentially stated that it will not make its next payment or any payments thereafter. To determine the financial implications of the event, the two parties must compute the market value of the swap. Suppose the value is now $1,100,000 and is positive to A. Then A, the bankrupt party, holds a claim against B of $1,100,000. The fact that A is bankrupt does not mean that it cannot have a claim against someone else, just as a bankrupt corporation can be owed money for inventory it has sold but on which it has not yet collected payment.

Of course, A could be bankrupt and B's claim against A could be the greater. In fact, with A bankrupt, there is a very good possibility that this scenario would be the case. Then, of course, B would simply be another of A's many creditors.

Exactly what happens to resolve these claims in each of these situations is a complex legal issue and is beyond the scope of our level of treatment. In addition, the bankruptcy laws vary somewhat around the world, so the potential exists for different treatments of the same situation. Most countries do recognize the legality of netting, however, so it would be rare that a party would be able to claim the full amount owed it without netting out the amount it owes.

The credit risk in a swap varies during its life. An interest rate or equity swap has no final principal payments. The credit risk in either of these swap types is greater during the middle of its life. This occurs because near the end of the life of the swap, not many payments remain, so there is not much money at risk. And at the beginning of the life of the swap, the credit risk is usually low because the parties would probably not engage in the swap if a great deal of credit risk already were present at the start. Therefore, the greatest potential for credit losses is during the middle of the life of the swap. For currency swaps, in which the notional principals are typically exchanged at the end of the life of the swap, the credit risk is concentrated between the middle and the end of its life.

The parties that engage in swaps are generally of good credit quality, but the fear of default is still a significant concern. Yet, perhaps surprisingly, the rates that all parties pay on swaps are the same, regardless of either party's credit quality. As we have illustrated here, a plain vanilla swap, in which one party pays a floating rate and the other pays a fixed rate, has the fixed rate determined by the term structure for that underlying rate. Therefore, if a party wanted to engage in a swap to pay LIBOR and receive a fixed rate, it would get the fixed rate based on the LIBOR term structure, regardless of its credit quality or that of the counterparty, provided that the two parties agreed to do the transaction. Implicit in the fixed rate, however, is the spread between LIBOR and the default-free rate. As we described earlier in the reading, swap rates are quoted with respect to a spread over the equivalent default-free rate. Thus, a one-year swap rate of 3.68 percent as in our example might be quoted as 50 basis points over the rate on a one-year U.S. Treasury note, implying that the one-year U.S. Treasury note rate was 3.18 percent. This differential is called the **swap spread**.

It is important to note that the swap spread is not a measure of the credit risk on a given swap but rather a reflection of the general level of credit risk in the global economy. The LIBOR term structure reflects the borrowing rate for London banks, which are generally highly rated but not default free. Whenever a recession approaches or credit concerns arise, this spread widens and fixed-rate payers on swaps end up paying more. Of course, floating-rate payers end up paying more as well, but the additional cost to them is less obvious up front because the floating rates change over the life of the swap.

So all parties pay the same rate, but clearly some parties are better credit risks than others. In addition, virtually no parties are default free, and many are of lower credit quality than the typical London bank on which LIBOR is based. How do parties manage the credit risk in swaps? There are a number of methods. For right now, however, we cover one such method that we have seen before with respect to forward contracts and that is routinely used in the futures market: marking to market.

Reconsider the interest rate swap we covered earlier in the reading in which the payments are made quarterly in the amount of 0.0092 per $1 notional principal. The swap lasts for one year, so there are four payments. Suppose the parties agree to mark the contract to market halfway through its life—that is, in six months, immediately after the payment is made. Suppose we are at that point and the term structure is as follows:

$$L_{180}(90) = 0.0390$$
$$L_{180}(180) = 0.0402$$

Note that we are at day 180, and the upcoming payments occur in 90 and 180 days. We thus need to calculate $B_{180}(270)$ and $B_{180}(360)$. These present value factors are

$$B_{180}(270) = \frac{1}{1 + 0.039(90/360)} = 0.9903$$

$$B_{180}(360) = \frac{1}{1 = 0.0402(180/360)} = 0.9803$$

Now we can compute the market value of the swap. The present value of the remaining fixed payments, plus the hypothetical notional principal, is $0.0092(0.9903 + 0.9803) + 1.0(0.9803) = 0.9984$.

Because the 90-day floating rate is 3.90 percent, the next floating payment will be $0.0390(90/360) = 0.00975$. Of course, we do not know the last floating payment, but it does not matter because the present value of the remaining floating payments, plus the hypothetical notional principal, is automatically 1.0 because we are on the coupon reset date. Therefore, the market value of the swap to the party receiving floating and paying fixed is the present value of the floating payments, 1.0, minus the present value of the fixed payments, 0.9984, or $1.0 - 0.9984 = 0.0016$.

If the two parties marked this swap to market, the party paying floating and receiving fixed would pay the other party a lump sum cash payment of $0.0016 per $1 notional principal. The two parties would then reprice the swap. The new payment would be

$$FS(0,n,m) = FS(0,2,90) = \frac{1 - 0.9803}{0.9903 + 0.9803} = 0.01$$

Thus, the fixed payment would be 0.01 for the rest of the swap.

Practice Problem 8

Consider a two-year swap to pay a fixed rate and receive a floating rate with semiannual payments. The fixed rate is 0.0462. Now, 360 days later, the term structure is

Days	Rate
180	10.1%
360	10.4%

The next floating payment will be 0.045. The swap calls for marking to market after 180 days, and, therefore, will now be marked to market. Determine the market value, identify which party pays which, and calculate the new fixed rate.

SOLUTION
First find the discount factors:

$$B_{360}(540) = \frac{1}{1 + 0.0101(180/360)} = 0.9519$$

$$B_{360}(720) = \frac{1}{1 + 0.104(360/360)} = 0.9058$$

The market value of the fixed payments plus $1 hypothetical notional principal is $0.0462(0.9519 + 0.9058) + 1.0(0.9058) = 0.9916$.

The market value of the floating payments plus $1 hypothetical notional principal is 1.045(0.9519) = 0.9947.

Therefore, the market value to the party paying fixed and receiving floating is 0.9947 − 0.9916 = 0.0031.

This amount would be paid by the party paying floating and receiving fixed. The new fixed rate would then be

$$\frac{1 - 0.9058}{0.9519 + 0.9058} = 0.0507$$

This rate would be quoted as an annual rate of 5.07% (360/180) = 10.14%.

As in the futures market, marking a swap contract to market results in the two parties terminating the contract and automatically engaging in a new swap. In essence, the arrangement commits the two parties to terminating the swap and re-establishing it on a predetermined schedule. This process reduces the credit risk by requiring one party to pay the other any amount due at a time prior to the expiration date of the swap. The effect is to reduce the extent to which the swap can go deeply underwater to one of the parties, who may be facing financial problems.

A number of other techniques can be used to control credit risk in swaps.

8   THE ROLE OF SWAP MARKETS

In each of the preceding three readings, we have discussed the role played by the markets represented by the various derivative instruments. The swap market is extremely large, consisting of dealers and end users engaging in customized transactions that involve a series of payments. As we showed in this reading, swaps can be equivalent to various other derivative instruments. Moreover, we used transactions in assets to replicate swaps. Hence, an obvious question is why swaps exist when the same results can be obtained using other instruments.

First let us ignore the obvious counter-question of why other instruments exist when swaps serve the same purpose. In the race to see which derivative instrument is more popular, swaps have clearly won. We can only surmise the reason why.

The tremendous popularity of swaps results largely from the popularity of interest rate swaps. For several reasons, these instruments have been embraced by corporations as tools for managing interest rate risk. One is that interest rate swaps, certainly the plain vanilla type, are simple instruments, rarely requiring technology, computational skills, or financial know-how beyond what exists in most corporate treasury offices. In short, they are easy to understand. In addition, interest rate swaps can easily be viewed as a pair of loans. Borrowing and lending money is second nature to corporations. Corporations view engaging in swaps as nothing more than an extension of their regular practice of borrowing and lending money. Many corporations are restricted in their use of options and futures, but they can usually justify swaps as nothing more than variations of loans. Also, swaps are so easily tailored to alter the interest rate patterns on most corporate loans that they seem to go hand in hand with the typical fixed- and floating-rate loans that corporations take out. Many corporations borrow money and combine the loan with a swap right from the start. Finally, we should note that some dealer firms have exploited the attractions of swaps by aggressive selling. In some cases, corporations entered into ill-advised and occasionally complex, exotic swaps. We do not suggest that most dealers have engaged in unethical actions (although some certainly have) but rather that, as in all sales-oriented activities, customers do not always get impartial advice from sales personnel. In some cases, corporations have used swaps to step over the line from good risk management into speculation on risks they know nothing about. In short, at least part of the success of swaps has probably not been for the right reasons.

But using swaps for the wrong reason does not sufficiently explain the success of these instruments. If it were the primary motivation for their use, swaps would die out as a risk management tool. Instead, swaps have grown in popularity. Swaps provide a mechanism for managing the risks associated with a series of payments. Although forward contracts and other instruments can manage that risk, a swap is more of a portfolio approach to managing risk—a package of risk management tools all rolled up into one. Given that risk often exists in a series, swaps are ideal instruments for managing it. Other instruments may be able to do the job, but they must be carefully constructed with a certain amount of financial ingenuity.

We have now completed Readings 74, 75, 76, and 77, each of which deals with specific types of derivatives. We have obtained a good description of each derivative and examined how to price and value them. We have briefly alluded to how they are used. In the following reading we shall examine strategies and applications using these instruments.

OPTIONAL SEGMENT
ENDS

SUMMARY

▶ Swaps are over-the-counter contracts in which two parties agree to pay a series of cash flows to each other. At least one series is floating or variable and related to an interest rate, exchange rate, equity price, or commodity price; the other can be fixed or floating. Swaps have zero value at the start and have payments made on scheduled payment or settlement dates and a final termination or expiration date. When swap payments are made in the same currency, the payments are usually netted. Swaps are subject to default on the part of either party.

▶ Swaps can be terminated by having one party pay the market value of the swap to the other party, by entering into a swap in which the variable payments offset, by selling the swap to another party, or by exercising a swaption to enter into an offsetting swap.

▶ In a currency swap, each party makes payments to the other in different currencies. A currency swap can have one party pay a fixed rate in one currency and the other pay a fixed rate in the other currency; have both pay a floating rate in their respective currencies; have the first party pay a fixed rate in one currency and the second party pay a floating rate in the other currency; or have the first party pay a floating rate in one currency and the second pay a fixed rate in the other currency. In currency swaps, the notional principal is usually exchanged at the beginning and at the end of the life of the swap, although this exchange is not mandatory.

▶ The payments on a currency swap are calculated by multiplying the notional principal by the fixed or floating interest rate times a day-count adjustment. This procedure is done in each currency, and the respective parties make their separate payments to each other. The payments are not netted.

▶ In a plain vanilla interest rate swap, one party makes payments at a fixed rate and the other makes payments at a floating rate, with no exchange of notional principal. A typical plain vanilla swap involves one party paying a fixed rate and the other paying a floating rate such as LIBOR. Swaps are often done by a party borrowing floating at a rate tied to LIBOR; that party then uses a pay-fixed, receive-floating swap to offset the risk of its exposure to LIBOR and effectively convert its loan to a fixed-rate loan.

▶ The payments on an interest rate swap are calculated by multiplying the notional principal by the fixed or floating interest rate times a day-count adjustment. The respective amounts are netted so that the party owing the greater amount makes a net payment to the other.

▶ The three types of equity swaps involve one party paying a fixed rate, a floating rate, or the return on another equity, while the other party pays an equity return. Therefore, an equity swap is a swap in which at least one party pays the return on a stock or stock index.

▶ The equity payment (or payments, if both sides of the swap are related to an equity return) on an equity swap is calculated by multiplying the return on the stock over the settlement period by the notional principal. If there is a fixed or floating payment, it is calculated in the same manner as in an interest rate swap. With payments in a single currency, the two sets of payments are netted.

▶ Swap pricing means to determine the fixed rate and any relevant terms, such as the foreign notional principal on a currency swap, at the start of the swap. Valuation means to determine the market value of the swap, which is the present value of one stream of payments less the present value of the other stream of payments. The market value of a swap is zero at the start but will change to positive for one party and negative for the other during the life of the swap, as market conditions change and time passes.

▶ Swaps can be viewed as combinations of assets. Currency swaps are like issuing a bond denominated in one currency and using the proceeds to buy a bond denominated in another currency. Interest rate swaps are like issuing a fixed-rate bond and using the proceeds to buy a floating-rate bond or vice versa. Equity swaps are like issuing a bond and using the proceeds to buy stock or vice versa. Equity swaps with both sides paying an equity return are like selling short one stock and using the proceeds to buy another stock. The stock position is not, however, a buy-and-hold position and requires some rebalancing.

▶ An interest rate swap is like a series of off-market FRAs, meaning that the rate on each FRA is set at the swap rate, not at the rate it would be set at if priced as an FRA with zero market value at the start. In addition, the first payment on a swap is just an exchange of known amounts of cash. Currency swaps and equity swaps are similar to forward contracts, but the connection is not as straightforward as in interest rate swaps.

▶ Interest rate swaps are like being long (short) interest rate calls and short (long) interest rate puts. Currency swaps and equity swaps are also similar to combinations of options, but the connection is not as straightforward.

▶ The fixed rate on an interest rate swap equates the present value of the fixed payments plus a hypothetical notional principal to the present value of the floating payments plus a hypothetical notional principal. The notional principals offset but permit these swaps to be treated like bonds. The fixed rate is then equivalent to the fixed rate on a par bond with the same payments as on the swap. The market value of the swap during its life is found by determining the difference in the market values of the floating- and fixed-rate bonds later during their lives under the new term structure.

▶ The fixed rates on a currency swap are the same as the fixed rates on plain vanilla interest rate swaps in the given countries. The foreign notional principal for a domestic notional principal of one unit is the inverse of the exchange rate. In other words, it is the foreign currency equivalent of the domestic notional principal. Because a currency swap is like issuing a bond in one currency and using the proceeds to buy a bond in another currency, the market value of a currency swap during its life is found by determining the difference in the market values of the two bonds during their lives using the new term structures in the two countries. The foreign bond value must be converted to its domestic equivalent by using the new exchange rate.

▶ The fixed rate on an equity swap is the same as the fixed rate on a plain vanilla interest rate swap. The market value of an equity swap involving fixed or floating payments during its life is found as the present value of the equity payments less the present value of the fixed or floating payments necessary to replicate the equity swap payment. The market value of an equity swap in which both sides make equity payments is the market value of a long position in one equity and a short position in the other, assuming the positions are liquidated at each settlement date and gains and losses are paid out.

▶ A swaption is an option to enter into a swap. The two types of interest rate swaptions are payer swaptions, which allow the holder to enter into a swap to pay the fixed rate and receive the floating rate, and receiver swaptions, which allow the holder to enter into a swap to receive the fixed rate and pay the floating rate. Swaptions are based on a specific underlying swap and have an exercise rate and an expiration date. At expiration, they can be exercised to enter into the underlying swap. Swaptions require an up-front premium.

▶ Swaptions exist to allow users the flexibility to enter into swaps at later dates but establish the terms in advance. If market conditions are not favorable to exercising a swaption, the holder can allow the swaption to expire and obtain more favorable terms by entering into a swap at the market rate. Swaptions are used by parties who anticipate a need to enter into a swap at a later date, who anticipate the need to terminate an already-existing swap, or who wish to speculate on interest rates.

▶ The payoffs of an interest rate swaption are like those of an option on a coupon-bearing bond. The option has an exercise price of par value, and the coupon rate is the exercise rate on the swaption. A payer swaption is like a put on the bond, and a receiver swaption is like a call on the bond.

▶ At expiration, an interest rate payer swaption is worth the maximum of zero or the present value of the difference between the market swap rate and the exercise rate, valued as an annuity extending over the remaining life of the underlying swap. To value a receiver swaption at expiration, we take the difference between the exercise rate and the market swap rate, adjusted for its present value over the life of the underlying swap. These figures must be multiplied by the notional principal.

▶ The market value of a swaption at expiration can be received in one of four ways: by exercising the swaption to enter into the underlying swap, by exercising the swaption and entering into an offsetting swap that keeps both swaps in force, by exercising the swaption and entering into an offsetting swap that eliminates both swaps and pays a series of payments equal to the net difference in the fixed rates on the two swaps, or by exercising the swaption and receiving a lump sum cash payment.

▶ A forward swap is a forward contract to enter into a swap. It commits both parties to entering into a swap at a later date at a fixed rate agreed on today. In contrast to a swaption, which is the right to enter into a swap, a forward swap is a binding commitment to enter into a swap.

▶ Credit risk arises in a swap due to the possibility that a party will not be able to make its payments. Current credit risk is the risk of a party being unable to make the upcoming payment. Potential credit risk is the risk of a party being unable to make future payments. Credit risk is faced only by the party that is owed the greater amount.

▶ The credit risk in an interest rate or equity swap is greatest during the middle of the swap's life. The risk is small at the beginning of the swap because the parties would not engage in the swap if the credit risk were significant at the start. The risk is low at the end of the life of the swap because of the small number of remaining payments. For currency swaps, the payment of notional principal shifts the credit risk more toward the end of the life of the swap. In addition, because the payments are typically not netted, the credit risk on currency swaps is greater than on interest rate swaps.

▶ The swap spread is the difference between the fixed rate on a swap and the yield on a default-free security of the same maturity as the swap. The spread indicates the average credit risk in the global economy but not the credit risk in a given swap.

▶ Netting reduces the credit risk in a swap by reducing the amount of money passing from any one party to another. The amount owed by a party is deducted from the amount due to a party, and only the net is paid. Marking a swap to market is a process in which the parties agree to periodically calculate the market value of the swap and have the party owing the greater amount pay the market value to the other party. The fixed rate is then reset on the swap until it is marked to market again or terminates. This procedure forces the party to which the swap is losing money to pay the other party before getting too deeply in debt.

▶ Swaps play an important role in the financial system by providing a simple means of managing a series of risks. Their popularity has arisen largely from corporate use in managing interest rate exposure.

PROBLEMS FOR READING 77

1. A U.S. company enters into a currency swap in which it pays a fixed rate of 5.5 percent in euros and the counterparty pays a fixed rate of 6.75 percent in dollars. The notional principals are $100 million and €116.5 million. Payments are made semiannually and on the basis of 30 days per month and 360 days per year.

   A. Calculate the initial exchange of payments that takes place at the beginning of the swap.

   B. Calculate the semiannual payments.

   C. Calculate the final exchange of payments that takes place at the end of the swap.

2. A British company enters into a currency swap in which it pays a fixed rate of 6 percent in dollars and the counterparty pays a fixed rate of 5 percent in pounds. The notional principals are £75 million and $105 million. Payments are made semiannually and on the basis of 30 days per month and 360 days per year.

   A. Calculate the initial exchange of payments that takes place at the beginning of the swap.

   B. Calculate the semiannual payments.

   C. Calculate the final exchange of payments that takes place at the end of the swap.

3. A U.S. company has entered into an interest rate swap with a dealer in which the notional principal is $50 million. The company will pay a floating rate of LIBOR and receive a fixed rate of 5.75 percent. Interest is paid semiannually, and the current LIBOR is 5.15 percent. Calculate the first payment and indicate which party pays which. Assume that floating-rate payments will be made on the basis of 180/360 and fixed-rate payments will be made on the basis of 180/365.

4. A German company that has issued floating-rate notes now believes that interest rates will rise. It decides to protect itself against this possibility by entering into an interest rate swap with a dealer. In this swap, the notional principal is €25 million and the company will pay a fixed rate of 5.5 percent and receive Euribor. The current Euribor is 5 percent. Calculate the first payment and indicate which party pays which. Assume that floating-rate payments will be made on the basis of 90/360 and fixed-rate payments will be made on the basis of 90/365.

5. An asset manager wishes to reduce his exposure to large-cap stocks and increase his exposure to small-cap stocks. He seeks to do so using an equity swap. He agrees to pay a dealer the return on a large-cap index, and the dealer agrees to pay the manager the return on a small-cap index. For each of the scenarios listed below, calculate the first overall payment and indicate which party makes the payment. Assume that payments are made semiannually. The notional principal is $100 million.

   A. The value of the small-cap index starts off at 689.40, and the large-cap index starts at 1130.20. In six months, the small-cap index is at 625.60 and the large-cap index is at 1251.83.

   B. The value of the small-cap index starts off at 689.40 and the large-cap index starts at 1130.20. In six months, the small-cap index is at 703.23 and the large-cap index is at 1143.56.

6. An asset manager wishes to reduce her exposure to small-cap stocks and increase her exposure to fixed-income securities. She seeks to do so using an equity swap. She agrees to pay a dealer the return on a small-cap index and the dealer agrees to pay the manager a fixed rate of 5.5 percent. For each of the scenarios listed below, calculate the overall payment six months later and indicate which party makes the payment. Assume that payments are made semiannually (180 days per period) and there are 365 days in each year. The notional principal is $50 million.

   A. The value of the small-cap index starts off at 234.10 and six months later is at 238.41.

   B. The value of the small-cap index starts off at 234.10 and six months later is at 241.27.

7. An asset manager wishes to reduce his exposure to fixed-income securities and increase his exposure to large-cap stocks. He seeks to do so using an equity swap. He agrees to pay a dealer a fixed rate of 4.5 percent, and the dealer agrees to pay the manager the return on a large-cap index. For each of the scenarios listed below, calculate the overall payment six months later and indicate which party makes it. Assume that payments are made semiannually (180 days per period) and there are 365 days in a year. The notional principal is $25 million.

   A. The value of the large-cap index starts off at 578.50 and six months later is at 622.54.

   B. The value of the large-cap index starts off at 578.50 and six months later is at 581.35.

4⅝	4⅛	⅜	
5½	5½	—	⅜
5½	2¹³⁄₁₆	—	¼
20⅝	21¹³⁄₁₆	+	⅞
17⅜	18⅛	+	⅞
	6½	—	½
6½	6½	—	
7¼	3¹⁄₃₂	—	⅛
	15⁄₁₆		
	9⁄₁₆	9⁄₁₆	
1¹⁄₃₂			
7¹⁵⁄₁₆	7¹³⁄₁₆	7¹⁵⁄₁₆	
2⅝	2¹¹⁄₃₂	2½	+
	2¾	2¼	2¼
	11¾	11¼	+
61½	12¼	11⅜	
87	33¾	33	33¼ —
	25⅝	24⁹⁄₁₆	25¾ +
602	11⅝	11⅞ +	
833	12		
16	10½	10½	10½ —
78	15⅞	15¹³⁄₁₆	15⅞ —
	9¹⁄₁₆	8¼	8⅜
5 4508			
430	11¼	10⅛	
		4⅞	4⅞

RISK MANAGEMENT APPLICATIONS OF OPTION STRATEGIES

by Don M. Chance

LEARNING OUTCOMES

The candidate should be able to:

a. determine the value at expiration, profit, maximum profit, maximum loss, breakeven underlying price at expiration, and general shape of the graph of the strategies of buying and selling calls and buying and selling puts, and explain each strategy's characteristics;

b. determine the value at expiration, profit, maximum profit, maximum loss, breakeven underlying price at expiration, and general shape of the graph of the covered call strategy and the protective put strategy, and explain each strategy's characteristics.

INTRODUCTION   1

In the previous reading, we examined strategies that employ forward and futures contracts. Recall that forward and futures contracts have linear payoffs and do not require an initial outlay. Options, on the other hand, have nonlinear payoffs and require the payment of cash up front. By having nonlinear payoffs, options permit their users to benefit from movements in the underlying in one direction and to not be harmed by movements in the other direction. In many respects, they offer the best of all worlds, a chance to profit if expectations are realized with minimal harm if expectations turn out to be wrong. The price for this opportunity is the cash outlay required to establish the position. From the standpoint of the holder of the short position, options can lead to extremely large losses. Hence, sellers of options must be well compensated in the form of an adequate up-front premium and must skillfully manage the risk they assume.

In this reading we examine the most widely used option strategies. The reading is divided into three parts. In the first part, we look at option strategies that are typically used in equity investing, which include standard strategies involving single options and strategies that combine options with the underlying. In the second part, we look at the specific strategies that are commonly used in managing interest rate risk. In the third part, we examine option strategies that are used primarily by dealers and sophisticated traders to manage the risk of option positions.

Let us begin by reviewing the necessary notation. These symbols are the same ones we have previously used. First recall that time 0 is the time at which the strategy is initiated and time T is the time the option expires, stated as a fraction of a year. Accordingly, the amount of time until expiration is simply $T - 0 = T$, which is (Days to expiration)/365. The other symbols are

c_0, c_T = price of the call option at time 0 and time T
p_0, p_T = price of the put option at time 0 and time T[1]
X = exercise price
S_0, S_T = price of the underlying at time 0 and time T
V_0, V_T = value of the position at time 0 and time T
Π = profit from the transaction: $V_T - V_0$
r = risk-free rate

Some additional notation will be introduced when necessary.

Note that we are going to measure the profit from an option transaction, which is simply the final value of the transaction minus the initial value of the transaction. Profit does not take into account the time value of money or the risk. Although a focus on profit is not completely satisfactory from a theoretical point of view, it is nonetheless instructive, simple, and a common approach to examining options. Our primary objective here is to obtain a general picture of the manner in which option strategies perform. With that in mind, discussing profit offers probably the best trade-off in terms of gaining the necessary knowledge with a minimum of complexity.

In this reading, we assume that the option user has a view regarding potential movements of the underlying. In most cases that view is a prediction of the direction of the underlying, but in some cases it is a prediction of the volatility of the underlying. In all cases, we assume this view is specified over a horizon that corresponds to the option's life or that the option expiration can be tailored to the horizon date. Hence, for the most part, these options should be considered customized, over-the-counter options.[2] Every interest rate option is a customized option.

---

[1] As in Reading 76, lower case indicates European options, and upper case indicates American options. In this reading, all options are European.

[2] If the options discussed were exchange-listed options, it would not significantly alter the material in this reading.

Because the option expiration corresponds to the horizon date for which a particular view is held, there is no reason to use American options. Accordingly, all options in this reading are European options. Moreover, we shall not consider terminating the strategy early. Putting an option in place and closing the position prior to expiration is certainly a legitimate strategy. It could reflect the arrival of new information over the holding period, but it requires an understanding of more complex issues, such as valuation of the option and the rate at which the option loses its time value. Thus, we shall examine the outcome of a particular strategy over a range of possible values of the underlying only on the expiration day.

Section 2 of this reading focuses on option strategies that relate to equity investments. Section 3 concentrates on strategies using interest rate options. In Section 4, we focus on managing an option portfolio.

OPTION STRATEGIES FOR EQUITY PORTFOLIOS

2

Many typical illustrations of option strategies use individual stocks, but we shall use options on a stock index, the Nasdaq 100, referred to simply as the Nasdaq. We shall assume that in addition to buying and selling options on the Nasdaq, we can also buy the index, either through construction of the portfolio itself, through an index mutual fund, or an **exchange-traded fund**.[3] We shall simply refer to this instrument as a stock. We are given the following numerical data:

$S_0 = 2000$, value of the Nasdaq 100 when the strategy is initiated

$T = 0.0833$, the time to expiration (one month = $1/12$)

The options available will be the following:[4]

Exercise Price	Call Price	Put Price
1950	108.43	56.01
2000	81.75	79.25
2050	59.98	107.39

Let us start by examining an initial strategy that is the simplest of all: to buy or sell short the underlying. Panel A of Exhibit 78-1 illustrates the profit from the transaction of buying a share of stock. We see the obvious result that if you buy the stock and it goes up, you make a profit; if it goes down, you incur a loss. Panel B shows the case of selling short the stock. Recall that this strategy involves borrowing the shares from a broker, selling them at the current price, and then

---

[3] Exchange-traded shares on the Nasdaq 100 are called Nasdaq 100 Trust Shares and QQQs, for their ticker symbol. They are commonly referred to as Qubes, trade on the Amex, and are the most active exchange-traded fund and often the most actively traded of all securities. Options on the Nasdaq 100 are among the most actively traded as well.

[4] These values were obtained using the Black–Scholes–Merton model. By using this model, we know we are working with reasonable values that do not permit arbitrage opportunities.

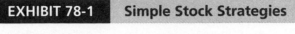

EXHIBIT 78-1   **Simple Stock Strategies**

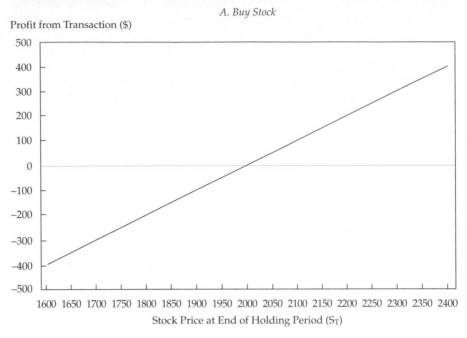

A. Buy Stock

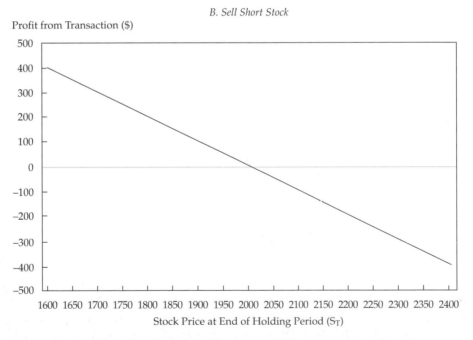

B. Sell Short Stock

buying them back at a later date. In this case, if you sell short the stock and it goes down, you make a profit. Conversely, if it goes up, you incur a loss. Now we shall move on to strategies involving options, but we shall use the stock strategies again when we combine options with stock.

In this section we examine option strategies in the context of their use in equity portfolios. Although these strategies are perfectly applicable for fixed-income portfolios, corporate borrowing scenarios, or even commodity risk management situations, they are generally more easily explained and understood in the context of investing in equities or equity indices.

To analyze an equity option strategy, we first assume that we establish the position at the current price. We then determine the value of the option at expiration for a specific value of the index at expiration. We calculate the profit as the value at expiration minus the current price. We then generate a graph to illustrate the value at expiration and profit for a range of index values at expiration. Although the underlying is a stock index, we shall just refer to it as the underlying to keep things as general as possible. We begin by examining the most fundamental option transactions, long and short positions in calls and puts.

2.1 Standard Long and Short Positions

2.1.1 Calls

Consider the purchase of a call option at the price c_0. The value at expiration, c_T, is $c_T = \max(0, S_T - X)$. Broken down into parts,

$$c_T = 0 \qquad \text{if } S_T \leq X$$
$$c_T = S_T - X \qquad \text{if } S_T > X$$

The profit is obtained by subtracting the option premium, which is paid to purchase the option, from the option value at expiration, $\Pi = c_T - c_0$. Broken down into parts,

$$\Pi = -c_0 \qquad \text{if } S_T \leq X$$
$$\Pi = S_T - X - c_0 \qquad \text{if } S_T > X$$

Now consider this example. We buy the call with the exercise price of 2000 for 81.75. Consider values of the index at expiration of 1900 and 2100. For $S_T = 1900$,

$$c_T = \max(0, 1900 - 2000) = 0$$
$$\Pi = 0 - 81.75 = -81.75$$

For $S_T = 2100$,

$$c_T = \max(0, 2100 - 2000) = 100$$
$$\Pi = 100 - 81.75 = 18.25$$

Exhibit 78-2 illustrates the value at expiration and profit when S_T, the underlying price at expiration, ranges from 1600 to 2400. We see that buying a call results in a limited loss of the premium, 81.75. For an index value at expiration greater than the exercise price of 2000, the value and profit move up one-for-one with the index value, and there is no upper limit.

It is important to identify the breakeven index value at expiration. Recall that the formula for the profit is $\Pi = \max(0, S_T - X) - c_0$. We would like to know the value of S_T for which $\Pi = 0$. We shall call that value S_T^*. It would be nice to be able to solve $\Pi = \max(0, S_T^* - X) - c_0 = 0$ for S_T^*, but that is not directly possible. Instead, we observe that there are two ranges of outcomes, one in which $\Pi = S_T^* - X - c_0$ for $S_T^* > X$, the case of the option expiring in-the-money, and the other in which $\Pi = -c_0$ for $S_T \leq X$, the case of the option expiring out-of-the-money. It is obvious from the equation and by observing

Exhibit 78-2 that in the latter case, there is no possibility of breaking even. In the former case, we see that we can solve for $S_T{}^*$. Setting $\Pi = S_T{}^* - X - c_0 = 0$, we obtain $S_T{}^* = X + c_0$.

Thus, the breakeven is the exercise price plus the option premium. This result should be intuitive: The value of the underlying at expiration must exceed the exercise price by the amount of the premium to recover the cost of the premium. In this problem, the breakeven is $S_T{}^* = 2000 + 81.75 = 2081.75$. Observe in Exhibit 78-2 that the profit line crosses the axis at this value.

In summarizing the strategy, we have the following results for the option buyer:

$$c_T = \max(0, S_T - X)$$
Value at expiration $= c_T$
Profit: $\Pi = c_T - c_0$
Maximum profit $= \infty$
Maximum loss $= c_0$
Breakeven: $S_T{}^* = X + c_0$

EXHIBIT 78-2	Buy Call

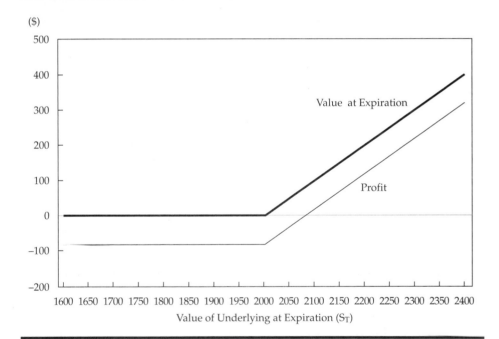

Call options entice naive speculators, but it is important to consider the *likely* gains and losses more than the *potential* gains and losses. For example, in this case, the underlying must go up by about 4.1 percent in one month to cover the cost of the call. This increase equates to an annual rate of almost 50 percent and is an unreasonable expectation by almost any standard. If the underlying does not move at all, the loss is 100 percent of the premium.

For the seller of the call, the results are just the opposite. The sum of the positions of the seller and buyer is zero. Hence, we can take the value and profit results for the buyer and change the signs. The results for the maximum profit and maximum loss are changed accordingly, and the breakeven is the same. Hence, for the option seller,

$c_T = \max(0, S_T - X)$
Value at expiration $= -c_T$
Profit: $\Pi = -c_T + c_0$
Maximum profit $= c_0$
Maximum loss $= \infty$
Breakeven: $S_T{}^* - X + c_0$

Exhibit 78-3 shows the results for the seller of the call. Note that the value and profit have a fixed maximum. The worst case is an infinite loss. Just as there is no upper limit to the buyer's potential gain, there is no upper limit to how much the seller can lose.

Call options are purchased by investors who are bullish. We now turn to put options, which are purchased by investors who are bearish.

EXHIBIT 78-3	Sell Call

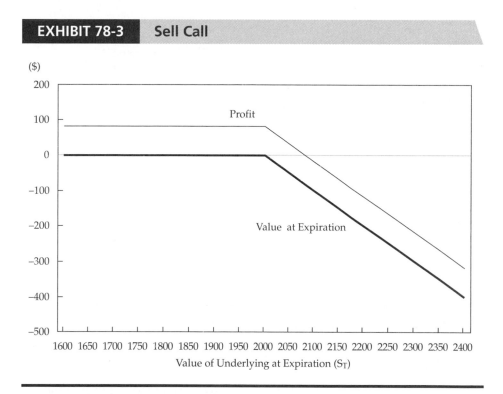

Practice Problem 1

Consider a call option selling for $7 in which the exercise price is $100 and the price of the underlying is $98.

A. Determine the value at expiration and the profit for a buyer under the following outcomes:

i. The price of the underlying at expiration is $102.

ii. The price of the underlying at expiration is $94.

B. Determine the value at expiration and the profit for a seller under the following outcomes:

  i. The price of the underlying at expiration is \$91.

  ii. The price of the underlying at expiration is \$101.

C. Determine the following:

  i. The maximum profit to the buyer (maximum loss to the seller)

  ii. The maximum loss to the buyer (maximum profit to the seller)

D. Determine the breakeven price of the underlying at expiration.

SOLUTIONS

A. Call buyer

  i. Value at expiration $= c_T = \max(0, S_T - X) = \max(0, 102 - 100) = 2$
  $\Pi = c_T - c_0 = 2 - 7 = -5$

  ii. Value at expiration $= c_T = \max(0, S_T - X) = \max(0, 94 - 100) = 0$
  $\Pi = c_T - c_0 = 0 - 7 = -7$

B. Call seller

  i. Value at expiration $= -c_T = -\max(0, S_T - X) = -\max(0, 91 - 100) = 0$
  $\Pi = -c_T + c_0 = -0 + 7 = 7$

  ii. Value at expiration $= -c_T = -\max(0, S_T - X) = -\max(0, 101 - 100) = -1$
  $\Pi = -c_T + c_0 = -1 + 7 = 6$

C. Maximum and minimum

  i. Maximum profit to buyer (loss to seller) $= \infty$

  ii. Maximum loss to buyer (profit to seller) $= c_0 = 7$

D. $S_T^* = X + c_0 = 100 + 7 = 107$

2.1.2 Puts

The value of a put at expiration is $p_T = \max(0, X - S_T)$. Broken down into parts,

$$p_T = X - S \qquad \text{if } S_T < X$$
$$p_T = 0 \qquad \text{if } S_T \geq X$$

The profit is obtained by subtracting the premium on the put from the value at expiration:

$$\Pi = p_T - p_0$$

Broken down into parts,

$$\Pi = X - S_T - p_0 \qquad \text{if } S_T < X$$
$$\Pi = -p_0 \qquad \text{if } S_T \geq X$$

For our example and outcomes of $S_T = 1900$ and 2100, the results are as follows:

$S_T = 1900$:

$$p_T = \max(0,2000 - 1900) = 100$$
$$\Pi = 100 - 79.25 = 20.75$$

$S_T = 2100$:

$$p_T = \max(0,2000 - 2100) = 0$$
$$\Pi = 0 - 79.25 = -79.25$$

These results are shown in Exhibit 78-4. We see that the put has a maximum value and profit and a limited loss, the latter of which is the premium. The maximum value is obtained when the underlying goes to zero.[5] In that case, $p_T = X$. So the maximum profit is $X - p_0$. Here that will be $2000 - 79.25 = 1920.75$.

The breakeven is found by breaking up the profit equation into its parts, $\Pi = X - S_T - p_0$ for $S_T < X$ and $\Pi = -p_0$ for $S_T \geq X$. In the latter case, there is no possibility of breaking even. It refers to the range over which the entire premium is lost. In the former case, we denote the breakeven index value as S_T^*, set the equation to zero, and solve for S_T^* to obtain $S_T^* = X - p_0$. In our example, the breakeven is $S_T^* = 2000 - 79.25 = 1920.75$.

EXHIBIT 78-4	Buy Put

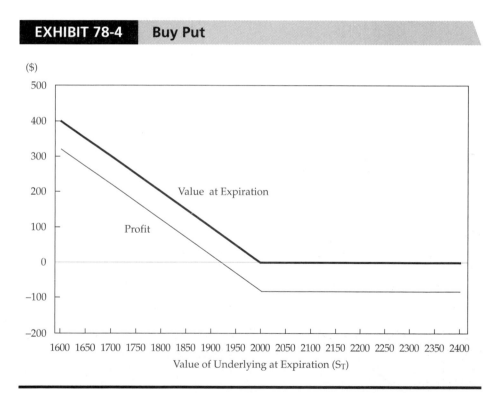

---

[5] The maximum value and profit are not visible on the graph because we do not show S_T all the way down to zero.

In summary, for the strategy of buying a put we have

$p_T = \max(0, X - S_T)$
Value at expiration $= p_T$
Profit: $\Pi = p_T - p_0$
Maximum profit $= X - p_0$
Maximum loss $= p_0$
Breakeven: $S_T^* = X - p_0$

Now consider the *likely* outcomes for the holder of the put. In this case, the underlying must move down by almost 4 percent in one month to cover the premium. One would hardly ever expect the underlying to move down at an annual rate of almost 50 percent. Moreover, if the underlying does not move downward at all (a likely outcome given the positive expected return on most assets), the loss is 100 percent of the premium.

For the sale of a put, we simply change the sign on the value at expiration and profit. The maximum profit for the buyer becomes the maximum loss for the seller and the maximum loss for the buyer becomes the maximum profit for the seller. The breakeven for the seller is the same as for the buyer. So, for the seller,

$p_T = \max(0, X - S_T)$
Value at expiration $= -p_T$
Profit: $\Pi = -p_T + p_0$
Maximum profit $= p_0$
Maximum loss $= X - p_0$
Breakeven: $S_T^* = X - p_0$

Exhibit 78-5 graphs the value at expiration and the profit for this transaction.

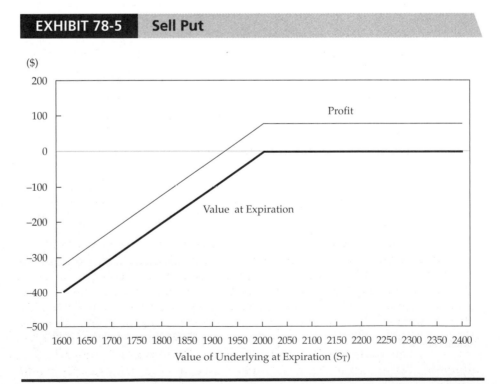

EXHIBIT 78-5   Sell Put

Practice Problem 2

Consider a put option selling for $4 in which the exercise price is $00 and the price of the underlying is $62.

A. Determine the value at expiration and the profit for a buyer under the following outcomes:

   i. The price of the underlying at expiration is $62.

   ii. The price of the underlying at expiration is $55.

B. Determine the value at expiration and the profit for a seller under the following outcomes:

   i. The price of the underlying at expiration is $51.

   ii. The price of the underlying at expiration is $68.

C. Determine the following:

   i. The maximum profit to the buyer (maximum loss to the seller)

   ii. The maximum loss to the buyer (maximum profit to the seller)

D. Determine the breakeven price of the underlying at expiration.

SOLUTIONS

A. Put buyer

   i. Value at expiration $= p_T = \max(0, X - S_T) = \max(0, 60 - 62) = 0$
   $\Pi = p_T - p_0 = 0 - 4 = -4$

   ii. Value at expiration $= p_T = \max(0, X - S_T) = \max(0, 60 - 55) = 5$
   $\Pi = p_T - p_0 = 5 - 4 = 1$

B. Put seller

   i. Value at expiration $= -p_T = -\max(0, X - S_T) = -\max(0, 60 - 51) = -9$
   $\Pi = -p_T + p_0 = -9 + 4 = -5$

   ii. Value at expiration $= -p_T = -\max(0, X - S_T) = -\max(0, 60 - 68) = 0$
   $\Pi = -p_T + p_0 = 0 + 4 = 4$

C. Maximum and minimum

   i. Maximum profit to buyer (loss to seller) $= X - p_0 = 60 - 4 = 56$

   ii. Maximum loss to buyer (profit to seller) $= p_0 = 4$

D. $S_T{}^* = X - p_0 = 60 - 4 = 56$

It may be surprising to find that we have now covered all of the information we need to examine all of the other option strategies. We need to learn only a few basic facts. We must know the formula for the value at expiration of a call and a put. Then we need to know how to calculate the profit for the purchase of a call and a put, but that calculation is simple: the value at expiration minus the initial value. If we know these results, we can calculate the value at expiration of the option and the profit for any value of the underlying at expiration. If we can do that, we can graph the results for a range of possible values of the underlying at expiration. Because graphing can take a long time, however, it is probably helpful to learn the basic shapes of the value and profit graphs for calls and puts. Knowing the profit equation and the shapes of the graphs, it is easy to determine the maximum profit and maximum loss. The breakeven can be determined by setting the profit equation to zero for the case in which the profit equation contains S_T. Once we have these results for the long call and put, it is an easy matter to turn them around and obtain the results for the short call and put. Therefore, little if any memorization is required. From there, we can go on to strategies that combine an option with another option and combine options with the underlying.

2.2 Risk Management Strategies with Options and the Underlying

In this section, we examine two of the most widely used option strategies, particularly for holders of the underlying. One way to reduce exposure without selling the underlying is to sell a call on the underlying; the other way is to buy a put.

2.2.1 Covered Calls

A **covered call** is a relatively conservative strategy, but it is also one of the most misunderstood strategies. A covered call is a position in which you own the underlying and sell a call. The value of the position at expiration is easily found as the value of the underlying plus the value of the short call:

$$V_T = S_T - \max(0, S_T - X)$$

Therefore,

$$V_T = S_T \qquad\qquad\qquad \text{if } S_T \leq X$$
$$V_T = S_T - (S_T - X) = X \qquad \text{if } S_T > X$$

We obtain the profit for the covered call by computing the change in the value of the position, $V_T - V_0$. First recognize that V_0, the value of the position at the start of the contract, is the initial value of the underlying minus the **call premium**. We are long the underlying and short the call, so we must subtract the call premium that was received from the sale of the call. The initial investment in the position is what we pay for the underlying less what we receive for the call. Hence, $V_0 = S_0 - c_0$. The profit is thus

$$\Pi = S_T - \max(0, S_T - X) - (S_0 - c_0)$$
$$= S_T - S_0 - \max(0, S_T - X) + c_0$$

With the equation written in this manner, we see that the profit for the covered call is simply the profit from buying the underlying, $S_T - S_0$, plus the profit from selling the call, $-\max(0, S_T - X) + c_0$. Breaking it down into ranges,

$$\Pi = S_T - S_0 + c_0 \qquad\qquad\qquad\qquad \text{if } S_T \leq X$$
$$\Pi = S_T - S_0 - (S_T - X) + c_0 = X - S_0 + c_0 \qquad \text{if } S_T > X$$

In our example, $S_0 = 2000$. In this section we shall use a call option with the exercise price of 2050. Thus $X = 2050$, and the premium, c_0, is 59.98. Let us now examine two outcomes: $S_T = 2100$ and $S_T = 1900$. The value at expiration when $S_T = 2100$ is $V_T = 2100 - (2100 - 2050) = 2050$, and when $S_T = 1900$, the value of the position is $V_T = 1900$.

In the first case, we hold the underlying worth 2100 but are short a call worth 50. Thus, the net value is 2050. In the second case, we hold the underlying worth 1900 and the option expires out-of-the-money.

In the first case, $S_T = 2100$, the profit is $\Pi = 2050 - 2000 + 59.98 = 109.98$. In the second case, $S_T = 1900$, the profit is $\Pi = 1900 - 2000 + 59.98 = -40.02$. These results are graphed for a range of values of S_T in Exhibit 78-6. Note that for all values of S_T greater than 2050, the value and profit are maximized. Thus, 2050 is the maximum value and 109.98 is the maximum profit.[6]

As evident in Exhibit 78-6 and the profit equations, the maximum loss would occur when S_T is zero. Hence, the profit would be $S_T - S_0 + c_0$. The profit is $-S_0 + c_0$ when $S_T = 0$. This means that the maximum loss is $S_0 - c_0$. In this example, $-S_0 + c_0$ is $-2000 + 59.98 = -1940.02$. Intuitively, this would mean that you purchased the underlying for 2000 and sold the call for 59.98. The underlying value went to zero, resulting in a loss of 2000, but the call expired with no value, so the gain from the option is the option premium. The total loss is 1940.02.

EXHIBIT 78-6	Covered Call (Buy Underlying, Sell Call)

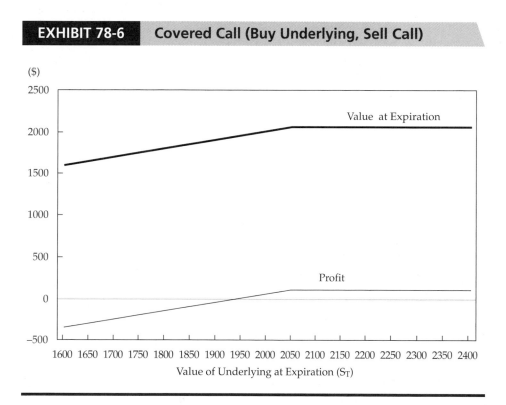

The breakeven underlying price is found by examining the profit equations and focusing on the equation that contains S_T. In equation form, $\Pi = S_T - S_0 + c_0$ when $S_T \leq X$. We let $S_T{}^*$ denote the breakeven value of S_T, set the equation to zero, and solve for $S_T{}^*$ to obtain $S_T{}^* = S_0 - c_0$. The breakeven and the maximum loss are identical. In this example, the breakeven is $S_T{}^* = 2000 - 59.98 = 1940.02$, which is seen in Exhibit 78-6.

---

[6] Note in Exhibit 78-6 that there is a large gap between the value at expiration and profit, especially compared with the graphs of buying and selling calls and puts. This difference occurs because a covered call is mostly a position in the underlying asset. The initial value of the asset, S_0, accounts for most of the difference in the two lines. Note also that because of the put–call parity relationship we covered in Reading 76, a covered call looks very similar to a short put.

To summarize the covered call, we have the following:

Value at expiration: $V_T = S_T - \max(0, S_T - X)$
Profit: $\Pi = V_T - S_0 + c_0$
Maximum profit $= X - S_0 + c_0$
Maximum loss $= S_0 - c_0$
Breakeven: $S_T^* = S_0 - c_0$

Because of the importance and widespread use of covered calls, it is worthwhile to discuss this strategy briefly to dispel some misunderstandings. First of all, some investors who do not believe in using options fail to see that selling a call on a position in the underlying reduces the risk of that position. Options do not automatically increase risk. The option part of this strategy alone, viewed in isolation, seems an extremely risky strategy. We noted in Section 2.1.1 that selling a call without owning the stock exposes the investor to unlimited loss potential. But selling a covered call—adding a short call to a long position in a stock—reduces the overall risk. Thus, any investor who holds a stock cannot say he is too conservative to use options.

Following on that theme, however, one should also view selling a covered call as a strategy that reduces not only the risk but also the expected return compared with simply holding the underlying. Hence, one should not expect to make a lot of money writing calls on the underlying. It should be apparent that in fact the covered call writer could miss out on significant gains in a strong bull market. The compensation for this willingness to give up potential upside gains, however, is that in a bear market the losses on the underlying will be cushioned by the option premium.

It may be disconcerting to some investors to look at the profit profile of a covered call. The immediate response is to think that no one in their right mind would invest in a strategy that has significant downside risk but a limited upside. Just owning the underlying has significant downside risk, but at least there is an upside. But it is important to note that the visual depiction of the strategy, as in Exhibit 78-6, does not tell the whole story. It says nothing about the likelihood of certain outcomes occurring.

For example, consider the covered call example we looked at here. The underlying starts off at 2000. The maximum profit occurs when the option expires with the underlying at 2050 or above, an increase of 2.5 percent over the life of the option. We noted that this option has a one-month life. Thus, the underlying would have to increase at an approximate annual rate of at least $2.5\%(12) = 30\%$ for the covered call writer to forgo all of the upside gain. There are not many stocks, indices, or other assets in which an investor would expect the equivalent of an annual move of at least 30 percent. Such movements obviously do occur from time to time, but they are not common. Thus, covered call writers do not often give up large gains.

But suppose the underlying did move to 2050 or higher. As we previously showed, the value of the position would be 2050. Because the initial value of the position is $2000 - 59.98 = 1940.02$, the rate of return would be 5.7 percent for one month. Hence, the maximum return is still outstanding by almost anyone's standards.[7]

Many investors believe that the initial value of a covered call should not include the value of the underlying if the underlying had been previously purchased. Suppose, for example, that this asset, currently worth 2000, had been

---

[7] Of course, we are not saying that the performance reflects a positive alpha. We are saying only that the upside performance given up reflects improbably high returns, and therefore the limits on the upside potential are not too restrictive.

bought several months ago at 1900. It is tempting to ignore the current value of the underlying; there is no current outlay. This view, however, misses the notion of opportunity cost. If an investor currently holding an asset chooses to write a call on it, she has made a conscious decision not to sell the asset. Hence, the current value of the asset should be viewed as an opportunity cost that is just as real as the cost to an investor buying the underlying at this time.

Sellers of covered calls must make a decision about the chosen exercise price. For example, one could sell the call with an exercise price of 1950 for 108.43, or sell the call with an exercise price of 2000 for 81.75, or sell the call with an exercise price of 2050 for 59.98. The higher the exercise price, the less one receives for the call but the more room for gain on the upside. There is no clear-cut solution to deciding which call is best; the choice depends on the risk preferences of the investor.

Finally, we should note that anecdotal evidence suggests that writers of call options make small amounts of money, but make it often. The reason for this phenomenon is generally thought to be that buyers of calls tend to be overly optimistic, but that argument is fallacious. The real reason is that the expected profits come from rare but large payoffs. For example, consider the call with exercise price of 2000 and a premium of 81.75. As we learned in Section 2.1, the breakeven underlying price is 2081.75—a gain of about 4.1 percent in a one-month period, which would be an exceptional return for almost any asset. These prices were obtained using the Black–Scholes–Merton model, so they are fair prices. Yet the required underlying price movement to profit on the call is exceptional. Obviously someone buys calls, and naturally, someone must be on the other side of the transaction. Sellers of calls tend to be holders of the underlying or other calls, which reduces the enormous risk they would assume if they sold calls without any other position.[8] Hence, it is reasonable to expect that sellers of calls would make money often, because large underlying price movements occur only rarely. Following this line of reasoning, however, it would appear that sellers of calls can consistently take advantage of buyers of calls. That cannot possibly be the case. What happens is that buyers of calls make money less often than sellers, but when they do make money, the leverage inherent in call options amplifies their returns. Therefore, when call writers lose money, they tend to lose big, but most call writers own the underlying or are long other calls to offset the risk.

Practice Problem 3

Consider a bond selling for $98 per $100 face value. A call option selling for $8 has an exercise price of $105. Answer the following questions about a covered call.

A. Determine the value of the position at expiration and the profit under the following outcomes:

  i. The price of the bond at expiration is $110.

  ii. The price of the bond at expiration is $88.

B. Determine the following:

  i. The maximum profit

  ii. The maximum loss

---

[8] Sellers of calls who hold other calls are engaged in transactions called spreads. We discuss several types of spreads in Section 2.3.

> **C.** Determine the breakeven bond price at expiration.
>
> **SOLUTIONS**
> **A. i.** $V_T = S_T - \max(0, S_T - X) = 110 - \max(0, 110 - 105)$
> $= 110 - 110 + 105 = 105$
> $\Pi = V_T - V_0 = 105 - (S_0 - c_0) = 105 - (98 - 8) = 15$
> **ii.** $V_T = S_T - \max(0, S_T - X) = 88 - \max(0, 88 - 105) = 88 - 0 = 88$
> $\Pi = V_T - V_0 = 88 - (S_0 - c_0) = 88 - (98 - 8) = -2$
> **B. i.** Maximum profit $= X - S_0 + c_0 = 105 - 98 + 8 = 15$
> **ii.** Maximum loss $= S_0 - c_0 = 98 - 8 = 90$
> **C.** $S_T^* = S_0 - c_0 = 98 - 8 = 90$

Covered calls represent one widely used way to protect a position in the underlying. Another popular means of providing protection is to buy a put.

2.2.2 Protective Puts

Because selling a call provides some protection to the holder of the underlying against a fall in the price of the underlying, buying a put should also provide protection. A put, after all, is designed to pay off when the price of the underlying moves down. In some ways, buying a put to add to a long stock position is much better than selling a call. As we shall see here, it provides downside protection while retaining the upside potential, but it does so at the expense of requiring the payment of cash up front. In contrast, a covered call generates cash up front but removes some of the upside potential.

Holding an asset and a put on the asset is a strategy known as a **protective put**. The value at expiration and the profit of this strategy are found by combining the value and profit of the two strategies of buying the asset and buying the put. The value is $V_T = S_T + \max(0, X - S_T)$. Thus, the results can be expressed as

$$V_T = S_T + (X - S_T) = X \quad \text{if } S_T \leq X$$
$$V_T = S_T \quad \text{if } S_T > X$$

When the underlying price at expiration exceeds the exercise price, the put expires with no value. The position is then worth only the value of the underlying. When the underlying price at expiration is less than the exercise price, the put expires in-the-money and is worth $X - S_T$, while the underlying is worth S_T. The combined value of the two instruments is X. When the underlying is worth less than the exercise price at expiration, the put can be used to sell the underlying for the exercise price.

The initial value of the position is the initial price of the underlying, S_0, plus the premium on the put, p_0. Hence, the profit is $\Pi = S_T + \max(0, X - S_T) - (S_0 + p_0)$. The profit can be broken down as follows:

$$\Pi = X - (S_0 + p_0) \quad \text{if } S_T \leq X$$
$$\Pi = S_T - (S_0 + p_0) \quad \text{if } S_T > X$$

In this example, we are going to use the put with an exercise price of 1950. Its premium is 56.01. Recalling that the initial price of the underlying is 2000, the value at expiration and profit for the case of $S_T = 2100$ are

$$V_T = 2100$$
$$\Pi = 2100 - (2000 + 56.01) = 43.99$$

For the case of $S_T = 1900$, the value at expiration and profit are

$$V_T = 1950$$
$$\Pi = 1950 - (2000 + 56.01) = -106.01$$

The results for a range of outcomes are shown in Exhibit 78-7. Note how the protective put provides a limit on the downside with no limit on the upside.[9] Therefore, we can say that the upper limit is infinite. The lower limit is a loss of 106.01. In the worst possible case, we can sell the underlying for the exercise price, but the up-front cost of the underlying and put are 2056.01, for a maximum loss of 106.01.

Now let us find the breakeven price of the underlying at expiration. Note that the two profit equations are $\Pi = S_T - (S_0 + p_0)$ if $S_T > X$ and $\Pi = X - (S_0 + p_0)$ if $S_T \leq X$. In the latter case, there is no value of the underlying that will allow us to break even. In the former case, $S_T > X$, we change the notation on S_T to S_T^* to denote the breakeven value, set this expression equal to zero, and solve for S_T^*:

$$S_T^* = S_0 + p_0$$

EXHIBIT 78-7   **Protective Put (Buy Underlying, Buy Put)**

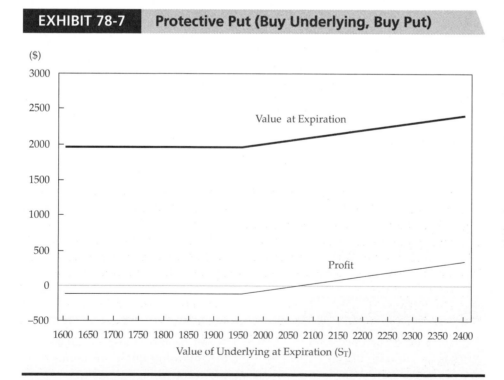

[9] Note that the graph for a protective put looks like the graph for a call. This result is due to put–call parity, as covered in Reading 76.

To break even, the underlying must be at least as high as the amount expended up front to establish the position. In this problem, this amount is $2000 + 56.01 = 2056.01$.

To summarize the protective put, we have the following:

Value at expiration: $V_T = S_T + \max(0, X - S_T)$
Profit: $\Pi = V_T - S_0 - p_0$
Maximum profit $= \infty$
Maximum loss $= S_0 + p_0 - X$
Breakeven: $S_T^* = S_0 + p_0$

A protective put can appear to be a great transaction with no drawbacks. It provides downside protection with upside potential, but let us take a closer look. First recall that this is a one-month transaction and keep in mind that the option has been priced by the Black–Scholes–Merton model and is, therefore, a fair price. The maximum loss of 106.01 is a loss of $106.01/2056.01 = 5.2\%$. The breakeven of 2056.01 requires an upward move of 2.8 percent, which is an annual rate of about 34 percent. From this angle, the protective put strategy does not look quite as good, but in fact, these figures simply confirm that protection against downside loss is expensive. When the protective put is fairly priced, the protection buyer must give up considerable upside potential that may not be particularly evident from just looking at a graph.

The purchase of a protective put also presents the buyer with some choices. In this example, the buyer bought the put with exercise price of 1950 for 56.01. Had he bought the put with exercise price of 2000, he would have paid 79.25. The put with exercise price of 2050 would have cost 107.39. The higher the price for which the investor wants to be able to sell the underlying, the more expensive the put will be.

The protective put is often viewed as a classic example of insurance. The investor holds a risky asset and wants protection against a loss in value. He then buys insurance in the form of the put, paying a premium to the seller of the insurance, the put writer. The exercise price of the put is like the insurance deductible because the magnitude of the exercise price reflects the risk assumed by the party holding the underlying. The higher the exercise price, the less risk assumed by the holder of the underlying and the more risk assumed by the put seller. The lower the exercise price, the more risk assumed by the holder of the underlying and the less risk assumed by the put seller. In insurance, the higher the deductible, the more risk assumed by the insured party and the less risk assumed by the insurer. Thus, a higher exercise price is analogous to a lower insurance deductible.

Like traditional insurance, this form of insurance provides coverage for a period of time. At the end of the period of time, the insurance expires and either pays off or not. The buyer of the insurance may or may not choose to renew the insurance by buying another put.

Practice Problem 4

Consider a currency selling for $0.875. A put option selling for $0.075 has an exercise price of $0.90. Answer the following questions about a protective put.

A. Determine the value at expiration and the profit under the following outcomes:

  i. The price of the currency at expiration is $0.00.

  ii. The price of the currency at expiration is $0.75.

B. Determine the following:

  i. The maximum profit

  ii. The maximum loss

C. Determine the breakeven price of the currency at expiration.

SOLUTIONS

A. **i.** $V_T = S_T + \max(0, X - S_T) = 0.96 + \max(0, 0.90 - 0.96) = 0.96$
$\Pi = V_T - V_0 = 0.96 - (S_0 + p_0) = 0.96 - (0.875 + 0.075) = 0.01$

  ii. $V_T = S_T + \max(0, X - S_T) = 0.75 + \max(0, 0.90 - 0.75) = 0.90$
$\Pi = V_T - V_0 = 0.90 - (S_0 + p_0) = 0.90 - (0.875 + 0.075) = -0.05$

B. **i.** Maximum profit $= \infty$

  ii. Maximum loss $= S_0 + p_0 - X = 0.875 + 0.075 - 0.90 = 0.05$

C. $S_T^* = S_0 + p_0 = 0.875 + 0.075 = 0.95$

Finally, we note that a protective put can be modified in a number of ways. One in particular is to sell a call to generate premium income to pay for the purchase of the put. This strategy is known as a collar. We shall cover collars in detail in Section 2.4.1 when we look at combining puts and calls. For now, however, let us proceed with strategies that combine calls with calls and puts with puts. These strategies are called spreads.

2.3 Money Spreads

A spread is a strategy in which you buy one option and sell another option that is identical to the first in all respects except either exercise price or time to expiration. If the options differ by time to expiration, the spread is called a time spread. Time spreads are strategies designed to exploit differences in perceptions of volatility of the underlying. They are among the more specialized strategies, and we do not cover them here. Our focus is on money spreads, which are spreads in which the two options differ only by exercise price. The investor buys an option with a given expiration and exercise price and sells an option with the same expiration but a different exercise price. Of course, the options are on the same underlying asset. The term *spread* is used here because the payoff is based on the difference, or spread, between option exercise prices.

2.3.1 Bull Spreads

A **bull spread** is designed to make money when the market goes up. In this strategy we combine a long position in a call with one exercise price and a short position in a call with a higher exercise price. Let us use X_1 as the lower of the two exercise prices and X_2 as the higher. Following the notation we introduced in Reading 76, the European call prices would be denoted as $c(X_1)$ and $c(X_2)$, but we shall simplify this notation somewhat in this reading by using the symbols c_1 and c_2, respectively. We found that the value of a call at expiration is $c_T = \max(0, S_T - X)$. So, the value of the spread at expiration is

$$V_T = \max(0, S_T - X_1) - \max(0, S_T - X_2)$$

Therefore,

$$
\begin{array}{ll}
V_T = 0 - 0 = 0 & \text{if } S_T \leq X_1 \\
V_T = S_T - X_1 - 0 = S_T - X_1 & \text{if } X_1 < S_T < X_2 \\
V_T = S_T - X_1 - (S_T - X_2) = X_2 - X_1 & \text{if } S_T \geq X_2
\end{array}
$$

The profit is obtained by subtracting the initial outlay for the spread from the above value of the spread at expiration. To determine the initial outlay, recall that a call option with a lower exercise price will be more expensive than a call option with a higher exercise price. Because we are buying the call with the lower exercise price and selling the call with the higher exercise price, the call we buy will cost more than the call we sell. Hence, the spread will require a net outlay of funds. This net outlay is the initial value of the position of $V_0 = c_1 - c_2$, which we call the net premium. The profit is $V_T - V_0$. Therefore,

$$\Pi = \max(0, S_T - X_1) - \max(0, S_T - X_2) - (c_1 - c_2)$$

In this manner, we see that the profit is the profit from the long call, $\max(0, S_T - X_1) - c_1$, plus the profit from the short call, $-\max(0, S_T - X_2) + c_2$. Broken down into ranges, the profit is

$$
\begin{array}{ll}
\Pi = -c_1 + c_2 & \text{if } S_T \leq X_1 \\
\Pi = S_T - X_1 - c_1 + c_2 & \text{if } X_1 < S_T < X_2 \\
\Pi = X_2 - X_1 - c_1 + c_2 & \text{if } S_T \geq X_2
\end{array}
$$

If S_T is below X_1, the strategy will lose a limited amount of money. The profit on the upside, if S_T is at least X_2, is also limited. When both options expire out-of-the-money, the investor loses the net premium, $c_1 - c_2$.

In this example, we use exercise prices of 1950 and 2050. Thus $X_1 = 1950$, $c_1 = 108.43$, $X_2 = 2050$, and $c_2 = 59.98$. Let us examine the outcomes in which the asset price at expiration is 2100, 2000, and 1900. In one outcome, the underlying is above the upper exercise price at expiration, and in one, the underlying is below the lower exercise price at expiration. Let us also examine one case between the exercise prices with S_T equal to 2000.

When $S_T = 2100$, the value at expiration is $V_T = 2050 - 1950 = 100$.
When $S_T = 2000$, the value at expiration is $V_T = 2000 - 1950 = 50$.
When $S_T = 1900$, the value at expiration is $V_T = 0$.

To calculate the profit, we simply subtract the initial value for the call with exercise price X_1 and add the initial value for the call with exercise price X_2.

When $S_T = 2100$, the profit is $\Pi = 100 - 108.43 + 59.98 = 51.55$.
When $S_T = 2000$, the profit is $\Pi = 50 - 108.43 + 59.98 = 1.55$.
When $S_T = 1900$, the profit is $\Pi = -108.43 + 59.98 = -48.45$.

When S_T is greater than 2100, we would obtain the same outcome as when S_T equals 2100. When S_T is less than 1900, we would obtain the same outcome as when S_T equals 1900.

| EXHIBIT 78-8 | Bull Spread (Buy Call with Exercise Price X_1, Sell Call with Exercise Price X_2) |

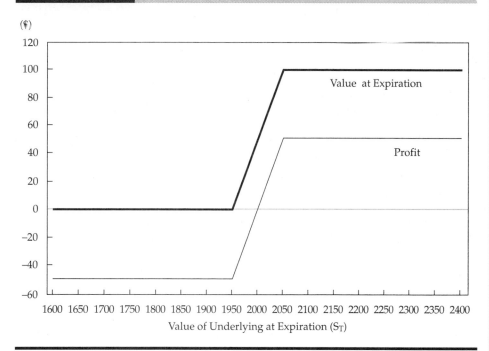

Exhibit 78-8 depicts these results graphically. Note how the bull spread provides a limited gain as well as a limited loss. Of course, just purchasing a call provides a limited loss. But when selling the call in addition to buying the call, the investor gives up the upside in order to reduce the downside. In the bull spread, the investor sells gains from the call beyond the higher exercise price. Thus, a bull spread has some similarities to the covered call. With a covered call, the long position in the underlying "covers" the short position in the call. In a bull spread, the long position in the call with the lower exercise price "covers" the short position in the call with the higher exercise price. For both strategies, the short call can be viewed as giving up the gains beyond its exercise price. The upside gain can also be viewed as paying a premium of $c_1 - c_2$ to buy the underlying for X_1 and sell it for X_2. Accordingly, the maximum gain is $X_2 - X_1 - c_1 + c_2 = 2050 - 1950 - 108.43 + 59.98 = 51.55$, as computed above. This amount represents a maximum return of about 106 percent.[10] The maximum loss is the net premium, 48.45, which is a 100 percent loss.

As can be seen from the graph and the profit equations, there is a breakeven asset price at expiration that falls between the two exercise prices. We let S_T^* be the breakeven asset price at expiration and set the profit for the case of $X_1 < S_T < X_2$ to zero:

$$S_T^* = X_1 + c_1 - c_2$$

To achieve a profit of zero or more, the asset price at expiration must exceed the lower exercise price by at least the net premium paid for the options. The long

---

[10] This calculation is based on the fact that the initial value of the position is $108.43 - 59.98 = 48.45$ and the maximum value is 100, which is a gain of 106.4 percent.

option must expire in-the-money by enough to cover the net premium. In our example,

$$S_T^* = 1950 + 108.43 - 59.98 = 1,998.45$$

What this result means is that the underlying must not move down by more than 0.08 percent.

To summarize the bull spread, we have

Value at expiration: $V_T = \max(0, S_T - X_1) - \max(0, S_T - X_2)$
Profit: $\Pi = V_T - c_1 + c_2$
Maximum profit $= X_2 - X_1 - c_1 + c_2$
Maximum loss $= c_1 - c_2$
Breakeven: $S_T^* = X_1 + c_1 - c_2$

Practice Problem 5

Consider two call options on a stock selling for $72. One call has an exercise price of $65 and is selling for $9. The other call has an exercise price of $75 and is selling for $4. Both calls expire at the same time. Answer the following questions about a bull spread:

A. Determine the value at expiration and the profit under the following outcomes:

   i. The price of the stock at expiration is $78.

   ii. The price of the stock at expiration is $69.

   iii. The price of the stock at expiration is $62.

B. Determine the following:

   i. The maximum profit

   ii. The maximum loss

C. Determine the breakeven stock price at expiration.

SOLUTIONS

A. i. $V_T = \max(0, S_T - X_1) - \max(0, S_T - X_2) = \max(0, 78 - 65) - \max(0, 78 - 75) = 13 - 3 = 10$
$\Pi = V_T - V_0 = V_T - (c_1 - c_2) = 10 - (9 - 4) = 5$

   ii. $V_T = \max(0, S_T - X_1) - \max(0, S_T - X_2) = \max(0, 69 - 65) - \max(0, 69 - 75) = 4 - 0 = 4$
$\Pi = V_T - V_0 = V_T - (c_1 - c_2) = 4 - (9 - 4) = -1$

   iii. $V_T = \max(0, S_T - X_1) - \max(0, S_T - X_2) = \max(0, 62 - 65) - \max(0, 62 - 75) = 0 - 0 = 0$
$\Pi = V_T - V_0 = 0 - (c_1 - c_2) = 0 - (9 - 4) = -5$

B. i. Maximum profit $= X_2 - X_1 - (c_1 - c_2) = 75 - 65 - (9 - 4) = 5$

   ii. Maximum loss $= c_1 - c_2 = 9 - 4 = 5$

C. $S_T^* = X_1 + c_1 - c_2 = 65 + 9 - 4 = 70$

Bull spreads are used by investors who think the underlying price is going up. There are also **bear spreads**, which are used by investors who think the underlying price is going down.

2.3.2 Bear Spreads

If one uses the opposite strategy, selling a call with the lower exercise price and buying a call with the higher exercise price, the opposite results occur. The graph is completely reversed: The gain is on the downside and the loss is on the upside. This strategy is called a **bear spread.** The more intuitive way of executing a bear spread, however, is to use puts. Specifically, we would buy the put with the higher exercise price and sell the put with the lower exercise price.

The value of this position at expiration would be $V_T = \max(0, X_2 - S_T) - \max(0, X_1 - S_T)$. Broken down into ranges, we have the following relations:

$$
\begin{aligned}
V_T &= X_2 - S_T - (X_1 - S_T) = X_2 - X_1 && \text{if } S_T \leq X_1 \\
V_T &= X_2 - S_T - 0 = X_2 - S_T && \text{if } X_1 < S_T < X_2 \\
V_T &= 0 - 0 = 0 && \text{if } S_T \geq X_2
\end{aligned}
$$

To obtain the profit, we subtract the initial outlay. Because we are buying the put with the higher exercise price and selling the put with the lower exercise price, the put we are buying is more expensive than the put we are selling. The initial value of the bear spread is $V_0 = p_2 - p_1$. The profit is, therefore, $V_T - V_0$, which is

$$
\Pi = \max(0, X_2 - S_T) - \max(0, X_1 - S_T) - p_2 + p_1
$$

We see that the profit is the profit from the long put, $\max(0, X_2 - S_T) - p_2$, plus the profit from the short put, $-\max(0, X_1 - S_T) + p_1$. Broken down into ranges, the profit is

$$
\begin{aligned}
\Pi &= X_2 - X_1 - p_2 + p_1 && \text{if } S_T \leq X_1 \\
\Pi &= X_2 - S_T - p_2 + p_1 && \text{if } X_1 < S_T < X_2 \\
\Pi &= -p_2 + p_1 && \text{if } S_T \geq X_2
\end{aligned}
$$

In contrast to the profit in a bull spread, the bear spread profit occurs on the downside; the maximum profit occurs when $S_T \leq X_1$. This profit reflects the purchase of the underlying at X_1, which occurs when the short put is exercised, and the sale of the underlying at X_2, which occurs when the long put is exercised. The worst outcome occurs when $S_T > X_2$, in which case both puts expire out-of-the-money and the net premium is lost.

In the example, we again use options with exercise prices of 1950 and 2050. Their premiums are $p_1 = 56.01$ and $p_2 = 107.39$. We examine the three outcomes we did with the bull spread: S_T is 1900, 2000, or 2100.

With $S_T = 1900$, the value at expiration is $V_T = 2050 - 1950 = 100$.
With $S_T = 2000$, the value at expiration is $V_T = 2050 - 2000 = 50$.
With $S_T = 2100$, the value at expiration is $V_T = 0$.

The profit is obtained by taking the value at expiration, subtracting the premium of the put with the higher exercise price, and adding the premium of the put with the lower exercise price:

When $S_T = 1900$, the profit is $\Pi = 100 - 107.39 + 56.01 = 48.62$.
When $S_T = 2000$, the profit is $\Pi = 50 - 107.39 + 56.01 = -1.38$.
When $S_T = 2100$, the profit is $\Pi = -107.39 + 56.01 = -51.38$.

| EXHIBIT 78-9 | Bear Spread (Buy Put with Exercise Price X_2, Sell Put with Exercise Price X_1) |

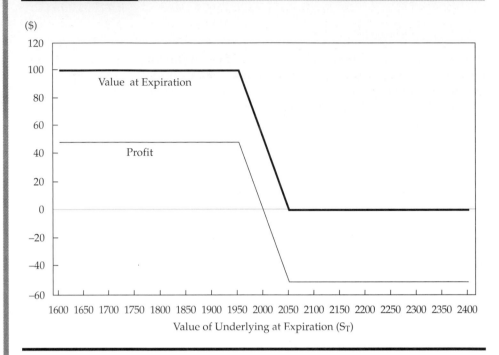

When S_T is less than 1900, the outcome is the same as when S_T equals 1900. When S_T is greater than 2100, the outcome is the same as when S_T equals 2100.

The results are graphed in Exhibit 78-9. Note how this strategy is similar to a bull spread but with opposite outcomes. The gains are on the downside underlying moves and the losses are on the upside underlying. The maximum profit occurs when both puts expire in-the-money. You end up using the short put to buy the asset and the long put to sell the asset. The maximum profit is $X_2 - X_1 - p_2 + p_1$, which in this example is $100 - 107.39 + 56.01 = 48.62$, a return of 94 percent.[11] The maximum loss of $p_2 - p_1$ occurs when both puts expire out-of-the-money, and in this case is $107.39 - 56.01 = 51.38$, a loss of 100 percent.

The breakeven asset price occurs between the two exercise prices. Let S_T^* be the breakeven asset price at expiration, set the profit equation for the middle case to zero, and solve for S_T^* to obtain $S_T^* = X_2 - p_2 + p_1$. In this case, the breakeven is $S_T^* = 2050 - 107.39 + 56.01 = 1,998.62$. The underlying need move down only as little as 0.07 percent to make a profit.

To summarize the bear spread, we have

Value at expiration: $V_T = \max(0, X_2 - S_T) - \max(0, X_1 - S_T)$
Profit: $\Pi = V_T - p_2 + p_1$
Maximum profit $= X_2 - X_1 - p_2 + p_1$
Maximum loss $= p_2 - p_1$
Breakeven: $S_T^* = X_2 - p_2 + p_1$

---

[11] The net premium is $107.39 - 56.01 = 51.38$, so the maximum value of 100 is a return of about 94 percent.

Practice Problem 6

Consider two put options on a bond selling for $92 per $100 par. One put has an exercise price of $85 and is selling for $3. The other put has an exercise price of $95 and is selling for $11. Both puts expire at the same time. Answer the following questions about a bear spread:

A. Determine the value at expiration and the profit under the following outcomes:

  i. The price of the bond at expiration is $98.

  ii. The price of the bond at expiration is $91.

  iii. The price of the bond at expiration is $82.

B. Determine the following:

  i. The maximum profit

  ii. The maximum loss

C. Determine the breakeven bond price at expiration.

SOLUTIONS

A. **i.** $V_T = \max(0, X_2 - S_T) - \max(0, X_1 - S_T) = \max(0, 95 - 98) - \max(0, 85 - 98) = 0 - 0 = 0$

  $\Pi = V_T - V_0 = V_T - (p_2 - p_1) = 0 - (11 - 3) = -8$

  ii. $V_T = \max(0, X_2 - S_T) - \max(0, X_1 - S_T) = \max(0, 95 - 91) - \max(0, 85 - 91) = 4 - 0 = 4$

  $\Pi = V_T - V_0 = V_T - (p_2 - p_1) = 4 - (11 - 3) = -4$

  iii. $V_T = \max(0, X_2 - S_T) - \max(0, X_1 - S_T) = \max(0, 95 - 82) - \max(0, 85 - 82) = 13 - 3 = 10$

  $\Pi = V_T - V_0 = 10 - (p_2 - p_1) = 10 - (11 - 3) = 2$

B. **i.** Maximum profit $= X_2 - X_1 - (p_2 - p_1) = 95 - 85 - (11 - 3) = 2$

  ii. Maximum loss $= p_2 - p_1 = 11 - 3 = 8$

C. $S_T^* = X_2 - p_2 + p_1 = 95 - 11 + 3 = 87$

The bear spread with calls involves selling the call with the lower exercise price and buying the one with the higher exercise price. Because the call with the lower exercise price will be more expensive, there will be a cash inflow at initiation of the position and hence a profit if the calls expire worthless.

Bull and bear spreads are but two types of spread strategies. We now take a look at another strategy, which combines bull and bear spreads.

2.3.3 *Butterfly Spreads*

In both the bull and bear spread, we used options with two different exercise prices. There is no limit to how many different options one can use in a strategy. As an example, the **butterfly spread** combines a bull and bear spread. Consider three different exercise prices, X_1, X_2, and X_3. Suppose we first construct a bull spread, buying the call with exercise price of X_1 and selling the call with exercise price of X_2. Recall that we could construct a bear spread using calls instead of puts. In that case, we would buy the call with the higher exercise price and sell the call with the lower exercise price. This bear spread is identical to the sale of a bull spread.

Suppose we sell a bull spread by buying the call with exercise price X_3 and selling the call with exercise price X_2. We have now combined a long bull spread and a short bull spread (or a bear spread). We own the calls with exercise price X_1 and X_3 and have sold two calls with exercise price X_2. Combining these results, we obtain a value at expiration of

$$V_T = max(0, S_T - X_1) - 2max(0, S_T - X_2) + max(0, S_T - X_3)$$

This can be broken down into ranges of

$$
\begin{aligned}
V_T &= 0 - 2(0) + 0 = 0 & \text{if } S_T \leq X_1 \\
V_T &= S_T - X_1 - 2(0) + 0 = S_T - X_1 & \text{if } X_1 < S_T < X_2 \\
V_T &= S_T - X_1 - 2(S_T - X_2) + 0 = -S_T + 2X_2 - X_1 & \text{if } X_2 \leq S_T < X_3 \\
V_T &= S_T - X_1 - 2(S_T - X_2) + S_T - X_3 = 2X_2 - X_1 - X_3 & \text{if } S_T \geq X_3
\end{aligned}
$$

If the exercise prices are equally spaced, $2X_2 - X_1 - X_3$ would equal zero.[12] In virtually all cases in practice, the exercise prices are indeed equally spaced, and we shall make that assumption. Therefore,

$$V_T = 2X_2 - X_1 - X_3 = 0 \qquad \text{if } S_T \geq X_3$$

To obtain the profit, we must subtract the initial value of the position, which is $V_0 = c_1 - 2c_2 + c_3$. Is this value positive or negative? It turns out that it will always be positive. The bull spread we buy is more expensive than the bull spread we sell, because the lower exercise price on the bull spread we buy (X_1) is lower than the lower exercise price on the bull spread we sell (X_2). Because the underlying is more likely to move higher than X_1 than to move higher than X_2, the bull spread we buy is more expensive than the bull spread we sell.

The profit is thus $V_T - V_0$, which is

$$\Pi = max(0, S_T - X_1) - 2max(0, S_T - X_2) + max(0, S_T - X_3) - c_1 + 2c_2 - c_3$$

Broken down into ranges,

$$
\begin{aligned}
\Pi &= -c_1 + 2c_2 - c_3 & \text{if } S_T \leq X_1 \\
\Pi &= S_T - X_1 - c_1 + 2c_2 - c_3 & \text{if } X_1 < S_T < X_2 \\
\Pi &= -S_T + 2X_2 - X_1 - c_1 + 2c_2 - c_3 & \text{if } X_2 \leq S_T < X_3 \\
\Pi &= -c_1 + 2c_2 - c_3 & \text{if } S_T \geq X_3
\end{aligned}
$$

Note that in the lowest and highest ranges, the profit is negative; a loss. It is not immediately obvious what happens in the middle two ranges. Let us look at our example. In this example, we buy the calls with exercise prices of 1950 and 2050 and sell two calls with exercise price of 2000. So, $X_1 = 1950$, $X_2 = 2000$, and $X_3 = 2050$. Their premiums are $c_1 = 108.43$, $c_2 = 81.75$, and $c_3 = 59.98$. Let us examine the outcomes in which $S_T = 1900$, 1975, 2025, and 2100. These outcomes fit into each of the four relevant ranges.

When $S_T = 1900$, the value at expiration is $V_T = 0 - 2(0) + 0 = 0$.
When $S_T = 1975$, the value at expiration is $V_T = 1975 - 1950 = 25$.
When $S_T = 2025$, the value at expiration is $V_T = -2025 + 2(2000) - 1950 = 25$.
When $S_T = 2100$, the value at expiration is $V_T = 0$.

---

[12] For example, suppose the exercise prices are equally spaced with $X_1 = 30$, $X_2 = 40$, and $X_3 = 50$. Then $2X_2 - X_3 - X_1 = 2(40) - 50 - 30 = 0$.

Now, turning to the profit,

When $S_T = 1900$, the profit will be $\Pi = 0 - 108.43 + 2(81.75) - 59.98 = -4.91$.
When $S_T = 1975$, the profit will be $\Pi = 25 - 108.43 + 2(81.75) - 59.98 = 20.09$.
When $S_T = 2025$, the profit will be $\Pi = 25 - 108.43 + 2(81.75) - 59.98 = 20.09$.
When $S_T = 2100$, the profit will be $\Pi = 0 - 108.43 + 2(81.75) - 59.98 = -4.91$.

Exhibit 78-10 depicts these results graphically. Note that the strategy is based on the expectation that the volatility of the underlying will be relatively low. The expectation must be that the underlying will trade near the middle exercise price. The maximum loss of 4.91 occurs if the underlying ends up below the lower strike, 1950, or above the upper strike, 2050. The maximum profit occurs if the underlying ends up precisely at the middle exercise price. This maximum profit is found by examining either of the middle two ranges with S_T set equal to X_2:

$$\Pi \text{ (maximum)} = S_T - X_1 - c_1 + 2c_2 - c_3$$
$$= X_2 - X_1 - c_1 + 2c_2 - c_3 \qquad \text{if } S_T = X_2$$
$$\Pi \text{ (maximum)} = -S_T + 2X_2 - X_1 - c_1 + 2c_2 - c_3$$
$$= X_2 - X_1 - c_1 + 2c_2 - c_3 \qquad \text{if } S_T = X_2$$

In this case, the maximum profit is Π (maximum) $= 2000 - 1950 - 108.43 + 2(81.75) - 59.98 = 45.09$, which is a return of 918 percent.[13]

EXHIBIT 78-10 **Butterfly Spread (Buy Calls with Exercise Price X_1 and X_3, Sell Two Calls with Exercise Price X_2)**

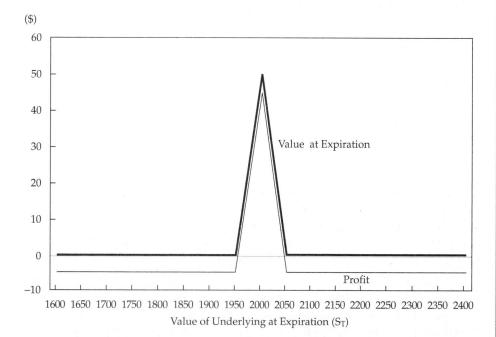

[13] This return is based on a maximum value of $2000 - 1950 = 50$ versus the initial value of 4.91, a return of 918 percent.

There are two breakeven prices, and they lie within the two middle profit ranges. We find them as follows:

For $X_1 < S_T < X_2$:

$$\Pi = S_T* - X_1 - c_1 + 2c_2 - c_3 = 0$$
$$S_T* = X_1 + c_1 - 2c_2 + c_3$$

For $X_2 \leq S_T < X_3$:

$$\Pi = -S_T* + 2X_2 - X_1 - c_1 + 2c_2 - c_3 = 0$$
$$S_T* = 2X_2 - X_1 - c_1 + 2c_2 - c_3$$

In this example, therefore, the breakeven prices are

$$S_T* = X_1 + c_1 - 2c_2 + c_3$$
$$= 1950 + 108.43 - 2(81.75) + 59.98 = 1954.91$$
$$S_T* = 2X_2 - X_1 - c_1 + 2c_2 - c_3$$
$$= 2(2000) - 1950 - 108.43 + 2(81.75) - 59.98 = 2045.09$$

These movements represent a range of roughly ±2.3 percent from the starting value of 2000. Therefore, if the underlying stays within this range, the strategy will be profitable.

In summary, for the butterfly spread

Value at expiration: $V_T = \max(0, S_T - X_1) - 2\max(0, S_T - X_2) +$
$$\max(0, S_T - X_3)$$
Profit: $\Pi = V_T - c_1 + 2c_2 - c_3$
Maximum profit $= X_2 - X_1 - c_1 + 2c_2 - c_3$
Maximum loss $= c_1 - 2c_2 + c_3$
Breakeven: $S_T* = X_1 + c_1 - 2c_2 + c_3$ and $S_T* = 2X_2 - X_1 - c_1 + 2c_2 - c_3$

As we noted, a butterfly spread is a strategy based on the expectation of low volatility in the underlying. Of course, for a butterfly spread to be an appropriate strategy, the user must believe that the underlying will be less volatile than the market expects. If the investor buys into the strategy and the market is more volatile than expected, the strategy is likely to result in a loss. If the investor expects the market to be more volatile than he believes the market expects, the appropriate strategy could be to sell the butterfly spread. Doing so would involve selling the calls with exercise prices of X_1 and X_3 and buying two calls with exercise prices of X_2.[14]

Alternatively, a butterfly spread can be executed using puts. Note that the initial value of the spread using calls is $V_0 = c_1 - 2c_2 + c_3$. Recall that from put–call parity, $c = p + S - X/(1 + r)^T$. If we use the appropriate subscripts and substitute $p_i + S - X_i/(1 + r)^T$ for c_i where $i = 1, 2$, and 3, we obtain $V_0 = p_1 - 2p_2 + p_3$. The positive signs on p_1 and p_3 and the negative sign on $2p_2$ mean that we could buy the puts with exercise prices X_1 and X_3 and sell two puts with exercise price of X_2 to obtain the same result. We would, in effect, be buying a bear spread with puts consisting of buying the put with exercise price of X_3 and selling the put with exercise price of X_2, and also selling a bear spread by selling the put with exercise price of X_2 and buying the put with exercise price of X_1. If the options are priced correctly, it does not really matter whether we use puts or calls.[15]

---

[14] A short butterfly spread is sometimes called a **sandwich spread**.

[15] If puts were underpriced, it would be better to buy the butterfly spread using puts. If calls were underpriced, it would be better to buy the butterfly spread using calls. Of course, other strategies could also be used to take advantage of any mispricing.

Practice Problem 7

Consider three put options on a currency that is currently selling for $1.45. The exercise prices are $1.30, $1.40, and $1.50. The put prices are $0.08, $0.125, and $0.18, respectively. The puts all expire at the same time. Answer the following questions about a butterfly spread.

A. Determine the value at expiration and the profit under the following outcomes:

   i. The price of the currency at expiration is $1.26.

   ii. The price of the currency at expiration is $1.35.

   iii. The price of the currency at expiration is $1.47.

   iv. The price of the currency at expiration is $1.59.

B. Determine the following:

   i. The maximum profit

   ii. The maximum loss

C. Determine the breakeven currency price at expiration.

SOLUTIONS

A. **i.** $V_T = \max(0, X_1 - S_T) - 2\max(0, X_2 - S_T) + \max(0, X_3 - S_T)$
$= \max(0, 1.30 - 1.26) - 2\max(0, 1.40 - 1.26) + \max(0, 1.50 - 1.26) = 0.04 - 2(0.14) + 0.24 = 0.0$
$\Pi = V_T - V_0 = V_T - (p_1 - 2p_2 + p_3) = 0.0 - [0.08 - 2(0.125) + 0.18] = -0.01$

   ii. $V_T = \max(0, X_1 - S_T) - 2\max(0, X_2 - S_T) + \max(0, X_3 - S_T)$
$= \max(0, 1.30 - 1.35) - 2\max(0, 1.40 - 1.35) + \max(0, 1.50 - 1.35) = 0.0 - 2(0.05) + 0.15 = 0.05$
$\Pi = V_T - V_0 = V_T - (p_1 - 2p_2 + p_3) = 0.05 - [0.08 - 2(0.125) + 0.18] = 0.04$

   iii. $V_T = \max(0, X_1 - S_T) - 2\max(0, X_2 - S_T) + \max(0, X_3 - S_T)$
$= \max(0, 1.30 - 1.47) - 2\max(0, 1.40 - 1.47) + \max(0, 1.50 - 1.47) = 0.0 - 2(0) + 0.03 = 0.03$
$\Pi = V_T - V_0 = V_T - (p_1 - 2p_2 + p_3) = 0.03 - [0.08 - 2(0.125) + 0.18] = 0.02$

   iv. $V_T = \max(0, X_1 - S_T) - 2\max(0, X_2 - S_T) + \max(0, X_3 - S_T)$
$= \max(0, 1.30 - 1.59) - 2\max(0, 1.40 - 1.59) + \max(0, 1.50 - 1.59) = 0.0 - 2(0) + 0.0 = 0.0$
$\Pi = V_T - V_0 = V_T - (p_1 - 2p_2 + p_3) = 0.0 - [0.08 - 2(0.125) + 0.18] = -0.01$

B. **i.** Maximum profit $= X_2 - X_1 - (p_1 - 2p_2 + p_3) = 1.40 - 1.30 - [0.08 - 2(0.125) + 0.18] = 0.09$

   ii. Maximum loss $= p_1 - 2p_2 + p_3 = 0.08 - 2(0.125) + 0.18 = 0.01$

C. $S_T^* = X_1 + p_1 - 2p_2 + p_3 = 1.30 + 0.08 - 2(0.125) + 0.18 = 1.31$
$S_T^* = 2X_2 - X_1 - p_1 + 2p_2 - p_3 = 2(1.40) - 1.30 - 0.08 + 2(0.125) - 0.18 = 1.49$

So far, we have restricted ourselves to the use of either calls or puts, but not both. We now look at strategies that involve positions in calls *and* puts.

2.4 Combinations of Calls and Puts

2.4.1 Collars

Recall that in Section 2.2 we examined the protective put. In that strategy, the holder of the underlying asset buys a put to provide protection against downside loss. Purchasing the put requires the payment of the put premium. One way to get around paying the put premium is to sell another option with a premium equal to the put premium, which can be done by selling a call with an exercise price above the current price of the underlying.

Although it is not necessary that the call premium offset the put premium, and the call premium can even be more than the put premium, the typical collar has the call and put premiums offset. When this offsetting occurs, no net premium is required up front. In effect, the holder of the asset gains protection below a certain level, the exercise price of the put, and pays for it by giving up gains above a certain level, the exercise price of the call. This strategy is called a **collar**. When the premiums offset, it is sometimes called a **zero-cost collar**. This term is a little misleading, however, as it suggests that there is no "cost" to this transaction. The cost takes the form of forgoing upside gains. The term "zero-cost" refers only to the fact that no cash is paid up front.

A collar is a modified version of a protective put and a covered call and requires different exercise prices for each. Let the put exercise price be X_1 and the call exercise price be X_2. With X_1 given, it is important to see that X_2 is not arbitrary. If we want the call premium to offset the put premium, the exercise price on the call must be set such that the price of the call equals the price of the put. We thus can select any exercise price of the put. Then the call exercise price is selected by determining which exercise price will produce a call premium equal to the put premium. Although the put can have any exercise price, typically the put exercise price is lower than the current value of the underlying. The call exercise price then must be above the current value of the underlying.[16]

So let X_1 be set. The put with this exercise price has a premium of p_1. We now need to set X_2 such that the premium on the call, c_2, equals the premium on the put, p_1. To do so, we need to use an option valuation model, such as Black–Scholes–Merton, to find the exercise price of the call that will make $c_2 = p_1$. Recall that the Black–Scholes–Merton formula is

$$c = S_0 N(d_1) - Xe^{-r^c T}N(d_2)$$

where

$$d_1 = \frac{\ln(S_0/X) + (r^c + \sigma^2/2)T}{\sigma\sqrt{T}}$$

$$d_2 = d_1 - \sigma\sqrt{T}$$

---

[16] It can be proven in general that the call exercise price would have to be above the current value of the underlying. Intuitively, it can be shown through put–call parity that if the call and put exercise prices were equal to the current value of the underlying, the call would be worth more than the put. If we lower the put exercise price below the price of the underlying, the put price would decrease. Then the gap between the call and put prices would widen further. We would then need to raise the call exercise price above the current price of the underlying to make its premium come down.

and where r^c is the continuously compounded risk-free rate and $N(d_1)$ and $N(d_2)$ are normal probabilities associated with the values d_1 and d_2. Ideally we would turn the equation around and solve for X in terms of c, but the equation is too complex to be able to isolate X on one side. So, we must solve for X by trial and error. We substitute in values of X until the option price equals c, where c is the call premium that we want to equal the put premium.

Consider the Nasdaq example. Suppose we use the put with exercise price of 1950. Its premium is 56.01. So now we need a call with a premium of 56.01. The call with exercise price of 2000 is worth 81.75. So to get a lower call premium, we need a call with an exercise price higher than 2000. By trial and error, we insert higher and higher exercise prices until the call premium falls to 56.01, which occurs at an exercise price of about 2060.[17] So now we have it. We buy the put with an exercise price of 1950 for 56.01 and sell the call with exercise price of 2060 for 56.01. This transaction requires no cash up front.

The value of the position at expiration is the sum of the value of the underlying asset, the value of the put, and the value of the short call:

$$V_T = S_T + \max(0, X_1 - S_T) - \max(0, S_T - X_2)$$

Broken down into ranges, we have

$$V_T = S_T + X_1 - S_T - 0 = X_1 \qquad \text{if } S_T \leq X_1$$
$$V_T = S_T + 0 - 0 = S_T \qquad \text{if } X_1 < S_T < X_2$$
$$V_T = S_T + 0 - (S_T - X_2) = X_2 \qquad \text{if } S_T \geq X_2$$

The initial value of the position is simply the value of the underlying asset, S_0. The profit is $V_T - V_0$:

$$\Pi = S_T + \max(0, X_1 - S_T) - \max(0, S_T - X_2) - S_0$$

Broken down into ranges, we have

$$\Pi = X_1 - S_0 \qquad \text{if } S_T \leq X_1$$
$$\Pi = S_T - S_0 \qquad \text{if } X_1 < S_T < X_2$$
$$\Pi = X_2 - S_0 \qquad \text{if } S_T \geq X_2$$

Using our example where $X_1 = 1950$, $p_1 = 56.01$, $X_2 = 2060$, $c_2 = 56.01$, and $S_0 = 2000$, we obtain the following values at expiration:

If $S_T = 1900$, $V_T = 1950$
If $S_T = 2000$, $V_T = 2000$
If $S_T = 2100$, $V_T = 2060$

The profit for $S_T = 1900$ is $\Pi = 1950 - 2000 = -50$.

If $S_T = 2000$, $\Pi = 2000 - 2000 = 0$
If $S_T = 2100$, $\Pi = 2060 - 2000 = 60$

A graph of this strategy is shown in Exhibit 78-11. Note that the lines are flat over the range of S_T up to the put exercise price of 1950 and in the range beyond the

---

[17] The other necessary information to obtain the exercise price of the call are that the volatility is 0.35, the risk-free rate is 0.02, and the dividend yield is 0.005. The actual call price at a stock price of 2060 is 56.18. At 2061, the call price is 55.82. Thus, the correct exercise price lies between 2060 and 2061; we simply round to 2060.

EXHIBIT 78-11   **Zero-Cost Collar (Buy Put with Exercise Price X₁, Sell Call with Exercise Price X₂, Put and Call Premiums Offset)**

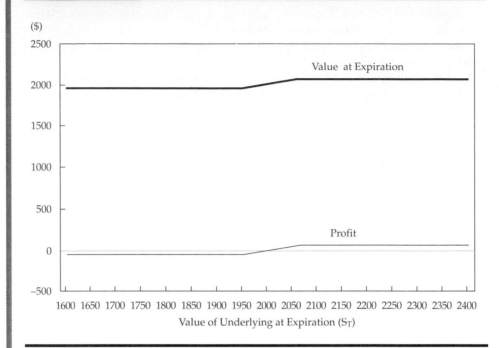

call exercise price of 2060. Below 1950, the put provides protection against loss. Above 2060, the short call forces a relinquishment of the gains, which are earned by the buyer of the call. In between these ranges, neither the put nor the call has value. The profit is strictly determined by the underlying and moves directly with the value of the underlying. The maximum profit is $X_2 - S_0$, which here is $2060 - 2000 = 60$, a return of 3 percent. The maximum loss is $S_0 - X_1$, which here is $2000 - 1950 = 50$, a loss of 2.5 percent. Keep in mind that these options have lives of one month, so those numbers represent one-month returns. The breakeven is simply the original underlying price of 2000.

In summary, for the collar

Value at expiration: $V_T = S_T + \max(0, X_1 - S_T) - \max(0, S_T - X_2)$
Profit: $\Pi = V_T - S_0$
Maximum profit $= X_2 - S_0$
Maximum loss $= S_0 - X_1$
Breakeven: $S_T^* = S_0$

Collars are also known as **range forwards** and risk reversals.[18] Asset managers often use them to guard against losses without having to pay cash up front for the protection. Clearly, however, they are virtually the same as bull spreads. The latter has a cap on the gain and a floor on the loss but does not involve actually holding the underlying. In Section 3.0, we shall encounter this strategy again in the form of an interest rate collar, which protects floating-rate borrowers against high interest rates.

---

[18] It is not clear why a collar is sometimes called a risk reversal. It is clear, however, why a collar is sometimes called a range forward. Like a forward contract, it requires no initial outlay other than for the underlying. Unlike a forward contract, which has a strictly linear payoff profile, the collar payoff breaks at the two exercise prices, thus creating a range.

Practice Problem 8

The holder of a stock worth $42 is considering placing a collar on it. A put with an exercise price of $40 costs $5.32. A call with the same premium would require an exercise price of $50.59.

A. Determine the value at expiration and the profit under the following outcomes:

   i. The price of the stock at expiration is $55.

   ii. The price of the stock at expiration is $48.

   iii. The price of the stock at expiration is $35.

B. Determine the following:

   i. The maximum profit

   ii. The maximum loss

C. Determine the breakeven stock price at expiration.

SOLUTIONS

A. **i.** $V_T = S_T + \max(0, X_1 - S_T) - \max(0, S_T - X_2) = 55 + \max(0, 40 - 55) - \max(0, 55 - 50.59) = 55 + 0 - (55 - 50.59) = 50.59$

      $\Pi = V_T - S_0 = 50.59 - 42 = 8.59$

   ii. $V_T = S_T + \max(0, X_1 - S_T) - \max(0, S_T - X_2) = 48 + \max(0, 40 - 48) - \max(0, 48 - 50.59) = 48 + 0 - 0 = 48$

      $\Pi = V_T - S_0 = 48 - 42 = 6$

   iii. $V_T = S_T + \max(0, X_1 - S_T) - \max(0, S_T - X_2) = 35 + \max(0, 40 - 35) - \max(0, 35 - 50.59) = 35 + 5 - 0 = 40$

      $\Pi = V_T - S_0 = 40 - 42 = -2$

B. **i.** Maximum profit $= X_2 - S_0 = 50.59 - 42 = 8.59$

   ii. Maximum loss $= S_0 - X_1 = 42 - 40 = 2$

C. $S_T{}^* = S_0 = 42$

Collars are one of the many directional strategies, meaning that they perform based on the direction of the movement in the underlying. Of course, butterfly spreads perform based on the volatility of the underlying. Another strategy in which performance is based on the volatility of the underlying is the straddle.

2.4.2 Straddle

To justify the purchase of a call, an investor must be bullish. To justify the purchase of a put, an investor must be bearish. What should an investor do if he believes the market will be volatile but does not feel particularly strongly about the direction? We discussed earlier that a short butterfly spread is one strategy. It benefits from extreme movements, but its gains are limited. There are other, more-complex strategies, such as time spreads, that can benefit from high volatility; however, one simple strategy, the **straddle,** also benefits from high volatility.

Suppose the investor buys both a call and a put with the same exercise price on the same underlying with the same expiration. This strategy enables the investor to profit from upside or downside moves. Its cost, however, can be quite heavy. In fact, a straddle is a wager on a large movement in the underlying.

The value of a straddle at expiration is the value of the call and the value of the put: $V_T = \max(0, S_T - X) + \max(0, X - S_T)$. Broken down into ranges,

$$V_T = X - S_T \qquad \text{if } S_T < X$$
$$V_T = S_T - X \qquad \text{if } S_T \geq X$$

The initial value of the straddle is simply $V_0 = c_0 + p_0$. The profit is $V_T - V_0$ or $\Pi = \max(0, S_T - X) + \max(0, X - S_T) - c_0 - p_0$. Broken down into ranges,

$$\Pi = X - S_T - c_0 - p_0 \qquad \text{if } S_T < X$$
$$\Pi = S_T - X - c_0 - p_0 \qquad \text{if } S_T \geq X$$

In our example, let $X = 2000$. Then $c_0 = 81.75$ and $p_0 = 79.25$.

> If $S_T = 2100$, the value of the position at expiration is
> $V_T = 2100 - 2000 = 100$.
> If $S_T = 1900$, the value of the position at expiration is
> $V_T = 2000 - 1900 = 100$.
> If $S_T = 2100$, the profit is $\Pi = 100 - 81.75 - 79.25 = -61$.
> If $S_T = 1900$, the profit is $\Pi = 100 - 81.75 - 79.25 = -61$.

Note the symmetry, whereby a move of 100 in either direction results in a change in value of 61. The put and call payoffs are obviously symmetric. It is also apparent that these outcomes are below breakeven.

Observe the results in Exhibit 78-12. Note that the value and profit are V-shaped, thereby benefiting from large moves in the underlying in either direction. Like the call option the straddle contains, the gain on the upside is unlimited. Like the put, the downside gain is not unlimited, but it is quite large. The underlying can go down no further than zero. Hence, on the downside the maximum profit is $X - c_0 - p_0$, which in this case is $2000 - 81.75 - 79.25 = 1839$. The maximum loss

EXHIBIT 78-12	Straddle (Buy Call and Put with Exercise Price X)

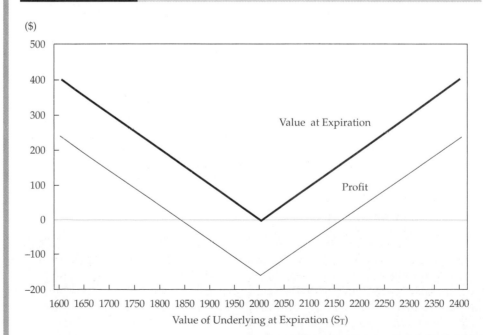

occurs if the underlying ends up precisely at the exercise price. In that case, neither the call nor the put expires with value and the premiums are lost on both. Therefore, the maximum loss is $c_0 + p_0$, which is $81.75 + 79.25 = 161$.

There are two breakevens. Using S_T* to denote the breakevens, we set each profit equation to zero and solve for S_T*:

If $S_T \geq X$,
$$\Pi = S_T* - X - c_0 - p_0 = 0$$
$$S_T* = X + c_0 + p_0$$

If $S_T < X$,
$$\Pi = X - S_T* - c_0 - p_0 = 0$$
$$S_T* = X - c_0 - p_0$$

The breakevens thus equal the exercise price plus or minus the premiums. So in this case, the breakevens are $2000 \pm 161 = 2161$ and 1839. A move of 161 is a percentage move of 8.1 percent over a one-month period. Hence, in this example, the purchase of a straddle is a bet that the underlying will move at nearly a 100 percent annual rate over a one-month period, quite a risky bet. An investor would make such a bet only when he felt that the underlying would be exceptionally volatile. An obvious time to use a straddle would be around major events such as earnings announcements. But because earnings announcements are known and anticipated events, the greater uncertainty surrounding them should already be reflected in the options' prices. Recall that the greater the volatility, the higher the prices of both puts and calls. Therefore, using a straddle in anticipation of an event that everyone knows is coming is not necessarily a good idea. Only when the investor believes the market will be more volatile than everyone else believes would a straddle be advised.

In summary, for a straddle

Value at expiration: $V_T = \max(0, S_T - X) + \max(0, X - S_T)$
Profit: $\Pi = V_T - (c_0 + p_0)$
Maximum profit $= \infty$
Maximum loss $= c_0 + p_0$
Breakeven: $S_T* = X \pm (c_0 + p_0)$

As we have noted, a straddle would tend to be used by an investor who is expecting the market to be volatile but does not have strong feelings one way or the other on the direction. An investor who leans one way or the other might consider adding a call or a put to the straddle. Adding a call to a straddle is a strategy called a **strap**, and adding a put to a straddle is called a **strip**. It is even more difficult to make a gain from these strategies than it is for a straddle, but if the hoped-for move does occur, the gains are leveraged. Another variation of the straddle is a **strangle**, in which the put and call have different exercise prices. This strategy creates a graph similar to a straddle but with a flat section instead of a point on the bottom.

Practice Problem 9

Consider a stock worth $49. A call with an exercise price of $50 costs $6.25 and a put with an exercise price of $50 costs $5.875. An investor buys a straddle.

A. Determine the value at expiration and the profit under the following outcomes:

  i. The price of the stock at expiration is $61.

  ii. The price of the stock at expiration is $37.

B. Determine the following:

  i. The maximum profit

  ii. The maximum loss

C. Determine the breakeven stock price at expiration.

SOLUTIONS

A. **i.** $V_T = \max(0, S_T - X) + \max(0, X - S_T) = \max(0, 61 - 50) + \max(0, 50 - 61) = 11 - 0 = 11$

  $\Pi = V_T - (c_0 + p_0) = 11 - (6.25 + 5.875) = -1.125$

  ii. $V_T = \max(0, S_T - X) + \max(0, X - S_T) = \max(0, 37 - 50) + \max(0, 50 - 37) = 0 + 13 = 13$

  $\Pi = V_T - S_0 = 13 - (6.25 + 5.875) = 0.875$

B. **i.** Maximum profit $= \infty$

  ii. Maximum loss $= c_0 + p_0 = 6.25 + 5.875 = 12.125$

C. $S_T^* = X \pm (c_0 + p_0) = 50 \pm (6.25 + 5.875) = 62.125, 37.875$

Now we turn to a strategy that combines more than one call and more than one put. It should not be surprising that we shall recognize this strategy as just a combination of something we have already learned.

2.4.3 Box Spreads

In Reading 76 we exploited an arbitrage opportunity with a neutral position three alternative ways: using put–call parity, using the binomial model, or using the Black–Scholes–Merton model. Exploiting put–call parity requires a position in the underlying. Using the binomial or Black–Scholes–Merton model requires that the model holds in the market. In addition, both models require a position in the underlying and an estimate of the volatility.

A **box spread** can also be used to exploit an arbitrage opportunity but it requires that neither the binomial nor Black–Scholes–Merton model holds, it needs no estimate of the volatility, and all of the transactions can be executed within the options market, making implementation of the strategy simpler, faster, and with lower transaction costs.

In basic terms, a box spread is a combination of a bull spread and a bear spread. Suppose we buy the call with exercise price X_1 and sell the call with exercise price X_2. This set of transactions is a bull spread. Then we buy the put with exercise price X_2 and sell the put with exercise price X_1. This is a bear spread. Intuitively, it should sound like a combination of a bull spread and a bear spread would leave the investor with a fairly neutral position, and indeed, that is the case.

The value of the box spread at expiration is

$$V_T = \max(0, S_T - X_1) - \max(0, S_T - X_2) + \max(0, X_2 - S_T) - \max(0, X_1 - S_T)$$

Broken down into ranges, we have

$$V_T = 0 - 0 + X_2 - S_T - (X_1 - S_T) = X_2 - X_1 \qquad \text{if } S_T \le X_1$$
$$V_T = S_T - X_1 - 0 + X_2 - S_T - 0 = X_2 - X_1 \qquad \text{if } X_1 < S_1 < X_2$$
$$V_T = S_T - X_1 - (S_T - X_2) + 0 - 0 = X_2 - X_1 \qquad \text{if } S_T \ge X_2$$

These outcomes are all the same. In each case, two of the four options expire in-the-money, and the other two expire out-of-the-money. In each case, the holder of the box spread ends up buying the underlying with one option, using either the long call at X_1 or the short put at X_1, and selling the underlying with another option, using either the long put at X_2 or the short call at X_2. The box spread thus results in buying the underlying at X_1 and selling it at X_2. This outcome is known at the start.

The initial value of the transaction is the value of the long call, short call, long put, and short put, $V_0 = c_1 - c_2 + p_2 - p_1$. The profit is, therefore, $\Pi = X_2 - X_1 - c_1 + c_2 - p_2 + p_1$.

In contrast to all of the other strategies, the outcome is simple. In all cases, we end up with the same result. Using the options with exercise prices of 1950 and 2050, which have premiums of $c_1 = 108.43$, $c_2 = 59.98$, $p_1 = 56.01$, and $p_2 = 107.39$, the value at expiration is always $2050 - 1950 = 100$ and the profit is always $\Pi = 100 - 108.43 + 59.98 - 107.39 + 56.01 = 0.17$. This value may seem remarkably low. We shall see why momentarily.

The initial value of the box spread is $c_1 - c_2 + p_2 - p_1$. The payoff at expiration is $X_2 - X_1$. Because the transaction is risk free, the present value of the payoff, discounted using the risk-free rate, should equal the initial outlay. Hence, we should have

$$(X_2 - X_1)/(1 + r)^T = c_1 - c_2 + p_2 - p_1$$

If the present value of the payoff exceeds the initial value, the box spread is underpriced and should be purchased.

In this example, the initial outlay is $V_0 = 108.43 - 59.98 + 107.39 - 56.01 = 99.83$. To obtain the present value of the payoff, we need an interest rate and time to expiration. The prices of these options were obtained using a time to expiration of one month and a risk-free rate of 2.02 percent. The present value of the payoff is

$$(X_2 - X_1)/(1 + r)^r = (2050 - 1950)/(1.0202)^{1/12} = 99.83$$

In other words, this box spread is correctly priced. This result should not be surprising, because we noted that we used the Black–Scholes–Merton model to price these options. The model should not allow arbitrage opportunities of any form.

Recall that the profit from this transaction is 0.17, a very low value. This profit reflects the fact that the box spread is purchased at 99.83 and matures to a value of 100, a profit of 0.17, which is a return of the risk-free rate for one month.[19] The reason the profit seems so low is that it is just the risk-free rate.

Let us assume that one of the long options, say the put with exercise price of 2050, is underpriced. Let its premium be 105 instead of 107.39. Then the net premium would be $108.43 - 59.98 + 105 - 56.01 = 97.44$. Again, the present

---

[19] That is, $99.83(1.0202)^{1/12} \approx 100$. Hence, the profit of 0.17 is about 2.02 percent, for one month.

value of the payoff is 99.83. Hence, the box spread would generate a gain in value clearly in excess of the risk-free rate. If some combination of the options was such that the net premium is more than the present value of the payoff, then the box spread would be overpriced. Then we should sell the X_1 call and X_2 put and buy the X_2 call and X_1 put. Doing so would generate an outlay at expiration with a present value less than the initial value.

So to summarize the box spread, we say that

Value at expiration: $V_T = X_2 - X_1$
Profit: $\Pi = X_2 - X_1 - (c_1 - c_2 + p_2 - p_1)$
Maximum profit = (same as profit)
Maximum loss = (no loss is possible, given fair option prices)

Breakeven: no breakeven; the transaction always earns the risk-free rate, given fair option prices.

Practice Problem 10

Consider a box spread consisting of options with exercise prices of 75 and 85. The call prices are 16.02 and 12.28 for exercise prices of 75 and 85, respectively. The put prices are 9.72 and 15.18 for exercise prices of 75 and 85, respectively. The options expire in six months and the discrete risk-free rate is 5.13 percent.

A. Determine the value of the box spread and the profit for any value of the underlying at expiration.

B. Show that this box spread is priced such that an attractive opportunity is available.

SOLUTIONS

A. The box spread always has a value at expiration of $X_2 - X_1$
= 85 − 75 = 10
$\Pi = V_T - (c_1 - c_2 + p_2 - p_1)$ = 10 − (16.02 − 12.28 + 15.18 − 9.72) = 0.80

B. The box spread should be worth $(X_2 - X_1)/(1 + r)^T$, or

$$(85 - 75)/(1.0513)^{0.5} = 9.75$$

The cost of the box spread is 16.02 − 12.28 + 15.18 − 9.72 = 9.20. The box spread is thus underpriced. At least one of the long options is priced too low or at least one of the short options is priced too high; we cannot tell which. Nonetheless, we can execute this box spread, buying the call with exercise price $X_1 = 75$ and put with exercise price $X_2 = 85$ and selling the call with exercise price $X_2 = 85$ and put with exercise price $X_1 = 75$. This would cost 9.20. The present value of the payoff is 9.75. Therefore, the box spread would generate an immediate increase in value of 0.55.

We have now completed our discussion of equity option strategies. Although the strategies are applicable, with minor changes, to fixed-income securities, we shall not explore that area here. We shall, however, look at interest rate option strategies, which require some significant differences in presentation and understanding compared with equity option strategies.

INTEREST RATE OPTION STRATEGIES

3

In Reading 76 we examined options, which included a group of options in which the underlying is an interest rate and the exercise price is expressed in terms of a rate. Recall that this group of options consists of calls, which pay off if the option expires with the underlying interest rate above the exercise rate, and puts, which pay off if the option expires with the underlying interest rate below the exercise rate. Interest rate call and put options are usually purchased to protect against changes in interest rates. For dollar-based interest rate derivatives, the underlying is usually LIBOR but is always a specific rate, such as the rate on a 90- or 180-day underlying instrument. An interest rate option is based on a specific notional principal, which determines the payoff when the option is exercised. Traditionally, the payoff does not occur immediately upon exercise but is delayed by a period corresponding to the life of the underlying instrument from which the interest rate is taken, an issue we review below.

Recall from Reading 76 that the payoff of an interest rate call option (Equation 76-1) is

$$(\text{Notional principal}) \max(0, \text{Underlying rate at expiration} - \text{Exercise rate})\left(\frac{\text{Days in underlying rate}}{360}\right)$$

where "days in underlying" refers to the maturity of the instrument from which the underlying rate is taken. In some cases, "days in underlying" may be the exact day count during a period. For example, if an interest rate option is used to hedge the interest paid over an m-day period, then "days in underlying" would be m. Even though LIBOR of 30, 60, 90, 180 days, etc., whichever is closest to m, might be used as the underlying rate, the actual day count would be m, the exact number of days. In such cases, the payment date is usually set at 30, 60, 90, 180, etc. days after the option expiration date. So, for example, 180-day LIBOR might be used as the underlying rate, and "days in underlying" could be 180 or perhaps 182, 183, etc. The most important point, however, is that the rate is determined on one day, the option expiration, and payment is made m days later. This practice is standard in floating-rate loans and thus is used with interest rate options, which are designed to manage the risk of floating-rate loans.

Likewise, the payoff of an interest rate put (Equation 78-2) is

$$(\text{Notional principal}) \max(0, \text{Exercise rate} - \text{Underlying rate at expiration})\left(\frac{\text{Days in underlying rate}}{360}\right)$$

Now let us take a look at some applications of interest rate options.

3.1 Using Interest Rate Calls with Borrowing

Let us examine an application of an interest rate call to establish a maximum interest rate for a loan to be taken out in the future. In brief, a company can buy an interest rate call that pays off from increases in the underlying interest rate beyond a chosen level. The call pay-off then compensates for the higher interest rate the company has to pay on the loan.

Consider the case of a company called Global Computer Technology (GCT), which occasionally takes out short-term loans in U.S. dollars with the rate tied to LIBOR. Anticipating that it will take out a loan at a later date, GCT recognizes the potential for an interest rate increase by that time. In this example, today is 14 April, and GCT expects to borrow $40 million on 20 August at LIBOR plus 200 basis points. The loan will involve the receipt of the money on 20 August with full repayment of principal and interest 180 days later on 16 February. GCT would like protection against higher interest rates, so it purchases an interest rate call on 180-day LIBOR to expire on 20 August. GCT chooses an exercise rate of 5 percent. This option gives it the right to receive an interest payment of the difference between the 20 August LIBOR and 5 percent. If GCT exercises the option on 20 August, the payment will occur 180 days later on 16 February when the loan is paid off. The cost of the call is $100,000, which is paid on 14 April. LIBOR on 14 April is 5.5 percent.

The transaction is designed such that if LIBOR is above 5 percent on 20 August, GCT will benefit and be protected against increases in interest rates. To determine how the transaction works, we need to know the effective rate on the loan. Note that the sequence of events is as follows:

14 April ⟶ 20 August ⟶ 16 February
GCT buys call   Call expires; loan starts   Loan repaid and call payoff made

So cash is paid for the call on 14 April. Cash proceeds from the loan are received on 20 August. On 16 February, the loan is repaid and the call payoff (if any) is made.

To evaluate the effectiveness of the overall transaction, we need to determine how the call affects the loan. Therefore, we need to incorporate the payment of the call premium on 14 April into the cash flow on the loan. So, it would be appropriate to compound the call premium from 14 April to 20 August. In effect, we need to know what the call, purchased on 14 April, effectively costs on 20 August. We compound its premium for the 128 days from 14 April to 20 August at the rate at which GCT would have to borrow on 14 April. This rate would be LIBOR on 14 April plus 200 basis points, or 7.5 percent. The call premium thus effectively costs

$$\$100{,}000\left[1 + 0.075\left(\frac{128}{360}\right)\right] = \$102{,}667$$

on 20 August.[20] On that date, GCT takes out the loan, thereby receiving $40 million. We should, however, reduce this amount by $102,667, because GCT effectively receives less money because it must buy the call. So, the loan proceeds are effectively $40,000,000 − $102,667 = $39,897,333.

Next we must calculate the amount of interest paid on the loan and the amount of any call payoff. Let us assume that LIBOR on 20 August is 8 percent. In that case, the loan rate will be 10 percent. The interest on the loan will be

$$\$40{,}000{,}000(0.10)\left(\frac{128}{360}\right) = \$2{,}000{,}000$$

This amount, plus $40 million principal, is repaid on 16 February. With LIBOR assumed to be 8 percent on 20 August, the option payoff is

---

[20] The interpretation of this calculation is that GCT's cost of funds is 7.5 percent, making the option premium effectively $102,667 by the time the loan is taken out.

$$\$40,000,000 \max(0, 0.08 - 0.05)\left(\frac{128}{360}\right) = \$40,000,000(0.03)\left(\frac{128}{360}\right)$$
$$= \$600,000$$

This amount is paid on 16 February. The effective interest paid on 16 February is thus $2,000,000 − $600,000 = $1,400,000. So, GCT effectively receives $39,897,333 on 20 August and pays back $40,000,000 plus $1,400,000 or $41,400,000 on 16 February. The effective annual rate is

$$\left(\frac{\$41,400,000}{\$39,897,333}\right)^{365/180} - 1 = 0.0779$$

Exhibit 78-13 presents a complete description of the transaction and the results for a range of possible LIBORs on 20 August. Exhibit 78-14 illustrates the effective loan rate compared with LIBOR on 20 August. We see that the strategy places an effective ceiling on the rate on the loan of about 7.79 percent while enabling GCT to benefit from decreases in LIBOR. Of course, a part of this maximum rate is the 200 basis point spread over LIBOR that GCT must pay.[21] In effect, the company's maximum rate without the spread is 5.79 percent. This reflects the exercise rate of 5.5 percent plus the effect of the option premium.

EXHIBIT 78-13	Outcomes for an Anticipated Loan Protected with an Interest Rate Call

Scenario (14 April)

Global Computer Technology (GCT) is a U.S. corporation that occasionally undertakes short-term borrowings in U.S. dollars with the rate tied to LIBOR. To facilitate its cash flow planning, it buys an interest rate call to put a ceiling on the rate it pays while enabling it to benefit if rates fall. A call gives GCT the right to receive the difference between LIBOR on the expiration date and the exercise rate it chooses when it purchases the option. The payoff of the call is determined on the expiration date, but the payment is not received until a certain number of days later, corresponding to the maturity of the underlying LIBOR. This feature matches the timing of the interest payment on the loan.

Action

GCT determines that it will borrow $40 million at LIBOR plus 200 basis points on 20 August. The loan will be repaid with a single payment of principal and interest 180 days later on 16 February.

To protect against increases in LIBOR between 14 April and 20 August, GCT buys a call option on LIBOR with an exercise rate of 5 percent to expire on 20 August with the underlying being 180-day LIBOR. The call premium is $100,000. We summarize the information as follows:

Loan amount:	$40,000,000
Underlying:	180-day LIBOR
Spread:	200 basis points over LIBOR
Current LIBOR:	5.5 percent
Expiration:	20 August (128 days later)
Exercise rate:	5 percent
Call premium:	$100,000

(Exhibit continued on next page …)

---

[21] It should be noted that the effective annual rate is actually more than 200 basis points. For example, if someone borrows $100 at 2 percent for 180 days, the amount repaid would be $100[1 + 0.02(180/360)] = $101. The effective annual rate would be $(\$101/\$100)^{365/180} - 1 = 0.0204$.

EXHIBIT 78-13   (continued)

Scenario (20 August)
LIBOR on 20 August is 8 percent.

Outcome and Analysis
For any LIBOR, the call payoff at expiration is given below and will be received 180 days later:

$$\$40{,}000{,}000 \max(0,\text{LIBOR} - 0.05)\left(\frac{180}{360}\right)$$

For LIBOR of 8 percent, the payoff is

$$\$40{,}000{,}000 \max(0,0.08 - 0.05)\left(\frac{180}{360}\right) = \$600{,}000$$

The premium compounded from 14 April to 20 August at the original LIBOR of 5.5 percent plus 200 basis points is

$$\$100{,}000\left[1 + (0.055 + 0.02)\left(\frac{128}{360}\right)\right] - \$102{,}667$$

So the call costs $100,000 on 14 April, which is equivalent to $102,667 on 20 August. The effective loan proceeds are $40,000,000 − $102,667 = $39,897,333. The loan interest is

$$\$40{,}000{,}000(\text{LIBOR on 20 August} + 200 \text{ basis points})\left(\frac{180}{360}\right)$$

For LIBOR of 8 percent, the loan interest is

$$\$40{,}000{,}000(0.08 + 0.02)\left(\frac{180}{360}\right) = \$2{,}000{,}000$$

The call payoff was given above. The loan interest minus the call payoff is the effective interest. The effective rate on the loan is

$$\left(\frac{\$40{,}000.000 \text{ plus effective interest}}{\$39{,}897{,}333}\right)^{365/180} - 1$$

$$= \left(\frac{\$40{,}000{,}000 + \$2{,}000{,}000 - \$600{,}000}{\$39{,}897{,}333}\right)^{365/180} - 1 = 0.0779$$

or 7.79 percent.

(Exhibit continued on next page …)

EXHIBIT 78-13	(continued)

The results are shown below for a range of LIBORs on 20 August.

LIBOR on 20 August	Loan Rate	Loan Interest Paid on 16 February	Call Payoff	Effective Interest	Effective Loan Rate
0.010	0.030	$600,000	$0	$600,000	0.0360
0.015	0.035	700,000	0	700,000	0.0412
0.020	0.040	800,000	0	800,000	0.0464
0.025	0.045	900,000	0	900,000	0.0516
0.030	0.050	1,000,000	0	1,000,000	0.0568
0.035	0.055	1,100,000	0	1,100,000	0.0621
0.040	0.060	1,200,000	0	1,200,000	0.0673
0.045	0.065	1,300,000	0	1,300,000	0.0726
0.050	0.070	1,400,000	0	1,400,000	0.0779
0.055	0.075	1,500,000	100,000	1,400,000	0.0779
0.060	0.080	1,600,000	200,000	1,400,000	0.0779
0.065	0.085	1,700,000	300,000	1,400,000	0.0779
0.070	0.090	1,800,000	400,000	1,400,000	0.0779
0.075	0.095	1,900,000	500,000	1,400,000	0.0779
0.080	0.100	2,000,000	600,000	1,400,000	0.0779
0.085	0.105	2,100,000	700,000	1,400,000	0.0779
0.090	0.110	2,200,000	800,000	1,400,000	0.0779

EXHIBIT 78-14	The Effective Rate on an Anticipated Future Loan Protected with an Interest Rate Call Option

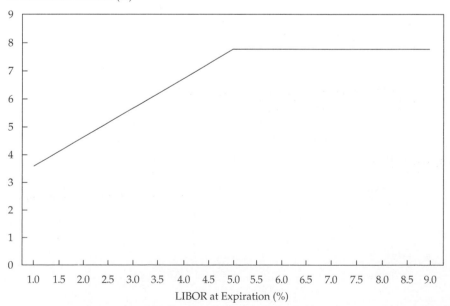

Effective Rate on Loan (%)

LIBOR at Expiration (%)

Practice Problem 11

On 10 January, ResTex Ltd. determines that it will need to borrow $5 million on 15 February at 90-day LIBOR plus 300 basis points. The loan will be an add-on interest loan in which ResTex will receive $5 million and pay it back plus interest on 16 May. To manage the risk associated with the interest rate on 15 February, ResTex buys an interest rate call that expires on 15 February and pays off on 16 May. The exercise rate is 5 percent, and the option premium is $10,000. The current 90-day LIBOR is 5.25 percent. Assume that this rate, plus 300 basis points, is the rate it would borrow at for any period of up to 90 days if the loan were taken out today. Interest is computed on the exact number of days divided by 360.

Determine the effective annual rate on the loan for each of the following outcomes:

i. 90-day LIBOR on 15 February is 6 percent.

ii. 90-day LIBOR on 15 February is 4 percent.

SOLUTION

First we need to compound the premium from 10 January to 15 February, which is 36 days. This calculation tells us the effective cost of the call as of the time the loan is taken out:

$$\$10,000\left[1 + (0.0525 + 0.03)\left(\frac{36}{360}\right)\right] = \$10,083$$

The loan proceeds will therefore be $5,000,000 − $10,083 = $4,989,917.

i. LIBOR is 6 percent. The loan rate will be 9 percent.

The interest on the loan will be $5,000,000(0.06 + 0.03)(90/360) = $112,500.

The option payoff will be $5,000,000 max(0,0.06 − 0.05)(90/360) = $12,500.

Therefore, the effective interest will be $112,500 − $12,500 = $100,000.

The effective rate on the loan will be $\left(\dfrac{\$5,000,000 + \$1,000,000}{\$4,989,917}\right)^{365/90} - 1 = 0.0925$.

Of course, a little more than 300 basis points of this amount is the spread.

ii. LIBOR is 4 percent. The loan rate will be 7 percent.

The interest on the loan will be $5,000,000(0.04 + 0.03)(90/360) = $87,500.

The option payoff will be $5,000,000 max(0,0.04 − 0.05)(90/360) = $0.00.

The effective interest will, therefore, be $87,500.

The effective rate on the loan will be $\left(\dfrac{\$5,000,000 + \$87,500}{\$4,989,917}\right)^{365/90} - 1 = 0.0817$.

Of course, a little more than 300 basis points of this amount is the spread.

Whereas interest rate call options are appropriate for borrowers, lenders also face the risk of interest rates changing. As you may have guessed, they make use of interest rate puts.

3.2 Using Interest Rate Puts with Lending

Now consider an application of an interest rate put to establish a minimum interest rate for a commitment to give a loan in the future. A lender can buy a put that pays off if the interest rate falls below a chosen level. The put payoff then compensates the bank for the lower interest rate on the loan.

For example, consider Arbitrage Bank Inc. (ABInc) which makes loan commitments to corporations. It stands ready to make a loan at LIBOR at a future date. To protect itself against decreases in interest rates between the time of the commitment and the time the loan is taken out, it buys interest rate puts. These options pay off if LIBOR is below the exercise rate at expiration. If LIBOR is above the exercise rate at expiration, the option expires unexercised and the lender benefits from the higher rate on the loan.

In this example, ABInc makes a commitment on 15 March to lend $50 million at 90-day LIBOR plus 2.5 percent on 1 May, which is 47 days later. Current LIBOR is 7.25 percent. It buys a put with an exercise rate of 7 percent for $62,500. Assume that the opportunity cost of lending in the LIBOR market is LIBOR plus a spread of 2.5 percent. Therefore, the effective cost of the premium compounded to the option's expiration is[22]

$$\$62,500\left[1 + (0.0725 + 0.025)\left(\frac{47}{360}\right)\right] = \$63,296$$

When it lends $50 million on 1 May, it effectively has an outlay of $50,000,000 + $63,296 = $50,063,296. The loan rate is set on 1 May and the interest, paid 90 days later on 30 July, is

$$\$50,000,000\left[\text{LIBOR on 1 May plus 250 basis points}\left(\frac{90}{360}\right)\right]$$

The put payoff is

$$\$50,000,000\max(0, 0.07 - \text{LIBOR on 1 May})\left(\frac{90}{360}\right)$$

The loan interest plus the put payoff make up the effective interest. The effective rate on the loan is

---

[22] The interpretation of this calculation is that the bank could have otherwise made a loan of $62,500, which would have paid back $63,296 on 1 May.

The effective rate on the loan will be

$$\left(\frac{\$100,000,000 + \$4,044,444}{\$100,481,968}\right)^{365/182} - 1 = 0.0724.$$

Of course, a little more than 100 basis points of this amount is the spread.

Interest rate calls and puts can be combined into packages of multiple options, which are widely used to manage the risk of floating-rate loans.

3.3 Using an Interest Rate Cap with a Floating-Rate Loan

As we have described previously in this book, many corporate loans are floating-rate loans. They require periodic interest payments in which the rate is reset on a regularly scheduled basis. Because there is more than one interest payment, there is effectively more than one distinct risk. If a borrower wanted to use an interest rate call to place a ceiling on the effective borrowing rate, it would require more than one call. In effect, it would require a distinct call option expiring on each interest rate reset date. As described in Reading 76, a combination of interest rate call options designed to align with the rates on a loan is called a **cap**. The component options are called **caplets**. Each caplet is distinct in having its own expiration date, but typically the exercise rate on each caplet is the same.

To illustrate the use of a cap, consider a company called Measure Technology (MesTech), which borrows in the floating-rate loan market. It usually takes out a loan for several years at a spread over LIBOR, paying the interest semiannually and the full principal at the end. On 15 April, MesTech takes out a $10 million three-year loan at 100 basis points over 180-day LIBOR from a bank called SenBank. Current 180-day LIBOR is 9 percent, which sets the rate for the first six-month period at 10 percent. Interest payments will be on the 15th of October and April for three years. This means that the day counts for the six payments will be 183, 182, 183, 182, 183, and 182.

To protect against increases in interest rates, MesTech purchases an interest rate cap with an exercise rate of 8 percent. The component caplets expire on 15 October, the following 15 April, and so forth until the last caplet expires on a subsequent 15 October. The loan has six interest payments, but because the first rate is already set, there are only five risky payments so the cap will contain five caplets. The payoff of each caplet will be determined on its expiration date, but the caplet payoff, if any, will actually be made on the next payment date. This enables the caplet payoff to line up with the date on which the loan interest is paid. The cap premium, paid up front on 15 April, is $75,000.

In the example of a single interest rate call, we looked at a range of outcomes several hundred basis points around the exercise rate. In a cap, however, many more outcomes are possible. Ideally we would examine a range of outcomes for each caplet. In the example of a single cap, we looked at the exercise rate and 8 rates above and below for a total of 17 rates. For five distinct rate resets, this same procedure would require 5^{17} or more than 762 billion different possibilities. So, we shall just look at one possible combination of rates.

We shall examine a set of outcomes in which LIBOR is

8.50 percent on 15 October
7.25 percent on 15 April the following year
7.00 percent on the following 15 October
6.90 percent on the following 15 April
8.75 percent on the following 15 October

The loan interest is computed as

$$\$10,000,000(\text{LIBOR on previous reset date} + 100 \text{ basis points})\left(\frac{\text{Days in settlement period}}{360}\right)$$

Thus, the first interest payment is

$$\$10,000,000(0.10)\left(\frac{183}{360}\right) = \$508,333$$

which is based on 183 days between 15 April and 15 October. This amount is certain, because the first interest rate has already been set. The remaining interest payments are based on the assumption we made above about the course of LIBOR over the life of the loan.

The results for these assumed rates are shown in the table at the end of Exhibit 78-17. Note several things about the effective interest, displayed in the last column. First, the initial interest payment is much higher than the other interest payments because the initial rate is somewhat higher than the remaining rates that prevailed over the life of the loan. Also, recall that the initial rate is already set, and it would make no sense to add a caplet to cover the initial rate, because the caplet would have to expire immediately in order to pay off on the first 15 October. If the caplet expired immediately, the amount MesTech would have to pay for it would be the amount of the caplet payoff, discounted for the deferral of the payoff. In other words, it would make no sense to have an option, or any derivative for that matter, that is purchased and expires immediately. Note also the variation in the effective interest payments, which occurs for two reasons. One is that, in contrast to previous examples, interest is computed over the exact number of days in the period. Thus, even if the rate were the same, the interest could vary by the effect of one or two days of interest. The other reason is that in some cases the caplets do expire with value, thereby reducing the effective interest paid.

EXHIBIT 78-17   Interest Rate Cap

Scenario (15 April)

Measure Technology (MesTech) is a corporation that borrows in the floating-rate instrument market. It typically takes out a loan for several years at a spread over LIBOR. MesTech pays the interest semiannually and the full principal at the end.

To protect against rising interest rates over the life of the loan, MesTech usually buys an interest rate cap in which the component caplets expire on the dates on which the loan rate is reset. The cap seller is a derivatives dealer.

Action

MesTech takes out a $10 million three-year loan at 100 basis points over LIBOR. The payments will be made semiannually. The lender is SenBank. Current LIBOR is

(Exhibit continued on next page …)

OPTIONAL SEGMENT

EXHIBIT 78-18   (continued)

6.90 percent on the following 15 April

8.75 percent on the following 15 October

Outcome and Analysis

The loan interest is computed as

$$\$10,000,000(\text{LIBOR on previous reset date} + 100 \text{ basis points})\left(\frac{\text{Day in settlement period}}{360}\right)$$

The floorlet payoff is

$$\$10,000,000 \max(0, 0.08 - \text{LIBOR on previous reset date})\left(\frac{\text{Days in settlement period}}{360}\right)$$

The effective interest is the interest due plus the floorlet payoff. The following table shows the payments on the loan and floor:

Date	LIBOR	Loan Rate	Days in Period	Interest Due	Floorlet Payoffs	Effective Interest
15 April	0.0900	0.1000				
15 October	0.0850	0.0950	183	$508,333		$508,333
15 April	0.0725	0.0825	182	480,278	$0	480,278
15 October	0.0700	0.0800	183	419,375	38,125	457,500
15 April	0.0690	0.0790	182	404,444	50,556	455,000
15 October	0.0875	0.0975	183	401,583	55,917	457,500
15 April			182	492,917	0	492,917

Practice Problem 14

Capitalized Bank (CAPBANK) is a lender in the floating-rate loan market. It uses fixed-rate financing on its floating-rate loans and buys floors to hedge the rate. On 1 May 2002, it makes a loan of $40 million at 180-day LIBOR plus 150 basis points. Interest will be paid on 1 November, the following 5 May, the following 1 November, and the following 2 May, at which time the principal will be repaid. The exercise rate is 4.5 percent, the floorlets expire on the rate reset dates, and the premium will be $120,000. Interest will be calculated based on the actual number of days in the period over 360. The current 180-day LIBOR is 5 percent.

Determine the effective interest payments CAPBANK will receive if LIBOR on the following dates is as given:

1 November: 4.875 percent

5 May: 4.25 percent

1 November: 5.125 percent

SOLUTION

The interest due for each period is computed as $40,000,000(LIBOR on previous reset date $+ 0.0150)$(Days in period$/360$). For example, the first interest payment is $40,000,000(0.05 + 0.0150)(184/360) = $1,328,889$, based on the fact that there are 184 days between 1 May and 1 November. Each floorlet payoff is computed as $40,000,000 \max(0,0.045 -$ LIBOR on previous reset date)(Days in period$/360$), where the "previous reset date" is the floorlet expiration. Payment is deferred until the date on which the interest is paid at the given LIBOR. For example, the floorlet expiring on 5 May is worth $40,000,000 \max(0,0.045 - 0.0425)(180/360) = $50,000$, which is paid on 1 November and is based on the fact that there are 180 days between 5 May and 1 November.

The effective interest is the actual interest plus the floorlet payoff. The payments are shown in the table below:

Date	LIBOR	Loan Rate	Days in Period	Interest Due	Caplet Payoff	Effective Interest
1 May	0.05	0.065				
1 November	0.04875	0.06375	184	$1,328,889		$1,328,889
5 May	0.0425	0.0575	185	1,310,417	$0	1,310,417
1 November	0.05125	0.06625	180	1,150,000	50,000	1,200,000
2 May			182	1,339,722	0	1,339,722

When studying equity option strategies, we combined puts and calls into a single transaction called a collar. In a similar manner, we now combine caps and floors into a single transaction, also called a collar.

3.5 Using an Interest Rate Collar with a Floating-Rate Loan

As we showed above, borrowers are attracted to caps because they protect against rising interest rates. They do so, however, at the cost of having to pay a premium in cash up front. A collar combines a long position in a cap with a short position in a floor. The sale of the floor generates a premium that can be used to offset the premium on the cap. Although it is not necessary that the floor premium completely offset the cap premium, this arrangement is common.[25] The exercise rate on the floor is selected such that the floor premium is precisely the cap premium. As with equity options, this type of strategy is called a zero-cost collar.

---

[25] It is even possible for the floor premium to be greater than the cap premium, thereby *generating cash* up front.

Recall, however, that this term is a bit misleading because it suggests that this transaction has no true "cost." The cost is simply not up front in cash. The sale of the floor results in the borrower giving up any gains from interest rates below the exercise rate on the floor. Therefore, the borrower pays for the cap by giving away some of the gains from the possibility of falling rates.

Recall that for equity investors, the collar typically entails ownership of the underlying asset and the purchase of a put, which is financed with the sale of a call. In contrast, an interest rate collar is more commonly seen from the borrower's point of view: a position as a borrower and the purchase of a cap, which is financed by the sale of a floor. It is quite possible, however, that a lender would want a collar. The lender is holding an asset, the loan, and wants protection against falling interest rates, which can be obtained by buying a floor, which itself can be financed by selling a cap. Most interest rate collars, however, are initiated by borrowers.

In the example we used previously, MesTech borrows $10 million at LIBOR plus 100 basis points. The cap exercise rate is 8 percent, and the premium is $75,000. We now change the numbers a little and let MesTech set the exercise rate at 8.625 percent. To sell a floor that will generate the same premium as the cap, the exercise rate is set at 7.5 percent. It is not necessary for us to know the amounts of the cap and floor premiums; it is sufficient to know that they offset.

Exhibit 78-19 shows the collar results for the same set of interest rate outcomes we have been previously using. Note that on the first 15 October, LIBOR is between the cap and floor exercise rates, so neither the caplet nor the floorlet expires in-the-money. On the following 15 April, 15 October, and the next 15 April, the rate is below the floor exercise rate, so MesTech has to pay up on the expiring floorlets. On the final 15 October, LIBOR is above the cap exercise rate, so MesTech gets paid on its cap.

EXHIBIT 78-19	Interest Rate Collar

Scenario (15 April)

Consider the Measure Technology (MesTech) scenario described in the cap and floor example in Exhibits 78-17 and 78-18. MesTech is a corporation that borrows in the floating-rate instrument market. It typically takes out a loan for several years at a spread over LIBOR. MesTech pays the interest semiannually and the full principal at the end.

To protect against rising interest rates over the life of the loan, MesTech usually buys an interest rate cap in which the component caplets expire on the dates on which the loan rate is reset. To pay for the cost of the interest rate cap, MesTech can sell a floor at an exercise rate lower than the cap exercise rate.

Action

Consider the $10 million three-year loan at 100 basis points over LIBOR. The payments are made semiannually. Current LIBOR is 9 percent, which means that the first rate will be at 10 percent. Interest is based on the exact number of days in the six-month period divided by 360. MesTech selects an exercise rate of 8.625 percent for the cap. Generating a floor premium sufficient to offset the cap premium requires a floor exercise rate of 7.5 percent. The caplets and floorlets will expire on 15 October, 15 April of the following year, and so on for three years, but the payoffs will occur on the following payment date to correspond with the interest payment based on LIBOR that determines the caplet and floorlet payoffs. Thus, we have the following information:

    Loan amount: $10,000,000

(Exhibit continued on next page ...)

EXHIBIT 78-19   (continued)

Underlying:	180-day LIBOR
Spread:	100 basis points over LIBOR
Current LIBOR:	9 percent
Interest based on:	actual days/360
Component options:	five caplets and floorlets expiring 15 October, 15 April, etc.
Exercise rate:	8.625 percent on cap, 7.5 percent on floor
Premium:	no net premium

Scenario (various dates throughout the loan)

Shown below is one particular set of outcomes for LIBOR:

8.50 percent on 15 October
7.25 percent on 15 April the following year
7.00 percent on the following 15 October
6.90 percent on the following 15 April
8.75 percent on the following 15 October

Outcome and Analysis

The loan interest is computed as

$$\$10,000,000(\text{LIBOR on previous reset date} + 100 \text{ basis points})\left(\frac{\text{Days in settlement period}}{360}\right)$$

The caplet payoff is

$$\$10,000,000\max(0,\text{LIBOR on previous reset date} - 0.08625)\left(\frac{\text{Days in settlement period}}{360}\right)$$

The floorlet payoff is

$$\$10,000,000\max(0,0.075 - \text{LIBOR on previous reset date})\left(\frac{\text{Days in settlement period}}{360}\right)$$

The effective interest is the interest due minus the caplet payoff minus the floorlet payoff. Note that because the floorlet was sold, the floorlet payoff is either negative (so we would subtract a negative number, thereby adding an amount to obtain the total interest due) or zero.

The following table shows the payments on the loan and collar:

Date	LIBOR	Loan Rate	Days in Period	Interest Due	Caplet Payoffs	Floorlet Payoffs	Effective Interest
15 April	0.0900	0.1000					
15 October	0.0850	0.0950	183	$508,333			$508,333
15 April	0.0725	0.0825	182	480,278	$0	$0	480,278
15 October	0.0700	0.0800	183	419,375	0	−12,708	432,083
15 April	0.0690	0.0790	182	404,444	0	−25,278	429,722
15 October	0.0875	0.0975	183	401,583	0	−30,500	432,083
15 April			182	492,917	6,319	0	486,598

A collar establishes a range, the cap exercise rate minus the floor exercise rate, within which there is interest rate risk. The borrower will benefit from falling rates and be hurt by rising rates within that range. Any rate increases above the cap exercise rate will have no net effect, and any rate decreases below the floor exercise rate will have no net effect. The net cost of this position is zero, provided that the floor exercise rate is set such that the floor premium offsets the cap premium.[26] It is probably easy to see that collars are popular among borrowers.

Practice Problem 15

Exegesis Systems (EXSYS) is a floating-rate borrower that manages its interest rate risk with collars, purchasing a cap and selling a floor in which the cost of the cap and floor are equivalent. EXSYS takes out a $35 million one-year loan at 90-day LIBOR plus 200 basis points. It establishes a collar with a cap exercise rate of 7 percent and a floor exercise rate of 6 percent. Current 90-day LIBOR is 6.5 percent. The interest payments will be based on the exact day count over 360. The caplets and floorlets expire on the rate reset dates. The rates will be set on the current date (5 March), 4 June, 5 September, and 3 December, and the loan will be paid off on the following 3 March.

Determine the effective interest payments if LIBOR on the following dates is as given:

4 June:	7.25 percent
5 September:	6.5 percent
3 December:	5.875 percent

SOLUTION
The interest due for each period is computed as $35,000,000(LIBOR on previous reset date + 0.02)(Days in period/360). For example, the first interest payment is $35,000,000(0.065 + 0.02)(91/360) = $752,014, based on the fact that there are 91 days between 5 March and 4 June. Each caplet payoff is computed as $35,000,000 max(0,LIBOR on previous reset date − 0.07)(Days in period/360), where the "previous reset date" is the caplet expiration. Payment is deferred until the date on which the interest is paid at the given LIBOR. For example, the caplet expiring on 4 June is worth $35,000,000 max(0,0.0725 − 0.07) (93/360) = $22,604, which is paid on 5 September and is based on the fact that there are 93 days between 4 June and 5 September. Each floorlet payoff is computed as $35,000,000 max(0,0.06 − LIBOR on previous reset date)(Days in period/360). For example, the floorlet expiring on 3 December is worth $35,000,000 max(0,0.06 − 0.05875)(90/360) = $10,938, based on the fact that there are 90 days between 3 December

---

[26] It is certainly possible that the floor exercise rate would be set first, and the cap exercise rate would then be set to have the cap premium offset the floor premium. This would likely be the case if a lender were doing the collar. We assume, however, the case of a borrower who wants protection above a certain level and then decides to give up gains below a particular level necessary to offset the cost of the protection.

and 3 March. The effective interest is the actual interest minus the caplet payoff plus the floorlet payoff. The payments are shown in the following table:

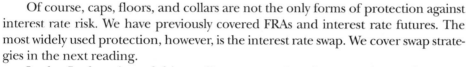

Date	LIBOR	Loan Rate	Days in Period	Interest Due	Caplet Payoff	Floorlet Payoff	Effective Interest
5 March	0.065	0.085					
4 June	0.0725	0.0925	91	$752,014			$752,014
5 September	0.065	0.085	93	836,354	$22,604	$0	813,750
3 December	0.05875	0.07875	89	735,486	0	0	735,486
3 March			90	689,063	0	−10,938	700,001

Of course, caps, floors, and collars are not the only forms of protection against interest rate risk. We have previously covered FRAs and interest rate futures. The most widely used protection, however, is the interest rate swap. We cover swap strategies in the next reading.

In the final section of this reading, we examine the strategies used to manage the risk of an option portfolio.

OPTION PORTFOLIO RISK MANAGEMENT STRATEGIES

So far we have looked at examples of how companies and investors use options. As we have described previously, many options are traded by dealers who make markets in these options, providing liquidity by first taking on risk and then hedging their positions in order to earn the bid–ask spread without taking the risk. In this section, we shall take a look at the strategies dealers use to hedge their positions.[27]

Let us assume that a customer contacts a dealer with an interest in purchasing a call option. The dealer, ready to take either side of the transaction, quotes an acceptable ask price and the customer buys the option. Recall from earlier in this reading that a short position in a call option is a very dangerous strategy, because the potential loss on an upside underlying move is open ended. The dealer would not want to hold a short call position for long. The ideal way to lay off the risk is to find someone else who would take the exact opposite position, but in most cases, the dealer will not be so lucky.[28] Another ideal possibility is for the dealer to lay off the risk using put–call parity. Recall that put–call parity says that $c = p + S - X/(1 + r)^T$. The dealer that has sold a call needs to buy a call to hedge the position. The put–call parity equation means that a long call is equivalent to a long put, a long position in the asset, and issuing a zero-coupon bond with a face value equal to the option exercise price and maturing on the

---

[27] For over-the-counter options, these dealers are usually the financial institutions that make markets in these options. For exchange-traded options, these dealers are the traders at the options exchanges, who may trade for their own accounts or could represent firms.

[28] Even luckier would be the dealer's original customer who might stumble across a party who wanted to sell the call option. The two parties could then bypass the dealer and negotiate a transaction directly between each other, which would save each party half of the bid–ask spread.

option expiration date. Therefore, if the dealer could buy a put with the same exercise price and expiration, buy the asset, and sell a bond or take out a loan with face value equal to the exercise price and maturity equal to that of the option's expiration, it would have the position hedged. Other than buying an identical call, as described above, this hedge would be the best because it is static: No change to the position is required as time passes.

Unfortunately, neither of these transactions can be commonly employed. The necessary options may not be available or may not be favorably priced. As the next best alternative, dealers **delta hedge** their positions using an available and attractively priced instrument. The dealer is short the call and will need an offsetting position in another instrument. An obvious offsetting instrument would be a long position of a certain number of units of the underlying. The size of that long position will be related to the option's delta. In Reading 76, we discussed the concept of an option's delta. Let us briefly review delta here. By definition,

$$\text{Delta} = \frac{\text{Change in option price}}{\text{Change in underlying price}}$$

Delta expresses how the option price changes relative to the price of the underlying. Technically, we should use an approximation sign ($\approx$) in the above equation, but for now we shall assume the approximation is exact. Let ΔS be the change in the underlying price and Δc be the change in the option price. Then Delta = $\Delta c/\Delta S$. Recall from Reading 76 that the delta usually lies between 0.0 and 1.0.[29] Delta will be 1.0 only at expiration and only if the option expires in-the-money. Delta will be 0.0 only at expiration and only if the option expires out-of-the-money. So most of the time, the delta will be between 0.0 and 1.0. Hence, 0.5 is often given as an "average" delta, but one must be careful because even before expiration the delta will tend to be higher than 0.5 if the option is in-the-money.

Now, let us assume that we construct a portfolio consisting of N_S units of the underlying and N_c call options. The value of the portfolio is, therefore,

$$V = N_S S + N_c c$$

The change in the value of the portfolio is

$$\Delta V = N_S \Delta S + N_c \Delta c$$

If we want to hedge the portfolio, then we want the change in V, given a change in S, to be zero. Dividing by ΔS, we obtain

$$\frac{\Delta V}{\Delta S} = N_S \frac{\Delta S}{\Delta S} + N_c \frac{\Delta c}{\Delta S}$$

$$= N_S + N_c \frac{\Delta c}{\Delta S}$$

---

[29] In the following text, we always make reference to the delta lying between 0.0 and 1.0, which is true for calls. For puts, the delta is between −1.0 and 0.0. It is common, however, to refer to a put delta of −1.0 as just 1.0, in effect using its absolute value and ignoring the negative. In all discussions in this reading, we shall refer to delta as ranging between 1.0 and 0.0, recalling that a put delta would range from −1.0 to 0.0.

Setting this result equal to zero and solving for N_c/N_S, we obtain

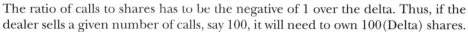

$$\frac{N_c}{N_S} = -\frac{1}{\Delta c/\Delta S}$$

The ratio of calls to shares has to be the negative of 1 over the delta. Thus, if the dealer sells a given number of calls, say 100, it will need to own 100(Delta) shares.

How does delta hedging work? Let us say that we sell call options on 200 shares (this quantity is 2 standardized call contracts on an options exchange) and the delta is 0.5. We would, therefore, need to hold $200(0.5) = 100$ shares. Say the underlying falls by \$1. Then we lose \$100 on our position in the underlying. If the delta is accurate, the option should decline by \$0.50. By having 200 options, the loss in value of the options collectively is \$100. Because we are short the options, the loss in value of the options is actually a gain. Hence, the loss on the underlying is offset by the gain on the options. If the dealer were long the option, it would need to sell short the shares.

This illustration may make delta hedging sound simple: Buy (sell) delta shares for each option short (long). But there are three complicating issues. One is that delta is only an approximation of the change in the call price for a change in the underlying. A second issue is that the delta changes if anything else changes. Two factors that change are the price of the underlying and time. When the price of the underlying changes, delta changes, which affects the number of options required to hedge the underlying. Delta also changes as time changes; because time changes continuously, delta also changes continuously. Although a dealer can establish a delta-hedged position, as soon as anything happens—the underlying price changes or time elapses—the position is no longer delta hedged. In some cases, the position may not be terribly out of line with a delta hedge, but the more the underlying changes, the further the position moves away from being delta hedged. The third issue is that the number of units of the underlying per option must be rounded off, which leads to a small amount of imprecision in the balancing of the two opposing positions.

In Reading 76, we took a basic look at the concept of delta hedging. In the following section, we examine how a dealer delta hedges an option position, carrying the analysis through several days with the additional feature that excess cash will be invested in bonds and any additional cash needed will be borrowed.

4.1 Delta Hedging an Option Over Time

In the previous section, we showed how to set up a delta hedge. As we noted, a delta-hedged position will not remain delta hedged over time. The delta will change as the underlying changes and as time elapses. The dealer must account for these effects.

Let us first examine how actual option prices are sensitive to the underlying and what the delta tells us about that sensitivity. Consider a call option in which the underlying is worth 1210, the exercise price is 1200, the continuously compounded risk-free rate is 2.75 percent, the volatility of the underlying is 20 percent, and the expiration is 120 days. There are no dividends or cash flows on the underlying. Substituting these inputs into the Black–Scholes–Merton model, the option is worth 65.88. Recall from our study of the Black–Scholes–Merton model that delta is the term "$N(d_1)$" in the formula and represents a normal probability associated with the value d_1, which is provided as part of the Black–Scholes–Merton formula. In this example, the delta is 0.5826.[30]

---

[30] All calculations were done on a computer for best precision.

Suppose that the underlying price instantaneously changes to 1200, a decline of 10. Using the delta, we would estimate that the option price would be

$$65.88 + (1200 - 1210)(0.5826) = 60.05$$

If, however, we plugged into the Black–Scholes–Merton model the same parameters but with a price of the underlying of 1200, we would obtain a new option price of 60.19—not much different from the previous result. But observe in Exhibit 78-20 what we obtain for various other values of the underlying. Two patterns become apparent: (1) The further away we move from the current price, the worse the delta-based approximation, and (2) the effects are asymmetric. A given move in one direction does not have the same effect on the option as the same move in the other direction. Specifically, for calls, the delta underestimates the effects of increases in the underlying and overestimates the effects of decreases in the underlying.[31] Because of this characteristic, the delta hedge will not be perfect. The larger the move in the underlying, the worse the hedge. Moreover, whenever the underlying price changes, the delta changes, which requires a rehedging or adjustment to the position. Observe in the last column of the table in Exhibit 78-20 we have recomputed the delta using the new price of the underlying. A dealer must adjust the position according to this new delta.

EXHIBIT 78-20	Delta and Option Price Sensitivity

S = 1210
X = 1200
r^c = 0.0275 (continuously compounded)
σ = 0.20
T = 0.328767 (based on 120 days/365)
No dividends
c = 65.88 (from the Black–Scholes–Merton model)

New Price of Underlying	Delta-Estimated Call Price[a]	Actual Call Price[b]	Difference (Actual − Estimated)	New Delta
1180	48.40	49.69	1.29	0.4959
1190	54.22	54.79	0.57	0.5252
1200	60.05	60.19	0.14	0.5542
1210	65.88	65.88	0.00	0.5826
1220	71.70	71.84	0.14	0.6104
1230	77.53	78.08	0.55	0.6374
1240	83.35	84.59	1.24	0.6635

[a] Delta-estimated call price = Original call price + (New price of underlying − Original price of underlying)Delta.
[b] Actual call price obtained from Black–Scholes–Merton model using new price of underlying; all other inputs are the same.

---

[31] For puts, delta underestimates the effects of price decreases and overestimates the effects of price increases.

Now let us consider the effect of time on the delta. Exhibit 78-21 shows the delta and the number of units of underlying required to hedge 1,000 short options when the option has 120 days, 119, etc. on down to 108. A critical assumption is that we are holding the underlying price constant. Of course, this constancy would not occur in practice, but to focus on understanding the effect of time on the delta, we must hold the underlying price constant. Observe that the delta changes slowly and the number of units of the underlying required changes gradually over this 12-day period. Another not-so-obvious effect is also present: When we round up, we have more units of the underlying than needed, which has a negative effect that hurts when the underlying goes down. When we round down, we have fewer units of the underlying than needed, which hurts when the underlying goes up.

EXHIBIT 78-21   **The Effect of Time on the Delta**

$S = 1210$

$X = 1200$

$r^c = 0.0275$ (continuously compounded)

$\sigma = 0.20$

$T = 0.328767$ (based on 120 days/365)

No dividends

$c = 65.88$ (from the Black–Scholes–Merton model)

Delta = 0.5826

Delta hedge 1,000 short options by holding $1,000(0.5826) = 582.6$ units of the underlying.

Time to Expiration (days)	Delta	Number of Units of Underlying Required
120	0.5826	582.6
119	0.5825	582.5
118	0.5824	582.4
117	0.5823	582.3
116	0.5822	582.2
115	0.5821	582.1
114	0.5820	582.0
113	0.5819	581.9
112	0.5818	581.8
111	0.5817	581.7
110	0.5816	581.6
109	0.5815	581.5
108	0.5814	581.4

The combined effects of the underlying price changing and the time to expiration changing interact to present great challenges for delta hedgers. Let us set up a delta hedge and work through a few days of it. Recall that for the option we have been working with, the underlying price is $1,200, the option price is $65.88, and the delta is 0.5826. Suppose a customer comes to us and asks to buy calls on 1,000 shares. We need to buy a sufficient number of shares to offset the sale of the 1,000 calls. Because we are short 1,000 calls, and this number is fixed, we need 0.5826 shares per call or about 583 shares. So we buy 583 shares to balance the 1,000 short calls. The value of this portfolio is

$$583(\$1,210) - 1,000(\$65.88) = \$639,550$$

So, to initiate this delta hedge, we would need to invest \$639,550. To determine if this hedge is effective, we should see this value grow at the risk-free rate. Because the Black–Scholes–Merton model uses continuously compounded interest, the formula for compounding a value at the risk-free rate for one day is $\exp(r^c/365)$, where r^c is the continuously compounded risk-free rate. One day later, this value should be $\$639,550 \exp(0.0275/365) = \$639,598$. This value becomes our benchmark.

Now, let us move forward one day and have the underlying go to \$1,215. We need a new value of the call option, which now has one less day until expiration and is based on an underlying with a price of \$1,215. The market would tell us the option price, but we do not have the luxury here of asking the market for the price. Instead, we have to appeal to a model that would tell us an appropriate price. Naturally, we turn to the Black–Scholes–Merton model. We recalculate the value of the call option using Black–Scholes–Merton, with the price of the underlying at \$1,215 and the time to expiration at $119/365 = 0.3260$. The option value is \$68.55, and the new delta is 0.5966. The portfolio is now worth

$$583(\$1,215) - 1,000(\$68.55) = \$639,795$$

This value differs from the benchmark by a small amount: $\$639,795 - \$639,598 = \$197$. Although the hedge is not perfect, it is off by only about 0.03 percent.

Now, to move forward and still be delta hedged, we need to revise the position. The new delta is 0.5966. So now we need $1,000(0.5966) = 597$ units of the underlying and must buy 14 units of the underlying. This purchase will cost $14(\$1,215) = \$17,010$. We obtain this money by borrowing it at the risk-free rate. So we issue bonds in the amount of \$17,010. Now our position is 597 units of the underlying, 1,000 short calls, and a loan of \$17,010. The value of this position is still

$$597(\$1,215) - 1,000(\$68.55) - \$17,010 = \$639,795$$

Of course, this is the same value we had before adjusting the position. We could not expect to generate or lose money just by rearranging our position. As we move forward to the next day, we should see this value grow by one day's interest to $\$639,795 \exp(0.0275/365) = \$639,843$. This amount is the benchmark for the next day.

Suppose the next day the underlying goes to \$1,198, the option goes to 58.54, and its delta goes to 0.5479. Our loan of \$17,010 will grow to $\$17,010 \exp(0.0275/365) = \$17,011$. The new value of the portfolio is

$$597(\$1,198) - 1,000(\$58.54) - \$17,011 = \$639,655$$

This amount differs from the benchmark by $\$639,655 - \$639,843 = -\$188$, an error of about 0.03 percent.

With the new delta at 0.5479, we now need 548 shares. Because we have 597 shares, we now must sell $597 - 548 = 49$ shares. Doing so would generate $49(\$1,198) = \$58,702$. Because the value of our debt was \$17,011 and we now have \$58,702 in cash, we can pay back the loan, leaving $\$58,702 - \$17,011$

= $41,691 to be invested at the risk-free rate. So now we have 548 units of the underlying, 1,000 short calls, and bonds of $41,691. The value of this position is

$$548(\$1,198) - 1,000(\$58.54) + \$41,691 = \$639,655$$

Of course, this is the same value we had before buying the underlying. Indeed, we cannot create or destroy any wealth by just rearranging the position.

Exhibit 78-22 illustrates the delta hedge, carrying it through one more day. After the third day, the value of the position should be $639,655 exp(0.0275/365) = $639,703. The actual value is $639,870, a difference of $639,870 − $639,703 = $167.

As we can see, the delta hedge is not perfect, but it is pretty good. After three days, we are off by $167, only about 0.03 percent of the benchmark.

In our example and the discussions here, we have noted that the dealer would typically hold a position in the underlying to delta-hedge a position in the option. Trading in the underlying would not, however, always be the preferred hedge vehicle. In fact, we have stated quite strongly that trading in derivatives is often easier and more cost effective than trading in the underlying. As noted previously, ideally a short position in a particular option would be hedged by holding a long position in that same option, but such a hedge requires that the dealer find another customer or dealer who wants to sell that same option. It is possible, however, that the dealer might be able to more easily buy a different option on the same underlying and use that option as the hedging instrument.

EXHIBIT 78-22	Delta Hedge of a Short Options Position

S = $1,210
X = $1,200
r^c = 0.0275 (continuously compounded)
σ = 0.20
T = 0.328767 (based on 120 days/365)
No dividends
c = $65.88 (from the Black–Scholes–Merton model)
Delta = 0.5826

Units of option constant at 1,000
Units of underlying required = 1000 × Delta
Units of underlying purchased = (Units of underlying required one day) − (Units of underlying required previous day)
Bonds purchased = −S(Units of underlying purchased)
Bond balance = (Previous balance) exp(r^c/365) + Bonds purchased
Value of portfolio = (Units of underlying)S + (Units of options)c + Bond balance

Day	S	c	Delta	Options Sold	Units of Underlying Required	Units of Underlying Purchased	Value of Bonds Purchased	Bond Balance	Value of Portfolio
0	$1,210	$65.88	0.5826	1,000	583	583	$0	$0	$639,550
1	1,215	68.55	0.5965	1,000	597	14	−17,010	−17,010	639,795
2	1,198	58.54	0.5479	1,000	548	−49	58,702	41,691	639,655
3	1,192	55.04	0.5300	1,000	530	−18	21,456	63,150	639,870

For example, suppose one option has a delta of Δ_1 and the other has a delta of Δ_2. These two options are on the same underlying but are not identical. They differ by exercise price, expiration, or both. Using c_1 and c_2 to represent their prices and N_1 and N_2 to represent the quantity of each option in a portfolio that hedges the value of one of the options, the value of the position is

$$V = N_1 c_1 + N_2 c_2$$

Dividing by ΔS, we obtain

$$\frac{\Delta V}{\Delta S} = N_1 \frac{\Delta c_1}{\Delta S} + N_2 \frac{\Delta c_2}{\Delta S}$$

To delta hedge, we set this amount to zero and solve for N_1/N_2 to obtain

$$\frac{N_1}{N_2} = -\frac{\Delta c_2}{\Delta c_1}$$

The negative sign simply means that a long position in one option will require a short position in the other. The desired quantity of Option 1 relative to the quantity of Option 2 is the ratio of the delta of Option 2 to the delta of Option 1. As in the standard delta-hedge example, however, these deltas will change and will require monitoring and modification of the position.[32]

Practice Problem 16

DynaTrade is an options trading company that makes markets in a variety of derivative instruments. DynaTrade has just sold 500 call options on a stock currently priced at $125.75. Suppose the trade date is 18 November. The call has an exercise price of $125, 60 days until expiration, a price of $10.89, and a delta of 0.5649. DynaTrade will delta-hedge this transaction by purchasing an appropriate number of shares. Any additional transactions required to adjust the delta hedge will be executed by borrowing or lending at the continuously compounded risk-free rate of 4 percent.

DynaTrade has begun delta hedging the option. Two days later, 20 November, the following information applies:

Stock price:	$122.75
Option price:	$9.09
Delta:	0.5176
Number of options:	500
Number of shares:	328
Bond balance:	−$6,072
Market value:	$29,645

---

[32] Because the position is long one option and short another, whenever the options differ by exercise price, expiration, or both, the position has the characteristics of a spread. In fact, it is commonly called a **ratio spread**.

A. At the end of 19 November, the delta was 0.6564. Based on this number, show how 328 shares of stock is used to delta hedge 500 call options.

B. Show the allocation of the $29,645 market value of DynaTrade's total position among stock, options, and bonds on 20 November.

C. Show what transactions must be done to adjust the portfolio to be delta hedged for the following day (21 November).

D. On 21 November, the stock is worth $120.50 and the call is worth $7.88. Calculate the market value of the delta-hedged portfolio and compare it with a benchmark, based on the market value on 20 November.

SOLUTIONS

A. If the stock moves up (down) $1, the 328 shares should change by $328. The 500 calls should change by $500(0.6564) = 328.20, rounded off to $328. The calls are short, so any change in the value of the stock position is an opposite change in the value of the options.

B. Stock worth $328(\$122.75) = \$40,262$

Options worth $-500(\$9.09) = -\$4,545$

Bonds worth $-\$6,072$

   Total of $29,645

C. The new required number of shares is $500(0.5176) = 258.80$. Round this number to 259. So we need to have 259 shares instead of 328 shares and must sell 69 shares, generating $69(\$122.75) = \$8,470$. We invest this amount in risk-free bonds. We had a bond balance of $-\$6,072$, so the proceeds from the sale will pay off all of this debt, leaving a balance of $\$8,470 - \$6,072 = \$2,398$ going into the next day. The composition of the portfolio would then be as follows:

   Shares worth $259(\$122.75) = \$31,792$

   Options worth $-500(\$9.09) = -\$4,545$

   Bonds worth $2,398

      Total of $29,645

D. The benchmark is $\$29,645 \exp(0.04/365) = \$29,648$. Also, the value of the bond one day later will be $\$2,398 \exp(0.04/365) = \$2,398$. (This is less than a half-dollar's interest, so it essentially leaves the balance unchanged.) Now we have

   Shares worth $259(\$120.50) = \$31,210$

   Options worth $-500(\$7.88) = -\$3,940$

   Bonds worth $2,398

      Total of $29,668

This is about $20 more than the benchmark.

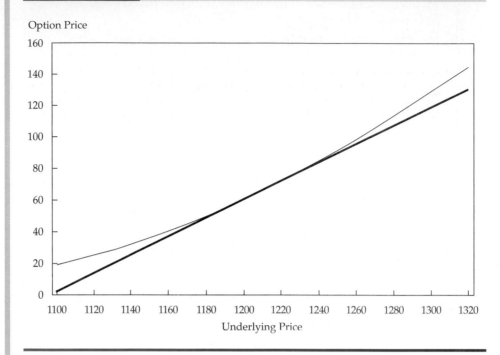

EXHIBIT 78-23   **Actual Option Price (−) and Delta-Estimated Option Price (−)**

As previously noted, the delta is a fairly good approximation of the change in the option price for a very small and rapid change in the price of the underlying. But the underlying does not always change in such a convenient manner, and this possibility introduces a risk into the process of delta hedging.

Note Exhibit 78-23, a graph of the actual option price and the delta-estimated option price from the perspective of day 0 in Exhibit 78-20. At the underlying price of $1,210, the option price is $65.88. The curved line shows the exact option price, calculated with the Black–Scholes–Merton model, for a range of underlying prices. The heavy line shows the option price estimated using the delta as we did in Exhibit 78-20. In that exhibit, we did not stray too far from the current underlying price. In Exhibit 78-23, we let the underlying move a little further. Note that the further we move from the current price of the underlying of $1,210, the further the heavy line deviates from the solid line. As noted earlier, the actual call price moves up more than the delta approximation and moves down less than the delta approximation. This effect occurs because the option price is convex with respect to the underlying price, a point we discussed in Section 7.3.1 of Reading 76. This convexity, which is quite similar to the convexity of a bond price with respect to its yield, means that a first-order price sensitivity measure like delta, or its duration analog for bonds, is accurate only if the underlying moves by a small amount. With duration, a second-order measure called convexity reflects the extent of the deviation of the actual pricing curve from the approximation curve. With options, the second-order measure is called **gamma**.

4.2 Gamma and the Risk of Delta

As noted, in Reading 76 we introduced the concept of the gamma, which is a measure of several effects. We already mentioned that it reflects the deviation of the exact option price change from the price change as approximated by the delta. It also measures the sensitivity of delta to a change in the underlying. In effect, it is the delta of the delta. Specifically,

$$\text{Gamma} = \frac{\text{Change in delta}}{\text{Change in underlying price}}$$

Like delta, gamma is actually an approximation, but we shall treat it as exact. Although a formula exists for gamma, we need to understand only the concept.

If a delta-hedged position were risk free, its gamma would be zero. The larger the gamma, the more the delta-hedged position deviates from being risk free. Because gamma reflects movements in the delta, let us first think about how delta moves. Focusing on call options, recall that the delta is between 0.0 and 1.0. At expiration, the delta is 1.0 if the option expires in-the-money and 0.0 if it expires out-of-the-money. During its life, the delta will tend to be above 0.5 if the option is in-the-money and below 0.5 if the option is out-of-the-money. As expiration approaches, the deltas of in-the-money options will move toward 1.0 and the deltas of out-of-the-money options will move toward 0.0.[33] They will, however, move slowly in their respective directions. The largest moves occur near expiration, when the deltas of at-the-money options move quickly toward 1.0 or 0.0. These rapid movements are the ones that cause the most problems for delta hedgers. Options that are **deep in-the-money** or **deep out-of-the-money** tend to have their deltas move closer to 1.0 or 0.0 well before expiration. Their movements are slow and pose fewer problems for delta hedgers. Thus, it is the rapid movements in delta that concern delta hedgers. These rapid movements are more likely to occur on options that are at-the-money and/or near expiration. Under these conditions, the gammas tend to be largest and delta hedges are hardest to maintain.

When gammas are large, some delta hedgers choose to also gamma hedge. This somewhat advanced strategy requires adding a position in another option, combining the underlying and the two options in such a manner that the delta is zero and the gamma is zero. Because it is a somewhat advanced and specialized topic, we do not cover the details of how this is done.

The delta is not the only important factor that changes in the course of managing an option position. The volatility of the underlying can also change.

4.3   Vega and Volatility Risk

As we covered in Reading 76, the sensitivity of the option price to the volatility is called the vega and is defined as

$$\text{Vega} = \frac{\text{Change in option price}}{\text{Change in volatility}}$$

As with delta and gamma, the relationship above is an approximation, but we shall treat it as exact. As we noted in Reading 76, an option price is very sensitive to the volatility of the underlying. Moreover, the volatility is the only unobservable variable required to value an option. Hence, volatility is the most critical variable. When we examined option-pricing models, we studied the Black–Scholes–Merton and binomial models. In neither of these models is the

---

[33] The deltas of options that are very slightly in-the-money will temporarily move down as expiration approaches. Exhibit 78-21 illustrates this effect. But they will eventually move up toward 1.0.

volatility allowed to change. Yet no one believes that volatility is constant; on some days the stock market is clearly more volatile than on other days. This risk of changing volatility can greatly affect a dealer's position in options. A delta-hedged position with a zero or insignificant gamma can greatly change in value if the volatility changes. If, for example, the dealer holds the underlying and sells options to delta hedge, an increase in volatility will raise the value of the options, generating a potentially large loss for the dealer.

Measuring the sensitivity of the option price to the volatility is difficult. The vega from the Black–Scholes–Merton or binomial models is a somewhat artificial construction. It represents how much the model price changes if one changes the volatility by a small amount. But in fact, the model itself is based on the assumption that volatility does not change. Forcing the volatility to change in a model that does not acknowledge that volatility can change has unclear implications.[34] It is clear, however, that an option price is more sensitive to the volatility when it is at-the-money.

Dealers try to measure the vega, monitor it, and in some cases hedge it by taking on a position in another option, using that option's vega to offset the vega on the original option. Managing vega risk, however, cannot be done independently of managing delta and gamma risk. Thus, the dealer is required to jointly monitor and manage the risk associated with the delta, gamma, and vega. We should be aware of the concepts behind managing these risks.

5   FINAL COMMENTS

Forward and futures strategies provide gains from movements of the underlying in one direction but result in losses from movements of the underlying in the other direction. The advantage of a willingness to incur losses is that no cash is paid at the start. Options offer the advantage of having one-directional effects: The buyer of an option gains from a movement in one direction and loses only the premium from movements in the other direction. The cost of this advantage is that options require the payment of cash at the start. Some market participants choose forwards and futures because they do not have to pay cash at the start. They can justify taking positions without having to come up with the cash to do so. Others, however, prefer the flexibility to benefit when their predictions are right and suffer only a limited loss when wrong. The trade-off between the willingness to pay cash at the start versus incurring losses, given one's risk preferences, is the deciding factor in whether to use options or forwards/futures.

All option strategies are essentially rooted in the transactions of buying a call or a put. Understanding a short position in either type of option means understanding the corresponding long position in the option. All remaining strategies are just combinations of options, the underlying, and risk-free bonds. We looked at a number of option strategies associated with equities, which can apply about equally to index options or options on individual stocks. The applicability of

---

[34] If this point seems confusing, consider this analogy. In the famous Einstein equation $E = mc^2$, E is energy, m is mass, and c is the constant representing the speed of light. For a given mass, we could change c, which would change E. The equation allows this change, but in fact the speed of light is constant at 186,000 miles per second. So far as scientists know, it is a universal constant and can never change. In the case of option valuation, the model assumes that volatility of a given stock is like a universal constant. We can change it, however, and the equation would give us a new option price. But are we allowed to do so? Unlike the speed of light, volatility does indeed change, even though our model says that it does not. What happens when we change volatility in our model? We do not know.

these strategies to bonds is also fairly straightforward. The options must expire before the bonds mature, but the general concepts associated with equity option strategies apply similarly to **bond option** strategies.

Likewise, strategies that apply to equity options apply in nearly the same manner to interest rate options. Nonetheless, significant differences exist between interest rate options and equity or bond options. If nothing else, the notion of bullishness is quite opposite. Bullish (bearish) equity investors buy calls (puts). In interest rate markets, bullish (bearish) investors buy puts (calls) on interest rates, because being bullish (bearish) on interest rates means that one thinks rates are going down (up). Interest rate options pay off as though they were interest payments. Equity or bond options pay off as though the holder were selling or buying stocks or bonds. Finally, interest rate options are very often combined into portfolios in the form of caps and floors for the purpose of hedging floating-rate loans. Standard option strategies such as straddles and spreads are just as applicable to interest rate options.

Recall that in Reading 76, we examined one other slightly different type of option, one in which the underlying is a futures contract. Despite some subtle differences between the option strategies examined in this reading and comparable strategies using options on futures, the differences are relatively minor and do not warrant separate coverage here. If you have a good grasp of the basics of the option strategies presented in this reading, you can easily adapt those strategies to ones in which the underlying is a futures contract.

As we have so often mentioned, interest rate swaps are the most widely used financial derivative. They are less widely used with currencies and equities than are forwards, futures, and options. Nonetheless, there are many applications of swaps to currencies and equities, and we shall certainly look at them. To examine swaps, however, we must return to the types of instruments with two-directional payoffs and no cash payments at the start. Indeed, as we showed in Reading 77, swaps are a lot like forward contracts, which themselves are a lot like futures.

OPTIONAL SEGMENT ENDS

SUMMARY

▶ The profit from buying a call is the value at expiration, $\max(0, S_T - X)$, minus c_0, the option premium. The maximum profit is infinite, and the maximum loss is the option premium. The breakeven underlying price at expiration is the exercise price plus the option premium. When one sells a call, these results are reversed.

▶ The profit from buying a put is the value at expiration, $\max(0, X - S_T)$, minus p_0, the option premium. The maximum profit is the exercise price minus the option premium, and the maximum loss is the option premium. The breakeven underlying price at expiration is the exercise price minus the option premium. When one sells a put, these results are reversed.

▶ The profit from a covered call—the purchase of the underlying and sale of a call—is the value at expiration, $S_T - \max(0, S_T - X)$, minus $S_0 - c_0$, the cost of the underlying minus the option premium. The maximum profit is the exercise price minus the original underlying price plus the option premium, and the maximum loss is the cost of the underlying less the option premium. The breakeven underlying price at expiration is the original price of the underlying minus the option premium.

▶ The profit from a protective put—the purchase of the underlying and a put—is the value at expiration, $S_T + \max(0, X - S_T)$, minus the cost of the underlying plus the option premium, $S_0 + p_0$. The maximum profit is infinite, and the maximum loss is the cost of the underlying plus the option premium minus the exercise price. The breakeven underlying price at expiration is the original price of the underlying plus the option premium.

▶ The profit from a bull spread—the purchase of a call at one exercise price and the sale of a call with the same expiration but a higher exercise price—is the value at expiration, $\max(0, S_T - X_1) - \max(0, S_T - X_2)$, minus the net premium, $c_1 - c_2$, which is the premium of the long option minus the premium of the short option. The maximum profit is $X_2 - X_1$ minus the net premium, and the maximum loss is the net premium. The breakeven underlying price at expiration is the lower exercise price plus the net premium.

▶ The profit from a bear spread—the purchase of a put at one exercise price and the sale of a put with the same expiration but a lower exercise price—is the value at expiration, $\max(0, X_2 - S_T) - \max(0, X_1 - S_T)$, minus the net premium, $p_2 - p_1$, which is the premium of the long option minus the premium of the short option. The maximum profit is $X_2 - X_1$ minus the net premium, and the maximum loss is the net premium. The breakeven underlying price at expiration is the higher exercise price minus the net premium.

▶ The profit from a butterfly spread—the purchase of a call at one exercise price, X_1, sale of two calls at a higher exercise price, X_2, and the purchase of a call at a higher exercise price, X_3—is the value at expiration, $\max(0, S_T - X_1) - 2\max(0, S_T - X_2), + \max(0, S_T - X_3)$, minus the net premium, $c_1 - 2c_2 + c_3$. The maximum profit is $X_2 - X_1$ minus the net premium, and the maximum loss is the net premium. The breakeven underlying prices at expiration are $2X_2 - X_1$ minus the net premium and X_1 plus the net premium. A butterfly spread can also be constructed by trading the corresponding put options.

▶ The profit from a collar—the holding of the underlying, the purchase of a put at one exercise price, X_1, and the sale of a call with the same expiration and a higher exercise price, X_2, and in which the premium on the put equals the premium on the call—is the value at expiration, $S_T + \max(0, X_1 - S_T) - \max(0, S_T - X_2)$, minus S_0, the original price of the underlying. The maximum profit is $X_2 - S_0$, and the maximum loss is $S_0 - X_1$. The breakeven underlying price at expiration is the initial price of the underlying.

▶ The profit from a straddle—a long position in a call and a put with the same exercise price and expiration—is the value at expiration, $\max(0, S_T - X) + \max(0, X - S_T)$, minus the premiums on the call and put, $c_0 + p_0$. The maximum profit is infinite, and the maximum loss is the sum of the premiums on the call and put, $c_0 + p_0$. The breakeven prices at expiration are the exercise price plus and minus the premiums on the call and put.

▶ A box spread is a combination of a bull spread using calls and a bear spread using puts, with one call and put at an exercise price of X_1 and another call and put at an exercise price of X_2. The profit is the value at expiration, $X_2 - X_1$, minus the net premiums, $c_1 - c_2 + p_2 - p_1$. The transaction is risk free, and the net premium paid should be the present value of this risk-free payoff.

▶ A long position in an interest rate call can be used to place a ceiling on the rate on an anticipated loan from the perspective of the borrower. The call provides a payoff if the interest rate at expiration exceeds the exercise rate, thereby compensating the borrower when the rate is higher than the exercise rate. The effective interest paid on the loan is the actual interest paid minus the call payoff. The call premium must be taken into account by compounding it to the date on which the loan is taken out and deducting it from the initial proceeds received from the loan.

▶ A long position in an interest rate put can be used to lock in the rate on an anticipated loan from the perspective of the lender. The put provides a payoff if the interest rate at expiration is less than the exercise rate, thereby compensating the lender when the rate is lower than the exercise rate. The effective interest paid on the loan is the actual interest received plus the put payoff. The put premium must be taken into account by compounding it to the date on which the loan is taken out and adding it to initial proceeds paid out on the loan.

▶ An interest rate cap can be used to place an upper limit on the interest paid on a floating-rate loan from the perspective of the borrower. A cap is a series of interest rate calls, each of which is referred to as a caplet. Each caplet provides a payoff if the interest rate on the loan reset date exceeds the exercise rate, thereby compensating the borrower when the rate is higher than the exercise rate. The effective interest paid is the actual interest paid minus the caplet payoff. The premium is paid at the start and is the sum of the premiums on the component caplets.

▶ An interest rate floor can be used to place a lower limit on the interest received on a floating-rate loan from the perspective of the lender. A floor is a series of interest rate puts, each of which is called a floorlet. Each floorlet provides a payoff if the interest rate at the loan reset date is less than the exercise rate, thereby compensating the lender when the rate is lower than the exercise rate. The effective interest received is the actual interest plus the floorlet payoff. The premium is paid at the start and is the sum of the premiums on the component floorlets.

▶ An interest rate collar, which consists of a long interest rate cap at one exercise rate and a short interest rate floor at a lower exercise rate, can be used to place an upper limit on the interest paid on a floating-rate loan. The floor, however, places a lower limit on the interest paid on the floating-rate loan. Typically the floor exercise rate is set such that the premium on the floor equals the premium on the cap, so that no cash outlay is required to initiate the transaction. The effective interest is the actual interest paid minus any payoff from the long caplet plus any payoff from the short floorlet.

▶ Dealers offer to take positions in options and typically hedge their positions by establishing delta-neutral combinations of options and the underlying or other options. These positions require that the sensitivity of the option position with respect to the underlying be offset by a quantity of the underlying or another option. The delta will change, moving toward 1.0 for in-the-money calls (-1.0 for puts) and 0.0 for out-of-the-money options as expiration approaches. Any change in the underlying price will also change the delta. These changes in the delta necessitate buying and selling options or the underlying to maintain the delta-hedged position. Any additional funds required to buy the underlying or other options are obtained by issuing risk-free bonds. Any additional funds released from selling the underlying or other options are invested in risk-free bonds.

▶ The delta of an option changes as the underlying changes and as time elapses. The delta will change more rapidly with large movements in the underlying and when the option is approximately at-the-money and near expiration. These large changes in the delta will prevent a delta-hedged position from being truly risk free. Dealers usually monitor their gammas and in some cases hedge their gammas by adding other options to their positions such that the gammas offset.

▶ The sensitivity of an option to volatility is called the vega. An option's volatility can change, resulting in a potentially large change in the value of the option. Dealers monitor and sometimes hedge their vegas so that this risk does not impact a delta-hedged portfolio.

PROBLEMS FOR READING 78

1. Consider a call option selling for $4 in which the exercise price is $50.

   A. Determine the value at expiration and the profit for a buyer under the following outcomes:
      i. The price of the underlying at expiration is $55.
     ii. The price of the underlying at expiration is $51.
    iii. The price of the underlying at expiration is $48.

   B. Determine the value at expiration and the profit for a seller under the following outcomes:
      i. The price of the underlying at expiration is $49.
     ii. The price of the underlying at expiration is $52.
    iii. The price of the underlying at expiration is $55.

   C. Determine the following:
      i. The maximum profit to the buyer (maximum loss to the seller)
     ii. The maximum loss to the buyer (maximum profit to the seller)

   D. Determine the breakeven price of the underlying at expiration.

2. Suppose you believe that the price of a particular underlying, currently selling at $99, is going to increase substantially in the next six months. You decide to purchase a call option expiring in six months on this underlying. The call option has an exercise price of $105 and sells for $7.

   A. Determine the profit under the following outcomes for the price of the underlying six months from now.
       i. $99
      ii. $104
     iii. $105
     iv. $109
       v. $112
     vi. $115

   B. Determine the breakeven price of the underlying at expiration. Check that your answer is consistent with the solution to Part A of this problem.

3. Consider a put option on the Nasdaq 100 selling for $106.25 in which the exercise price is 2100.

   A. Determine the value at expiration and the profit for a buyer under the following outcomes:
      i. The price of the underlying at expiration is 2125.
     ii. The price of the underlying at expiration is 2050.
    iii. The price of the underlying at expiration is 1950.

   B. Determine the value at expiration and the profit for a seller under the following outcomes:
      i. The price of the underlying at expiration is 1975.
     ii. The price of the underlying at expiration is 2150.

   C. Determine the following:
      i. The maximum profit to the buyer (maximum loss to the seller)
     ii. The maximum loss to the buyer (maximum profit to the seller)

   D. Determine the breakeven price of the underlying at expiration.

4. Suppose you believe that the price of a particular underlying, currently selling at $99, will decrease considerably in the next six months. You decide to purchase a put option expiring in six months on this underlying. The put option has an exercise price of $95 and sells for $5.

    A. Determine the profit for you under the following outcomes for the price of the underlying six months from now:

        i. $100

        ii. $95

        iii. $93

        iv. $90

        v. $85

    B. Determine the breakeven price of the underlying at expiration. Check that your answer is consistent with the solution to Part A of this problem.

    C. **i.** What is the maximum profit that you can have?

        ii. At what expiration price of the underlying would this profit be realized?

5. You simultaneously purchase an underlying priced at $77 and write a call option on it with an exercise price of $80 and selling at $6.

    A. What is the term commonly used for the position that you have taken?

    B. Determine the value at expiration and the profit for your strategy under the following outcomes:

        i. The price of the underlying at expiration is $70.

        ii. The price of the underlying at expiration is $75.

        iii. The price of the underlying at expiration is $80.

        iv. The price of the underlying at expiration is $85.

    C. Determine the following:

        i. The maximum profit

        ii. The maximum loss

        iii. The expiration price of the underlying at which you would realize the maximum profit

        iv. The expiration price of the underlying at which you would incur the maximum loss

    D. Determine the breakeven price at expiration.

6. Suppose you simultaneously purchase an underlying priced at $77 and a put option on it, with an exercise price of $75 and selling at $3.

    A. What is the term commonly used for the position that you have taken?

    B. Determine the value at expiration and the profit for your strategy under the following outcomes:

        i. The price of the underlying at expiration is $70.

        ii. The price of the underlying at expiration is $75.

        iii. The price of the underlying at expiration is $80.

        iv. The price of the underlying at expiration is $85.

        v. The price of the underlying at expiration is $90.

    C. Determine the following:

        i. The maximum profit

        ii. The maximum loss

        iii. The expiration price of the underlying at which you would incur the maximum loss

    D. Determine the breakeven price at expiration.

ANALYSIS OF ALTERNATIVE INVESTMENTS

STUDY SESSION

Study Session 18   Alternative Investments

TOPIC LEVEL LEARNING OUTCOME

The candidate should be able to demonstrate a working knowledge of the analysis of alternative investments, including mutual funds, exchange rated funds, real estate, venture capital, hedge funds, closely held companies, distressed securities, and commodities and commodity derivatives.

4⅛ 4¹¹⁄₁₆ $-$ 3⅞
5½ 5½ $-$ 3⅞
5½ 5½ $-$ ¹⁄₁₆
20⅝ 21¹³⁄₁₆ $-$ ¼
17⅜ 18⅛ $+$ ⅞
18½ 6½ 6½ $-$ ½
7¼ 6½ 31¹⁄₃₂ $-$ ⅛
15⁄₁₆
1 9⁄₁₆ 9⁄₁₆
1¹⁄₃₂ 9⁄₁₆
7¹⁵⁄₁₆ 7¹³⁄₁₆ 7¹⁵⁄₁₆
2⅝ 2¹¹⁄₃₂ 2½ $+$
2¾ 2¼ 2¼
6⅛ 12¹⁄₁₆ 11⅜ 11¾ $+$
87 33¾ 33 33¹⁄₁₆ $-$
602 25⅝ 24⁹⁄₁₆ 25⅜ $+$
833 12 11⅝ 11¾ $+$
16 10½ 10½ 10½ $-$
78 15⅞ 15¹³⁄₁₆ 15⅞ $-$
4608 9¹⁄₁₆ 8¼ 8⅞ $+$
430 11¼ 10⅛ ...

STUDY SESSION 18
ALTERNATIVE INVESTMENTS

READING ASSIGNMENT

Reading 79   Alternative Investments

This study session describes the common types of alternative investments, methods for their valuation, unique risks and opportunities associated with them, and the relationship that alternatives have to more traditional investments.

Although finding a single definition of an "alternative" investment is difficult, certain features (e.g., limited liquidity, infrequent valuations, and unique legal structures) are typically associated with alternative investments. This study session discusses these features and how to evaluate their impact on the investment returns and decisions in more detail. The readings provide an overview of some of the major categories of alternative investments, including real estate, private equity, venture capital, hedge funds, closely held companies, distressed securities, and commodities.

Each one of these categories has several unique characteristics, and the readings discuss valuation methods for illiquid assets (such as direct real estate or closely held companies), performance measurement for venture capital investments, differences between various hedge fund strategies, and various implementation vehicles for investments in alternative assets.

LEARNING OUTCOMES

Reading 79: Alternative Investments
The candidate should be able to:

a. distinguish between an open end and a closed end fund;

b. explain how the net asset value of a fund is calculated;

c. explain the nature of various fees charged by investment companies;

d. distinguish among style, sector, index, global, and stable value strategies in equity investment;

e. distinguish among exchange traded funds (ETFs), traditional mutual funds, and closed end funds;

f. explain the advantages and risks of ETFs;

g. describe the forms of real estate investment and explain their characteristics as an investable asset class;

h. describe the various approaches to the valuation of real estate;

i. calculate the net operating income (NOI) from a real estate investment;

j. calculate the value of a property using the sales comparison and income approaches;

k. calculate the after-tax cash flows, net present value, and yield of a real estate investment;

l. explain the various stages in venture capital investing;

m. discuss venture capital investment characteristics and the challenges to venture capital valuation and performance measurement;

n. calculate the net present value (NPV) of a venture capital project, given the project's possible payoff and conditional failure probabilities;

o. discuss the descriptive accuracy of the term "hedge fund," define hedge fund in terms of objectives, legal structure, and fee structure, and describe the various classifications of hedge funds;

p. discuss the benefits and drawbacks to fund of funds investing;

q. discuss the leverage and unique risks of hedge funds;

r. discuss the performance of hedge funds, the biases present in hedge fund performance measurement, and explain the effect of survivorship bias on the reported return and risk measures for a hedge fund data base;

s. explain how the legal environment affects the valuation of closely held companies;

t. describe alternative valuation methods for closely held companies and distinguish among the bases for the discounts and premiums for these companies;

u. discuss distressed securities investing and the similarities between venture capital investing and distressed securities investing;

v. discuss the role of commodities as a vehicle for investing in production and consumption;

w. discuss the motivation for investing in commodities, commodities derivatives, and commodity-linked securities;

x. discuss the sources of return on a collateralized commodity futures position.

ALTERNATIVE INVESTMENTS
by Bruno Solnik and Dennis McLeavey

LEARNING OUTCOMES

The candidate should be able to:

a. distinguish between an open end and a closed end fund;

b. explain how the net asset value of a fund is calculated;

c. explain the nature of various fees charged be investment companies;

d. distinguish among style, sector, index, global, and stable value strategies in equity investment;

e. distinguish among exchange traded funds (ETFs), traditional mutual funds, and closed end funds;

f. explain the advantages and risks of ETFs;

g. describe the forms of real estate investment and explain their characteristics as an investable asset class;

h. describe the various approaches to the valuation of real estate;

i. calculate the net operating income (NOI) from a real estate investment;

j. calculate the value of a property using the sales comparison and income approaches;

k. calculate the after-tax cash flows, net present value, and yield of a real estate investment;

l. explain the various stages in venture capital investing;

m. discuss venture capital investment characteristics and the challenges to venture capital valuation and performance measurement;

n. calculate the net present value (NPV) of a venture capital project, given the project's possible payoff and conditional failure probabilities;

o. discuss the descriptive accuracy of the term "hedge fund," define hedge fund in terms of objectives, legal structure, and fee structure, and describe the various classifications of hedge funds;

p. discuss the benefits and drawbacks to fund of funds investing;

q. discuss the leverage and unique risks of hedge funds;

International Investments, Fifth Edition, by Bruno Solnik and Dennis McLeavey, Copyright © 2004. Reprinted with permission of Pearson Education, publishing as Pearson Addison Wesley.

r. discuss the performance of hedge funds, the biases present in hedge fund performance measurement, and explain the effect of survivorship bias on the reported return and risk measures for a hedge fund data base;

s. explain how the legal environment affects the valuation of closely held companies;

t. describe alternative valuation methods for closely held companies and distinguish among the bases for the discounts and premiums for these companies;

u. discuss distressed securities investing and the similarities between venture capital investing and distressed securities investing;

v. discuss the role of commodities as a vehicle for investing in production and consumption;

w. discuss the motivation for investing in commodities, commodities derivatives, and commodity-linked securities;

x. discuss the sources of return on a collateralized commodity futures position.

1 INTRODUCTION

Alternative investments complement stocks, bonds, and other traditional financial instruments traded on international financial markets. There is a large variety of alternative investments, and the list evolves over time. Both alternative assets (such as real estate) and alternative strategies (hedge funds) are classified as alternative investments. Alternative investments generally have lower liquidity, sell in less efficient markets, and require a longer time horizon than publicly traded stocks and bonds. Sharpe, Alexander, and Bailey (1999) provide a nice summary of the common features of alternative investments:

▶ Illiquidity
▶ Difficulty in determining current market values
▶ Limited historical risk and return data
▶ Extensive investment analysis required

When present, liquidity can make alternative investments, such as real estate, attractive; but are there cases in which the general illiquidity of alternative investments can be attractive? Alternative investments beckon investors to areas of the market where alpha[1] is more likely to be found than in more liquid and efficient markets. Illiquidity, limited information, and less efficiency do not suit all investors, but can be attractive features to those looking for likely places to add value through investment expertise.

---

[1] *Alpha* is risk-adjusted return in excess of the required rate of return, but, more colloquially, stands for positive excess risk-adjusted return, the goal of active managers.

Terhaar, Staub, and Singer (2003) discuss two additional features of alternative investments:

▶ A liquidity premium compensates the investor for the investor's inability to continuously rebalance the alternative investments in the portfolio.

▶ A segmentation premium compensates investors for the risk of alternative assets that, by nature, are generally not priced in a fully integrated global market.

It is difficult to give a broad characterization of alternative investments, but they are often equity investments in some nonpublicly traded asset. In some cases, however, they may look more like an investment strategy than an asset class. Whatever the nature of alternative investments, specialized intermediaries often link the investor to the investments. Whether the investor invests directly or through an intermediary, he must know the investment's characteristics. In the case of investing through an intermediary, he must make sure that the incentive structure for any intermediary suits his investor needs.

Finally, alternative investments can be characterized as raising unique legal and tax considerations. A financial advisor would coordinate with an attorney and a tax accountant before recommending any specific real estate investment. Also, many forms of alternative investments involve special legal structures that avoid some taxes (exchange traded funds) or avoid some regulations (hedge funds).

INVESTMENT COMPANIES   2

Investment companies are financial intermediaries that earn fees to pool and invest investors' funds, giving the investors rights to a proportional share of the pooled fund performance. Both managed and unmanaged companies pool investor funds in this manner. Unmanaged investment companies (unit investment trusts in the United States) hold a fixed portfolio of investments (often tax exempt) for the life of the company and usually stand ready to redeem the investor's shares at market value. Managed investment companies are classified according to whether or not they stand ready to redeem investor shares. Open-end investment companies (mutual funds) offer this redemption feature, but closed-end funds do not. **Closed-end investment companies** issue shares that are then traded in the secondary markets.

2.1 Valuing Investment Company Shares

The basis for valuing investment company shares is net asset value (NAV). NAV is the per-share value of the investment company's assets minus its liabilities. Liabilities may come from fees owed to investment managers, for example. Share value equals NAV for unmanaged and open-end investment companies because they stand ready to redeem their shares at NAV. The price of a closed end investment company's shares is determined in the secondary markets in which they trade, and, consequently, can be at a premium or discount to NAV.

2.2 Fund Management Fees

Investment companies charge fees, some as one-time charges and some as annual charges. By setting an initial selling price above the NAV, the unmanaged company charges a fee for the effort of setting up the fund. For managed funds, loads are simply sales commissions charged at purchase (front-end) as a percentage of the investment. A redemption fee (back-end load) is a charge to exit the fund. Redemption fees discourage quick trading turnover and are often set up so that the fees decline the longer the shares are held (in this case, the fees are sometimes called contingent deferred sales charges). Loads and redemption fees provide sales incentives but not portfolio management performance incentives.

Annual charges are composed of operating expenses including management fees, administrative expenses, and continuing distribution fees (12b-1 fees in the U.S.). The ratio of operating expenses to average assets is often referred to as the fund's "expense ratio." Distribution fees are fees paid back to the party that arranged the initial sale of the shares and are thus another type of sales incentive fee. Only management fees can be considered a portfolio management incentive fee. Example 79-1 is an illustration of the effects of investment company fees on fund performance.

Example 79-1

Investment Company Fees: Effects on Performance

An investor is considering the purchase of TriGroup International Equity Fund (TRIEF) for her portfolio. Like many U.S.-based mutual funds today, TRIEF has more than one class of shares. Although all classes hold the same portfolio of securities, each class has a different expense structure. This particular mutual fund has three classes of shares, A, B, and C. The expenses of these classes are summarized in the following table:

Expense Comparison for Three Classes of TRIEF

	Class A	Class B*	Class C
Sales charge (load) on purchases	3%	None	None
Deferred sales charge (load) on redemptions	None	5% in the first year, declining by 1 percentage point each year thereafter	1% for the initial two years

	Class A	Class B*	Class C
Annual expenses:			
Distribution fee	0.25%	0.50%	0.50%
Management fee	0.75%	0.75%	0.75%
Other expenses	0.25%	0.25%	0.25%
	1.25%	1.50%	1.50%

*Class B shares automatically convert to Class A shares 72 months (6 years) after purchase, reducing future annual expenses.

The time horizon associated with the investor's objective in purchasing TRIEF is six years. She expects equity investments with risk characteristics similar to TRIEF to earn 8 percent per year, and she decides to make her selection of fund share class based on an assumed 8 percent return each year, gross of any of the expenses given in the preceding table.

A. Based on only the information provided here, determine the class of shares that is most appropriate for this investor. Assume that expense percentages given will be constant at the given values. Assume that the deferred sales charges are computed on the basis of NAV.

B. Suppose that, as a result of an unforeseen liquidity need, the investor needs to liquidate her investment at the end of the first year. Assume an 8 percent rate of return has been earned. Determine the relative performance of the three fund classes, and interpret the results.

C. Based on your answers to A and B, discuss the appropriateness of these share classes as it relates to an investor's time horizon; for example, a one-, six- and ten-year horizon.

SOLUTIONS

A. To address this question, we compute the terminal value of $1 invested at the end of year 6. The share class with the highest terminal value, net of all expenses, would be the most appropriate for this investor, as all classes are based on the same portfolio and thus have the same portfolio risk characteristics.

Class A. $1 \times (1 - 0.03) = \$0.97$ is the amount available for investment at $t = 0$, after paying the front-end sales charge. Because this amount grows at 8 percent for six years, reduced by annual expenses of 0.0125, the terminal value per $1 invested after six years is $\$0.97 \times 1.08^6 \times (1 - 0.0125)^6 = \$1.4274$.

Class B. After six years, $1 invested grows to $\$1 \times 1.08^6 \times (1 - 0.015)^6 = \$1.4493$. According to the table, the deferred sales charge disappears after year 5; therefore, the terminal value is $1.4493.

Class C. After six years, $1 invested grows to $\$1 \times 1.08^6 \times (1 - 0.015)^6 = \$1.4493$. There is no deferred sales charge in the sixth year, so $1.4493 is the terminal value.

In summary, the ranking by terminal value after six years is Class B and Class C ($1.4493), followed by Class A ($1.4274). Class B or Class C appears to be the most appropriate for this investor with a six-year horizon.

B. For Class A shares, the terminal value per $1 invested is $\$0.97 \times 1.08 \times (1 - 0.0125) = \$1.0345$. For Class B shares, it is $\$1 \times 1.08 \times (1 - 0.015) \times (1 - 0.05) = \$1.0106$, reflecting a 5 percent redemption charge; for Class C shares, it is $\$1 \times 1.08 \times (1 - 0.015) \times (1 - 0.01) = \$1.0532$, reflecting a 1 percent redemption charge. Thus, the ranking is Class C ($1.0532), Class A ($1.0345), and Class B ($1.0106).

C. Although Class B is appropriate given a six-year investment horizon, it is a costly choice if the fund shares need to be liquidated soon after investment. That eventuality would need to be assessed by the investor we are discussing. Class B, like Class A, is more attractive the longer the holding period, in general. Because Class C has higher annual expenses than Class A and Class B (after six years), it becomes less attractive the longer the holding period, in general.

After 10 years Class B shares would return $\$1 \times 1.08^{10} \times (1 - 0.015)^6 \times (1 - 0.0125)^4 = \$1.8750$, reflecting conversion to Class A after six years. Class C would return $\$1 \times 1.08^{10} \times (1 - 0.0150)^{10} = \$1.8561$. Class A shares would return the smallest amount, $\$0.97 \times 1.08^{10} \times (1 - 0.0125)^{10} = \$1.8466$. Though Class A underperforms Class C for a ten-year investment horizon, one could verify that Class A outperforms Class C for an investment horizon of 13 years or more. Also, in practice, the sales charge for Class A shares may be lower for purchases over certain sizes, making them more attractive in such comparisons.

2.3 Investment Strategies

Investment companies primarily invest in equity. Investment strategies can be characterized as style, sector, index, global, or stable value strategies. Style strategies focus on the underlying characteristics common to certain investments. Growth is a different style than value, and large capitalization investing is a different style than small stock investing. A growth strategy may focus on high price-to-earnings stocks, and a value strategy on low price-to-earnings stocks. Clearly, there are many styles.[2] A sector investment fund focuses on a particular industry. An index fund tracks an index. In the simplest implementation, the fund owns the securities in the index in exactly the same proportion as the market value weights of those securities in the index. A global fund includes securities from around the world and might keep portfolio weights similar to world market capitalization weights. An international fund is one that does not include the home country's securities, whereas a global fund includes the securities from the home country. A stable value fund invests in securities such as short-term fixed income instruments and guaranteed investment contracts which are guaranteed by the issuing insurance company and pay principal and a set rate of interest.

2.4 Exchange Traded Funds

Exchange traded funds (ETFs) are index-based investment products that allow investors to buy or sell exposure to an index through a single financial instrument. ETFs are funds that trade on a stock market like shares of any individual companies. Gastineau (2001) gives a good introduction to ETFs. They can be traded at any time during market hours, can be sold short or margined. But they are shares of a portfolio, not of an individual company. They represent shares of ownership in either open-end funds or unit investment trusts that hold portfo-

---

[2] See, for example, Richard Bernstein, *Style Investing*, Wiley, 1995, and Richard Michaud, *Investment Styles, Market Anomalies, and Global Stock Selection*, The Research Foundation of AIMR, 1999.

lios of stocks or bonds in custody, which are designed to track the price and yield performance of their underlying indexes—broad market, sector/industry, single country/region (multiple countries), or fixed income. Although many investors regard ETFs simply as a form of diversified equity investment, their novelty and legal specificity suggested their inclusion in this reading.

2.4.1 Recent Developments of ETFs

ETFs first appeared as TIP 35 (Toronto Index Participation Fund) in Canada in 1989, and appeared in the United States in 1993 with the introduction of Standard & Poor's 500 (S&P 500) Depositary Receipts. The first Asian ETF, the Hong Kong Tracker Fund, was launched in 1999. The first ETF launched in Europe, Euro STOXX 50, did not appear until 2000. Japan did not trade ETFs until 2001, when eight were listed. Their popularity has grown so quickly that they have become one of the most successful financial products of the decade.

According to Merrill Lynch (2002), there were 102 ETFs listed in the United States as of June 2002, 14 in Canada, 106 in Europe, and approximately 24 in Asia, including Japan—a total of 246.[3] Total global assets under management approached $130 billion, 75 percent of which are invested in U.S.-listed products. Although ETFs had a slow trading start in the United States, the trading volume of ETFs has grown rapidly in the last few years. According to Goldman Sachs (2002), the total shares outstanding for U.S. ETFs amounts to 1.9 million shares, with total assets of $92 billion, while average daily trading volume reached $7.0 billion, or 146.6 million shares per day, in mid-2002. ETFs based on international indexes have shown a strong growth and now represent almost 10 percent of total U.S.-listed ETF assets. The latest additions to the universe of ETFs are fixed-income ETFs, which started trading in July 2002 on the American Stock Exchange.

In Europe, the first ETF was launched by Merrill Lynch in April 2000 to track the Euro STOXX 50, which is the most actively replicated index in Europe. Listings of multiple ETFs on the same underlying index are common in Europe. In general, ETFs traded in Europe fall into four categories: single-country ETFs, regional ETFs based mostly on some pan-European or Eurozone indexes, European-sector ETFs, and global ETFs. The most popular ETFs are based on Euro STOXX 50, CAC 40, and the DAX. Although assets under management ($8 billion in mid-2002) and average daily volumes are still small compared with U.S. figures, the growth in terms of volume and number of outstanding products has been impressive. The daily trading volume grew from $6 million in the third quarter of 2000 to over $250 million in the first quarter of 2002 (Mussavian and Hirsch, 2002).

In Asia, the growth in ETFs comes primarily from Japan. Merrill Lynch (2002) estimates that the total assets under management in Asian ETFs were in excess of $13.9 billion in mid-2002.

2.4.2 ETF Structure

The usual ETF structure adopted worldwide is that of open-end funds with special characteristics, such as the "in-kind" process for creation and redemption of shares described subsequently (see Gastineau, 2001). Details of the legal structure vary depending on the country where the ETF is incorporated. In the United States, ETFs have adopted three different legal structures:

[3] Complete listings of ETFs can be found at www.indexfunds.com.

▶ *Managed investment companies:* Managed investment companies are open-ended investment companies registered under the Investment Company Act of 1940. They offer the most flexible ETF structure. The index can be tracked using various techniques, such as holding only a sample of the underlying securities in the index, lending of securities, and trading in derivatives. Dividends paid on the securities can be immediately reinvested in the fund. Sector SPDRs, iShares, and WEBS use this legal structure.

▶ *Unit investment trusts:* Unit investment trusts (UITs) are also registered investment companies, but they operate under more constraints, because they do not have a manager per se (but trustees). UITs are required to be fully invested in all underlying securities forming the index and must hold dividends received on securities in cash until the ETF pays a dividend to shareholders. This could result in a slight cash drag on performance. UITs are not permitted to lend securities and do not generally use derivatives. S&P 500 SPDR, Midcap 400 SPDR and NASDAQ-100 QQQ use this legal structure.

▶ *Grantor trusts:* Grantor trusts are not registered investment companies. Accordingly, owning a grantor trust is substantially similar to holding a basket of securities. A grantor trust often takes the form of an American Depositary Receipt (ADR) and trades as such. Because a grantor trust is fully invested in the basket of securities, no investment discretion is exercised by the trust. This is basically an unmanaged (and unregistered) investment company with a limited life. The trust passes all dividends on the underlying securities to shareholders as soon as practicable. Securities lending and use of derivatives are generally not practiced. HOLDRs use this legal structure. Grantor trusts are a structure that allows investors to indirectly own an unmanaged basket of stocks rather than tracking an index, and some do not classify them as ETFs.

We will now introduce the unique "in-kind" creation and redemption process used by open-end and UIT ETFs. This in-kind process is a major distinguishing feature of ETFs. Creation/redemption units are created in large multiples of individual ETF shares, for example, 50,000 shares. These units are available to exchange specialists (*authorized participants* or *creation agents*) that are authorized by the fund and who will generally act as market makers on the individual ETF shares. The fund publishes the index tracking portfolio that it is willing to accept for in-kind transactions. When there is excess demand for ETF shares, an authorized participant will create a *creation unit* (a large block of ETF shares) by depositing with the trustee of the fund the specified portfolio of stocks used to track the index. In return, the authorized participant will receive ETF shares that can be sold to investors on the stock market. The redemption process is the same but in reverse. If there is an excess number of ETF shares sold by investors, an authorized participant will decide to redeem ETF shares; it will do so by exchanging with the fund a *redemption unit* (a large block of ETF shares) for a portfolio of stocks held by the fund and used to track the index. Exhibit 79-1 depicts the ETF structure and the creation/redemption process.

As opposed to traditional open-end funds, the in-kind redemption means that no capital gain will be realized in the fund's portfolio on redemption. If the redemption were in cash, the fund would have to sell stocks held in the fund's portfolio. If their price had appreciated, the fund would realize a capital gain, and the tax burden would have to be passed to all existing fund shareholders. This is not the case with ETFs. This in-kind transfer for redemptions does not create a tax burden for the remaining ETF shareholders under current U.S. tax law, unlike the capital gains distributions on traditional mutual fund shareholders that could result from the sale of securities to meet redemption demand.[4] As in any **open-end fund**, individual ETF shareholders[5] can require in-cash redemption based on the NAV. Redemption in cash by individual ETF shareholders is discouraged in two ways:

▶ Redemption is based on the NAV computed a couple of days after the shareholder commits to redemption. So, the redemption value is unknown when the investor decides to redeem. This is a common feature of mutual funds.

▶ A large fee is assessed on in-cash redemptions.

It is more advantageous for individual shareholders to sell their shares on the market than to redeem them in cash. Arbitrage[6] by authorized participants ensures that the listed price is close to the fund's NAV, and the sale can take place immediately based on observed share prices and at a low transaction cost. Authorized participants maintain a market in the ETF share by posting bid-and-ask prices with a narrow spread, or by entering in an electronic order book buy-and-sell limit orders, which play the same role. The transaction cost of ETFs can be estimated as the sum of the commission charged by the broker plus half this bid–ask spread.

| EXHIBIT 79-1 | Creation/Redemption Process of Exchange Traded Funds |

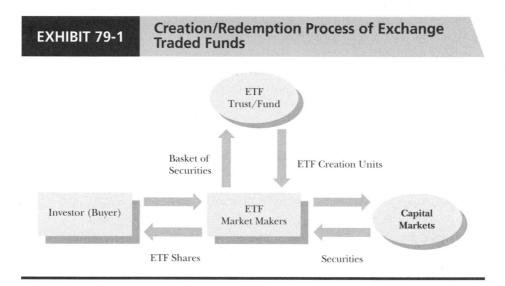

In comparing the ETF structure presented in Exhibit 79-1 with that of the traditional mutual fund structure, it is clear that market makers in the ETF structure play an instrumental role in the creation and redemption process. In the traditional mutual fund structure, an increase in demand for the shares of the mutual fund is met by the mutual fund, which simply issues new shares to the investor, and the fund manager will take the cash to the capital markets and buy securities appropriate to the fund's objective. When the customer wants to sell the mutual fund shares, the fund manager may need to raise cash by selling securities back to the capital markets. In contrast, when a customer wants to buy ETF shares, the order is not directed to the fund but to the market makers on the exchange. The market maker will exchange ETF shares for cash with the customer (via broker/dealer) and, when necessary, replenish the supply of ETFs through the creation process outlined earlier.

---

[4] As pointed out by Chamberlain and Jordan (2002), there are situations in which capital gains distributions are generated for the ETF, such as capital gains resulting from selling securities directly to the capital markets due to an index reconstitution. Thus, zero capital gains distributions are not guaranteed.

[5] But authorized participants commit to redeem only in kind.

[6] ETFs usually publish an indicative intraday NAV every 15 seconds that is available from major data providers.

2.4.3 Advantages/Disadvantages of ETFs

ETFs are used by a wide spectrum of investors, both individual and institutional, in a wide variety of investment strategies. This is because ETFs have the following advantages:

▶ Diversification can be obtained easily with a single ETF transaction. With equity-oriented ETFs, investors can gain instant exposure to different market capitalizations, style (value or growth), sector or industries, countries or geographic regions. With fixed income ETFs, they can gain exposure to different maturity segments and bond market sectors. Thus, ETFs provide a convenient way to diversify.

▶ Although ETFs represent interests in a portfolio of securities, they trade similarly to a stock on an organized exchange. For example, ETFs can be sold short and also bought on margin.

▶ ETFs trade throughout the whole trading day at market prices that are updated continuously, rather than only trading once a day at closing market prices, as do the traditional open-end mutual funds.

▶ For many ETFs, there exist futures and options contracts on the same index, which is convenient for risk management.

▶ Portfolio holdings of ETFs are transparent. The ETF sponsor publishes the constituents of the fund on a daily basis. This should closely resemble the constituents of the underlying index. This is in contrast to other funds, for which the manager publishes only the list of assets in the fund from time to time.

▶ ETFs are cost effective. There are no load fees. Moreover, because the ETFs are passively managed, the expense ratio (which includes management fee for open-end funds, trustee fee for UITs, and custody fee for HOLDRs) can be kept low relative to actively managed funds. The expense ratio is comparable to that of an index mutual fund. For example, management fee can be as low as 8 basis points for the most successful U.S. ETFs, and up to 90 basis points for sector and international products (Mussavian and Hirsch, 2002). ETFs have a cost advantage over traditional mutual funds because there is no shareholder accounting at the fund level.

▶ ETFs have an advantage over closed-end index funds because their structure can prevent a significant premium/discount. Although supply and demand determine the market price of an ETF just like any other security, arbitrage helps keep the traded price of an ETF much more in line with its underlying value. By simultaneously buying (or selling) the ETF basket of securities and selling (or buying) the ETF shares in the secondary market, and creating (or redeeming) ETF shares to be delivered against the sale, market makers can capture the price discrepancy and make an arbitrage profit. Thus, UIT and open-end ETFs have the capability to avoid trading at large premiums and discounts to the NAVs. This is in contrast to closed-end index funds, which offer a fixed supply of shares, and as demand changes, they frequently trade at appreciable discounts from—and sometimes premiums to—their NAVs.

▶ The exposure to capital gains distribution taxes is lower than for traditional funds, so the consequences of other shareholders' redemptions are limited. As mentioned, capital gains resulting from in-kind transfer for redemptions do not create a tax burden for the remaining ETF shareholders. For this reason, capital gains tax liability is expected to be lower for ETF shareholders than for mutual fund shareholders.

► Dividends are reinvested immediately for open-end ETFs (but not for UIT ETFs), whereas for index mutual funds, timing of dividend reinvestment varies.

However, ETFs are not necessarily the most efficient alternative for investing in a market segment.

► In many countries, actively traded ETFs track a narrow-based market index, including only stocks with large market capitalization. So, no ETF is available for mid or low market-cap stocks. This is not the case in the United States, where a variety of ETF products trade actively.

► Many investors do not require the intraday trading opportunity provided by ETFs, because they have a long investment horizon.

► Some ETFs do not have large trading volumes and the bid–ask spread can be quite large. For example, some U.S. ETFs based on some sector indexes or on some foreign indexes (e.g., emerging markets) do not trade actively, and directly investing in a managed fund can be a less costly alternative, especially for large investors. Sector and international ETFs have an expense ratio that can be substantial (close to 1 percent) compared with that of a managed portfolio.

► For large institutional investors, the alternative to international ETFs is to invest directly in an indexed, or actively managed, international portfolio; the costs could be less, and the tax situation equivalent or better.

2.4.4 Types of ETFs

ETFs can be grouped by investment category, based on their investment target (broad domestic market index, style, sector/industry, country or region). For a given investment target, ETFs can be created based on different indexes of the same market, as well as by different sponsors. The number of ETFs keeps growing, and the diversity of investment targets increases, although all ETFs launched are not successful. We only cite some notable examples under each of the following categories:

► *Broad domestic market index:* In many countries, the most active ETFs are those launched on the major local stock index. Hong Kong Tracker Fund was the first ETF listed in Asia and the largest ever IPO in Asia excluding Japan. In Japan, Nikkei 225 and TOPIX ETFs have amassed significant assets under management, and there are several competing sponsors offering ETFs on the same indexes. In Europe, ETFs based on the French CAC 40 index and the German DAX 30 index are, by far, the most actively traded. In the United States, there are many market indexes followed by investors, so there are many competing ETFs; the most notable examples in this category include S&P 500 Depositary Receipts (SPDRs or "spiders"), Nasdaq-100 Index Tracking Stock (QQQs or "cubes"), and Diamonds Trust Series (DIAs or "diamonds"). There are also ETFs based on very broad U.S. market indexes, such as the Russell 1000, Russell 3000, or Wilshire 5000 indexes. It is fair to say that ETFs based on local market indexes now exist in most countries, including in many emerging countries.

► *Style:* Some ETFs track a specific investment style. This type of ETF is mostly found in the United States, because investors from other countries are less accustomed to style investing. ETFs exist on growth and value indexes developed by S&P/BARRA and Russell. Investors can also find ETFs specialized by market capitalization (large, mid, and small cap).

▶ *Managing cash flows:* Investment managers can take advantage of ETFs' liquidity during periods of cash inflows and outflows. A portfolio manager can establish a position in an ETF that corresponds to the portfolio's benchmark or investment strategy, investing inflows into the ETF and liquidating the position as needed to meet redemptions or invest in specific stocks or bonds.

▶ *Completing overall investment strategy:* Fund or money managers can use ETFs to quickly establish or increase exposure to an industry or sector to "fill holes" in an overall investment strategy.

▶ *Bridging transitions in fund management:* Pension plan assets can often lie dormant during times of investment manager appointments, replacements, or shifts. Institutions can use ETFs as a cost-effective method to keep assets invested in the interim.

▶ *Managing portfolio risk:* Because ETFs can be sold short in a declining equity market (or rising interest rate market for fixed-income ETFs), portfolio managers can use ETFs to hedge overall portfolio risk or sector/industry exposure.

▶ *Applying relative value, long/short strategies:* Institutions can take advantage of ETF features to apply long/short strategies aimed at increasing returns. For example, an institution can establish a long position in a broad market, country, sector, or bond index expected to outperform while shorting an index expected to underperform. Doubling the size of the long position versus the short position can leverage the total position. Market makers can use ETFs to exploit price discrepancies between ETFs, the underlying index, the futures, and/or options.

3   REAL ESTATE

Real estate is usually considered to be buildings and buildable land, including offices, industrial warehouses, multifamily buildings, and retail space. Real estate is a form of tangible asset, one that can be touched and seen, as opposed to financial claims that are recorded as pieces of paper. Other forms of tangible assets are available for investment purposes. These include natural resources, timber, containers, artwork, and many others. We will focus on real estate, which is, by far, the most common form of investment in tangible assets.

Real estate as an investment has several unique characteristics as well as several characteristics common to other types of investments. Even the definition of real estate isolates it as a unique investment. Real estate is an immovable asset—land (earth surface) and the permanently attached improvements to it. Graaskamp defines real estate as artificially delineated space with a fourth dimension of time referenced to a fixed point on the face of the earth.[7] This astrophysical definition stresses the idea that ownership rights to earth areas can be divided up not only in the three dimensions of space, but also in a time dimension, as well as divided up among investors. One plot of land with its building can be divided into above ground (e.g., buildings) and below ground (e.g., minerals), into areas within the building (e.g., rooms), and into periods of time (timesharing). Different investors can own the different divisions. Many classifications can be adopted for real estate. Real estate can be classified by usage (office space, multifamily housing, retail space) and location. It can also be classified into four quadrants

---

[7] Jarchow (1991), p. 42.

by form of ownership, public or private, and by form of financing, debt or equity.[8] Clearly, it is not possible to adopt a simple classification of real estate, because this asset class covers so many different investment products.

Real estate is an important investment category. In many countries, domestic real estate is a common investment vehicle for pension funds and life insurance companies. It is not uncommon to have private European investors owning and renting directly a few real estate units, such as houses, condominium apartments, or parking spaces. But there are some obstacles for institutions and individuals wishing to invest in foreign real estate. First, it is difficult to monitor properties located abroad. Second, taxes, paperwork, and unforeseen risks may make foreign real estate investment impractical on a large scale, although investments can be made through specialized managers in the countries of interest. To be sure, private deals can be arranged for special projects, but these are well beyond the scope of this book. There is, however, a definite trend toward the development of negotiable forms for real property interest. In many countries, pooled funds have been created with the specific purpose of real estate investment. Mortgage-backed Eurobonds are rapidly growing in popularity. Many institutional investors, especially in Europe, have started to invest in international real estate. The time may not be too far off when real estate will be a normal component of international investment strategies.

3.1 Forms of Real Estate Investment

There are several forms of real estate investment: free and clear equity, leveraged equity, mortgages, and aggregation vehicles.

3.1.1 Free and Clear Equity

"Free and clear equity," sometimes called "fee simple," refers to full ownership rights for an indefinite period of time, giving the owner the right, for example, to lease the property to tenants and resell the property at will. This is straightforward purchase of some real estate property.

3.1.2 Leveraged Equity

Leveraged equity refers to the same ownership rights but subject to debt (a promissory note) and a pledge (mortgage) to hand over real estate ownership rights if the loan terms are not met. A mortgage is a pledge of real estate ownership rights to another party as security for debt owed to that party. Thus, leveraged equity involves equity ownership plus a debt and a requirement to transfer ownership of the equity in case of default on the debt. The debt and the mortgage are usually packaged together into a mortgage loan.

3.1.3 Mortgages

Mortgages (or more precisely, mortgage loans) themselves are another real estate investment vehicle, representing a type of debt investment. Investing in a mortgage provides the investor with a stream of bondlike payments. These payments include net interest, net of mortgage servicing fees, and a scheduled repayment of principal. This is a form of real estate investment because the creditor may end up owning the property being mortgaged. Mortgage loans often include a clause of

---

[8] See, for example, Hudson-Wilson (2001).

early repayment (at a cost) at the option of the debtor. So, the debtholder may also receive excess principal repayments, called mortgage prepayments. These prepayments produce uncertainty in the amount and timing of mortgage cash flows.

To diversify risks, a typical investor does not invest in one mortgage, but in securities issued against a pool of mortgages. An intermediary buys a pool of mortgages and then issues securities backed by the mortgages, but with the securities passing through the net mortgage payments to the investors.

3.1.4 Aggregation Vehicles

Aggregation vehicles aggregate investors and serve the purpose of giving investors collective access to real estate investments. *Real estate limited partnerships (RELPs)* allow investors (the limited partners) to participate in real estate projects while preserving limited liability (the initial investment) and leaving management to the general partners who are real estate experts. *Commingled funds* are pools of capital created largely by like-minded institutional investors organized together by an intermediary to invest chiefly in real estate investment projects. The investors share in the investment rewards according to the amount of capital they invest. Commingled funds can be either open or closed end. Closed-end funds have a set termination date, typically allow no new investors after initiation of the fund, and typically buy and hold a real estate portfolio for the life of the fund, with no reinvestment as sales occur. By contrast, open-end funds have indefinite lives, accept new investors, and revise their real estate portfolios over time. Finally, *real estate investment trusts (REITs)* are a type of closed-end investment company. They issue shares that are traded on a stock market, and they invest in various types of real estate. Thus, they aggregate individual investors and provide them easy access to real estate and diversification within real estate. Of course, the risk and return characteristics of REITs depend on the type of investment they make. Mortgage REITs, which invest primarily in mortgages, are more akin to a bond investment, while equity REITs, which invest primarily in commercial or residential properties using leverage, are more akin to an investment in leveraged equity real estate. The shares of REITs trade freely on the stock market, so they are liquid investments, but their share price can trade at a discount (or premium) to the NAV of the properties in their portfolio.

3.2 Valuation Approaches

Real estate assets are quite different from securities traded on a financial market: "Because the real estate market is not an auction market offering divisible shares in every property, and information flows in the market are complex, these features place a premium on investment judgment. Managers who want to own some of IBM simply buy some shares. Managers who want to participate in the returns on, say, a $300 million office building, must take a significant position in the property."[9] Following are some characteristics of real estate as an investable asset class:

► Properties are immovable, basically indivisible, and unique assets, as contrasted to fungible (perfectly interchangeable) and divisible assets such as currencies. Though unique, even art is movable and thus not as unique as real estate.

► Properties are only approximately comparable to other properties.

► Properties are generally illiquid, due to their immobility and indivisibility.

---

[9] Firstenberg, Ross, and Zisler (1988).

> ▶ There is no national, or international, auction market for properties. Hence, the "market" value of a given property is difficult to assess.

> ▶ Transaction costs and management fees for real estate investments are high.

> ▶ Real estate markets suffer inefficiencies because of the nature of real estate itself and because information is not freely available.

Valuation of real estate focuses on intrinsic value just as does the valuation of any asset. In real estate, the term *appraisal* is used for the process of estimating the market and the investment value of the property. The market value estimate is independent of the particular investor, but the investment value depends on the particular use that the investor plans for the property.

To estimate a property's value, a real estate appraiser generally uses one of three approaches or a combination of the approaches. The approaches are the cost approach, the sales comparison approach, and the income approach. An investor can further take into account her specific tax situation to value the property using a discounted after-tax cash flow approach. These four approaches are used worldwide.

3.2.1 The Cost Approach

The cost approach is analogous to the use of replacement cost of total assets in the calculation of Tobin's Q for equity valuation. What would it cost to replace the building in its present form? Of course, an estimate of the land value must be added to the building replacement cost estimate. The replacement cost approach is relatively easy to implement because it is based on current construction costs, but it suffers from severe limitations. First, an appraisal of the land value is required and that is not always an easy task. Second, the market value of an existing property could differ markedly from its construction cost. An office building could be very valuable because it has some prestigious and stable tenants that pay high rents, not because of the value of the construction. Conversely, an office building in poor condition, with a large vacancy rate and in a bad neighborhood, could be worth much less than its replacement cost.

3.2.2 The Sales Comparison Approach

The sales comparison approach is similar to the "price multiple comparables" approach in equity valuation. Market value is estimated relative to a benchmark value. The benchmark value may be the market price of a similar property, or the average or median value of the market prices of similar properties, in transactions made near the time of the appraisal. The benchmark-based estimate needs to be adjusted for changing market conditions, the possibility that the benchmark itself is mispriced, and the unique features of the property relative to the benchmark. Properties with comparable characteristics might not have traded recently.

One formal variation of the sales comparison approach is the method of *hedonic price estimation*. In this method, the major characteristics of a property that can affect its value are identified. The characteristics of a residential property that are relevant to its value can be the age of the building, its size, its location, its vacancy rate, its amenities, and so on. Individual properties are given a quantitative rating for each of the characteristics. For example, location could be ranked from 1 (very bad) to 10 (very good). The sales price for all recent transactions of the properties in the benchmark are then regressed on their characteristics ratings. This is a regression in which there is one observation for each transaction. The dependent (left-hand side) variable is the transaction price, and the independent (right-hand side) variables are the ratings for each of the characteristics. The estimated slope coefficients are the valuation of each characteristic in the transaction price. The result is a benchmark monetary value associated with each characteristic's rating. It is then possible to estimate the selling price of a specific property by taking into account its rating on each feature. Although this has become a standard technique in residential property appraisal, it has also been applied to income producing property.[10]

Example 79-2

Sales Comparison Approach: Hedonic Price Model

A real estate company has prepared a simple hedonic model to value houses in a specific area. A summary list of the house's characteristics that can affect pricing are:

▶ the number of main rooms,
▶ the surface area of the garden,
▶ the presence of a swimming pool, and
▶ the distance to a shopping center.

A statistical analysis of a large number of recent transactions in the area allowed the company to estimate the following slope coefficients:

Characteristics	Units	Slope Coefficient in Pounds per Unit
Number of rooms	Number	20,000
Surface area of the garden	Square feet	5
Swimming pool	0 or 1	20,000
Distance to shopping center	In miles	−10,000

A typical house in the area has five main rooms, a garden of 10,000 square feet, a swimming pool, and a distance of one mile to the nearest shopping center. The transaction price for a typical house was £160,000.

You wish to value a house that has seven rooms, a garden of 10,000 square feet, a swimming pool, and a distance of two miles to the nearest shopping center. What is the appraisal value based on this sales comparison approach of hedonic price estimation?

SOLUTION
The appraised value is given by the equation

$$Value = 20{,}000 \times (\# \text{ Rooms}) + 5 \times (\text{Garden surface}) + 20{,}000 \times (\text{Pool}) - 10{,}000 \times (\text{Distance to shopping center})$$
$$= 20{,}000 \times 7 + 5 \times 10{,}000 + 20{,}000 \times 1 - 10{,}000 \times 2$$
$$= £190{,}000$$

---

[10] See Söderberg (2002), pp. 157–180.

This specific house has an appraised value of £190,000. Compared to the typical house in the area, it has two more rooms but is one mile farther from the nearest shopping center.

3.2.3 The Income Approach

The income approach to real estate valuation values property using a perpetuity discount type of model. The perpetuity is the annual net operating income (NOI). This perpetual stream is discounted at a market required rate of return (the market capitalization or cap rate). NOI is gross potential income minus expenses, which include estimated vacancy and collection losses, insurance, taxes, utilities, and repairs and maintenance. Technically, the market cap rate is the rate used by the market in recent transactions to capitalize future income into a present market value. For a constant and perpetual stream of annual NOI, we have

$$\text{Appraisal price} = \frac{\text{NOI}}{\text{Market cap rate}}$$

And the market cap rate is calculated on the benchmark transactions as

$$\text{Market cap rate} = \frac{\text{Benchmark NOI}}{\text{Benchmark transaction price}}$$

Benchmark may refer to a single comparable property or the median or mean of several comparable properties, with any appropriate adjustments.

It must be stressed that the income approach makes the simplifying assumption of a constant and perpetual amount of annual income. The income approach can also be adjusted for the special cases of a constant growth rate in rentals or a constant growth rate in rentals coupled with long-term leases. Valuation with a constant growth rate in rentals parallels the constant growth dividend discount model. Inflation could make NOI grow at the inflation rate over time. As long as inflation can be passed through, it will not affect valuation, because the market cap rate also incorporates the inflation rate. In the long-term lease case, the growth in rentals is not fully reflected in the NOI growth rate. The rent remains fixed over the term of the lease, while costs grow at the inflation rate. This is analogous to the inflation pass-through question raised in equity valuation (see Reading 61). If expected inflation will cause operating expenses to rise, how much of the inflation can the owner pass through to the tenants? Longer lease terms delay the pass-through. Another limitation of this approach is that all calculations are performed before tax.

Example 79-3

The Income Approach

An investor wants to evaluate an apartment complex using the income approach. Recent sales in the area consist of an office building and an apartment complex. He gathers the following data on the apartment complex, as well as on recent sales in the area. All income items are on an annual basis. According to the income approach, what is the value of the apartment complex?

	Apartment Investment under Consideration	Office Building Recently Sold	Apartment Complex Recently Sold
Gross potential rental income	$120,000		
Estimated vacancy and collection losses	6%		
Insurance and taxes	$10,000		
Utilities	$7,000		
Repairs and maintenance	$12,000		
Depreciation	$14,000		
Interest on proposed financing	$11,000		
Net operating income		$300,000	$60,000
Sales price		$2,000,000	$500,000

SOLUTION

The NOI for the apartment complex is gross potential rental income minus estimated vacancy and collection costs minus insurance and taxes minus utilities minus repairs and maintenance.

NOI = 120,000 − 0.06 × 120,000 − 10,000 − 7,000 − 12,000 = 83,800

The other apartment complex is the comparable property, and that has a capitalization rate of

NOI/(Transaction price) = 60,000/500,000 = 0.12

Applying this cap rate to the apartment complex under consideration gives an appraisal price of

NOI/(Cap rate) = 83,800/0.12 = $698,333

Note that we do not use the financing costs to determine the NOI, because we wish to appraise the value of the property independently of its financing. Neither do we subtract depreciation. The implicit assumption is that repairs and maintenance will allow the investor to keep the building in good condition forever.

3.2.4 The Discounted After-Tax Cash Flow Approach

Supplementing the cost, sales comparison, and income approach used for market value appraisals, the discounted after-tax cash flow approach is a check on investment valuation. If the investor can deduct depreciation and any interest payments from NOI, then the investor's after-tax cash flows depend on the investor's marginal tax rate. Hence, the value of a property for a specific investor depends on the investor's marginal tax rate. Once these cash flows and after-tax proceeds from future property disposition are estimated, the net present value of the property to an equity investor is obtained as the present value of the cash flows, discounted at the investor's required rate of return on equity, minus the amount of equity required to make the investment.

For an equity investment to be worthwhile, its expected net present value must be positive. Alternatively, the investment's yield (internal rate of return) should exceed the investor's required rate of return.

Example 79-4

The Discounted Cash Flow Approach

An analyst is assigned the task of evaluating a real estate investment project. The purchase price is $700,000, which is financed 20 percent by equity and 80 percent by a mortgage loan at a 10 percent pretax interest rate. According to the applicable country's tax rules, the interest on real estate financing for this project is tax deductible. The mortgage loan has a long maturity and level annual payments of $59,404. This includes interest payments on the remaining principal at a 10 percent interest rate and a variable principal repayment that steps up with time. The analyst calculated NOI in the first year to be $83,800. NOI is expected to grow at a rate of 5 percent every year.

The analyst faces the following valuation tasks: determining the first year's after-tax cash flow, determining interim after-tax cash flows, determining the final year's after-tax cash flow, and calculating two measures of the project's profitability, the investment's net present value (NPV) and the investment's yield (internal rate of return).

i. Determine the first year's after-tax cash flow, using the following data:

Net operating income (NOI) for first year	$83,800
Straight-line depreciation	18,700
Mortgage payment	59,404
Purchase price	700,000
80% financing at a 10% interest rate	
NOI growth rate	5%
Marginal income tax rate	31%

ii. Determine the second year's after-tax cash flow, using the preceding table and with a growth rate of 5% in NOI.

iii. The property is sold at the end of the fifth year. Determine the after-tax cash flow for that property sale year, using the following data (the after-tax cash flow without property sale has been calculated as previously).

After-tax cash flow without property sale	$33,546
Straight-line depreciation	18,700
Mortgage payment	59,404
Cumulative mortgage principal repayments by end of fifth year	20,783
Purchase price	700,000
80% financing at 10% interest rate	

NOI growth factor	5%
Marginal income tax rate	31%
Capital gains tax rate	20%
Forecasted sales price	$875,000
Property sales expense as a percentage of sales price	6%

Use the information below to answer Parts iv and v.

The following data summarize the after-tax cash flows for all five years of the project's life (the table includes the results we have calculated previously for years 1, 2, and 5, as well as results for years 3 and 4):

Year	1	2	3	4	5
Cash flow	21.575	24,361	27.280	30,339	273,629

The analyst now turns to evaluating whether the project should be undertaken. She estimates the required rate of return for an equity investment in projects of similar risk as 16 percent. The purchase price for the property is $700,000. The financing plan calls for 80 percent debt financing, so the equity investment is only $140,000. The investor's cost of equity for projects with this level of risk is 16 percent, but a sensitivity analysis on cost of equity helps provide some perspective for the analyst. She decides to conduct a sensitivity analysis, calculating the present value of the year 1 to year 5 after-tax cash flows using a range of discount rates other than 16 percent; the results appear in the following table:

Discount Rate	Present Value
0.10	$250,867
0.14	$216,161
0.18	$187,637
0.22	$164,012
0.26	$144,303
0.30	$127,747
0.34	$113,750

iv. Determine the real estate project's NPV, using the analyst's required rate of return, and make a purchase recommendation based only on this analysis.

v. Determine an approximate yield for the real estate project, and make a purchase recommendation based only on this analysis.

SOLUTION TO i

Because interest is tax deductible here, calculate the first year's interest, and then calculate after-tax net income. The amount borrowed is $560,000 = 700,000 \times 0.8$. The first year's interest at 10 percent is then $56,000 = 0.1 \times $560,000$. After-tax net income is then ($83,800 - $18,700 - $56,000) \times (1 - 0.31) = $6,279$.

To get after-tax cash flow from after-tax net income, depreciation must be added and the principal repayment component of the $59,404 mortgage payment must be subtracted. The principal repayment is the mortgage payment minus the interest payment, or $3,404 = $59,404 - $56,000$. Thus, the after-tax cash flow is $21,575 = $6,279 + $18,700 - $3,404$.

SOLUTION TO ii

First we calculate the new NOI, equal to $87,990 = $83,800 \times (1.05)$.

Second, we calculate after-tax net income. We need to calculate the second year's interest payment on the mortgage balance after the first year's payment. This mortgage balance is the original principal balance minus the first year's principal repayment, or $556,596. The interest on this balance is then $55,660. After-tax net income is then ($87,990 - $18,700 - $55,660) \times (1 - 0.31) = $9,405$.

Third, the second year's principal repayment is the mortgage payment minus the interest payment, or $3,744 = $59,404 - $55,660$.

Finally, then calculate the second year's after-tax cash flow, which equals the second year's after-tax net income plus depreciation minus the principal repayment, or $24,361 = $9,405 + $18,700 - $3,744$.

SOLUTION TO iii

The after-tax cash flow for the property sale year is equal to the sum of the after-tax cash flow without the property sale plus the after-tax cash flow from the property sale. When a property is sold, the outstanding mortgage principal balance (the outstanding mortgage, for short) must be paid to the lender. In the following calculations, we incorporate that effect into the after-tax cash flow from the property sale.

To begin, we calculate the capital gains on the sale of the property. To do that, first determine the ending book value as the original purchase price minus five years' worth of depreciation, or $606,500 = $700,000 - 5 \times $18,700$. The net sale price is equal to the forecasted sale price, $875,000, minus sales expenses of 6 percent, or $52,500. Capital gains taxes are paid on the difference between the net sales price and the book value, or a difference of $216,000 = ($875,000 - $52,500) - $606,500$. The capital gains taxes are then $43,200 = 0.2 \times $216,000$. The after-tax cash flow from the property sale is then the net sales price minus the outstanding mortgage minus the capital gains taxes. The outstanding mortgage is the original mortgage minus five years' worth of principal repayments, or $539,217 = $560,000 − $20,783. Thus the after-tax cash flow from the property sale is $240,083 = ($875,000 − $52,500) − $539,217 − $43,200. The after-tax cash flow for the property sale year is then $273,629 = $33,546 + $240,083.

SOLUTION TO iv

At a cost of equity of 16 percent, the present value of the cash flow is $201,215 = $21,575/1.16 + $24,361/1.16^2 + $27,280/1.16^3 + $30,339/1.16^4 + $273,629/1.16^5. The investment requires equity of $140,000 = 0.2 × $700,000. Thus, the NPV is $61,215 = $201,215 − $140,000. The analyst recommends this investment because it has a positive NPV.

SOLUTION TO v

We can address the question using the results of the analyst's sensitivity analysis. The yield or internal rate of return is the discount rate that makes the project's NPV equal to zero. The yield must be between 26 percent and 30 percent because discounting at 26 percent gives a present value ($144,303) that is larger than the initial investment (of $140,000), or a positive NPV, while discounting at 30 percent gives a present value ($127,747) that is smaller than the initial investment, or a negative NPV. Consequently, the project's yield must lie between 26 percent and 30 percent. Actually, the internal rate of return of this project is slightly below 27 percent. The analyst recommends the investment because the investment's yield exceeds the investor's required rate of return (16 percent).

3.3 Real Estate in a Portfolio Context

Some real estate indexes have been developed to attempt to measure the average return on real estate investment. Good-quality indexes with a long-term historical record exist in the United States and United Kingdom, but they are more recent or even nonexistent in other countries.

Real estate returns consist of income and capital gain or loss. The income on a property can usually be measured in a straightforward fashion. The value appreciation is more difficult to assess. The most common method is to use changes in appraised value. Appraisal of each property is conducted by specialists fairly infrequently (typically once a year). Appraisals are generally based on the approaches discussed previously. In practice, appraisal prices exhibit remarkable inertia. The value of a real estate portfolio is further smoothed because properties are appraised infrequently, so their prices remain constant between appraisals.

Following are the major U.S. real estate indexes, based on appraisal values:

▶ The *Frank Russell Company (FRC)* and the *National Council of Real Estate Investment Fiduciaries (NCREIF)* indexes. These are quarterly indexes, starting in 1978 and broken down by regions and property types.

▶ The *Commingled Real Estate Equity Fund (CREF)* index, published by Evaluation Associates. This is a quarterly index of major tax-exempt funds, starting in 1969.

Another method of measuring price appreciation is to use a reference to REITs. The total return on a REIT is made up of the income paid to shareholders, as well as of the stock market appreciation of the REIT share price. Various REIT indexes are used to proxy the average total return on real estate investments. They are easier to construct, because they are simply some weighted average of market-traded shares. The major REIT indexes are as follows:

▶ The *National Association of Real Estate Investment Trusts (NAREIT),* a monthly equal-weighted index of some one hundred REITs, starting in 1972.

▶ REIT indexes published by various institutions, for example, Wilshire or Goldman Sachs.

The two types of indexes provide very different performance and risk characteristics, which have been studied by Firstenberg, Ross, and Zisler (1988), Goetzmann and Ibbotson (1990), and Gyourko and Keim (1993). Appraisal-based indexes are much less volatile than REIT indexes. For example, Goetzman and Ibbotson found that a REIT index had an annual standard deviation of 15.4 percent, comparable to that of the S&P 500 index, but six times larger than that of the CREF index, of 2.6 percent. Furthermore, appraisal-based indexes and REIT indexes have very little correlation. Appraisal-based indexes exhibit persistent returns (returns are correlated over time), showing the inertia in appraisals. REIT indexes are strongly correlated with the rest of the stock market.

In summary, real estate returns can be calculated using either appraisal indexes or REIT indexes. Appraisals do not provide continuous price data and they do not provide market prices but only market price estimates. REIT indexes provide continuous market prices of REITs but not of the underlying real estate. Thus, they reflect the amount of leverage used in the REITs. Therefore neither approach to calculating returns is entirely satisfactory. In any case, the issue in investment is one of forecasting returns, standard deviations, and correlations. For example, in analyzing a particular real estate project, an investor would supplement cash flow forecasts and discounted cash flow analysis with considerations of how the project's cash flows will covary with his existing portfolio. An individual investor will not receive diversification benefits from a real estate project whose returns are highly correlated with his own business employment income.

A few studies have looked at real estate from a global viewpoint. These studies examine the proposed portfolio benefits of real estate, risk reduction (through diversification) and inflation protection. Eichholtz (1996) looked at the diversification benefits of real estate shares quoted in many countries. He found that international diversification strongly reduces the risk of a real estate portfolio. However, Mull and Soenen (1997) showed that REITs are strongly correlated with other U.S. stocks, so that foreign investors who buy U.S. REITs do not gain much diversification benefit, beyond the U.S. stock market exposure. Liu, Hartzell, and Hoesli (1997) looked at real estate securities traded on seven national stock markets and concluded that their correlation with inflation is low, so they do not provide a good hedge against inflation. Quan and Titman (1997) studied commercial real estate values in 17 countries, where property values and rents are calculated using an appraisal-based approach. Commercial real estate prices and stock prices are both affected by the general level of economic activity, so they should be strongly correlated. Pooling their international data, Quan and Titman did find that the relation between stock returns and changes in real estate values is very strong.

Although research studies have not provided overwhelming evidence to support the risk reduction and inflation protection benefits of real estate, such studies are always limited by the use of either appraisal indexes or REIT indexes.

Judgment is needed in assessing the impact of real estate on a portfolio. First, what are the projected cash flows and what are the predicted covariances of the cash flows with the current portfolio? Second, what are the inflation pass-through characteristics of the real estate investment?

4 PRIVATE EQUITY: VENTURE CAPITAL

Venture capital is one of the main categories of private equity investing. Private equity investments are equity investments that are not traded on exchanges. Venture capital investments are private equity investments in business ventures from idea stage through expansion of a company already producing and selling a product and through preparation for exit from the investment via buyout or initial public offering. Venture capital investing may be done at stages along the way, but eventual exit is a primary consideration. By its very nature, such investing requires a horizon of several years and the willingness to accept several failures for every success in the venture capital portfolio: The possibly enormous return on the winning venture must compensate for many likely failed ventures.

Institutional and individual investors usually invest in private equity through limited partnerships. Limited partnerships allow investors (the limited partners) to participate in a portfolio of venture capital projects while preserving limited liability (the initial investment) and leaving management to the general partners who are private equity experts. Typically, the general partners are associated with a firm that specializes in private equity or with the private equity department of a financial institution. Funds of funds are also offered that pool investments in several ventures.

CONCEPTS IN ACTION   Global Investing: Mounting Overseas Interest Keeps U.S. Real Estate Prices Above Water

As stock markets continue to offer weak returns, foreign investors have poured money into US real estate at a fast pace this year, attracted by superior yields and the transparency and liquidity of the market.

Jacques Gordon, international director of investment strategy and research for LaSalle Investment Management, said US real estate has always been attractive to foreign money, but the magnitude of the sums incoming has been particularly noteworthy this year.

Much of the attraction is based on the higher yields from US properties, which average between 7 and 8 per cent compared with 4 to 5 per cent in Europe.

Real Capital Analytics, a real estate monitoring group, estimates foreign investors will have acquired nearly $9bn of US commercial property by the end of 2002, double the $4.5bn seen in 2001.

Overseas money is largely being spent on office space in metropolitan areas such as New York and Washington. Foreigners bought $6.7bn of office properties, representing 16 per cent of total office investments in the US in 2002. German-based Jamestown Immobilien is just about to close a $745m deal to buy the Axa Financial Center on Sixth Avenue in New York.

Of greatest interest to foreigners have been "trophy" buildings in the central business districts of big cities. That heightened interest has boosted property prices to new records, despite rising vacancies and falling rents.

This discrepancy in the fundamentals is raising concerns for the future profitability of current investments, especially in light of continuing weakness in the US economy. "There is a disconnect between the price of commercial real estate and if there is a renewed recession that disconnect cannot persist," said Hugh Kelly, professor of real estate at New York University.

But Mr Gordon said that although record prices are being paid for office properties, he sees limited risk to the downside, given that the amounts being paid are only about 10 per cent higher than previous records.

"Although record amounts are being paid, it is not anything like the tech frenzy we saw in the stock market. [The record prices] do not trouble me in the sense that there's a bubble about to burst," Mr Gordon said.

Interest in the US market has been heaviest from Germany, accounting for 51 per cent of total foreign capital in US real estate this year. Germans invested $4.9bn in US property in 2002 compared with just $2.7bn a year earlier.

The main reason for the increased interest is that money is flowing at an unprecedented rate into German open-ended and closed-end funds, and analysts say investing large sums in high-profile buildings in the US is an easy way to invest the funds quickly and efficiently.

Markus Derkum of Jamestown, a real estate investment company that raises money in Germany for investments in the US, says weak stock-market performance already saw German investors turning to US real estate in 2001. He said the terrorist attacks in the World Trade Center and the Pentagon in September only caused a minor blip on the flow.

"We thought nobody would touch US real estate any more, especially the international capital. We were wrong," he said.

In 2001, foreign acquisitions in apartment, industrial and retail properties totaled $1bn and that is set to jump to $2.2bn this year.

Non-German European investors account for about 22 per cent of the foreign interest in the US, and Middle Eastern investors, Israeli and Arab, account for about 14 per cent. Canadians invested 8 per cent of total foreign investment and Australians, with 5 per cent, have this year emerged as a significant new source of capital, particularly in the retail sector.

Source: Global Investing, Zarina Rijnen, *Financial Times*, 10 December 2002.

4.1 Stages of Venture Capital Investing

Schilit (1996) provides a good review of the various stages of venture capital investing. Several rounds of financing take place, and these can be characterized by where they occur in the development of the venture itself. Here, Schilit's classification review is adapted and blended with other common industry terminology.[11] Each stage of financing is matched by investments, so that aggregate investment activity is often reported by the amount in different stage funds.

1. *Seed-stage* financing is capital provided for a business idea. The capital generally supports product development and market research.

2. *Early-stage* financing is capital provided for companies moving into operation and before commercial manufacturing and sales have occurred.

   ▶ *Start-up* is capital provided for companies just moving into operation but without any commercial product or service sales. The capital generally supports product development and initial marketing.

   ▶ *First-stage* financing is capital provided to initiate commercial manufacturing and sales.

[11] See, for example, Thomson Venture Economics, the National Venture Capital Association (in the United States), the European Venture Capital Association, and the British Venture Capital Association.

3. *Formative-stage* financing includes seed stage and early stage.

4. *Later-stage* financing is capital provided after commercial manufacturing and sales have begun but before any initial public offering.

   ▶ *Second-stage* financing refers to capital used for initial expansion of a company already producing and selling a product but perhaps not yet profitably.

   ▶ *Third-stage* financing is capital provided for major expansion, such as physical plant expansion, product improvement, or a major marketing campaign.

   ▶ *Mezzanine* (bridge) financing is capital provided to prepare for the step of going public and represents the bridge between the expanding company and the initial public offering (IPO).

Expansion-stage financing includes second and third stage. *Balanced-stage* financing is a term used to refer to all the stages, seed through mezzanine.

CONCEPTS IN ACTION   Venture Capital Investments Continue to Decline in Q3 2002: Economic Realities Return Investing to pre-1998 levels

Stage of Development

Expansion stage companies continue to receive the most venture capital, receiving 56% of all capital invested and 55% of the number of deals in the third quarter. At the same time, investors continued to fund earlier stage companies. In Q3, companies in the "formative" stages of development (early stage and startup/seed) received similar levels as last quarter, 23% of dollars invested and 30% of the number of deals. This stability in earlier stage investing indicates venture capital firms continue to take longer-term views.

   Later stage investing became more dominant in the third quarter, representing 20% of the dollars invested and 15% of the number of deals compared to 13% of the dollars invested and 9% of the number of deals in Q2. This increase in later stage deals demonstrates that venture capitalists have remained committed to their existing portfolio companies and continue to finance their development during this difficult economic period.

   According to Jesse Reyes, vice president at Thomson Venture Economics, "Venture funds that focus on later stage deals are finding fewer traditional later stage opportunities—that is, deals a couple of years from exit—because the time to exit has lengthened. As a result, VCs are finding that the only new investments that fit their focus are expansion stage deals that require even more time to mature before exit is a possibility."

Source: PricewaterhouseCoopers, Venture Economics, National Venture Capital Association MoneyTree™ Survey.

4.2 Investment Characteristics

Venture capital investing has several characteristics, some of which are common to alternative investing in general, but many of which are unique:

   ▶ *Illiquidity:* Venture capital investments do not provide an easy or short-term path for cashing out. Liquidation or divestment of each venture within a portfolio is dependent on the success of the fund manager in creating a buyout or initial public offering (IPO) opportunity. One particular risk is that inexperienced venture fund managers will "grandstand" and bring ventures to the market too early, especially when the IPO market is good. Conversely, a poor IPO market may mean that otherwise successful ventures may afford no immediate path to liquidity.

▶ *Long-term commitment required:* Venture capital requires a long-term commitment because of the time lag to liquidity. If the average investor is averse to illiquidity, this will create a liquidity risk premium on venture capital. Thus, an investor with a longer than average time horizon can expect to profit from this liquidity risk premium. It is not surprising that university endowments (with their long horizons) have sought venture capital vehicles.

▶ *Difficulty in determining current market values:* Because there is no continuous trading of the investments within a venture fund portfolio, there is no objective way of determining the current market value of the portfolio. This poses a problem for reporting the market value exposure of the current venture capital portion of an investor's portfolio.

▶ *Limited historical risk and return data:* Because there is no continuous market in venture capital, historical risk and return data have limitations.

▶ *Limited information:* Because entrepreneurs operate in previously uncharted territory, there is little information on which to base estimates of cash flows or the probability of success of their ventures

▶ *Entrepreneurial/management mismatches:* Although surely profit motivated, some entrepreneurs may be more wedded to the success of their favorite idea than to the financial success of the venture. During the early life of a firm, there are also two major problems that may arise. First, the entrepreneur may not be a good manager, so the existence or creation of a good management team is critical. Second, rapid growth produces a change in the type of managerial expertise required, so that entrepreneurs/managers who can succeed with small ventures need the ability to adapt to the different demands of larger companies, or the investors must be in a position to replace them.

▶ *Fund manager incentive mismatches:* Fund managers may be rewarded by size of their fund rather than by performance of their fund. Investors interested in performance must look for fund managers whose incentives are aligned with theirs.

▶ *Lack of knowledge of how many competitors exist:* Because entrepreneurs operate in uncharted territory, there is often little way for them or for analysts to know how many other entrepreneurs are developing substitute ideas or products at the same time. Thus, competitive analysis for venture capital investments is even more difficult than for investments in established companies in established industries.

▶ *Vintage cycles:* Some years are better than others. Both entry and exit are factors here. If too many entrepreneurial firms enter at the prompt of increased venture capital availability, the economics of perfect competition will prevail and returns will be weak. On the exit side, poor financial market conditions can cause venture capital to dry up, and perhaps some firms that could be successful will not find the financing needed for their success. Thus, some years provide better firm planting and growing conditions than others.

▶ *Extensive operations analysis and advice may be required:* More than financial engineering skill is required of fund managers. Venture capital investments require extensive investment analysis, but they also require extensive operating management experience. Thus, a venture capital manager who can add value will be the one who has both financial and operating experience, and knowledge of the emerging industry in which the entrepreneur is operating. The venture capital manager must be able to act as both a financial and an operations management consultant to the venture. Reflecting David Swensen's philosophy[12] at the Yale Endowment, the investor is well advised to choose a fund manager who knows the business and can add value.

4.3 Types of Liquidation/Divestment[13]

Exit strategies are critical for venture capital investing. The main types of liquidation/divestment are trade sales, initial public offerings (IPOs) followed by the sale of quoted equity, and write-offs. Trade sales are sales or mergers of the private company for cash or stock of the acquirer. An IPO is the initial issuance of shares registered for public trading. Shares are distributed to the private equity investors who can sell them in the marketplace only after the expiration of a lock-up period. (In rare cases, a sale or merger of the private company follows the IPO.) Write-offs are voluntary liquidations that may or may not produce any proceeds. In addition to the main types of liquidation, there are also cases of bankruptcy as well as the situation in which the founder/entrepreneur buys out the outside venture capital investors and takes the company back to a privately held company without institutional shareholders.

Participating in a venture capital fund, investors get distributions of public stock or cash from realized venture capital investments. The fund may require additional investments (drawdowns) from limited partners and may make cash or share distributions at random times during the life of the fund. Investors might also be able to sell their interests if they can find a buyer. Also, at the end of the fund's life, there are often illiquid, barely alive companies (living dead) that are transferred to a liquidating vehicle with minimal fees. A very few funds have an evergreen type of structure, which rolls old fund investments into a new fund that has new cash commitments.

In the following Concepts in Action, note that divestment by flotation and sale of quoted equity together constitute the second main exit mechanism (exit via a public market).

CONCEPTS IN ACTION European Divestment Reported Through the Third Quarter of 2002

Excluding write-offs, the highest amount divested at cost this year was in quarter three. A total of €1.5bn was divested at cost in Q3, up from €1.3bn in Q2 and just over €1bn in Q1. A total of 502 companies were divested in Q3, down from the 774 divested in Q2. Trade sales remained the most significant route to exit and accounted for 28.8% of total divestment at cost (€434m), a 5% decrease in amount on the previous quarter. At €342m, write-offs remained significant in Q3, but fell by 18% on the previous quarter. IPOs as an exit were still a rare option, but the slow trickle of activity (2 companies divested through IPO in Q3) showed that some practitioners still managed to use the IPO, even in the prevailing difficult climate. Between Q1 and Q3 of 2002, a total of €3.9bn was divested at cost.

---

[12] See pages 17 and 18 in Lerner (2000).

[13] This section has benefited from correspondence with Dean Takahashi.

	Q3 2002				
	Amount at Cost (€m)	%	No of Divestments	%	No of Co.s
Divestment by Trade Sale	433.6	28.8	118	17.5	81
Divestment by Flotation (IPO)	5.1	0.3	6	0.9	2
Sale of Quoted Equity	62.0	4.1	99	14.7	58
Divestment by Write-Off	342.0	22.7	194	28.8	177
Other	664.7	44.1	257	38.1	184
Total	**1,507.5**	**100.0**	**674**	**100.0**	**502**

Source: Reprinted with permission from European Venture Capital & Private Equity Association, Thomson Economics and PricewaterhouseCoopers.

(Quarterly Activity Indicator, Q3 2002).

4.4 Valuation and Performance Measurement

In the venture capital area, valuation and performance measurement is a difficult exercise. This is true at the level of a single venture project, but also at the level of an investment in a venture capital fund.

4.4.1 Valuation and Project Risk

Valuing a prospective venture capital project is a challenging task. Although some valuation methods can be applied, quantifying future cash flows is difficult. Investing in a particular venture capital project is motivated by an anticipated large payoff at time of exit. But many projects will fail along the way. In addition to the normal risk of equity investments, the particular risk of venture capital stems from the increased uncertainty created by possibly inexperienced entrepreneurs with innovative products or product ideas and uncertain time to success, even if successful. Some of the unique risks of venture capital projects come from their investment characteristics, as described. Of course, the risk of a portfolio of venture capital investments is less than the risk of any individual venture project, because of risk diversification.

So, there are three main parameters that enter into valuing a venture capital project:

▶ An assessment of the expected payoff at time of exit, if the venture is successful;

▶ An assessment of the time it will take to exit the venture successfully; and

▶ An assessment of the probability of failure.

This is illustrated in Example 79-5.

Example 79-5

Venture Capital Valuation And Risk

An investor estimates that investing $1 million in a particular venture capital project will pay $16 million at the end of seven years if it succeeds; however, she realizes that the project may fail at any time between now and the end of seven years. The investor is considering an equity investment in the project and her cost of equity for a project with this level of risk is 18 percent. In the following table are the investor's estimates of some probabilities of failure for the project. First, 0.25 is the probability of failure in year 1. For year 2, 0.25 is the probability that the project fails in the second year, given that it has survived through year 1. For year 3, 0.20 is the probability that the project fails, given that it has survived through year 2, and so forth.

Year	1	2	3	4	5	6	7
Failure probability	0.25	0.22	0.20	0.20	0.20	0.20	0.20

i. Determine the probability that the project survives to the end of the seventh year.

ii. Determine the expected NPV of the project.

iii. Make a recommendation.

SOLUTION

i. The probability that the project survives to the end of the first year is $(1 - 0.25) = 1$ minus the probability of failure in the first year; the probability that it survives the end of second year is the product of the probability it survives the first year times the probability it survives the second year, or $(1 - 0.25)\ (1 - 0.22)$. Using this pattern, the probability that the firm survives to end of the seventh year is $(1 - 0.25)\ (1 - 0.22)\ (1 - 0.20)^5 = (0.75)\ (0.78)\ (0.80)^5 = 0.192$ or 19.2%.

ii. The NPV of the project, given that it survives to the end of the seventh year and thus earns $16 million, equals $4.02 million $= -\$1$ million $+ \$16$ million$/1.18^7$. The NPV of project given that it fails is $-\$1$ million. Thus, the project's expected NPV is a probability-weighted average of these two amounts, or $(0.192)(\$4.02$ million$) + (0.808)(-\$1$ million$) = -\$36,160$.

iii. Based on its negative NPV, the recommendation is to decline the investment.

The payoff structure of actual projects is generally more complex than that of Example 79-5. Practitioners may use a multiple-scenario approach to valuation. In this approach, payoffs are simulated under each scenario (from optimistic to pessimistic) and weighted by the probability of occurrence of the scenario.

4.4.2 Performance Measurement

Investors in a venture capital fund need to evaluate the performance of their investment, not only at time of liquidation, but also during the life of their investment. This is usually done by calculating an internal rate of return based on cash flows since inception and the end-of-period valuation of the unliquidated remaining holdings (residual value or net asset value). The European Venture Capital Association (www.evca.com), the British Venture Capital Association (www.bvca.co.uk), and AIMR have valuation guidelines bearing on this.

There are several challenges to performance measurement in the venture capital area. Lerner (2000) points these out in a discussion of future directions for an endowment fund:

► The difficulty in determining precise valuations. Venture capital funds do not have market prices to value their holdings, so they use some arbitrary technique to value their portfolios of ongoing projects. For example, some managers apply an average internal rate of return to the historical investment costs of their ongoing projects. Of course, the actual exit value is used at the time of exit of a project, or a zero value is used if a project failed.

► The lack of meaningful benchmarks against which fund manager and investment success can be measured.

► The long-term nature of any reliable performance feedback in the venture capital asset class.

HEDGE FUNDS AND ABSOLUTE RETURN STRATEGIES

5

The early 1990s saw the explosive development of *hedge funds*. Even though the attraction of these funds was tempered by many huge losses suffered in 1994 and 1998, the hedge fund industry continued to prosper. The number of global hedge funds, estimated to be 1,373 in 1988 grew to an estimated 7,000 at the end of 2001. The assets under management of hedge funds grew from $42 billion in 1988 to $311 billion in 1998, and to about $600 billion by the end of 2001.[14] The asset base of U.S. and non-U.S. hedge funds are of the same order of magnitude.

CONCEPTS IN ACTION Losses in Private Equity Business Reach $10bn

Financial services companies' private equity operations have lost more than $10bn in total since the bear market in technology began in 2000, according to their financial reports.

Many institutions—including Deutsche Bank, which has lost $1.7bn, and GE Capital Services, which has taken a $592m hit to earnings—are planning to leave the business, while those that remain are radically changing their practices.

The banks with the largest private equity operations, JP Morgan Chase and Credit Suisse First Boston—both of which have assets of more than $20bn in their groups—remain committed to their business.

But JP Morgan, which has lost at least $1.8bn during the downturn, will have a much reduced presence in the market.

---

[14] The source for this is Van Hedge Fund Advisors International at www.vanhedge.com, accessed on 12 December 2002.

In a memo last week, Bill Harrison, chief executive, reiterated his support for the private equity group, but also set a multi-year target of halving private equity exposure to 10 percent of common equity from 20 percent.

He also noted that the private equity group would have to seek more outside money to support their efforts. The bank recently launched a private equity fund with $1.7bn of outside money, but that fell well short of the initial $5bn target.

JP Morgan also intends to sell its interests in other people's private equity partnerships. Both JP Morgan and CSFB, among others, bought into the idea of investing in buyout funds to cement their growing relationships with buyout firms, which are important Wall Street clients.

But the fall in some funds injected unwanted volatility into banks' income statements and bankers now acknowledge those positions were less useful in attracting buyout business.

Banks have reacted to those losses by turning to the secondary and securitization markets in an effort to find an exit. JP Morgan sold more than $1bn of partnerships 18 months ago and CSFB is in the process of concluding a $100m sale.

Deutsche Bank plans to securitize its investments in other private equity partnerships, as well as allowing its own group to launch a management buyout.

Many firms have found it difficult to divest their private equity exposures, however.

Secondary private equity funds have raised billions of dollars to buy unwanted private equity partnerships.

But after a year when the average buyout fund declined 11 percent in value and the average venture capital fund has fallen 27 percent, according to Thomson Venture Economics, secondary funds are cautious about what they will pay for other people's portfolios.

Source: Robert Clow, *Financial Times: Companies & Markets,* 13 December 2002, p. 19.

Although individual investors have been the traditional client bases of hedge funds, institutional investors, especially endowments and foundations, have started to invest en masse. We start this section by a description of the different types of hedge funds available, including funds of funds. A discussion of the leverage and unique risk characteristics of hedge funds will complete this description. Hedge funds follow strategies that promise a large absolute return, and deserve a close investigation of the actual performance and risk of those strategies. We therefore present the case for investing in hedge funds in some detail, but also provide the caveats.

CONCEPTS IN ACTION Endowments, Foundations Move More to Hedge Funds

WILTON, Conn.—Endowments and foundations increased their allocations to hedge funds in the year ended June 30, a Commonfund report shows.

Among those that altered their asset allocations during the year, hedge fund exposure rose to 35% of the average alternatives portfolio from 22%.

Increased use of hedge funds helped boost alternative investments to 15% of total assets as of June 30, from 11% a year earlier among the funds that changed their asset allocations.

Of the 97 endowments and foundations surveyed, 29% reported changes in the asset allocation in the previous year.

The $197 million University of Connecticut foundation in Storrs is among those hiking hedge fund exposure. The foundation doubled its hedge fund allocation to 10% of total assets following an asset allocation study by Wilshire Associates, Santa Monica, Calif.

"We've been adding diversification," said Kevin Edwards, director of treasury services.

Of those institutions that made changes, the average allocation to domestic equities dropped three percentage points to 47%; the average allocation to international equities dropped one point to 10%.

John Griswold, executive director of Commonfund Institute, said while he's pleased endowments and foundations largely "are sticking to their guns" on asset allocation, he expects more shifts soon.

"This fall, there will be meetings of committees with a lot of concern," he said.

This is the second consecutive year that endowments and foundations showed negative returns. The average return was −5.4% for the year ended June 30 and −3% for the previous one-year period. For the year ended June 30, 2000, the average return was 13.2%.

The smaller the fund, the worse the return, the survey shows. Respondents with assets between $51 million and $100 million reported an average return of −7.4%, while those assets between $101 million and $500 million reported an average −6.1% return.

By contrast, funds with more than $1 billion in assets returned an average −3.4% for the year ended June 30.

The findings are from the interim edition of Commonfund's benchmark study, an annual survey of higher-education endowments and foundations. The interim study covers 97 endowments and foundations that were surveyed through an Internet questionnaire. The final results of the study will be released in 2003.

Source: Mike Kennedy, *Pensions & Investments,* 30 September 2002, p. 33. Reprinted with permission, *Pensions & Investments,* September 30, 2002. Copyright Crain Communications Inc.

5.1 Definition

5.1.1 Objective

It is difficult to provide a general definition of hedge funds. The original concept of a hedge fund was to offer plays *against* the markets, using shortselling, futures, and other derivative products. Today, funds using the "hedge fund" appellation follow all kinds of strategies and cannot be considered a homogeneous asset class. Some funds are highly leveraged; others are not. Some engage in hedging activities, and others do not. Some focus on making macroeconomic bets on commodities, currencies, interest rates, and so on. Some are mostly "technical" funds trying to take advantage of the mispricing of some securities within their market. Futures funds belong to the world of hedge funds. In fact, the common denominator of hedge funds is not their investment strategy but the *search for absolute returns.*

Money management has progressively moved toward a focus on performance *relative to preassigned benchmarks.* An institutional money manager's performance is generally evaluated relative to some market index that is assigned as a mandate. In turn, these benchmarks guide (some would say "unduly constrain") the money manager's investment policy. The risk of deviating from the performance of the benchmark has become huge, given all of the publicity surrounding relative performance in a very competitive money management industry. The development of hedge funds can be seen as a reaction against this trend, with the search for absolute return in all directions. In practice, this means that hedge funds might have more appropriately been termed *isolation* funds. They generally try to isolate specific bets for the purpose of generating alpha. One can infer the particular bet from each hedge fund position. Hedge fund managers seek freedom to achieve high absolute returns and wish to be rewarded for their performance. These objectives are apparent in the legal organization and the fee structure of hedge funds. These two aspects are probably the only uniform characteristics of hedge funds.

5.1.2 Legal Structure

Hedge funds are typically set up as a *limited partnership,* as a limited liability corporation (in the United States), or as an *offshore corporation.* These legal structures allow the fund manager to take short and long positions in any asset, to use all kinds of derivatives, and to leverage the fund without restrictions. Hedge funds based in the United States most often take the form of a limited partnership organized under section 3(c)(1) of the Investment Company Act, thereby gaining exemption from most U.S. Securities and Exchange Commission (SEC) regulations. The fund is limited to no more than 100 partners, who must be "accredited investors,"[15] and is prohibited from advertising. Some U.S. hedge funds are organized under section 3(c)(7) of the Investment Company Act, and are also exempt from most SEC regulations. In that case, the fund is limited to no more than 500 investors, who must be "qualified purchasers,"[16] and is prohibited from advertising. Given the small number of partners, a minimum investment is typically more than $200,000. Institutional investors can become partners. U.S. hedge funds are typically incorporated in a "fund-friendly" state, such as Delaware. *Offshore funds* have also proved to be an attractive legal structure. These are incorporated in locations such as the British Virgin Islands, Cayman Islands, Bermuda, or other locations attractive from a fiscal and legal point of view. A hedge fund might consider using "feeders" (vehicles that have an ownership interest in the hedge fund) that enable the hedge fund to solicit funds from investors in every imaginable tax and legal domain—one feeder for ordinary U.S. investors; another for tax-free pensions; another for Japanese who want their profits hedged in yen; still another for European institutions, which invest only in shares that are listed on an exchange (i.e., a dummy listing on the Irish Stock Exchange). These feeders don't keep the money; they are used as paper conduits that channel the money to a central fund, typically a Cayman Islands partnership.

5.1.3 Fee Structure

The manager is compensated through a *base* management fee based on the value of assets under management (at one time as much as 2 to 3 percent, now more typically 1 percent of the asset base) plus an *incentive fee* proportional to the realized profits (ranging from 15 percent to 30 percent, typically 20 percent of total profits).[17] The base fee is paid whatever the performance of the fund. The incentive fee cannot be negative, so a negative return on the funds implies a zero incentive fee. The incentive fee is sometimes applied to profits measured above a risk-free rate applied to the assets. In other words, the hedge fund return has to be greater than the risk-free rate before the incentive fee is activated. The fee structure sometimes includes a "high water mark" stating that following a year in which the fund declined in value, the hedge fund would first have to recover those losses before any incentive fee would be paid. Example 79-6 shows the effect of a hedge fund's fee structure on its net return.

---

[15] An accredited investor under the Securities and Exchange Act is an individual with a net worth in excess of $1 million or an annual income in excess of $200,000; or an entity with total assets of $5 million or more.

[16] A qualified purchaser (or qualified investor) is an individual with at least $5 million in investments or an entity with at least $25 million in investments.

[17] Besides the management and incentive fees that almost all hedge funds charge their clients, hedge funds may charge other fees, such as surrender fees, ticket charges, and financing fees.

Example 79-6

Hedge Fund Fee

A hedge fund has an annual fee of 1 percent base management fee plus a 20 percent incentive fee applied to profits above the risk-free rate, taken to be the Treasury Bill rate. Hence the incentive fee is applied to annual profits after deduction of the Treasury bill rate applied to the amount of assets under management at the start of the year. The gross return during the year is 40 percent. What is the net return (the return after fees) for an investor, if the risk-free rate is 5 percent?

SOLUTION

Fee $= 1\% + 20\% \times (40\% - 5\%) = 8\%$

Net return $= 40\% - 8\% = 32\%$

5.2 Classification

Hedge funds have become quite global, as evidenced by the wide array of global investments used by these hedge funds and the international diversity of their client base. Some classifications of hedge funds by investment strategy is provided in the media and by hedge funds databases. These classifications are somewhat arbitrary, exhibit a large degree of overlap, and differ extensively across sources. Following is one possible classification system:

▶ *Long/short funds* are the traditional types of hedge funds, taking short and long bets in common stocks. They vary their short and long exposures according to forecasts, use leverage, and now operate on numerous markets throughout the world. These funds often maintain net positive or negative market exposures; so they are not necessarily market-neutral. In fact, a subgroup within this category is funds that have a systematic short bias, known as dedicated short funds, or short-seller funds. Long/short funds represent a large amount of hedge fund assets.

▶ *Market-neutral funds* are a form of long/short funds that attempt to be hedged against a general market movement. They take bets on valuation differences of individual securities within some market segment. This could involve simultaneous long and short positions in closely related securities with a zero net exposure to the market itself. A market-neutral long-short portfolio is constructed so that the total value of the positions held long equals the total value of the positions sold short (dollar neutrality) and so that the total sensitivity of the long positions equals and offsets the total sensitivity of the short positions (beta neutrality). The long position would be in stocks considered undervalued, and the short position would be in stocks considered overvalued. Leverage is generally used, so that the investment in the long position (or the short position) is a multiple of the hedge fund equity. Another alternative is to use derivatives to hedge market risk. For example, a manager could buy some bond deemed to be underpriced with a simultaneous short position in bond futures or other fixed-income derivatives. This type of fund is sometimes called a fixed-income arbitrage fund. Other types of arbitrage make use of complex securities with option-like clauses, such as convertibles, warrants, or collateralized mortgage obligations (CMOs). Among the various techniques used by market-neutral funds are

- equity long/short,
- fixed-income hedging,
- pairs trading,
- warrant arbitrage,
- mortgage arbitrage,
- convertible bond arbitrage,
- **closed-end fund** arbitrage, and
- statistical arbitrage.

It must be stressed that despite their labels ("arbitrage," "neutral"), these funds are not riskless because hedges can never be perfect. Loss can be incurred if the model used is imperfect, and can be high because hedge funds tend to be highly leveraged.

Example 79-7

Long/Short Market-Neutral Strategy

A hedge fund has a capital of $10 million and invests in a market-neutral long/short strategy on the British equity market. Shares can be borrowed from a primary broker with a cash margin deposit equal to 18 percent of the value of the shares. No additional costs are charged to borrow the shares. The hedge fund has drawn up a list of shares regarded as under-valued (list A) and a list of shares regarded as overvalued (list B). The hedge fund expects that shares in list A will outperform the British index by 5 percent over the year, while shares in list B will underperform the British index by 5 percent over the year. The hedge fund wishes to retain a cash cushion of $1 million for unforeseen events. What specific invest-ment actions would you suggest?

SOLUTION

The hedge fund would sell short shares from list B and use the proceeds to buy shares from list A for an equal amount such that the overall beta of the portfolio with respect to the market equals zero. Some capital needs to be invested in the margin deposit. The hedge funds could take long/short positions for $50 million:

- Keep $1 million in cash.
- Deposit $9 million in margin.
- Borrow $50 million of Shares B from a broker, and sell those shares short.
- Use the sale proceeds to buy $50 million worth of shares A.

The positions in shares A and B are established so that the portfolio's beta is zero. Also, note that the invested assets of $50 million equals $50 million divided by 0.10. The ratio of invested assets to equity capital is roughly 5:1.

If expectations materialize, the return for investors in the hedge fund will be high. The long/short portfolio of shares should have a gain over the year of 10 percent on $50 million, whatever the movement in the general market index. This $5 million gain will translate into an annual return before fees of 50 percent on the invested capital of $10 million. This calculation does not take into account the return on invested cash ($1 million) and assumes that the dividends on long positions will offset dividends on short positions.

▶ *Global macro funds* take bets on the direction of a market, a currency, an interest rate, a commodity, or any macroeconomic variable. These funds tend to be highly leveraged and make extensive use of derivatives. There are many subgroups in this category, including the following:

  ▶ *Futures funds* (or *managed futures funds*) are commodity pools that include commodity trading advisor funds (CTAs). They take bets on directional moves in the positions they hold (long and short) in a single asset class, such as currency, fixed income, or commodities and tend to use many actively traded futures contracts.

  ▶ *Emerging-market funds* primarily take bets on all types of securities in emerging markets. The securities markets in these economies are typically less efficient and less liquid than those in developed markets. There typically is not an organized lending market for securities, so it is difficult to sell short most issues. Emerging market investments tend to be fairly volatile and greatly influenced by economic and political factors.

▶ *Event-driven funds* take bets on some event specific to a company or a security. Typically the events are special situations or opportunities to capitalize on price fluctuations. These include the following, among others:

  ▶ *Distressed securities funds:* The manager invests in the debt and/or equity of companies having financial difficulty. Such companies are generally in bankruptcy reorganization or are emerging from reorganization or appear likely to declare bankruptcy in the near future. Because of their distressed situations, the manager can buy such companies' securities at deeply discounted prices. The manager stands to make money should the company successfully reorganize and return to profitability. The manager may take short positions in companies whose situations he believes will worsen, rather than improve, in the short term.

  ▶ *Risk arbitrage in mergers and acquisitions:* Before the effective date of a merger, the stock of the acquired company will typically sell at a discount to its acquisition value as officially announced. A hedge fund manager simultaneously buys stock in a company being acquired and sells stock in its acquirers. Even though a merger has been accepted by the board of directors of the two companies, there is always a chance that the merger will not go through, possibly because of objections by regulatory authorities. This is a reason for the existence of the discount. If the takeover falls through, fund managers can be left with large losses.

group of buyers and extending full financing, price levels achieve an artificial buoyancy.

In such a setting, disasters can happen easily. Askin was trying to make as much money as possible for himself and his investors. Dealers who were eager to deal and extend credit a short time before, in March suddenly demanded repayment from Askin's highly leveraged funds—leaving the end investor in the lurch. An intimate circle of over-the-counter buyers and sellers, which seemed small and comfortable weeks before, suddenly turned into pitiless adversaries.

Another lesson is the importance of knowing how specific money managers value portfolios. Askin's holdings were so highly structured that some bonds had taken as long as a week to create. With this degree of complexity, first, investors were unable to create shadow portfolios; then, changes to a few elements of the formula resulted in large shifts in prices.

Askin could and did argue with dealers about pricing—until he finally took matters into his own hands. By late December, Askin reportedly was using his own "internal manager marks" to price his portfolio.

Such situations are a danger not only to highly sophisticated institutional investors like the ones who bet on Askin Capital's three hedge funds, but to any fund sponsors who invest in specialized corners of the OTC markets. Despite the complexities of Askin's "market neutral" strategy, the crisis that enveloped his funds—an interest rate shift, sparking a turnaround in expectations for mortgages—is all too familiar in the burgeoning CMO market.

Source: Jinny St Goar, *Pension Sponsor,* June 1994.

However, the study of performance and risk of all of these hedge fund indexes yields a strong case for investing in hedge funds:

▶ Hedge funds tend to have a net return (after fees) that is higher than equity markets and bond markets. For example, Exhibit 79-2 reports the average U.S. hedge fund net returns for various indexes over the period January 1996 to September 2002, as calculated by CISDM. The mean annual return for U.S. hedge funds is 10.92 percent based on the HFR Fund Weighted Composite index, compared with 5.86 percent for the S&P 500, and 7.24 percent for the Lehman Brothers government/corporate bond index.

▶ Hedge funds tend to have lower risk (measured by the volatility of return or standard deviation) than equity investments. Their investment strategies appear to provide more stable return than traditional equity investments. This is shown on Exhibit 79-2.

▶ The Sharpe ratio is the reward-to-risk ratio measured as the mean return in excess of the risk-free rate and divided by the standard deviation. Services that follow hedge funds frequently report this metric which may not be appropriate, however, when returns have option-like characteristics as discussed later. Over the period 1996–2002, the Sharpe ratio of hedge funds (represented by all indexes) was higher than that of equity investments and that of bonds (except for the HFR fund of funds index).

▶ The correlation of hedge funds with conventional investments is generally low, though still positive. In periods of bear equity markets, hedge funds tend to produce returns that are positive (or less negative than equity). Note, however, in Exhibit 79-2, that the correlation of major fund indexes with the S&P 500 is still positive and fairly large over the period 1996–2002. Exhibit 79-3 reports the correlations of hedge fund subindexes (including a CTA subindex) with the S&P 500 index and the Lehman Brothers government/corporate bond index over the same 1996–2002 period. Although some correlations with the S&P 500 are low, especially for market-neutral funds (only 0.15), the correlation for equity hedge funds is a fairly large 0.70. The correlations of hedge fund subindexes with the bond markets are low and mostly negative, with the CTA dollar-weighted index being the highest at 0.45.

EXHIBIT 79-2	Net Return and Risk of Hedge Funds and Conventional Investments *January 1996 to September 2002, Annualized*					
	HFR Fund Weighted Composite	HFR Fund of Funds	EACM 100	CSFB/ Tremont	S&P 500	Lehman Government/ Corporate Bond Index
Annualized Return	10.92%	8.29%	9.96%	11.55%	5.86%	7.24%
Standard Deviation	8.59%	7.00%	4.93%	9.34%	17.49%	3.99%
Sharpe Ratio	0.74	0.54	1.10	0.75	0.08	0.68
Correlation with HFR Fund Weighted Composite	1.00	0.91	0.88	0.77	0.73	−0.11
Correlation with HFR Fund of Funds	0.91	1.00	0.94	0.91	0.56	0.04
Correlation with EACM 100	0.88	0.94	1.00	0.88	0.52	0.01
Correlation with CSFB/ Tremont	0.77	0.91	0.88	1.00	0.51	0.13
Correlation with S&P 500	0.73	0.56	0.52	0.51	1.00	−0.04
Correlation with Lehman Government/Corporate Bond Index	−0.11	−0.04	0.01	0.13	−0.04	1.00

Source: CISDM, University of Massachusetts at Amherst, Winter 2002.

EXHIBIT 79-3	Correlation of Hedge Fund Subindexes with S&P 500 Index and Lehman Government/Corporate Bond Index *January 1996 to September 2002*	
Hedge Fund Subindex	Correlation with S&P 500	Correlation with Lehman Government/ Corporate Bond Index
HFR Convertible Arbitrage	0.35	−0.08
HFR Equity Hedged	0.70	−0.08
HFR Fixed Income Arbitrage	−0.13	−0.12
HFR Emerging Markets	0.61	−0.20
HFR Event Driven	0.66	−0.14
HFR Merger Arbitrage	0.52	−0.15
HFR Equity Market Neutral	0.15	0.18
HFR Macro	0.40	0.21
CISDM CTA Dollar Weighted	−0.11	0.45

Source: CISDM, University of Massachusetts at Amherst, Winter 2002.

5.5.2 Talent

The fee structure and flexibility of hedge funds attract talented fund managers. Someone having an outstanding investment idea can apply it in a hedge fund with few constraints. The investment idea can be leveraged to generate high returns for investors and for the manager. So, the search for an attractive hedge fund is based on its track record and also on the perceived talent of the manager to generate superior performance.

5.6 Caveats

Investors should exercise caution when using the historical track record of hedge funds in reaching asset allocation decisions. The hedge fund industry does not adhere to rigorous performance presentation standards. Biases in historical performance data can make it difficult to interpret hedge fund performance; past winners may also not repeat.

5.6.1 Biases

The performance data from hedge fund databases and indexes suffer from serious biases that are listed here. Both performance and risk measures are affected.

► *Self-selection bias:* Hedge fund managers decide themselves whether they want to be included in a database. Managers that have funds with an unimpressive track record will not wish to have that information exposed.

► *Instant history bias:* When a hedge fund enters a database, it brings with it its track record. Because only hedge funds with good track records enter the database, this creates a positive bias in past performance in the database, as stressed by Fung and Hsieh (2002).

► *Survivorship bias: Return:* In the investment industry, unsuccessful funds and managers tend to disappear over time. Only successful ones search for new clients and present their track records. This creates a survivor bias. This problem is acute with hedge funds because they often do not have to comply with performance presentation standards. It is not uncommon to see hedge fund managers present the track records of only their successful funds, omitting those that have been closed. If a fund begins to perform poorly, perhaps even starting to go out of business, it may stop reporting its performance entirely, thus inflating the reported average performance of hedge funds. Hedge fund indexes and databases may only include funds that have survived. Funds with bad performance disappear and are removed from the database that is used by investors to select among existing funds. Some data bases are now available that may be free from survivorship bias as defunct hedge funds are left in the data base; however, funds that simply stop reporting still pose a problem.

► *Survivorship bias: Risk:* Biases also affect risk measures. A similar survivorship bias applies to risk measures. Investors shy away from high risk, as well as from negative returns. Hedge funds that exhibited highly volatile returns in the past tend to disappear. Only strategies that have experienced low volatility in the past survive. So, reported volatility of existing funds will tend to be low. There is no guarantee that the same strategy will also be low risk in the future. Examples abound of hedge funds that were regarded as low risk but lost all of their capital.

► *Smoothed pricing: Infrequently traded assets:* Some assets trade infrequently. This is the case for many alternative assets that are not exchange-traded, such as real estate or private equity. This is also the case for illiquid exchange-traded securities or OTC instruments often used by hedge funds. Because prices used are often not up-to-date market prices, but estimates of fair value, their volatility is reduced (smoothing effect). The infrequent nature of price updates for alternative investments, induces a significant downward bias to the measured risk of the assets. In addition, correlations of alternative investment returns with conventional equity and fixed income returns, and correlations among the alternative investments, are often artificially low simply because of the smoothing effect and the absence of market-observable returns. The bias can be very large,[20] so the true risk is much larger than the reported estimates.

Example 79-9

Biases in Reported Performance

A manager without any expertise has decided to launch five long/**short hedge** funds with some seed money. The investment strategies of the five funds are quite different. Actually, the investment strategy of fund A is just the opposite of that of fund E. After a couple of years, some have performed well and some badly, as could be expected by pure chance. The annualized gross returns on the five funds are listed in the following table. All have an annualized standard deviation of 10 percent and the annual risk-free rate is 3 percent. The manager decides to close funds A, B, and C and to enter funds D and E in a well-known hedge fund database. The marketing pitch of the manager is that the funds have superior performance (Sharpe ratio of 1.7 and 2.7). What do you think?

Fund Name	Mean Annual Return	Standard Deviation	Sharpe Ratio
Fund A	−30%	10%	−3.3
Fund B	−20%	10%	−2.3
Fund C	0%	10%	−0.3
Fund D	+20%	10%	1.7
Fund E	+30%	10%	2.7

SOLUTION

The performance on the funds is purely random. But only the good-performing funds are included in the hedge fund database. The performance reported for a selection of funds is misleading. There is obvious survivorship and self-selection bias. Similarly, the performance of the hedge fund index is biased upward and misleading.

---

[20] See, for example, Asness, Krail, and Liew (2001).

▶ *Option-like investment strategies:* Traditional risk measures used in performance appraisal assume that portfolio returns are drawn from normal or, at least symmetric, distributions. Many investment strategies followed by hedge funds have some option-like features that violate these distributional assumptions. For example, hedge funds following so-called arbitrage strategies will generally make a small profit when asset prices converge to their estimated fair value, but they run the risk of a huge loss if their arbitrage model fails. Standard deviation or traditional value at risk (VaR) measures understate the true risk of losses, and the Sharpe ratio can be an inappropriate performance measure.

▶ *Fee structure and gaming:* It is also important to remember the high fees charged by hedge funds: Typically a fixed fee of 1 percent plus an incentive fee of 20 percent of the total return, if positive. This compensation structure is option-like. Clearly, fund managers are paid to take risks. One can argue that they have strong incentives to take a huge amount of risk if their recent performance has been bad. However, one can also argue that because of the high water mark provision, hedge fund managers may not want to ruin their chance to stage a comeback by taking more risk as their performance diminishes. In either case, past risk measures may be misleading for forecasting future performance and risk for a fund that has performed badly in the recent past.

5.6.2 *Persistence of Performance*

Because of various biases, judging the average performance of the hedge fund industry by using the indexes discussed can be difficult. To appraise individual hedge funds, investors should look at their persistence of performance. Before a specific hedge fund is purchased, investors should judge whether their good track record will persist in the future. A similar attitude must be adopted when considering an FOF.[21]

Talented hedge fund managers can exploit market inefficiencies that cannot be exploited by conventional asset managers and/or design innovative investment strategies that may yield excellent returns. But, again, two caveats are in order. First, the size of the hedge fund industry is huge (some $600 billion by the end of 2001), and the leverage used means that the industry is a very large player in capital markets. But the existence of pricing inefficiencies, for which many managers search, is necessarily limited. Thus there is a very large pool of capital chasing after what is likely to be a limited supply of pricing inefficiencies. Second, any successful strategy will quickly be imitated by many other investors, thereby reducing its future profitability.

To summarize, investors need to exercise great caution in interpreting the reported performance of hedge funds; the risks in hedge fund investments are easily underestimated.

---

[21] In a study that may come as a surprise to proponents of hedge funds, Brown, Goetzmann, and Ibbotson (1999) found "no evidence of performance persistence in raw returns or risk-adjusted returns, even when we break funds down according to their returns-based style classification." They conclude that "the hedge fund arena provides no evidence that past performance forecasts future performance." It's important to note, however, that this study covers a relatively short time period and that determining accurate and comparable performance figures in the hedge fund arena is extremely complex.

CLOSELY HELD COMPANIES AND INACTIVELY TRADED SECURITIES

6

Investments in closely held companies and inactively traded securities require analysis of legal, financial, and ownership considerations with account taken of the effects of illiquidity. Closely held companies are those that are not publicly traded. Inactively traded securities are securities of companies that are infrequently traded; they generally do not trade on major exchanges. Illiquidity, limited information availability, and minority ownership issues are common to such companies.

6.1 Legal Environment

Closely held companies may be organized in various legal forms, such as special tax-advantaged corporations (subchapter S corporations in the United States), regular corporations, general partnerships, limited partnerships, and sole proprietorships. These forms have tax implications, as well as ownership differences, for the investor. Ownership is a bundle of rights, and these rights differ, depending on the business form. Because valuations can be required to provide evidence in litigation—for example, minority shareholder claims—much case law defines terms such as *intrinsic value, fundamental value,* and *fair value.* These definitions may vary in different jurisdictions. Even what is judged as evidence for a valuation can vary. There has long been a tension between the theory of value as based on projected cash flows and the acceptance of the *hard* evidence of recent cash flows. In a real sense, then, valuation of closely held and inactively traded securities requires extensive knowledge of the law and the purposes of the valuation.[22]

6.2 Valuation Alternatives

The basic types of valuation are the cost approach, the comparables approach, and the income approach.

6.2.1 The Cost Approach

This approach attempts to determine what it would cost to replace the company's assets in their present form.

6.2.2 The Comparables Approach

In the company comparison approach, market value is estimated relative to a benchmark value. The benchmark value may be the market price of a similar but actively traded company, or the average or median value of the market prices of similar companies, in transactions made near the time of the appraisal. The benchmark-based estimate needs to be adjusted for changing market conditions, the possibility that the benchmark itself is mispriced, and the unique features of the company relative to the benchmark. Companies with comparable characteristics might not have traded recently.

---

[22] See Pratt, Reilly, and Schweihs (1996) for an extensive treatment of the analysis and appraisal of closely held companies.

6.2.3 *The Income Approach*

For business valuation, Pratt, Reilly, and Schweihs (1996) essentially define the income approach as one of appropriately discounting any anticipated future economic income stream.

6.3 Bases for Discounts/Premiums

Because closely held companies and inactively traded securities are illiquid, some discount must be made for that illiquidity. For infrequently traded stocks, share prices should reflect a liquidity discount compensating investors for illiquidity in the market for the shares. Shares of closely held companies lack a public market (lack marketability) and so their valuation should reflect a marketability discount to account for the extra return investors should require on those shares. In addition to a discount for lack of marketability for a closely held company, the analyst may also need to apply a discount for minority interest, or a premium for control. The minority interest discount is applied if the interest will not be able to influence corporate strategy and other business decisions. To estimate a marketability discount, minority discount, or control premium, the analyst must carefully define the amount or base to which the discount or premium should be applied.

To estimate a marketability discount for a closely held company, the analyst identifies a publicly traded comparable company with a liquid market. The comparable's market value of equity is the base to which the marketability discount is applied.

To estimate a minority interest discount for a company, the base is an estimate of that company's value of equity inclusive of the value arising from ownership of all rights of control. To estimate a control premium, the base is an estimate of that company's value of equity not reflecting control (the value of equity from a minority shareholder perspective).

7   DISTRESSED SECURITIES/BANKRUPTCIES

Distressed securities are securities of companies that have filed or are close to filing for bankruptcy court protection, or that are seeking out-of-court debt restructuring to avoid bankruptcy.[23] The legal framework of bankruptcy proceedings differs across countries. In the United States, two types of bankruptcy protection are available: protection for liquidation (called Chapter 7) and protection for reorganization (called Chapter 11). Valuation of such securities requires legal, operational, and financial analysis.

To understand distressed securities, one must appreciate the inherent divergence of interests between the stockholders and bondholders of a company. Stockholders own the successful company, but bondholders have a prior claim to the assets of the bankrupt company. In reorganizations, bondholders' prior claim can allow them to negotiate for ownership in the postbankruptcy company, thus diluting the original shareholders' claims. Investing in distressed securities, then, usually means investing in distressed company bonds with a view toward equity ownership in the eventually reconstituted company. In this regard, such investments have characteristics somewhat similar to those of venture capital investing. For example, they are illiquid and require a long horizon, as well as intense investor participation in guiding the venture to a successful outcome.

[23] See Tremont Advisers, 2002.

Another similarity, though, is the possibility of mispricing. Hooke (1998) reports on the disappointment of some traditional distressed-securities investors that these investments are attracting attention and efficient prices; but he suggests that business volatility and high leverage will guarantee many problem companies with inevitable value discrepancies (mispricing).

Distressed-security investing may be viewed as the ultimate in value investing. A distressed company with low enterprise value (EV) to earnings before interest, taxes, depreciation, and amortization (EBITDA) will attract the attention of an investor looking for positive, postrestructuring cash flows. The primary question for any distressed security is the question of the distress source. Is the company operationally sound but financially hampered by too much gearing (leverage), or is the company weak operationally? If the company is weak operationally, is it a candidate to be turned around by cost cutting and improvement in the business cycle or else by new management and/or a new competitive strategy? Distressed-security investing requires intense industry analysis, as well as analysis of business strategies and of the management team that will conduct the restructuring.

COMMODITY MARKETS AND COMMODITY DERIVATIVES

8

Commodities present an unusual investment alternative. Investing in commodities complements the investment opportunities offered by shares of corporations that extensively use those commodities in their production process. Investing directly in agricultural products and other commodities gives the investor a share in the commodity components of the country's production and consumption. Money managers and average investors, however, usually prefer commodity derivatives (financial instruments that derive their value from the value of the underlying commodity) rather than commodities themselves. The average investor does not want to store grains, cattle, crude oil, or metals. A common investment objective is to purchase indirectly those real assets that should provide a good hedge against inflation risk. There are several indirect ways to invest in commodities:

▶ Futures contracts: A commodity futures contract is a standardized, exchange-traded agreement between two parties in which the buyer agrees to buy a commodity from the seller at a future date at a price agreed upon today.

▶ Bonds indexed on some commodity price.

▶ Stocks of companies producing the commodity.

CONCEPTS IN ACTION UAL Strategy Chief Outlines Plans

Competitive costs, services for range of customers will form basis of revival

The business plan that UAL Corp.'s United Airlines hopes will be the foundation for its emergence from bankruptcy-court protection features competitive costs and a suite of discrete air-service products designed to make the airline "relevant" to as many customers as possible.

In a message to employees, Doug Hacker, UAL's new executive vice president of strategy, said the company intends to develop a "mainline" jet service that has the lowest costs among its peers. United will court international travelers through increased reliance on its airline partners in the Star Alliance, he said.

To serve small domestic cities, United intends to continue to build up small-jet flights offered by its regional affiliates. And to cater to leisure fliers, it expects to operate a separate airline that offers "a low-cost, no-frills" product in markets dominated by leisure customers and low-cost competition, Mr. Hacker said.

Lenders set conditions

UAL, the world's second-largest carrier, filed for protection from its creditors Monday in U.S. Bankruptcy Court in Chicago. As part of its filing, the company said it arranged $1.5 billion in interim financing to help it operate while under court protection. The lenders, who next week will extend an initial $800 million of that funding, insist that the airline meet strict financial benchmarks if it is to receive the balance.

Mr. Hacker, who served for several years as UAL's chief financial officer before leaving to head a United subsidiary, on Wednesday was named to the new post as strategy chief. Yesterday, he presented an overview of United's business plan to leaders of the carrier's union. In a telephone message to employees, he noted that the terms of the interim bankruptcy financing require lower labor costs "under very tight time frames."

In discussions with union leaders yesterday, it wasn't clear whether the company spelled out specific savings targets. A United spokesman last night declined to discuss details on the business plan or the savings targets.

Possible low-fare product

"We want to make the United brand relevant to as many customers as we can," Mr. Hacker told employees. "We'll do that through a family of products that meets customers' different needs."

Glenn Tilton, UAL's chairman and chief executive, has hinted in recent days that United would revive a product similar to its low-fare shuttle service that operated in the Western U.S. in the late 1990s to help the carrier fight off competition from Southwest Airlines. Mr. Tilton also hinted in employee meetings the past few days in the airline's hubs that UAL may seek government aid to facilitate its exit from Chapter 11.

The Air Transportation Stabilization Board, whose refusal to grant government-loan backing forced the airline into bankruptcy, has indicated it would consider a revised application from United for loan guarantees to back up financing to help the airline emerge from reorganization.

Source: Susan Carey, *The Wall Street Journal,* 13 December 2002, p. A2.

Investing in commodity futures is the most common strategy. Commodity trading advisers (CTAs) offer *managed futures funds* that take positions in exchange-traded derivatives on commodities and financials.[24]

8.1 Commodity Futures

Futures contracts are the easiest and cheapest way to invest in commodities. Commodities can be grouped into three major categories:

▶ *Agricultural products,* including fibers (wool, cotton), grains (wheat, corn, soybeans), food (coffee, cocoa, orange juice), and livestock (cattle, hogs, pork bellies). These are often called soft commodities by professionals.

▶ *Energy,* including crude oil, heating oil, and natural gas

▶ *Metals,* such as copper, aluminum, gold, silver, and platinum

Numerous commodity indexes have been developed. Some traditional indexes are broadly based, with a global economic perspective; they aim to track the evolution of input prices. Other indexes have been developed as *investable*

---

[24] See Jaeger (2002) p. 18.

indexes. They are based on the most liquid commodity futures contracts, so they can easily be replicated by taking positions in individual commodities. For example, the Goldman Sachs Commodity Index (GSCI) is a world-production weighted index of 26 commodities with liquid futures contracts. Futures contracts on the GSCI trade in Chicago. The composition and weights of the various commodity indexes differ widely, and so do their performances.

8.2 Motivation and Investment Vehicles

Commodities are sometimes treated as an asset class because they represent a direct participation in the real economy. The motivation for investing in commodities ranges from the diversification benefits achievable by a passive investor to the speculative profits sought by an *active* investor. The design of the investment vehicle used reflects these different motivations.

8.2.1 Passive Investment

A passive investor would buy commodities for their risk-diversification benefits. When inflation accelerates, commodity prices go up, whereas bond and stock prices tend to go down. A passive investor would typically invest through a collateralized position in a futures contract. Many banks and money managers offer collateralized futures funds based on one of the investable commodity indexes. A collateralized position in futures is a portfolio in which an investor takes a long position in futures for a given amount of underlying value and simultaneously invests the same amount in government securities, such as Treasury bills. The various investable indexes and collateralized futures indexes are published both in excess-return and in total-return form. The indexes reported assume that the *total return* on the index is continuously reinvested. The *excess return* is the return above the risk-free rate. The total return is the risk-free rate plus the excess return.

Example 79-10

Collateralized Futures

Assume that the futures price is currently $100. If $100 million is added to the fund, the manager will take a long position in the futures contract for $100 million of underlying value and simultaneously buy $100 million worth of Treasury bills (part of this will be deposited as margin). If the futures price drops to $95 the next day, the futures position will be marked to market, and the manager will have to sell $5 million of the Treasury bills to cover the loss. Conversely, if the futures price rises to $105, the manager will receive a marked-to-market profit of $5 million, which will be invested in additional Treasury bills. Discuss the sources of total return from such an investment.

SOLUTION

The total return on the collateralized futures position comes from the change in futures price and the interest income on the Treasury bills.

Generally, the volatility of commodity futures is higher than that of domestic or international equity, but commodities have a negative correlation with stock and bond returns and a desirable positive correlation with inflation. Nevertheless, the excellent long-term performance of some commodity indexes requires a word of caution. The commodities and weights selected to enter indexes reflect a selection bias when they include data from time periods prior to the initiation of the index, which biases any back-calculated performance.

8.3 Active Investment

Besides making inflation bets, another motivation for investing in commodities is that they provide good performance in periods of economic growth. In periods of rapid economic growth, commodities are in strong demand to satisfy production needs, and their prices go up. Because of productivity gains, the prices of finished goods are unlikely to rise as fast as those of raw materials. This suggests an active management strategy in which specific commodities are bought and sold at various times. Managed futures are proposed by a large number of institutions.

As with any investments, the return–risk characteristics of managed futures must be analyzed carefully. Schneeweis (2002) discusses the proposed attraction of managed futures: the possibility of positive returns in months when the market does well and in the months when it does poorly. Jaeger (2002) proposes several principles for the risk management of managed futures portfolios:

▶ Diversification

▶ Liquidity monitoring, because diversification into a larger universe of contracts can include illiquid contracts

▶ Volatility dependent allocation where the weight of the different contracts in the portfolio is determined by their historical or implied volatility

▶ Quantitative risk management techniques such as value at risk (VaR) and stress tests

▶ Risk budgeting on various aggregation levels to detect undesired risk concentrations

▶ Limits on leverage

▶ Use of derivatives to hedge any unwanted currency risk

▶ Care in model selection with respect to data mining, in and out of sample performance, and adequate performance adjustments for risk

8.4 The Example of Gold

Gold has always played a special role in investments. It is a commodity traded worldwide, but more important, it has been regarded by many Europeans and Asians as the ultimate store of value. It is considered an international monetary asset that offers protection in case of a major disruption. Furthermore, central banks and most non-U.S. investors regard gold as a monetary asset because it has been the core of domestic and international monetary systems for many centuries. This section focuses on gold investment because of the historical importance of gold in investment strategies, and as an example of a real asset investment. Of course, precious stones, stamps, or paintings could also be profitable long-term investments, but they usually require high transaction costs; moreover, each stone or painting is in a sense unique, which reduces its marketability. Gold is offered in a wide variety of investment vehicles that can be used in passive or active strategies. Gold-linked investments include gold bullion, coins, bonds, mining equity, futures, and options on gold and on mining equity or bonds.

8.4.1 The Motivation for Investing In Gold

The traditional role of gold as the ultimate hedge and store of value is well known. For centuries, Europeans and Asians alike have regarded gold as the best possible protection against inflation and social, political, or economic crises because it can easily be traded worldwide at any time, and its real value increases during crises. Europeans and others who have suffered revolutions, invasions, and periods of hyperinflation need no correlation coefficients to be convinced of this attractive portfolio hedge characteristic. For example, gold kept its real value during the U.S. stock market crash from 1929 to 1932 and the London Stock Exchange collapse in equity and bonds from 1973 to 1975. Furthermore, the central role gold has played in domestic and international monetary systems for thousands of years makes it, in part, a monetary asset with exceptional liquidity. Other real assets, such as diamonds or stamps, do not have this characteristic.

In general, gold often allows investors to diversify against the kinds of risks that affect all stock markets simultaneously. For example, in 1973 and 1974, the price of bullion tripled when stock markets worldwide dropped dramatically during the oil crisis; the NYSE dropped approximately 50 percent.

A theoretical comment is in order here. In modern portfolio theory, a small or negative beta implies that the expected return on gold should be small. For example, a negative beta caused by a negative correlation between gold and the market portfolio implies that in the capital asset pricing model (CAPM) framework, the expected return on gold should be less than the risk-free interest rate. Indeed, it can be claimed that we should expect a modest long-term performance in gold and a greater return on the other assets in the portfolio; however, gold assets will reduce the risk of the portfolio in the event of adverse economic conditions. The question for a prudent portfolio manager, then, is whether these hedge benefits are worth the implicit cost she must pay in the form of a smaller expected long-term return for a small part of the portfolio.

8.4.2 Gold Price Determinants

The following material is intended to indicate the kind of information and methods that analysts and investment managers use to analyze real asset investments. Commodities other than gold could also serve as examples.

Gold is a tangible international asset in limited supply. Gold can be extracted at a cost but cannot be produced artificially. Although gold is immune to the effects of weather, water, and oxygen, it suffers from human habits. The tradition of hiding gold treasures in the ground is consistent with the observation that gold is the ultimate physical store of value during major disruptions such as civil unrest, coup d'état, and war. During World War II, most Europeans dug a hole in their gardens or cellars to hide their gold holdings. Part of this hidden gold is never recovered if the owner dies. Most of the gold used in dentistry also disappears with the owner. Despite these losses, the stock of gold keeps slowly increasing with the amount extracted.

In a sense, the price of gold should be easy to forecast: The product is well defined. The supply sources are well identified, and reserves can be reasonably estimated. The major demands are clearly identified: carat jewelry, industrial needs, coins, and investment.

Supply and demand clearly determine the price of gold. It is therefore necessary to study the various components of supply and demand to forecast the price of gold. A different model may be required for each component. For example, Western mine production is affected by technological considerations, South African extraction policy, and political situations in sensitive countries. Russia's gold sales depend on their need for hard currencies. Official sales may also be induced by monetary and balance of payments problems. Industrial demand depends on technological innovation and the discovery of cheaper substitutes. Jewelry demand is sensitive to short-term gold price movements, as well as fashion; the investment motivation is often present in jewelry purchases. Investment demand for bullion and coins is a component of the total demand affecting gold price but is also determined by expectations of future price movements.

So, although gold is a single, well-identified, extensively researched product, its analysis and valuation is not a simple exercise. This difficulty may add another dimension to gold's mystical attraction.

8.5 Commodity-Linked Securities

Holding commodities provides no income, so the sole return to the owner is through price increase. Investors can also select securities that are linked to some commodity prices and also provide some income. This can be an attractive alternative for investors who wish to, or must, hold financial investments rather than real assets. The two major types of commodity-linked securities are bonds and equity. The indexation clause is explicit for commodity-linked bonds but implicit for equity. Again, we focus on the example of gold.

8.5.1 Commodity-Linked Bonds

There are many examples of commodity-linked bonds in the world capital markets.[25] In periods of high inflation, governments have often been forced to offer loans with coupons or principal indexed to either the price of a specific good or a global inflation index. Inflation-indexed gilts became popular in the United Kingdom during the 1980s. The capital and coupons of these bonds are indexed to British retail prices.

In 1997, the U.S. Treasury started to offer Inflation-Indexed Securities, also known as Treasury Inflation Protected Securities (TIPS).[26] The first such security was a 10-year bond, issued with a real yield of 3.45 percent. The principal value is adjusted for changes in the consumer price index (CPI) on each semiannual coupon payment date. So, the nominal coupon, equal to the real yield times the CPI-adjusted principal, increases with inflation. At maturity, the CPI-adjusted principal is reimbursed. In the United States, some government agencies, municipalities, and corporations have also issued inflation-indexed bonds. Often, the inflation adjustment to the principal is paid out immediately rather than at final maturity. This structure has been adopted because seeing their nominal credit exposure on non-government issues accumulate automatically over time worried investors.

---

[25] Jacquillat and Roll (1979) provide an empirical analysis of the benefits of commodity-linked bonds. Schwartz (1982) provides a theoretical model for an index-linked bond with an option to repay the bond at face value or at an index-linked price. Such a model was tested on a silver-linked bond issued by Sunshine Mining in Brauer and Ravichandran (1986). An interesting analysis of oil-linked securities is provided by Gibson and Schwartz (1990).

[26] McFall Lamm (1998) and Anderson and Moore (1998) provide an analysis of TIPS.

Several countries have issued inflation-indexed bonds, and corporations and governments have issued bonds indexed to a variety of specific prices, such as oil prices. Gold bonds, and bonds with warrants on gold, have been an attractive alternative to holding gold ingots.

8.5.2 Commodity-Linked Equity

The value of some companies is directly affected by commodity prices. This is clearly the case with the so-called *energy companies*. For example, companies in the oil and gas industries are affected by the evolution of oil prices. The link between commodity prices and stock prices is more evident for small, undiversified companies that specialize in one type of activity, for example, oil and gas exploration and production. However, large oil companies tend to be quite diversified across activities and the link between commodity prices and stock prices is weaker. An integrated exploration, production, and refining company will be less affected by oil price increases than a company operating in only one of the industry segments.

Gold mining companies are another example of commodity-linked equity. Gold mining shares differ from commodity-linked bonds in that the indexation clause is not fixed by contract but depends on mining economics. In fact, the mining industry is probably the simplest activity to describe in a valuation model. The economics of mining can be described by a simple discounted cash flow model. The principal relationship in the model is the cost structure of the mine as measured by the ratio of costs to revenues. The cost to remove an ounce or a gram of gold from so-called storage and refine it depends on several factors: technology, wage rates, power rates, and the grade and depth of the mine. Revenues depend on the world price of gold. Any movement in the market price of gold will directly affect the cash flows of a mine and therefore its market value; the higher the ratio of costs to revenues, the more sensitive will be the cash flows to gold price movements. However, note that the correlation between gold mine share prices and the price of gold is far from perfect. Gold mine values are influenced by factors other than gold prices; for example, social and political factors have strongly affected South African share prices over time.

SUMMARY

▶ Alternative investments usually involve illiquidity, difficulty in the determination of current market values, limited historical risk and return data, the requirement for extensive investment analysis, a liquidity risk premium, and a segmentation risk premium. Alternative assets are assets not traded on exchanges. Alternative strategies are strategies that mostly use traded assets for the purpose of isolating bets and generating alpha.

▶ An open-end fund stands ready to redeem investor shares at market value, but a closed-end fund does not. A load fund has sales commission charges, and a **no-load fund** does not. Sales fees may also appear in annual distribution fees.

▶ The net asset value of a fund is calculated as the per-share value of the investment company's assets minus liabilities.

▶ Mutual funds may charge several different fees: Loads and redemption fees provide sales incentives; distribution and operating fees are annual fees; the part of the operating fee that is allocated to the fund manager can be considered an investment performance incentive.

▶ An exchange traded fund (ETF) is a special type of fund that tracks some market index but that is traded on a stock market as any common share.

▶ A mutual fund's purchases and sales of stocks held in the fund lead to taxable gains at the level of the fund, but this is not the case for an ETF because of its in-kind creation and redemption process.

▶ The advantages of ETFs are diversification; trading similarly to a stock; management of their risk augmented by futures and options contracts on them; transparency; cost effectiveness; avoidance of significant premiums or discounts to NAV; tax savings from payment of in-kind redemption; and immediate dividend reinvestment for open-end ETFs. The disadvantages are only a narrow-based market index tracked in some countries; intraday trading opportunity is not important for long-horizon investors; large bid–ask spreads on some ETFs; and possibly better cost structures and tax advantages to direct index investing for large institutions.

▶ Some characteristics of real estate as an investable asset class are that each property is immovable, basically indivisible, and unique; not directly comparable to other properties; illiquid; and bought and sold intermittently in a generally local marketplace, with high transaction costs and market inefficiencies.

▶ The main approaches to real estate valuation are the cost approach, the sales comparison approach, the income approach, and the discounted after-tax cash flow approach.

▶ The net operating income from a real estate investment is gross potential income minus expenses, which include estimated vacancy and collection costs, insurance, taxes, utilities, and repairs and maintenance.

▶ The value of a property can be calculated as the cost to replace the building in its present form in the cost approach; an adjusted value from a benchmark of comparable sales in the sales comparison approach; or a hedonic price estimate from a regression model in the sales comparison approach; and capitalized net operating income in the income approach.

▶ The net present value of a property to an equity investor is obtained as the present value of the after tax cash flows, discounted at the investor's required rate of return on equity, minus the amount of equity required to make the investment.

► Venture capital investing is done in many stages from seed through mezzanine.

► Venture capital investment characteristics include illiquidity; long-term commitment required; difficulty in determining current market values; limited historical risk and return data, limited information; entrepreneurial/ management mismatches; fund manager incentive mismatches; lack of knowledge of how many competitors exist; vintage cycles; and the requirement for extensive operations analysis and advice. The challenges to venture capital performance measurement are the difficulty in determining precise valuations, the lack of meaningful benchmarks, and the long-term nature of any performance feedback.

► The expected net present value of a venture capital project with a single, terminal payoff and a single, initial investment can be calculated, given its possible payoff and its conditional failure probabilities, as the present value of the expected payoff minus the required initial investment.

► The term *hedge fund* is not fully descriptive, because the hedged position is generally designed to isolate a bet rather than to reduce risk. Hedge funds can be defined as funds that seek absolute returns; have a legal structure avoiding some government regulations; and have option-like fees, including a base management fee and an incentive fee proportional to realized profits.

► The net performance of a hedge fund can be calculated by subtracting its fees from its gross performance.

► Hedge funds can be classified in a variety of ways. One classification of hedge funds comprises the categories: long/short, market neutral, global macro, and event driven.

► The advantages of fund of funds investing are availability to the small investor, access to funds closed to new investors, diversification, managerial expertise, and a due diligence process. The disadvantages to fund of funds investing are high fees, little evidence of persistent performance, and the absolute return loss through diversification.

► High leverage is often present in hedge funds as part of the trading strategy and is an essential part of some strategies in which the arbitrage return is so small that leverage is needed to amplify the profit. The unique risks of hedge funds are liquidity risk, pricing risk, counterparty credit risk, settlement risk, short squeeze risk, and financing squeeze risk.

► In terms of performance, hedge funds are generally viewed as having a net return higher than available for equity or bond investments, lower standard deviation of return than equity investments, a Sharpe ratio that is comparable to bonds and higher than that of equity investments, and a low correlation with conventional investments. The biases present in hedge fund performance reporting include self-selection bias, instant history bias, survivorship bias on return, survivorship bias on risk, smoothed pricing on infrequently traded assets, option-like investment strategies, and fee structure–induced gaming.

► For closely held companies and inactively traded securities, a discount is used for lack of liquidity, lack of marketability, and for a minority interest, but a control premium is added for controlling ownership. The base for the marketability discount is the market value of equity for a comparable publicly traded company.

► Distressed-securities investing usually means investing in distressed company bonds with a view to equity ownership in the eventually reconstituted company. Such investments are similar to venture capital investments because they are illiquid; they require a long investment horizon; they require intense investor participation/consulting; and they offer the possibility of alpha because of mispricing.

▶ As a vehicle for investing in production and consumption, commodities complement the investment opportunities offered by shares of corporations that extensively use these as raw materials in their production processes. Investing directly in agricultural products and other commodities gives the investor exposure to the commodity components of the country's production and consumption.

▶ Commodity trading advisors (CTAs) offer managed futures funds that take positions in exchange traded derivatives on commodities and financials.

▶ The return on a collateralized futures position comes from the change in the futures price plus the interest income on risk-free government securities.

▶ The motivation for investing in commodities, commodity derivatives, and commodity-linked securities is that they may have negative correlation with stock and bond returns and a desirable positive correlation with inflation. In the case of commodity-linked securities, the investor can receive some income rather than depending solely on commodity price changes.

▶ The risk of managed futures can be managed through diversification, liquidity monitoring, volatility dependent allocation, quantitative techniques such as VaR, risk budgeting on various aggregation levels, limits on leverage, use of derivatives, and care in model selection.

PROBLEMS FOR READING 79

Use the following information for Problems 1 and 2. Global Leveraged Equity Fund (GLEF) has three classes of shares, each holding the same portfolio of securities but having a different expense structure. The following table summarizes the expenses of these classes of shares.

Expense Comparison for Four Classes of GLEF

	Class A	Class B*	Class C
Sales charge (load) on purchases	5%	None	None
Deferred sales charge (load) on redemptions	None	4% in the first year, declining by 1% each year thereafter	1% for the initial 2 years only
Annual expenses:			
Distribution fee	0.25%	0.50%	0.50%
Management fee	0.50%	0.50%	0.50%
Other expenses	0.50%	0.50%	0.50%
	1.25%	1.50%	1.50%

*Class B shares automatically convert to Class A shares 72 months (6 years) after purchase.

Assume that expense percentages given will be constant at the given values. Assume that the deferred sales charges are computed on the basis of NAV.

An investor is considering the purchase of GLEF shares. The investor expects equity investments with risk characteristics similar to GLEF to earn 9 percent per year. He decides to make his selection of fund share class based on an assumed 9 percent return each year, gross of any of the expenses given in the preceding table.

1. Decide which class of shares of GLEF is best for the investor if he plans to liquidate his investment toward the end of
   A. Year 1
   B. Year 3
   C. Year 5
   D. Year 15

2. You have analyzed the relative performance of different classes of GLEF shares for liquidation in several years. Specifically, you have looked at liquidation in years 1, 3, 5, and 15. Your results are as follows. (The > symbol implies that the class preceding the sign performs better than the class following and the = symbol implies equal performance of the two classes.)

   ▶ Liquidation in year 1: Class C > Class B > Class A
   ▶ Liquidation in year 3: Class C > Class B > Class A
   ▶ Liquidation in year 5: Class B = Class C > Class A
   ▶ Liquidation in year 15: Class B > Class C > Class A

Provide an intuitive explanation for the pattern of relative performance that you observe.

3. Using the price data for several houses recently sold in a particular area, a real estate firm has identified the main characteristics that affect the prices of houses in that area. The characteristics identified include the living area, the number of bathrooms, whether the house has a fireplace, and how old the house is. The estimated slope coefficient for each of these characteristics and the constant term are as follows:

Characteristic	Units	Coefficient in Euros per Unit
Intercept	—	140,000
Living area	Square meters	210
Number of bathrooms	Number	10,000
Fireplace	0 or 1	15,000
Age of the house	Years	−6,000

Use these above estimates to value a five-year-old house with a living area of 500 square meters, three bathrooms, and a fireplace.

4. A real estate firm is evaluating an office building, using the income approach. The real estate firm has compiled the following information for the office building. All information is on an annual basis.

Gross potential rental income	$350,000
Estimated vacancy and collection losses*	4%
Insurance and taxes	$26,000
Utilities	$18,000
Repairs and maintenance	$23,000
Depreciation	$40,000
Interest on proposed financing	$18,000

*As a percentage of gross potential rental income

There have been two recent sales of office buildings in the area. The first building had a net operating income of $500,000 and was sold at $4 million. The second building had a net operating income of $225,000 and was sold at $1.6 million.

A. Compute the net operating income for the office building to be valued.

B. Use the income approach to compute the appraisal price of the office building.

5. An analyst is evaluating a real estate investment project using the discounted cash flow approach. The purchase price is $3 million, which is financed 15 percent by equity and 85 percent by a mortgage loan. It is expected that the property will be sold in five years. The analyst has estimated the following after-tax cash flows during the first four years of the five-year life of the real estate investment project.

Year	1	2	3	4
Cash flow	$60,000	$75,000	$91,000	$108,000

For the fifth year, that is, the year when the property would be sold by the investor, the after-tax cash flow without the property sale is estimated to be $126,000 and the after-tax cash flow from the property sale is estimated to be $710,000.

Compute the NPV of this project. State whether the investor should undertake the project. The investor's cost of equity for projects with level of risk comparable to this real estate investment project is 18 percent.

6. An investment firm is evaluating a real estate investment project, using the discounted cash flow approach. The purchase price is $1.5 million, which is financed 20 percent by equity and 80 percent by a mortgage loan at a 9 percent pre-tax interest rate. The mortgage loan has a long maturity and constant annual payments of $120,000. This includes interest payments on the remaining principal at a 9 percent interest rate and a variable principal repayment that steps up with time. The net operating income (NOI) in the first year is estimated to be $170,000. NOI is expected to grow at a rate of 4 percent every year. The interest on real estate financing for the project is tax deductible. The marginal income tax rate for the investment firm is 30 percent. Using straight-line depreciation, the annual depreciation of the property is $37,500.

A. Compute the after-tax cash flows in years 1, 2, and 3 of the project.

B. It is expected that the property will be sold at the end of three years. The projected sale price is $1.72 million. The property's sales expenses are 6.5 percent of the sale price. The capital gains tax rate is 20 percent. Compute the after-tax cash flow from the property sale in year 3.

C. The investor's cost of equity for projects with level of risk comparable to this real estate investment project is 19 percent. Recommend whether to invest in the project or not, based on the NPV of the project.

7. Would you suggest using real estate appraisal-based indexes in a global portfolio optimization?

8. Suppose the estimated correlation matrix of the Wilshire 5000 U.S. stock index and two real estate indexes, the Federal Russell Company index (FRC) and the National Association of Real Estate Investment Trusts (NAREIT) is as follows:

	Wilshire 5000	NAREIT	FRC
Wilshire 5000	1.00	0.79	0.18
NAREIT	0.79	1.00	0.02
FRC	0.18	0.02	1.00

Based on this above matrix, compare the expected price behavior of the two real estate indexes.

9. An investor is evaluating a venture capital project that will require an investment of $1.4 million. The investor estimates that she will be able to exit the venture successfully in eight years. She also estimates that there is an 80 percent chance that the venture will not survive until the end of the eighth year.

If the venture does survive until then, she expects to exit the project then, and it is equally likely that the payoff at the time of exit will be either $25 million or $35 million. The investor is considering an equity investment in the project, and her cost of equity for a project with similar risk is 20 percent.

A. Compute the net present value of the venture capital project.

B. Recommend whether to accept or reject the project.

10. VenCap, Inc. is a venture capital financier. It estimates that investing €4.5 million in a particular venture capital project can return €60 million at the end of six years if it succeeds; however, it realizes that the project may fail at any time between now and the end of six years. The following table has VenCap's estimates of probabilities of failure for the project. First, 0.28 is the probability of failure in year 1. The probability that the project fails in the second year, given that it has survived through year 1, is 0.25. The probability that the project fails in the third year, given that it has survived through year 2, is 0.22; and so forth. VenCap is considering an equity investment in the project, and its cost of equity for a project with this level of risk is 22 percent.

Year	1	2	3	4	5	6
Failure probability	0.28	0.25	0.22	0.18	0.18	0.10

Compute the expected net present value of the venture capital project and recommend whether VenCap should accept or reject the project.

11. Consider a hedge fund that has an annual fee structure of 1.5 percent base management fee plus a 15 percent incentive fee applied to profits above the risk-free rate. If the risk-free rate is 5.5 percent, compute the net percentage return for an investor if the gross return during the year is

A. 35%

B. 5%

C. −6%

12. A hedge fund currently has assets of $2 billion. The annual fee structure of this fund consists of a fixed fee of 1 percent of portfolio assets plus a 20 percent incentive fee. The fund applies the incentive fee to the gross return each year in excess of the portfolio's previous high watermark, which is the maximum portfolio value since the inception of the fund. The maximum value the fund has achieved so far since its inception was a little more than a year ago when its value was $2.1 billion. Compute the fee that the manager would earn in dollars if the return on the fund this year turns out to be

A. 29%

B. 4.5%

C. −1.8%

13. Consider a hedge fund whose annual fee structure has a fixed fee and an incentive fee with a high watermark provision. The fund manager earns an incentive fee only if the fund is above the high watermark of the maximum portfolio value since the inception of the fund. Discuss the positive and negative implications of the high watermark provision for the investors of the hedge fund.

14. The shares of an Italian firm have been trading earlier around €6. Recently, a Spanish firm entered into talks with the Italian firm to acquire it. The Spanish firm offered two of its shares for every three shares of the Italian firm. The boards of directors of both firms have approved the merger, and ratification by shareholders is expected soon. The shares of the Spanish firm are currently trading at €12.50, and the shares of the Italian firm are trading at €8.

A. Should the shares of the Italian firm trade at a discount? Explain.

B. What position do you think a hedge fund that specializes in risk arbitrage in mergers and acquisitions will take in the two firms? Assume that the hedge fund's position will involve 250,000 shares of the Italian firm.

C. It turns out that the European Union commission does not approve the merger because it fears that the merged firm will have a monopolistic position in its industry. After this announcement, the shares of the Italian firm fell to €6.10 each. The shares of the Spanish firm are still trading at €12.50 each. Discuss the consequences for the hedge fund. Ignore the cost of securities lending and margins deposit.

15. Global group manages hedge funds, and has three hedge funds invested in the stock market of a particular emerging country. These three hedge funds have very different investment strategies. As expected, the 2000 returns on the three funds were quite different. Over the year 2000, an index based on the overall stock market of the emerging country went up by 20 percent. Here are the performances of the three funds before management fees set at 15 percent of gross profits:

Fund	Gross Return
A	50%
B	20%
C	−10%

At year end, most clients had left fund C, and Global group closed this fund. At the start of 2001, Global group launched an aggressive publicity campaign among portfolio managers, stressing the remarkable return on fund A. If potential clients asked whether the firm had other hedge funds invested in the particular emerging market, it mentioned the only other fund, fund B, and claimed that the group's average gross performance during 2000 was 35 percent.

A. Compare the average gross return and the average net return on the three hedge funds with the percentage increase in the stock market index.

B. Comment on the publicity campaign launched by Global group.

16. An analyst is examining the performance of hedge funds. He looks at the 90 hedge funds that are in existence today, and notes that the average annual return on these funds during the last 10 years is 25.17 percent. The standard deviation of these returns is 17.43 percent and the Sharpe ratio is 1.15. The analyst also observes that the average of the annual returns on a stock market index during the last 10 years is 14.83 percent. The standard deviation of these returns is 11.87 percent and the Sharpe ratio is 0.81. The analyst concludes that the hedge funds have substantially outperformed the stock market index. Discuss why the comparison by the analyst could be misleading.

17. Consider the four major commodities traded on a commodity futures exchange today (year 10). The following table lists the average annualized price movements from year 1 to year 10, as well as the production volumes, expressed in the local currency unit, today (year 10) and ten years ago (year 1).

Commodity	Average Return	Annual Production Year 1	Annual Production Year 10
A	20%	10	50
B	20%	5	20
C	−10%	50	10
D	0%	35	20

The futures exchange has now decided to create a commodity index based on the four commodities, with weights equal to their current relative importance in economic production. These indexes are back-calculated till year 1 using today's weights.

A. Would such an index give unbiased indications over the past 10 years?

B. What suggestions do you have regarding weights that can be used to back-calculate the indexes?

18. The beta of gold relative to the market portfolio is −0.3. The risk-free rate is 7 percent, and the market risk premium is 4 percent.

A. What is the expected return on gold based on the capital asset pricing model (CAPM)?

B. Give an intuitive explanation for the magnitude of the expected return on gold.

APPENDIX

Appendix A Solutions to End-of-Reading Problems and Practice Questions

SOLUTIONS FOR READING 73

1. **B.** A call option is not binding on both parties in the same sense that the other financial instruments are. The call option gives the holder a right but does not impose an obligation.

2. **B.** If the market falls, the buyer of a forward contract could pay more for the index, as determined by the price that was contracted for at the inception of the contract, than the index is worth when the contract matures. Although it is possible that a rise in interest rates could cause the market to fall, this might not always happen and thus is a secondary consideration.

3. **D.** Forward contracts are usually private transactions that do not have an intermediary such as a clearinghouse to guarantee performance by both parties. This type of transaction requires a high degree of creditworthiness for both parties.

4. **B.** Forward contracts are usually less liquid than futures contracts because they are typically private transactions tailored to suit both parties, unlike futures contracts, which are usually for standardized amounts and are exchange traded.

5. **A.** A swap is most like a series of forward contracts. An example is a swap in which one party makes a set of fixed-rate payments over time in exchange for a set of floating-rate payments based on some notional amount.

6. **C.** Unlike a contingent claim, a forward commitment typically requires no premium to be paid up front. An intuitive way to look at this is to realize that a forward commitment is binding on both parties, so any up-front fees would cancel, while a contingent claim is binding only on the party in the short position. For this, the party in the short position demands (and receives) compensation.

7. **C.** Because the holder of a contingent claim (the party in the long position) has a right but not an obligation, she will only exercise when it is in her best interest to do so and not otherwise. This will happen only when she stands to gain and never when she stands to lose.

8. **A.** The notional principal is the amount of the underlying asset covered by the derivative contract.

9. **A.** The most widely used derivative contracts are written on underlying assets that are financial, such as Treasury instruments and stock indices.

10. **A.** Arbitrage, or the absence of it, is the basis for pricing most derivative contracts. Consequently, it is relatively unusual, although certainly not impossible, for derivative markets to be used to generate arbitrage profits.

11. **B.** One reason derivative markets have flourished is that they have relatively low transaction costs. For example, buying a risk-free Treasury security and a futures contract on the S&P 500 Index to replicate payoffs to the index is cheaper than buying the 500 stocks in the index in their proper proportions to get the same payoff.

12. **C.** In the absence of arbitrage opportunities, an investor bearing no risk should expect to earn the risk-free rate.

13. **C.** The six-month forward price of gold should be $250 \times [1 + (0.10/2)] = 250 \times (1.05) = \$262.50$.

Analysis of Derivatives for the CFA® Program, by Don M. Chance, Copyright © 2003 by Association for Investment Management and Research. Reprinted with permission.

14. C. Efficient markets are characterized by the absence, or the rapid elimination, of arbitrage opportunities.

15. C. Stock B should be priced at $24.00 today. To see this, imagine selling 2.4 shares of A short for $24.00, and buying one share of B. Now, in the next period, suppose B is worth $30.00. Then selling B permits you to buy 2.4 shares of A (at $12.50 per share) to return the shares sold short. Alternatively, if B is worth $18.00, selling B permits you to still buy 2.4 shares of A (at $7.50) to return them. The same no-profit situation holds if you sell one share of B and buy 2.4 shares of A. An alternative explanation lies in the fact that in each of the two outcomes, the price of B is 2.4 times the price of A. Thus, the price of B today must be 2.4 times the price of A.

SOLUTIONS FOR READING 74

1. **A.** Discount yield $= 0.0174 = \left(\dfrac{10{,}000 - \text{Price}}{10{,}000}\right)\left(\dfrac{360}{153}\right)$

   Price $= \$9{,}926.05$

   B. Discount yield $= \left(\dfrac{10{,}000 - 9{,}950}{10{,}000}\right)\left(\dfrac{360}{69}\right) = 0.0261$

2. $\$20{,}000{,}000\,[1 + 0.0435(60/360)] = \$20{,}145{,}000$

3. **A.** Taking a short position will hedge the interest rate risk for Company A. The gain on the contract will offset the reduced interest rate that can be earned when rates fall.

   B. This is a 3×6 FRA.

   C. $\$15{,}000{,}000\left[\dfrac{(0.045 - 0.05)(90/360)}{1 + 0.045(90/360)}\right] = -\$18{,}541.41$

   The negative sign indicates a gain to the short position, which Company A holds.

4. **A.** These instruments are called off-the-run FRAs.

   B. $\$20{,}000{,}000\left[\dfrac{(0.04 - 0.0475)(137/360)}{1 + 0.04(137/360)}\right] = -\$56{,}227.43$

   Because the party is long, this amount represents a loss.

5. The contract is settled in cash, so the settlement would be €20,000,000(0.875 − 0.90) = −$500,000. This amount would be paid by Sun Microsystems to the dealer. Sun would convert euros to dollars at the spot rate of $0.90, receiving €20,000,000 × (0.90) = $18,000,000. The net cash receipt is $17,500,000, which results in an effective rate of $0.875.

SOLUTIONS FOR READING 75

1. **A.** Parsons would close out his position in April by offsetting his long position with a short position. To do so, he would re-enter the market and offer for sale a June futures contract on the Nasdaq 100 index. When he has a buyer, he has both a long and a short position in the June futures contract on the Nasdaq 100 index. From the point of view of the clearinghouse, he no longer has a position in the contract.

   B. Smith would close out her position in August by offsetting her short position with a long position. To do so, she would re-enter the market and purchase a September futures contract on the S&P 500. She then has both a short and a long position in the September futures contract on the S&P 500. From the point of view of the clearinghouse, she no longer has a position in the contract.

2. The difference between initial and maintenance margin requirements for one gold futures contract is $2,000 − $1,500 = $500. Because one gold futures contract is for 100 troy ounces, the difference between initial and maintenance margin requirements per troy ounce is $500/100, or $5.

   A. Because Evans has a long position, he would receive a maintenance margin call if the price were to *fall* below $320 − $5, or $315 per troy ounce.

   B. Because Tosca has a short position, he would receive a maintenance margin call if the price were to *rise* above $323 + $5, or $328 per troy ounce.

3. *Trader with a long position:* This trader loses if the price falls. The maximum loss would be incurred if the futures price falls to zero, and this loss would be $0.75/lb × 25,000 lbs, or $18,750. Of course, this scenario is only theoretical, not realistic.

   Trader with a short position: This trader loses if the price increases. Because there is no limit on the price increase, there is no theoretical upper limit on the loss that the trader with a short position could incur.

4. **A.** The difference between the initial margin requirement and the maintenance margin requirement is $2. Because the initial futures price was $212, a margin call would be triggered if the price falls below $210.

   B.

Day	Beginning Balance	Funds Deposited	Futures Price	Price Change	Gain/Loss	Ending Balance
0	0	200	212			200
1	200	0	211	−1	−20	180
2	180	0	214	3	60	240
3	240	0	209	−5	−100	140
4	140	60	210	1	20	220
5	220	0	204	−6	−120	100
6	100	100	202	−2	−40	160

On day 0, you deposit $200 because the initial margin requirement is $10 per contract and you go long 20 contracts ($10 per contract times 20 contracts equals $200). At the end of day 3, the balance is down to $140, $20 below the $160 maintenance margin requirement ($8 per contract times 20 contracts). You must deposit enough money to bring the balance up to the initial margin requirement of $200. So, the next day (day 4), you deposit $60. The price change on day 5 causes a gain/loss of −$120, leaving you with a balance of $100 at the end of day 5. Again, this amount is less than the $160 maintenance margin requirement. You must deposit enough money to bring the balance up to the initial margin requirement of $200. So on day 6, you deposit $100.

C. By the end of day 6, the price is $202, a decrease of $10 from your purchase price of $212. Your loss so far is $10 per contract times 20 contracts, or $200.

You could also look at your loss so far as follows. You initially deposited $200, followed by margin calls of $60 and $100. Thus, you have deposited a total of $360 so far and have not withdrawn any excess margin. The ending balance, however, is only $160. Thus, the total loss incurred by you so far is $360 − $160, or $200.

5. A.

Day	Beginning Balance	Funds Deposited	Futures Price	Price Change	Gain/Loss	Ending Balance
0	0	2,700.00	96-06			2,700.00
1	2,700.00	0	96-31	25/32	−781.25	1,918.75
2	1,918.75	781.25	97-22	23/32	−718.75	1,981.25
3	1,981.25	718.75	97-18	−4/32	125.00	2,825.00
4	2,825.00	0	97-24	6/32	−187.50	2,637.50
5	2,637.50	0	98-04	12/32	−375.00	2,262.50
6	2,262.50	0	97-31	−5/32	156.25	2,418.75

On day 0, Moore deposits $2,700 because the initial margin requirement is $2,700 per contract and she has gone short one contract. At the end of day 1, the price has increased from 96-06 to 96-31—that is, the price has increased from $96,187.50 to $96,968.75. Because Moore has taken a short position, this increase of $781.25 is an adverse price movement for her, and the balance is down by $781.25 to $1,918.75. Because this amount is less than the $2,000 maintenance margin requirement, she must deposit additional funds to bring her account back to the initial margin requirement of $2,700. So, the next day (day 2), she deposits $781.25. Another adverse price movement takes place on day 2 as the price further increases by $718.75 to $97,687.50. Her ending balance is again below the maintenance margin requirement of $2,000, and she must deposit enough money to bring her account back to the initial margin requirement of $2,700. So, the next day (day 3), she deposits $718.75. Subsequently, even though her balance falls below the initial margin requirement, it does not go below the maintenance margin requirement, and she does not need to deposit any more funds.

B. Moore bought the contract at a futures price of 96-06. By the end of day 6, the price is 97-31, an increase of 1 25/32. Therefore, her loss so far is 1.78125 percent of $100,000, which is $1,781.25.

You could also look at her loss so far as follows: She initially deposited $2,700, followed by margin calls of $781.25 and $718.75. Thus, she has deposited a total of $4,200 so far, and has not withdrawn any excess margin. Her ending balance is $2,418.75. Thus, the total loss so far is $4,200 − $2,418.75, or $1,781.25.

6. A. Because the IMM index price is 95.23, the annualized LIBOR rate priced into the contract is $100 − 95.23 = 4.77$ percent. With each contract based on $1 million notional principal of 90-day Eurodollars, the actual futures price is $\$1,000,000[1 − 0.0477(90/360)] = \$988,075$.

B. Because the IMM index price is 95.25, the annualized LIBOR rate priced into the contract is $100 − 95.25 = 4.75$ percent. The actual futures price is $\$1,000,000[1 − 0.0475(90/360)] = \$988,125$. So, the change in actual futures price is $\$988,125 − \$988,075 = \$50$.

You could also compute the change in price directly by noting that the IMM index price increased by 2 basis points. Because each basis point move in the rate moves the actual futures price by $25, the increase in the actual futures price is $2 \times \$25$, or $50.

SOLUTIONS FOR READING 76

1. **A.** $S_T = 579.32$
   i. Call payoff, $X = 450$: $\text{Max}(0,579.32 - 450) \times 100 = \$12,932$
   ii. Call payoff, $X = 650$: $\text{Max}(0,579.32 - 650) \times 100 = 0$
   B. $S_T = 579.32$
   i. Put payoff, $X = 450$: $\text{Max}(0,450 - 579.32) \times 100 = 0$
   ii. Put payoff, $X = 650$: $\text{Max}(0,650 - 579.32) \times 100 = \$7,068$

2. **A.** $S_T = \$0.95$
   i. Call payoff, $X = 0.85$: $\text{Max}(0,0.95 - 0.85) \times 100,000 = \$10,000$
   ii. Call payoff, $X = 1.15$: $\text{Max}(0,0.95 - 1.15) \times 100,000 = \$0$
   B. $S_T = \$0.95$
   i. Put payoff, $X = 0.85$: $\text{Max}(0,0.85 - 0.95) \times 100,000 = \$0$
   ii. Put payoff, $X = 1.15$: $\text{Max}(0,1.15 - 0.95) \times 100,000 = \$20,000$

3. **A.** $S_T = 0.0653$
   i. Call payoff, $X = 0.05$: $\text{Max}(0,0.0653 - 0.05) \times (180/360) \times 10,000,000 = \$76,500$
   ii. Call payoff, $X = 0.08$: $\text{Max}(0,0.0653 - 0.08) \times (180/360) \times 10,000,000 = 0$
   B. $S_T = 0.0653$
   i. Put payoff, $X = 0.05$: $\text{Max}(0,0.05 - 0.0653) \times (180/360) \times 10,000,000 = 0$
   ii. Put payoff, $X = 0.08$: $\text{Max}(0,0.08 - 0.0653) \times (180/360) \times 10,000,000 = \$73,500$

4. **A.** $S_T = \$1.438$
   i. Call payoff, $X = 1.35$: $\text{Max}(0,1.438 - 1.35) \times 125,000 = \$11,000$
   ii. Call payoff, $X = 1.55$: $\text{Max}(0,1.438 - 1.55) \times 125,000 = \$0$
   B. $S_T = \$1.438$
   i. Put payoff, $X = 1.35$: $\text{Max}(0,1.35 - 1.438) \times 125,000 = \$0$
   ii. Put payoff, $X = 1.55$: $\text{Max}(0,1.55 - 1.438) \times 125,000 = \$14,000$

5. **A.** $S_T = 1136.76$
   i. Call payoff, $X = 1130$: $\text{Max}(0,1136.76 - 1130) \times 1,000 = \$6,760$
   ii. Call payoff, $X = 1140$: $\text{Max}(0,1136.76 - 1140) \times 1,000 = 0$
   B. $S_T = 1136.76$
   i. Put payoff, $X = 1130$: $\text{Max}(0,1130 - 1136.76) \times 1,000 = 0$
   ii. Put payoff, $X = 1140$: $\text{Max}(0,1140 - 1136.76) \times 1,000 = \$3,240$

6. **A.** $S_0 = 1240.89$, $T = 75/365 = 0.2055$, $X = 1225$ or 1255, call options
   i. $X = 1225$
   Maximum value for the call: $c_0 = S_0 = 1240.89$
   Lower bound for the call: $c_0 = \text{Max}[0,1240.89 - 1225/(1.03)^{0.2055}] = 23.31$
   ii. $X = 1255$
   Maximum value for the call: $c_0 = S_0 = 1240.89$
   Lower bound for the call: $c_0 = \text{Max}[0,1240.89 - 1255/(1.03)^{0.2055}] = 0$
   B. $S_0 = 1240.89$, $T = 75/365 = 0.2055$, $X = 1225$ or 1255, put options
   i. $X = 1225$
   Maximum value for the put: $p_0 = 1225/(1.03)^{0.2055} = 1217.58$
   Lower bound for the put: $p_0 = \text{Max}[0,1225/(1.03)^{0.2055} - 1240.89] = 0$

ii. X = 1255

Maximum value for the put: $p_0 = 1255/(1.03)^{0.2055} = 1247.40$

Lower bound for the put: $p_0 = Max[0,1255/(1.03)^{0.2055} - 1240.89]$
= 6.51

7. A. $S_0 = 1.05$, T = 60/365 = 0.1644, X = 0.95 or 1.10, American-style options

i. X = \$0.95

Maximum value for the call: $C_0 = S_0 = \$1.05$

Lower bound for the call: $C_0 = Max[0,1.05 - 0.95/(1.055)^{0.1644}] = \$0.11$

Maximum value for the put: $P_0 = X = \$0.95$

Lower bound for the put: $P_0 = Max(0,0.95 - 1.05) = \$0$

ii. X = \$1.10

Maximum value for the call: $C_0 = S_0 = \$1.05$

Lower bound for the call: $C_0 = Max[0,1.05 - 1.10/(1.055)^{0.1644}] = \$0$

Maximum value for the put: $P_0 = X = \$1.10$

Lower bound for the put: $P_0 = Max(0,1.10 - 1.05) = \$0.05$

B. $S_0 = 1.05$, T = 60/365 = 0.1644, X = 0.95 or 1.10, European-style options

i. X = \$0.95

Maximum value for the call: $c_0 = S_0 = \$1.05$

Lower bound for the call: $c_0 = Max[0,1.05 - 0.95/(1.055)^{0.1644}] = \$0.11$

Maximum value for the put: $p_0 = 0.95/(1.055)^{0.1644} = \$0.94$

Lower bound for the put: $p_0 = Max[0,0.95/(1.055)^{0.1644} - 1.05] = \$0$

ii. X = \$1.10

Maximum value for the call: $c_0 = S_0 = \$1.05$

Lower bound for the call: $c_0 = Max[0,1.05 - 1.10/(1.055)^{0.1644}] = \$0$

Maximum value for the put: $p_0 = 1.10/(1.055)^{0.1644} = \$1.09$

Lower bound for the put: $p_0 = Max[0,1.10/(1.055)^{0.1644} - 1.05] = \$0.04$

8. We can illustrate put–call parity by showing that for the fiduciary call and the protective put, the current values and values at expiration are the same.

Call price, $c_0 = \$6.64$

Put price, $p_0 = \$2.75$

Exercise price, X = \$30

Risk-free rate, r = 4 percent

Time to expiration = 219/365 = 0.6

Current stock price, $S_0 = \$33.19$

Bond price, $X/(1 + r)^T = 30/(1 + 0.04)^{0.6} = \$29.30$

Transaction	Current Value	Value at Expiration $S_T = 20$	$S_T = 40$
Fiduciary call			
Buy call	6.64	0	40 − 30 = 10
Buy bond	29.30	30	30
Total	35.94	30	40
Protective put			
Buy put	2.75	30 − 20 = 10	0
Buy stock	33.19	20	40
Total	35.94	30	40

The values in the table above show that the current values and values at expiration for the fiduciary call and the protective put are the same. That is, $c_0 + X/(1 + r)^T = p_0 + S_0$.

SOLUTIONS FOR READING 77

1. **A.** The payments at the beginning of the swap are as follows:
The U.S. company (domestic party) pays the counterparty $100 million.
The counterparty pays the U.S. company €116.5 million.

   B. The semiannual payments are as follows:
The U.S. company (domestic party) pays the counterparty
€116,500,000(0.055)(180/360) = €3,203,750.
The counterparty pays the U.S. company $100,000,000(0.0675) ×
(180/360) = $3,375,000.

   C. The payments at the end of the swap are as follows:
The U.S. company (domestic party) pays the counterparty €116.5 million.
The counterparty pays the U.S. company $100 million.

2. **A.** The payments at the beginning of the swap are as follows:
The British company (domestic party) pays the counterparty £75 million.
The counterparty pays the British company $105 million.

   B. The semiannual payments are as follows:
The British company (domestic party) pays the counterparty
$105,000,000(0.06)(180/360) = $3,150,000.
The counterparty pays the British company £75,000,000(0.05) ×
(180/360) = £1,875,000.

   C. The payments at the end of the swap are as follows:
The British company (domestic party) pays the counterparty $105 million.
The counterparty pays the British company £75 million.

3. The fixed payments are $50,000,000(0.0575)(180/365) = $1,417,808.
The floating payments are $50,000,000(0.0515)(180/360) = $1,287,500.
The net payment is $130,308, made by the party paying fixed—that is, the
dealer pays the company.

4. The fixed payments are €25,000,000(0.055)(90/365) = €339,041.
The floating payments are €25,000,000(0.05)(90/360) = €312,500.
The net payment is €26,541, made by the party paying fixed—that is, the
company pays the dealer.

5. **A.** The small-cap equity payment is $\left(\dfrac{625.60}{689.40} - 1\right)(100,000,000)$
$= -\$9,254,424$.
The asset manager owes $9,254,424 to the dealer.

   The large-cap equity payment is $\left(\dfrac{1251.83}{1130.20} - 1\right)(100,000,000)$
$= \$10,761,812$.
The asset manager owes this amount to the dealer.
The overall payment made by the asset manager to the dealer is
$9,254,424 + $10,761,812 = $20,016,236.

   B. The small-cap equity payment is $\left(\dfrac{703.23}{689.40} - 1\right)(100,000,000)$
$= \$2,006,092$.
The dealer owes the asset manager this amount.

   The large-cap equity payment is $\left(\dfrac{1143.56}{1130.20} - 1\right)(100,000,000)$
$= \$1,182,092$.

The asset manager owes this amount to the dealer.

The overall payment made by the dealer to the asset manager is
$2,006,092 - $1,182,092 = $824,000.

6. A. The small-cap equity payment is $\left(\dfrac{238.41}{234.10} - 1\right)(50,000,000) = \$920,547.$

The asset manager owes the dealer this amount.

The fixed interest payment is $(50,000,000)(0.055)(180/365)$
$= \$1,356,164.$

The dealer owes this amount to the asset manager.

So the dealer pays to the asset manager $1,356,164 - $920,547
$= \$435,617.$

B. The small-cap equity payment is $\left(\dfrac{241.27}{234.10} - 1\right)(50,000,000)$
$= \$1,531,397.$

The asset manager owes the dealer this amount.

The fixed interest payment is $(50,000,000)(0.055)(180/365)$
$= \$1,356,164.$

The dealer owes this amount to the asset manager.

So the asset manager pays to the dealer $1,531,397 - $1,356,164
$= \$175,233.$

7. A. The large-cap equity payment is $\left(\dfrac{622.54}{578.50} - 1\right)(25,000,000)$
$= \$1,903,198.$

The dealer owes this amount to the asset manager.

The fixed interest payment is $(25,000,000)(0.045)(180/365)$
$= \$554,795.$

The asset manager owes this amount to the dealer.

So the dealer pays to the asset manager $1,903,198 - $554,795
$= \$1,348,403.$

B. The large-cap equity payment is $\left(\dfrac{581.35}{578.50} - 1\right)(25,000,000) = \$123,163.$

The dealer owes this amount to the asset manager.

The fixed interest payment is $(25,000,000)(0.045)(180/365)$
$= \$554,795.$

The asset manager owes this amount to the dealer.

So the asset manager pays to the dealer $554,795 - $123,163
$= \$431,632.$

SOLUTIONS FOR READING 78

1. A. Call buyer

   i. $c_T = \max(0, S_T - X) = \max(0, 55 - 50) = 5$
   $\Pi = c_T - c_0 = 5 - 4 = 1$

   ii. $c_T = \max(0, S_T - X) = \max(0, 51 - 50) = 1$
   $\Pi = c_T - c_0 = 1 - 4 = -3$

   iii. $c_T = \max(0, S_T - X) = \max(0, 48 - 50) = 0$
   $\Pi = c_T - c_0 = 0 - 4 = -4$

   B. Call seller

   i. Value $= -c_T = -\max(0, S_T - X) = -\max(0, 49 - 50) = 0$
   $\Pi = -c_T + c_0 = -0 + 4 = 4$

   ii. Value $= -c_T = -\max(0, S_T - X) = -\max(0, 52 - 50) = -2$
   $\Pi = -c_T + c_0 = -2 + 4 = 2$

   iii. Value $= -c_T = -\max(0, S_T - X) = -\max(0, 55 - 50) = -5$
   $\Pi = -c_T + c_0 = -5 + 4 = -1$

   C. Maximum and minimum

   i. Maximum profit to buyer (loss to seller) $= \infty$
   ii. Maximum loss to buyer (profit to seller) $= c_0 = 4$

   D. $S_T^* = X + c_0 = 50 + 4 = 54$

2. A.

   i. $c_T = \max(0, S_T - X) = \max(0, 99 - 105) = 0$
   $\Pi = c_T - c_0 = 0 - 7 = -7$

   ii. $c_T = \max(0, S_T - X) = \max(0, 104 - 105) = 0$
   $\Pi = c_T - c_0 = 0 - 7 = -7$

   iii. $c_T = \max(0, S_T - X) = \max(0, 105 - 105) = 0$
   $\Pi = c_T - c_0 = 0 - 7 = -7$

   iv. $c_T = \max(0, S_T - X) = \max(0, 109 - 105) = 4$
   $\Pi = c_T - c_0 = 4 - 7 = -3$

   v. $c_T = \max(0, S_T - X) = \max(0, 112 - 105) = 7$
   $\Pi = c_T - c_0 = 7 - 7 = 0$

   vi. $c_T = \max(0, S_T - X) = \max(0, 115 - 105) = 10$
   $\Pi = c_T - c_0 = 10 - 7 = 3$

   B. $S_T^* = X + c_0 = 105 + 7 = 112$

   Clearly, this result is consistent with our solution above, where the profit is exactly zero in Part A(v), in which the price at expiration is 112.

3. A. Put buyer

   i. $p_T = \max(0, X - S_T) = \max(0, 2100 - 2125) = 0$
   $\Pi = p_T - p_0 = 0 - 106.25 = -106.25$

   ii. $p_T = \max(0, X - S_T) = \max(0, 2100 - 2050) = 50$
   $\Pi = p_T - p_0 = 50 - 106.25 = -56.25$

   iii. $p_T = \max(0, X - S_T) = \max(0, 2100 - 1950) = 150$
   $\Pi = p_T - p_0 = 150 - 106.25 = 43.75$

   B. Put seller

   i. Value $= -p_T = -\max(0, X - S_T) = -\max(0, 2100 - 1975) = -125$
   $\Pi = -p_T + p_0 = -125 + 106.25 = -18.75$

   ii. Value $= -p_T = -\max(0, X - S_T) = -\max(0, 2100 - 2150) = 0$
   $\Pi = -p_T + p_0 = -0 + 106.25 = 106.25$

   C. Maximum and minimum

   i. Maximum profit to buyer (loss to seller) $= X - p_0 = 2100 - 106.25$
   $= 1993.75$

   ii. Maximum loss to buyer (profit to seller) $= p_0 = 106.25$

   D. $S_T^* = X - p_0 = 2100 - 106.25 = 1993.75$

4. A. **i.** $p_T = \max(0, X - S_T) = \max(0, 95 - 100) = 0$
      $\Pi = p_T - p_0 = 0 - 5 = -5$

     ii. $p_T = \max(0, X - S_T) = \max(0, 95 - 95) = 0$
      $\Pi = p_T - p_0 = 0 - 5 = -5$

    iii. $p_T = \max(0, X - S_T) = \max(0, 95 - 93) = 2$
      $\Pi = p_T - p_0 = 2 - 5 = -3$

    iv. $p_T = \max(0, X - S_T) = \max(0, 95 - 90) = 5$
      $\Pi = p_T - p_0 = 5 - 5 = 0$

     v. $p_T = \max(0, X - S_T) = \max(0, 95 - 85) = 10$
      $\Pi = p_T - p_0 = 10 - 5 = 5$

   B. $S_T^* = X - p_0 = 95 - 5 = 90$
Clearly, this result is consistent with our solution above, where the profit is exactly zero in Part A(iv), in which the price at expiration is 90.

   C. **i.** Maximum profit (to put buyer) $= X - p_0 = 95 - 5 = 90$.
     ii. This profit would be realized in the unlikely scenario of the price of the underlying falling all the way down to zero.

5. A. This position is commonly called a covered call.

   B. **i.** $V_T = S_T - \max(0, S_T - X) = 70 - \max(0, 70 - 80) = 70 - 0 = 70$
      $\Pi = V_T - V_0 = 70 - (S_0 - c_0) = 70 - (77 - 6) = 70 - 71 = -1$

     ii. $V_T = S_T - \max(0, S_T - X) = 75 - \max(0, 75 - 80) = 75 - 0 = 75$
      $\Pi = V_T - V_0 = 75 - (S_0 - c_0) = 75 - (77 - 6) = 4$

    iii. $V_T = S_T - \max(0, S_T - X) = 80 - \max(0, 80 - 80) = 80 - 0 = 80$
      $\Pi = V_T - V_0 = 80 - (S_0 - c_0) = 80 - (77 - 6) = 9$

    iv. $V_T = S_T - \max(0, S_T - X) = 85 - \max(0, 85 - 80) = 85 - 5 = 80$
      $\Pi = V_T - V_0 = 80 - (S_0 - c_0) = 80 - (77 - 6) = 9$

   C. **i.** Maximum profit $= X - S_0 + c_0 = 80 - 77 + 6 = 9$
     ii. Maximum loss $= S_0 - c_0 = 77 - 6 = 71$
    iii. The maximum profit would be realized if the expiration price of the underlying is at or above the exercise price of \$80.
    iv. The maximum loss would be incurred if the underlying price drops to zero.

   D. $S_T^* = S_0 - c_0 = 77 - 6 = 71$

6. A. This position is commonly called a protective put.

   B. **i.** $V_T = S_T + \max(0, X - S_T) = 70 + \max(0, 75 - 70) = 70 + 5 = 75$
      $\Pi = V_T - V_0 = 75 - (S_0 + p_0) = 75 - (77 + 3) = 75 - 80 = -5$

     ii. $V_T = S_T + \max(0, X - S_T) = 75 + \max(0, 75 - 75) = 75 + 0 = 75$
      $\Pi = V_T - V_0 = 75 - (S_0 + p_0) = 75 - (77 + 3) = 75 - 80 = -5$

    iii. $V_T = S_T + \max(0, X - S_T) = 80 + \max(0, 75 - 80) = 80 + 0 = 80$
      $\Pi = V_T - V_0 = 80 - (S_0 + p_0) = 80 - (77 + 3) = 80 - 80 = 0$

    iv. $V_T = S_T + \max(0, X - S_T) = 85 + \max(0, 75 - 85) = 85 + 0 = 85$
      $\Pi = V_T - V_0 = 85 - (S_0 + p_0) = 85 - (77 + 3) = 85 - 80 = 5$

     v. $V_T = S_T + \max(0, X - S_T) = 90 + \max(0, 75 - 90) = 90 + 0 = 90$
      $\Pi = V_T - V_0 = 90 - (S_0 + p_0) = 90 - (77 + 3) = 90 - 80 = 10$

   C. **i.** Maximum profit $= \infty$
     ii. Maximum loss $= -(X - S_0 - p_0) = -(75 - 77 - 3) = 5$
    iii. The maximum loss would be incurred if the expiration price of the underlying were at or below the exercise price of \$75.

   D. $S_T^* = S_0 + p_0 = 77 + 3 = 80$

SOLUTIONS FOR READING 79

1. Let us compute the terminal value of $1 invested. The share class with the highest terminal value net of all expenses would be the most appropriate, because all classes are based on the same portfolio and thus have the same portfolio risk characteristics.

   A. Class A. $1 × (1 − 0.05) = $0.95 is the amount available for investment at $t = 0$, after paying the front-end sales charge. Because this amount grows at 9 percent per year, reduced by annual expenses of 0.0125, the terminal value per $1 invested after 1 year is $0.95 × 1.09 × (1 − 0.0125) = $1.0226.

   Class B. Ignoring any deferred sales charge, after 1 year, $1 invested grows to $1 × 1.09 × (1 − 0.015) = $1.0737. According to the table, the deferred sales charge would be 4 percent; therefore, the terminal value is $1.0737 × 0.96 = $1.0308.

   Class C. Ignoring any deferred sales charge, after 1 year, $1 invested grows to $1 × 1.09 × (1 − 0.015) = $1.0737. According to the table, the deferred sales charge would be 1 percent; therefore, the terminal value is $1.0737 × 0.99 = $1.063.

   Class C is the best.

   B. Class A. The terminal value per $1 invested after three years is $0.95 × $1.09^3 × (1 − 0.0125)^3 = 1.1847.

   Class B. Ignoring any deferred sales charge, after three years, $1 invested grows to $1 × $1.09^3 × (1 − 0.015)^3 = 1.2376. The deferred sales charge would be 2 percent; therefore, the terminal value is $1.2376 × 0.98 = $1.2128.

   Class C. There would be no deferred sales charge. Thus, after three years, $1 invested grows to $1 × $1.09^3 × (1 − 0.015)^3 = 1.2376.

   Class C is the best.

   C. Class A. The terminal value per $1 invested after five years is $0.95 × $1.09^5 × (1 − 0.0125)^5 = 1.3726.

   Class B. There would be no deferred sales charge. So, the terminal value per $1 invested after five years is $1 × $1.09^5 × (1 − 0.015)^5$ = $1.4266.

   Class C. There would be no deferred sales charge. So, the terminal value per $1 invested after 5 years is $1 × $1.09^5 × (1 − 0.015)^5$ = $1.4266.

   Classes B and C are the best.

   D. Class A. The terminal value per $1 invested after 15 years is $0.95 × $1.09^{15} × (1 − 0.0125)^{15} = 2.8653.

   Class B. There would be no deferred sales charge. So, the terminal value per $1 invested after 15 years is $1 × $1.09^{15} × (1 − 0.015)^6 ×$ $(1 − 0.0125)^9 = 2.9706.

   Class C. There would be no deferred sales charge. So, the terminal value per $1 invested after 15 years is $1 × $1.09^{15} × (1 − 0.015)^{15} =$ $2.9036.

   Class B is the best.

2. Class A performs quite poorly unless the investment horizon is very long. The reason is the high sales charge of 5 percent on purchases. Even though the annual expenses for class A are low, that is not enough to offset the

International Investments, Fifth Edition, by Bruno Solnik and Dennis McLeavey, Copyright © 2004. Reprinted with permission of Pearson Education, publishing as Pearson Addison Wesley.

high sales charge on purchases until a very long investment horizon. One could verify that Class A outperforms Class C for an investment horizon of 21 years or more.

Class B performs worse than Class C at very short-term horizons because of its higher deferred sales charges. However, after its deferred sales charges disappear, the relative performance of Class B starts improving. After six years, Class B shares convert to Class A with its lower annual expenses. At longer horizons, Class B starts to outperform Class C due to its annual expenses, which are lower than that of Class C.

Class C performs well at shorter investment horizons because it has no initial sales charge and it has a low deferred sales charge.

3. The estimated model is

House value in euros $= 140,000 + (210 \times \text{Living area}) + (10,000 \times \text{Number of bathrooms}) + (15,000 \times \text{Fireplace}) - (6,000 \times \text{Age})$

So, the value of the specific house is

$140,000 + (210 \times 500) + (10,000 \times 3) + (15,000 \times 1) - (6,000 \times 5)$
$= €260,000$

4. **A.** The net operating income for the office building is gross potential rental income minus estimated vacancy and collection costs minus insurance and taxes minus utilities minus repairs and maintenance.

$\text{NOI} = 350,000 - 0.04 \times 350,000 - 26,000 - 18,000 - 23,000$
$= \$269,000$

B. The capitalization rate of the first office building recently sold in the area is

$\text{NOI}/(\text{Transaction price}) = 500,000/4,000,000 = 0.125$

The capitalization rate of the second office building recently sold in the area is

$\text{NOI}/(\text{Transaction price}) = 225,000/1,600,000 = 0.141$

The average of the two capitalization rates is 0.133.

Applying this capitalization rate to the office building under consideration, which has an NOI of $269,000, gives an appraisal value of:

$\text{NOI}/(\text{Capitalization rate}) = 269,000/0.133 = \$2,022,556$

5. The after-tax cash flow for the property sale year is $126,000 + $710,000 = $836,000. At a cost of equity of 18 percent, the present value of the after-tax cash flows in years 1 through 5 is as follows.

$\$60,000/1.18 + \$75,000/1.18^2 + \$91,000/1.18^3 + \$108,000/1.18^4 + \$836,000/1.18^5 = \$581,225$

The investment requires equity of $0.15 \times \$3,000,000 = \$450,000$. Thus, the NPV = $581,225 - $450,000 = $131,225. The recommendation based on NPV would be to accept the project, because the NPV is positive.

6. A. The amount borrowed is 80 percent of $1.5 million, which is $1.2 million. The first year's interest = 9% of $1.2 million = $108,000. So,

After-tax net income in year 1 = (NOI − Depreciation − Interest) × (1 − Marginal tax rate) = ($170,000 − $37,500 − $108,000) × (1 − 0.30) = $17,150

After-tax cash flow = After-tax net income + Depreciation − Principal repayment

And,

Principal repayment = Mortgage payment − Interest = $120,000 − $108,000 = $12,000

So,

After-tax cash flow in year 1 = $17,150 + $37,500 − $12,000 = $42,650

New NOI in year 2 = 1.04 × $170,000 = $176,800. We need to calculate the second year's interest payment on the mortgage balance after the first year's payment. This mortgage balance is the original principal balance minus the first year's principal repayment, or $1,200,000 − $12,000 = $1,188,000. The interest on this balance is $106,920. So,

After-tax net income = ($176,800 − $37,500 − $106,920) × (1 − 0.30) = $22,666

Principal repayment = $120,000 − $106,920 = $13,080

So,

After-tax cash flow in year 2 = $22,666 + $37,500 − $13,080 = $47,086

New NOI in year 3 = 1.04 × $176,800 = $183,872. We need to calculate the third year's interest payment on the mortgage balance after the second year's payment. This mortgage balance is the original principal balance minus the first two years' principal repayments, or $1,200,000 − $12,000 − $13,080 = $1,174,920. The interest on this balance is $105,743. So,

After-tax net income = ($183,872 − $37,500 − $105,743) × (1 − 0.30) = $28,440

Principal repayment = $120,000 − $105,743 = $14,257

So,

After-tax cash flow in year 3 = $28,440 + $37,500 − $14,257 = $51,683

B. Ending book value = Original purchase price − Total depreciation during three years = $1,500,000 − 3 × $37,500 = $1,387,500.

The net sale price = $1,720,000 × (1 − 0.065) = $1,608,200

Capital gains tax = 0.20 × ($1,608,200 − $1,387,500) = $44,140

After-tax cash flow from property sale = Net sales price − Outstanding mortgage − Capital gains tax

And,

> Outstanding mortgage = Original mortgage − Three years' worth of principal repayments,

or

> $1,200,000 − ($12,000 + $13,080 + $14,257) = $1,160,663

So,

> After-tax cash flow from the property sale = $1,608,200 − $1,160,663 − $44,140 = $403,397

C. The total after-tax cash flow for the property sale year is $51,683 + $403,397 = $455,080. At a cost of equity of 19 percent, the present value of the after-tax cash flows in years 1 through 3 is as follows:

> $42,650/1.19 + $47,086/1.19^2 + $455,080/1.19^3 = $339,142

The investment requires equity of 0.20 × $1,500,000 = $300,000. Thus, the NPV = $339,142 − $300,000 = $39,142. The recommendation based on NPV would be to accept the project, because the NPV is positive.

7. No, one would not suggest using real estate appraisal–based indexes in a global portfolio optimization. Real estate appraisal values are a smoothed series. One of the reasons for this smoothness is that the appraisals are done quite infrequently. Another reason is that the appraised values typically show relatively few changes. Due to these two reasons, an appraisal-based index understates volatility. This spuriously low volatility would inflate the attractiveness of real estate.

8. Clearly, the two real estate indexes have very different price behaviors. Their correlation is almost null. As expected, the NAREIT *index* exhibits a strong correlation with U.S. stocks because the REIT share prices are strongly influenced by the stock market. In contrast, the FRC index, which is much less volatile, is not highly correlated with the stock market.

9. **A.** There are three possibilities.

   ▶ Project does not survive until the end of the eighth year
   ▶ Project survives and the investor exits with a payoff of $25 million
   ▶ Project survives and the investor exits with a payoff of $35 million

   There is an 80 percent chance that the project will not survive until the end of the eighth year. That is, there is a 20 percent chance that the project will survive, and the investor will exit the project then. If the project survives, it is equally likely that the payoff at the time of exit will be either $25 million or $35 million.
      The project's NPV is the present value of the expected payoffs minus the required initial investment of $1.4 million.

   > NPV = 0.8 × $0 + 0.2 × [(0.5 × $25 million + 0.5 × $35 million)/1.2^8] − $1.4 million = −$0.004592 million or −$4,592

   B. Because the expected NPV of the project is negative, the project should be rejected.

10. The probability that the venture capital project survives to the end of the first year is $(1 - 0.28)$, 1 minus the probability of failure in the first year; the probability that it survives to the end of the second year is the product of the probability it survives the first year times the probability it survives the second year, or $(1 - 0.28)(1 - 0.25)$. So, the probability that the project survives to end of the sixth year is $(1 - 0.28)(1 - 0.25)(1 - 0.22)(1 - 0.18)(1 - 0.18)(1 - 0.10) = (0.72)(0.75)(0.78)(0.82)(0.82)(0.90) = 0.255$, or 25.5%. The probability that the project fails is $1 - 0.255 = 0.745$, or 74.5%.

The net present value of the project, if it survives to the end of the sixth year and thus earns €60 million, is $-$€4.5 million $+$ €60 million$/$ $1.22^6 =$ €13.70 million. The net present value of the project if it fails is $-$€4.5 million. Thus, the project's expected NPV is a probability-weighted average of these two amounts, or $(0.255)($€13.70 million$) + (0.745)(-$€4.5 million$) =$ €141,000.

Based on the project's positive net present value, VenCap should accept the investment.

11. A. Fee $= 1.5\% + 15\% \times (35\% - 5.5\%) = 1.5\% + 4.425\% = 5.925\%$.

Net return $= 35\% - 5.925\% = 29.1\%$

B. Because the gross return is less than the risk-free rate, the incentive fee is zero. The only fee incurred is the base management fee of 1.5 percent.

Net return $= 5\% - 1.5\% = 3.5\%$

C. Again, the incentive fee is zero.

Net return $= -6\% - 1.5\% = -7.5\%$

12. A. Fixed fee $= 1\%$ of \$2 billion $=$ \$20 million.

If the return is 29 percent, the new value of the fund would be \$2 billion $\times 1.29 =$ \$2.58 billion. This new value would be \$2.58 billion $-$ \$2.1 billion $=$ \$0.48 billion above the high watermark. So, the incentive fee $= 20\% \times$ \$0.48 billion $=$ \$0.096 billion, or \$96 million.

Total fee $=$ \$20 million $+$ \$96 million $=$ \$116 million

B. Fixed fee $= 1\%$ of \$2 billion $=$ \$20 million.

If the return is 4.5 percent, the new value of the fund would be \$2 billion $\times 1.045 =$ \$2.09 billion. Because this new value is below the high watermark of \$2.1 billion, no incentive fee would be earned.

Total fee $=$ \$20 million

C. Fixed fee $= 1\%$ of \$2 billion $=$ \$20 million.
If the return is -1.8%, no incentive fee would be earned.

Total fee $=$ \$20 million

13. Clearly, high watermark provision has the positive implication for the investors that they would have to pay the manager an incentive fee only when they make a profit. Further, the hedge fund manager would need to make up any earlier losses before becoming eligible for the incentive fee payment. However, a negative implication is that the option-like characteristic of the high watermark provision (the incentive fee being zero everywhere below the benchmark and increasing above the benchmark) may induce risk-taking behavior when the fund is below the high watermark. The manager may take more risky positions when the fund is below the high watermark in order to get to above the high watermark and earn an incentive fee. The worst case for the manager is a zero incentive fee, regardless of how far below the benchmark the fund turns out to be. Another negative implication is that the incentive fees, if the fund exceeds the high watermark, are set quite high (typically at 20 percent), which reduces long-run asset growth.

14. **A.** The Spanish firm will give two of its shares, which are worth €25, for three of the Italian firm's shares, which are worth €24. Thus, the shares of the Italian firm are trading at a discount. The reason for the discount is that there is a possibility that the merger may not go through. If the merger does not go through, the shares of the Italian firm are likely to fall back to the premerger announcement level. An investor currently buying shares of the Italian firm is taking the risk that the merger will indeed occur.

   B. The hedge fund will take a hedged position by selling two shares of the Spanish firm short for every three shares of the Italian firm that it buys. So, the hedge fund will buy 250,000 shares of the Italian firm by selling $(2/3) \times 250,000 = 166,666.67$, that is, 166,667 shares of the Spanish firm. The proceeds from the short sale are $166,667 \times €12.50 = €2,083,338$, which is €83,338 more than the cost of buying the shares of the Italian firm, which is $250,000 \times €8 = €2,000,000$.

   C. Because the merger did not go through and the stock price of the Italian firm fell, the hedge fund incurs a substantial loss. The loss is $250,000 \times (€8 - €6.10) = €475,000$.

15. **A.** Net return on fund A = $50\% \times (1 - 0.15) = 42.5\%$

   Net return on fund B = $20\% \times (1 - 0.15) = 17\%$

   Net return on fund C = -10%

   So, average net return = $(42.5\% + 17\% - 10\%)/3 = 16.5\%$

   Average gross return = $(50\% + 20\% - 10\%)/3 = 20\%$

   Thus, the average gross return on the three hedge funds is the same as the percentage increase in the stock market index, and the average net return is lower.

   B. The publicity campaign launched by Global group illustrates the problem of survivorship bias in performance measure of hedge funds. Although the average gross return on the three hedge funds is the same as the percentage increase in the stock market index, the performance reported by Global group seems much better because it is based on only the funds that survive. That is, the average performance reported by Global group is inflated.

16. The measurement of the performance of the hedge funds suffers from survivorship bias. The 90 hedge funds that the analyst has examined include only those funds that have survived during the last 10 years. Thus, any poorly performing funds that have been discontinued due to low return or high volatility, or both, have been excluded. Accordingly, the average return on hedge funds has been overstated, while the volatility has been understated. Consequently, the Sharpe ratio for the hedge funds has been overstated. Furthermore, the Sharpe ratio may be a misleading measure of risk-adjusted performance for hedge funds because of the optionality in their investment strategies.

17. **A.** The construction of the index is okay in year 10 but not in the earlier years. By using today's weights in construction of the index in earlier years, the exchange is overweighing those commodities that have become important over the period, and have simultaneously gone up in price.

B. For each year, use the relative economic importance of the commodities in that year as the weights for that year. That is, use year 1 weights for the index calculated in year 1, and so on.

18. **A.** The expected return on gold, as theoretically derived by the CAPM, is

$$E(R_{gold}) = 7\% + \beta_{gold} \times 4\%$$
$$= 7\% - 0.3\ (4\%) = 5.8\%$$

B. Given its negative beta, gold is likely to perform well when the overall market performs poorly. Thus, our investment in gold is likely to offset some of the loss on the rest of the portfolio. Investors should be willing to accept an overall lower expected return on gold because, in periods of financial distress, gold tends to do well.

GLOSSARY

Abnormal rate of return The amount by which a security's actual return differs from its expected rate of return which is based on the market's rate of return and the security's relationship with the market.

Above full-employment equilibrium A macroeconomic equilibrium in which real GDP exceeds potential GDP.

Absolute dispersion The amount of variability present without comparison to any reference point or benchmark.

Absolute frequency The number of observations in a given interval (for grouped data).

Accelerated method A method of depreciation that allocates relatively large amounts of the depreciable cost of an asset to earlier years and reduced amounts to later years.

Accrual accounting The system of recording financial transactions as they come into existence as a legally enforceable claim, rather than when they settle.

Accrued interest (1) Interest earned but not yet due and payable. This is equal to the next coupon to be paid on a bond multiplied by the time elapsed since the last payment date and divided by the total coupon period. Exact conventions differ across bond markets. (2) Interest earned but not yet paid.

Additional information Information that is required or recommended under the GIPS standards and is not considered as "supplemental information" for the purposes of compliance.

Addition rule for probabilities A principle stating that the probability that A or B occurs (both occur) equals the probability that A occurs, plus the probability that B occurs, minus the probability that both A and B occur.

Additions Enlargements to the physical layout of a plant asset.

Add-on interest A procedure for determining the interest on a bond or loan in which the interest is added onto the face value of a contract.

Administrative fees All fees other than the trading expenses and the investment management fee. Administrative fees include custody fees, accounting fees, consulting fees, legal fees, performance measurement fees, or other related fees. These administrative fees are typically outside the control of the investment management firm and are not included in either the gross-of-fees return or the net-of-fees return. However, there are some markets and investment vehicles where administrative fees are controlled by the firm. (See the term "bundled fee.")

Aggregate demand The relationship between the quantity of real GDP demanded and the price level.

Aggregate hours The total number of hours worked by all the people employed, both full time and part time, during a year.

Aggregate production function The relationship between the quantity of real GDP supplied and the quantities of labor and capital and the state of technology.

Allocative efficiency A situation in which we cannot produce more of any good without giving up some of another good that we value more highly.

Alpha A term commonly used to describe a manager's abnormal rate of return, which is the difference between the return the portfolio actually produced and the expected return given its risk level.

Alternative hypothesis The hypothesis accepted when the null hypothesis is rejected.

American Depository Receipts (ADRs) Certificates of ownership issued by a U.S. bank that represent indirect ownership of a certain number of shares of a specific foreign firm. Shares are held on deposit in a bank in the firm's home country.

American option An option contract that can be exercised at any time until its expiration date. (1) An option contract that can be exercised at any time until its expiration date. (2) An option that can be exercised on any day through the expiration day. Also referred to as American-style exercise.

American terms With reference to U.S. dollar exchange rate quotations, the U.S. dollar price of a unit of another currency.

Amortization The periodic allocation of the cost of an intangible asset to the periods it benefits.

Amortizing and accreting swaps A swap in which the notional principal changes according to a formula related to changes in the underlying.

Analysis of variance (ANOVA) The analysis of the total variability of a dataset (such as observations on the dependent variable in a regression) into components representing different sources of variation; with reference to regression, ANOVA provides the inputs for an F-test of the significance of the regression as a whole.

Annual percentage rate The cost of borrowing expressed as a yearly rate.

Annuity A finite set of level sequential cash flows.

Annuity due An annuity having a first cash flow that is paid immediately.

Anomalies Security price relationships that appear to contradict a well-regarded hypothesis; in this case, the efficient market hypothesis.

A priori probability A probability based on logical analysis rather than on observation or personal judgment.

Arbitrage (1) The simultaneous purchase of an undervalued asset or portfolio and sale of an over-valued but equivalent asset or portfolio, in order to obtain a riskless profit on the price differential. Taking advantage of a market inefficiency in a risk-free manner. (2) A trading strategy designed to generate a guaranteed profit from a transaction that requires no capital commitment or risk bearing on the part of the trader. A simple example of an arbitrage trade would be the simultaneous purchase and sale of the same security in different markets at different prices. (3) The condition in a financial market in which equivalent assets or combinations of assets sell for two different prices, creating an opportunity to profit at no risk with no commitment of money. In a well-functioning financial market, few arbitrage opportunities are possible. Equivalent to the law of one price. (4) A risk-free operation that earns an expected positive net profit but requires no net investment of money.

Arbitrage pricing theory (APT) A theory that posits that the expected return to a financial asset can be described by its relationship with several common risk factors. The multifactor APT can be contrasted with the single-factor CAPM.

Arithmetic mean (AM) The sum of the observations divided by the number of observations.

Arrears swap A type of interest rate swap in which the floating payment is set at the end of the period and the interest is paid at that same time.

Asian call option A European-style option with a value at maturity equal to the difference between the stock price at maturity and the average stock price during the life of the option, or $0, whichever is greater.

Asset allocation The process of deciding how to distribute an investor's wealth among different asset classes for investment purposes.

Asset class Securities that have similar characteristics, attributes, and risk/return relationships.

Asset impairment Loss of revenue-generating potential of a long-lived asset before the end of its useful life; the difference between an asset's carrying value and its fair value, as measured by the present value of the expected cash flows.

Assets under management (AUM) The total market value of the assets managed by an investment firm.

At-the-money option An option for which the strike (or exercise) price is close to (at) the current market price of the underlying asset.

Automatic fiscal policy A change in fiscal policy that is triggered by the state of the economy.

Automatic stabilizers Mechanisms that stabilize real GDP without explicit action by the government.

Autonomous expenditure The sum of those components of aggregate planned expenditure that are not influenced by real GDP. Autonomous expenditure equals investment, government purchases, exports, and the autonomous parts of consumption expenditure and imports.

Average cost pricing rule A rule that sets price to cover cost including normal profit, which means setting the price equal to average total cost.

Average fixed cost Total fixed cost per unit of output—total fixed cost divided by output.

Average product The average product of a resource. It equals total product divided by the quantity of the resource employed.

Average tax rate A person's total tax payment divided by his or her total income.

Average total cost Total cost per unit of output.

Average variable cost Total variable cost per unit of output.

Backwardation A condition in the futures markets in which the benefits of holding an asset exceed the costs, leaving the futures price less than the spot price.

Balance of payments (1) A summary of all economic transactions between a country and all other countries for a specific time period, usually a year. The balance-of-payments account reflects all payments and liabilities to foreigners (debits) and all payments and obligations received from foreigners (credits). (2) A record of all financial flows crossing the borders of a country during a given time period (a quarter or a year).

Balance of payments accounts A country's record of international trading, borrowing, and lending.

Balance of trade *See* Trade balance.

Balance sheet A financial statement that shows what assets the firm controls at a fixed point in time and how it has financed these assets.

Balanced budget A government budget in which tax revenues and expenditures are equal.

Balanced budget multiplier The magnification on aggregate demand of a *simultaneous* change in government purchases and taxes that leaves the budget balance unchanged.

Balanced fund A mutual fund with, generally, a three-part investment objective: (1) to conserve the investor's principal, (2) to pay current income, and (3) to increase both principal and income. The fund aims to achieve this by owning a mixture of bonds, preferred stocks, and common stocks.

Bank discount basis A quoting convention that annualizes, on a 360-day year, the discount as a percentage of face value.

Barriers to entry Legal or natural constraints that protect a firm from potential competitors.

Barter The direct exchange of one good or service for other goods and services.

Basic earnings per share Total earnings divided by the weighted average number of shares actually outstanding during the period.

Basis The difference between the spot price of the underlying asset and the futures contract price at any point in time (e.g., the *initial* basis at the time of contract origination, the *cover* basis at the time of contract termination).

Basis swap (1) An interest rate swap involving two floating rates. (2) A swap in which both parties pay a floating rate.

Bayes' formula A method for updating probabilities based on new information.

Bear spread An option strategy that involves selling a put with a lower exercise price and buying a put with a higher exercise price. It can also be executed with calls.

Behavioral finance Involves the analysis of various psychological traits of individuals and how these traits affect how they act as investors, analysts, and portfolio managers.

Below full-employment equilibrium A macroeconomic equilibrium in which potential GDP exceeds real GDP.

Benchmark An independent rate of return (or hurdle rate) forming an objective test of the effective implementation of an investment strategy.

Benchmark bond A bond representative of current market conditions and used for performance comparison.

Benchmark error Situation where an inappropriate or incorrect benchmark is used to compare and assess portfolio returns and management.

Benchmark portfolio A comparison standard of risk and assets included in the policy statement and similar to the investor's risk preference and investment needs, which can be used to evaluate the investment performance of the portfolio manager.

Bernoulli random variable A random variable having the outcomes 0 and 1.

Bernoulli trial An experiment that can produce one of two outcomes.

Beta A standardized measure of systematic risk based upon an asset's covariance with the market portfolio.

Betterments Improvements that do not add to the physical layout of a plant asset.

Bid-ask spread The difference between the quoted ask and the bid prices.

Big tradeoff A tradeoff between equity and efficiency.

Bill-and-hold basis Sales on a bill-and-hold basis involve selling products but not delivering those products until a later date.

Binomial model A model for pricing options in which the underlying price can move to only one of two possible new prices.

Binomial option pricing model A valuation equation that assumes the price of the underlying asset changes through a series of discrete upward or downward movements.

Binomial random variable The number of successes in n Bernoulli trials for which the probability of success is constant for all trials and the trials are independent.

Binomial tree (1) A diagram representing price movements of the underlying in a binomial model. (2) The graphical representation of a model of asset price dynamics in which, at each period, the asset moves up with probability p or down with probability $(1 - p)$.

Black market An illegal trading arrangement in which the price exceeds the legally imposed price ceiling.

Black-Scholes option pricing model A valuation equation that assumes the price of the underlying asset changes continuously through the option's expiration date by a statistical process known as *geometric Brownian motion.*

Bond A long-term debt security with contractual obligations regarding interest payments and redemption.

Bond-equivalent basis A basis for stating an annual yield that annualizes a semiannual yield by doubling it.

Bond-equivalent yield The yield to maturity on a basis that ignores compounding.

Bond option An option in which the underlying is a bond; primarily traded in over-the-counter markets.

Bond price volatility The percentage changes in bond prices over time.

Book value of equity (or book value) (1) Shareholders' equity (total assets minus total liabilities) minus the value of preferred stock; common shareholders' equity. (2) The accounting value of a firm.

Book value per share Book value of equity divided by the number of common shares outstanding.

Box spread An option strategy that combines a bull spread and a bear spread having two different exercise prices, which produces a risk-free payoff of the difference in the exercise prices.

Brady bonds Bonds issued by emerging countries under a debt-reduction plan named after Mr. Brady, former U.S. Secretary of the Treasury.

Brand name A registered name that can be used only by its owner to identify a product or service.

Broker (1) An agent who executes orders to buy or sell securities on behalf of a client in exchange for a commission. (2) *See* Futures commission merchants.

Budget deficit A government's budget balance that is negative—expenditures exceed tax revenues.

Budget surplus A government's budget balance that is positive—tax revenues exceed expenditures.

Bull spread An option strategy that involves buying a call with a lower exercise price and selling a call with a higher exercise price. It can also be executed with puts.

Bundled fee A fee that combines multiple fees into one "bundled" fee. Bundled fees can include any combination of management, transaction, custody, and other administrative fees. Two specific examples of bundled fees are the wrap fee and the all-in fee.

All-in fee Due to the universal banking system in some countries, asset management, brokerage, and custody are often part of the same company. This allows banks to offer a variety of choices to customers regarding how the fee will be charged. Customers are offered numerous fee models in which fees may be bundled together or charged separately. All-in fees can include any combination of investment management, trading expenses, custody, and other administrative fees.

Wrap fee Wrap fees are specific to a particular investment product. The U.S. Securities and Exchange Commission (SEC) defines a wrap fee account (now more commonly known as a separately managed account or SMA) as "any advisory program under which a specified fee or fees not based upon transactions in a client's account is charged for investment advisory services (which may include portfolio management or advice concerning the selection of other investment advisers) and execution of client transactions." A typical separately managed account has a contract or contracts (and fee) involving a sponsor (usually a broker or independent provider) acting as the investment advisor, an investment management firm typically as the subadvisor, other services (custody, consulting, reporting, performance, manager selection, monitoring, and execution of trades), distributor, and the client (brokerage customer). Wrap fees can be all-inclusive, asset-based fees (which may include any combination of management, transaction, custody, and other administrative fees).

Business cycle The periodic but irregular up-and-down movement in production.

Business risk The variability of operating income arising from the characteristics of the firm's industry. Two sources of business risk are sales variability and operating leverage.

Butterfly spread An option strategy that combines two bull or bear spreads and has three exercise prices.

Buy-and-hold strategy A passive portfolio management strategy in which securities (bonds or stocks) are bought and held to maturity.

Call An option that gives the holder the right to buy an underlying asset from another party at a fixed price over a specific period of time.

Call market A market in which trading for individual stocks only takes place at specified times. All the bids and asks available at the time are combined and the market administrators specify a single price that will possibly clear the market at that time.

Call option Option to buy an asset within a certain period at a specified price called the *exercise price.*

Call premium Amount above par that an issuer must pay to a bondholder for retiring the bond before its stated maturity.

Call provisions Specifies when and how a firm can issue a call for bonds outstanding prior to their maturity.

Cap (1) A contract on an interest rate, whereby at periodic payment dates, the writer of the cap pays the difference between the market interest rate and a specified cap rate if, and only if, this difference is positive. This is equivalent to a stream of call options on the interest rate. (2) A combination of interest rate call options designed to hedge a borrower against rate increases on a floating-rate loan.

Capital The tools, equipment, buildings, and other constructions that businesses now use to produce goods and services.

Capital account (1) The record of transactions with foreigners that involve either (a) the exchange of ownership rights to real or financial assets or (b) the extension of loans. (2) A component of the balance of payments that reflects unrequited (or unilateral) transfers corresponding to capital flows entailing no compensation (in the form of goods, services, or assets). Examples include investment capital given (without future repayment) in favor of poor countries, debt forgiveness, and expropriation losses.

Capital accumulation The growth of capital resources.

Capital appreciation A return objective in which the investor seeks to increase the portfolio value, primarily through capital gains, over time to meet a future need rather than dividend yield.

Capital asset pricing model (CAPM) A theory concerned with deriving the expected or required rates of return on risky assets based on the assets' systematic risk relative to a market portfolio.

Capital budgeting The process of planning expenditures on assets whose cash flows are expected to extend beyond one year.

Capital Employed (Real Estate) The denominator of the return expressions, defined as the "weighted-average equity" (weighted-average capital) during the measurement period. Capital employed should not include any income or capital return accrued during the measurement period. Beginning capital is adjusted by weighting the cash flows (contributions and distributions) that occurred during the period. Cash flows are typically weighted based on the actual days the flows are in or out of the portfolio. Other weighting methods are acceptable; however, once a methodology is chosen, it should be consistently applied.

Capital expenditure An expenditure for the purchase or expansion of a long-term asset, recorded in an asset account.

Capital market line (CML) The line from the intercept point that represents the risk-free rate tangent to the original efficient frontier; it becomes the new efficient frontier since investments on this line dominate all the portfolios on the original Markowitz efficient frontier.

Capital preservation A return objective in which the investor seeks to minimize the risk of loss; generally a goal of the risk-averse investor.

Capital return (real estate) The change in the market value of the real estate investments and cash/cash equivalent assets held throughout the measurement period (ending market value less beginning market value) adjusted for all capital expenditures (subtracted) and the net proceeds from sales (added). The return is computed as a percentage of the capital employed through the measurement period. Synonyms: capital appreciation return, appreciation return.

Capital stock The total quantity of plant, equipment, buildings, and inventories.

Capital structure A company's specific mixture of long-term financing.

Caplet Each component call option in a cap.

Capped swap A swap in which the floating payments have an upper limit.

Carried interest (private equity) The profits that general partners earn from the profits of the investments made by the fund (generally 20–25%). Also known as "carry."

Carrying value The unexpired part of an asset's cost. Also called *book value*.

Cartel A group of firms that has entered into a collusive agreement to restrict output and increase prices and profits.

Carve-Out A single or multiple asset class segment of a multiple asset class portfolio.

Cash For purposes of the statement of cash flows, both cash and cash equivalents.

Cash equivalents Short-term (90 days or less), highly liquid investments, including money market accounts, commercial paper, and U.S. Treasury bills.

Cash flow additivity principle The principle that dollar amounts indexed at the same point in time are additive.

Cash-generating efficiency A company's ability to generate cash from its current or continuing operations.

Cash price or spot price The price for immediate purchase of the underlying asset.

Cash settlement (1) A procedure for settling futures contracts in which the cash difference between the futures price and the spot price is paid instead of physical delivery. (2) A procedure used in certain derivative transactions that specifies that the long and short parties engage in the equivalent cash value of a delivery transaction.

CD equivalent yield *See* Money market yield.

Central bank A bank's bank and a public authority that regulates a nation's depository institutions and controls the quantity of money.

Central limit theorem A result in statistics that states that the sample mean computed from large samples of size n from a population with finite variance will follow an approximate normal distribution with a mean equal to the population mean and a variance equal to the population variance divided by n.

Certificates of deposit (CDs) Instruments issued by banks and S&Ls that require minimum deposits for specified terms and that pay higher rates of interest than deposit accounts.

Ceteris paribus Other things being equal—all other relevant things remaining the same.

Change in demand   A change in buyers' plans that occurs when some influence on those plans other than the price of the good changes. It is illustrated by a shift of the demand curve.

Change in supply   A change in sellers' plans that occurs when some influence on those plans other than the price of the good changes. It is illustrated by a shift of the supply curve.

Change in the quantity demanded   A change in buyers' plans that occurs when the price of a good changes but all other influences on buyers' plans remain unchanged. It is illustrated by a movement along the demand curve.

Characteristic line   Regression line that indicates the systematic risk (beta) of a risky asset.

Cheapest to deliver   A bond in which the amount received for delivering the bond is largest compared with the amount paid in the market for the bond.

Classical   A macroeconomist who believes that the economy is self-regulating and that it is always at full employment.

Clean price   The price of a bond obtained as the total price of the bond minus accrued interest. Most bonds are traded on the basis of their clean price.

Closed-end fund (private equity)   A type of investment fund where the number of investors and the total committed capital is fixed and not open for subscriptions and/or redemptions.

Closed-end investment company   An investment company that issues only a limited number of shares, which it does not redeem (buy back). Instead, shares of a closed-end fund are traded in securities markets at prices determined by supply and demand.

Coefficient of variation (CV)   The ratio of a set of observations' standard deviation to the observations' mean value.

Collar   (1) A combination of a cap and a floor. (2) An option strategy involving the purchase of a put and sale of a call in which the holder of an asset gains protection below a certain level, the exercise price of the put, and pays for it by giving up gains above a certain level, the exercise price of the call. Collars also can be used to provide protection against rising interest rates on a floating-rate loan by giving up gains from lower interest rates.

Collateralized mortgage obligation (CMO)   A debt security based on a pool of mortgage loans that provides a relatively stable stream of payments for a relatively predictable term.

Collateral trust bonds   A mortgage bond wherein the assets backing the bond are financial assets like stocks and bonds.

Collusive agreement   An agreement between two (or more) producers to restrict output, raise the price, and increase profits.

Combination   A listing in which the order of the listed items does not matter.

Command system   A method of organizing production that uses a managerial hierarchy.

Commercial bank   A firm that is licensed by the Comptroller of the Currency in the U.S. Treasury or by a state agency to receive deposits and make loans.

Commercial paper   Unsecured short-term corporate debt that is characterized by a single payment at maturity.

Commission brokers   Employees of a member firm who buy or sell securities for the customers of the firm.

Committed capital (private equity)   Pledges of capital to a venture capital fund. This money is typically not received at once but drawn down over three to five years, starting in the year the fund is formed. Also known as "commitments."

Common stock   An equity investment that represents ownership of a firm, with full participation in its success or failure. The firm's directors must approve dividend payments.

Comparative advantage   A person or country has a comparative advantage in an activity if that person or country can perform the activity at a lower opportunity cost than anyone else or any other country.

Competitive bid   An underwriting alternative wherein an issuing entity (governmental body or a corporation) specifies the type of security to be offered (bonds or stocks) and the general characteristics of the issue, and the issuer solicits bids from competing investment banking firms with the understanding that the issuer will accept the highest bid from the bankers.

Competitive environment   The level of intensity of competition among firms in an industry, determined by an examination of five competitive forces.

Competitive market   A market that has many buyers and many sellers, so no single buyer or seller can influence the price.

Competitive strategy   The search by a firm for a favorable competitive position within an industry within the known competitive environment.

Complement   A good that is used in conjunction with another good.

Complement   With reference to an event S, the event that S does not occur.

Completely diversified portfolio   A portfolio in which all unsystematic risk has been eliminated by diversification.

Composite   Aggregation of individual portfolios representing a similar investment mandate, objective, or strategy.

Composite creation date   The date when the firm first groups the portfolios to create a composite. The composite creation date is not necessarily the earliest date for which performance is reported for the composite. (See composite inception date.)

Composite definition   Detailed criteria that determine the allocation of portfolios to composites. Composite definitions must be documented in the firm's policies and procedures.

Composite description   General information regarding the strategy of the composite. A description may be more abbreviated than the composite definition but includes all salient features of the composite.

Compounding   The process of accumulating interest on interest.

Computer-Assisted Execution System (CAES)   A service created by Nasdaq that automates order routing and execution for securities listed on domestic stock exchanges and involved on the Intermarket Trading System (ITS).

Conditional expected value   (1) Expected value of a variable conditional on some available information set. The expected value changes over time with changes in the information set. (2) The expected value of a stated event given that another event has occurred.

Conditional probability   The probability of an event given (conditioned on) another event.

Conditional variance   (1) Variance of a variable conditional on some available information set. (2) The variance of one variable, given the outcome of another.

Confidence interval   A range that has a given probability that it will contain the population parameter it is intended to estimate.

Consistency   A desirable property of estimators; a consistent estimator is one for which the probability of estimates close to the value of the population parameter increases as sample size increases.

Consistent   With reference to estimators, describes an estimator for which the probability of estimates close to the value of the population parameter increases as sample size increases.

Consolidated Quotation System (CQS)   An electronic quotation service for issues listed on the NYSE, the AMEX, or regional exchanges and traded on the Nasdaq InterMarket.

Constant maturity swap or CMT swap   A swap in which the floating rate is the rate on a security known as a constant maturity treasury or CMT security.

Constant maturity treasury or CMT   A hypothetical U.S. Treasury note with a constant maturity. A CMT exists for various years in the range of 2 to 10.

Constant returns to scale   Features of a firm's technology that leads to constant long-run average cost as output increases. When constant returns to scale are present, the *LRAC* curve is horizontal.

Consumer Price Index (CPI)   An index that measures the average of the prices paid by urban consumers for a fixed "basket" of the consumer goods and services.

Consumer surplus   The value of a good minus the price paid for it, summed over the quantity bought.

Consumption expenditure   The total payment for consumer goods and services.

Contango   A situation in a futures market where the current contract price is greater than the current spot price for the underlying asset.

Contestable market   A market in which firms can enter and leave so easily that firms in the market face competition from potential entrants.

Continuously compounded return   The natural logarithm of 1 plus the holding period return, or equivalently, the natural logarithm of the ending price over the beginning price.

Continuous market   A market where stocks are priced and traded continuously by an auction process or by dealers when the market is open.

Continuous random variable   A random variable for which the range of possible outcomes is the real line (all real numbers between − and +) or some subset of the real line.

Continuous time   Time thought of as advancing in extremely small increments.

Contract price   The transaction price specified in a forward or futures contract.

Convenience yield   (1) An adjustment made to the theoretical forward or futures contract delivery price to account for the preference that consumers have for holding spot positions in the underlying asset. (2) The nonmonetary return offered by an asset when the asset is in short supply, often associated with assets with seasonal production processes.

Conversion value   The value of the convertible security if converted into common stock at the stock's current market price.

Convertible bonds   A bond with the added feature that the bondholder has the option to turn the bond back to the firm in exchange for a specified number of common shares of the firm.

Convexity   (1) A measure of the change in duration with respect to changes in interest rates. (2) A measure of the degree to which a bond's price-yield curve departs from a straight line. This characteristic affects estimates of a bond's price volatility for a given change in yields.

Cooperative equilibrium   The outcome of a game in which the players make and share the monopoly profit.

Copyright   A government-sanctioned exclusive right granted to the inventor of a good, service, or productive process to produce, use, and sell the invention for a given number of years.

Correlation   A number between –1 and +1 that measures the co-movement (linear association) between two random variables.

Correlation analysis   The analysis of the strength of the linear relationship between two data series.

Correlation coefficient   A standardized measure of the relationship between two variables that ranges from − 1.00 to + 1.00.

Cost averaging   The periodic investment of a fixed amount of money.

Cost of carry   (1) The cost associated with holding some asset, including financing, storage, and insurance costs. Any yield received on the asset is treated as a negative carrying cost. (2) The net amount that would be required to store a commodity or security for future delivery, usually calculated as physical storage costs plus financial capital costs less dividends paid to the underlying asset. (3) The costs of holding an asset.

Cost of carry model   A model for pricing futures contracts in which the futures price is determined by adding the cost of carry to the spot price.

Cost-push inflation   An inflation that results from an initial increase in costs.

Council of Economic Advisers   The President's council whose main work is to monitor the economy and keep the President and the public well informed about the current state of the economy and the best available forecasts of where it is heading.

Counterparty   A participant to a derivative transaction.

Country risk   Uncertainty due to the possibility of major political or economic change in the country where an investment is located. Also called *political risk.*

Coupon   Indicates the interest payment on a debt security. It is the coupon rate times the par value that indicates the interest payments on a debt security.

Covariance   (1) A measure of the degree to which two variables, such as rates of return for investment assets, move together over time relative to their individual mean returns. (2) A measure of

the extent to which the returns on two assets move together. (3) A measure of the co-movement (linear association) between two random variables.

Covariance matrix   A matrix or square array whose entries are covariances; also known as a variance–covariance matrix.

Covered call   An option strategy involving the holding of an asset and sale of a call on the asset.

Credit analysis   An active bond portfolio management strategy designed to identify bonds that are expected to experience changes in rating. This strategy is critical when investing in high-yield bonds.

Credit risk or default risk   The risk of loss due to nonpayment by a counterparty.

Credit union   A depository institution owned by a social or economic group such as firm's employees that accepts savings deposits and makes mostly consumer loans.

Creditor nation   A country that during its entire history has invested more in the rest of the world than other countries have invested in it.

Cross elasticity of demand   The responsiveness of the demand for a good to the price of a substitute or complement, other things remaining the same. It is calculated as the percentage change in the quantity demanded of the good divided by the percentage change in the price of the substitute or complement.

Cross-sectional analysis   An examination of a firm's performance in comparison to other firms in the industry with similar characteristics to the firm being studied.

Cross-sectional data   Observations over individual units at a point in time, as opposed to time-series data.

Crowding-out effect   The tendency for a government budget deficit to decrease in investment.

Cumulative distribution function   A function giving the probability that a random variable is less than or equal to a specified value.

Cumulative relative frequency   For data grouped into intervals, the fraction of total observations that are less than the value of the upper limit of a stated interval.

Currency   The bills and coins that we use today.

Currency appreciation   The rise in the value of one currency in terms of another currency.

Currency depreciation   The fall in the value of one currency in terms of another currency.

Currency drain   An increase in currency held outside the banks.

Currency option   An option that allows the holder to buy (if a call) or sell (if a put) an underlying currency at a fixed exercise rate, expressed as an exchange rate.

Current account A record of the payments for imports of goods and services, receipts from exports of goods and services, the interest income, and net transfers.

Current account (1) The record of all transactions with foreign nations that involve the exchange of merchandise goods and services, current income derived from investments, and unilateral gifts. (2) A component of the balance of payments covering all current transactions that take place in the normal business of the residents of a country, such as exports and imports, services, income, and current transfers.

Current credit risk The risk associated with the possibility that a payment currently due will not be made.

Current income A return objective in which the investor seeks to generate income rather than capital gains; generally a goal of an investor who wants to supplement earnings with income to meet living expenses.

Current P/E *See* Trailing P/E.

Current yield A bond's yield as measured by its current income (coupon) as a percentage of its market price.

Customer list A list of customers or subscribers.

Cyclical businesses Businesses with high sensitivity to business- or industry-cycle influences.

Cyclical company A firm whose earnings rise and fall with general economic activity.

Cyclical stock A stock with a high beta; its gains typically exceed those of a rising market and its losses typically exceed those of a falling market.

Cyclical surplus or deficit The actual surplus or deficit minus the structural surplus or deficit.

Cyclical unemployment The fluctuations in unemployment over the business cycle.

Daily settlement *See* Marking to market.

Data mining The practice of determining a model by extensive searching through a dataset for statistically significant patterns.

Day trader A trader holding a position open somewhat longer than a scalper but closing all positions at the end of the day.

Deadweight loss A measure of inefficiency. It is equal to the decrease in consumer surplus and producer surplus that results from an inefficient level of production.

Debentures Bonds that promise payments of interest and principal but pledge no specific assets. Holders have first claim on the issuer's income and unpledged assets. Also known as *unsecured bonds.*

Debtor nation A country that during its entire history has borrowed more from the rest of the world than it has lent to it.

Deciles Quantiles that divide a distribution into 10 equal parts.

Declining-balance method An accelerated method of depreciation in which depreciation is computed by applying a fixed rate to the carrying value (the declining balance) of a tangible long-lived asset.

Declining trend channel The range defined by security prices as they move progressively lower.

Deep in the money Options that are far in-the-money.

Deep out of the money Options that are far out-of-the-money.

Default risk The risk that an issuer will be unable to make interest and principal payments on time.

Default risk premium An extra return that compensates investors for the possibility that the borrower will fail to make a promised payment at the contracted time and in the contracted amount.

Defensive competitive strategy Positioning the firm so that its capabilities provide the best means to deflect the effect of the competitive forces in the industry.

Defensive stock A stock whose return is not expected to decline as much as that of the overall market during a bear market (a beta less than one).

Deflation A process in which the price level falls—a negative inflation.

Degree of confidence The probability that a confidence interval includes the unknown population parameter.

Degrees of freedom (df) The number of independent observations used.

Delivery A process used in a deliverable forward contract in which the long pays the agreed-upon price to the short, which in turn delivers the underlying asset to the long.

Delivery option The feature of a futures contract giving the short the right to make decisions about what, when, and where to deliver.

Delta The change in the price of the option with respect to a one dollar change in the price of the underlying asset; this is the option's *hedge ratio,* or the number of units of the underlying asset that can be hedged by a single option contract.

Delta hedge (1) A dynamic hedging strategy using options with continuous adjustment of the number of options used, as a function of the delta of the option. (2) An option strategy in which a position in an asset is converted to a risk-free position with a position in a specific number of options.

The number of options per unit of the underlying changes through time, and the position must be revised to maintain the hedge.

Demand   The relationship between the quantity of a good that consumers plan to buy and the price of the good when all other influences on buyers' plans remain the same. It is described by a demand schedule and illustrated by a demand curve.

Demand curve   A curve that shows the relationship between the quantity demanded of a good and its price when all other influences on consumers' planned purchases remain the same.

Demand for labor   The relationship between the quantity of labor demanded and the real wage rate when all other influences on firm's hiring plans remain the same.

Demand-pull inflation   An inflation that results from an initial increase in aggregate demand.

Dependent   With reference to events, the property that the probability of one event occurring depends on (is related to) the occurrence of another event.

Dependent variable   The variable whose variation about its mean is to be explained by the regression; the left-hand-side variable in a regression equation.

Depletion   The exhaustion of a natural resource through mining, cutting, pumping, or other extraction, and the way in which the cost is allocated.

Depository institution   A firm that takes deposits from households and firms and makes loans to other households and firms.

Depreciable cost   The cost of an asset less its residual value.

Depreciation   The decrease in the capital stock that results from wear and tear and obsolescence.
The periodic allocation of the cost of a tangible long-lived asset (other than land and natural resources) over its estimated useful life.

Derivatives   (1) Securities bearing a contractual relation to some underlying asset or rate. Options, futures, forward, and swap contracts, as well as many forms of bonds, are derivative securities. (2) A financial instrument that offers a return based on the return of some other underlying asset.

Derivatives dealers   The commercial and investment banks that make markets in derivatives. Also referred to as market makers.

Derivative security   An instrument whose market value ultimately depends upon, or derives from, the value of a more fundamental investment vehicle called the underlying asset or security.

Derived demand   The demand for a productive resource, which is derived from the demand for the goods and services produced by the resource.

Descriptive statistics   The study of how data can be summarized effectively.

Diff swaps   A swap in which the payments are based on the difference between interest rates in two countries but payments are made in only a single currency.

Diluted earnings per share   Total earnings divided by the number of shares that would be outstanding if holders of securities such as executive stock options and convertible bonds exercised their options to obtain common stock.

Diminishing marginal returns   The tendency for the marginal product of an additional unit of a factor of production is less than the marginal product of the previous unit of the factor.

Diminishing marginal utility   The decrease in marginal utility as the quantity consumed increases.

Direct method   The procedure for converting the income statement from an accrual basis to a cash basis by adjusting each item on the income statement.

Discount   (1) A bond selling at a price below par value due to capital market conditions. (2) To reduce the value of a future payment in allowance for how far away it is in time; to calculate the present value of some future amount. Also, the amount by which an instrument is priced below its face value.

Discounting   The conversion of a future amount of money to its present value.

Discount interest   A procedure for determining the interest on a loan or bond in which the interest is deducted from the face value in advance.

Discouraged workers   People who are available and willing to work but have not made specific efforts to find a job within the previous four weeks.

Discrete random variable   A random variable that can take on at most a countable number of possible values.

Discrete time   Time thought of as advancing in distinct finite increments.

Discretionary fiscal policy   A policy action that is initiated by an act of Congress.

Discretionary policy   A policy that responds to the state of the economy in a possibly unique way that uses all the information available, including perceived lessons from past "mistakes."

Diseconomies of scale   Features of a firm's technology that leads to rising long-run average cost as output increases.

Dispersion   (1) The variability around the central tendency. (2) A measure of the spread of the annual returns of individual portfolios within a composite. Measures may include, but are not limited to, high/low, inter-quartile range, and standard deviation (asset weighted or equal weighted).

Disposable income Aggregate income minus taxes plus transfer payments.

Distinct business entity A unit, division, department, or office that is organizationally and functionally segregated from other units, divisions, departments, or offices and retains discretion over the assets it manages and autonomy over the investment decision-making process. Possible criteria that can be used to determine this include: (a) being a legal entity; (b) having a distinct market or client type (e.g., institutional, retail, private client, etc.); (c) using a separate and distinct investment process

Dividend discount model (DDM) A technique for estimating the value of a stock issue as the present value of all future dividends.

Dominant strategy equilibrium A Nash equilibrium in which the best strategy of each player is to cheat (deny) regardless of the strategy of the other player.

Double-declining-balance method An accelerated method of depreciation in which a fixed rate equal to twice the straight-line percentage is applied to the carrying value (the declining balance) of a tangible long-lived asset.

Down transition probability The probability that an asset's value moves down in a model of asset price dynamics.

Dumping The sale by a foreign firm of exports at a lower price that the cost of production.

Duopoly A market structure in which two producers of a good or service compete.

DuPont system A method of examining ROE by breaking it down into three component parts: (1) profit margin, (2) total asset turnover, and (3) financial leverage.

Duration (1) A measure of an option-free bond's average maturity. Specifically, the weighted average maturity of all future cash flows paid by a security, in which the weights are the present value of these cash flows as a fraction of the bond's price. More importantly, a measure of a bond's price sensitivity to interest rate movements (*see* Modified duration). (2) A measure of the interest rate sensitivity of a bond's market price taking into consideration its coupon and term to maturity. (3) A measure of the size and timing of the cash flows paid by a bond. It quantifies these factors by summarizing them in the form of a single number. For bonds without option features attached, duration is interpreted as a weighted average maturity of the bond.

Dutch Book Theorem A result in probability theory stating that inconsistent probabilities create profit opportunities.

Dynamic comparative advantage A comparative advantage that a person or country possesses as a result of having specialized in a particular activity and then, as a result of learning-by-doing, having become the producer with the lowest opportunity cost.

Earnings momentum A strategy in which portfolios are constructed of stocks of firms with rising earnings.

Earnings multiplier model A technique for estimating the value of a stock issue as a multiple of its earnings per share.

Earnings surprise A company announcement of earnings that differ from analysts' prevailing expectations.

Earnings yield Earnings per share divided by price; the reciprocal of the P/E ratio.

EBITDA Earnings before interest, taxes, depreciation, and amortization.

Economic depreciation The change in the market value of capital over a given period.

Economic efficiency A situation that occurs when the firm produces a given output at the least cost.

Economic growth The expansion of production possibilities that results from capital accumulation and technological change.

Economic information Data on prices, quantities, and qualities of goods and services and factors of production.

Economic model A description of some aspect of the economic world that includes only those features of the world that are needed for the purpose at hand.

Economic profit A firm's total revenue minus its opportunity cost.

Economic rent The income received by the owner of a factor of production over and above the amount required to induce that owner to offer the factor for use.

Economics The social science that studies the *choices* that individuals, businesses, governments, and entire societies make and how they cope with *scarcity* and the *incentives* that influence and reconcile those choices.

Economic theory A generalization that summarizes what we think we understand about the economic choices that people make and the performance of industries and entire economies.

Economic value added (EVA)   Internal management performance measure that compares net operating profit to total cost of capital. Indicates how profitable company projects are as a sign of management performance.

Economies of scale   Features of a firm's technology that leads to a falling long-run average cost as output increases.

Economies of scope   Decreases in average total cost that occur when a firm uses specialized resources to produce a range of goods and services.

Effective annual rate   The amount by which a unit of currency will grow in a year with interest on interest included.

Effective annual yield (EAY)   An annualized return that accounts for the effect of interest on interest; EAY is computed by compounding 1 plus the holding period yield forward to one year, then subtracting 1.

Effective duration   Direct measure of the interest rate sensitivity of a bond (or any financial instrument) based upon price changes derived from a pricing model.

Efficiency   A desirable property of estimators; an efficient estimator is the unbiased estimator with the smallest variance among unbiased estimators of the same parameter.

Efficient capital market   A market in which security prices rapidly reflect all information about securities.

Efficient frontier   The set of portfolios that has the maximum rate of return for every given level of risk, or the minimum risk for every potential rate of return.

Efficient market   A market in which the actual price embodies all currently available relevant information. Resources are sent to their highest valued use.

Elastic demand   Demand with a price elasticity greater than 1; other things remaining the same, the percentage change in the quantity demanded exceeds the percentage change in price.

Elasticity of demand   The responsiveness of the quantity demanded of a good to a change in its price, other things remaining the same.

Elasticity of supply   The responsiveness of the quantity supplied of a good to a change in its price, other things remaining the same.

Empirical probability   The probability of an event estimated as a relative frequency of occurrence.

Employment Act of 1946   A landmark Congressional act that recognized a role for government actions to keep unemployment, keep the economy expanding, and keep inflation in check.

Employment-to-population ratio   The percentage of people of working age who have jobs.

Ending market value (private equity)   The remaining equity that a limited partner has in a fund. Also referred to as net asset value or residual value.

Entrepreneurship   The human resource that organizes labor, land, and capital. Entrepreneurs come up with new ideas about what and how to produce, make business decisions, and bear the risks that arise from their decisions.

Equation of exchange   An equation that states that the quantity of money multiplied by the velocity of circulation equals GDP.

Equilibrium price   The price at which the quantity demanded equals the quantity supplied.

Equilibrium quantity   The quantity bought and sold at the equilibrium price.

Equity forward   A contract calling for the purchase of an individual stock, a stock portfolio, or a stock index at a later date at an agreed-upon price.

Equity options   Options on individual stocks; also known as stock options.

Equity swap   A swap transaction in which one cash flow is tied to the return to an equity portfolio position, often an index such as the Standard and Poor's 500, while the other is based on a floating-rate index.

Error term   The portion of the dependent variable that is not explained by the independent variable(s) in the regression.

Estimate   The particular value calculated from sample observations using an estimator.

Estimated (or fitted) parameters   With reference to regression analysis, the estimated values of the population intercept and population slope coefficient(s) in a regression.

Estimated rate of return   The rate of return an investor anticipates earning from a specific investment over a particular future holding period.

Estimated useful life   The total number of service units expected from a long-term asset.

Estimation   With reference to statistical inference, the subdivision dealing with estimating the value of a population parameter.

Estimator   An estimation formula; the formula used to compute the sample mean and other sample statistics are examples of estimators.

Eurobonds   Bonds denominated in a currency not native to the country in which they are issued.

Eurodollar   A dollar deposited outside the United States.

European option   An option contract that can only be exercised on its expiration date.

European-style option or European option   An option exercisable only at maturity.

European terms With reference to U.S. dollar exchange rate quotations, the price of a U.S. dollar in terms of another currency.

European Union (EU) A formal association of European countries founded by the Treaty of Rome in 1957. Formerly known as the EEC.

Event study Research that examines the reaction of a security's price to a specific company, world event, or news announcement.

Ex-ante Before the fact.

Excess kurtosis Degree of peakedness (fatness of tails) in excess of the peakedness of the normal distribution.

Excess reserves A bank's actual reserves minus its required reserves.

Exchange for physicals (EEP) A permissible delivery procedure used by futures market participants, in which the long and short arrange a delivery procedure other than the normal procedures stipulated by the futures exchange.

Exchange rate risk Uncertainty due to the denomination of an investment in a currency other than that of the investor's own country.

Exchange-traded fund (ETF) A tradable depository receipt that gives investors a pro rata claim to the returns associated with a portfolio of securities (often designed to mimic an index, such as the Standard & Poor's 500) held in trust by a financial institution.

Exercise (or exercising the option) The process of using an option to buy or sell the underlying.

Exercise price The transaction price specified in an option contract; also known as the *strike price*.

Exercise price (or strike price or striking price, or strike) (1) The transaction price specified in an option contract. *See also* Strike price. (2) The fixed price at which an option holder can buy or sell the underlying.

Exercise rate or strike rate The fixed rate at which the holder of an interest rate option can buy or sell the underlying.

Exhaustive Covering or containing all possible outcomes.

Expansion A business cycle phase between a trough and a peak—phase in which real GDP increases.

Expected rate of return The return that analysts' calculations suggest a security should provide, based on the market's rate of return during the period and the security's relationship to the market.

Expected return The rate of return that an investor expects to get on an investment.

Expected utility The average utility arising from all possible outcomes.

Expected value The probability-weighted average of the possible outcomes of a random variable.

Expenditure A payment or obligation to make future payment for an asset or a service.

Expiration date The date on which a derivative contract expires.

Expiry The expiration date of a derivative security.

Exports The goods and services that we sell to people in other countries.

Extended DuPont System A method of examining *ROE* by breaking it down into five component parts.

External benefits Benefits that accrue to people other than the buyer of the good.

External cash flow Cash, securities, or assets that enter or exit a portfolio.

External costs Costs that are not borne by the producer of the good but borne by someone else.

External diseconomies Factors outside the control of a firm that raise the firm's costs as the industry produces a larger output.

External economies Factors beyond the control of a firm that lower the firm's costs as the industry produces a larger output.

Externality A cost or a benefit that arises from production and falls on someone other than the producer of or cost of a benefit that arises from consumption and falls on someone other than the consumer.

External valuation (real estate) An external valuation is an assessment of market value performed by a third party who is a qualified, professionally designated, certified, or licensed commercial property valuer/appraiser. External valuations must be completed following the valuation standards of the local governing appraisal body.

Extraordinary repairs Repairs that affect the estimated residual value or estimated useful life of an asset thereby increasing its carrying value.

Face value (1) The amount paid on a bond at redemption and traditionally printed on the bond certificate. This face value excludes the final coupon payment. Sometimes referred to as par value. (2) The promised payment at maturity separate from any coupon payment.

Factors of production The productive resources that businesses use to produce goods and services.

Federal budget The annual statement of the expenditures and tax revenues of the government of the United States together with the laws and regulations that approve and support those expenditures and taxes.

Federal funds rate The interest rate that banks charge each other on overnight loans of reserves.

Federal Open Market Committee The main policy-making organ of the Federal Reserve System.

Federal Reserve System The central bank of the United States.

Feedback-rule policy   A rule that specifies how policy actions respond to changes in the state of the economy.

Fee Schedule   The firm's current investment management fees or bundled fees for a particular presentation. This schedule is typically listed by asset level ranges and should be appropriate to the particular prospective client.

Fiduciary   A person who supervises or oversees the investment portfolio of a third party, such as in a trust account, and makes investment decisions in accordance with the owner's wishes.

Fiduciary call   A combination of a European call and a risk-free bond that matures on the option expiration day and has a face value equal to the exercise price of the call.

Financial account   A component of the balance of payments covering investments by residents abroad and investments by nonresidents in the home country. Examples include direct investment made by companies, portfolio investments in equity and bonds, and other investments and liabilities.

Financial innovation   The development of new financial products—new ways of borrowing and lending.

Financial risk   (1) The variability of future income arising from the firm's fixed financing costs, for example, interest payments. The effect of fixed financial costs is to magnify the effect of changes in operating profit on net income or earnings per share. (2) Risk relating to asset prices and other financial variables.

Financing activities   Business activities that involve obtaining resources from stockholders and creditors and providing the former with a return on their investments and the latter with repayment.

Firm   (1) For purposes of the GIPS standards, the term "firm" refers to the entity defined for compliance with the GIPS standards. See the term "distinct business entity." (2) An economic unit that hires factors of production and organizes those factors to produce and sell goods and services.

Fiscal imbalance   The present value of the government's commitments to pay benefits minus the present value of its tax revenues.

Fiscal policy   The government's attempt to achieve macroeconomic objectives such as full employment, sustained economic growth, and price level stability by setting and changing taxes, making transfer payments, and purchasing goods and services.

Fixed exchange rate   An exchange rate that is set at a determined amount by government policy.

Fixed exchange rate regime   A system in which the exchange rate between two currencies remains fixed at a preset level, known as official parity.

Fixed-income forward   A forward contract in which the underlying is a bond.

Fixed-income investments   Loans with contractually mandated payment schedules from firms or governments to investors.

Fixed-rule policy   A rule that specifies an action to be pursued independently of the state of the economy.

Flat trend channel   The range defined by security prices as they maintain a relatively steady level.

Flexible exchange rates   Exchange rates that are determined by the market forces of supply and demand. They are sometimes called floating exchange rates.

Flexible exchange rate system   A system in which exchange rates are determined by supply and demand.

Floating-rate loan   A loan in which the interest rate is reset at least once after the starting date.

Floor   (1) A contract on an interest rate, whereby the writer of the floor periodically pays the difference between a specified floor rate and the market interest rate if, and only if, this difference is positive. This is equivalent to a stream of put options on the interest rate. (2) A combination of interest rate put options designed to hedge a lender against lower rates on a floating-rate loan.

Floor brokers   Independent members of an exchange who act as brokers for other members.

Floored swap   A swap in which the floating payments have a lower limit.

Floorlet   Each component put option in a floor.

Flow   A quantity per unit of time.

Foreign bond   A bond issued by a foreign company on the local market and in the local currency (e.g., Yankee bonds in the United States, Bulldog bonds in the United Kingdom, or Samurai bonds in Japan).

Foreign exchange expectation   A relation that states that the forward exchange rate, quoted at time 0 for delivery at time 1, is equal to the expected value of the spot exchange rate at time 1. When stated relative to the current spot exchange rate, the relation states that the forward discount (premium) is equal to the expected exchange rate movement.

Foreign exchange market   The market in which the currency of one country is exchanged for the currency of another.

Foreign exchange rate   The price at which one currency exchanges for another.

Forward contract An agreement between two parties in which one party, the buyer, agrees to buy from the other party, the seller, an underlying asset at a later date for a price established at the start of the contract.

Forward discount A situation where, from the perspective of the domestic country, the spot exchange rate is smaller than the forward exchange rate with a foreign country.

Forward P/E *See* Leading P/E.

Forward premium A situation where, from the perspective of the domestic country, the spot exchange rate is larger than the forward exchange rate with a foreign country.

Forward price or forward rate The fixed price or rate at which the transaction scheduled to occur at the expiration of a forward contract will take place. This price is agreed on at the initiation date of the contract.

Forward rate A short-term yield for a future holding period implied by the spot rates of two securities with different maturities.

Forward rate agreement (FRA) A forward contract calling for one party to make a fixed interest payment and the other to make an interest payment at a rate to be determined at the contract expiration.

Four-firm concentration ratio A measure of market power that is calculated as the percentage of the value of sales accounted for by the four largest firms in an industry.

Franchise The right or license to an exclusive territory or market.

Franchise factor A firm's unique competitive advantage that makes it possible for a firm to earn excess returns (rates of return above a firm's cost of capital) on its capital projects. In turn, these excess returns and the franchise factor cause the firm's stock price to have a *P/E* ratio above its base *P/E* ratio that is equal to $1/k$.

Free cash flow to equity This cash flow measure equals cash flow from operations minus capital expenditures and debt payments.

Free-rider problem The absence of an incentive for people to pay for what they consume.

Frequency distribution A tabular display of data summarized into a relatively small number of intervals.

Frequency polygon A graph of a frequency distribution obtained by drawing straight lines joining successive points representing the class frequencies.

Frictional unemployment The unemployment that arises from normal labor turnover—from people entering and leaving the labor force and from the ongoing creation and destruction of jobs.

Full-costing A method of accounting for the costs of exploring and developing oil and gas resources in which all costs are recorded as assets and depleted over the estimated life of the producing resources.

Full-costing method A method of accounting for the costs of exploring and developing oil and gas resources in which all costs are recorded as assets and depleted over the estimated life of the producing resources.

Full employment A situation in which the quantity of labor demanded equal the quantity supplied. At full employment, there is no cyclical unemployment—all unemployment is frictional and structural.

Full price (or dirty price) (1) The total price of a bond, including accrued interest. (2) The price of a security with accrued interest.

Futures commission merchants (FCMs) Individuals or companies that execute futures transactions for other parties off the exchange.

Futures contract A variation of a forward contract that has essentially the same basic definition but with some additional features, such as a clearing-house guarantee against credit losses, a daily settlement of gains and losses, and an organized electronic or floor trading facility.

Future value (FV) The amount to which a payment or series of payments will grow by a stated future date.

Game theory A tool that economists use to analyze strategic behavior—behavior that takes into account the expected behavior of others and the mutual recognition of independence.

Gamma A numerical measure of how sensitive an option's delta is to a change in the underlying.

GDP deflator One measure of the price level, which is the average of current-year prices as a percentage of base-year prices.

General Agreement on Tariffs and Trade An international agreement signed in 1947 to reduce tariffs on international trade.

Generally accepted accounting principles (GAAP) Accounting principles formulated by the Financial Accounting Standards Board and used to construct financial statements.

Generational accounting An accounting system that measures the lifetime tax burden and benefits of each generation.

Generational imbalance The division of the fiscal imbalance between the current and future generations, assuming that the current generation will enjoy the existing levels of taxes and benefits

Generic *See* Plain-vanilla.

Geometric mean (GM) A measure of central tendency computed by taking the nth root of the product of n non-negative values.

Goods and services   The objects that people value and produce to satisfy their wants.

Goodwill   The excess of the cost of a group of assets (usually a business) over the fair market value of the assets if purchased individually.

Government budget deficit   The deficit that arises when federal government spends more than it collects in taxes.

Government budget surplus   The surplus that arises when the federal government collects more in taxes than it spends.

Government debt   The total amount of borrowing that the government has borrowed. It equals the sum of past budget deficits minus budget surpluses.

Government purchases   Goods and services bought by the government.

Government purchases multiplier   The magnification effect of a change in government purchases of goods and services on aggregate demand.

Government sector surplus or deficit   An amount equal to net taxes minus government purchases of goods and services.

Great Depression   A decade (1929–1939) of high unemployment and stagnant production throughout the world economy.

Gross domestic product (GDP)   The market value of all the final goods and services produced within a country during a given time period—usually a year.

Gross-Of-Fees Return   The return on assets reduced by any trading expenses incurred during the period.

Gross investment   The total amount spent on purchases of new capital and on replacing depreciated capital.

Group depreciation   The grouping of similar items to calculate depreciation.

Growth company   A company that consistently has the opportunities and ability to invest in projects that provide rates of return that exceed the firm's cost of capital. Because of these investment opportunities, it retains a high proportion of earnings, and its earnings grow faster than those of average firms.

Growth stock   A stock issue that generates a higher rate of return than other stocks in the market with similar risk characteristics.

Harmonic mean   A type of weighted mean computed by averaging the reciprocals of the observations, then taking the reciprocal of that average.

Hedge   A trading strategy in which derivative securities are used to reduce or completely offset a counterparty's risk exposure to an underlying asset.

Hedge fund   An investment vehicle designed to manage a private, unregistered portfolio of assets according to any of several strategies. The investment strategy often employs arbitrage trading and significant financial leverage (e.g., short selling, borrowing, derivatives) while the compensation arrangement for the manager typically specifies considerable profit participation.

Hedge ratio   The number of derivative contracts that must be transacted to offset the price volatility of an underlying commodity or security position.

Herfindahl-Hirschman Index   A measure of market power that is calculated as the square of the market share of each firm (as a percentage) summed over the largest 50 firms (or over all firms if there are fewer than 50) in a market.

High-yield bond   A bond rated below investment grade. Also referred to as *speculative-grade bonds* or *junk bonds.*

Histogram   A bar chart of data that have been grouped into a frequency distribution.

Holding period return (HPR)   The return that an investor earns during a specified holding period; a synonym for total return.

Holding period yield (HPY)   (1) The total return from an investment for a given period of time stated as a percentage. (2) The return that an investor earns during a specified holding period; holding period return with reference to a fixed-income instrument.

Human capital   The value of skills and knowledge possessed by the workforce.

Hurdle rate   The discount rate (cost of capital) which the IRR must exceed if a project is to be accepted.

Hypothesis   With reference to statistical inference, a statement about one or more populations.

Hypothesis testing   With reference to statistical inference, the subdivision dealing with the testing of hypotheses about one or more populations.

Implicit rental rate   The firm's opportunity cost of using its own capital.

Implied repo rate   The rate of return from a cash-and-carry transaction implied by the futures price relative to the spot price.

Implied volatility   The volatility that option traders use to price an option, implied by the price of the option and a particular option-pricing model.

Imports   The goods and services that we buy from people in other countries.

Incentive   A reward that encourages or a penalty that discourages an action.

Incentive system   A method of organizing production that uses a market-like mechanism inside the firm.

Income effect   The effect of a change in income on consumption, other things remaining the same.

Income elasticity of demand   The responsiveness of demand to a change in income, other things remaining the same. It is calculated as the percentage change in the quantity demanded divided by the percentage change in income.

Income statement   A financial statement that shows the flow of the firm's sales, expenses, and earnings over a period of time.

Incremental cash flows   The changes or increments to cash flows resulting from a decision or action.

Indenture   The legal agreement that lists the obligations of the issuer of a bond to the bondholder, including payment schedules, call provisions, and sinking funds.

Independent   With reference to events, the property that the occurrence of one event does not affect the probability of another event occurring.

Independent variable   A variable used to explain the dependent variable in a regression; a right-hand-side variable in a regression equation.

Index amortizing swap   An interest rate swap in which the notional principal is indexed to the level of interest rates and declines with the level of interest rates according to a predefined schedule. This type of swap is frequently used to hedge securities that are prepaid as interest rates decline, such as mortgage-backed securities.

Indexing   An investment strategy in which an investor constructs a portfolio to mirror the performance of a specified index.

Indirect method   The procedure for converting the income statement from an accrual basis to a cash basis by adjusting net income for items that do not affect cash flows, including depreciation, amortization, depletion, gains, losses, and changes in current assets and current liabilities.

Individual transferable quota (ITQ)   A production limit that is assigned to an individual who is free to transfer the quota to someone else.

Induced taxes   Taxes that vary with real GDP.

Industry life cycle analysis   An analysis that focuses on the industry's stage of development.

Inelastic demand   A demand with a price elasticity between 0 and 1; the percentage change in the quantity demanded is less than the percentage change in price.

Infant-industry argument   The argument that it is necessary to protect a new industry to enable it to grow into a mature industry that can compete in world markets.

Inferior good   A good for which demand decreases as income increases.

Inflation   A process in which the price level is rising and money is losing value.

Inflationary gap   The amount by which real GDP exceeds potential GDP.

Inflation rate   The percentage change in the price level from one year to the next.

Information   An attribute of a good market that includes providing buyers and sellers with timely, accurate information on the volume and prices of past transactions and on all currently outstanding bids and offers.

Informationally efficient market   A more technical term for an efficient capital market that emphasizes the role of information in setting the market price.

Information ratio   Statistic used to measure a portfolio's average return in excess of a comparison, benchmark portfolio divided by the standard deviation of this excess return.

Initial margin requirement   The margin requirement on the first day of a transaction as well as on any day in which additional margin funds must be deposited.

Initial public offering (IPO)   A new issue by a firm that has no existing public market.

Intangible assets   Long-term assets with no physical substance whose value is based on rights or advantages accruing to the owner.

Intellectual property rights   Property rights for discoveries owned by the creators of knowledge.

Interest   The income that capital earns.

Interest-on-interest   Bond income from reinvestment of coupon payments.

Interest rate   A rate of return that reflects the relationship between differently dated cash flows; a discount rate.

Interest rate call   An option in which the holder has the right to make a known interest payment and receive an unknown interest payment.

Interest rate cap or cap   A series of call options on an interest rate, with each option expiring at the date on which the floating loan rate will be reset, and with each option having the same exercise rate. A cap in general can have an underlying other than an interest rate.

Interest rate collar   A combination of a long cap and a short floor, or a short cap and a long floor. A collar in general can have an underlying other than an interest rate.

Interest rate floor or floor   A series of put options on an interest rate, with each option expiring at the date on which the floating loan rate will be reset, and with each option having the same exercise rate. A floor in general can have an underlying other than the interest rate.

Interest rate forward *See* Forward rate agreement.

Interest rate option An option in which the underlying is an interest rate.

Interest rate parity The relationship that must exist in an efficient market between the spot and forward foreign exchange rates between two countries and the interest rates in those countries.

Interest rate put An option in which the holder has the right to make an unknown interest payment and receive a known interest payment.

Interest rate risk The uncertainty of returns on an investment due to possible changes in interest rates over time.

Interest rate swap An agreement calling for the periodic exchange of cash flows, one based on an interest rate that remains fixed for the life of the contract and the other that is linked to a variable-rate index.

Intergenerational data mining A form of data mining that applies information developed by previous researchers using a dataset to guide current research using the same or a related dataset.

Intermarket Trading System (ITS) A computerized system that connects competing exchanges and dealers who trade stocks listed on an exchange. Its purpose is to help customers find the best market for these stocks at a point in time.

Internal liquidity (solvency) ratios Financial ratios that measure the ability of the firm to meet future short-term financial obligations.

Internal rate of return (IRR) The discount rate that makes net present value equal 0; the discount rate that makes the present value of an investment's costs (outflows) equal to the present value of the investment's benefits (inflows).

Internal Rate of Return (Private Equity) (IRR) IRR is the annualized implied discount rate (effective compounded rate) that equates the present value of all the appropriate cash inflows (paid-in capital, such as drawdowns for net investments) associated with an investment with the sum of the present value of all the appropriate cash outflows (such as distributions) accruing from it and the present value of the unrealized residual portfolio (unliquidated holdings). For an interim cumulative return measurement, any IRR depends on the valuation of the residual assets.

Internal Valuation (Real Estate) An internal valuation is an advisor's or underlying third-party manager's best estimate of market value based on the most current and accurate information available under the circumstances. An internal valuation could include industry practice techniques, such as discounted cash flow, sales comparison, replacement cost, or a review of all significant events (both general market and asset specific) that could have a material impact on the investment. Prudent assumptions and estimates must be used, and the process must be applied consistently from period to period, except where a change would result in better estimates of market value.

International Fisher relation The assertion that the interest rate differential between two countries should equal the expected inflation rate differential over the term of the interest rates.

Interval With reference to grouped data, a set of values within which an observation falls.

Interval scale A measurement scale that not only ranks data but also gives assurance that the differences between scale values are equal.

In the money An option that has positive intrinsic value.

In-the-money option (1) An option that has a positive value if exercised immediately. For example, a call when the strike price is below the current price of the underlying asset, or a put when the strike price is above the current price of the underlying asset. (2) An option that has positive intrinsic value. (3) Options that, if exercised, would result in the value received being worth more than the payment required to exercise.

Intrinsic value The portion of a call option's total value equal to the greater of either zero or the difference between the current value of the underlying asset and the exercise price; for a put option, intrinsic value is the greater of either zero or the exercise price less the underlying asset price. For a stock, it is the value derived from fundamental analysis of the stock's expected returns or cash flows.

Inverse floater A floating-rate note or bond in which the coupon is adjusted to move opposite to a benchmark interest rate.

Inverse relationship A relationship between variables that move in opposite directions.

Invested Capital (Private Equity) The amount of paid-in capital that has been invested in portfolio companies.

Investing activities Business activities that involve the acquisition and sale of marketable securities and long-term assets and the making and collecting of loans.

Investment The current commitment of dollars for a period of time in order to derive future payments that will compensate the investor for the time the

funds are committed, the expected rate of inflation, and the uncertainty of future payments.

Investment   The purchase of new plant, equipment, and buildings and additions to inventories.

Investment Advisor (Private Equity)   Any individual or institution that supplies investment advice to clients on a per fee basis. The investment advisor inherently has no role in the management of the underlying portfolio companies of a partnership/fund.

Investment company   A firm that sells shares of the company and uses the proceeds to buy portfolios of stock, bonds, or other financial instruments.

Investment decision process   Estimation of intrinsic value for comparison with market price to determine whether or not to invest.

Investment demand   The relationship between investment and real interest rate, other things remaining the same.

Investment horizon   The time period used for planning and forecasting purposes or the future time at which the investor requires the invested funds.

Investment management company   A company separate from the investment company that manages the portfolio and performs administrative functions.

Investment Management Fee   The fee payable to the investment management firm for the on-going management of a portfolio. Investment management fees are typically asset based (percentage of assets), performance based (based on performance relative to a benchmark), or a combination of the two but may take different forms as well.

Investment Multiple (TVPI Multiple) (Private Equity)   The ratio of total value to paid-in-capital. It represents the total return of the investment to the original investment not taking into consideration the time invested. Total value can be found by adding the residual value and distributed capital together.

Investment strategy   A decision by a portfolio manager regarding how he or she will manage the portfolio to meet the goals and objectives of the client. This will include either active or passive management and, if active, what style in terms of top-down or buttom-up or fundamental versus technical.

IRR   The discount rate which forces the PV of a project's inflows to equal the PV of its costs.

IRR rule   An investment decision rule that accepts projects or investments for which the IRR is greater than the opportunity cost of capital.

January effect   A frequent empirical anomaly where risk-adjusted stock returns in the month of January are significantly larger than those occurring in any other month of the year.

Job search   The activity of looking for acceptable vacant jobs.

Joint probability   The probability of the joint occurrence of stated events.

Keynesian   An economist who believes that left alone, the economy would rarely operate at full employment and that to achieve full employment, active help from fiscal policy and monetary policy is required.

Kurtosis   The statistical measure that indicates the peakedness of a distribution.

Labor   The work time and work effort that people devote to producing goods and services.

Labor force   The sum of the people who are employed and who are unemployed.

Labor force participation rate   The percentage of the working-age population who are members of the labor force.

Labor productivity   Real GDP per hour of work.

Labor union   An organized group of workers whose purpose is to increase wages and to influence other job conditions.

Laffer curve   The relationship between the tax rate and the amount of tax revenue collected.

Land   The gifts of nature that we use to produce goods and services.

Law of demand   Other things remaining the same, the higher the price of a good, the smaller is the quantity demanded of it.

Law of diminishing returns   As a firm uses more of a variable input, with a given quantity of other inputs (fixed inputs), the marginal product of the variable input eventually diminishes.

Law of one price   The condition in a financial market in which two financial instruments or combinations of financial instruments can sell for only one price. Equivalent to the principle that no arbitrage opportunities are possible.

Law of supply   Other things remaining the same, the higher the price of a good, the greater is the quantity supplied of it.

Leading indicators   A set of economic variables whose values reach peaks and troughs in advance of the aggregate economy.

Leading P/E (or forward P/E or prospective P/E)   A stock's current price divided by next year's expected earnings.

Learning-by-doing   People become more productive in an activity (learn) just by repeatedly producing a particular good or service (doing).

Leasehold   A right to occupy land or buildings under a long-term rental contract.

Leasehold improvements   Improvements to leased property that become the property of the lessor at the end of the lease.

Legal monopoly   A market structure in which there is one firm and entry is restricted by the granting of a public franchise, government license, patent, or copyright.

Leptokurtic   Describes a distribution that is more peaked than a normal distribution.

License   The right to use a formula, technique, process, or design.

Likelihood   The probability of an observation, given a particular set of conditions.

Limit down   A limit move in the futures market in which the price at which a transaction would be made is at or below the lower limit.

Limited Partnership (Private Equity)   The legal structure used by most venture and private equity funds. Usually fixed life investment vehicles. The general partner or management firm manages the partnership using the policy laid down in a partnership agreement. The agreement also covers terms, fees, structures, and other items agreed between the limited partners and the general partner.

Limit move   A condition in the futures markets in which the price at which a transaction would be made is at or beyond the price limits.

Limit order   An order that lasts for a specified time to buy or sell a security when and if it trades at a specified price.

Limit pricing   The practice of setting the price at the highest level that inflicts a loss on an entrant.

Limit up   A limit move in the futures market in which the price at which a transaction would be made is at or above the upper limit.

Linear association   A straight-line relationship, as opposed to a relationship that cannot be graphed as a straight line.

Linear interpolation   The estimation of an unknown value on the basis of two known values that bracket it, using a straight line between the two known values.

Linear regression   Regression that models the straight-line relationship between the dependent and independent variable(s).

Linear relationship   A relationship between two variables that is illustrated by a straight line.

Liquid   Term used to describe an asset that can be quickly converted to cash at a price close to fair market value.

Liquidity premium   A premium added to the equilibrium interest rate on a security if that security cannot be converted to cash on short notice and at close to "fair market value."

Liquidity risk   Uncertainty due to the ability to buy or sell an investment in the secondary market.

Living wage   An hourly wage rate that enables a person who works a 40-hour week to rent adequate housing for not more than 30 percent of the amount earned.

Locked limit   A condition in the futures markets in which a transaction cannot take place because the price would be beyond the limits.

London InterBank Offer Rate (LIBOR)   (1) The rate at which international banks lend on the Eurocurrency market. This is the rate quoted to a top-quality borrower. The most common maturities are one month, three months, and six months. There is a LIBOR for the U.S. dollar and a few other major currencies. LIBOR is determined by the British Banking Association in London. *See* also Euribor. (2) The Eurodollar rate at which London banks lend dollars to other London banks; considered to be the best representative rate on a dollar borrowed by a private, high-quality borrower.

Long   The buyer of a derivative contract. Also refers to the position of owning a derivative.

Longitudinal data   Observations on characteristic(s) of the same observational unit through time.

Long position   The buyer of a commodity or security or, for a forward contract, the counterparty who will be the eventual buyer of the underlying asset.

Long run   A period of time in which the quantities of all resources can be varied.

Long-run aggregate supply curve   The relationship between the real GDP supplied and the price level in the long run when real GDP equals potential GDP.

Long-run average cost curve   The relationship between the lowest attainable average total cost and output when both capital and labor are varied.

Long-run industry supply curve   A curve that shows how the quantity supplied by an industry varies as the market price varies after all the possible adjustments have been made, including changes in plant size and the number of firms in the industry.

Long-run macroeconomic equilibrium   A situation that occurs when real GDP equals potential GDP—the economy is on its long-run aggregate supply curve.

Long-run Phillips curve   A curve that shows the relationship between inflation and unemployment when the actual inflation rate equals the expected inflation rate.

Long-term assets   Assets that have a useful life of more than one year, are used in the operation of a business, and are not intended for resale. Less commonly called *fixed assets*.

Long-term equity anticipatory securities (LEAPS)   Options originally created with expirations of several years.

Look-ahead bias   A bias caused by using information that was unavailable on the test date.

Lower bound   The lowest possible value of an option.

Lucas wedge The accumulated loss of output that results from a slowdown in the growth rate of real GDP per person.

M1 A measure of money that consists of currency and traveler's checks plus checking deposits owned by individuals and businesses.

M2 A measure of money that consists of M1 plus time deposits, savings deposits, and money market mutual funds and other deposits.

Macroeconomic long run. A time frame that is sufficiently long for real GDP to return to potential GDP so that full employment prevails.

Macaulay duration A measure of the time flow of cash from a bond where cash flows are weighted by present values discounted by the yield to maturity.

Macroeconomics The study of the performance of the national economy and the global economy.

Macroeconomic short run A period during which some money prices are sticky and real GDP might be below, above, or at potential GDP and unemployment might be above, below, or at the natural rate of unemployment.

Maintenance margin The required proportion that the investor's equity value must be to the total market value of the stock. If the proportion drops below this percent, the investor will receive a margin call.

Maintenance margin requirement The margin requirement on any day other than the first day of a transaction.

Management fee The compensation an investment company pays to the investment management company for its services. The average annual fee is about 0.5 percent of fund assets.

Margin (1) The percent of cost a buyer pays in cash for a security, borrowing the balance from the broker. This introduces leverage, which increases the risk of the transaction. (2) The amount of money that a trader deposits in a margin account. The term is derived from the stock market practice in which an investor borrows a portion of the money required to purchase a certain amount of stock. In futures markets, there is no borrowing so the margin is more of a down payment or performance bond.

Margin account The collateral posted with the futures exchange clearinghouse by an outside counterparty to insure its eventual performance; the *initial* margin is the deposit required at contract origination while the *maintenance* margin is the minimum collateral necessary at all times.

Marginal benefit The benefit that a person receives from consuming one more unit of a good or service. It is measured as the maximum amount that a person is willing to pay for one more unit of the good or service.

Marginal benefit curve A curve that shows the relationship between the marginal benefit of a good and the quantity of that good consumed.

Marginal cost The opportunity cost of producing one more unit of a good or service. It is the best alternative forgone. It is calculated as the increase in total cost divided by the increase in output.

Marginal cost pricing rule A rule that sets the price of a good or service equal to the marginal cost of producing it.

Marginal probability *See* Unconditional probability.

Marginal product The increase in total product that results from a one-unit increase in the variable input, with all other inputs remaining the same. It is calculated as the increase in total product divided by the increase in the variable input employed, when the quantities of all other inputs are constant.

Marginal product of labor The additional real GDP produced by an additional hour of labor when all other influences on production remain the same.

Marginal propensity to consume The fraction of a change in disposable income that is consumed. It is calculated as the change in consumption expenditure divided by the change in disposable income.

Marginal revenue The change in total revenue that results from a one-unit increase in the quantity sold. It is calculated as the change in total revenue divided by the change in quantity sold.

Marginal revenue product The change in total revenue that results from employing one more unit of a resource (labor) while the quantity of all other resources remains the same. It is calculated as the increase in total revenue divided by the increase in the quantity of the resource (labor).

Marginal social benefit The marginal benefit enjoyed by society—by the consumer of a good or service (marginal private benefit) plus the marginal benefit enjoyed by others (marginal external benefit).

Marginal social cost The marginal cost incurred by the entire society—by the producer and by everyone else on whom the cost falls—and is the sum of marginal private cost and the marginal external cost.

Marginal tax rate The part of each additional dollar in income that is paid as tax.

Margin call A request by an investor's broker for additional capital for a security bought on margin if the investor's equity value declines below the required maintenance margin.

Marked to market The settlement process used to adjust the margin account of a futures contract for daily changes in the price of the underlying asset.

Near-term, high-priority goal A short-term financial investment goal of personal importance, such as accumulating funds for making a house down payment or buying a car.

Needs-tested spending Government spending on programs that pay benefits to suitably qualified people and businesses.

Negative relationship A relationship between variables that move in opposite directions.

Negotiated sales An underwriting arrangement wherein the sale of a security issue by an issuing entity (governmental body or a corporation) is done using an investment banking firm that maintains an ongoing relationship with the issuer. The characteristics of the security issue are determined by the issuer in consultation with the investment banker.

Neoclassical growth theory A theory of economic growth that proposes that real GDP grows because technological change induces a level of saving and investment that makes capital per hour of labor grow.

Net asset value The market value of the assets owned by a fund.

Net borrower A country that is borrowing more from the rest of the world than it is lending to it.

Net exports The value of exports minus the value of imports.

Net investment Net increase in the capital stock—gross investment minus depreciation.

Net lender A country that is lending more to the rest of the world than it is borrowing from it.

Net-of-Fees Return The gross-of-fees return reduced by the investment management fee.

Net present value The present value of the future flow of marginal revenue product generated by capital minus the cost of the capital.

Net present value (NPV) A measure of the excess cash flows expected from an investment proposal. It is equal to the present value of the cash *inflows* from an investment proposal, discounted at the required rate of return for the investment, minus the present value of the cash *outflows* required by the investment, also discounted at the investment's required rate of return. If the derived net present value is a positive value (i.e., there is an excess net present value), the investment should be acquired since it will provide a rate of return above its required returns.

Net taxes Taxes paid to governments minus transfer payments received from governments.

Netting When parties agree to exchange only the net amount owed from one party to the other.

New issue Common stocks or bonds offered by companies for public sale.

New Keynesian A Keynesian who holds the view that not only is the money wage rate sticky but that prices of goods and services are also sticky.

Node Each value on a binomial tree from which successive moves or outcomes branch.

No-load fund A mutual fund that sells its shares at net asset value without adding sales charges.

Nominal GDP The value of the final goods and services produced in a given year valued at the prices that prevailed in that same year. It is a more precise name for GDP.

Nominal risk-free interest rate The sum of the real risk-free interest rate and the inflation premium.

Nominal scale A measurement scale that categorizes data but does not rank them.

Nominal yield A bond's yield as measured by its coupon rate.

Noncash investing and financing transactions Significant investing and financing transactions involving only long-term assets, long-term liabilities, or stockholders' equity that do not affect current cash inflows or outflows.

Nonlinear relation An association or relationship between variables that cannot be graphed as a straight line.

Nonparametric test A test that is not concerned with a parameter, or that makes minimal assumptions about the population from which a sample comes.

Nonrenewable natural resources Natural resources that can be used only once and that cannot be replaced once they have been used.

Nontariff barrier Any action other than a tariff that restricts international trade.

Normal backwardation The condition in futures markets in which futures prices are lower than expected spot prices.

Normal contango The condition in futures markets in which futures prices are higher than expected spot prices.

Normal good A good for which demand increases as income increases.

Normal profit The expected return for supplying entrepreneurial ability.

North American Free Trade Agreement An agreement, which became effective on January 1, 1994, to eliminate all barriers to international trade between the United States, Canada, and Mexico after a 15-year phasing in period.

Notes Intermediate-term debt securities with maturities longer than 1 year but less than 10 years.

Notional principal The principal value of a swap transaction, which is not exchanged but is used as a scale factor to translate interest rate differentials into cash settlement payments.

NPV rule An investment decision rule that states that an investment should be undertaken if its NPV is positive but not undertaken if its NPV is negative.

Null hypothesis The hypothesis to be tested.

Objective probabilities Probabilities that generally do not vary from person to person; includes a priori and objective probabilities.

Objectives The investor's goals expressed in terms of risk and return and included in the policy statement.

Obsolescence The process of becoming out of date, which is a factor in the limited useful life of tangible assets.

Offensive competitive strategy A strategy whereby a firm attempts to use its strengths to affect the competitive forces in the industry and, in so doing, improves the firm's relative position in the industry.

Official reserves The amount of reserves owned by the central bank of a government in the form of gold, Special Drawing Rights, and foreign cash or marketable securities.

Official settlements account A record of the change in a country's official reserves.

Off-market FRA A contract in which the initial value is intentionally set at a value other than zero and therefore requires a cash payment at the start from one party to the other.

Offsetting A transaction in exchange-listed derivative markets in which a party re-enters the market to close out a position.

Okun gap The gap between real GDP and potential GDP, and so is another name for the output gap.

Oligopoly A market structure in which a small number of firms compete.

One-sided hypothesis test (or one-tailed hypothesis test) A test in which the null hypothesis is rejected only if the evidence indicates that the population parameter is greater than (smaller than) θ_0. The alternative hypothesis also has one side.

Open-End Fund (Private Equity) A type of investment fund where the number of investors and the total committed capital is not fixed (i.e., open for subscriptions and/or redemptions).

Open market operation The purchase or sale of government securities—U.S. Treasury bills and bonds—by the Federal Reserve System in the open market.

Operating activities Business activities that involve the cash effects of transactions and other events that enter into the determination of net income.

Operating efficiency ratios Financial ratios intended to indicate how efficiently management is utilizing the firm's assets in terms of dollar sales generated per dollar of assets. Primary examples would be: total asset turnover, fixed asset turnover, or equity turnover.

Operating leverage The use of fixed-production costs in the firm's operating cost structure. The effect of fixed costs is to magnify the effect of a change in sales on operating profits.

Operating profitability ratios Financial ratios intended to indicate how profitable the firm is in terms of the percent of profit generated from sales. Alternative measures would include: operating profit (EBIT)/net sales; pretax profit (EBT)/ net sales; and net profit/sales.

Opportunity cost The highest-valued alternative that we give up to something.

Optimal portfolio The portfolio on the efficient frontier that has the highest utility for a given investor. It lies at the point of tangency between the efficient frontier and the curve with the investor's highest possible utility.

Option A financial instrument that gives one party the right, but not the obligation, to buy or sell an underlying asset from or to another party at a fixed price over a specific period of time. Also referred to as contingent claims.

Option-adjusted spread A type of yield spread that considers changes in the term structure and alternative estimates of the volatility of interest rates.

Option contract An agreement that grants the owner the right, but not the obligation, to make a future transaction in an underlying commodity or security at a fixed price and within a predetermined time in the future.

Option premium The initial price that the option buyer must pay to the option seller to acquire the contract.

Option premium (or option price or premium) (1) The price of an option. (2) The initial price that the option buyer must pay to the option seller to acquire the contract. (3) The amount of money a buyer pays and seller receives to engage in an option transaction.

Ordinal scale A measurement scale that sorts data into categories that are ordered (ranked) with respect to some characteristic.

Ordinary annuity An annuity with a first cash flow that is paid one period from the present.

OTC Electronic Bulletin Board (OTCBB) A regulated quotation service that displays real-time quotes, last-sale prices, and volume information for a specified set of over-the-counter (OTC) securities that are not traded on the formal Nasdaq market.

Outcome   A possible value of a random variable.

Out-of-sample test   A test of a strategy or model using a sample outside the time period on which the strategy or model was developed.

Out-of-the-money option   (1) An option that has no value if exercised immediately. For example, a call when the strike price is above the current price of the underlying asset, or a put when the strike price is below the current price of the underlying asset. (2) An option that has no intrinsic value. (3) Options that, if exercised, would require the payment of more money than the value received and therefore would not be currently exercised.

Overnight index swap (OIS)   A swap in which the floating rate is the cumulative value of a single unit of currency invested at an overnight rate during the settlement period.

Overweighted   A condition in which a portfolio, for whatever reason, includes more of a class of securities than the relative market value alone would justify.

Paid-In Capital (Private Equity)   The amount of committed capital a limited partner has actually transferred to a venture fund. Also known as the cumulative drawdown amount.

Paired comparisons test   A statistical test for differences based on paired observations drawn from samples that are dependent on each other.

Paired observations   Observations that are dependent on each other.

Pairs arbitrage trade   A trade in two closely related stocks involving the short sale of one and the purchase of the other.

Panel data   Observations through time on a single characteristic of multiple observational units.

Parameter   A descriptive measure computed from or used to describe a population of data, conventionally represented by Greek letters.

Parameter instability   The problem or issue of population regression parameters that have changed over time.

Parametric test   Any test (or procedure) concerned with parameters or whose validity depends on assumptions concerning the population generating the sample.

Par value   *See* Principal.
The principal amount repaid at maturity of a bond. Also called face value.

Patent   A government-sanctioned exclusive right granted to the inventor of a good, service, or productive process to produce, use, and sell the invention for a given number of years.

Patent   An exclusive right granted by the federal government for a period of 20 years to make a particular product or use a specific process.

Payback   The time required for the added income from the convertible security relative to the stock to offset the conversion premium.

Payer swaption   A swaption that allows the holder to enter into a swap as the fixed-rate payer and floating-rate receiver.

Payment date   The date on which a firm actually mails dividend checks.

Payoff   The value of an option at expiration.

Payoff matrix   A table that shows the payoffs for every possible action by each player for every possible action by each other player.

Pegged exchange rate regime   A system in which a country's exchange rate in relation to a major currency is set at a target value (the peg) but allowed to fluctuate within a small band around the target.

Percentiles   Quantiles that divide a distribution into 100 equal parts.

Perfect competition   A market in which there are many firms each selling an identical product; there are many buyers; there are no restrictions on entry into the industry; firms in the industry have no advantage over potential new entrants; and firms and buyers are well informed about the price of each firm's product.

Perfectly elastic demand   Demand with an infinite price elasticity; the quantity demanded changes by an infinitely large percentage in response to a tiny price change.

Perfectly inelastic demand   Demand with a price elasticity of zero; the quantity demanded remains constant when the price changes.

Perfect price discrimination   Price discrimination that extracts the entire consumer surplus.

Performance appraisal   (1) The assessment of an investment record for evidence of investment skill. (2) The evaluation of risk-adjusted performance; the evaluation of investment skill.

Performance measurement   The calculation of returns in a logical and consistent manner.

Permutation   An ordered listing.

Perpetuity   (1) An investment without any maturity date. It provides returns to its owner indefinitely. (2) A perpetual annuity, or a set of never-ending level sequential cash flows, with the first cash flow occurring one period from now.

Personal trust   An amount of money set aside by a grantor and often managed by a third party, the trustee. Often constructed so one party receives income from the trust's investments and another party receives the residual value of the trust after the income beneficiaries' death.

Phillips curve A curve that shows a relationship between inflation and unemployment.

Physical deterioration A decline in the useful life of a depreciable asset resulting from use and from exposure to the elements.

Plain-vanilla Refers to a security, especially a bond or a swap, issued with standard features. Sometimes called generic.

Plain vanilla swap An interest rate swap in which one party pays a fixed rate and the other pays a floating rate, with both sets of payments in the same currency.

Platykurtic Describes a distribution that is less peaked than the normal distribution.

Point estimate A single numerical estimate of an unknown quantity, such as a population parameter.

Policy statement A statement in which the investor specifies investment goals, constraints, and risk preferences.

Pooled estimate An estimate of a parameter that involves combining (pooling) observations from two or more samples.

Population All members of a specified group.

Population mean The arithmetic mean value of a population; the arithmetic mean of all the observations or values in the population.

Population standard deviation A measure of dispersion relating to a population in the same unit of measurement as the observations, calculated as the positive square root of the population variance.

Population variance A measure of dispersion relating to a population, calculated as the mean of the squared deviations around the population mean.

Portfolio An individually managed pool of assets. A portfolio may be a subportfolio, account, or pooled fund.

Position trader A trader who typically holds positions open overnight.

Positive relationship A relationship between two variables that move in the same direction.

Potential GDP The quantity of real GDP at full employment.

Posterior probability An updated probability that reflects or comes after new information.

Potential credit risk The risk associated with the possibility that a payment due at a later date will not be made.

Poverty A situation in which a household's income is too low to be able to buy the quantities of food, shelter, and clothing that are deemed necessary.

Power of a test The probability of correctly rejecting the null—that is, rejecting the null hypothesis when it is false.

Predatory pricing Setting a low price to drive competitors out of business with the intention of setting a monopoly price when the competition has gone.

Preferences A description of a person's likes and dislikes.

Preferred stock An equity investment that stipulates the dividend payment either as a coupon or a stated dollar amount. The firm's directors may withhold payments.

Premium A bond selling at a price above par value due to capital market conditions.

Present value The amount of money that, if invested today, will grow to be as large as a given future amount when the interest that it will earn is taken into account.

Present value (PV) (1) The current worth of future income after it is discounted to reflect the fact that revenues in the future are valued less highly than revenues now. (2) The current worth of a future cash flow. Obtained by discounting the future cash flow at the market-required rate of return. (3) The current (discounted) value of a future cash flow or flows.

Price ceiling A regulation that makes it illegal to charge a price higher than a specified level.

Price continuity A feature of a liquid market in which there are small price changes from one transaction to the next due to the depth of the market.

Price discovery A feature of futures markets in which futures prices provide valuable information about the price of the underlying asset.

Price discrimination The practice of selling different units of a good or service for different prices or of charging one customer different prices for different quantities bought.

Price/earnings (P/E) ratio The number by which expected earnings per share is multiplied to estimate a stock's value; also called the *earnings multiplier*.

Price effect The effect of a change in the price on the quantity of a good consumed, other things remaining the same.

Price elasticity of demand A units-free measure of the responsiveness of the quantity demanded of a good to a change in its price, when all other influences on buyers' plans remain the same.

Price floor A regulation that makes it illegal to charge a price lower than a specified level.

Price level The average level of prices as measured by a price index.

Price limits Limits imposed by a futures exchange on the price change that can occur from one day to the next.

Price momentum   A portfolio strategy in which you acquire stocks that have enjoyed above-market stock price increases.

Price multiple   The ratio of a stock's market price to some measure of value per share.

Price relative   A ratio of an ending price over a beginning price; it is equal to 1 plus the holding period return on the asset.

Price risk   The component of interest rate risk due to the uncertainty of the market price of a bond caused by changes in market interest rates.

Price taker   A firm that cannot influence the price of the good or service it produces.

Price-weighted index   An index calculated as an arithmetic mean of the current prices of the sampled securities.

Primary market   The market in which newly issued securities are sold by their issuers, who receive the proceeds.

Principal-agent problem   The problem of devising compensation rules that induce an agent to act in the best interest of a principal.

Prior probabilities   Probabilities reflecting beliefs prior to the arrival of new information.

Private Equity   Private equity includes, but is not limited to, organizations devoted to venture capital, leveraged buyouts, consolidations, mezzanine and distressed debt investments, and a variety of hybrids, such as venture leasing and venture factoring.

Private information   Information that is available to one person but is too costly for anyone else to obtain.

Private placement   A new issue sold directly to a small group of investors, usually institutions

Private sector surplus or deficit   An amount equal to saving minus investment.

Probability   A number between 0 and 1 describing the chance that a stated event will occur.

Probability density function   A function with non-negative values such that probability can be described by areas under the curve graphing the function.

Probability distribution   A distribution that specifies the probabilities of a random variable's possible outcomes.

Probability function   A function that specifies the probability that the random variable takes on a specific value.

Producer surplus   The price of a good minus the opportunity cost of producing it, summed over the quantity sold.

Product differentiation   Making a product slightly different from the product of a competing firm.

Production efficiency   A situation in which the economy cannot produce more of one good without producing less of some other good.

Production function   The relationship between real GDP and the quantity of labor when all other influences on production remain the same.

Production method   A method of depreciation that assumes depreciation is solely the result of use and that allocates depreciation based on the units of use or output during each period of an asset's useful life.

Production possibilities frontier   The boundary between the combinations of goods and services that can be produced and the combinations that cannot.

Production quota   An upper limit to the quantity of a good that may be produced in a specified period.

Productivity growth slowdown   A slowdown in the growth rate of output per person.

Profit   The income earned by entrepreneurship.

Property rights   Social arrangements that govern the ownership, use, and disposal of resources or factors of production, goods, and services that are enforceable in the courts.

Prospective P/E   *See* Leading P/E.

Protective put   An option strategy in which a long position in an asset is combined with a long position in a put.

Public good   A good or service that is both nonrival and nonexcludable—it can be consumed simultaneously by everyone and from which no one can be excluded.

Purchasing power parity   The equal value of different monies.

Purchasing power parity (PPP)   A theory stating that the exchange rate between two currencies will exactly reflect the purchasing power of the two currencies.

Pure discount instruments   Instruments that pay interest as the difference between the amount borrowed and the amount paid back.

Put   An option that gives the holder the right to sell an underlying asset to another party at a fixed price over a specific period of time.

Put option   A contract giving the right to sell an asset at a specified price, on or before a specified date.

Put–call–forward parity   The relationship among puts, calls, and forward contracts.

Put-call parity   The relationship that must exist in an efficient market between the prices for put and call options having the same underlying asset, exercise price, and expiration date.

p-Value   The smallest level of significance at which the null hypothesis can be rejected; also called the marginal significance level.

Quality financial statements   Financial statements that most knowledgeable observers (analysts, portfolio managers) would consider conservatively prepared in terms of sales, expenses, earnings, and asset valuations. The results reported would reflect reasonable estimates and indicate what truly happened during the period and the legitimate value of assets and liabilities on the balance sheet.

Quantile (or fractile)   A value at or below which a stated fraction of the data lies.

Quantity demanded   The amount of a good or service that consumers plan to buy during a given time period at a particular price.

Quantity of labor demanded   The labor hours hired by the firms in the economy.

Quantity of labor supplied   The number of labor hours that all households in the economy plan to work.

Quantity supplied   The amount of a good or service that producers plan to sell during a given time period at a particular price.

Quantity theory of money   The proposition that in the long run, an increase in the quantity of money brings an equal percentage increase in the price level.

Quartiles   Quantiles that divide a distribution into four equal parts.

Quintiles   Quantiles that divide a distribution into five equal parts.

Quota   A quantitative restriction on the import of a particular good, which specifies the maximum amount that can be imported in a given time period.

Random number   An observation drawn from a uniform distribution.

Random number generator   An algorithm that produces uniformly distributed random numbers between 0 and 1.

Random variable   A quantity whose future outcomes are uncertain.

Random walk theory   (1) The theory that current stock prices already reflect known information about the future. Therefore, the future movement of stock prices will be determined by surprise occurrences. This will cause them to change in a random fashion. (2) A theory stating that all current information is reflected in current security prices and that future price movements are random because they are caused by unexpected news.

Range   The difference between the maximum and minimum values in a dataset.

Range forward   A trading strategy based on a variation of the put-call parity model where, for the same underlying asset but different exercise prices, a call option is purchased and a put option is sold (or vice versa).

Rational expectation   The most accurate forecast possible, a forecast that uses all the available information, including knowledge of the relevant economic forces that influence the variable being forecasted.

Ratio scales   A measurement scale that has all the characteristics of interval measurement scales as well as a true zero point as the origin.

Real business cycle theory   A theory that regards random fluctuations in productivity as the main source of economic fluctuations.

Real Estate   Real estate Investments include: (a) Wholly owned or partially owned properties, (b) Commingled funds, property unit trusts, and insurance company separate accounts, (c) Unlisted, private placement securities issued by private real estate investment trusts (REITs) and real estate operating companies (REOCs), and (d) Equity-oriented debt, such as participating mortgage loans or any private interest in a property where some portion of return to the investor at the time of investment is related to the performance of the underlying real estate.

Real estate investment trusts (REITs)   Investment funds that hold portfolios of real estate investments.

Real income   A household's income expressed as a quantity of goods that the household can afford to buy.

Real interest rate   The nominal interest rate adjusted for inflation; the nominal interest rate minus the inflation rate.

Realization Multiple (Private Equity)   The realization multiple (DPI) is calculated by dividing the cumulative distributions by the paid-in-capital.

Realized capital gains   Capital gains that result when an appreciated asset is sold; realized capital gains are taxable.

Real options   Options embedded in a firm's real assets that give managers valuable decision-making flexibility, such as the right to either undertake or abandon an investment project.

Real rate of interest   The money rate of interest minus the expected rate of inflation. The real rate of interest indicates the interest premium, in terms of real goods and services, that one must pay for earlier availability.

Real risk-free rate (RRFR) The basic interest rate with no accommodation for inflation or uncertainty. The pure time value of money.

Real wage rate The quantity of goods ands services that an hour's work can buy. It is equal to the money wage rate divided by the price level.

Receiver swaption A swaption that allows the holder to enter into a swap as the fixed-rate receiver and floating-rate payer.

Recession There are two common definitions of recession. They are (1) A business cycle phase in which real GDP decreases for at least two successive quarters. (2) A significant decline in activity spread across the economy, lasting for more than a few months, visible in industrial production, employment, real income, and wholesale-retail trade.

Recessionary gap The amount by which potential GDP exceeds real GDP.

Reference base period The period in which the CPI is defined to be 100.

Registered competitive market makers (RCMMs) Members of an exchange who are allowed to use their memberships to buy or sell for their own account within the specific trading obligations set down by the exchange.

Registered traders Members of the stock exchange who are allowed to use their memberships to buy and sell for their own account, which means they save commissions on their trading but they provide liquidity to the market, and they abide by exchange regulations on how they can trade.

Regression coefficients The intercept and slope coefficient(s) of a regression.

Regulation Rules administrated by a government agency to influence economic activity by determining prices, product standards and types, and conditions under which new firms may enter an industry.

Regulatory risk The risk associated with the uncertainty of how derivative transactions will be regulated or with changes in regulations.

Relative dispersion The amount of dispersion relative to a reference value or benchmark.

Relative frequency With reference to an interval of grouped data, the number of observations in the interval divided by the total number of observations in the sample.

Relative price The ratio of the price of one good or service to the price of another good or service. A relative price is an opportunity cost.

Renewable natural resources Natural resources that can be used repeatedly without depleting what is available for future use.

Rent The income that land earns.

Rent ceiling A regulation that makes it illegal to charge a rent higher than a specified level.

Rent seeking Any attempt to capture a consumer surplus, a producer surplus, or an economic profit.

Replacement value The market value of a swap.

Required rate of return The return that compensates investors for their time, the expected rate of inflation, and the uncertainty of the return.

Required reserve ratio The ratio of reserves to deposits that banks are required, by regulation, to hold.

Reserve ratio The fraction of a bank's total deposits that are held in reserves.

Reserves Cash in a bank's vault plus the bank's deposits at Federal Reserve banks.

Ricardo-Barro effect The equivalence of financing government purchases by taxes or by borrowing.

Residual value The estimated net scrap, salvage, or trade-in value of a tangible asset at the estimated date of its disposal. Also called *salvage value* or *disposal value*.

Resistance level A price at which a technician would expect a substantial increase in the supply of a stock to reverse a rising trend.

Return prediction studies Studies wherein investigations attempt to predict the time series of future rates of return using public information. An example would be predicting above-average returns for the stock market based on the aggregate dividend yield—e.g., high dividend yield indicates above average future market returns.

Revenue bond A bond that is serviced by the income generated from specific revenue-producing projects of the municipality.

Revenue expenditure An expenditure for ordinary repairs and maintenance of a long-term asset, which is recorded by a debit to an expense account.

Rising trend channel The range defined by security prices as they move progressively higher.

Risk averse The assumption about investors that they will choose the least risky alternative, all else being equal.

Risk-free asset An asset with returns that exhibit zero variance.

Risk management The process of identifying the level of risk an entity wants, measuring the level of risk the entity currently has, taking actions that bring the actual level of risk to the desired level of risk, and monitoring the new actual level of risk so that it continues to be aligned with the desired level of risk.

Risk-neutral probabilities Weights that are used to compute a binomial option price. They are the probabilities that would apply if a risk-neutral investor valued an option.

Risk-neutral valuation The process by which options and other derivatives are priced by treating investors as though they were risk neutral.

Risk premium (1) The difference between the expected return on an asset and the risk-free interest rate. (2) The increase over the nominal risk-free rate that investors demand as compensation for an investment's uncertainty. (3) The expected return on an investment minus the risk-free rate.

Risk premium (RP) The increase over the nominal risk-free rate that investors demand as compensation for an investment's uncertainty.

Risky asset An asset with uncertain future returns.

Rival A good or services or a resource is rival if its use by one person decreases the quantity available for someone else.

Robust The quality of being relatively unaffected by a violation of assumptions.

Runs test A test of the weak-form efficient market hypothesis that checks for trends that persist longer in terms of positive or negative price changes than one would expect for a random series.

Safety-first rules Rules for portfolio selection that focus on the risk that portfolio value will fall below some minimum acceptable level over some time horizon.

Sample A subset of a population.

Sample excess kurtosis A sample measure of the degree of a distribution's peakedness in excess of the normal distribution's peakedness.

Sample kurtosis A sample measure of the degree of a distribution's peakedness.

Sample mean The sum of the sample observations, divided by the sample size.

Sample selection bias Bias introduced by systematically excluding some members of the population according to a particular attribute—for example, the bias introduced when data availability leads to certain observations being excluded from the analysis.

Sample skewness A sample measure of degree of asymmetry of a distribution.

Sample standard deviation The positive square root of the sample variance.

Sample statistic or statistic A quantity computed from or used to describe a sample.

Sample variance A sample measure of the degree of dispersion of a distribution, calculated by dividing the sum of the squared deviations from the sample mean by the sample size (n) minus 1.

Sampling (1) A technique for constructing a passive index portfolio in which the portfolio manager buys a representative sample of stocks that comprise the benchmark index. (2) The process of obtaining a sample.

Sampling distribution The distribution of all distinct possible values that a statistic can assume when computed from samples of the same size randomly drawn from the same population.

Sampling error The difference between the observed value of a statistic and the quantity it is intended to estimate.

Sampling plan The set of rules used to select a sample.

Sandwich spread An option strategy that is equivalent to a short butterfly spread.

Saving The amount of income that households have left after they have paid their taxes and bought their consumption goods and services.

Savings and loan association (S&L) A depository institution that receives checking deposits and savings deposits and that makes personal, commercial, and home-purchase loans.

Savings bank A depository institution, owned by its depositors, that accepts savings deposits and makes mortgage loans.

Saving supply The relationship between saving and the real interest rate, other things remaining the same.

Scalper A trader who offers to buy or sell futures contracts, holding the position for only a brief period of time. Scalpers attempt to profit by buying at the bid price and selling at the higher ask price.

Scarcity Our inability to satisfy all our wants.

Scatter diagram A diagram that plots the value of one economic variable against the value of another.

Scatter plot A two-dimensional plot of pairs of observations on two data series.

Scenario analysis A risk management technique involving the examination of the performance of a portfolio under specified situations. Closely related to stress testing.

Search activity The time spent looking for someone with whom to do business.

Seasoned equity issues New equity shares offered by firms that already have stock outstanding.

Seats Memberships in a derivatives exchange.

Secondary market The market in which outstanding securities are bought and sold by owners other than the issuers. Purpose is to provide liquidity for investors.

Sector rotation strategy An active strategy that involves purchasing stocks in specific industries or stocks with specific characteristics (low *P/E*, growth, value) that are anticipated to rise in value more than the overall market.

Security market line (SML)   The line that reflects the combination of risk and return of alternative investments. In CAPM, risk is measured by systematic risk (beta).

SelectNet   An order-routing and trade-execution system for institutional investors (brokers and dealers) that allows communication through the Nasdaq system rather than by phone.

Self-interest   The choices that you think are the best for you.

Semideviation   The positive square root of semivariance (sometimes called semistandard deviation).

Semilogarithmic   Describes a scale constructed so that equal intervals on the vertical scale represent equal rates of change, and equal intervals on the horizontal scale represent equal amounts of change.

Semivariance   The average squared deviation below the mean.

Separation theorem   The proposition that the investment decision, which involves investing in the market portfolio on the capital market line, is separate from the financing decision, which targets a specific point on the CML based on the investor's risk preference.

Settlement date or payment date   The date on which the parties to a swap make payments.

Settlement period   The time between settlement dates.

Settlement price   The price determined by the exchange clearinghouse with which futures contract margin accounts are marked to market.

Settlement risk   When settling a contract, the risk that one party could be in the process of paying the counterparty while the counterparty is declaring bankruptcy.

Shareholders' equity   Total assets minus total liabilities.

Sharpe measure   A relative measure of a portfolio's benefit-to-risk ratio, calculated as its average return in excess of the risk-free rate divided by the standard deviation of portfolio returns.

Sharpe ratio   (1) The ratio of mean excess return (return minus the risk-free rate) to standard deviation of returns (or excess returns). (2) The average return in excess of the risk-free rate divided by the standard deviation of return; a measure of the average excess return earned per unit of standard deviation of return.

Shortfall risk   The risk that portfolio value will fall below some minimum acceptable level over some time horizon.

Short hedge   A short position in a forward or futures contract used to offset the price volatility of a long position in the underlying asset.

Short position   The seller of a commodity or security or, for a forward contract, the counterparty who will be the eventual seller of the underlying asset.

Short run   The short run in microeconomics has two meanings. For the firm, it is the period of time in which the quantity of at least one input is fixed and the quantities of the other inputs can be varied. The fixed input is usually capital—that is, the firm has a given plant size. For the industry, the short run is the period of time in which each firm has a given plant size and the number of firms in the industry is fixed.

Short-run aggregate supply curve   A curve that shows the relationship between the quantity of real GDP supplied and the price level in the short run when the money wage rate, other resource prices, and potential GDP remain constant.

Short-run industry supply curve   A curve that shows the quantity supplied by the industry at each price varies when the plant size of each firm and the number of firms in the industry remain the same.

Short-run macroeconomic equilibrium   A situation that occurs when the quantity of real GDP demanded equals quantity of real GDP supplied—at the point of intersection of the *AD* curve and the *SAS* curve.

Short-run Phillips curve   A curve that shows the tradeoff between inflation and unemployment, when the expected inflation rate and the natural rate of unemployment remain the same.

Short sale   The sale of borrowed securities with the intention of repurchasing them later at a lower price and earning the difference.

Should   Encouraged (recommended) to follow the recommendation of the GIPS standards but not required.

Shutdown point   The output and price at which the firm just covers its total variable cost. In the short run, the firm is indifferent between producing the profit-maximizing output and shutting down temporarily.

Signal   An action taken by an informed person (or firm) to send a message to uninformed people or an action taken outside a market that conveys information that can be used by that market.

Simple interest   The interest earned each period on the original investment; interest calculated on the principal only.

Simple random sample   A subset of a larger population created in such a way that each element of the population has an equal probability of being selected to the subset.

Simulation trial   A complete pass through the steps of a simulation.

Single-price monopoly   A monopoly that must sell each unit of its output for a same price to all its customers.

Sinking fund   (1) Bond provision that requires the bond to be paid off progressively rather than in full at maturity. (2) Bond provision that requires the issuer to redeem some or all of the bond systematically over the term of the bond rather than in full at maturity.

Skewed   Not symmetrical.

Skewness   A quantitative measure of skew (lack of symmetry); a synonym of skew.

Slope   The change in the value of the variable measured on the y-axis divided by the change in the value of the variable measured on the x-axis.

Small-firm effect   A frequent empirical anomaly where risk-adjusted stock returns for companies with low market capitalization (i.e., share price multiplied by number of outstanding shares) are significantly larger than those generated by high market capitalization (large cap) firms.

Small-Order Execution System (SOES)   A quotation and execution system for retail (nonprofessional) investors who place orders with brokers who must honor their prevailing bid-ask for automatic execution up to 1,000 shares.

Social interest   Choices that are the best for society as a whole.

Soft dollars   A form of compensation to a money manager generated when the manager commits the investor to paying higher brokerage fees in exchange for the manager receiving additional services (e.g., stock research) from the broker.

Software   Capitalized costs associated with computer programs developed for sale, lease, or internal use and amortized over the estimated economic life of the programs.

Sovereign risk   The risk that a government may default on its debt.

Spearman rank correlation coefficient   A measure of correlation applied to ranked data.

Specialist   The major market maker on U.S. stock exchanges who acts as a broker or dealer to ensure the liquidity and smooth functions of the secondary stock market.

Speculative company   A firm with a great degree of business and/or financial risk, with commensurate high earnings potential.

Speculative stock   A stock that appears to be highly overpriced compared to its intrinsic valuation.

Spending phase   Phase in the investment life cycle during which individuals' earning years end as they retire. They pay for expenses with income from social security and returns from prior investments and invest to protect against inflation.

Spot price   Current market price of an asset. Also called cash price.

Spot rate   The required yield for a cash flow to be received at some specific date in the future—for example, the spot rate for a flow to be received in one year, for a cash flow in two years, and so on.

Spread   An option strategy involving the purchase of one option and sale of another option that is identical to the first in all respects except either exercise price or expiration.

Spurious correlation   A correlation that misleadingly points towards associations between variables.

Stagflation   The combination of recession and inflation.

Standard deviation   A measure of variability equal to the square root of the variance.

Standardizing   A transformation that involves subtracting the mean and dividing the result by the standard deviation.

Standard normal distribution (or unit normal distribution)   The normal density with mean (μ) equal to 0 and standard deviation (σ) equal to 1.

Stated annual interest rate or quoted interest rate   A quoted interest rate that does not account for compounding within the year.

Statement of cash flows   A financial statement that shows how a company's operating, investing, and financing activities have affected cash during an accounting period.

Statistic   A quantity computed from or used to describe a sample of data.

Statistical inference   Making forecasts, estimates, or judgments about a larger group from a smaller group actually observed; using a sample statistic to infer the value of an unknown population parameter.

Statistically significant   A result indicating that the null hypothesis can be rejected; with reference to an estimated regression coefficient, frequently understood to mean a result indicating that the corresponding population regression coefficient is different from 0.

Statistics   The science of describing, analyzing, and drawing conclusions from data; also, a collection of numerical data.

Stock   A quantity that exists at a point in time.

Stock dividend   A dividend paid in the form of additional shares rather than in cash.

Stock split   An action taken by a firm to increase the number of shares outstanding, such as doubling the number of shares outstanding by giving each stockholder two new shares for each one formerly held.

Storage costs or carrying costs   The costs of holding an asset, generally a function of the physical characteristics of the underlying asset.

Straddle   An option strategy involving the purchase of a put and a call with the same exercise price. A straddle is based on the expectation of high volatility of the underlying.

Straight-line method   A method of depreciation that assumes depreciation depends only on the passage of time and that allocates an equal amount of depreciation to each accounting period in an asset's useful life.

Strangle   A variation of a straddle in which the put and call have different exercise prices.

Strap   An option strategy involving the purchase of two calls and one put.

Strategies   All the possible actions of each player in a game.

Stratified random sampling   A procedure by which a population is divided into subpopulations (strata) based on one or more classification criteria. Simple random samples are then drawn from each stratum in sizes proportional to the relative size of each stratum in the population. These samples are then pooled.

Stress testing   A risk management technique in which the risk manager examines the performance of the portfolio under market conditions involving high risk and usually high correlations across markets. Closely related to scenario analysis.

Stress testing/scenario analysis   A set of techniques for estimating losses in extremely unfavorable combinations of events or scenarios.

Strike price   Price at which an option can be exercised (same as exercise price).

Strip   An option strategy involving the purchase of two puts and one call.

Structural change   Economic trend occurring when the economy is undergoing a major change in organization or in how it functions.

Structural surplus or deficit   The budget balance that would occur if the economy were at full employment and real GDP were equal to potential GDP.

Structural unemployment   The unemployment that arises when changes in technology or international competition change the skills needed to perform jobs or change the locations of jobs.

Structured note   (1) A bond or note issued with some unusual, often option-like, clause. (2) A bond with an embedded derivative designed to create a payoff distribution that satisfies the needs of a specific investor clientele. (3) A variation of a floating-rate note that has some type of unusual characteristic such as a leverage factor or in which the rate moves opposite to interest rates.

Style analysis   An attempt to explain the variability in the observed returns to a security portfolio in terms of the movements in the returns to a series of benchmark portfolios designed to capture the essence of a particular security characteristic such as size, value, and growth.

Subjective probability   A probability drawing on personal or subjective judgment.

Subsidy   A payment that the government makes to a producer.

Substitute   A good that can be used in place of another good.

Substitution effect   The effect of a change in price of a good or service on the quantity bought when the consumer (hypothetically) remains indifferent between the original and the new consumption situations—that is, the consumer remains on the same indifference curve.

Successful efforts accounting   A method of accounting for the costs of exploring and developing oil and gas resources in which successful exploration is recorded as an asset and depleted over the estimated life of the resource and all unsuccessful efforts are immediately written off as losses.

Sunk cost   The past cost of buying a plant that has no resale value.

Supplemental Information   Any performance-related information included as part of a compliant performance presentation that supplements or enhances the required and/or recommended disclosure and presentation provisions of the GIPS standards.

Supply   The relationship between the quantity of a good that producers plan to sell and the price of the good when all other influences on sellers' plans remain the same. It is described by a supply schedule and illustrated by a supply curve.

Supply curve   A curve that shows the relationship between the quantity supplied and the price of a good when all other influences on producers' planned sales remain the same.

Supply of labor   The relationship between the quantity of labor supplied and the real wage rate when all other influences on work plans remain the same.

Supply-side effects The effects of fiscal policy on employment, potential GDP, and aggregate supply.

Support level A price at which a technician would expect a substantial increase in price and volume for a stock to reverse a declining trend that was due to profit taking.

Survivorship bias The bias resulting from a test design that fails to account for companies that have gone bankrupt, merged, or are otherwise no longer reported in a database.

Sustainable growth rate A measure of how fast a firm can grow using internal equity and debt financing and a constant capital structure. Equal to retention rate _ ROE.

Swap (1) A contract whereby two parties agree to a periodic exchange of cash flows. In certain types of swaps, only the net difference between the amounts owed is exchanged on each payment date. (2) An agreement between two parties to exchange a series of future cash flows.

Swap spread The difference between the fixed rate on an interest rate swap and the rate on a Treasury note with equivalent maturity; it reflects the general level of credit risk in the market.

Swaption (1) An option to enter into a swap contract at a later date. (2) An option to enter into a swap.

SWOT analysis An examination of a firm's Strengths, Weaknesses, Opportunities, and Threats. This analysis helps an analyst evaluate a firm's strategies to exploit its competitive advantages or defend against its weaknesses.

Symmetry principle A requirement that people in similar situations be treated similarly.

Synthetic call The combination of puts, the underlying, and risk-free bonds that replicates a call option.

Synthetic forward contract The combination of the underlying, puts, calls, and risk-free bonds that replicates a forward contract.

Synthetic put The combination of calls, the underlying, and risk-free bonds that replicates a put option.

Systematic risk The variability of returns that is due to macroeconomic factors that affect all risky assets. Because it affects all risky assets, it cannot be eliminated by diversification.

Systematic sampling A procedure of selecting every kth member until reaching a sample of the desired size. The sample that results from this procedure should be approximately random.

Tangible assets Long-term assets that have physical substance.

Tangible book value per share Common shareholders' equity minus intangible assets from the balance sheet, divided by the number of shares outstanding.

Tap Procedure by which a borrower can keep issuing additional amounts of an old bond at its current market value. This procedure is used for bond issues, notably by the British and French governments, as well as for some short-term debt instruments.

Target semideviation The positive square root of target semivariance.

Target semivariance The average squared deviation below a target value.

Tariff A tax that is imposed by the importing country when an imported good crosses its international boundary.

Tax incidence The division of the burden of a tax between the buyer and the seller.

Tax multiplier The magnification effect of a change in taxes on aggregate demand.

Tax wedge The gap between the before-tax and after-tax wage rates.

Taylor rule A rule that adjusts the federal funds rate to target the inflation rate and to take into account deviations of the inflation rate from its target and deviations of real GDP from potential GDP.

Technical analysis Estimation of future security price movements based on past price and volume movements.

Technological change The development of new goods and better ways of producing goods and services.

Technological efficiency A situation that occurs when the firm produces a given output by using the least amount of inputs.

Technology Any method of producing a good or service.

t-Distribution A symmetrical distribution defined by a single parameter, degrees of freedom, that is largely used to make inferences concerning the mean of a normal distribution whose variance is unknown.

Temporary New Account A tool that firms can use to remove the effect of significant cash flows on a portfolio. When a significant cash flow occurs in a portfolio, the firm may treat this cash flow as a "temporary new account," allowing the firm to implement the mandate of the portfolio without the impact of the cash flow on the performance of the portfolio.

Termination date The date of the final payment on a swap; also, the swap's expiration date.

Terms of trade The quantity of goods and services that a country exports to pay for its imports of goods and services.

Term structure of interest rates The relationship between term to maturity and yield to maturity for a sample of comparable bonds at a given time. Popularly known as the *yield curve.*

Term to maturity Specifies the date or the number of years before a bond matures or expires.

Test statistic A quantity, calculated based on a sample, whose value is the basis for deciding whether or not to reject the null hypothesis.

Theta The rate at which an option's time value decays.

Third market Over-the-counter trading of securities listed on an exchange.

Thrift institutions Thrift institutions include savings and loan associations, savings banks, and credit unions.

Tick The minimum price movement for the asset underlying a forward or futures contract; for Treasury bonds, one tick equals 1/32 of 1 percent of par value.

Time-period bias The possibility that when we use a time-series sample, our statistical conclusion may be sensitive to the starting and ending dates of the sample.

Time-series analysis An examination of a firm's performance data over a period of time.

Time-series data Observations of a variable over time.

Time-series graph A graph that measures time (for example, months or years) on the x-axis and the variable or variables in which we are interested on the y-axis.

Time to expiration The time remaining in the life of a derivative, typically expressed in years.

Time value decay The loss in the value of an option resulting from movement of the option price toward its payoff value as the expiration day approaches.

Time-weighted rate of return (1) The compound rate of growth of one unit of currency invested in a portfolio during a stated measurement period; a measure of investment performance that is not sensitive to the timing and amount of withdrawals or additions to the portfolio. (2) Calculation that computes period-by-period returns on an investment and removes the effects of external cash flows, which are generally client-driven, and best reflects the firm's ability to manage assets according to a specified strategy or objective.

Total cost The cost of all the productive resources that a firm uses.

Total Firm Assets Total firm assets are all assets for which a firm has investment management responsibility. Total firm assets include assets managed outside the firm (e.g., by subadvisors) for which the firm has asset allocation authority.

Total fixed cost The cost of the firm's fixed inputs.

Total probability rule for expected value A rule explaining the expected value of a random variable in terms of expected values of the random variable conditional on mutually exclusive and exhaustive scenarios.

Total product The total output produced by a firm in a given period of time.

Total return A return objective in which the investor wants to increase the portfolio value to meet a future need by both capital gains and current income reinvestment.

Total revenue The value of a firm's sales. It is calculated as the price of the good multiplied by the quantity sold.

Total revenue test A method of estimating the price elasticity of demand by observing the change in total revenue that results from a change in the price, when all other influences on the quantity sold remain the same.

Total variable cost The cost of all the firm's variable inputs.

Tracking error (1) The standard deviation of the difference in returns between an active investment portfolio and its benchmark portfolio; also called tracking error volatility. (2) The condition in which the performance of a portfolio does not match the performance of an index that serves as the portfolio's benchmark. (3) A synonym for tracking risk and active risk; also, the total return on a portfolio (gross of fees) minus the total return on a benchmark.

Tracking risk The standard deviation of the differences between a portfolio's returns and its benchmark's returns; a synonym of active risk.

Trade balance The balance of a country's exports and imports; part of the current account.

Trade Date Accounting The transaction is reflected in the portfolio on the date of the purchase or sale, and not on the settlement date. Recognizing the asset or liability within at least 3 days of the date the transaction is entered into (Trade Date, T + 1, T + 2 or T + 3) all satisfy the trade date accounting requirement for purposes of the GIPS standards. (See settlement date accounting.)

Trademark A registered symbol that can be used only by its owner to identify a product or service.

Tradeoff An exchange—giving up one thing to get something else.

Trading effect The difference in performance of a bond portfolio from that of a chosen index due to short-run changes in the composition of the portfolio.

Trading Expenses The costs of buying or selling a security. These costs typically take the form of brokerage commissions or spreads from either internal or external brokers. Custody fees charged per transaction should be considered custody fees and not direct transaction costs. Estimated trading expenses are not permitted.

Trading rule A formula for deciding on current transactions based on historical data.

Trading turnover The percentage of outstanding shares traded during a period of time.

Trailing P/E (or current P/E) A stock's current market price divided by the most recent four quarters of earnings per share.

Tranche Refers to a portion of an issue that is designed for a specific category of investors. French for "slice."

Transaction cost The cost of executing a trade. Low costs characterize an operationally efficient market.

Transaction Expenses (Private Equity) Include all legal, financial, advisory, and investment banking fees related to buying, selling, restructuring, and recapitalizing portfolio companies.

Transactions costs The costs that arise from finding someone with whom to do business, of reaching an agreement about the price and other aspects of the exchange, and of ensuring that the terms of the agreement are fulfilled. The opportunity costs of conducting a transaction.

Treasury bill A negotiable U.S. government security with a maturity of less than one year that pays no periodic interest but yields the difference between its par value and its discounted purchase price.

Treasury bond A U.S. government security with a maturity of more than 10 years that pays interest periodically.

Treasury note A U.S. government security with maturities of 1 to 10 years that pays interest periodically.

Tree diagram A diagram with branches emanating from nodes representing either mutually exclusive chance events or mutually exclusive decisions.

Trend The general tendency for a variable to move in one direction.

Trimmed mean A mean computed after excluding a stated small percentage of the lowest and highest observations.

t-Test A hypothesis test using a statistic (t-statistic) that follows a t-distribution.

Two-sided hypothesis test (or two-tailed hypothesis test) A test in which the null hypothesis is rejected in favor of the alternative hypothesis if the evidence indicates that the population parameter is either smaller or larger than a hypothesized value.

Type I error The error of rejecting a true null hypothesis.

Type II error The error of not rejecting a false null hypothesis.

Unbiasedness Lack of bias. A desirable property of estimators, an unbiased estimator is one whose expected value (the mean of its sampling distribution) equals the parameter it is intended to estimate.

Uncertainty A situation in which more than one event might occur but it is not known which one.

Unconditional probability (or marginal probability) The probability of an event not conditioned on another event.

Uncovered interest rate parity The assertion that expected currency depreciation should offset the interest differential between two countries over the term of the interest rate.

Underlying (1) Refers to a security on which a derivative contract is written. (2) An asset that trades in a market in which buyers and sellers meet, decide on a price, and the seller then delivers the asset to the buyer and receives payment. The underlying is the asset or other derivative on which a particular derivative is based. The market for the underlying is also referred to as the spot market.

Underweighted A condition in which a portfolio, for whatever reason, includes less of a class of securities than the relative market value alone would justify.

Unemployment rate The percentage of the people in the labor force who are unemployed.

Unit elastic demand Demand with a price elasticity of 1; the percentage change in the quantity demanded equals the percentage change in price.

Unit normal distribution *See* Standard normal distribution.

Univariate distribution A distribution that specifies the probabilities for a single random variable.

Unrealized capital gains Capital gains that reflect the price appreciation of currently held unsold assets.

Unsystematic risk Risk that is unique to an asset, derived from its particular characteristics. It can be eliminated in a diversified portfolio.

Unweighted index An indicator series affected equally by the performance of each security in the sample regardless of price or market value. Also referred to as an *equal-weighted series*.

Unwind The negotiated termination of a forward or futures position before contract maturity.

Up transition probability The probability that an asset's value moves up.

U.S. interest rate differential A gap equal to the U.S. interest rate minus the foreign interest rate.

U.S. Official reserves   The government's holdings of foreign currency.

Utilitarianism   A principle that states that we should strive to achieve "the greatest happiness for the greatest number of people."

Utility   The benefit or satisfaction that a person gets from the consumption of a good or service.

Utility of wealth   The amount of utility that a person attaches to a given amount of wealth.

Value   The maximum amount that a person is willing to pay for a good. The value of one more unit of the good or service is its marginal benefit.

Valuation   The process of determining the value of an asset or service.

Valuation analysis   An active bond portfolio management strategy designed to capitalize on expected price increases in temporarily undervalued issues.

Valuation process   Part of the investment decision process in which you estimate the value of a security.

Value at risk (VaR)   (1) A money measure of the minimum loss that is expected over a given period of time with a given probability. (2) A probability-based measure of loss potential for a company, a fund, a portfolio, a transaction, or a strategy over a specified period of time. (3) A money measure of the minimum value of losses expected during a specified time period at a given level of probability.

Value chain   The set of transformations to move from raw material to product or service delivery.

Value stocks   Stocks that appear to be undervalued for reasons besides earnings growth potential. These stocks are usually identified based on high dividend yields, low *P/E* ratios, or low price-to-book ratios.

Value-weighted index   An index calculated as the total market value of the securities in the sample. Market value is equal to the number of shares or bonds outstanding times the market price of the security.

Variance   The expected value (the probability-weighted average) of squared deviations from a random variable's expected value.

Variation margin   Profits or losses on open positions in futures and option contracts that are paid or collected daily.

Vega   The relationship between option price and volatility.

Velocity of circulation   The average number of times a dollar of money is used annually to buy the goods and services that make up GDP.

Venture Capital (Private Equity)   Risk capital in the form of equity and/or loan capital that is provided by an investment institution to back a business venture that is expected to grow in value.

Vintage Year (Private Equity)   The year that the venture capital or private equity fund or partnership first draws down or calls capital from its investors.

Volatility   (1) A measure of the uncertainty about the future price of an asset. Typically measured by the standard deviation of returns on the asset. (2) As used in option pricing, the standard deviation of the continuously compounded returns on the underlying asset.

Voluntary export restraint   An agreement between two governments in which the government of the exporting country agrees to restrain the volume of its own exports.

Wages   The income that labor earns.

Warrant   An instrument that allows the holder to purchase a specified number of shares of the firm's common stock from the firm at a specified price for a given period of time.

Weak-form efficient market hypothesis   The belief that security prices fully reflect all security market information.

Wealth   The market value of all the things that people own.

Weighted-average cost of capital   A weighted average of the after-tax required rates of return on a company's common stock, preferred stock, and long-term debt, where the weights are the fraction of each source of financing in the company's target capital structure.

Weighted mean   An average in which each observation is weighted by an index of its relative importance.

Winsorized mean   A mean computed after assigning a stated percent of the lowest values equal to one specified low value, and a stated percent of the highest values equal to one specified high value.

Working-age population   The total number of people aged 16 years and over who are not in jail, hospital, or some other form of institutional care.

Working capital management   The management of a company's short-term assets (such as inventory) and short-term liabilities (such as money owed to suppliers).

World Trade Organization   An international organization that places greater obligations on its member countries to observe the GATT rules.

Yankee bonds   Bonds sold in the United States and denominated in U.S. dollars but issued by a foreign firm or government.

Yield   The promised rate of return on an investment under certain assumptions.

Yield spread   The difference between the promised yields of alternative bond issues or market segments at a given time relative to yields on Treasury issues of equal maturity.

Yield to maturity   The total yield on a bond obtained by equating the bond's current market value to the discounted cash flows promised by the bond. Also called actuarial yield.

Yield to worst   Given a bond with multiple potential maturity dates and prices due to embedded call options, the practice is to calculate a yield to maturity for each of the call dates and prices and select the lowest yield (the most conservative possible yield) as yield to worst.

Zero-cost collar   A transaction in which a position in the underlying is protected by buying a put and selling a call with the premium from the sale of the call offsetting the premium from the purchase of the put. It can also be used to protect a floating-rate borrower against interest rate increases with the premium on a long cap offsetting the premium on a short floor.

$4\frac{5}{8}$ $4\frac{11}{16}$ $\frac{5}{8}$

$5\frac{1}{2}$ $5\frac{1}{2}$ —

$5\frac{1}{2}$ $2\frac{13}{16}$ — $\frac{1}{16}$

$20\frac{5}{8}$ $21\frac{3}{16}$ — $\frac{7}{8}$

$17\frac{3}{8}$ $18\frac{1}{8}$ + $\frac{1}{2}$

$6\frac{1}{2}$ $6\frac{1}{2}$ — $\frac{1}{8}$

$31\frac{1}{32}$ —

$\frac{15}{16}$

$\frac{9}{16}$

$\frac{9}{16}$

$7\frac{15}{16}$ $7\frac{13}{16}$ $7\frac{15}{16}$

$2\frac{5}{8}$ $2\frac{11}{32}$ $2\frac{1}{2}$ +

$2\frac{3}{4}$ $2\frac{1}{4}$ $2\frac{1}{4}$

$12\frac{1}{16}$ $11\frac{3}{8}$ $11\frac{7}{8}$ +

$33\frac{3}{4}$ 33 $33\frac{1}{16}$ —

$25\frac{5}{8}$ $24\frac{9}{16}$ $25\frac{3}{8}$ +

12 $11\frac{5}{8}$ $11\frac{7}{8}$ +

$10\frac{1}{2}$ $10\frac{1}{2}$ $10\frac{1}{2}$ —

$15\frac{7}{8}$ $15\frac{13}{16}$ $15\frac{7}{8}$ —

$9\frac{1}{16}$ $8\frac{1}{4}$

$11\frac{1}{4}$ $10\frac{1}{8}$

electronic money, V2: 346–347
electronic trading (e-trading), V6: 16, 0, 2
　bond markets and, V5: 471
　traders, V6: 91
Elliot, V3: 83, 414, 446, 447
embedded options, V5: 394–396, 407, 495–496, 616–620, 617n3
Emerging Issues Task Force (EITF), V3: 15, 17, 405
emerging-market funds, V6: 411
emerging market overinvestment, V4: 149n21
emerging markets, government bonds and, V5: 441
EMH. *See* efficient market hypothesis (EMH)
empirical probability, V1: 318
employee stock options, V5: 218
employees, versus independent contractors, V1: 70–71
employers
　disclosure of conflicts to, V1: 90–91
　duties to, V1: 13, 68–79, 9 4
employment, V2: 269
　full employment, V2: 383, 410
　trade protection and, V2: 482
Employment Act (of 1946), V2: 403–404
employment-to-population ratio, V2: 270–271
EnCana (Canada), V4: 186
end-of-period valuation, V6: 405
end users, V6: 34
endogenous growth theory, V5: 226, 227
endowment funds, V6: 405, 406
energy commodities, V6: 424–425
energy companies, V6: 429
Ennis Business Forms, V5: 357–359
Enron, V2: 88, 9 6, 109–111; V4: 209; V5: 214–216
enterprise value (EV), V5: 209; V6: 423
entrants, V2: 276
entrepreneurial/management mismatches, V6: 401
entrepreneurship, V2: 232
entry and exit, V2: 147–148, 151, 191
　ease of entry, V5: 168, 236
environment of international capital structures, V4: 155–159
environmental projects, V4: 9–10
environmental standards, V2: 484
EOQ (economic order quantity), V3: 333
ePIPER, V4: 299
EPS. *See* earnings per share (EPS)
EQK Realty Investors, V3: 516–519

equality of opportunity, V2: 49
equation format for cash flows, V4: 32–34
equation format for economic profit (EP), V4: 66
equation of exchange, V2: 361–363
equilibrium, V2: 59–60, 156
　foreign exchange market, V2: 505–507, 543
　free trade equilibrium, V2: 473
　macroeconomic equilibrium, V2: 303–310
　money market equilibrium, V2: 354–355
　rent-seeking equilibrium, V2: 174–175
equipment acquisition costs, V3: 363
equity, V6: 428–429
　Commingled Real Estate Equity Fund (CREF) index, V6: 396
　commodity-linked, V6: 429
　forward markets, V6: 37, 39, 53–56
　free and clear, V6: 387
　investments, V6: 393
　leveraged, V6: 387
　long-term equity anticipatory securities, V6: 154
　losses in private, V6: 405–406
　portfolios, V6: 293–295
　private equity/venture capital
　　global investing, V6: 398–399
　　investment characteristics, V6: 400–402
　　stages of venture capital investing, V6: 399–400
　　types of liquidation/divestment, V6: 402–403
　　valuation and performance measurement, V6: 403–405
　swaps, V6: 235n1, 253, 265–269
　TriGroup International Equity Fund (TRIEF), V6: 376–377
equity analysis. *See* equity concepts/techniques
equity book value, V5: 221
equity capital, V2: 330; V3: 261
equity capital requirements, V2: 330
equity concepts/techniques
　equity analysis
　　currency changes and stock prices, V5: 254–255
　　franchise value/growth, V5: 249–252
　　global financial ratio analysis, V5: 243–247
　　industry/country valuation, V5: 241–243
　　inflation and stock prices, V5: 252–254

　　market efficiency in stock valuation, V5: 247
　　valuation models, V5: 247–249
　global industry analysis
　　country analysis, V5: 222–228
　　examples, V5: 237–241
　　return expectations, V5: 228–233
　　risk elements, V5: 233–237
　global risk, V5: 255–258
　international analysis, V5: 206–209
　introduction, V5: 205–206
　national accounting standards
　　overview, V5: 209–210
　　earnings/stock prices, V5: 220–221
　　global standards, V5: 213–220
　　historical setting, V5: 210–211
　　international differences, V5: 221–222
　　international harmonization, V5: 211–213
　summary, V5: 259
equity financing. *See also* cost of common equity (r_e)
　capital budgeting and, V4: 4:10
equity method, V5: 216
equity risk premium (ERP), V4: 92
equity turnover, V3: 221
equity valuation, V5: 126
equivalent annual annuity (EAA) approach, V4: 42–43, 43n10
Erichmann Gold Mine, V4: 59
Ernst & Young LLP, V3: 36, 38
ERR (exchange rate risks), V5: 170, 320–321
error term, V1: 518
escalation bias, V5: 84
escrowed-to-maturity bonds, V5: 453
estimated parameters, V1: 519
estimated rates of return, V4: 315–316
estimated useful life, V3: 365
estimated values vs. market prices, V5: 122–123
estimates and estimation, V1: 430.
　See also pooled estimates; sampling
　confidence intervals, V1: 431–437
　historical volatility of, V6: 213–214
　issues, V4: 296–297
　point estimators, V1: 430–431
　role of, V1: 429, 452–453
estimation period of capital estimation, V4: 98
estimators, V1: 430, 432n13
ETFs. *See* exchange traded funds (ETFs)
ethics. *See also* professional conduct
　CFA Institute on, V1: 5–8, 11–14, 15
　disassociation from violations to, V1: 16–17, 18

summary, V5: 598–599

yield measures, traditional, V5: 557, 558–565, 566–567, 568, 569–572

yield to maturity (YTM), V1: 231; V4: 87, 9; V5: 568n5

Z

z-alternative, V1: 433–434, 437

Z-spreads, V5: 580–584

z-test, V1: 466–470

Zacks, V5: 319n18

Zamsky, Steven, V5: 246

Zarnowitz, Victor, V1: 506n5

Zarowin, V3: 48

Zeale Corporation, V4: 82

Zeller, V5: 193

Zephyr Associates, V4: 299

zero-beta model and SML, V4: 322–323

zero-cost collar transactions, V6: 159, 320, 322, 347–348

zero-coupon bonds

arbitrage-free approach and, V5: 540

benchmark rate curves, V5: 547

bonds, V5: 384, 417

commercial paper, V5: 463

debt securities valuation, V5: 534–535

forward contracts, V6: 40

Treasuries, V5: 439–440, 490

zero-coupon debt, V3: 515–519

zero economic profit, V2: 194–195

zero-value contracts, V6: 100

zero variance, V4: 305

zero-volatility OAS, V5: 585–586

Zhang, Gouhua, V4: 49–52

Zhao, Quanshui, V4: 109

Zurich Capital Management, V6: 415